CIMA

Paper F2

Financial Management

Study Text

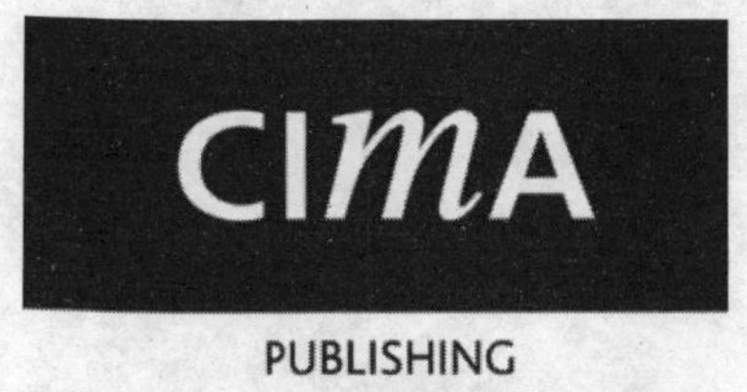

PUBLISHING

WORKING TOGETHER FOR YOU

PUBLISHING

CIMA Publishing is an imprint of Elsevier
The Boulevard, Langford Lane, Kidlington, Oxford, OX5 1GB, UK
225 Wyman Street, Waltham, MA02451, USA
Kaplan Publishing UK, Unit 2 The Business Centre, Molly Millars Lane, Wokingham, Berkshire RG41 2QZ

British Library Cataloguing in Publication Data
A catalogue record for this book is available from the British Library

ISBN: 978-0-85732-575-4

Printed and bound in Great Britain

12 13 14 10 9 8 7 6 5 4 3 2 1

Contents

chapter

Intro

Paper Introduction

How to Use the Materials

These Official CIMA learning materials brought to you by Elsevier/CIMA Publishing and Kaplan Publishing have been carefully designed to make your learning experience as easy as possible and to give you the best chances of success in your *Financial Management* examinations.

The product range contains a number of features to help you in the study process. They include:

- a detailed explanation of all syllabus areas;
- extensive 'practical' materials, including readings from relevant journals;
- generous question practice, together with full solutions;
- a specimen paper, complete with solutions.

This Study Text has been designed with the needs of home-study and distance-learning candidates in mind. Such students require very full coverage of the syllabus topics, and also the facility to undertake extensive question practice. However, the Study Text is also ideal for fully taught courses.

The main body of the text is divided into a number of chapters, each of which is organised on the following pattern:

- *Detailed learning outcomes.* You should assimilate these before beginning detailed work on the chapter, so that you can appreciate where your studies are leading.
- *Step-by-step topic coverage.* This is the heart of each chapter, containing detailed explanatory text supported, where appropriate, by worked examples and exercises. You should work carefully through this section, ensuring that you understand the material being explained and can tackle the examples and exercises successfully. Remember that in many cases knowledge is cumulative; if you fail to digest earlier material thoroughly, you may struggle to understand later chapters.
- *Readings and activities.* Most chapters are illustrated by more practical elements, such as relevant journal articles or other readings, together with comments and questions designed to stimulate discussion.

- *Question practice.* The test of how well you have learned the material is your ability to tackle questions. Make a serious attempt at producing your own answers, but at this stage don't be too concerned about attempt the questions under exam conditions. In particular, it is more important to absorb the material thoroughly by completing a full solution than to observe the time limits that would apply in the actual exam.
- *Solutions.* Avoid the temptation merely to 'audit' the solutions provided. It is an illusion to think that this provides the same benefits as you would gain from a serious attempt of your own. However, if you are struggling to get started on a question you should read the introductory guidance provided at the beginning of the solution, and then make your own attempt before referring back to the full solution.

Having worked through the chapters you are ready to begin your final preparations for the examination. The final section of this Study Text provides you with a specimen paper. You should attempt this under strict exam conditions before fully reviewing the solutions provided.

If you work conscientiously through this official CIMA Study Text according to the guidelines above you will be giving yourself an excellent chance of exam success. Good luck with your studies.

Icon Explanations

Definition - these sections explain important areas of knowledge which must be understood and reproduced in an exam environment.

Key Point - Identifies topics that are key to success and are often examined.

Supplementary reading - identifies a more detailed explanation of key terms. These sections will help to provide a deeper understanding of core areas. Reference to this text is vital when self studying.

Illustration - to help develop an understanding of particular topics. The illustrative examples are useful in preparing for the Test Your Understanding exercises.

Test Your Understanding - following key points and definitions are exercises which give the opportunity to assess the understanding of these core areas.

Exclamation Mark - this symbol signifies a topic which can be more difficult to understand, when reviewing these areas care should be taken.

Study technique

Passing exams is partly a matter of intellectual ability, but however accomplished you are in that respect you can improve your chances significantly by the use of appropriate study and revision techniques. In this section we briefly outline some tips for effective study during the earlier stages of your approach to the exam.

Planning

To begin with, formal planning is essential to get the best return from the time you spend studying. Estimate how much time in total you are going to need for each subject you are studying. Remember that you need to allow time for revision as well as for initial study of the material. You may find it helpful to read 'Pass First Time!' second edition by David R. Harris, ISBN 9781856177986. This book will provide you with proven study techniques. Chapter by chapter it covers the building blocks of successful learning and examination techniques. This is the ultimate guide to passing your CIMA exams, written by a past CIMA examiner and shows you how to earn all the marks you deserve, and explains how to avoid the most common pitfalls. You may also find "The E Word: Kaplan's Guide to Passing Exams" by Stuart Pedley-Smith, ISBN: 9780857322050, helpful. Stuart Pedley-Smith is a senior lecturer at Kaplan Financial and a qualified accountant specialising in financial management. His natural curiosity and wider interests have led him to look beyond the technical content of financial management to the processes and journey that we call education. He has become fascinated by the whole process of learning and the exam skills and techniques that contribute towards success in the classroom. This book is for anyone who has to sit and exam and wants to give themselves a better chance of passing. It is easy to read, written in a common sense style and full of anecdotes, facts, and practical tips. It also contains synopses of interviews with people involved in the learning and examining process.

With your study material before you, decide which chapters you are going to study each week, and which weeks you will devote to revision and final question practice.

Prepare a written schedule summarising the above and stick to it!

It is essential to know your syllabus. As your studies progress, you will become more familiar with how long it takes to cover topics in sufficient depth. Your timetable may need to be adapted to allocate enough time for the whole syllabus.

Students are advised to refer to the notice of examinable legislation published regularly in CIMA's magazine (Financial Management), the students e-newsletter (Velocity) and on the CIMA website, to ensure they are up-to-date.

Tips for effective studying

(1) Aim to find a quiet and undisturbed location for your study, and plan as far as possible to use the same period of time each day. Getting into a routine helps to avoid wasting time. Make sure that you have all the materials you need before you begin so as to minimise interruptions.

(2) Store all your materials in one place, so that you do not waste time searching for items around the house. If you have to pack everything away after each study period, keep them in a box, or even a suitcase, which will not be disturbed until next time.

(3) Limit distractions. To make the most effective use of your study periods you should be able to apply total concentration, so turn off the TV, set your phones to message mode, and put up your 'do not disturb' sign.

(4) Your timetable will tell you which topic to study. However, before diving in and becoming engrossed in the fine points, make sure you have an overall picture of all the areas that need to be covered by the end of that session. After an hour, allow yourself a short break and move away from your books. With experience, you will learn to assess the pace you need to work at. You should also allow enough time to read relevant articles from newspapers and journals, which will supplement your knowledge and demonstrate a wider perspective.

(5) Work carefully through a chapter, making notes as you go. When you have covered a suitable amount of material, vary the pattern by attempting a practice question. Preparing an answer plan is a good habit to get into, while you are both studying and revising, and also in the examination room. It helps to impose a structure on your solutions and avoid rambling. When you have finished your attempt, make notes of any mistakes you made, or any areas that you failed to cover or covered more briefly.

(6) Make notes as you study, and discover the techniques that work best for you. Your notes may be in the form of lists, bullet points, diagrams, summaries, 'mind maps' or the written word, but remember that you will need to refer back to them at a later date, so they must be intelligible. If you are on a taught course, make sure you highlight any issues you would like to follow up with your lecturer.

(7) Organise your notes. Make sure that all your notes, calculations etc., can be effectively filed and easily retrieved later.

The Examination

Examination format

The examination is a three hour written paper, plus 20 minutes of pre-examination question paper reading time. All questions are compulsory. It will contain both computational and discursive elements.

Some questions will adopt a scenario/case study approach.

An individual question may often involve elements that relate to different areas of the syllabus. For example, an analysis and interpretation question could include matters relating to substance or financial instruments.

Questions may ask candidates to comment on the appropriateness or acceptability of management's opinion or chosen accounting treatment.

Questions will test an understanding of accounting principles and concepts and how these are applied to practical examples.

The examination paper will have the following sections:

Section A – 50 marks

Five compulsory medium answer questions, each worth 10 marks. Short scenarios may be given, to which some or all questions relate.

Section B – 50 marks

One or two compulsory questions. Short scenarios may be given, to which questions relate.

Paper based examination tips

Spend the first few minutes of the examination reading the paper.

Divide the time you spend on questions in proportion to the marks on offer. One suggestion **for this examination** is to allocate 1.8 minutes to each mark available, so a 10-mark question should be completed in approximately 18 minutes.

Unless you know exactly how to answer the question, spend some time planning your answer. Stick to the question and tailor your answer to what you are asked. Pay particular attention to the verbs in the question.

Spend the last five minutes reading through your answers and making any additions or corrections.

If you **get completely stuck** with a question, leave space in your answer book and return to it later.

If you do not understand what a question is asking, state your assumptions. Even if you do not answer in precisely the way the examiner hoped, you should be given some credit, if your assumptions are reasonable.

You should do everything you can to make things easy for the marker. The marker will find it easier to identify the points you have made if your answers are legible.

- **Medium answer questions**: These might ask for numerical answers, but could also ask you to write a definition of a word or phrase, or to use a formula.
- **Essay questions**: Make a quick plan in your answer book and under each main point list all the relevant facts you can think of. Then write out your answer developing each point fully. Your essay should have a clear structure; it should contain a brief introduction, a main section and a conclusion. Be concise. It is better to write a little about a lot of different points than a great deal about one or two points.

- **Computations**: It is essential to include all your workings in your answers. Many computational questions require the use of a standard format: company income statement, statement of financial position and statement of cash flows for example. Be sure you know these formats thoroughly before the examination and use the layouts that you see in the answers given in this resource. If you are asked to comment or make recommendations on a computation, you must do so. There are important marks to be gained here. Even if your computation contains mistakes, you may still gain marks if your reasoning is correct.
- **Reports, memos and other documents**: Some questions ask you to present your answer in the form of a report or a memo or other document. Use the correct format – there could be easy marks to gain here.

Examinable legislation

For the most up-to-date list of examinable documents please visit the student section of the CIMA website: http://www.cimaglobal.com/Students/2010-professional-qualification/Management-level/F2-study-resources/.

IFRSs 10-12

The IASB issued these three standards in May 2011: IFRS 10 *Consolidated Financial Statements*, IFRS 11 *Joint Arrangements* and IFRS 12 *Disclosure of Interests in Other Entities*. The issuance of these standards completes the IASB's improvements to the accounting requirements for off balance sheet activities and joint arrangements and brings the accounting treatment of IFRS and US GAAP broadly in line.

IFRS 10 replaces all of the consolidation guidance previously contained in IAS 27 *Consolidated and Separate Financial Statements* (and SIC 12 *Consolidation - Special Purposes Entities*). The old standard has been reissued and is now IAS 27 *Separate Financial Statements.*

IFRS 11 *Joint* Arrangements replaces IAS 31 *Interests in Joint* Ventures. It addresses inconsistencies in accounting treatements by eliminating the option of proportionate consolidation for joint ventures and requires that all joint ventures are now accounted for using the equity method in accordance with IAS 28. As a result of this IAS 28 *Investments in Associates* has now been reissued and renamed IAS 28 *Investments in Associates and Joint Ventures.*

IFRS 12 *Disclosure of Interests in Other Entities* requires entities to disclose the nature of, and risks associated with, its interests in other entities. It replaces all of the disclosure requirements previously contained in IAS's 27, 28 and 31.

IFRS 13

IFRS 13 was also published in May 2011 with the objective of establishing a single framework for measuring fair values. It is the result of a joint project between the IASB and US FASB and introduces a new definition for fair value, based principally on market prices.

IAS 19 revised

A further project recently completed by the IASB was on improvements to the accounting for pension schemes and it resulted in revisions to IAS 19. The revised standard removes the option to defer recognition of actuarial gains and losses and now requires all entities to account for such items through other comprehensive income, thereby improving consistency of treatment.

IAS 1 revised

IAS 1 has recently been amended and now requires entities to group items in other comprehensive income into two categories: items that are potentially reclassifiable to profit or loss and items that are not.

PAPER F2
FINANCIAL MANAGEMENT

Syllabus overview

Paper F2 extends the scope of Paper F1 Financial Operations to more advanced topics in financial accounting (preparation of full consolidated financial statements and issues of principle in accounting standards dealing with more complex areas) and to developments in external reporting. With the advanced level of financial accounting and reporting achieved in this paper, the analysis and interpretation of accounts becomes more meaningful and this constitutes a substantial element.

Syllabus structure

The syllabus comprises the following topics and study weightings:

A	Group Financial Statements	35%
B	Issues in Recognition and Measurement	20%
C	Analysis and Interpretation of Financial Accounts	35%
D	Developments in External Reporting	10%

Assessment strategy

There will be a written examination paper of three hours, plus 20 minutes of pre-examination question paper reading time. The examination paper will have the following sections:

Section A – 50 marks
Five compulsory medium answer questions, each worth ten marks. Short scenarios may be given, to which some or all questions relate.

Section B – 50 marks
One or two compulsory questions. Short scenarios may be given, to which questions relate.

F2 – A. GROUP FINANCIAL STATEMENTS (35%)

Learning outcomes On completion of their studies students should be able to:		**Indicative syllabus content**
Lead	**Component**	
1. prepare the full consolidated statements of a single company and the consolidated statements of financial position and comprehensive income for a group (in relatively complex circumstances).	(a) prepare a complete set of consolidated financial statements in a form suitable for publication for a group of companies; (b) demonstrate the impact on group financial statements where: there is a minority interest; the interest in a subsidiary or associate is acquired or disposed of part way through an accounting period (to include the effective date of acquisition and dividends out of pre-acquisition profits); shareholdings, or control, are acquired in stages; intra-group trading and other transactions occur; the value of goodwill is impaired; (c) apply the concept of a joint venture and how various types are accounted for.	• Relationships between investors and investees, meaning of control and circumstances in which a subsidiary is excluded from consolidation. [4–8], [10] • The preparation of consolidated financial statements (including the group cash flow statement and statement of changes in equity) involving one or more subsidiaries, sub-subsidiaries and associates (IAS 1 (revised), 7 and 27, IFRS 3). [4–8], [10] • The treatment in consolidated financial statements of minority interests, pre and post- acquisition reserves, goodwill (including its impairment), fair value adjustments, intra-group transactions and dividends, piece-meal and mid-year acquisitions, and disposals to include sub-subsidiaries and mixed groups. [4–8], [10] • The accounting treatment of associates and joint ventures (IAS 28 and 31) using the equity method and proportional consolidation method. [4–8], [10]
2. explain the principles of accounting for capital schemes and foreign exchange rate changes.	(a) explain the principles of accounting for a capital reconstruction scheme or a demerger; (b) explain foreign currency translation principles, including the difference between the closing rate/net investment method and the historical rate method; (c) explain the correct treatment for foreign loans financing foreign equity investments.	• Accounting for reorganisations and capital reconstruction schemes. [7] • Foreign currency translation (IAS 21), to include overseas transactions and investments in overseas subsidiaries. [9]

F2 – B. ISSUES IN RECOGNITION AND MEASUREMENT (20%)

Learning outcomes **On completion of their studies students should be able to:**		**Indicative syllabus content**
Lead	**Component**	
1. discuss accounting principles and their relevance to accounting issues of contemporary interest.	(a) discuss the problems of profit measurement and alternative approaches to asset valuations; (b) discuss measures to reduce distortion in financial statements when price levels change; (c) discuss the principle of substance over form applied to a range of transactions; (d) discuss the possible treatments of financial instruments in the issuer's accounts (i.e. liabilities versus equity, and the implications for finance costs); (e) discuss circumstances in which amortised cost, fair value and hedge accounting are appropriate for financial instruments, the principles of these accounting methods and considerations in the determination of fair value; (f) discuss the recognition and valuation issues concerned with pension schemes (including the treatment of actuarial deficits and surpluses) and share-based payments.	• The problems of profit measurement and the effect of alternative approaches to asset valuation; current cost and current purchasing power bases and the real terms system; Financial Reporting in Hyperinflationary Economies (IAS 29). [12] • The principle of substance over form and its influence in dealing with transactions such as sale and repurchase agreements, consignment stock, debt factoring, securitised assets, loan transfers and public and private sector financial collaboration. [16] • Financial instruments classified as liabilities or shareholders funds and the allocation of finance costs over the term of the borrowing (IAS 32 and 39). [13] • The measurement, including methods of determining fair value, and disclosure of financial instruments (IAS 32 and 39, IFRS 7). [13] • Retirement benefits, including pension schemes – defined benefit schemes and defined contribution schemes, actuarial deficits and surpluses (IAS 19). [15] • Share-based payments (IFRS 2): types of transactions, measurement bases and accounting; determination of fair value. [14]

F2 – C. ANALYSIS AND INTERPRETATION OF FINANCIAL ACCOUNTS (35%)

Learning outcomes **On completion of their studies students should be able to:**		**Indicative syllabus content**
Lead	**Component**	
1. produce a ratio analysis from financial statements and supporting information.	(a) interpret a full range of accounting ratios; (b) discuss the limitations of accounting ratio analysis and analysis based on financial statements.	• Ratios in the areas of performance, profitability, financial adaptability, liquidity, activity, shareholder investment and financing, and their interpretation. [2] • Calculation of Earnings per Share under IAS 33, to include the effect of bonus issues, rights issues and convertible stock. [3] • The impact of financing structure, including use of leasing and short-term debt, on ratios, particularly gearing. [2] • Limitations of ratio analysis (e.g. comparability of businesses and accounting policies). [2]
2. evaluate performance and position.	(a) analyse financial statements in the context of information provided in the accounts and corporate report; (b) evaluate performance and position based on analysis of financial statements; (c) discuss segmental analysis, with inter-firm and international comparisons taking account of possible aggressive or unusual accounting policies and pressures on ethical behaviour; (d) discuss the results of an analysis of financial statements and its limitations.	• Interpretation of financial statements via the analysis of the accounts and corporate reports. [2] • The identification of information required to assess financial performance and the extent to which financial statements fail to provide such information. [2] • Interpretation of financial obligations included in financial accounts (e.g. redeemable debt, earn-out arrangements, contingent liabilities). [2] • Segment analysis: inter-firm and international comparison (IFRS 8). [2] • The need to be aware of aggressive or unusual accounting policies ("creative accounting"), e.g. in the areas of cost capitalisation and revenue recognition, and threats to the ethics of accountants from pressure to report "good results". [2] • Reporting the results of analysis. [2]

F2 – D. DEVELOPMENTS IN EXTERNAL REPORTING (10%)

Learning outcomes On completion of their studies students should be able to:		**Indicative syllabus content**
Lead	**Component**	
1. discuss contemporary developments in financial and non-financial reporting.	(a) discuss pressures for extending the scope and quality of external reports to include prospective and non-financial matters, and narrative reporting generally; (b) explain how information concerning the interaction of a business with society and the natural environment can be communicated in the published accounts; (c) discuss social and environmental issues which are likely to be most important to stakeholders in an organisation; (d) explain the process of measuring, recording and disclosing the effect of exchanges between a business and society – human resource accounting; (e) discuss major differences between IFRS and US GAAP, and the measures designed to contribute towards their convergence.	• Increasing stakeholder demands for information that goes beyond historical financial information and frameworks for such reporting, including, as an example of national requirements and guidelines, the UK's Business Review and the Accounting Standard Board's best practice standard, RS1, and the Global Reporting Initiative. [11] • Environmental and social accounting issues, differentiating between externalities and costs internalised through, for example, capitalisation of environmental expenditure, recognition of future environmental costs by means of provisions, taxation and the costs of emissions permit trading schemes. [11] • Non-financial measures of social and environmental impact. [11] • Human resource accounting. [11] • Major differences between IFRS and US GAAP, and progress towards convergence. [11]

MATHS TABLES AND FORMULAE

Present value table

Present value of $1, that is $(1 + r)^{-n}$ where r = interest rate; n = number of periods until payment or receipt.

Periods (n)	Interest rates (r)									
	1%	2%	3%	4%	5%	6%	7%	8%	9%	10%
1	0.990	0.980	0.971	0.962	0.952	0.943	0.935	0.926	0.917	0.909
2	0.980	0.961	0.943	0.925	0.907	0.890	0.873	0.857	0.842	0.826
3	0.971	0.942	0.915	0.889	0.864	0.840	0.816	0.794	0.772	0.751
4	0.961	0.924	0.888	0.855	0.823	0.792	0.763	0.735	0.708	0.683
5	0.951	0.906	0.863	0.822	0.784	0.747	0.713	0.681	0.650	0.621
6	0.942	0.888	0.837	0.790	0.746	0.705	0.666	0.630	0.596	0.564
7	0.933	0.871	0.813	0.760	0.711	0.665	0.623	0.583	0.547	0.513
8	0.923	0.853	0.789	0.731	0.677	0.627	0.582	0.540	0.502	0.467
9	0.914	0.837	0.766	0.703	0.645	0.592	0.544	0.500	0.460	0.424
10	0.905	0.820	0.744	0.676	0.614	0.558	0.508	0.463	0.422	0.386
11	0.896	0.804	0.722	0.650	0.585	0.527	0.475	0.429	0.388	0.350
12	0.887	0.788	0.701	0.625	0.557	0.497	0.444	0.397	0.356	0.319
13	0.879	0.773	0.681	0.601	0.530	0.469	0.415	0.368	0.326	0.290
14	0.870	0.758	0.661	0.577	0.505	0.442	0.388	0.340	0.299	0.263
15	0.861	0.743	0.642	0.555	0.481	0.417	0.362	0.315	0.275	0.239
16	0.853	0.728	0.623	0.534	0.458	0.394	0.339	0.292	0.252	0.218
17	0.844	0.714	0.605	0.513	0.436	0.371	0.317	0.270	0.231	0.198
18	0.836	0.700	0.587	0.494	0.416	0.350	0.296	0.250	0.212	0.180
19	0.828	0.686	0.570	0.475	0.396	0.331	0.277	0.232	0.194	0.164
20	0.820	0.673	0.554	0.456	0.377	0.312	0.258	0.215	0.178	0.149

Periods (n)	Interest rates (r)									
	11%	12%	13%	14%	15%	16%	17%	18%	19%	20%
1	0.901	0.893	0.885	0.877	0.870	0.862	0.855	0.847	0.840	0.833
2	0.812	0.797	0.783	0.769	0.756	0.743	0.731	0.718	0.706	0.694
3	0.731	0.712	0.693	0.675	0.658	0.641	0.624	0.609	0.593	0.579
4	0.659	0.636	0.613	0.592	0.572	0.552	0.534	0.516	0.499	0.482
5	0.593	0.567	0.543	0.519	0.497	0.476	0.456	0.437	0.419	0.402
6	0.535	0.507	0.480	0.456	0.432	0.410	0.390	0.370	0.352	0.335
7	0.482	0.452	0.425	0.400	0.376	0.354	0.333	0.314	0.296	0.279
8	0.434	0.404	0.376	0.351	0.327	0.305	0.285	0.266	0.249	0.233
9	0.391	0.361	0.333	0.308	0.284	0.263	0.243	0.225	0.209	0.194
10	0.352	0.322	0.295	0.270	0.247	0.227	0.208	0.191	0.176	0.162
11	0.317	0.287	0.261	0.237	0.215	0.195	0.178	0.162	0.148	0.135
12	0.286	0.257	0.231	0.208	0.187	0.168	0.152	0.137	0.124	0.112
13	0.258	0.229	0.204	0.182	0.163	0.145	0.130	0.116	0.104	0.093
14	0.232	0.205	0.181	0.160	0.141	0.125	0.111	0.099	0.088	0.078
15	0.209	0.183	0.160	0.140	0.123	0.108	0.095	0.084	0.079	0.065
16	0.188	0.163	0.141	0.123	0.107	0.093	0.081	0.071	0.062	0.054
17	0.170	0.146	0.125	0.108	0.093	0.080	0.069	0.060	0.052	0.045
18	0.153	0.130	0.111	0.095	0.081	0.069	0.059	0.051	0.044	0.038
19	0.138	0.116	0.098	0.083	0.070	0.060	0.051	0.043	0.037	0.031
20	0.124	0.104	0.087	0.073	0.061	0.051	0.043	0.037	0.031	0.026

Cumulative present value of $1 per annum,

Receivable or Payable at the end of each year for n years $\frac{1-(1+r)^{-n}}{r}$

Periods	Interest rates (r)									
(n)	1%	2%	3%	4%	5%	6%	7%	8%	9%	10%
1	0.990	0.980	0.971	0.962	0.952	0.943	0.935	0.926	0.917	0.909
2	1.970	1.942	1.913	1.886	1.859	1.833	1.808	1.783	1.759	1.736
3	2.941	2.884	2.829	2.775	2.723	2.673	2.624	2.577	2.531	2.487
4	3.902	3.808	3.717	3.630	3.546	3.465	3.387	3.312	3.240	3.170
5	4.853	4.713	4.580	4.452	4.329	4.212	4.100	3.993	3.890	3.791
6	5.795	5.601	5.417	5.242	5.076	4.917	4.767	4.623	4.486	4.355
7	6.728	6.472	6.230	6.002	5.786	5.582	5.389	5.206	5.033	4.868
8	7.652	7.325	7.020	6.733	6.463	6.210	5.971	5.747	5.535	5.335
9	8.566	8.162	7.786	7.435	7.108	6.802	6.515	6.247	5.995	5.759
10	9.471	8.983	8.530	8.111	7.722	7.360	7.024	6.710	6.418	6.145
11	10.368	9.787	9.253	8.760	8.306	7.887	7.499	7.139	6.805	6.495
12	11.255	10.575	9.954	9.385	8.863	8.384	7.943	7.536	7.161	6.814
13	12.134	11.348	10.635	9.986	9.394	8.853	8.358	7.904	7.487	7.103
14	13.004	12.106	11.296	10.563	9.899	9.295	8.745	8.244	7.786	7.367
15	13.865	12.849	11.938	11.118	10.380	9.712	9.108	8.559	8.061	7.606
16	14.718	13.578	12.561	11.652	10.838	10.106	9.447	8.851	8.313	7.824
17	15.562	14.292	13.166	12.166	11.274	10.477	9.763	9.122	8.544	8.022
18	16.398	14.992	13.754	12.659	11.690	10.828	10.059	9.372	8.756	8.201
19	17.226	15.679	14.324	13.134	12.085	11.158	10.336	9.604	8.950	8.365
20	18.046	16.351	14.878	13.590	12.462	11.470	10.594	9.818	9.129	8.514

Periods	Interest rates (r)									
(n)	11%	12%	13%	14%	15%	16%	17%	18%	19%	20%
1	0.901	0.893	0.885	0.877	0.870	0.862	0.855	0.847	0.840	0.833
2	1.713	1.690	1.668	1.647	1.626	1.605	1.585	1.566	1.547	1.528
3	2.444	2.402	2.361	2.322	2.283	2.246	2.210	2.174	2.140	2.106
4	3.102	3.037	2.974	2.914	2.855	2.798	2.743	2.690	2.639	2.589
5	3.696	3.605	3.517	3.433	3.352	3.274	3.199	3.127	3.058	2.991
6	4.231	4.111	3.998	3.889	3.784	3.685	3.589	3.498	3.410	3.326
7	4.712	4.564	4.423	4.288	4.160	4.039	3.922	3.812	3.706	3.605
8	5.146	4.968	4.799	4.639	4.487	4.344	4.207	4.078	3.954	3.837
9	5.537	5.328	5.132	4.946	4.772	4.607	4.451	4.303	4.163	4.031
10	5.889	5.650	5.426	5.216	5.019	4.833	4.659	4.494	4.339	4.192
11	6.207	5.938	5.687	5.453	5.234	5.029	4.836	4.656	4.486	4.327
12	6.492	6.194	5.918	5.660	5.421	5.197	4.988	7.793	4.611	4.439
13	6.750	6.424	6.122	5.842	5.583	5.342	5.118	4.910	4.715	4.533
14	6.982	6.628	6.302	6.002	5.724	5.468	5.229	5.008	4.802	4.611
15	7.191	6.811	6.462	6.142	5.847	5.575	5.324	5.092	4.876	4.675
16	7.379	6.974	6.604	6.265	5.954	5.668	5.405	5.162	4.938	4.730
17	7.549	7.120	6.729	6.373	6.047	5.749	5.475	5.222	4.990	4.775
18	7.702	7.250	6.840	6.467	6.128	5.818	5.534	5.273	5.033	4.812
19	7.839	7.366	6.938	6.550	6.198	5.877	5.584	5.316	5.070	4.843
20	7.963	7.469	7.025	6.623	6.259	5.929	5.628	5.353	5.101	4.870

FORMULAE

Annuity
Present value of an annuity of $1 per annum receivable or payable for *n* years, commencing in one year, discounted at *r*% per annum:

$$PV = \frac{1}{r}\left[1 - \frac{1}{[1+r]^n}\right]$$

Perpetuity
Present value of $1 per annum receivable or payable in perpetuity, commencing in one year, discounted at *r*% per annum:

$$PV = \frac{1}{r}$$

Growing Perpetuity
Present value of $1 per annum, receivable or payable, commencing in one year, growing in perpetuity at a constant rate of *g*% per annum, discounted at *r*% per annum:

$$PV = \frac{1}{r-g}$$

chapter

1

CIMA verb hierarchy

Chapter learning objectives

CIMA VERB HIERARCHY

CIMA place great importance on the choice of verbs in exam question requirements. It is thus critical that you answer the question according to the definition of the verb used.

1 Managerial level verbs

In managerial level exams you will mainly meet verbs from levels 2, 3 and 4. Very occasionally you will also see level 1 verbs but these should not account for more than 5-10% of the marks in total.

Level 2 – COMPREHENSION

What you are expected to understand

VERBS USED	DEFINITION
Describe	Communicate the key features of.
Distinguish	Highlight the differences between.
Explain	Make clear or intelligible/state the meaning or purpose of.
Identify	Recognise, establish or select after consideration.
Illustrate	Use an example to describe or explain something.

Level 3 – APPLICATION

How you are expected to apply your knowledge

VERBS USED	DEFINITION
Apply	Put to practical use.
Calculate	Ascertain or reckon mathematically.
Demonstrate	Prove with certainty or exhibit by practical means.
Prepare	Make or get ready for use.
Reconcile	Make or prove consistent/compatible.
Solve	Find an answer to.
Tabulate	Arrange in a table.

Level 4 – ANALYSIS

How you are expected to analyse the detail of what you have learned.

VERBS USED	DEFINITION
Analyse	Examine in detail the structure of.
Categorise	Place into a defined class or division.
Compare and contrast	Show the similarities and/or differences between.
Construct	Build up or compile.
Discuss	Examine in detail by argument.
Interpret	Translate into intelligible or familiar terms.
Prioritise	Place in order of priority or sequence for action.
Produce	Create or bring into existence.

2 Further guidance on managerial level verbs that cause confusion

Verbs that cause students confusion at this level are as follows:

Level 2 verbs

- **The difference between "describe" and "explain"**

  An explanation is a set of statements constructed to describe a set of facts which clarifies the **causes**, **context**, and **consequences** of those facts.

  For example, if asked to **describe** the features of activity based costing (ABC) you could talk, amongst other things, about how costs are grouped into cost pools (e.g. quality control), cost drivers identified (e.g. number of inspections) and an absorption rate calculated based on this cost driver (e.g. cost per inspection). This tells us what ABC looks like.

  However if asked to **explain** ABC, then you would have to talk about why firms were dissatisfied with previous traditional costing methods and switched to ABC (causes), what types of firms it is more suitable for (context) and the implications for firms (consequences) in terms of the usefulness of such costs per unit for pricing and costing.

  More simply, to describe something is to answer "what" type questions whereas to explain looks at "what" and "why" aspects.

- **The verb "to illustrate"**

  The key thing about illustrating something is that you may have to decide on a relevant example to use. This could involve drawing a diagram, performing supporting calculations or highlighting a feature or person in the scenario given. Most of the time the question will be structured so calculations performed in part (a) can be used to illustrate a concept in part (b).

  For example, you could be asked to explain and illustrate what is meant by an "adverse variance".

Level 3 verbs

- **The verb "to apply"**

  Given that all level 3 verbs involve application, the verb "apply" is rare in the real exam. Instead one of the other more specific verbs are used instead.

- **The verb "to reconcile"**

  This is a numerical requirement and usually involves starting with one of the figures, adjusting it and ending up with the other.

  For example, in a bank reconciliation you start with the recorded cash at bank figure, adjust it for unpresented cheques, etc, and (hopefully!) end up with the stated balance in the cash "T account".

- **The verb "to demonstrate"**

  The verb "to demonstrate" can be used in two main ways.

  Firstly it could mean to prove that a given statement is true or consistent with circumstances given. For example, the Finance Director may have stated in the question that the company will not exceed its overdraft limit in the next six months. The requirement then asks you to demonstrate that the Director is wrong. You could do this by preparing a cash flow forecast for the next six months.

  Secondly you could be asked to demonstrate **how** a stated model, framework, technique or theory **could be used** in the particular scenario to achieve a specific result - for example, how a probability matrix could be used to make a production decision. Ensure in such questions that you do not merely describe the model but use it to generate the desired outcome.

Level 4 verbs

- **The verb "to analyse"**

To analyse something is to examine it in detail in order to discover its meaning or essential features. This will usually involve breaking the scenario down and looking at the fine detail, possibly with additional calculations, and then stepping back to see the bigger picture to identify any themes to support conclusions.

For example, if asked to analyse a set of financial statements, then the end result will be a set of statements about the performance of the business with supporting evidence. This could involve the following:

(1) You could break down your analysis into areas of profitability, liquidity, gearing and so on.

(2) Under each heading look at key figures in the financial statements, identifying trends (e.g. sales growth) and calculating supporting ratios (e.g. margins).

(3) Try to explain what the figures mean and why they have occurred (e.g. why has the operating margin fallen?)

(4) Start considering the bigger picture - are the ratios presenting a consistent message or do they contradict each other? Can you identify common causes?

(5) Finally you would then seek to pull all this information together and interpret it to make some higher level comments about overall performance.

The main error students make is that they fail to draw out any themes and conclusions and simply present the marker with a collection of uninterpreted, unexplained facts and figures.

- **The verb "to discuss"**

To discuss something is very similar to analysing it, except that discussion usually involves two or more different viewpoints or arguments as the context, rather than a set of figures, say. To discuss viewpoints will involve looking at their underlying arguments, examining them critically, trying to assess whether one argument is more persuasive than the other and then seeking to reach a conclusion.

For example, if asked to discuss whether a particular technique could be used by a company, you would examine the arguments for and against, making reference to the specific circumstances in the question, and seek to conclude.

- **The verb "to prioritise"**

  To prioritise is to place objects in an order. The key issue here is to decide upon the criteria to use to perform the ordering. For example, prioritising the external threats facing a firm could be done by considering the scale of financial consequences, immediacy, implications for the underlying business model and so on.

  The main mistake students make is that they fail to justify their prioritisation - why is this the most important issue?

chapter

2

Analysis and interpretation of financial accounts

Chapter learning objectives

On completion of their studies students should be able to:

- Calculate and interpret a full range of accounting ratios;
- Analyse financial statements in the context of information provided in the accounts and corporate report to evaluate performance and position;
- Prepare a concise report on the results of an analysis of financial statements;
- Explain and discuss the limitations of accounting ratio analysis and analysis based on financial statements;
- Discuss segmental analysis, with inter-firm and international comparisons taking account of possible aggressive or unusual accounting policies and pressures on ethical behaviour.

1 Session content

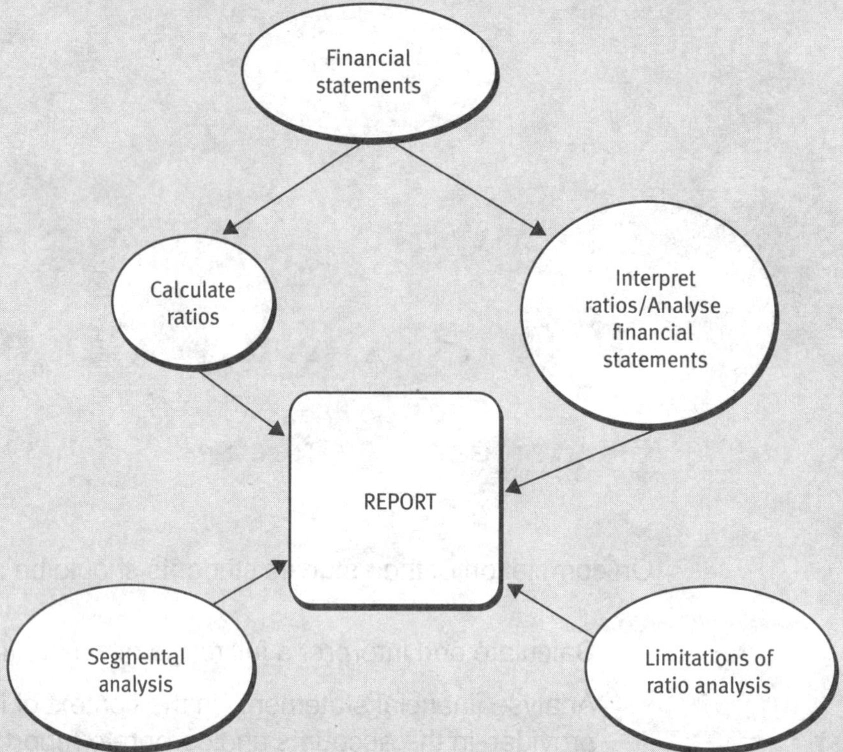

2 Interpretation and analysis

The IASB's conceptual framework states:

The objective of financial reporting is to provide financial information about the reporting entity that is useful to existing and potential investors, lenders and other creditors in making decisions about providing resources to the entity.

Interpretation and analysis of the financial statements is the process of arranging, examining and comparing the results in order that users are equipped to make such decisions.

The interpretation process is assisted by adopting an analytical approach. The main components of an appropriate approach are:

- identification of the user of the analysis;
- an understanding of the nature of the business, industry and organisation;
- identification of relevant sources of data for analysis;
- numerical analysis of the data available;
- interpretation of the results of the analysis;
- writing the report detailing the analysis of the results and recommendations.

3 Identify the user of the analysis

Examination questions will usually identify the type of user for whom a report is being prepared, so it is important to recognise the differences between users and their needs. It is important that any analysis and interpretation exercise is oriented towards the needs of the particular user who requires a report.

There is a wide range of user groups that may be interested in an entity's financial statements. Historically the financial statements have been prepared for investors. However, other users will also be interested in them.

Users of financial statements

Present and potential investors

Both present and potential investors are interested in information that is useful in making buy/sell/hold decisions. Will the entity be able to generate cash in the future? How risky is the investment? Does its financial performance exceed that of other potential investee entities? How much is the investment likely to yield in capital growth and/or dividend? Analysis of the financial statements can help to answer these questions. There is a range of ratios of particular interest to the investor group; these are examined in detail later in this chapter. In addition, return on capital employed (ROCE) and related performance and asset management ratios are likely to be of interest to this group of users.

Lenders and potential lenders

Lenders are principally interested in assessing whether or not the loans that they have made are likely to be repaid, and whether or not the related interest charge will be paid in full and on time. Potential lenders require analysis of financial statements in order to assist them in deciding whether or not to lend. Lender groups are likely to be particularly interested in ratios such as interest cover and gearing, and will be interested in the nature and longevity of other categories of loan to the entity.

Suppliers and other creditors

This group is interested in information that helps them to decide whether or not to supply goods or services to an entity. Availability of cash will be of particular interest, together with such evidence as is available in general-purpose financial statements about the entity's record in paying its creditors on time. Working capital ratios, and the working capital cycle, may be appropriate calculations to undertake when analysing financial statements for the benefit of this class of user.

Employees

In large organisations employees are likely to be particularly interested in one part of the entity's operations. They may, therefore, find segmental information to be useful. More generally, they need to be able to assess the stability and performance of the entity in order to gauge how reliable it is likely to be as a source of employment in the longer term. Employees are likely to be interested in disclosures about retirement benefits and remuneration.

Customers

Customers may be in a vulnerable position if there are few potential suppliers in a market for goods. They may therefore be interested in assessing the risks which threaten their supplier. Potentially they may be interested in takeover opportunities in order to ensure the continuing supply of a particular raw material.

Governments and their agencies

The governmental group is in a position to require special-purpose reports. Tax computations would fall into this category. However, general-purpose reports may also be of use, for example in gathering statistics on particular industries.

The general public

Members of the public may have special interests in the activities of certain entities, especially where, say, an individual entity dominates the local employment market. Pressure groups and their members would also fall under the umbrella category of 'general public', and their needs will vary according to their special interest. Environmental issues are of increasing concern to many people, and it is likely that pressure groups will take a particular interest in firms that are perceived as polluters. Analysis of the financial statements for this type of user would tend to focus on any additional voluntary disclosures made about the entity's environmental policies, on provisions and contingent liabilities related to environmental damage, and on capital investment (e.g. investment in new plant).

4 Understand the entity

It is often thought that financial analysis involves purely the application of a standard set of numerical calculations to a set of published accounts. This is only one part of the task. In order to interpret those calculations it is important to understand the entity's current position.

The history of the entity underlies the current position and future outlook. Furthermore, the owners and their individual characteristics will influence factors such as the level of risk in the entity and dividend policy. Knowledge of the quality, qualifications and experience of management will assist in evaluating the performance and position of the entity.

Financial analysis requires an understanding of the products, services and operating characteristics of the entity. This will assist in understanding data such as revenue, profitability, inventories and working capital.

The entity operates within an industry consisting of entities with similar operating characteristics. If the analysis requires comparison of the entity with the industry norms, it is important to identify the key characteristics of the industry and to establish benchmarks such as gross profit ratios, receivables collection days etc.

5 Identify relevant sources of data

In practice, the analyst needs to consider carefully the possible sources of information available about an entity, starting with the annual report. This will contain financial information but there may be additional voluntary disclosures that will be helpful to the analyst, such as the entity's environmental impact, employment reports, graphs, pie charts and ratio calculations.

In the Financial Management examination it will not be possible, because of time restrictions, to carry out an analysis in great depth, and there are obvious limitations on the amount of information that can be provided in an examination question. The information provided for analysis in a question is likely to include one or more of the following:

- income statement data for one or more years;
- cash flow statement data for one or more years;
- industry wide ratios and benchmarks;
- statement of financial position data for one or more years;
- budget data, and variance analysis;
- data regarding a competitor, potential subsidiary or customer applying for credit.

Working with this information and with any descriptive background provided in the question, we need to gain an understanding of the entity and the relationships between the data. Where information in the form of extracts from the financial statements is given, it is often possible (and is often specifically required by the requirements of the question) to calculate a set of financial ratios as the basis for further analysis and comment. The rest of this chapter examines numerical data analysis in the form of the most frequently used accounting ratios.

6 Calculation of ratios

Test your understanding 1 - Profitability ratios

Below are the financial statements for T for the years ended 30 June 20X5 and 20X6:

Income statements	**20X6**	**20X5**
	$000	$000
Revenue	180,000	150,000
Cost of sales	(65,000)	(60,000)
Gross profit	115,000	90,000
Operating expenses	(39,900)	(28,500)
Profit from operations	75,100	61,500
Finance costs	(12,000)	(10,000)
Profit before tax	63,100	51,500
Tax	(17,300)	(13,600)
Profit for the year	45,800	37,900

Dividends of $25m were paid to shareholders in each year.

Statements of financial position

		20X6		**20X5**
		$000		$000
Property, plant and equipment		266,200		190,000
Current assets				
Inventory	15,000		12,000	
Receivables	49,300		37,500	
Bank	–		500	
		64,300		50,000
		330,500		240,000
Share capital		12,000		10,000
Share premium		5,000		4,000
Revaluation reserve		30,000		–
Retained earnings		99,700		78,900
		146,700		92,900

		20X6	20X5
Non-current liabilities			
Loan		150,000	125,000
Current liabilities			
Trade payables	11,700	10,600	
Overdraft	9,100	–	
Taxation	13,000	11,500	
		33,800	22,100
		330,500	240,000

Required:

For each of the two years, calculate the following ratios for T and suggest reasons why the ratios have changed.

	20X6	20X5
Gross profit margin		
$\frac{\text{Gross profit}}{\text{Revenue}} \times 100\%$		
Operating profit margin		
$\frac{\text{Operating profit}}{\text{Revenue}} \times 100\%$		
Net profit margin		
$\frac{\text{Net profit}}{\text{Revenue}} \times 100\%$		
Return on capital employed		
$\frac{\text{Profit before interest}}{\text{Capital employed}} \times 100\%$		
Asset utilisation		
$\frac{\text{Revenue}}{\text{Capital employed}}$		

Capital employed = equity + borrowings

Analysing profitability ratios and data

Start by looking at the first line in the income statement: *revenue*. Has it gone up or down and what is the percentage increase or decrease? A change in revenue may be due to a change in selling price or sales volume or both.

Gross profit margin is the percentage of revenue retained after costs of sale are deducted. Entities will aim to sell many products with a low margin or potentially fewer products with a high margin. A change in gross profit margin may be due to a change in product mix, for example selling more of a product with a higher margin or conversely bringing a new product to market with a low margin to gain market share.

The *operating profit margin* is the trading or operating profit in relation to revenue, expressed as a percentage. The difference between gross profit margin and operating profit margin is the operating costs of the entity such as administration costs, telephone costs and advertising costs. You need to use any background information provided to assess how these expenses may differ to the prior year or to another entity.

Net profit margin expresses the relationship between net profit and sales. Net profit for this purpose would be profit after deduction of finance cost. It may be calculated on either pre-tax or post-tax profit.

Non-current asset policies (see Illustration 1) can have a substantial effect on ratios and comparison between entities. For example, there may be differences in whether an entity owns or leases assets and whether assets are measured at historical cost or are revalued. Depreciation charges will be higher for revalued assets. Depreciation may be categorised as a cost of sale or operating expense.

Exceptional items such as a profit on disposal of a non-current asset should be removed from the analysis to enable comparisons to be made.

Return on capital employed (ROCE) is a very useful measure when analysing performance. It assesses the efficiency with which the entity uses its assets to produce revenue and profits. You should consider any changes in capital employed and for example, whether an increase occurred towards the end of an accounting period and hence there has not yet been an opportunity for the entity to use the capital to generate increased revenue.

Asset turnover or asset utilisation is another measure of how much revenue is produced by the capital invested.

Further analysis of profitability

Revenue

Problems can arise in making a valid interpretation of movements in revenue. For example:

- Accounting policies on revenue recognition may vary between entities. There may be inconsistencies between accounting periods, especially where the entity derives some or all of its revenue from long-term contracts.
- Inflation may account for some of the increase in price.
- A detailed breakdown of revenue for the entity may not be available. To some extent IFRS 8 Operating Segments (see later in the chapter for more details) requires revenue details for different segments of the entity. However there are problems in using segmental data, for example, segments may not be consistently defined.

Understanding the reasons for movements in revenue may help to explain movements in costs such as cost of sales, advertising, selling and distribution costs and telephone charges. If revenue increases, then a similar increase in these revenue-related costs could be expected. Conversely, an increase in, say, marketing and advertising expenditure might help to explain an increase in revenue.

Gross profit margin

This ratio is expected to be more or less constant from one year to the next within an entity. Even if there is an increase in direct costs, an efficient entity could be expected to pass on the increases in the form of increased sales prices. However, this may not be the case in reality.

The gross profit margin requires a detailed breakdown in order to gain an understanding of movements. Ideally, the analyst requires information relating to opening and closing inventories, purchases, direct wages and overheads. Further information as to the following items would be required in order to evaluate gross profit margin fully:

- breakdown by product, geographical area or other segment;
- inventory valuation policies;
- overhead allocation methods;
- purchasing details such as bulk discounts, purchasing errors, wastage or theft;
- selling prices of different products over the period.

Obviously, much of this information is not available from an entity's annual report. Some entities do not even report gross profits.

Operating profit margin

Operating profit is the profit from the trading activities of the business; it comprises profits after operating costs, but before finance costs, tax, investment income and any share of profits from an associate. Note that IAS 1 revised does not encourage the reporting of operating profit as a separate line item, although there is nothing to prevent entities providing additional information. It is likely, though that in many cases it will not be possible to calculate operating profit margin.

Net profit margin

Where comparing net profit year on year, it is important to allow for any exceptional charges or credits. Also, it would be sensible to take into account any large adjustments in respect of under- or over-provided tax provisions.

Return on capital employed

Return on capital employed (ROCE) is a measurement that is frequently used in the analysis of financial statements. This shows the overall performance of the entity, expressed as a percentage return on the total investment. It measures management's efficiency in generating profits from the resources available.

For the purposes of the ROCE measurement, capital employed is equity (including share capital, reserves and NCI) and interest bearing borrowings.

It is important in this type of calculation that the numerator and denominator should be consistent. Therefore, in calculating ROCE, the numerator should include profit before any deductions for finance costs. If capital employed includes a bank overdraft, the profit figure used in the calculation should exclude interest paid and payable on the overdraft.

Exam questions will often include an Associate in the financial statements being analysed. To deal with this you should exclude the share of profit of the associate from the profit figure (the numerator) and should deduct the carrying value of the investment in associate from the capital employed (the denominator). An example of this can be seen in TYU 4 later in this chapter.

Asset turnover / asset utilisation

This calculation is usually expressed as a simple ratio, rather than as a percentage. It shows how much revenue is produced per unit of capital invested.

This ratio shows the productivity of assets in generating sales. It should be noted that this ratio is not always useful or informative. Where an entity is using assets that are nearing the end of their useful lives, having been subject to annual depreciation charges over a relatively long period, the ratio is likely to be rather high. Similarly, where an entity uses the historical cost convention, unmodified by revaluation, asset values are also likely to be relatively low, an effect which is more intrusive as the assets age. Also, in labour-intensive entities, where the non-current asset base is low, the ratio tends to lack significance.

Note that, where possible, the average asset figure over the year should be used in the denominator of the fraction. This is likely to give a more consistent and representative result. External users of annual reports do not have access to monthly information with which to calculate an average, but opening and closing figures often give a reasonable approximation.

EBITDA

EBITDA is an acronym for earnings before interest, tax, depreciation and amortisation.

In recent years many large entities have adopted EBITDA as a key measure of financial performance. Sceptics suggest that they do this in order to publicise a higher measure of earnings than profit from operations (this type of measurement is sometimes cynically referred to as EBB – earnings before the bad bits).

However, it does make some sense to measure EBITDA, provided that the user fully understands what is included and what is left out. Depreciation and amortisation are accounting adjustments, not representing cash flows, that are determined by management. It can therefore be argued that excluding these items in assessing earnings eliminates a major area where management bias can operate.

Unfortunately, EBITDA is consequently often misunderstood as being a measurement of cash flow, which of course it is not. Even though two categories of non-cash adjustment are eliminated, financial statements are prepared on an accruals basis. EBITDA makes no adjustments in respect of accruals or working capital movements, and so is emphatically not a cash flow measurement.

Illustration 1 - Effect of non-current asset policies on ratios

The following information has been extracted from the financial statements of A for the year ended 30 September 20X4:

	A	B	C
Income statement	$000	$000	$000
Revenue	200	200	200
Operating costs	(160)	(190)	(170)
Profit from operations	40	10	30
Statement of financial position			
Share capital	50	50	50
Retained earnings	90	60	50
Revaluation reserve		210	
Capital employed	140	320	100
Operating profit margin	20%	5%	15%
Asset utilisation	1.43	0.63	2
Return on capital employed	28.6%	3.1%	30%

Entity A

A had purchased an asset costing $200,000 4 years ago. The asset is being depreciated on the straight-line basis over 10 years. Therefore, $20,000 of depreciation has been charged to this year's income statement and the asset has a carrying value of $120,000 in the statement of financial position.

B and C as entities hold a similar asset to A but have adopted the following treatments in their financial statements. They are identical to A in all other respects.

Entity B

B revalued the asset to its current value of $350,000 at the start of the current year. As a result a revaluation gain of $210,000 has been recognised and depreciation has been increased to $50,000 per annum, i.e. additional depreciation of $30,000 has been charged to the income statement in the current year.

The revaluation has caused the operating profit margin to fall due to the extra depreciation. Asset utilisation has also fallen due to the revaluation reserve being included in capital employed.

Hence the entity looks to be generating a lower return.

Entity C

C has been leasing the asset under an operating lease agreement, paying an annual rental of $30,000 which has been charged to operating expenses.

This causes the operating profit margin to fall due to the lease payments being higher than depreciation. However, the asset utilisation is higher than A since the asset is not included on the statement of financial position but is still being used by the business to generate sales.

Test your understanding 2 - Liquidity ratios

Required:

Using the financial statements provided for T in TYU 1, calculate the following ratios for T and suggest why the ratios may have changed.

	20X6	20X5
Current ratio		
$\frac{\text{Current assets}}{\text{Current liabilities}}$		
Quick ratio		
$\frac{\text{(Current assets – Inventory)}}{\text{Current liabilities}}$		

Inventory holding period

$$\frac{\text{Inventory}}{\text{Cost of sales}} \times 365 \text{ days}$$

Receivables collection period

$$\frac{\text{Receivables}}{\text{Revenue}} \times 365 \text{ days}$$

Payables payment period

$$\frac{\text{Trade payables}}{\text{Cost of Sales}} \times 365 \text{ days}$$

Analysing liquidity ratios and data

The analysis of the liquidity of an entity should start with a review of the actual *bank balance* in absolute terms. Has the bank balance increased or decreased significantly? It could be that the overdraft is near to its permitted limit or that high cash resources indicate a good takeover prospect.

The *current ratio* compares current assets to current liabilities. A ratio greater than 1 indicates there are more current assets than current liabilities. The current ratio guides us to the extent the entity is able to meet its current liabilities as they fall due.

The *quick ratio* compares current assets, excluding inventory, to current liabilities. The quick ratio gives a better indicator of liquidity if the inventory of an entity is difficult to realise into cash, for example, a whisky distillery that requires a number of months to mature before being sold.

The *inventory holding period* indicates how much working capital is tied up in goods in the warehouse by giving an average number of days that inventory is held before being sold. An entity must balance the need to supply goods on time to customers with the risk of obsolescence.

The *receivables collection period* tells us the number of days it takes on average to receive payment from credit customers. It should be based on the credit agreement with customers. Cash should be collected efficiently whilst bearing in mind customers in a strong negotiating position.

The *payables payment period* is the length of time it takes to pay suppliers for goods bought on credit. This is effectively a free source of finance but the business should make sure suppliers are paid on a timely basis to avoid the risk of stock-outs.

When an entity is growing rapidly there may be a risk of *overtrading,* i.e. expanding the entity without adequate long term finance. Inventory, receivables and payables increase but there is a decline in cash and the entity may be unable to pay its suppliers as debts fall due.

You must also be aware of liquidity issues not reflected on the statement of financial position, for example contingent liabilities.

Further analysis of liquidity

Short term liquidity

The quick ratio recognises that the time taken to convert inventory into cash in many entities is significantly longer than other current assets and so gives a more conservative view of liquidity. However, it is important to select ratios suitable for the circumstances of the entity. If inventory is an insignificant amount (as it would be, for example, in most service entities), there is little point in calculating the quick ratio.

There is no standard number that should be expected in these calculations; it should depend on the industry and should be linked to other areas of the analysis. The higher the ratio, the more liquid the entity, but high liquidity can itself be a problem. It may mean that the entity is unable to utilise cash effectively by investing it profitably.

The working capital cycle

The length of the working capital cycle can assist in determining the immediate effects of the financial position on the bank balance.

The working capital cycle comprises cash, receivables, inventory and payables. The entity uses cash to buy inventory. Additional inventory may be purchased on credit.

Inventories are sold and become receivables. Receivables pay and then the entity has cash available to repay payables or buy further inventory.

The total length of the working capital cycle is the inventory turnover days plus the receivables days less the payables days, which approximates to the total time it takes to purchase the inventory, sell the inventory and receive cash.

Inventory holding period

The ratio gives the number of days that inventory, on average, has remained in the warehouse. If only a closing figure is available for inventory, then that can be used. However, the result must be treated with some caution, as the closing figure may be unrepresentative, particularly if the nature of the entity's business is seasonal.

Receivables days

A retail or cash-based entity may have zero or very low receivables days. Note that, where an entity sells for both cash and on credit, it will be necessary to split revenue into the two types.

Payables days

Current payables comprise a form of finance which is free, or almost free. However, there may be costs in terms of loss of prompt payment discount, and loss of supplier goodwill where excessive time is taken to pay. Efficiency is measured relative to industry norms, receivables days and supplier terms.

To calculate the working capital cycle, if figures are not available for credit sales and credit purchases (as may well be the case if the data source is a set of published accounts) an approximation may be obtained by using total revenue and cost of sales respectively, but the results of such ratio calculations must be treated with caution.

Test your understanding 3 - Capital structure ratios

Required:

Using the financial statements provided for T in TYU 1, calculate the following ratios for T and suggest why the ratios may have changed.

	20X6	20X5
Gearing		
$\frac{\text{Debt}}{\text{Debt + Equity}}$		
Gearing (alternative)		
$\frac{\text{Debt}}{\text{Equity}}$		

Interest cover

$$\frac{\text{Profit before interest}}{\text{Finance costs}}$$

Dividend cover

$$\frac{\text{Net profit}}{\text{Dividends}}$$

Analysing capital structure ratios and data

Gearing is an important measure of risk and a guide to the long term solvency of the entity. It is calculated by taking long term debt as a percentage of total capital employed, i.e. long term debt plus shareholders' funds. Alternatively it can be calculated by taking debt as a percentage of equity, or shareholders' funds. Make your calculation clear in the exam.

It is important to assess the gearing ratio against the *industry average* and to ensure that the debt finance is put to good use to generate revenue and profits.

The interest charged on debt finance should be compared to *interest rates* available to the entity from other sources. Also, debt is often *secured on assets* for security so there needs to be sufficient assets for this to be possible.

Interest cover indicates the number of times profits will cover the interest charge; the higher the ratio, the better. When looking at interest cover, the *stability of profits* is important as the interest must be paid consistently out of available profits otherwise the entity may default on its debt and may have to repay it at short notice.

Dividend cover indicates the number of times profits will cover the dividend; the higher the ratio, the better as shareholders may expect a sustainable dividend payment.

Further analysis of capital structure

The gearing (or leverage) ratio is an important measure of risk.

It is important to analyse, particularly for users such as shareholders and creditors, the ability to satisfy debts falling due after one year. There are two elements to consider: repayment of capital and payment of interest. The statement of financial position shows the current liquidity and capital structure of the entity, that is the short-term liquidity and the level of fixed prior charge capital.

The income statement shows the profitability of the business generally, indicating its ability to generate cash, some of which may be available to repay debt.

The capital structure of the entity provides information about the relative risk that is accepted by shareholders and creditors. As long-term debt increases relative to shareholders' funds, then more risk is assumed by long-term creditors and so they would require higher rewards, thereby decreasing resources available for the shareholders. As risk increases, creditors require higher interest in order to compensate for the higher risk.

However, the use of debt by management in their capital structure can assist in increasing profits available to shareholders. Cash received into the entity from lenders will be used to generate revenue and profits. As interest costs are fixed, any profits generated in excess of the interest costs will accrue to the shareholders. There is, however, a negative side to the use of debt in the entity. If the cash from the debt does not raise sufficient profits then the fixed interest cost must be paid first and so profits available to shareholders are decreased, and may be extinguished completely.

Gearing

Gearing is calculated by taking long term debt as a percentage of total capital employed, i.e. long term debt plus shareholders' funds. Long-term debt includes debentures, mortgages and other long-term debt, including preference shares. Any bank overdraft would be included to the extent that it is actually a source of long-term finance. Shareholders' funds comprises equity share capital and reserves.

Interest cover

Although the use of debt may generate higher profits for shareholders there is a limit to its use. This may be gauged from the income statement by focusing on the profitability and interest repayments in the interest cover ratio.

Illustration 2 - High gearing can be beneficial to shareholders

	Alpha		Beta	
	20X1	**20X2**	**20X1**	**20X2**
Income statements	$	$	$	$
Profit from operations	20,000	25,000	20,000	25,000
Finance cost	(1,000)	(1,000)	(4,000)	(4,000)
Profit before tax	19,000	24,000	16,000	21,000
Income tax	(5,700)	(7,200)	(4,800)	(6,300)
Profit for the year	13,300	16,800	11,200	14,700
Dividends paid (5c per share)	2,000	2,000	500	500
Statements of financial position				
10% Loan notes	10,000	10,000	40,000	40,000
Share capital $1 ordinary shares	40,000	40,000	10,000	10,000
Reserves	50,000	53,500	50,000	53,500
Capital employed	100,000	103,500	100,000	103,500

Beta is more highly geared than Alpha in 20X1, but both companies have the same amount of capital employed in total and generate the same returns overall:

	Alpha	Beta
	20X1	**20X1**
Gearing (Debt/ debt + equity)	10%	40%
ROCE (Operating profit/ debt + equity)	20%	20%

In 20X2 there is a 25% increase in the operating profits of both companies. However the shareholders of Beta benefit more than the shareholders of Alpha:

	Alpha		Beta	
	20X1	**20X2**	**20X1**	**20X2**
Return on equity (Net profit/ equity)	14.8%	18.0%	18.7%	23.1%
Increase on prior year		+21.6%		+23.5%
Earnings per share (see chapter 3) (Net profit/ no. of shares)	33.25c	42c	112c	147c
Increase on prior year		+26.3%		+31.25%

Analysing investor ratios and data

When appraising an entity as a potential investment, all the ratios discussed above may be used. This information may be supplemented by further ratios specifically for investors.

The market price of an ordinary share is often used in this analysis.

Price earnings ratio

A common benchmark for investors analysing different entities is the use of the price/earnings (P/E) ratio:

$$\frac{\text{Current market price per share}}{\text{Earnings per share}}$$

Earnings per share is basically the earnings available for distribution divided by the number of ordinary shares in issue. The calculation of earnings per share is covered in detail in Chapter 3.

The P/E ratio calculation produces a number which can be useful for assessing the relative risk of an investment.

Illustration 3 - P/E ratios

	V	W
Current market price per share	396c	288c
Most recent earnings per share	13.4c	35.6c
P/E ratio	29.6	8.1

W has much higher earnings per share than V, but the price of one share in W is lower than one share in V, giving rise to two very different P/E ratios. Generally, the lower the P/E ratio the greater the indication of risk for the investor.

The rational expectations of buyers and sellers in the stock market tend to be incorporated in the price of the share. The P/E ratios of these entities tend to suggest that the market considers investment in W to be riskier than investment in V.

There may be reasons to account for this difference, for example:

- The numerator of the fraction is current (an up-to-date market price can be obtained easily during the market's opening hours), but the EPS figure is the latest available which, for a listed entity in many markets, can be up to 6 months old. The EPS of either entity may therefore be quite significantly out of date.
- W may have issued a profits warning, or might have suffered adverse events, such as, for example, the loss of a major contract or the resignation of a key director. These events may have depressed the share price.
- W may be in a sector which is unfashionable or relatively undervalued.
- W may have had a difficult recent history with a volatile pattern of earnings. On the whole, markets prefer companies with a smooth profit record.

As usual, the process of analysis leads to demands for more information. A better picture could be obtained of V and W if share price graphs for the last year, for example, were available, so that the analyst could see whether the share prices quoted above are near to average or not.

Dividend related ratios

Growth potential and the ability to generate future wealth in the entity may depend on the amount of profits retained. This relationship may be measured using the *profit retention ratio*:

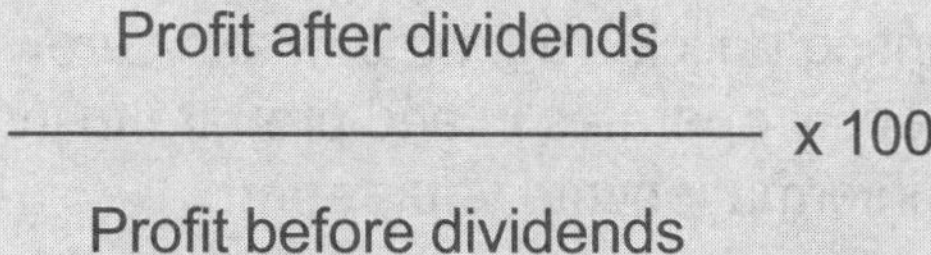

$$\frac{\text{Profit after dividends}}{\text{Profit before dividends}} \times 100$$

The higher the proportion of earnings retained, the higher the growth potential. Cash is retained in the entity for growth as opposed to being paid to shareholders.

When analysing financial statements from an investor's point of view it is important to identify the objectives of the investor. Does the investor require high capital growth, usually associated with high risk, or a lower risk fixed dividend payment and low capital growth?

Dividend yield will indicate the return on capital investment, relative to market price:

$$\frac{\text{Dividend per share}}{\text{Market price per share}} \times 100$$

Dividend cover measures the ability of the entity to maintain the existing level of dividend and is used in conjunction with the dividend yield:

$$\frac{\text{Earnings per share}}{\text{Dividends per share}}$$

The higher the dividend cover, the more likely it is that the dividend yield can be maintained.

7 Approach to a question

It is important in your studies and ultimately in the examination to develop an approach to analysis questions to make sure your answer is coherent and addresses the specific requirement you are given in the question.

You should use the approach detailed below when answering this style of question.

(1) Read the requirement, ensuring you identify any specific requirements, e.g. discuss which entity is most suitable to acquire. Identify the user of the report and what their needs are.

(2) Read the information, identifying specific information, e.g. what entity does, accounting policies adopted. Make sure you understand what industry the entity operates in and prepare to incorporate the background information into your report.

(3) Perform a high level analytical review of the financial information provided:

Statement of financial position

Non-current assets	Revaluations, additions
Current assets & current liabilities	Significant movements
Non-current liabilities	Loans issued, repaid
Share capital	Share issues
Reserves	Revaluations

Income statement

Revenue/ net profit	Growth or decline, in line or disparity
Gross/ operating profit	Growth or decline in line with revenue
Interest	Relationship with loans, overdraft
Additional information provided	How will it be useful to requirement?

(4) Calculate ratios as an appendix to your report. See below for advice on using ratios in the exam.

(5) Prepare report - see next section.

It is important that candidates read the additional information in the context of the scenario presented. This often provides further insight into the obstacles facing/changes to the entity under scrutiny. At the very least this should guide observations (and, if required, the choice of ratios calculated) to ensure responses are applied, rather than just robotic. It is also important that candidates do not hypothesise about a subject, only to find their assumptions are contradicted by the additional information.

Using ratios in the exam

When answering a Financial Management question it is important to be able to calculate ratios with a fair degree of accuracy from the information provided. However, students should bear in mind the following points:

- Only a proportion of the marks will be awarded for calculation, and this proportion may be relatively small. Generally, the majority of the marks will be awarded for the analysis and interpretation of data given in the question. Therefore, it is important not to get too absorbed in the calculations themselves; they are a means to an end. So far the calculations have been introduced; the next sections look at the interpretation and analysis of financial statements.
- Where a question asks for calculation of, say, 'relevant ratios', it is best to be fairly selective. Calculating the full range of ratios, as given in this chapter, may be inappropriate for the circumstances of the question. Time can be wasted in calculating ratios that are really not very useful.
- Some ratios may be of limited use, or may even be misleading in the context of service entities. For example, care should be taken in respect of return on capital ratios in entities with a low level of conventional non-current assets but a high level of unrecognised intellectual capital 'assets'.
- It is appropriate to round to no more than one decimal place.

- The selection of ratios is important. Do not just select the same ratios that were used in a different question or favoured ratios; this will inevitably lead to a vague/generalised response. Select ratios that are appropriate to the circumstances of the scenario and the audience of your report. For example: if you are responding to a bank then liquidity and gearing ratios are likely to be of prime importance. If you are responding to a potential shareholder then dividend ratios and EPS are likely to be key.

8 Preparing a report

Format

If the requirement asks for a report then ensure that you format your answer in a report style, i.e. use headings for To, From, Date and Subject. When addressing your report to somebody, think about who the report is for and what their needs are.

Introduction

Add a brief introduction to identify the purpose of the report using the requirement given in the question.

Body of the report

This is the most important part of your answer. Use the points below to make it as clear and succinct as possible whilst ensuring you remember to state why something has changed in the entity. Make sure you use the word because...! (See examiner's article on www.cimaglobal.com "Examiner's guide to passing F2.")

- Structure your answer with headings, e.g. performance, liquidity, capital structure or financial position and performance
- Use short paragraphs and sentences, but use proper English! Make one well explained point per paragraph.
- Explain why ratios have changed and the implication/ recommendations/ timescales involved.
- Ensure your discussion refers to the information in the scenario.

Conclusion

Make sure you add a brief conclusion, particularly if there is a question identified in the requirement, e.g. should we invest?

Appendix

Calculate any ratios required on a separate page. These ratios can be referred to in your report.

9 Limitations of analysis of financial statements

There are limitations to the analysis that can be performed when given an annual report or in examination questions. Sometimes it may be necessary to discuss these limitations.

It is important to answer the question requirement carefully, i.e. are you asked for limitations of financial information or the limitations of using ratios for analysis? It is also important to make your answer specific to the entity in question, if you are provided with one.

Limitations of financial reporting information

- Only provide historic data.
- Only provide financial information.
- Filed at least 3 months after reporting date reducing its relevance.
- Limited information to be able to identify trends over time.
- Lack of detailed information.
- Historic cost accounting does not take into account inflation.

Difficulties in drawing comparisons between different entities

- Comparisons affected by changes in the entity's business, for example selling an operation.
- Different accounting policies between different entities, e.g. revaluations.
- Different accounting practices between different entities, e.g. debt factoring, lease v buy decisions.
- Different entities within the same industry may have different activities.
- Non co-terminous accounting periods.
- Different entities may not be comparable in terms of size.
- Comparisons between entities operating in different countries will be influenced by different legal and regulatory systems, the relative strength and weakness of the national economy and exchange rate fluctuations.

Limitations of ratio analysis

- Where ratios have been provided, there may be discrepancies between how they have been calculated for each entity/period, e.g. gearing.
- Distortions when using year-end figures, particularly in seasonal industries and when entities have different accounting dates.
- Distortions due to not being able to use most appropriate figures, e.g. total sales revenue rather than credit sales when calculating receivables days.
- It is difficult to identify reasons behind ratio movements without significant additional information.

Creative accounting

- Timing of transactions may be delayed/speeded up to improve results, e.g. not investing in non-current assets to ensure ROCE does not fall.
- Profit smoothing using choices allowed, e.g. inventory valuation method.
- Classification of items, e.g. expenses v non-current assets; ordinary v exceptional.
- Off-balance sheet financing to improve gearing and ROCE.
- Revenue recognition policies.
- Managing market expectations.

These are, of course, generic limitations that are not necessarily applicable to all entities in all circumstances. In an exam situation limitations must be applied to the unique traits of an entity, for example: if you are asked to compare two entities it makes sense to consider whether they use the same accounting policies (e.g. depreciation rates) and business methods (e.g. acquiring or leasing assets). Please refer to the following expandable text sections for further guidance on these areas.

Limitations of financial reporting information

The objective of financial statements is set out in the IASB's Conceptual Framework for Financial Reporting, published in September 2010:

"The objective of general purpose financial reporting is to provide financial information about the reporting entity that is useful to existing and potential investors, lenders and other creditors in making decisions about providing resources to the entity."

A rather substantial limitation of financial statements, is, however, then explained in the following paragraphs:

"... general purpose financial reports do not and cannot provide all of the information that existing and potential investors, lenders and other creditors need. Those users need to consider pertinent information from other sources, for example, general economic conditions and expectations, political events and political climate, and industry and company outlooks.

Other parties, such as regulators and members of the public other than investors, lenders and other creditors, may also find general purpose financial reports useful. However, those reports are not primarily directed to these other groups."

It appears that although financial statements may be useful to a wide range of users, their usefulness is limited. The principal drawback is the fact that financial statements are oriented towards events that have already taken place. However, there are other significant limitations of the information contained in a set of financial statements. These can be summarised under the following principal headings.

Timeliness

By the time financial statements are received by users, 2 or 3 months or longer may have elapsed since the year end date. The earliest of the transactions that contribute to the income and expense items accumulated in the income statement will have taken place probably 15 or more months previously.

In some jurisdictions there may be a requirement for large, listed entities to produce half-yearly or even quarterly financial statements. Where these are available, the timeliness problem is reduced. However, the comprehensiveness of the information may be limited in comparison to what is produced in the annual report. For example, quarterly statements may include only an income statement without a statement of financial position or statement of changes in equity. Also, it is possible that they will have not been subject to verification in the form of audit.

Comparability

Comparisons over time for one entity

Comparisons over time between the financial statements of the same entity may prove to be invalid, or only partially valid, because significant changes have taken place in the entity. The disclosure provisions of IFRS 5 Non-current Assets Held for Sale and Discontinued Operations may assist the analyst if the entity plans to sell an operation. However, it may not be possible to discern the effect of other significant changes. For example, an entity that makes an investment in a new non-current item, say a major addition to its production facilities coupled with a significant increase in working capital, is not obliged to disclose any information about how well or badly the new investment has performed.

The analyst may, for example, be able to see that the entity's profitability overall has decreased, but the explanations could be as follows:

- The investment has proved to be very successful, but its success is offset by the rapidly declining profitability of other parts of the entity's productive capacity. As these elements are gradually replaced over the next 2 or 3 years, profitability is likely to increase overall.
- The investment has proved to be less successful than expected and is producing no better a return than the worn-out machinery it replaced.
- Although productive capacity has increased, the quality of goods overall has declined, and the entity has not been able to maintain its margins.

Financial statements simply do not provide sufficient information to permit the analyst to see these finer points of detail.

Comparisons over time and inflation

Comparability over time is often threatened by the effects of price inflation. This can, paradoxically, be particularly insidious where the general rate of inflation in the economy is comparatively low because analysts and others are not conscious of the effect. For example, suppose that the rate of price inflation applicable to a particular entity has been around 2.5 per cent per year over a 5-year period. Sales in 20X3 were reported at $100,000. A directly comparable level of sales in 20X4 would be $102,500 ($100,000 x 1.025). Therefore, sales in 20X4 would have to have increased to more than $102,500 before any real increase could be claimed. However, the analyst, seeing the two figures alongside each other on the income statement, and knowing that inflation is running at a low level, may very well not take this factor into account.

Differences in accounting policy and accounting practices

Changes in accounting policy and accounting practices may affect comparability over time in the same entity. Also, when comparing the financial statements of two or more entities, it is really quite likely that there will be some differences in accounting policy and/or practice between them.

The type of differences which make comparisons difficult include the following:

- Different approaches to valuation of non-current assets, as permitted under IAS 16 Property, Plant and Equipment. An entity that revalues its non-current assets on a regular basis, as permitted by that standard, is likely to have higher carrying values for its assets than an entity that carries non-current assets at depreciated historical cost. Also, the depreciation charges of the revaluing entity are likely to be higher. The two entities are therefore not strictly comparable.
- Different classifications of expenses in the income statement. At the margins it is not always easy to decide whether or not expenses should be classified as part of cost of sales or operating expenses. If entities classify similar expenses under the different headings their gross profit margins will not be comparable.
- More or less conservative approaches to judgements about the impairment of assets. Impairment review inevitably involves some degree of estimation.

Only the first of these three items relates, strictly speaking, to an accounting policy difference. The other two relate to variations in respect of judgemental issues. Where there is a difference in formal accounting policies adopted it is, at least, possible to discern this from the financial statements and to make some kind of adjustment to achieve comparability. However, judgemental matters are almost impossible to adjust for.

Entities in the same sector

Entities may appear to be comparable in that they operate in the same business sector. However, each entity has unique features, and a particular entity may not be strictly comparable with any other. Segment disclosure does allow for a more detailed approach to comparisons, although as we will see later in the chapter:

- Not all entities are required by accounting standards to make segment disclosures.
- Identifying segments is, necessarily, a judgmental matter. It is quite possible that one entity would identify a particular part of its business as a reportable segment, whereas another would not make the same judgement.

Non co-terminous accounting periods

Financial statements are prepared to a particular date annually. The annual financial statements of an entity with a year end of 31 December are not strictly comparable with those of an entity with a June year end. The difference is only 6 months, but significant events may have occurred in the industry or the economy as a whole that affect the statements prepared to the later date but not those prepared to the earlier date.

Size of the entity

It may be inappropriate to compare two entities of very different sizes, or to compare a listed with a non-listed entity. A large entity may be able to take advantage of economies of scale that are unavailable to the small entity, but that is not to say that the smaller entity is inefficient. It may, relatively speaking, be a better manager of the resources available to it. Conversely, a smaller entity may be able to react more rapidly to changes in economic conditions, because it can be easier to effect radical change in that environment.

Listed entities are subject to a great deal of additional regulation and their activities are far more likely than those of an unlisted entity to attract media coverage. Their share prices are widely advertised and are sensitive to alterations in market perceptions. It can be less acceptable for a listed entity to take risks or any course of action that might affect a regular flow of dividends to shareholders. By contrast, an unlisted entity whose shares are held by a limited number of people may be able to make investment decisions that result in a curtailment of dividends in the short term in exchange for projected higher returns in the long-term. So, operational flexibility varies between entities, and this may mean that their financial statements are not really comparable, or at least, that comparisons must be treated with caution.

Verification

Although regulations relating to audit vary from one country to another, it is likely that, in most jurisdictions, the financial statements of larger entities are audited. However, smaller entities' financial statements may not be subject to audit, and so the analyst has no external report on their validity or the fairness of their presentation.

International issues

Where the financial statements of entities based in different countries are being compared, there may be further sources of difference in addition to those already covered in this section.

- The entities may be subject to differing tax regimes.
- The financial statements may be based on different legal and regulatory systems. For example, traditionally, German, French and Spanish financial statements have been prepared in accordance with tax regulation (so, e.g. the depreciation allowances provided for in the financial statements are exactly those allowable for tax purposes). The preparation of British and Irish financial statements, by contrast, is focused much more upon the objective of achieving a true and fair view, and the link between accounts for tax purposes and accounts for filing and presentation purposes has been relatively weak.
- The relative strengths and weaknesses of a national economy, and of the exchange rate relating to its national currency, may produce cyclical differences in the profitability of business entities. These effects may have the result of reducing comparability of the financial statements of two entities located in different countries.

Provision of non-financial information

It was noted earlier in this section: '… financial reports do not and cannot provide all the information that existing and potential investors, lenders and other creditors need to make decisions' (the IASB's Conceptual Framework for Financial Reporting). Major listed entities have tended, in recent years, to provide more non-financial information in their financial statements, and it is increasingly common to find disclosures relating to, for example, environmental issues. However, there is a dearth of regulation relating to non-financial disclosure, and users cannot rely on finding a consistent level of high quality information in annual reports. This concept is explored further in chapter 11 "Developments in external reporting."

Limitations of ratio analysis

Calculation method

The only accounting ratio to have a prescribed method of calculation is earnings per share which is regulated through IAS 33 Earnings per share (see chapter 3). In respect of some of the other accounting ratios, there may be more than one valid method of calculation. There are, for example, two perfectly valid approaches to the calculation of gearing. When making comparisons between financial statements it is important to ensure that the same method of calculation is used consistently, otherwise the comparison will not be valid.

Reliability

Many ratios are calculated using average figures. Often the average is based on only two figures: the opening and closing. However, these may not be representative of a true average figure, and so any ratios calculated on the basis of such a figure will be unreliable. This effect is noticeable in entities with seasonal operations. For example, suppose that an artificial Christmas tree business starts building up its inventory from a low point at the beginning of February, gradually accumulating in order to build up to a maximum level at the beginning of November. Eighty-five per cent of its annual sales total is made in November and December.

If the entity has an accounting year end of 31 January (which would make sense as there's not much going on at the time of year), inventory will be at its lowest level. (Opening inventory + closing inventory)/2 will certainly produce an average inventory figure but it will not be representative of the entity's level of activity in the intervening months.

The idea of the norm

Sometimes we attempt to set norms for ratios: for example, that the current ratio should ideally be around 2, or 1.5 or 2.5. However, setting norms is both unrealistic and unhelpful. Some types of successful entity can, and do, operate successfully with a substantial excess of current liabilities over current assets. Such entities typically sell for cash, so don't have receivables, turn over their inventory very quickly (perhaps because it's perishable) but manage to take the maximum amounts of credit from their suppliers.

Inappropriate use of ratios

Not all ratios are useful or applicable in all business situations and the analyst must take care over the selection of ratios to use. For example, an entity may have a mixture of cash and credit sales, but it would normally not be possible to distinguish between them armed only with the information included in the annual financial statements. However, seeing a line for revenue and a line for receivables, the analyst (or student) might assume that it was therefore sensible to work out the number of days sales represented by receivables. The ratio would be inaccurate and the analyst could be seriously misled by it.

Limited usefulness of ratios

Mostly, the calculation and analysis of ratios simply leads to more questions and these cannot necessarily be answered where information is limited. Ratios, and more importantly their analysis, may contribute to an understanding of a entity's business operations but quite often they simply lead to more questions.

A related point is that stand-alone ratios are generally of very limited use. The analyst may be able to calculate that a business's gross profit percentage is 14.3 per cent for a particular year. In isolation, that piece of information is really quite useless. It's reassuring to know that the entity has actually made a positive gross profit, but without comparators, it's hard to say much more than that.

Creative accounting

Defining the nature and scope of creative accounting is not straightforward. Despite the best efforts of accounting regulators there remains wide scope for the use of judgement in matters such as the determination of useful lives of assets and allowances for irrecoverable receivables.

The term 'creative accounting' is commonly used to suggest a rather suspicious approach to accounting. It carries connotations of manipulation of figures, deliberate structuring of series of transactions and exploitation of loopholes in the rules.

Methods employed by creative accountants

Financial statements can be manipulated in many ways, some more acceptable than others. Methods include the following:

Altering the timing of transactions

For example, the despatch of sales orders could be hurried up or delayed just before the year end to either increase or decrease sales for the reporting period. Other examples include delaying sales of non-current assets and the timing of research and development expenditure. If an entity needs to improve its results it may decide upon a lower level of research and development activity in the short term in order to reduce costs. Delaying the replacement of worn-out assets falls into the same category. Some people would regard this type of 'manipulation' as falling outside the definition of creative accounting.

Artificial smoothing

This approach involves the exploitation of the elements of choice that exist in accounting regulation. Although the IASB has worked hard to reduce the number of allowed alternative treatments, there remains some scope for artificial adjustments in respect of, for example, the choice of inventory valuation method, the estimated useful lives of non-current assets, and the choice between valuation of non-current assets at revalued amounts or depreciated historical cost that is permitted by IAS 16 Property, Plant and Equipment.

A change in accounting policy would, of course, have to be noted in the year in which it occurs, but its effects are not so easily discernible after that first year.

Classification

One of the grey areas that persists in accounting is the classification of debit items as either expenses of the current year or as non-current assets. If items are classified as non-current assets they do not impact (unless they are depreciated) on the reported income for the period.

One of the best known cases of mis-classification in recent years occurred in the US long-distance phone company WorldCom. Over a 3-year period the entity improperly reported $3.8 billion of expenses as non-current assets, thus providing a considerable boost to reported earnings. The entity is also reported as having manipulated provisions in order to increase reported earnings. In this particular case, the scale of the irregularities has been such that senior officers are currently being prosecuted for fraud.

Other areas of the financial statements which provide opportunities for creative accounting via classification include the categorisation of expenses and income as exceptional and the decisions about classification as reportable segments where the entity is required to undertake segment reporting.

Exclusion of liabilities

Under-reporting liabilities in the statement of financial position can help to improve accounting ratios. For example, the calculation of gearing would be affected and total capital employed would be reduced, so that return on total capital employed would appear to be higher. Entities have sometimes been able to take advantage of loopholes in accounting regulation to arrange off-balance sheet financing in the form of subsidiary undertakings that are technically excluded from consolidation. This was demonstrated in the Enron case, where so-called Special Purpose Entities were set up to provide finance to the business; these SPEs were, however, excluded from consolidation so that their liabilities did not appear in the group financial statements. Regulations have been revised to make this more difficult, with the recent introduction of IFRS 10: *Consolidated Financial Statements* being an example. However, off-balance sheet financing remains a problem.

The analyst must read the notes to the financial statements carefully to be aware of any contingencies. A contingent liability is where the probability of occurrence is less than 50% but it is not remote. Where an item is noted as a contingent liability together with a note of the estimated financial impact, it may be useful to calculate the impact on the entity's liquidity and to work out accounting ratios both with and without the item.

Recognition of revenue

Aggressive accounting often exploits revenue recognition rules. Some examples of inappropriate revenue recognition include:

- recognising revenue from sales that are made conditionally (i.e. where the purchaser has the right to return the goods for an extended period, or where experience shows that returns are likely);
- failing to apportion subscription revenue over the appropriate accounting periods but instead recognising it immediately;
- recognising revenue on goods shipped to agents employed by the entity;
- recognising the full amount of revenue when only partial shipments of goods have been made.

Managing market expectations

This final category of manipulation has nothing to do with massaging an entity's figures, but it does involve the way the entity presents itself to the world. Reporting by listed entities, especially in the US market, is driven very much by analysts's expectations. It may be easlier to massage their expectations rather than to improve the reported results by use of creative accounting techniques. Directors of listed entities meet analysts in briefing meetings where they have the opportunity to influence analysts' expectations by forecasting fairly poor figures. When the entity then proceeds to turn in a better result than expected, the market's view of the shares may be enhanced. This is a psychological game of bluffing which may backfire on the reporting entity if analysts become aware of what it is doing.

The motivation to use creative accounting

Various research studies have examined the issue of managerial motivation to use creative accounting. The following have been identified as significant factors:

Tax avoidance

If income can be understated or expenses overstated, then it may be possible to avoid tax.

Increasing shareholder confidence

Creative accounting can be used to ensure an appropriate level of profits over a long period. Ideally, this would show a steady upward trajectory without nasty surprises for the shareholders, and so would help to avoid volatility in share prices, and would make it easier to raise further capital via share issues.

Personal gain

Where managerial bonuses are linked to profitability there is a clear motivation for managers to ensure that profits hit the necessary threshold to trigger a bonus payment.

Indirect personal gain

There is a market in managerial expertise in which demand often appears to outstrip supply. A manager's personal reputation in the marketplace will almost certainly be enhanced by association with entities that have strong earnings records. So, although the pay-off may not be either immediate or obvious, there is likely over the longer term to be a reward in terms of enhanced reputation and consequent higher earning power.

Following the pack

If managers perceive that every other entity in their sector is adopting creative accounting practices, they may feel obliged to do the same.

Meeting covenants

Sometimes, lenders insist on special covenant arrangements as a condition of making a loan: for example, they may stipulate that an entity's current ratio should not fall below 1.5:1, or that gearing never exceeds 35 per cent. In such cases, if the entity cannot meet those covenants that it has agreed to, the lender may be able to insist upon immediate repayment or to put the entity into liquidation. Where an entity is in danger of failing to meet its covenants, there is an obvious incentive for managers (especially if they genuinely feel that the difficulty is short-term in nature) to massage the figures so that the covenant is, apparently, satisfied.

10 Additional information

In practice and in examinations it is likely that the information available in the financial statements is not enough to produce a detailed and thorough analysis of the entity. This is particularly the case given the limitations of financial reporting information discussed in the previous section.

You may require additional information, financial and non-financial, to develop a better understanding of the entity's business and its industry. In the examination it is imperative that you relate any additional information requested to the entity in the question and to the user for whom the report is being prepared. You should ensure that the information you are suggesting would be reasonably available to the user (i.e. don't suggest that a minority shareholder would be able to access board minutes).

The following examples of additional information are for illustrative purposes only. There are questions in the exam practice kit to further this knowledge and to develop your higher skills.

You may require additional *financial* information such as:

- budgeted figures
- other management information
- industry averages
- figures for a similar entity
- figures for the entity over a longer period of time.

You may also require other *non-financial* information such as:

- market share
- key employee information
- sales mix information
- product range information
- the size of the order book
- the long-term plans of management.

11 Practice questions

Use the following Test Your Understandings to develop the skills required in analysis questions. You need to learn how to *analyse* and *evaluate* the companies. See chapter 1 for more information on the verbs used in question requirements and how to meet the level of skill required.

Test your understanding 4 - March 2011 exam question

A friend has approached you looking for some advice. He has been offered the position of Sales Director within an entity, DFG, which supplies the building trade. He commented that he had reviewed the information on DFG's website and there were lots of positive messages about the entity's future, including how it had secured a new supplier relationship in 20X1 resulting in a significant improvement in margins.

He has been offered a lucrative remuneration package to implement a new aggressive sales strategy, but has been with his current employer for six years and wants to ensure his future would be secure. He has provided you with the finalised financial statements for DFG for the year ended 31 December 20X1, with comparatives.

The financial statements of DFG are provided below:

Statements of financial position at 31 December

	20X1		20X0	
	$m	$m	$m	$m
Non-current assets				
Property, plant and equipment	254		198	
Investment in associate	24		–	
		278		198
Current assets				
Inventories	106		89	
Receivables	72		48	
Cash and cash equivalents	–		6	
		178		143
Total assets		456		341
Equity				
Share capital ($1 equity shares)	45		45	
Retained earnings	146		139	
Revaluation reserve	40		–	
		231		184
Non-current liabilities				
Long-term borrowings		91		91
Current liabilities				
Trade and other payables	95		66	
Short-term borrowings	39		–	
		134		66
		456		341

Statement of comprehensive income for the year ended 31 December

	20X1	20X0
	$m	$m
Revenue	252	248
Cost of sales	(203)	(223)
Gross profit	49	25
Distribution costs	(18)	(13)
Administrative expenses	(16)	(11)
Share of profit of associate	7	–
Finance costs	(12)	(8)
Profit before tax	10	(7)
Income tax expense	(3)	2
Profit for the year	7	(5)
Other comprehensive income:		
Revaluation gain on PPE	40	–
Total other comprehensive income	40	–
Total comprehensive income for the year	47	(5)

Additional information

(1) **Long term borrowings**

The long term borrowings are repayable in 20X3.

(2) **Contingent liability**

The notes to the financial statements include details of a contingent liability of $30 million. A major customer, a house builder, is suing DFG, claiming that it supplied faulty goods. The customer had to rectify some of its building work when investigations discovered that a building material, which had recently been supplied by DFG, was found to contain a hazardous substance. The initial assessment from the lawyer is that DFG is likely to lose the case although the amount of potential damages could not be measured with sufficient reliability at the year-end date.

(3) **Revaluation**

DFG decided on a change of accounting policy in the year and now includes its land and buildings at their revalued amount. The valuation was performed by an employee of DFG who is a qualified valuer.

Required:

(a) Analyse the financial performance of DFG for the year to 31 December 20X1 and its financial position at that date and briefly discuss DFG's suitability as a secure employer for your friend *(8 marks are available for the calculation of relevant ratios)*.

(20 marks)

(b) Explain the potential limitations of using traditional ratio analysis as a means of decision making, using DFG's situation to illustrate your answer.

(5 marks)

(Total: 25 marks)

Test your understanding 5 - DM

DM, a listed entity, has just published its financial statements for the year ended 31 December 20X4. DM operates a chain of 42 supermarkets in one of the six major provinces of its country of operation. During 20X4, there has been speculation in the financial press that the entity was likely to be a takeover target for one of the larger national chains of supermarkets that is currently under-represented in DM's province. A recent newspaper report has suggested that DM's directors are unlikely to resist a takeover. The six board members are all nearing retirement and all own significant minority shareholdings in the business.

You have been approached by a private shareholder in DM. She is concerned that the directors have a conflict of interests and that the financial statements for 20X4 may have been manipulated.

The income statement and summarised statement of changes in equity of DM, with comparatives, for the year ended 31 December 20X4, and a statement of financial position, with comparatives, at that date are as follows:

Income statements

	20X4	**20X3**
	$m	$m
Revenue	1,255	1,220
Cost of sales	(1,177)	(1,145)
Gross profit	78	75
Operating expenses	(21)	(29)
Profit from operations	57	46
Finance cost	(10)	(10)
Profit before tax	47	36
Income tax	(14)	(13)
Net profit	33	23

Summarised statements of changes in equity

	20X4	**20X3**
	$m	$m
Opening balance	276	261
Profit for the period	33	23
Dividends	(8)	(8)
Closing balance	301	276

Statements of financial position

	20X4		20X3	
	$m	$m	$m	$m
Non-current assets				
Plant, property and equipment	580		575	
Goodwill	100		100	
		680		675
Current assets				
Inventory	47		46	
Receivables	12		13	
Cash	46		12	
		105		71
		785		746
Equity				
Share capital	150		150	
Retained earnings	151		126	
		301		276
Non-current liabilities				
Interest-bearing borrowings	142		140	
Deferred tax	25		21	
		167		161
Current liabilities				
Trade and other payables	297		273	
Short-term borrowings	20		36	
		317		309
		785		746

Notes:

(1) DM's directors have undertaken a reassessment of the useful lives of non-current tangible assets during the year. In most cases, they estimate that the useful lives have increased and the depreciation charges in 20X4 have been adjusted accordingly.

(2) Six new stores have been opened during 20X4, bringing the total to 42.

(3) Four key ratios for the supermarket sector (based on the latest available financial statements of 12 listed entities in the sector) are as follows:

(i) Annual sales per store: $27.6m

(ii) Gross profit margin: 5.9%

(iii) Net profit margin: 3.9%

(iv) Non-current asset turnover (including both tangible and intangible non-current assets): 1.93.

Required:

(a) Prepare a report, addressed to the investor, analysing the performance and position of DM based on the financial statements and supplementary information provided above. The report should also include comparisons with the key sector ratios, and it should address the investor's concerns about the possible manipulation of the 20X4 financial statements.

(b) Explain the limitations of the use of sector comparatives in financial analysis.

Test your understanding 6 - Expand

You are the management accountant of Expand, a company incorporated in Dollarland. The company is seeking to grow by acquisition and has identified two potential investment opportunities. One of these, Hone, is also a company incorporated in Dollarland. The other, Over, is a company incorporated in Francland.

You have been presented with financial information relating to both companies. The financial information is extracted from their published financial statements. In both cases, the financial statements conform to domestic accounting standards. The financial statements of Hone were drawn up in dollars ($) while those of Over were drawn up in Francs. The information relating to Over has been expressed in dollars by taking the figures in Francs and dividing by 1.55 – the dollar/franc exchange rate at 31 December 20X2. The financial information is given below.

Income statements

Year ended	Hone 31 March 20X3	31 March 20X2	Over 31 Dec 20X2	31 Dec 20X1
	$m	$m	$m	$m
Revenue	600	550	620	560
Cost of sales	(300)	(250)	(320)	(260)
Gross profit	300	300	300	300
Other operating expenses	(120)	(105)	(90)	(85)
Profit from operations	180	195	210	215
Finance cost	(20)	(18)	(22)	(20)
Profit before tax	160	177	188	195
Income tax expense	(50)	(55)	(78)	(90)
Profit for the period	110	122	110	105

Statements of changes in equity

Year ended	Hone 31 March 20X3	31 March 20X2	Over 31 Dec 20X2	31 Dec 20X1
	$m	$m	$m	$m
Balance brought forward	470	418	265	240
Profit for the period	110	122	110	105
Dividends	(70)	(70)	(80)	(80)
Balance carried forward	510	470	295	265

Statements of financial position

	Hone		Over	
	31 March 20X3	31 March 20X2	31 Dec 20X2	31 Dec 20X1
	$m	$m	$m	$m
Non-current assets	600	570	455	440
Inventories	60	50	55	50
Trade receivables	80	75	90	80
Cash	10	20	15	15
	750	715	615	585
Share capital	150	150	110	110
Reserves	360	320	185	155
	510	470	295	265
Interest-bearing borrowings	150	150	240	240
Current liabilities	90	95	80	80
	750	715	615	585

Expand is more concerned with the profitability of potential investment opportunities than with liquidity. You have been asked to review the financial statements of Hone and Over with this concern in mind.

Required:

(a) Prepare a short report to the directors of Expand that, based on the financial information provided, assesses the relative profitability of Hone and Over.

(b) Discuss the validity of using this financial information as a basis to compare the profitability of the two companies.

12 Analysis of the statement of cash flows

The cash flow of an entity is regarded by many users as being of primary importance in understanding its operations. After all, an entity that cannot generate sufficient cash will, sooner or later, fail.

The statement of cash flows provides valuable information for the analysis of an entity's operations and position. Students should note that the analysis of cash flow statements is examinable in Financial Management.

The statement of cash flows prepared in accordance with IAS 7 categorises cash flow under three principal headings: cash flows from operating activities, investing activities and financing activities. As well as comparing these totals from year to year, cash flows in the following areas should be reviewed:

- cash generation from trading operations
- dividend and interest payments
- investing activities
- financing activities
- net cash flow

There are also useful ratios that can be calculated, see expandable text below.

Cash generation from trading operations

The figure should be compared to the operating profit. The reconciliation note to the statement of cash flows is useful in this regard. Overtrading may be indicated by:

- high profits and low cash generation
- large increases in inventory, receivables and payables.

Dividend and interest payments

These can be compared to cash generated from trading operations to see whether the normal operations can sustain such payments. In most years they should.

Investing activities

The nature and scale of an entity's investment in non-current assets is clearly shown.

A simple test may be to compare investment and depreciation.

- If investment > depreciation, the entity is investing at a greater rate than its current assets are wearing out – this suggests expansion.
- If investment = depreciation, the entity is investing in new assets as existing ones wear out. The entity appears stable.
- If investment < depreciation the non-current asset base of the entity is not being maintained. This is potentially worrying as non-current assets are generators of profit.

Financing activities

The changes in financing (in pure cash terms) are clearly shown. Gearing can be considered at this point. It would be useful to comment on the impact that such changes will have on the gearing ratio.

Cash flow

The statement clearly shows the end result in cash terms of the entity's operations in the year. Do not overstate the importance of this figure alone, however. A decrease in cash in the year may be for very sound reasons (e.g. there was surplus cash last year) or may be mainly the result of timing (e.g. a new loan was raised just after the end of the accounting period).

Cash flow ratios

Return on capital employed: cash

$$\frac{\text{Cash generated from operations}}{\text{Capital employed}} \times 100$$

For many external users, cash is a more significant indicator than profit and this ratio should be calculated where the information is available.

Cash generated from operations to total debt

$$\frac{\text{Cash generated from operations}}{\text{Total long term borrowings}}$$

This gives an indication of an entity's ability to meet its long-term obligations. The inverse ratio can also be calculated:

$$\frac{\text{Total long-term borrowings}}{\text{Cash generated from operations}}$$

This provides an indication of how many years it would take to repay the long-term borrowings if all of the cash generated from operations were to be used for this purpose.

Net cash from operating activities to capital expenditure

$$\frac{\text{Net cash from operating activities}}{\text{Net capital expenditure}} \times 100$$

This gives some idea of the extent to which the entity can finance its capital expenditure out of cash flows from operating activities. If it cannot meet its capital expenditure from this source, then some kind of longer-term financing is likely to be required. However, this ratio could be misleading unless calculated and compared for several years.

Test your understanding 7 - March 2011 exam question

FGH has been trading for a number of years and is currently going through a period of expansion of its core business area.

The statement of cash flows for the year ended 31 December 20X0 for FGH is presented below.

	$000	$000
Cash flows from operating activities		
Profit before tax	2,200	
Adjustments for:		
Depreciation	380	
Gain on sale of investments	(50)	
Loss on sale of property, plant and equipment	45	
Investment income	(180)	
Interest costs	420	
	2,815	
Increase in trade receivables	(400)	
Increase in inventories	(390)	
Increase in payables	550	
Cash generated from operations		2,575
Interest paid		(400)
Income taxes paid		(760)
Net cash from operating activities		1,415

Cash flows from investing activities		
Acquisition of subsidiary, net of cash acquired	(800)	
Acquisition of property, plant and equipment	(340)	
Proceeds from sale of equipment	70	
Proceeds from sale of investments	150	
Interest received	100	
Dividends received	80	
Net cash used in investing activities		(740)
Cash flows from financing activities		
Proceeds of share issue	300	
Proceeds from long term borrowings	300	
Dividend paid to equity shareholders of the parent	(1,000)	
Net cash used in financing activities		(400)
Net increase in cash and cash equivalents		275
Cash and cash equivalents at the beginning of the period		110
Cash and cash equivalents at the end of the period		385

Required:

Analyse the above statement of cash flows for FGH, highlighting the key features of each category of cash flows.

(Total: 10 marks)

13 Segmental analysis

One of the limitations mentioned above is that different entities may have different segments to their business. Comparing entities as a whole may not be appropriate if the segments account for different proportions of the overall business and the activities of each segment are not similar.

It is also beneficial for users to be aware of how the individual segments of an entity contribute to its overall financial performance and position and how changes in its segments may impact on the business as whole.

IFRS 8 *Operating Segments* addresses these issues and requires entities to disclose certain segmental information.

The requirements of IFRS 8 only apply to publicly listed entities, although non-listed entities are encouraged to comply.

Identification of operating segments

Operating segments are identified on the basis of internal reports that are regularly reviewed by the chief operating decision maker.

IFRS 8 defines an operating segment as a component of an entity:

- that engages in business activities from which it may earn revenues and incur expenses (including intra-group revenues and expenses);
- whose operating results are reviewed regularly by the entity's chief operating decision maker to make decisions about resources to be allocated to the segment and assess its performance; and
- for which discrete financial information is available.

Not all operations of an entity will necessarily be an operating segment. For example, the corporate headquarters does not earn revenue therefore is not an operating segment.

However, the definition does include business segments whose activities are principally concerned with trading intra-group.

Reportable segments

IFRS 8 sets quantitative thresholds for reporting. Entities should report information about an operating segment that meets the 10% rule:

10% rule

Segments should be classed as reportable segments if they account for more than 10% of total revenue, more than 10% of total profit or hold more than 10% of total assets.

75% rule

If, after allocating segments according to the 10% rule, the revenue of reportable segments is less than 75% of the total revenue of the entity, additional segments will be classified as reportable segments even though they do not meet the 10% rule.

Benefits of segmental information

More appropriate assessment of performance of entity

Separate segments may have wide ranges of profitability, cash flows, growth, future prospects and risks. Without information on these segments, users would not be able to identify these differences and it would be impossible to properly assess performance and future prospects of the entity.

IFRS 8 requires information to be provided on the revenue, expense, profits, assets and liabilities of each segment. With this information, users can calculate the profit margins, asset utilisation and return on net assets of each segment and so further analyse the performance of each segment.

IFRS 8 is designed to allow users to see the type and categories of information that are used at the highest levels in the entity for decision-making. There is the further advantage that disclosure, while in many cases extensive, should not be excessively costly because it is based upon information reported and used within the entity.

Limitations of segmental information

Defining segments

One of the criticisms of IFRS 8 is that it allows an entity's managers to determine what is a reportable segment. Managers, therefore, are potentially able to conceal information by judicious selection of segments. A further, related, criticism is that comparability of segment information between entities suffers because segment identification is likely to differ between entities. However, it should be recognised that comparability between entities is often problematic, and users should in any case be very cautious when comparing entities even if they appear, superficially, to be quite similar in their operations.

Measurement of segment information

IFRS 8 also does not define segment revenue, segment expense, segment result, segment assets or segment liabilities, but does require an explanation of how segment profit or loss, segment assets and segment liabilities are measured for each operating segment.

As a consequence, entities will have more discretion in determining what is included in segment profit or loss under IFRS 8, limited only by their internal reporting practices.

Apportionment of 'common' items

Allocations of revenues, expenses, gains and losses are included only if they are included when the chief operating decision maker reviews the information. The same goes for assets and liabilities which can be difficult to apportion.

IFRS 8 does not prescribe how centrally incurred expenses should be allocated or whether they should be allocated at all. IFRS 8 simply states that amounts should be allocated on a reasonable basis.

This results in increased subjectivity and these allocations can significantly affect segment results.

Disclosure requirements for segmental reporting

Reporting of comparatives

As with other financial information included in the annual report of an entity, segment disclosures should include comparatives for the previous year. It is possible that an operating segment could meet the reporting criteria in one year but not in another. Where a segment ceases to meet the reporting criteria information about it should continue to be disclosed provided that management judge it to be of continuing significance.

Conversely, where a segment is newly identified and reported because it meets the reporting criteria for the first time, the previous year's comparatives should be reported for it, even though the segment was not significant in the prior period.

Disclosure requirements

General information about operating segments must be disclosed as follows:

(1) The factors used to identify the reportable segments, including the basis on which they have been identified – for example, geographical areas, types of product or service.

(2) The types of product or services from which each reportable segment derives its revenues.

The entity must disclose for each segment measures of profit or loss AND total assets. The extent of other disclosures depends to some extent on the nature and content of information that is reviewed by the 'chief operating decision maker' (probably the CEO or equivalent). A measure of liabilities must be disclosed for each segment if that information is regularly made available to the chief operating decision maker. If the following information is regularly reviewed by the chief operating decision maker it must be disclosed:

- Revenues from external customers
- Revenues from transactions with other operating segments
- Interest revenue
- Interest expense
- Depreciation and amortisation
- Material items of income and expense
- Interests in profit or loss of associates and joint ventures
- Income tax expense or income
- Material non-cash items other than depreciation or amortisation
- The amount of investment in associates and joint ventures
- The amounts of additions to non-current assets (with some exclusions).

Reconciliations

Reconciliations are required to be disclosed as follows:

- The total of the reportable segments' revenues to the entity's revenue
- The total of the reportable segments' profits or losses to the entity's profit or loss before tax and discontinued operations
- The total of the reportable segments' assets to the entity's assets
- The total of the reportable segments' liabilities to the entity's liabilities (if reported)
- The total of the reportable segments' amounts in respect of every other reportable item of information.

Information about products and services

In addition to the information requirements set out above, an entity must make the following disclosures (unless these are already made via the disclosures described above):

- Information about products and services: the revenues from external customers for each product and service, or similar groups of products and services.
- Information about geographical areas:
  (1) Revenues from external customers attributable to the entity's country of domicile and the total of revenues attributable to all foreign countries.
  (2) Non-current assets located in the entity's country of domicile and the total of non-current assets located in all foreign countries.
- Information about major customers:
  (1) If revenues in respect of a single customer amount to 10% or more of total revenues this should be disclosed (there is no requirement to disclose the name of the customer).
  (2) In respect of information about products, services and geographical areas, the disclosure requirement is waived if the cost to develop the information would be 'excessive'.

Test your understanding 8 - Boston

Shown below are the summarised financial statements for Boston, a publicly listed entity, for the years ended 31 March 20X8 and 20X9, together with some segment information analysed by class of business for the year ended 31 March 20X9 only:

Income statements

	Carpeting	Hotels	House building	Total 31 March 20X9	Total 31 March 20X8
	$m	$m	$m	$m	$m
Revenue	90	130	280	500	450
Cost of sales (note (i))	(30)	(95)	(168)	(293)	(260)
Gross profit	60	35	112	207	190
Operating expenses	(25)	(15)	(32)	(72)	(60)
Segment result	35	20	80	135	130
Unallocated corporate expenses				(60)	(50)
Profit from operations				75	80
Finance costs				(10)	(5)
Profit before tax				65	75
Income tax expense				(25)	(30)
Profit for the period				40	45

Statements of financial position

	Carpeting	Hotels	House building	Total 31 March 20X9	Total 31 March 20X8
	$m	$m	$m	$m	$m
Tangible non-current assets	40	140	200	380	332
Current assets	40	40	75	155	130
Segment assets	80	180	275	535	462
Unallocated bank balance				15	–
Consolidated total assets				550	462
Ordinary share capital				100	80
Share premium				20	–
Retained earnings				232	192
				352	272
Segment current liabilities					
Tax	4	9	12	25	30
Other	4	51	53	108	115
Unallocated loans				65	40
Unallocated bank overdraft				–	5
Consolidated equity and total liabilities				550	462

The following notes are relevant:

(i) Depreciation for the year to 31 March 20X9 was $35 million. During the year a hotel with a carrying amount of $40 million was sold at a loss of $12 million. Depreciation and the loss on the sale of non-current assets are charged to cost of sales. There were no other non-current asset disposals. As part of the entity's overall acquisition of new non-current assets, the hotel segment acquired $104 million of new hotels during the year.

(ii) The above figures are based on historical cost values. The fair values of the segment net assets are:

	Carpeting	Hotel	House building
	$m	$m	$m
31 March 20X8	80	150	250
31 March 20X9	97	240	265

(iii) The following ratios (which can be taken to be correct) have been calculated based on the overall group results:

Year ended:	31 March 20X9	31 March 20X8
Return on capital employed	18.0%	25.6%
Gross profit margin	41.4%	42.2%
Operating profit margin	15.0%	17.8%
Net asset turnover	1.4 times	1.7 times
Current ratio	1.3:1	0.9:1
Gearing	15.6%	12.8%

(iv) The following segment ratios (which can be taken to be correct) have been calculated for the year ended 31 March 20X9 only:

	Carpeting	Hotel	House building
Segment return on net assets	48.6%	16.7%	38.1%
Segment net asset turnover	1.3 times	1.1 times	1.3 times
Gross profit margin	66.7%	26.9%	40%
Net profit margin	38.9%	15.4%	28.6%
Current ratio (excluding bank)	5:1	0.7:1	1.2:1

Required:

Using the ratios provided, write a report to the Board of Boston analysing the entity's financial performance and position for the year ended 31 March 20X9.

Note: Your answer should make reference to the segmental information and consider the implication of the fair value information.

Test your understanding 9 - March 2012 exam question

A quote from a colleague: "I never look at the operating segment information in a set of financial statements when I am making investment decisions - it's just lots and lots of numbers I won't understand. It must cost entities a significant amount of money to produce the information, which must outweigh the benefits it provides."

Required:

(a) Discuss the benefits that could be gained by investors from reviewing the operating segment disclosures when making future decisions on investment.

(5 marks)

(b) Discuss the limitations of using operating segment information when making investment decisions.

(3 marks)

(c) Discuss how the requirements of IFRS 8 *Operating Segments* assist entities in minimising the costs of producing these disclosures.

(2 marks)

(Total: 10 marks)

14 Chapter summary

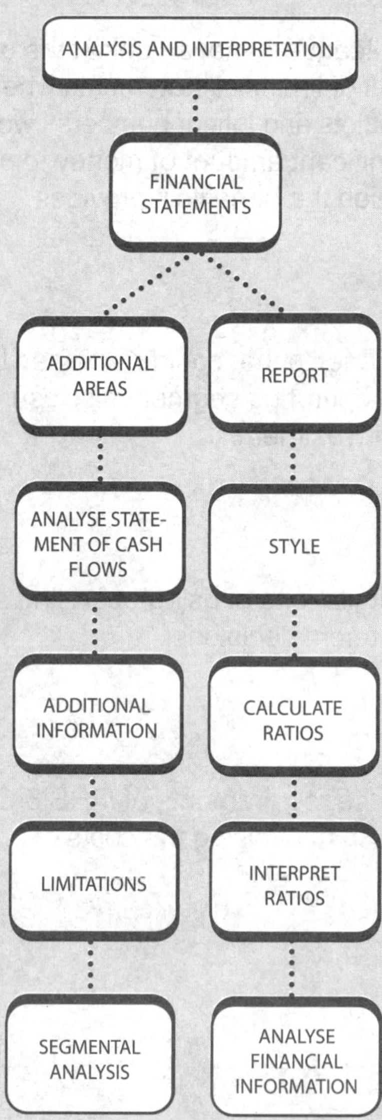

Test your understanding answers

Test your understanding 1 - Profitability ratios

Profitability

		20X6	**20X5**
Gross profit margin	Gross profit / Revenue	115/180= 63.9%	90/150 = 60%
Operating profit margin	Operating profit / Revenue	75.1/180 = 41.7%	61.5/150 = 41%
Net profit margin	Net profit / Revenue	45.8/180= 25.4%	37.9/150 = 25.3%
Return on capital employed	Profit before interest / Capital Employed	75.1/(146.7+150) = 25.3%	61.5/(92.9+125) = 28.2%
Asset utilisation	Revenue / Capital Employed	180/(146.7+150) = 0.61 times	150/(92.9+125) = 0.69 times

Possible reasons why T's ratios have changed:

Gross profit margin increased:

- Increase in sales due to increasing volume sold and so economies of scale result in lower costs per unit sold;
- Increase in sales price per unit;
- Changes in product mix.

Operating profit margin unchanged:

- Increase in expenses such as advertising to boost revenue;
- Increased depreciation charges following acquisitions of non-current assets;
- Poor control of costs since revenue increased by 20% but operating expenses increased by 40%.

Net profit margin unchanged:

- Increase in finance costs in line with increase in revenue;
- Increased borrowing to fund expansion has resulted in increased finance costs.

Return on capital employed and asset utilisation fallen:

- No reduction in operating profit margin and so fall is due to fall in asset utilisation;
- Revaluation of non-current assets will reduce asset utilisation (and ROCE) but not a "real" deterioration in efficiency;
- Significant increase in non-current assets during year. If acquired near year-end, will not have generated returns as yet.
- Have also revalued non-current assets and this will increase capital employed but have no effect on revenue.

Test your understanding 2 - Liquidity ratios

Liquidity

		20X6	20X5
Current ratio	Current assets / Current liabilities	64.3/33.8 = 1.9:1	50/22.1 = 2.3:1
Quick ratio	(Current assets – Inventory) / Current liabilities	49.3/33.8 = 1.5:1	38/22.1 = 1.7:1
Inventory holding period	Inventory / Cost of sales × 365 days	15/65 × 365 = 84 days	12/60 × 365 = 73 days
Receivables collection period	Receivables / Revenue × 365 days	49.3/180 × 365 =100 days	37.5/150 × 365 = 91 days
Payables payment period	Trade payables / Cost of Sales × 365 days	11.7/65 × 365 = 66 days	10.6/60 × 365 = 65 days

Possible reasons why T's ratios have changed:

Inventory holding period increased:

- Build up of inventory levels as a result of increased capacity following expansion of non-current assets;
- Increasing inventory levels in response to increased demand for product.
- Expectation of higher demand after year end.

Receivables collection period increased:

- Deliberate policy to attract customers;
- Poor credit control procedures.

Payables payment period largely unchanged.

Overall liquidity situation deteriorated:

- Current and quick ratios have both fallen but not yet at levels that give cause for concern. However, T is showing signs of liquidity issues with significant overdraft at year end. This is partially due to increasing inventory holding and receivables collection periods but suppliers being paid as quickly as last year. It appears that the increase in non-current assets has also been partially funded via the overdraft.

Test your understanding 3 - Capital structure ratios

Capital structure

		20X6	20X5
Gearing	Debt / (Debt + Equity)	150/(150+146.7) = 50.6%	125/(125+92.9) =57.4%
Gearing (alternative)	Debt / Equity	150/146.7 = 1.0:1	125/92.9 = 1.3:1
Interest cover	Profit before interest / Finance costs	75.1/12 = 6.26 times	61.5/10 = 6.15 times
Dividend cover	Net profit / Dividends	45.8/25 = 1.8 times	37.9/25 = 1.5 times

Gearing fallen:

- Primarily due to revaluation of non-current assets. Without revaluation, gearing in line with previous year;
- Increase in loan, but also an increase in equity financing;
- Additional finance been used to increase non-current assets and on other measures to expand company e.g. increased advertising expenditure;
- Gearing ratio appears quite high, but interest cover also high and so not an immediate cause for concern.

Dividend cover is adequate and improving.

Test your understanding 4 - March 2011 exam question

(a) **To friend**

Report on financial performance and position

The revenue has only marginally increased in the year by 1.6%, however profit margins have all increased significantly. In particular the gross profit margin has increased from 10% to 19%, which is likely to be as a result of reduced purchase prices from the new supplier contract that was secured in the year. Whilst this is a very positive and important step for DFG (given its low margin in the previous year) it will be important to establish whether this reduced cost also means a reduced level of quality. If quality is being compromised then this increase in margin may be short-lived as customers may be driven away in the longer term.

In addition, the switch in supplier may be responsible for the lawsuit. It is a risky strategy to pursue aggressive revenue and margin targets at the expense of supplying good quality products. Although a contingent liability of $30 million is included in the notes, the lawyer's assessment is that DFG is likely to lose the court case and the payout may be more. There is already serious pressure on the entity's finances and the entity may not survive if the payout is any more or if other customers decide to sue. There is a potential issue of going concern that would need clarification before you arrive at a final decision concerning employment.

Both administration and distribution costs have increased significantly when compared to a 1.6% increase in revenue. Whilst these costs are not that large in relation to revenues, it will be important to establish that management have good control over expenses for the long term.

The increase in TCI is largely due to the revaluation gain reported within other comprehensive income. The valuation was performed by an internal member of staff, which is perhaps not as ideal as someone external, however you noted that these financial statements were finalised and so I assume they have been audited and that the valuations are fair. One note of caution though is why the directors have chosen this year to change the policy - could it be an attempt to boost income and reduce gearing to make further borrowing easier, especially as the long term borrowings will need to be repaid or re-negotiated relatively soon. However, it maybe shows good commercial sense to ensure that assets that are to be used as security for finance are at the most up-to-date valuation.

The overall liquidity of DFG is on the low side at 1.3:1 and has fallen significantly from 20X0. One contributing factor to the worsening liquidity is the significant increase in inventories in the year. This could be as a result of bad publicity about below standard goods and customer orders being cancelled. There is then an increased risk of obsolete inventories. This is reinforced by the inventories days which have increased from146 days to 191 days. Receivables days have also increased from 71 days to 104 days, and this could be as a result of disputed invoices. DFG may then have a problem with slow/non-payment of these debts. Payables days have increased from 108 days to 171 days and this could be resulting from a deliberate attempt by DFG to improve cash flow by delaying payment or extended credit terms given by the new supplier to attract DFG's business.

The cash position of DFG is clearly a concern as the cash has moved from a positive balance to an overdraft and the long term borrowings are soon to be repaid or re-negotiated. This coupled with the poor working capital management would indicate that DFG must raise some additional funding if it is to survive. The gearing ratio shows deterioration on the previous year, despite an increase in equity from the revaluation. However, it is likely to be the lack of interest cover that would put lenders off. It is unlikely that DFG could afford to pay interest on any additional funding.

I would recommend investigating DFG in more detail before making your decision. Losing the court case and having a large settlement to pay could result in the entity collapsing and despite the fact that details of this are only in the notes, the seriousness of this should not be overlooked. The entity may struggle to survive anyway as there is a lack of cash and funding options (and it should be noted that DFG did not pay a dividend in 20X1). The increases in profitability are not enough of an indicator of a stable/growing entity - especially an entity involved in the building trade which is known for its sensitivity to the economy around it.

(b) **Limitations of ratio analysis**

The financial statements provide only historic information and reflect a point in time (i.e. the year end). However, the situation of the entity in question could have progressed significantly by the time you are analysing the information. For example, with the contingent liability for the court case, it could have progressed or be settled and the financial statements will not have reflected that.

The ratio analysis conducted on DFG showed an improvement in profitability margins, in cost of sales particularly, however it looks likely that quality has been compromised in favour of better margins and the result of that has been the filing of a law suit against DFG.

This is something that threatens the future of the business but is not reflected in the ratios calculated.

Changes in accounting policies can impact ratio calculations. DFG has changed the accounting policy for subsequent measurement of PPE from depreciated historic cost to revalued amount. The revaluation in the year then improves the gearing ratio and reduces non-current asset turnover but is due only to a change of policy rather than changes to the underlying environment.

Appendix A

Relevant ratios that could be selected and calculated:

	20X1	**20X0**
Gross profit margin	49/252 x 100 = 19.4%	25/248 x 100 = 10.1%
Operating profit margin	(49-18-16)/252 x 100 = 6.0%	(25-13-11)/248 x 100 = 0.4%
Net profit margin	7/252 x 100 = 2.8%	(5)/248 x 100 = (2.0)%
Gearing	(91+39)/231 x 100 = 56.3%	91/184 x 100 = 49.5%
Current ratio	178/134 = 1.3:1	143/66 = 2.2:1
Quick ratio	(178-106)/134 = 0.5:1	(143-89)/66 = 0.8:1
Receivable days	72/252 x 365 days = 104 days	48/248 x 365 days = 71 days
Payable days	95/203 x 365 days = 171 days	66/223 x 365 days = 108 days
Inventories days	106/203 x 365 days = 191 days	89/223 x 365 days = 146 days
Return on capital employed	(49-18-16)/(231+91-24) = 15/298 x 100 = 5.0%	(25-13-11)/(184+91) = 1/275 x 100 = 0.4%
Non-current asset turnover	252/254 = 0.99	248/198 = 1.3
Interest cover	(10+12)/12 = 1.8	((7)+8)/8 = 0.1

Tutorial note

When selecting your ratios, ensure that you calculate a range of ratios to cover the requirements of the question. A typical question will ask for an analysis of performance and position, as is the case here. Profitability ratios will assist with the analysis of performance and a mix of liquidity, working capital and capital structure ratios will provide the necessary detail to analyse position. Failure to calculate a specific type of ratio will restrict your ability to answer the question. Make sure that you stick to the number of marks available however. If there are 8 marks for ratio calculations then you should only calculate eight ratios in total (there will be 1 mark per ratio - a half mark per calculation with two calculations per ratio - one for each year/entity).

Test your understanding 5 - DM

(a) **REPORT**

To: A private shareholder

From: Management accountant

Date: XX/XX/20XX

Subject: Performance and position of DM

As requested, I have analysed the performance and position of DM. My analysis is based on extracts from the financial statements for the year ended 31 December 20X4 with comparative figures for the year ended 31 December 20X3. A number of key measures have been calculated and these are set out in the attached Appendix.

Sales

The company has opened six new stores during the year. However, sales have only increased very slightly in 20X4 and annual sales per store have fallen. This may be because the new stores have only opened part way through the year and have therefore not contributed a full year's revenue. Alternatively, the new stores may be taking sales away from existing stores thereby diluting this ratio.

Annual sales per store are still above the industry average. On the face of it, this is a good sign. However, it is possible that DM has large stores relative to the rest of the sector.

Profitability

Gross profit margin has increased very slightly during the year and this is a little above the industry average. However, although net profit margin has increased significantly during the year, this is still below the industry average. The increase in net profit margin has occurred because operating expenses have fallen by over a quarter in 20X4. The operating profit margin has risen from 3.8% in 20X3 to 4.5% in 20X4.

Given the information available, the most likely cause of this fall is the increase in asset lives and the resulting reduction in the depreciation expense. As might be expected, the company has a considerable investment in property, plant and equipment and depreciation would normally be a significant expense. An increase in asset lives is relatively unusual and it is possible that the directors have used this method to deliberately improve the operating and the net profit margins. (They may have been particularly concerned that the net profit margin has obviously been well below the industry average.)

On the other hand, the directors may have carried out their review of asset lives in good faith or there could be another legitimate reason why operating expenses have fallen. For example, the 20X3 figure may have been inflated by a significant 'one off' expense.

It is impossible to prove that the profit figure has been manipulated on the basis of the very limited information available. Information about the reasons for the fall in operating expenses and the review of asset lives and about the property, plant and equipment held by the company would be extremely useful.

Other matters

Non-current asset turnover has improved slightly, but is still below the industry average. This suggests that the company uses its assets less efficiently than others in the same sector. However, increasing the asset lives will have reduced the ratio for 20X4; it is possible that the company's asset turnover would have approached the sector average had the review not been carried out. Given that six new stores have opened in 20X4, it is surprising that property, plant and equipment has only increased by $5 million in the year. It is possible that most of the investment in new property was made during 20X3.

The current ratio for both years is extremely low. Supermarkets often do have relatively low current and quick ratios, but no average figure for the industry is available, so it is difficult to tell whether this is normal for the type of operation. Short-term liquidity appears not to be a problem because the company has a positive cash balance which has increased in the year. However, the appearance of the statement of financial position suggests that this has been achieved by delaying payment to suppliers. Trade and other payables have increased by nearly 9%, while revenue and cost of sales have only increased by approximately 3%.

The debt/equity ratio has fallen in the year and gearing does not appear to be a problem.

Conclusion

DM's profit margins appear to be reasonable for a company in its industry sector. Although its net profit margin is below the industry average, this is improving. There are no apparent short-term liquidity problems.

It is possible that at least some of this improvement has been achieved by deliberately reducing the operating expenses for the year. If, as seems likely, the directors wish to sell their interests in the company in the near future, improved results will help to secure a better price.

However, it is impossible to be certain that this has happened without much more detailed information about the reason for the fall in operating expenses. There may be a legitimate explanation for the improvement in the company's profit margins.

Appendix

	20X4	**20X3**	**Key sector ratio**
Annual sales per store	1,255/ 42 = $29.9m	1,220/ 36 = $33.9m	$27.6m
Gross profit margin	78/ 1,255 x 100% = 6.2%	75/ 1,220 x 100% = 6.1%	5.9%
Operating profit margin	57/ 1,255 x 100% = 4.5%	46/ 1,220 x 100% = 3.8%	–
Net profit margin	33/ 1,255 x 100% = 2.6%	23/ 1,220 x 100% = 1.9%	3.9%
Non-current asset turnover	1,255/ 680 = 1.85 times	1,220/ 675 = 1.81 times	1.93 times
Current ratio	105/ 317 = 0.33:1	71/ 309 = 0.23:1	–
Debt/ equity	142/ 301 = 47.2%	140/ 276 = 50.7%	–

(b) **Limitations of the use of sector comparatives**

It can often be useful to compare ratios for an individual company with averages for the sector. However, this type of analysis has a number of limitations:

- Some accounting ratios can be calculated in different ways. Therefore a sector average may be based on ratios that have not been calculated consistently.
- The figures in the financial statements are affected by the accounting policies adopted and by accounting estimates. Accounting estimates (such as the useful lives of assets) require judgement. Some international accounting standards still allow a choice of accounting policies.

- Entities in the same sector may operate under different business environments. For example, DM operates in one of six provinces. Conditions may be very different in the other five; so DM's financial performance and position may not be strictly comparable with companies operating in other provinces.
- Sector comparatives are normally based on an average of several entities. The average can be distorted by one entity that is significantly out of line with the others. Also, the smaller the number of entities, the less reliable the average figure will be. For example, 12 entities is quite a small number.
- Published sector averages may exclude some important ratios. For example, it would be useful to know the average current ratio and debt/equity ratio for DM's industry sector.

Test your understanding 6 - Expand

(a)

REPORT

To: The directors of Expand

From: The Management Accountant

Date: XX-XX-XX

Subject: Profitability of Hone and Over

This report assesses the relative profitability of Hone and Over, based on each company's most recent published financial statements translated, where necessary, into dollars. Detailed calculations of accounting ratios are shown in the appendix to this report.

Based on the financial information provided, it appears that Over is the more profitable company, since it has a higher return on capital employed. However it should be noted that the profitability of both companies has fallen somewhat over the last year.

Return on capital employed can be broken down into its component parts of operating profit percentage and asset turnover. Since the asset turnover for both companies has been fairly steady, the decline in profitability can be traced to a fall in operating profit percentage for both companies.

A key difference between the two companies is the higher operating expenses reported by Hone. This may be partly explained by Hone's higher depreciation charge paid on its greater amount of non-current assets held.

Over appears to pay a lower interest rate on its borrowings than Hone, which may explain why Over carries a higher level of borrowings in its statement of financial position than Hone. Since borrowings represent a cheap source of finance, this fact has contributed to Over's better relative profitability. However the tax rate paid by Over appears to be greater than the rate paid by Hone.

In conclusion the information provided shows that Over generates a greater return of profits from the capital employed in its business, so Over is relatively more profitable than Hone. However, before any decision is taken to invest in either of these companies, more investigations should be carried out, particularly in respect of any forecast future earnings and information concerning the future prospects of the companies. Historical information alone is insufficient to decide on a possible investment in a company now.

Appendix – Key accounting ratios assessing profitability

	Hone		Over	
	Mar 20X3	*Mar 20X2*	*Dec 20X2*	*Dec 20X1*
Return on capital employed	$\frac{180}{660}$ = 27%	$\frac{195}{620}$ = 31%	$\frac{210}{535}$ = 39%	$\frac{215}{505}$ = 43%
Gross profit percentage	$\frac{300}{600}$ = 50%	$\frac{300}{550}$ = 55%	$\frac{300}{620}$ = 48%	$\frac{300}{560}$ = 54%
Operating profit percentage	$\frac{180}{600}$ = 30%	$\frac{195}{550}$ = 35%	$\frac{210}{620}$ = 34%	$\frac{215}{560}$ = 38%
Asset turnover	$\frac{600}{660}$ = 0.91	$\frac{550}{620}$ = 0.89	$\frac{620}{535}$ = 1.16	$\frac{560}{505}$ = 1.11
Interest rate paid on borrowings	$\frac{20}{150}$ = 13.3%	$\frac{18}{150}$ = 12%	$\frac{22}{240}$ = 9.2%	$\frac{20}{240}$ = 8.3%
Effective tax rate	$\frac{50}{160}$ = 31.3%	$\frac{55}{177}$ = 31.1%	$\frac{78}{188}$ = 41.5%	$\frac{90}{195}$ = 46.2%

(b) There are serious limitations in using the financial information provided as a basis to compare the profitability of the two companies. First, we must consider the translation of the Over results. This has been done using a single exchange rate that is in force at 31 December 20X2. It would have been better to translate the 31 December 20X1 balance sheet using the exchange rate at that date, and to have used average exchange rates for 20X1 and 20X2 to translate the income statements respectively for 20X1 and 20X2.

A further problem arises in that the two companies have different year-end dates. If both companies earn their profits evenly over each year, then this will not be a problem. However it is more likely that there will be seasonal variations in the financial performance of each company, in which case the statement of financial position comparisons in particular will not be comparing like with like.

A further problem arises in that each company has drawn up their financial statements in accordance with the domestic accounting standards of the country in which they operate. No information is given of how similar the GAAP in Dollarland is to the GAAP in Francland. Different accounting practices could have a major effect on the reported profitability of the companies, such that a direct comparison is not valid.

Finally, we have no information on whether the two companies operate in a similar business sector. If they operate in different sectors (e.g. house building and publishing), then one would expect the financial statements to present a different pattern of operations. A direct comparison would only be valid if the two sets of statements were prepared in the same currency, for the same accounting periods, in accordance with the same accounting practices, and for companies in the same business sector in the same country. The analysis in part (a) is a long way short of this ideal.

Signed: The Management Accountant

Test your understanding 7 - March 2011 exam question

FGH has managed to generate significant cash from operating activities which is a positive sign for any business wishing to be a going concern, particularly since it appears that FGH is expanding. In addition to the inflow of cash from trading, the directors have clearly made some good investment decisions as income of $180,000 has been included in the year and also profit of $50,000 has been earned from the sale of these investments.

It does look as if FGH needs to improve working capital as receivables have increased in the year and it looks like the entity has in turn withheld payment to payables with an increase of $550,000. The increase in receivables may be a deliberate attempt to secure new customers by offering them favourable credit terms but it is essential that good working capital management is not compromised. The increase in inventories has probably arisen in order to meet future expected demand from the expansion. It should also be noted that FGH has acquired a subsidiary during the year, although the effect of the subsidiary on the working capital balances will have been adjusted for in the completion of the statement of cash flows.

The expansion is shown in two areas of investment, with the acquisition of a subsidiary and in the purchase of property, plant and equipment. The sale of property, plant and equipment for $70,000 resulted in a loss of $45,000. It's possible that the expansion has resulted in the need for new equipment and hence management have taken the view to sell some of the old equipment whilst there is still a second hand market for it. The sale of investments for $150,000 has probably been undertaken in order to generate funds for the expansion. The only note of caution is that these investments seem to be profitable and hence given that a proportion has been sold during the year, future income from investments will be reduced.

It is clear from the cash flows from financing that FGH appears to have the backing of its shareholders. A share issue has been supported and the shareholders have been rewarded with a significant dividend in the year. A good sign is that FGH has managed to fund the expansion without increasing the overall gearing of the business, as equal amounts of debt and equity have been raised as new finance. It indicates good stewardship of assets when long term expansion is financed by long term financing. FGH appear to have used a mixture of long term financing and retained earnings generated in the year, together with the sale of some investments to fund the expansion. However, this is not to the detriment of shareholders as they have still received a significant dividend during the year and it's possible that the new investments in a subsidiary and PPE will generate greater returns in the future than the investments which have been sold. In times of expansion, however, a more modest dividend may have negated the need for long term financing and the interest costs associated with it.

Test your understanding 8 - Boston

Report on the financial performance of Boston for the year ended 31 March 20X9

To: The Board of Boston

From: A N Other

Date: XX/XX/XX

Profitability (note figures are rounded to 1 decimal place)

The most striking feature of the current year's performance is the deterioration in the ROCE, down from 25.6% to only 18.0%. This represents an overall fall in profitability of 30% ((25.6 – 18.0)/25.6 x 100). An examination of the other ratios provided shows that this is due to a decline in both profit margins and asset utilisation.

A closer look at the profit margins shows that the decline in gross margin is relatively small (42.2% down to 41.4%), whereas the fall in the operating profit margin is down by 2.8 percentage points, representing a 15.7% decline in profitability (i.e. 2.8% on 17.8%). This has been caused by increases in operating expenses of $12m and unallocated corporate expenses of $10m. These increases represent more than half of the net profit for the period and further investigation into the cause of these increases should be made.

The company is generating only $1.40 of sales per $1 of net statement of financial position assets this year compared to a figure of $1.70 in the previous year. This decline in asset utilisation represents a fall of 17.6% ((1.7 – 1.4)/1.7 x 100).

Liquidity/solvency

From the limited information provided, a poor current ratio of 0.9:1 in 20X8 has improved to 1.3:1 in the current year. Despite the improvement, it is still below the accepted norm. At the same time gearing has increased from 12.8% to 15.6%.

The statement of financial position shows the company has raised $65 million in new capital. This was in the form of $40m in equity (total increase in share capital and share premium) and $25m in loans. The disproportionate increase in the loans is the cause of the increase in gearing; however, at 15.6% this is still not a highly geared company.

The increase in finance has been used mainly to purchase new non-current assets, but it has also improved liquidity, mainly by reversing an overdraft of $5 million to a bank balance in hand of $15 million.

A common feature of new investment is that there is often a delay between making the investment and benefiting from the returns. This may be the case with Boston, and it may be that in future years the increased investment will be rewarded with higher returns. Another aspect of the investment that may have caused the lower return on assets is that the investment is likely to have occurred part way through the year (maybe even near the year end). This means that the income statement may not include returns for a full year, whereas in future years it will.

Segment issues

Segment information is intended to help the users to better assess the performance of an enterprise by looking at the detailed contribution made by the differing activities that comprise the enterprise as a whole.

Referring to the segment ratios it appears that the carpeting segment is giving the greatest contribution to overall profitability, achieving a 48.6% return on its segment assets, whereas the equivalent return for house building is 38.1% and for hotels it is only 16.7%.

The main reason for the better return from carpeting is due to its higher segment net profit margin of 38.9% compared to hotels at 15.4% and house building at 28.6%. Carpeting's higher segment net profit is in turn a reflection of its underlying very high gross margin (66.7%). The segment net asset turnover of the hotels (1.1 times) is also very much lower than the other two segments (1.3 times).

It should be noted that hotel profits have been reduced due to the loss of $12 million on the sale of a hotel. This should potentially be treated as an exceptional item and excluded from the analysis for comparability purposes.

It seems that the hotel segment is also responsible for the group's fairly poor liquidity ratios. Ignoring the bank balances, the segment current liabilities are 50% greater than its current assets ($60m compared to $40m); the opposite of this would be a more acceptable current ratio.

These figures are based on historical values. Most commentators argue that the use of fair values is more consistent and thus provides more reliable information on which to base assessments (they are less misleading than the use of historical values). If fair values are used, all segments understandably show lower returns and poorer performance (as fair values are higher than historical values), but the figures for the hotels are proportionately much worse, falling by a half of the historic values (as the fair values of the hotel segment are exactly double the historical values).

Fair value adjusted figures may even lead one to question the future of the hotel activities. However, before jumping to any conclusions an important issue should be considered. Although the reported profit of the hotels is poor, the market values of its segment assets have increased by a net $90 million. New net investment in hotel capital expenditure is $64 million ($104m – $40m disposal); this leaves an increase in value of $26 million. The majority of this appears to be from market value increases. Whilst this is not a realised profit, it is nevertheless a significant and valuable gain (equivalent to 65% of the group reported net profit).

Conclusion

Although the company's overall performance has deteriorated in the current year, it is clear that at least some areas of the business have had considerable new investment which may take some time to bear fruit. This applies to the hotel segment in particular and may explain its poor performance, which is also partly offset by the strong increase in the market value of its assets.

Appendix

Further segment ratios:

	Carpeting	Hotels	House building
Return on net assets at fair value			
35/97 x 100%	36.1%		
20/240 x 100%		8.3%	
80/265 x 100%			30.2%
Asset turnover on fair values (times)			
90/97	0.9		
130/240		0.5	
280/265			1.1

Test your understanding 9 - March 2012 exam question

(a) **Benefits of operating segment information to investors**

Investors are normally looking for information that can help them estimate the future performance of an entity, in order to decide whether to make an investment, stay invested or to dispose of an investment. While the financial statements give the performance of the entity as a whole, the operating segment disclosures provide information on the performance and resources of the parts of the business that the management consider to be separately identifiable. Investors can then see the parts of the business that are expanding or declining, those with high or low margins and the resources that each is using to generate those returns.

Entities are growing in complexity and often operate across many business sectors, eg wholesale, retail, financial services. The risks associated with these sectors will be different and so to accurately assess the future risks facing an entity, users will need more than the combined figures in the financial statements. Entities may also operate in different geographical areas and be subject to different economic environments and again different risks. Operating segment disclosures provide information about where resources are based and from where revenues are generated.

IFRS 8 intends that the information provided in the operating segment disclosures reflects the information that the chief operating decision maker uses to make decisions about the business and so investors could be getting an inside view of the entity.

(b) **Limitations of using operating segment information**

Under IFRS 8, the entity's managers determine the reportable segments that exist in the entity. This is based on how the segments are viewed internally. Segments may be selected differently by each entity which reduces the comparability of segmental disclosures across entities.

Also, not all of the financial information can easily be allocated to segments - eg head office expenses and finance costs. This again makes it difficult for users to get a complete picture of the performance of segments and reduces comparability as allocation of costs and revenues may differ between entities.

(c) IFRS 8 and costs of preparing information

IFRS 8 requires that operating segment disclosures be based on the information that the entity produces for internal purposes in order to make decisions on how resources will be allocated, which areas to expand etc. If the information is already being internally produced it should not therefore cost much to comply with the IFRS 8 disclosures. The guidance provided by the standards is that operating segment disclosures should reflect the information that would typically be reviewed by the chief operating decision-maker in the organisation.

chapter

3

Earnings per share

Chapter learning objectives

On completion of their studies students should be able to:

- Calculate earnings per share under IAS 33 to include the effect of bonus issues, rights issues and convertible stock.

1 Session content

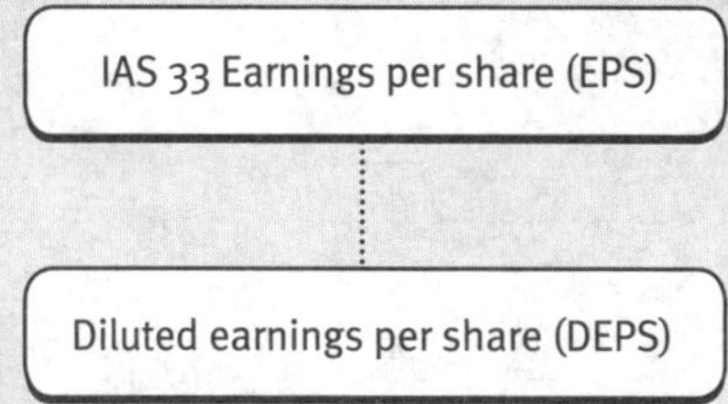

2 Earnings per share

Earnings per share (EPS) is widely regarded as the most important indicator of a company's performance.

It is also used in the calculation of the price-earnings ratio, a ratio closely monitored by analysts for listed companies. The price earnings ratio is equal to market price per share divided by earnings per share and gives an indicator of the level of confidence in the company by the market.

Consequently, EPS is the topic of its own accounting standard, IAS 33, which details rules on its calculation and presentation to ensure consistent treatment and comparability between companies.

Basic EPS

The basic EPS calculation is:

$$\text{EPS} = \frac{\text{Earnings}}{\text{Number of shares}}$$

This is expressed as dollars or cents per share (typically cents in exam questions).

- Earnings: Net profit attributable to ordinary equity shareholders of the parent entity, i.e. group profit after tax less non-controlling interests (see chapter 4) and irredeemable preference share dividends.
- Number of shares: Weighted average number of ordinary shares on a time weighted basis.

Issue of shares at full market price

Time apportion the number of shares issued during the period.

Illustration 1 - Weighted average number of shares

A has earnings of $300,000 during the year ended 31 December 20X6. On 1 January 20X6 A had share capital of 100,000 $1 shares. On 1 March 20X6 a further 60,000 shares were issued at $3.25 per share.

Required:

What is the basic EPS figure for the year ended 31 December 20X6?

Solution

$$EPS = \frac{\text{Earnings}}{\text{Number of shares}}$$

$$EPS = \frac{\$300,000}{(100,000 \times 2/12) + (160,000 \times 10/12)}$$

$$EPS = \frac{\$300,000}{150,000}$$

EPS = $2 per share

Example 1 - New issue of shares at market price

A company issued 200,000 shares at full market price ($3.00) on 1 July 20X8. There was no issue of shares in the year ended 31 December 20X7.

Relevant information

	20X8	**20X7**
Profit attributable to the ordinary shareholders for the year ending 31 December	$550,000	$460,000
Number of ordinary shares in issue at 31 December	1,000,000	800,000

Required:

Calculate the EPS for each of the years.

Example 1 answer

$$\text{20X7} \qquad \text{Number of shares} = \frac{\$460{,}000}{800{,}000} = 57.5c$$

Issue at full market price

Date	Actual number of shares	Fraction of year	Total
1 Jan 20X8	800,000	6/12	400,000
1 July 20X8	1,000,000	6/12	500,000
Number of shares in EPS calculation			900,000

$$\text{20X8} \qquad \text{Number of shares} = \frac{\$550{,}000}{900{,}000} = 61.1c$$

Since the 200,000 shares have only generated additional resources towards the earning of profits for half a year, the number of new shares is adjusted proportionately. Note that the approach is to use the earnings figure for the period without adjustment, but divide by the average number of shares weighted on a time basis.

Test your understanding 1

Gerard's earnings for the year ended 31 December 20X4 are $2,208,000. On 1 January 20X4, the issued share capital of Gerard was 8,280,000 ordinary shares of $1 each. The company issued 3,312,000 shares at full market value on 30 June 20X4.

Required:

Calculate the EPS for Gerard for 20X4.

Bonus issue

A bonus issue (or capitalisation issue or scrip issue):

- does not provide additional resources to the issuer.
- means that the shareholder owns the same proportion of the business before and after the issue.

In the calculation of EPS:

- the bonus shares are deemed to have been issued at the start of the year.
- comparative figures are restated to allow for the proportional increase in share capital caused by the bonus issue.

The EPS calculation becomes:

$$\text{EPS} = \frac{\text{Earnings}}{\text{No. of shares before bonus x bonus fraction}}$$

$$\text{Bonus fraction} = \frac{\text{No. of shares after bonus issue}}{\text{No. of shares before bonus issue}}$$

E.g. Company B holds 100,000 shares and makes a 1 for 10 bonus issue. 100,000/10 = 10,000 new shares issued.

$$\text{Bonus fraction} = \frac{110,000}{100,000} = \frac{11}{10}$$

- to adjust the comparative figures, multiply the previous year's basic EPS by the inverse of the bonus fraction, i.e. 100,000/110,000 or 10/11.

Illustration 2 - bonus issue

A company makes a bonus issue of one new share for every five existing shares held on 1 July 20X8.

	20X8	**20X7**
Profit attributable to the ordinary shareholders for the year ending 31 December	\$550,000	\$460,000
Number of ordinary shares in issue at 31 December	1,200,000	1,000,000

Required:

Calculate the EPS in 20X8 accounts, i.e. the current year EPS and comparatives for 20X7.

Solution

Calculation of EPS in 20X8 accounts.

$$20X8 \qquad \frac{\$550{,}000}{1{,}200{,}000} = 45.8c$$

$$20X7 \qquad \frac{\$460{,}000}{1{,}200{,}000} = 38.3c$$

In the example above, the computation for the comparative has been reworked in full. However, if last year's EPS is given then calculate the comparative EPS by multiplying this by the bonus fraction inverted.

Last year's EPS = 46c (\$460,000/1m)

The bonus fraction is:

$$\frac{1{,}200{,}000}{1{,}000{,}000} \quad \text{or} \quad \frac{6}{5}$$

Therefore, the comparative restated is

46c x 5/6 = 38.3c

Test your understanding 2

At 1 April 20X2, Dorabella had 7 million $1 ordinary shares in issue. It made a bonus issue of one share for every seven held on 31 August 20X2. Its earnings for the year were $1,150,000.

Dorabella's EPS for the year ended 31 March 20X2 was 10.7c.

Required:

Calculate the EPS for the year ending 31 March 20X3, together with the comparative EPS for 20X2 that would be presented in the 20X3 accounts.

Rights issue

Rights issues:

- contribute additional resources; and
- are normally priced below full market price.

Therefore, they combine the characteristics of issues at full market price and bonus issues.

Determining the weighted average capital, therefore, involves two steps as follows:

(1) adjust for the bonus element in the rights issue, by multiplying capital in issue before the rights issue by the following fraction:

$$\frac{\text{Actual cum rights price (CRP)}}{\text{Theoretical ex rights price (TERP)}}$$

- The cum rights price will be given to you in the exam question. It is the share price on the last trading day before the rights issue, i.e. the price of a share 'including' the rights.
- The theoretical ex-rights price is the theoretical share price after the rights issue has occurred. This must be calculated.

(2) calculate the weighted average capital in the issue on a time apportioned basis.

Illustration 3 - Theoretical ex rights price

C is making a 1 for 4 rights issue at $1.90 per share.

The cum rights price of C's shares is $2.00.

Required:

Calculate the theoretical ex rights price.

Solution

	Number of shares	x	Price	=	Value
Before rights	4	x	2.00	=	8.00
Rights issue	1	x	1.90	=	1.90
	——				——
After rights		x	?		

We are looking for the theoretical ex rights price (TERP), i.e. the price of a share after the rights issue, denoted by a question mark above.

Simply calculate the total value after the issue and divide it by the total number of shares after the issue.

	Number of shares	x	Price	=	Value
Before rights	4	x	2.00	=	8.00
Rights issue	1	x	1.90	=	1.90
	——				——
After rights	5	x	?		9.90

TERP = 9.90/ 5 = 1.98

The fraction to therefore apply (to the shares before the rights issue) to adjust for the bonus element is:

CRP/TERP = 2/1.98

Example 3 - Rights issue

A company issued one new share for every two existing shares held by way of rights at $1.50 per share on 1 July 20X8. Pre-issue market price was $3.00 per share.

Relevant information

	20X8	20X7
Profit attributable to the ordinary shareholders for the year ending 31 December	$550,000	$460,000
Number of ordinary shares in issue at 31 December	1,200,000	800,000

Required:

Calculate the EPS for 31 December 20X8 and the comparative for 20X7, assuming that there had been no share issues in 20X7.

Example 3 answer

20X8

$$\frac{\text{Earnings}}{\text{Weighted average number of shares (W1)}} = \frac{\$550{,}000}{1{,}080{,}000} = 50.9 \text{ cents}$$

20X7

The prior year EPS must be adjusted to reflect the bonus element in the rights issue.

$$\text{EPS} = 57.5\text{c (W3)} \times \frac{\$2.50 \text{ (W2)}}{\$3.00} = 47.9 \text{ cents}$$

NB: To restate the EPS for the previous year simply multiply EPS by the inverse of the rights issue bonus fraction.

(W1) **20X8 Weighted average number of shares**

The number of shares before the rights issue must be adjusted for the bonus element in the rights issue using the theoretical ex rights price.

6/12 × 800,000 × 3.00/2.50 (W2)	480,000
6/12 × 1,200,000	600,000
	1,080,000

(W2) **Theoretical ex rights price**

	2 shares	@ $3.00	$6.00
	1 share	@ $1.50	$1.50
	3 shares		$7.50
Theoretical ex rights price	= $7.50/3		$2.50

(W3)

20X7 EPS	=	$460,000 / 800,000
	=	57.5 cents

Test your understanding 3

On 31 December 20X1, the issued share capital of a company consisted of 4,000,000 ordinary shares of 25c each. On 1 July 20X2 the company made a rights issue in the proportion of 1 for 4 at 50c per share when the shares were quoted at $1. Its trading results for the last two years were as follows:

Year ended	**31 December**	
	20X2	**20X1**
	$	$
Profit after tax	425,000	320,000

There had been no shares issued during the year ended 31 December 20X1.

Required:

Show the calculation of basic EPS to be presented in the financial statements for the year ended 31 December 20X2 (including the comparative figure).

Test your understanding 4 - Rose

Extracts from Rose's financial statements for the year ended 30 April 20X4 and comparatives are shown below:

Income statement

	Year ending 30.4.X4	Year ending 30.4.X3
	$m	$m
Profit before tax	800	650
Income tax expense	(350)	(290)
Profit after tax	450	360

At 1 May 20X3 Rose has 900 million $1 ordinary shares in issue. There had been no share issues during the year ended 30 April 20X3.

Required:

Calculate the basic EPS, with comparatives, in each of the following situations:

(a) No changes in shares in the year ended 30 April 20X4.

(b) An issue of 50 million shares at full market price took place on 1 December 20X3.

(c) A bonus issue of 1 share for every 9 held was made on 1 September 20X3.

(d) On 1 July 20X3, a rights issue took place of 1 share for every 4 held at $2. The market value of each share immediately before the rights issue was $2.50.

3 Diluted earnings per share (DEPS)

Introduction

Equity share capital may change in the future owing to circumstances which exist now. The provision of a diluted EPS figure attempts to alert shareholders to the potential impact of these changes on the EPS figure.

Examples of dilutive factors are:

- the conversion terms for convertible bonds;
- the conversion terms for convertible preference shares;
- the exercise price for options and the subscription price for warrants.

When the potential ordinary shares are issued the total number of shares in issue will increase and this can have a dilutive effect on EPS i.e. it may fall. It will fall where the increase in shares outweighs any increase in profits e.g. due to a reduction in finance costs.

Basic principles of calculation

To deal with potential ordinary shares, adjust basic earnings and number of shares assuming convertibles, options, etc. had converted to equity shares on the first day of the accounting period, or on the date of issue, if later.

DEPS is calculated as follows:

$$\frac{\text{Earnings + notional extra earnings}}{\text{Number of shares + notional extra shares}}$$

Importance of DEPS

The basic EPS figure could be misleading to users if at some future time the number of shares in issue will increase without a proportionate increase in resources. For example, if an entity has issued bonds convertible at a later date into ordinary shares, on conversion the number of ordinary shares will rise, no fresh capital will enter the entity and earnings will therefore only rise by the savings made by no longer having to pay the post-tax amount of interest on the bonds. Often the earnings increase is proportionately less than the increase in the shares in issue. This effect is referred to as 'dilution' and the shares to be issued are called 'dilutive potential ordinary shares'.

IAS 33 therefore requires an entity to disclose the DEPS, as well as the basic EPS, calculated using current earnings but assuming that the worst possible future dilution has already happened. Existing shareholders can look at the DEPS to see the effect on current profitability of commitments already entered into to issue ordinary shares in the future.

For the purpose of calculating DEPS, the number of ordinary shares should be the weighted average number of ordinary shares calculated as for basic EPS, plus the weighted average number of ordinary shares which would be issued on the conversion of all the dilutive potential ordinary shares into ordinary shares. Dilutive potential ordinary shares are deemed to have been converted into ordinary shares at the beginning of the period or, if later, the date of the issue of the potential ordinary shares.

Convertibles

The principles of convertible bonds and convertible preference shares are similar and will be dealt with together.

If the convertible bonds/preference shares had been converted:

- the interest/dividend would be saved therefore earnings would be higher;
- the number of shares would increase.

Note: There will be an interest saving on bonds but not on preference dividends as they are not tax deductible.

Note: If there is an option to convert the debt into a variable number of ordinary shares depending on when conversion takes place, the maximum possible number of additional shares is used in the calculation.

Example 4 - Convertibles

A company has the following balances:

- $500,000 in 10% cumulative irredeemable preference shares of $1
- $1,000,000 in ordinary shares of 25c = 4,000,000 shares.

Income taxes are 30%.

On 1 April 20X1, the company issued convertible unsecured bonds for cash. Assuming the conversion was fully subscribed there would be an increase of 1,550,000 ordinary shares in issue.

The liability element of the bonds is $1,250,000 and the effective interest rate is 8%, resulting in an annual gross interest charge of $100,000.

Trading results for the years ended 31 December were as follows:

	20X2	20X1
	$	$
Profit before interest and tax	1,100,000	991,818
Interest on convertible unsecured bonds	(100,000)	(75,000)
Profit before tax	1,000,000	916,818
Income tax	(300,000)	(275,045)
Profit after tax	700,000	641,773

Required:

Calculate the basic and diluted EPS for 20X2 and 20X1.

Example 4 answer

	20X2	20X1
Basic EPS	$	$
Profit after tax	700,000	641,773
Less: Preference dividend	(50,000)	(50,000)
Earnings	650,000	591,773
EPS based on 4,000,000 shares	16.25c	14.8c

DEPS

Earnings as above	650,000	591,773
Notional extra earnings:		
Interest on the convertible unsecured bonds (only 9 months in 20X1)	100,000	75,000
Less: Income tax on interest at 30%	(30,000)	(22,500)
Adjusted earnings	720,000	644,273
EPS based on 5,550,000 shares (20X1 – 5,162,500)	13.0c	12.5c

The weighted average number of shares issued and issuable for 20X1 would have been 4,000,000 plus three quarters of 1,550,000, i.e. 5,162,500 (the convertibles issued on 1 April 20X1).

Convertible preference shares are dealt with on the same basis, except that often they do not qualify for tax relief so there is no tax saving foregone to be adjusted for.

Test your understanding 5

A company had 8.28 million shares in issue at the start of the year and made no new issue of shares during the year ended 31 December 20X4, but on that date it had in issue convertible loan stock 20X6-20X9.

Assuming the conversion was fully subscribed there would be an increase of 2,070,000 ordinary shares in issue. The liability element of the loan stock is $2,300,000 and the effective interest rate is 10%.

Assume a tax rate of 30%.The earnings for the year were $2,208,000.

Required:

Calculate the basic EPS and fully diluted EPS for the year ended 31 December 20X4.

Options and warrants to subscribe for shares

An option or warrant gives the holder the right to buy shares at some time in the future at a predetermined price.

The cash received by the entity when the option is exercised will be less than the market price of the shares, as the option will only be exercised if the exercise price is lower than the market price. The increase in resources does not match the increase there would be in resources if the issue of shares were at market value. The options will therefore have a dilutive effect on EPS.

The total number of shares issued on the exercise of the **option** or **warrant** is split into two:

- the number of shares that would have been issued if the cash received had been used to buy shares at fair value (using the average price of the shares during the period);
- the remainder, which are treated like a **bonus issue** (i.e. as having been issued for no consideration).

The number of shares issued for no consideration is added to the number of shares when calculating the DEPS.

The extra number of shares is equal to:

$$\text{No. of options} \times \frac{FV - EP}{FV}$$

FV = fair value of the share price

EP = exercise price of the shares

Example 5 - Options

On 1 January 20X7, a company has 4 million ordinary shares in issue and issues options over another million shares. The net profit for the year is $500,000.

During the year to 31 December 20X7 the average fair value of one ordinary share was $3 and the exercise price for the shares under option was $2.

Required:

Calculate basic EPS and DEPS for the year ended 31 December 20X7.

Example 5 answer

$$\text{Basic EPS} = \frac{\$500{,}000}{4{,}000{,}000} = 12.5c$$

Options

	$
Earnings	500,000
Number of shares	
Basic	4,000,000
Options (W1)	333,333
	4,333,333

$$\text{The DEPS is therefore } \frac{\$500{,}000}{4{,}333{,}333} = 11.5c$$

(W1) **Number of free shares issued**

$$\text{Free shares} = \text{No. of options} \times \frac{FV - EP}{FV}$$

$$\text{Free shares} = 1{,}000{,}000 \times \frac{3.00 - 2.00}{3.00} = 333{,}333$$

Test your understanding 6

A company had 8.28 million shares in issue at the start of the year and made no issue of shares during the year ended 31 December 20X4, but on that date there were outstanding options to purchase 920,000 ordinary $1 shares at $1.70 per share. The average fair value of ordinary shares was $1.80. Earnings for the year ended 31 December 20X4 were $2,208,000, giving rise to a basic EPS of 26.7c.

Required:

Calculate the fully DEPS for the year ended 31 December 20X4.

Test your understanding 7

On 1 January the issued share capital of Pillbox was 12 million preference shares of $1 each and 10 million ordinary shares of $1 each. Assume where appropriate that the income tax rate is 30%. The earnings for the year ended 31 December were $5,950,000.

You are given the following circumstances (a)–(f):

(a) there was no change in the issued share capital of the company during the year ended 31 December

(b) the company made a bonus issue on 1 October of one ordinary share for every four shares in issue at 30 September

(c) the company issued 1 million shares on 1 August at full market value of $4

(d) the company made a rights issue of $1 ordinary shares on 1 October in the proportion of 1 for every 3 shares held, at a price of $3. The middle market price for the shares on the last day of quotation cum rights was $4 per share

(e) the company made no new issue of shares during the year ended 31 December, but on that date it had in issue convertible bonds. Assuming the conversion was fully subscribed there would be an increase of 2,340,000 ordinary shares in issue. The liability element of the bond is $2,600,000 and the effective interest rate is 10%.

(f) the company made no issue of shares during the year ended 31 December, but on that date there were outstanding options to purchase 74,000 ordinary $1 shares at $2.50 per share. Share price during the year was $4.

Required:

Calculate separately the basic EPS in respect of the year ended 31 December for each of the circumstances (a)-(d) and the diluted EPS in respect of circumstances (e) and (f).

4 Chapter summary

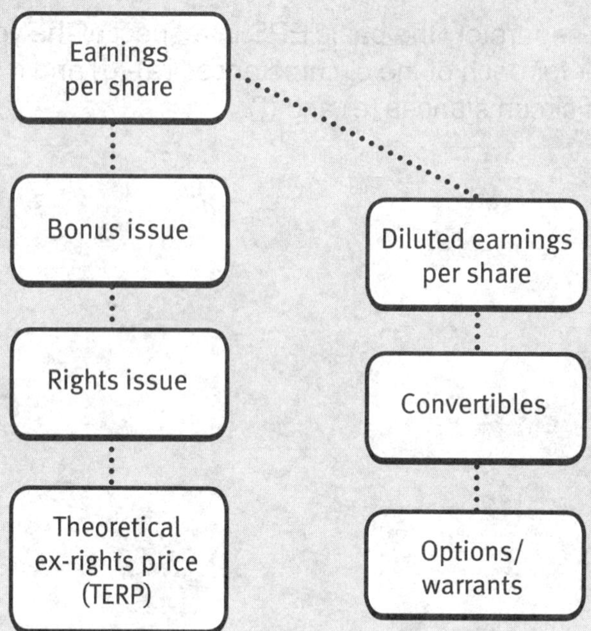

Test your understanding answers

Test your understanding 1

Issue at full market price

Date	Actual number of shares	Fraction of year	Total
1 January 20X4	8,280,000	6/12	4,140,000
30 June 20X4	11,592,000 (W1)	6/12	5,796,000
Number of shares in EPS calculation			9,936,000

(W1) **New number of shares**

Original number	8,280,000
New issue	3,312,000
New number	11,592,000

The earnings per share for 20X4 would now be calculated as:

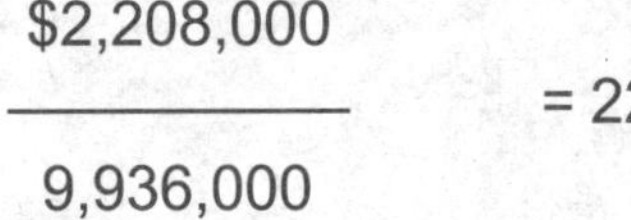

$$\frac{\$2{,}208{,}000}{9{,}936{,}000} = 22.2c$$

Test your understanding 2

The number of shares issued on 31 August 20X2 is 7,000,000 x 1/7 = 1,000,000

The EPS for 20X3 is 1,150,000 / 8,000,000 × 100 c = 14.4c

The bonus fraction is (7+1)/7 = 8/7

20X2 adjusted comparative = 10.7 × 7/8 (bonus fraction inverted) = 9.4c.

Test your understanding 3

20X2 EPS

$$\text{EPS} = \frac{\$425{,}000}{4{,}722{,}222\ (\text{W1})} = 9.0\text{c per share}$$

20X1 EPS

Applying correction factor to calculate adjusted comparative figure of EPS:

$$8\text{c (W3)} \times \frac{\text{Theoretical ex rights price}}{\text{Actual cum rights price}} = 8\text{c} \times \frac{90\text{c (W2)}}{100\text{c}} = 7.2\text{c per share}$$

(W1) **Current year weighted average number of shares**

The number of shares before the rights issue must be adjusted for the bonus element in the rights issue using the theoretical ex rights price.

6/12 × 4,000,000 × 1/0.90 (W2)	2,222,222
6/12 × 5,000,000	2,500,000
	4,722,222

(W2) **Theoretical ex rights price**

			$
Prior to rights issue	4 shares	worth 4 × $1 =	4.00
Taking up rights	1 share	cost 50c =	0.50
	5		4.50

i.e. theoretical ex rights price of each share is $4.50 ÷ 5 = 90c

(W3) **Prior year EPS**

Last year, reported EPS was $320,000 ÷ 4,000,000 = 8c

Test your understanding 4 - Rose

	20X4	20X3
(a) No change	$\frac{450}{900} = 50c$	$\frac{360}{900} = 40c$
(b) Issue at market price	$\frac{450}{(900 \times 7/12) + (950 \times 5/12)} = 48.9c$	$\frac{360}{900} = 40c$
(c) Bonus issue	$\frac{450}{(900 \times 10/9)} = 45c$	$40c \times \frac{9}{10} = 36c$
(d) Rights issue	$\frac{450}{(900 \times 2.50/2.40 \times 2/12) + (900 \times 5/4 \times 10/12)}$ = 41.1c	$\frac{40c \times 2.40}{2.50} = 38.4c$

(a) No changes: If there are no changes during the year EPS is simply equal to earnings divided by the number of shares.

(b) Share issued at full market price: Calculate the weighted average number of shares based on when the new shares were issued. No adjustment is necessary to the comparative because the new shares generate additional resources which should bring additional profits.

(c) Bonus issue: Calculate EPS as though the bonus shares had always been in issue by multiplying the number of shares before the issue by the bonus fraction. The comparative is multiplied by the inverse of the bonus fraction to adjust it for comparison between the years.

(d) Rights issue: Adjust for the rights issue bonus fraction (cum rights price / TERP). The TERP is calculated below. The number of shares are then time weighted. The comparative is multiplied by the inverse of the rights issue bonus fraction.

(W1) **Theoretical ex rights price**

			$
Prior to rights issue	4 shares	worth 4 × $2.50 =	10.00
Taking up rights	1 share	cost $2.00 =	2.00
	—		——
	5		12.00
	—		——

i.e. theoretical ex rights price of each share is $12 ÷ 5 = $2.40

The fraction to apply to the pre-issue number of shares is:

$$\frac{2.50}{2.40}$$

Test your understanding 5

Basic EPS = $2,208,000 / 8,280,000 = 26.7c

If this loan stock was converted to shares the impact on earnings would be as follows.

	$	$
Basic earnings		2,208,000
Add notional interest saved		
($2,300,000 × 10%)	230,000	
Less tax relief foregone $230,000 × 30%	(69,000)	
		161,000
Revised earnings		2,369,000
Number of shares if loan converted		
Basic number of shares		8,280,000
Notional extra shares		2,070,000
Revised number of shares		10,350,000

$$\text{DEPS} = \frac{\$2,369,000}{10,350,000} = 22.9\text{c}$$

Test your understanding 6

	$
Earnings	2,208,000
Number of shares	
Basic	8,280,000
Options (W1)	51,111
	8,331,111

The DEPS is therefore $\frac{\$2,208,000}{8,331,111}$ = 26.5c

(W1) **Number of free shares issued**

Free shares = No. of shares under option x $\frac{FV - EP}{FV}$

Free shares = 920,000 x $\frac{1.80 - 1.70}{1.80}$ = 51,111

Test your understanding 7

(a) EPS (basic) = 59.5c

Earnings	$5,950k
Shares	10,000k
EPS	59.5c

(b) EPS (basic) = 47.6c

Earnings	$5,950k
Shares (10m × 5/4)	12,500k
EPS	47.6c

(c) EPS (basic) = 57.1c

Earnings	$5,950k
Shares	10,416k
EPS	57.1c
Pre (7/12 ×10m)	5,833k
Post (5/12 ×11m)	4,583k
	10,416k

(d) EPS (basic) = 52.5c

Earnings	$5,950k
Shares	11,333k
EPS	52.5c
Pre (9/12 × 10m × 4.00/3.75)	8,000k
Post (3/12 × 10m × 4/3)	3,333k
	11,333k
Actual cum rights price	$4.00
TERP (1 x 3.00 + 3 x 4.00)/4	$3.75

(e) EPS (basic) = 59.5c

EPS (fully diluted) = 49.7c

Earnings (5.95m + (10% × 2.6m × 70%))	\$6,132k
Shares (10m + 2.34m)	12,340k
EPS	49.7c

(f) EPS (basic) = 59.5c

EPS (fully diluted) = 59.3c

Earnings	\$5,950k
Shares (10m + (74k x (4 - 2.50)/ 4))	10,028k
EPS	59.3c

chapter

4

Consolidated statement of financial position

Chapter learning objectives

On completion of their studies students should be able to:

- Explain the relationships between investors and investees and the meaning of control;
- Identify the circumstances in which a subsidiary is excluded from consolidation;
- Prepare consolidated financial statements for a group of companies;
- Explain the treatment in consolidated financial statements of non-controlling interests, pre- and post-acquisition reserves, goodwill (including its impairment), fair value adjustments, intra-group transactions and dividends.

1 Session content

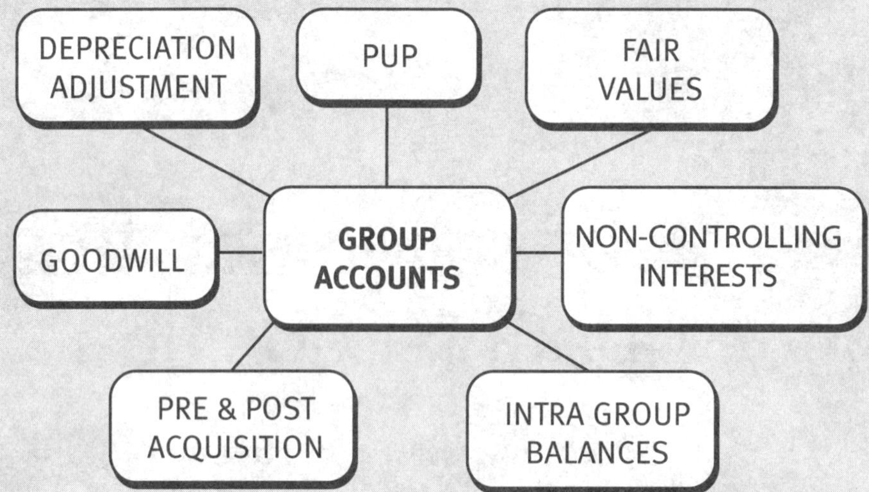

2 What is a group?

IFRS 10 - Consolidated financial statements

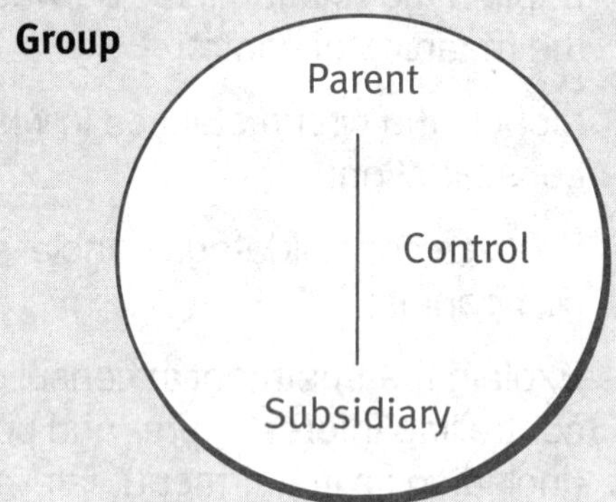

A group will exist where one company (the parent) **controls** another company (the subsidiary).

IFRS 10 *Consolidated Financial* Statements was published in May 2011, setting out a new definition of control and giving guidance on how to identify whether control exists.

An investor (the parent) **controls** an investee (the subsidiary) when the investor is exposed, or has rights, to variable returns from its involvement with the investee and has the ability to affect those returns through its power over the investee.

Power is defined as existing rights that give the current ability to direct the relevant activities.

In accordance with IFRS 10, an investor controls an investee if and only if the investor has all of the following elements:

- power over the investee (see definition of power above);

- exposure, or rights, to variable returns from its involvement with the investee; and
- the ability to use its power over the investee to affect the amount of the investor's returns.

Consolidated financial statements should be prepared when the parent has control over the subsidiary (for examination purposes control is usually established based on ownership of more than 50% of the voting rights).

Note that the basic principles and the mechanics of consolidation have not been changed, only the definition of control on which consolidation is based.

Exemption from preparation of group accounts

A parent need not present consolidated financial statements if it meets all of the following conditions:

- it is a wholly owned subsidiary or a partially-owned subsidiary and its owners, including those not otherwise entitled to vote, have been informed about, and do not object to, the parent not presenting consolidated financial statements;
- its debt or equity instruments are not traded in a public market;
- it did not file its financial statements with a securities commission or other regulatory organisation for the purpose of issuing any class of instruments in a public market;
- its ultimate parent company produces consolidated financial statements available for public use that comply with IFRS.

3 Acquisition accounting

This requires the following rules to be followed:

- Add the parent and subsidiary's assets, liabilities, income and expenses in full;
- Recognise the non-controlling interest's holding in the subsidiary;
- Recognise goodwill in accordance with IFRS 3 (revised) *Business Combinations* as the difference between the parent's cost of investment in the subsidiary together with the value of the non-controlling interest's holding and the fair value of the subsidiary's net assets;
- The share capital of the group is only the share capital of the parent;
- Adjustments are made to record the subsidiary's net assets at fair value at the date of acquisition;
- Intra-group balances and transactions must be eliminated in full;

- Profits/losses on intra-group transactions are eliminated in full (the PUP adjustment);
- Uniform accounting policies must be used.

Standard consolidated statement of financial position (CSFP) workings

(W1) **Group structure**

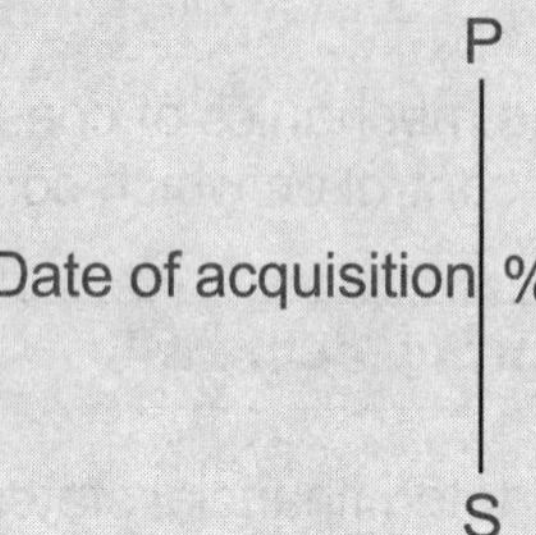

(W2) **Net assets of subsidiary**

	Acquisition Date		Reporting Date
Share capital	X		X
Retained earnings	X		X
Other reserves	X		X
Fair value adjustments	X		X
Depreciation adjustment	-		(X)
PUP adjustment (if sub is seller)	-		(X)
	X		X
		Difference = post-acquisition reserves	

(W3) **Goodwill**

Fair value of P's holding (cost of investment)	X
NCI holding at fair value or proportion of net assets	X
Fair value of sub's net assets at acquisition (W2)	(X)
Goodwill at acquisition	X
Impairment	(X)
Goodwill at reporting date	X

(W4) **Non-controlling interests**

NCI holding at acquisition (W3) (at fair value or proportion of net assets)	X
NCI% x post acquisition reserves (W2)	X
NCI% x impairment (W3) (fair value method only)	(X)
	X

(W5) **Group reserves**

	Retained earnings	**Other reserves**
Parent's reserves	X	X
Sub (P% × post-acquisition reserves (W2))	X	X
Impairment (W3) (use P% for fair value method)	(X)	–
	X	X

4 Non-controlling interest and goodwill

In paper F1 (Financial Operations), only fully owned (100%) subsidiaries were examinable. The F2 syllabus requires knowledge of how to consolidate non-fully owned subsidiaries.

By definition, a subsidiary is an entity that is controlled by another entity – the parent. Control is normally achieved by the parent owning a majority i.e. more than 50% of the equity shares of the subsidiary.

Non-controlling interest (NCI) shareholders own the shares in the subsidiary not owned by the parent entity.

NCI shareholders are considered to be shareholders of the group and thus their ownership interest in the subsidiary's net assets is reflected within equity.

Additionally, when calculating goodwill at acquisition the value of the NCI's holding is added to the value of the parent's holding in the subsidiary so that the value of the subsidiary as a whole (100%) is compared against all of its net assets.

IFRS 3 (2008) allows two methods to be used to value the NCI's holding at the date of acquisition:

- Fair value
- Proportion of net assets

IFRS 3 (2008) permits groups to choose their policy on how to value NCI on an acquisition by acquisition basis. In other words, it is possible for a group to have some subsidiaries where the fair value method is being adopted, but other subsidiaries where the proportion of net assets method is adopted. An exam question will state which method is to be used.

Fair value method

The fair value of the non-controlling interest's holding may be calculated using the market value of the subsidiary's shares at the date of acquisition or other valuation techniques if the subsidiary's shares are not traded in an active market. In exam questions, it is likely that you will be told the fair value of the NCI's holding (or given the subsidiary's share price in order to be able to calculate it).

Proportion of net assets method

Under this method, the NCI's holding is measured by calculating their share of the fair value of the subsidiary's net assets at acquisition.

Example 1

Sherriff purchased 60% of Nottingham's 3,000 shares on 1 January 20X9. Sherriff paid $5,500 cash for their investment. At 1 January 20X9, the fair value of Nottingham's net assets was $5,000. Nottingham's share price at this date was $2.25.

Required:

Calculate the goodwill arising on the acquisition of Nottingham, valuing the NCI's holding:

(a) Using the fair value method

(b) Using the proportion of net assets method

Example 1 answer

Goodwill

	Fair value method	Proportion of net assets method
	$	$
Fair value of P's holding	5,500	5,500
NCI's holding (W1/ W2)	2,700	2,000
Fair value S's net assets	(5,000)	(5,000)
Goodwill at acquisition	3,200	2,500

(W1) **NCI's holding – fair value method**

The subsidiary's share price is provided and so this is used to value the NCI's 40% holding in Nottingham.

The NCI owns:

40% x 3,000 shares = 1,200 shares

The fair value of this shareholding is:

1,200 x $2.25 = $2,700

(W2) **NCI's holding – proportion of net assets method**

The NCI's 40% holding is simply valued by taking this proportion of the subsidiary's net assets at acquisition of $5,000.

40% x $5,000 = $2,000

Test your understanding 1 - Wellington

Wellington purchased 80% of the equity share capital of Boot for $1,200,000 on 1 April 20X8. Boot's share capital is made up of 200,000 $1 shares and it had retained earnings of $800,000 at the date of acquisition. The book value of Boot's net assets was deemed to be equal to their fair value. The fair value of the NCI's holding as at 1 April 20X8 was $250,000.

Required:

Calculate the goodwill arising on the acquisition of Boot, valuing the NCI's holding:

(a) Using the fair value method

(b) Using the proportion of net assets method

Goodwill and NCI

Under the previous IFRS 3, it was only permitted to recognise the NCI's holding using the proportion of net assets method. This method resulted in only the goodwill attributable to the parent shareholders being recognised in the consolidated accounts. Using the information from TYU 1, consider the following alternative calculation of goodwill under this method:

	$000
Fair value of P's holding	1,200
P% x sub's net assets at acquisition (80% x 1,000)	(800)
Goodwill at acquisition	400

In the above calculation, rather than adding in the NCI's share (20%) of the subsidiary's net assets and then subtracting 100% of these net assets, just the parent's share (80%) has been deducted from the fair value of the parent's holding. This achieves the same answer for goodwill but more clearly demonstrates why valuing the NCI's holding at the proportion of net assets is equivalent to only the goodwill attributable to the parent's holding being recognised. Consequently this method is also referred to as the "partial" method of calculating goodwill.

This method was considered inconsistent with the treatment of the other assets of the subsidiary. Since the group controls the assets of the subsidiary, they are fully consolidated in the group accounts, i.e. 100% is added in line by line. Goodwill is an asset of the subsidiary in exactly the same way that property, inventory, etc, are assets of the subsidiary. So if property and inventory are consolidated in full, goodwill should be treated in the same way.

Therefore when IFRS 3 was revised in 2008, the option of valuing the NCI's holding at fair value was introduced. This recognises that the value of the NCI's holding should also reflect the goodwill attributable to their holding. Again, using the information from TYU 1, this can perhaps be more clearly illustrated using the following alternative goodwill calculation under the fair value method:

	$000	$000
Fair value of P's holding	1,200	
P% x sub's net assets at acquisition (80% x 1,000)	(800)	
Goodwill attributable to P shareholders		400
Fair value of NCI's holding	250	
NCI% x sub's net assets at acquisition (20% x 1,000)	(200)	
		50
Goodwill at acquisition		450

In this alternative calculation, the subsidiary's net assets have simply been deducted in two separate stages rather than on a single line as has been done in the answer to TYU 1.

These alternative calculations for goodwill will achieve the correct answers, but for exam purposes it is more appropriate to use the format as used in the answer to TYU 1. Not only is this format in accordance with IFRS 3 revised, it is also the format used by your examiner. It also results in you only having to learn one proforma for the calculation of goodwill with the only difference being how the NCIs are valued.

It is worth noting that the fair value of the NCI's holding is not normally proportionate to the fair value of the parent's holding. Again, using TYU 1 to illustrate, the parent's holding of 80% is four times that of the NCI's 20% holding. However, the fair value of the parent's holding of $1,200,000 is more than four times that of the NCI's holding which has a fair value of $250,000. This is because the parent's 80% holding provides control of the subsidiary and so the value of an 80% holding is proportionately more as it includes a premium for obtaining control.

Test your understanding 2 - Ruby

Ruby purchased 75% of the equity share capital of Sapphire for $2,500,000 on 1 April 20X8. Sapphire's share capital is made up of 500,000 $1 shares and it had retained earnings of $1,500,000 at the date of acquisition. The book value of Sapphire's net assets was deemed to be equal to their fair value. The fair value of the NCI's holding as at 1 April 20X8 should be calculated by reference to the subsidiary's share price. The market value of a Sapphire share at 1 April 20X8 was $6.

Required:

Calculate the goodwill arising on the acquisition of Sapphire, valuing the NCI's holding:

(a) Using the fair value method

(b) Using the proportion of net assets method

5 Impairment of goodwill

IFRS 3 (r2008) requires that goodwill is tested at each reporting date for impairment. This means that goodwill is reviewed to ensure that its value is not overstated in the consolidated statement of financial position.

In the exam, you will either be told the amount of the impairment loss or you will be told to calculate it as a percentage of the goodwill. You will not be required to calculate the impairment loss by carrying out an impairment review.

If an impairment loss exists, goodwill is written down and the loss is charged against profits in the consolidated income statement.

This charge against profits will result in a reduction in the equity section of the CSFP. How the impairment loss is charged against equity in the CSFP will depend on the method adopted for valuing the NCI's holding, or in other words, the method used to calculate goodwill.

Fair value method

As discussed in the expandable text "Goodwill and NCI", valuing the NCI holding at fair value is equivalent to recognising goodwill in full, i.e. goodwill attributable to both the parent and NCI shareholders is recognised.

Consequently, any impairment loss is charged to both the parent and NCI shareholders in the equity section of the CSFP in accordance with their ownership ratio of the subsidiary.

To record the impairment loss:

- Reduce Goodwill W3 by the full amount of the impairment loss;
- Reduce NCIs W4 by the NCI% of the impairment loss;
- Reduce Retained earnings W5 by the P% of the impairment loss.

Proportion of net assets method

As discussed in the expandable text above, valuing the NCI holding at their proportion of the subsidiary's net assets is equivalent to recognising only the goodwill attributable to the parent shareholders.

Consequently, any impairment loss is only charged to the parent shareholders in the equity section of the CSFP.

To record the impairment loss:

- Reduce Goodwill W3 by the amount of the impairment loss;
- Reduce Retained earnings W5 by the amount of the impairment loss.

Example 2

P acquired 75% of the equity share capital of S on 1 April 20X2, paying $900,000 in cash. At this date, the retained earnings of S were $300,000. Below are the statements of financial position of P and S as at 31 March 20X4:

	P	**S**
	$000	$000
Non-current assets	1,650	750
Investment in S	900	–
Current assets	450	650
	3,000	1,400
Equity		
Share capital	1,500	500
Retained earnings	900	400
Non current liabilities	100	50
Current liabilities	500	450
	3,000	1,400

It is group policy to value NCIs using the fair value method. The fair value of the NCI holding in S at 1 April 20X2 was $275,000.

As at 31 March 20X4, goodwill was impaired by $60,000.

Required:

(a) Prepare a consolidated statement of financial position as at 31 March 20X4.

(b) How would the CSFP change if the proportion of net assets method were used to value the NCI holding at acquisition?

Example 2 answer

(a) Firstly, draw up the group structure to understand what the relationship is between the companies. This is a good habit to form as it will be very useful when the group becomes more complicated.

(W1) **Group structure**

P

75% 1 April 20X2, i.e. 2 years since acquisition

S

Now that it has been identified that a group exists i.e. that the parent controls the subsidiary, it is worth setting up a proforma for your answer and adding across the parent and subsidiary's assets and liabilities. This will achieve some easy marks in an exam question.

Note:

- The share capital of the group is always only the share capital of the parent and so this can be inserted straight into the answer.
- The investment in S in the parent's individual statement of financial position will be taken to the goodwill calculation and so can be left out of the proforma. Instead insert a line for "goodwill" and reference this to W3.
- Include a line in the equity section for non-controlling interests and reference this to W4.

– Retained earnings in the equity section should be referenced to W5.

Consolidated statement of financial position as at 31 March 20X4

		$000
Non-current assets	(1,650 + 750)	2,400
Goodwill (W3)		
Current assets	(450 + 650)	1,100
		——
		——
Equity		
Share capital		1,500
Retained earnings (W5)		
Non-controlling interest (W4)		
Non-current liabilities	(100 + 50)	150
Current liabilities	(500 + 450)	950
		——
		——

Now we can continue with the standard workings, W2 through to W5.

(W2) **Net assets of subsidiary**

	Acquisition Date		**Reporting Date**
Share capital	500		500
Retained earnings	300		400
	——		——
	800		900
	——	100 = post acquisition reserves	——

Remember the accounting equation:

Equity = Assets – Liabilities

i.e. Equity = Net Assets

Therefore, although this working is referred to as the net assets working, it is actually the equity section of the subsidiary's statement of financial position. The figures in the reporting date column are copied straight from the SFP in the question. It may be assumed that the share capital of the subsidiary does not change and so was also $500,000 at acquisition two years ago. The retained earnings of the subsidiary at acquisition is given in the first paragraph of the scenario.

The increase in net assets of $100,000 represents post-acquisition gains recorded by the subsidiary. Since the subsidiary has only one reserve of retained earnings, this gain is post-acquisition profit. (If the subsidiary had other reserves, such as a revaluation reserve, post-acquisition gains could be made up of both a revaluation gain and profit.)

These post-acquisition gains belong to the shareholders of the subsidiary, i.e. 75% to the parent and 25% to the NCI shareholders and are allocated accordingly in workings 4 and 5.

(W3) **Goodwill**

	$000
Fair value of P's holding (cost of investment)	900
NCI holding at fair value	275
Fair value of sub's net assets at acquisition (W2)	(800)
Goodwill at acquisition	375
Impairment	(60)
Goodwill at reporting date	315

The fair value of the parent's holding is taken either from the line "Investment in S" in the parent's SFP or from the narrative information given. The question states that it is the group's policy to value the NCI's holding at fair value and the figure of $275,000 is given.

The question states that goodwill has been impaired by $60,000 and so the balance of goodwill to be recorded in the CSFP at the reporting date is $315,000.

(W4) **Non-controlling interests**

	$000
NCI holding at acquisition (W3)	275
NCI% x post acquisition reserves (25% x 100 (W2))	25
NCI% x impairment (25% x 60 (W3))	(15)
	285

The NCI holding at acquisition is measured at its fair value of $275,000 as given in the question. Since acquisition the subsidiary has made gains of $100,000, as shown in W2. The NCI shareholders are entitled to 25% of these gains. Thus their holding has increased in value by $25,000.

However, because the NCI holding has been valued at acquisition under the fair value method, the NCI shareholders are charged with their 25% share of the $60,000 impairment loss arising on goodwill. This reduces their share of the group's equity to $285,000 at the reporting date.

(W5) **Group reserves**

	Retained earnings
Parent's reserves	900
Sub (75% × 100 (W2))	75
Impairment (75% x 60 (W3))	(45)
	930

The only reserve in this question is retained earnings i.e. accumulated profits. The retained earnings figure in the CSFP represents the accumulated profits belonging to the parent shareholders. This is made up of the parent entity's retained earnings plus their share (75%) of the subsidiary's post acquisition profits less their share of any impairment losses on goodwill. Since the NCIs have been valued using the fair value method, the parent shareholders are charged with their 75% share of the impairment loss.

Now that we have completed the workings, the figures can be transferred to the answer and so the CSFP can be completed:

Consolidated statement of financial position as at 31 March 20X4

		$000
Non-current assets	(1,650 + 750)	2,400
Goodwill (W3)		315
Current assets	(450 + 650)	1,100
		3,815
Equity		
Share capital		1,500
Retained earnings (W5)		930
		2,430
Non-controlling interest (W4)		285
		2,715
Non-current liabilities	(100 + 50)	150
Current liabilities	(500 + 450)	950
		3,815

It is perhaps worth noting that the net assets i.e. assets ($3,815,000) less liabilities ($150,000 + $950,000) of the group at the reporting date are $2,715,000.

This represents the net assets that are under the control of the group.

The net assets i.e. equity are owned by the shareholders of the group and this is reflected within the equity section of the CSFP. A group is owned by two sets of shareholders – the parent shareholders and the NCI shareholders. The parent's share of equity is $2,430,000 whilst the NCI's share is $285,000.

(b) If the proportion of net assets method were used, this would change the goodwill & NCI calculations. Since goodwill is impaired this method would also change retained earnings as the parent shareholders would now suffer the full amount of the impairment loss.

Note: It is being assumed that the question would still state that the impairment loss arising on goodwill is $60,000. (In reality, if goodwill were being measured using the proportion of net assets method, this would result in a different impairment loss compared to that arising under the fair value method.)

W3, W4, W5 and the CSFP would become as follows:

(W3) **Goodwill**

	$000
Fair value of P's holding (cost of investment)	900
NCI holding at proportion of net assets (25% x 800 (W2))	200
Fair value of sub's net assets at acquisition (W2)	(800)
Goodwill at acquisition	300
Impairment	(60)
Goodwill at reporting date	240

(W4) **Non-controlling interests**

	$000
NCI holding at acquisition (W3)	200
NCI% x post acquisition reserves (25% x 100 (W2))	25
	225

(W5) **Group reserves**

	Retained earnings
Parent's reserves	900
Sub (75% × 100 (W2))	75
Impairment (W3)	(60)
	915

Consolidated statement of financial position as at 31 March 20X4

		$000
Non-current assets	(1,650 + 750)	2,400
Goodwill (W3)		240
Current assets	(450 + 650)	1,100
		3,740
Equity		
Share capital		1,500
Retained earnings (W5)		915
		2,415
Non-controlling interest (W4)		225
		2,640
Non-current liabilities	(100 + 50)	150
Current liabilities	(500 + 450)	950
		3,740

Tutorial note

There are a variety of workings that can be used to arrive at the final figures for inclusion in the consolidated statement of financial position. The above method combines the calculation of net assets at acquisition with the calculation of post-acquisition reserves within W2. The examiner's solutions will typically show the calculation of net assets at acquisition as part of the goodwill working and then the calculation of post-acquisition reserves will be separately calculated as part of the retained earnings working. The calculations are effectively the same, but with a slightly different layout.

Test your understanding 3

P acquired 80% of the equity share capital of S on 1 April 20X2, paying $2.5m in cash. At this date, the retained earnings of S were $950,000. Below are the statements of financial position of P and S as at 31 March 20X4:

	P	**S**
	$000	$000
Non-current assets	3,500	2,400
Investment in S	2,500	–
Current assets	1,000	600
	7,000	3,000
Equity		
Share capital	4,000	1,000
Retained earnings	2,150	1,450
Non current liabilities	200	150
Current liabilities	650	400
	7,000	3,000

It is group policy to value NCIs using the fair value method. The fair value of the NCI holding in S at 1 April 20X2 was $600,000.

As at 31 March 20X4, goodwill has been impaired by $150,000.

Required:

Prepare a consolidated statement of financial position as at 31 March 20X4.

Test your understanding 4

P acquired 75% of the equity share capital of S on 1 April 20X5, paying $6.5m in cash. At this date, the retained earnings of S were $2.5m. Below are the statements of financial position of P and S as at 31 March 20X8:

	P	S
	$000	$000
Non-current assets	14,000	9,500
Investment in S	6,500	–
Current assets	4,500	3,000
	25,000	12,500
Equity		
Share capital	10,000	5,000
Retained earnings	10,800	4,500
Non current liabilities	750	600
Current liabilities	3,450	2,400
	25,000	12,500

As at 31 March 20X8, 20% of the goodwill as at acquisition should be written off as an impairment loss.

Required:

Prepare a consolidated statement of financial position as at 31 March 20X8, on the basis that it is group policy to measure NCIs:

(a) at fair value with the fair value of the NCI holding at 1 April 20X5 being $2m

(b) at their proportion of the subsidiary's net assets

6 Goodwill and fair values

As mentioned in section 3, goodwill is treated in accordance with IFRS 3 (revised) Business Combinations.

Goodwill is a residual amount calculated by comparing, at acquisition, the value of the subsidiary as a whole and the fair value of its identifiable net assets at this time. A residual amount may exist as a result of the subsidiary's:

- Positive reputation;
- Loyal customer base;
- Staff expertise etc

Goodwill is capitalised as an intangible asset on the consolidated statement of financial position (CSFP). It is subject to an annual impairment review to ensure its value is not overstated on the CSFP.

Goodwill is calculated as:

Fair value of P's holding (cost of investment)	X
NCI holding at fair value or proportion of net assets	X
Fair value of sub's net assets at acquisition (W2)	(X)
Goodwill at acquisition	X
Impairment	(X)
Goodwill at reporting date	X

Fair value is defined in IFRS 13 *Fair Value Measurement* as "the price that would be received to sell an asset ot paid to transfer a liability in an orderly transaction between market participants at the measurement date".

It is worth emphasising that goodwill is measured at the date of acquisition i.e. the date on which the parent achieves control of the subsidiary. Therefore the components of the goodwill calculation are all measured as at the date of acquisition.

Occasionally, the consideration paid for the subsidiary may be less than the fair value of the identifiable net assets at acquisition. This may arise when the previous shareholders have been forced to sell the subsidiary and so are selling their holding at a bargain price. This situation gives rise to "negative goodwill" at acquisition and represents a credit balance. It is viewed as a gain on a "bargain purchase" and so is credited directly to profits and so the group's retained earnings.

Section 4 has already discussed how the NCI's holding is valued at acquisition. Sections 7 and 8 explain how to measure the fair value of the parent's holding and the fair value of the subsidiary's net assets.

7 Fair value of parent's holding

The value of the parent's holding in the subsidiary comprises the fair value at the date of acquisition of all consideration given by the parent company in return for their holding in the subsidiary. It is effectively the parent's cost of the investment in the subsidiary and is recognised within "Investments" in their individual statement of financial position.

It can be made up of several forms of consideration:

Cash	X
Shares issued by parent company (at market value)	X
Deferred consideration (at present value of future cash flows)	X
Contingent consideration (at fair value)	X
	——
Fair value of P's holding	X
	——

Note that directly attributable costs incurred in acquiring the subsidiary such as professional or legal fees are not included. They are expensed to the parent's Income Statement. This is because they are not part of what the parent gives in return for the shareholding in the subsidiary and so do not represent part of the value of that shareholding.

Additionally, provisions for future losses or expenses are not part of the value of the parent's holding in the subsidiary. However, they may be provided for in the parent's individual financial statements in accordance with IAS 37 Provisions if the recognition criteria are met.

Deferred consideration

This is consideration, normally cash, which will be paid in the future.

It is measured at its present value at acquisition for inclusion within the goodwill calculation, i.e. the future cash flow is discounted.

It is recorded in the parent's individual financial statements by:

Dr Investments

Cr Deferred consideration liability

Every year after acquisition, the liability will need to be increased to reflect that that payment is one year closer and so the present value has increased. This is referred to as unwinding the discount. The increase in the liability is charged as a finance cost. Therefore, the entry recorded in the parent's individual financial statements is:

Dr Finance cost (and so reduces the parent's retained earnings)

Cr Deferred consideration liability

Contingent consideration

Contingent consideration is consideration that may be paid in the future if certain future events occur or conditions are met. For example, cash may be paid in the future if certain profit targets are met.

Contingent consideration is measured at its fair value at the date of acquisition, to be consistent with how other forms of consideration are measured.

In exam questions, the fair value will be given or you will be told how to calculate it.

Adjustments to the value of contingent consideration arising from events after the acquisition date, e.g. a profit target not being met, are normally charged/credited to profits.

Example 3

Malawi has acquired 80% of the shares in Blantyre. The consideration consisted of:

(1) Cash paid $25,460.

(2) Malawi issued 10,000 shares to the shareholders of Blantyre, each with a nominal value of $1 and a market value of $4.

(3) Cash of $20,000 to be paid one year after the date of acquisition.

(4) Cash of $100,000 may be paid one year after the date of acquisition, if Blantyre achieves a certain profit target. It is thought that there is only a 40% chance that this will occur. The fair value of this consideration is to be measured as the present value of the expected value.

(5) Legal fees associated with the acquisition amounted to $15,000.

A discount rate of 10% should be used.

Required:

Calculate the fair value of Malawi's holding in Blantyre to be used in the goodwill calculation.

Example 3 answer

Goodwill

Fair value of P's holding (cost of investment)	$
Cash	25,460
Shares (10,000 x $4)	40,000
Deferred consideration ($20,000 x 0.909)	18,180
Contingent consideration ($100,000 x 40% x 0.909)	36,360
	120,000
NCI holding at fair value or proportion of net assets	X
Fair value of sub's net assets at acquisition	(X)
Goodwill on acquisition	X
Impairment	(X)
Goodwill at reporting date (in CSFP)	X

The cash payment of $20,000 in one year's time is deferred consideration as it is guaranteed that it will be paid. The future cash flow of $20,000 is discounted back to present value by applying the discount factor as obtained from discount tables (see Formulae & Tables at front of text) using an interest rate of 10% in 1 year's time.

The cash payment of $100,000 in one year's time is contingent consideration as it is dependent on Blantrye achieving a profit target. The question states that the fair value is to be the present value of the expected value. The expected value is 40% x $100,000 = $40,000 as it takes into account the expected probability of the profit target being achieved. This is then discounted to present value by applying the appropriate discount factor using an interest rate of 10% in 1 year's time.

Test your understanding 5

Duck has invested in 60% of Wicket's 10,000 $1 equity shares. Duck paid $5,000 cash consideration and issued 2 shares for every 3 shares acquired. At the date of acquisition the market value of a Duck share was $2.25.

Duck agreed to pay $3,000 cash 2 years after acquisition. A further $1,000 cash will be paid 3 years after acquisition if Wicket achieves a certain profit target. The fair value of this contingent consideration was deemed to be $700.

At acquisition the fair value of the NCI holding was measured at $10,000 and the fair value of Wicket's net assets was $15,000.

Assume a discount rate of 10%.

Required:

Using the fair value method, calculate the goodwill arising on the acquisition of Wicket.

8 Fair value of subsidiary's net assets

At acquisition, the subsidiary's net assets must be measured at fair value for inclusion within the consolidated financial statements.

The group must recognise the identifiable assets acquired and liabilities assumed of the subsidiary.

- An asset or liability may only be recognised if it meets the definition of an asset or liability as at the acquisition date.

  For example, costs relating to restructuring the subsidiary that will arise after acquisition do not meet the definition of a liability at the date of acquisition.

- An asset is identifiable if it either:
  - Is capable of being separated (regardless of whether the subsidiary intends to sell it); or
  - Arises from contractual or other legal rights.

Consequently certain intangible assets such as brand names, patents and customer relationships that are not recognised in the subsidiary's individual financial statements may be recognised on consolidation if they are identifiable.

Contingent liabilities are not recognised in the subsidiary's individual financial statements. (In accordance with IAS 37 they are simply disclosed by note.) On consolidation, however, a contingent liability will be recognised as a liability if it's fair value can be measured reliably, i.e. it is recognised even if it is not probable.

In the majority of exam questions, you are told the fair value of the subsidiary's assets / liabilities or are told the adjustment required to certain items. However, it may be required that you will need to calculate the fair value of certain assets / liabilities, in which case IFRS 3 provides guidance on how to do this.

Measuring fair value

IFRS 3 provides the following guidance on measuring the fair value of certain assets / liabilities:

Item	**Valuation**
Property, plant and equipment	Market value. If there is no evidence of market value, depreciated replacement cost should be used
Intangible assets	Market value. If none exists, an amount that reflects what the acquirer would have paid otherwise.
Inventories	(i) Finished goods should be valued at selling prices less the sum of disposal costs and a reasonable profit allowance. (ii) Work in progress should be valued at ultimate selling prices less the sum of completion costs, disposal costs and a reasonable profit allowance. (iii) Raw materials should be valued at current replacement costs.
Receivables, payables and loans	Present value of future cash flows expected to be received or paid. Discounting is unlikely to be necessary for short-term receivables or payables.

Example 4

Brussels acquired 75% of Madrid. It is group policy to measure NCIs using the proportion of net assets method.

The consideration comprised cash of $5m, 1.5m shares with a nominal value of $1 and a fair value of $1.50 and further cash consideration of $1m to be paid one year after acquisition.

At acquisition, the statement of financial position of Madrid showed equity share capital of $3m and retained earnings of $3.25m. Included in this total is:

- freehold land with a book value of $400,000 but a market value of $950,000.
- machinery with a book value of $1.2m. No reliable market value exists for these items. They would cost $1.5m to replace as new. The machinery has an expected life of 10 years and Madrid's machines are 4 years old.
- The fair value of all other assets and liabilities is approximately equal to book value.

Madrid's brand name was internally generated and so is not recognised in their statement of financial position. However, valuation experts have estimated its fair value to be $500,000.

The directors of Brussels intend to close down one of the divisions of Madrid and wish to provide for operating losses up to the date of closure which are forecast as $729,000.

An investment in plant and machinery will be required to bring the remaining production line of Madrid up to date. This will amount to $405,000 in the next 12 months.

Assume a discount rate of 10%.

Required:

Calculate the goodwill arising on the acquisition of Madrid.

Example 4 answer

The subsidiary's net assets are recorded in W2 and so this is the working in which to process any fair value adjustments. Start by setting up W2 by filling in the subsidiary's share capital and retained earnings at acquisition. Note that since the question only requires the calculation of goodwill, only the net assets at acquisition are required.

(W2) **Net assets of subsidiary**

	Acquisition
	$000
Share capital	3,000
Retained earnings	3,250
	____
	____

Now consider the adjustments required to adjust the net assets from their book values to their fair values.

Land – this requires an upwards adjustment of $550,000 (fair value of $950,000 less book value of $400,000)

Machinery – the fair value is not given and so needs to be calculated. It will be measured as the depreciated replacement cost. Madrid's machines have an expected life of 10 years and are 4 years old. Therefore, their remaining life is 6 years.

Depreciated replacement cost = 6 / 10 x $1,500,000 = $900,000

Since their book value is $1.2m and their fair value is $0.9m, a downwards fair value adjustment of $300,000 is required.

Brand – an upwards adjustment of $500,000 is required as its book value is currently zero but its fair value is $500,000. Note that the brand can be recognised on consolidation as the fact that it has a fair value indicates it is separable.

The provision for future operating losses does not represent a liability at acquisition since there is no past event giving rise to an obligation. Similarly, the future investment in machinery does not represent assets that exist at acquisition and so cannot be recognised.

Now process these adjustments in W2 to complete the working:

(W2) **Net assets of subsidiary**

	Acquisition
	$000
Share capital	3,000
Retained earnings	3,250
Fair value adjustments	
Land	550
Machinery	(300)
Brand	500
Fair value of sub's net assets	7,000

Now complete the goodwill proforma, remembering to calculate the fair value of the parent's holding as the fair value of the consideration given by Brussels. This will include having to discount the deferred consideration to present value.

Also, it is group policy to measure the NCI holding as their proportion of the subsidiary's net assets, i.e. their 25% share of the fair value of the subsidiary's net assets of $7 million from W2.

Goodwill

Fair value of P's holding (cost of investment)	$000
Cash	5,000
Shares (1.5m x $1.50)	2,250
Deferred consideration ($1m x 0.909)	909
	8,159
NCI holding at proportion of net assets (25% x 7,000 (W2))	1,750
Fair value of sub's net assets at acquisition (W2)	(7,000)
Goodwill on acquisition	2,909

Recording fair value adjustments

The fair value of the subsidiary's net assets at acquisition represents the "cost" of the net assets to the group at the date of acquisition. Recording fair value adjustments is therefore in accordance with the historic cost concept.

It also ensures an accurate measurement of goodwill. Assuming the fair value of the subsidiary's net assets is higher than their book value, goodwill would be overstated if the fair value adjustment were not recognised.

To record fair value adjustments:

- Adjust W2 in both columns (unless the asset / liability no longer exists at the reporting date)
- Reflect reporting date adjustment on face of CSFP

Impact on depreciation

Fair value adjustments often involve adjustments to non-current asset values which will consequently involve an adjustment to depreciation.

Depreciation in the group accounts must be based on the carrying value of the related non-current asset in the group accounts. Therefore if the non-current asset values are adjusted at acquisition then so must depreciation charges be adjusted in the post acquisition period.

To record depreciation adjustments

- Adjust W2 in reporting date column only
- Reflect adjustment on the face of CSFP

Example 5

The following summarised statements of financial position are provided for Wensum and Yare at 31 December 20X4.

	Wensum	Yare
	$000	$000
Non-current assets	1,900	750
Investment in Yare	550	–
Current assets	650	450
	3,100	1,200
Share capital ($1)	2,000	500
Retained earnings	700	220
Current liabilities	400	480
	3,100	1,200

Wensum purchased 300,000 shares in Yare on 1 January 20X3 for $550,000 when Yare's retained earnings were $150,000.

At this date Yare's non-current assets had a fair value of $600,000. Their book value at this time was $550,000. The assets had a remaining useful economic life of 10 years.

It is group policy to measure the NCI holding at fair value. The fair value of the NCI holding in Yare at 1 January 20X3 was $340,000. No impairment loss has arisen on goodwill.

Required:

Prepare the consolidated statement of financial position at 31 December 20X4.

Example 5 answer

Firstly, draw up the group structure. In this situation you are not given the % of shares that the parent owns in the subsidiary. Instead this is calculated using the number of shares the parent has acquired.

(W1) **Group structure**

W

300,000/ 500,000 = 60% 1 Jan 20X3, i.e. 2 years since acquisition

Y

Now set up a proforma for your answer, adding across the parent and subsidiary's assets and liabilities. Also fill in share capital and reference the remaining lines to the standard workings.

However, do not cast across and complete the total column for non-current assets since this total will change due to the fair value adjustment.

Consolidated statement of financial position as at 31 December 20X4

		$000
Non-current assets	(1,900 + 750	
Goodwill	(W3)	
Current assets	(650 + 450)	1,100
Equity		
Share capital		2,000
Retained earnings	(W5)	
Non-controlling interest	(W4)	
Current liabilities	(400 + 480)	880

Now we can continue with W2, remembering to record the fair value adjustment and consequent depreciation adjustment.

(W2) **Net assets of subsidiary**

	Acquisition	Reporting date
	$000	$000
Share capital	500	500
Retained earnings	150	220
Fair value adjustment (600 – 550)	50	50
Depreciation adj (50 x 2/10)	–	(10)
	700	760

60
Post acquisition profit

The question states that the non-current assets have a fair value of $600,000 and a book value of $550,000 at acquisition. Hence an upwards fair value adjustment of $50,000 is recorded in both columns of W2.

The question states that the assets have a remaining life of 10 years. From W1, we know that 2 years have passed since acquisition. Consequently, depreciation needs to be charged on the fair value adjustment for the 2 years since acquisition, resulting in additional depreciation of $10,000.

It is worth now updating the proforma CSFP with these adjustments as additional marks will be gained in the exam and it will be easy to forget to record these adjustments if this is left until the end.

Consolidated statement of financial position as at 31 December 20X4

		$000
Non-current assets	(1,900 + 750 + 50 – 10)	2,690
Goodwill	(W3)	
Current assets	(650 + 450)	1,100
Equity		
Share capital		2,000
Retained earnings	(W5)	
Non-controlling interest	(W4)	
Current liabilities	(400 + 480)	880

Now that W2 is completed, continue with W3, W4 and W5.

(W3) **Goodwill**

	$000
Fair value of P's holding (cost of investment)	550
NCI holding at fair value	340
Fair value of sub's net assets at acquisition (W2)	(700)
Goodwill at acquisition	190
Impairment	–
Goodwill at reporting date	190

(W4) **Non-controlling interest**

	$000
NCI holding at acquisition (W3)	340
NCI% x post acquisition reserves (40% x 60 (W2))	24
	364

(W5) **Reserves**

	Retained earnings
Parent's reserves	700
Sub (60% × 60 (W2))	36
	736

Finally the figures can be transferred to the answer and so the CSFP can be completed:

Consolidated statement of financial position as at 31 December 20X4

		$000
Non-current assets	(1,900 + 750 + 50 – 10)	2,690
Goodwill	(W3)	190
Current assets	(650 + 450)	1,100
		3,980
Equity		
Share capital		2,000
Retained earnings	(W5)	736
Non-controlling interest	(W4)	364
Current liabilities	(400 + 480)	880
		3,980

Test your understanding 6 - King and Lear

The following summarised statements of financial position are provided for King and Lear as at 31 December 20X7:

	King	Lear
	$000	$000
Non-current assets	2,000	1,000
Investment in Lear	1,200	–
Current assets	200	450
	3,400	1,450
Equity		
Share capital ($1)	2,000	750
Retained earnings	1,250	300
Current liabilities	150	400
	3,400	1,450

King purchased 60% of Lear's equity shares 1 January 20X5 for $1.2m when Lear's retained earnings were $100,000.

At this date Lear's non-current assets had a fair value of $1m and the assets had a remaining useful economic life of 5 years. Their book value at the date of acquisition was $850,000.

It is group policy to measure the NCI holding at fair value. The fair value of the NCI holding in Lear at 1 January 20X5 was $700,000.

As at 31 December 20X7, an impairment loss of $50,000 has arisen on goodwill.

Required:

Prepare the consolidated statement of financial position at 31 December 20X7.

Test your understanding 7 - Romeo and Juliet

The following summarised statements of financial position are provided for Romeo and Juliet as at 31 December 20X9:

	Romeo	Juliet
	$000	$000
Non-current assets	3,500	2,000
Investment in Lear	2,500	–
Current assets	1,250	750
	7,250	2,750
Equity		
Share capital ($1)	4,000	1,000
Retained earnings	2,250	1,250
Current liabilities	1,000	500
	7,250	2,750

Romeo purchased 80% of Juliet's equity shares 1 January 20X8 for $2.5m when Juliet's retained earnings were $800,000.

At this date Juliet's non-current assets had a fair value of $200,000 in excess of their book value and the assets had a remaining useful economic life of 10 years.

It is group policy to measure the NCI holding at their proportion of the subsidiary's net assets.

As at 31 December 20X9, an impairment loss of $30,000 has arisen on goodwill.

Required:

Prepare the consolidated statement of financial position at 31 December 20X9.

9 Intra-group balances

Intra-group balances must be eliminated in full, since the group as a single entity cannot owe balances to/from itself.

Intra-group balances may arise in the following situations:

- P and S trading with each other, resulting in current account balances i.e. receivables and payables
- Intra-group loans, resulting in an investment and loan balance

Adjust

- Face of CSFP by reducing the relevant asset and liability

Current account balances may disagree. This is most likely to be due to cash in transit or goods in transit.

Cash in transit

Cash has been sent by one group company, but has not been received and so is not recorded in the books of the other group company. The following adjustment will be required:

Cr Receivables (with the higher amount)
Dr Bank (with the amount in transit i.e. the difference)
Dr Payables (with the lower amount)

Goods in transit

Goods have been sent by one company, but have not been received and so are not recorded in the books of the other group company. The following adjustment will be required:

Cr Receivables (with the higher amount)
Dr Inventory (with the amount in transit i.e. the difference)
Dr Payables (with the lower amount)

Example 6

The following extracts are provided from the statements of financial position of P and S at the year-end:

	P	S
	$000	$000
Current assets		
Inventory	100	50
Receivables	270	80
Cash	120	40
Current liabilities		
Payables	160	90

P's statement of financial position includes a receivable of $40,000 being due from S.

Shortly before the year-end, S sent a cheque for $4,000 to P. P did not receive this cheque until after the year-end.

Also, P had dispatched goods to S with a value of $6,000 but S had not received them by the year-end.

Required:

What balances will be shown in the consolidated statement of financial position (CSFP) of the P group for the above items?

Example 6 answer

Consolidated statement of financial position

		$000
Current assets		
Inventory	100 + 50 + 6	156
Receivables	270 + 80 − 40	310
Cash	120 + 40 + 4	164
Current liabilities		
Payables	160 + 90 − 30	220

Start by adding across P and S's assets and liabilities for the consolidated statement of financial position.

For the cash in transit, neither entity is currently recognising the cash so this needs to be amended i.e. add $4,000 to cash.

Similarly, for the goods in transit, neither entity is currently recognising the inventory so this needs to be amended i.e. add $6,000 to inventory.

The intercompany receivable of $40,000 given in the scenario needs to be eliminated i.e. reduce receivables by $40,000.

The intercompany payable needs to be eliminated i.e. reduce payables. The amount that this needs reducing by is calculated as a balancing figure:

			$000
Dr	Cash	↑	4
Dr	Inventory	↑	6
Cr	Receivables	↓	40
Dr	Payables	↓	30

Test your understanding 8

The following summarised statements of financial position are provided for P and S as at 31 December 20X8:

	P	S
	$000	$000
Non-current assets	5,400	2,000
Investment in S	3,700	-
Current assets		
Inventory	750	140
Receivables	650	95
Cash	400	85
	10,900	2,320
Equity		
Share capital $1	7,000	1,400
Share premium	1,950	280
Retained earnings	1,050	440
Current liabilities		
Payables	900	200
	10,900	2,320

P acquired 90% of S five years ago when the balance on the retained earnings of S was $300,000.

Some of the non-current assets of S had a fair value of $1.2m at the date of acquisition by P. Their book value at this time was $1m. These non-current assets will be depreciated on a straight line basis over 20 years from the date of acquisition.

P and S traded with each other and at the reporting date, P owed S $25,000. This balance is stated after P had recorded that they had sent a cheque for $5,000 to S shortly before the year-end which S had not received by the reporting date.

It is group policy to record the NCI holding at their proportion of the subsidiary's net assets. At the reporting date, goodwill had been impaired by $500,000.

Required:

Prepare the consolidated statement of financial position at 31 December 20X8.

10 Provision for unrealised profits (PUP/ PURP)

PUPs in inventory

P and S may sell goods to each other, resulting in a profit being recorded in the selling company's financial statements. If these goods are still held by the purchasing company at the year-end, the goods have not been sold outside of the group. The profit is therefore unrealised from the group's perspective and should be removed.

The adjustment is also required to ensure that inventory is stated at the cost to the group i.e. the cost when the goods were first acquired by the group, not the cost to the purchasing company after the intra-group transfer.

Adjust

- **W2** Net assets at reporting date column **if S sells** the goods or **W5 if P sells** the goods.
- Inventory on the face of the CSFP.

Illustration 1

Parent sells to subsidiary

P sells goods to S for $400 at cost plus 25%. All goods remain in the inventory of S at the end of the year.

$$\text{Profit made on the sale } \frac{25}{125} \times 400 = 80.$$

Individual financial statements

P records profit	80
S records inventory	400

Group financial statements should show:

Profit	0
Inventory	320

PUP adjustment

Dr Group retained earnings (W5)	↓ 80
Cr Group inventory (CSFP)	↓ 80

The group profit figure for the parent will be reduced as it is the parent that recorded the profit in this case.

It is important to note that the adjustment takes place in the group accounts only. The individual accounts are correct as they stand and will not be adjusted as a result.

Subsidiary sells to parent

Individual financial statements

S records profit	80
P records inventory	400

PUP adjustment

Dr Sub's net assets at reporting date (W2)	↓ 80
Cr Group inventory (CSFP)	↓ 80

The subsidiary's profit will be reduced as it is the subsidiary that recorded the profit in this case. The reduction in the subsidiary's profits needs to be shared between the parent and NCI shareholders in W4 & W5. By adjusting W2 this split will automatically flow through to W4 and W5. S's profits are shared between the parent and the non-controlling interest shareholders

Cost structures

The cost structure of the intra-group sale may be given to you in one of two ways.

Mark up on cost

This occurs most frequently in questions. If, for example, goods are sold for $440 and there is a 25% mark up on cost, you need to calculate the profit included within the $440.

	%	$	
Revenue	125	440	
Cost of sales	100		
Gross profit	25	88	= 440 x 25/125

The PUP is $88.

Gross profit margin

The gross profit margin gives the profit as a percentage of revenue. Using the same figures as above but with a gross profit margin of 25%.

	%	$	
Revenue	100	440	
Cost of sales	75		
Gross profit	25	110	= 440 x 25/100

The PUP is $110.

Test your understanding 9

P sells goods to S for $520 at a margin of 20%. 40% of these goods were sold on by S to external parties by the year end.

Required:

What is the PUP adjustment in the group accounts?

Test your understanding 10

S sells goods to P at a mark-up of 33 1/3%. The selling price is $360. All goods remained unsold at the year end.

Required:

What is the PUP adjustment?

Example 8

The following statements of financial position exist at 30 June 20X6:

	P	S
	$000	$000
Non-current assets	4,000	2,000
Investment in S	2,000	
Current assets		
Inventory	500	150
Other current assets	1,500	300
	8,000	2,450
Ordinary share capital	6,000	1,500
Retained earnings	1,600	750
Current liabilities	400	200
	8,000	2,450

P acquired 70% of S when the balance on S's reserves stood at $250,000.

During the year, P sold goods to S for $120,000 at a mark-up of 20%. Half of these goods remain in inventory at the year end.

The NCI holding at acquisition should be measured using the proportion of net assets method.

Required:

(a) Prepare the consolidated statement of financial position of the P group.

(b) How would the CSFP change if S had sold the goods to P (all other information remaining the same)?

Example 8 answer

When answering the question using exam technique you would be well advised to follow these steps:

(1) Draw up the group structure including the date of acquisition if known.

(2) Draw up a proforma consolidated SFP adding across line by line the assets and liabilities of the parent and subsidiary. It is advisable to leave the brackets open at this stage so that you can later insert adjustments such as fair value, depreciation, PUPs and intercompany balances. Also insert the parent's share capital figure and reference other figures to the standard workings.

(3) Start on W2 Net assets of the subsidiary, remembering to include fair value and depreciation adjustments. If a PUP exists where the sub is the seller, this adjustment will also be included in W2. Remember to also include any adjustments on the face of the CSFP.

(4) If calculations are required eg for a PUP, add extra workings as required starting from W6.

(5) Then proceed through W3, W4 and W5. If a PUP exists where the parent is the seller, this adjustment will be included in W5. Remember to also include the adjustment on the face of the CSFP.

(6) Complete the CSFP proforma by transferring the numbers from your workings for goodwill, non-controlling interests equity and retained earnings.

Consolidated statement of financial position as at 30 June 20X6

		$000
Non-current assets	(4,000 + 2,000)	6,000
Goodwill	(W3)	775
Current assets		
Inventory	(500 + 150 – 10 (W6))	640
Other current assets	(1,500 + 300)	1,800
		9,215
Equity		
Share capital		6,000
Retained earnings	(W5)	1,940
		7,940
Non-controlling interest	(W4)	675
		8,615
Current liabilities	(400 + 200)	600
		9,215

(W1) **Group structure**

P
| 70%
S

(W2) **Net assets of subsidiary**

	Acquisition	Reporting date
	$000	$000
Share capital	1,500	1,500
Retained earnings	250	750
	1,750	2,250

500
Post acq'n profit

(W3) **Goodwill**

	$000
Fair value of P's holding (cost of investment)	2,000
NCI holding at proportion of net assets (30% x 1,750 (W2))	525
Fair value of sub's net assets at acquisition (W2)	(1,750)
Goodwill at acquisition / reporting date	775

(W4) **Non-controlling interest**

	$000
NCI holding at acquisition (W3)	525
NCI% x post acquisition reserves (30% x 500 (W2))	150
	675

(W5) **Reserves**

	Retained earnings
	$000
Parent's reserves	1,600
Sub (70% × 500 (W2))	350
PUP (W6)	(10)
	1,940

(W6) **PUP**

Profit in inventory = $120,000 x 20/120 x 1/2 = $10,000

(b) The calculation of the PUP adjustment in W6 would remain the same.

If the sub were the seller, the adjustment of $10,000 would be deducted from the net assets at the reporting date column in W2. This would subsequently change the post acquisition profit of the subsidiary and so would change W4 and W5.

In other words, the reduction in S's profits of $10,000 would be charged to both the NCI and parent shareholders in their ownership ratio of 70% : 30%.

The PUP adjustment would still be removed from inventory in the CSFP.

The answer would become:

Consolidated statement of financial position as at 30 June 20X6

		$000
Non-current assets	(4,000 + 2,000)	6,000
Goodwill	(W3)	775
Current assets		
Inventory	(500 + 150 – 10 (W6))	640
Other current assets	(1,500 + 300)	1,800
		9,215
Equity		
Share capital		6,000
Retained earnings	(W5)	1,943
		7,943
Non-controlling interest	(W4)	672
		8,615
Current liabilities	(400 + 200)	600
		9,215

(W1) **Group structure**

P
| 70%
S

(W2) **Net assets of subsidiary**

	Acquisition	Reporting date
	$000	$000
Share capital	1,500	1,500
Retained earnings	250	750
PUP (W6)		(10)
	1,750	2,240

490
Post acq'n profit

(W3) **Goodwill**

	$000
Fair value of P's holding (cost of investment)	2,000
NCI holding at proportion of net assets (30% x 1,750 (W2))	525
Fair value of sub's net assets at acquisition (W2)	(1,750)
Goodwill at acquisition / reporting date	775

(W4) **Non-controlling interest**

	$000
NCI holding at acquisition (W3)	525
NCI% x post acquisition reserves (30% x 490 (W2))	147
	672

(W5) **Reserves**

	Retained earnings
	$000
Parent's reserves	1,600
Sub (70% × 490 (W2))	343
	1,943

(W6) **PUP**

Profit in inventory = $120,000 x 20/120 x 1/2 = $10,000

Test your understanding 11

The following summarised statements of financial position are provided for P and S as at 30 June 20X8:

	P	**S**
	$000	$000
Non-current assets	8,500	5,000
Investment in S	6,500	–
Current assets		
Inventory	1,600	850
Receivables	1,350	950
Cash	850	400
	18,800	7,200
Equity		
Share capital $1	10,000	4,000
Share premium	2,000	500
Retained earnings	5,050	1,400

Current liabilities		
Payables	1,750	1,300
	18,800	7,200

P acquired 75% of S two years ago when the balance on the retained earnings of S was $800,000.

S sells goods to P at a profit margin of 20%. As a result at the reporting date, P's records showed a payable due to S of $50,000. However this disagreed to S's receivables balance of $60,000 due to cash in transit.

At the reporting date, P held $100,000 of goods in inventory that had been purchased from S.

It is group policy to record the NCI holding at fair value, which was deemed to be $1.25m at the date of acquisition. No impairment losses have arisen on goodwill.

Required:

Prepare the consolidated statement of financial position at 30 June 20X8.

Test your understanding 12

The following summarised statements of financial position are provided for P and S as at 30 June 20X8:

	P	S
	$000	$000
Non-current assets	16,700	10,200
Investment in S	12,000	–
Current assets		
Inventory	5,750	3,400
Receivables	4,250	2,950
Cash	2,500	1,450
	41,200	18,000
Equity		
Share capital $1	20,000	5,000
Retained earnings	12,600	7,900

Current liabilities		
Payables	8,600	5,100
	41,200	18,000

P acquired 80% of S three years ago when the balance on the retained earnings of S was $5,800,000.

At the date of acquisition it was determined that non-current assets of S had a fair value of $500,000 in excess of their book value. Their remaining useful life was 10 years at this time.

P sells goods to S at a mark-up of 25%. As a result at the reporting date, S's records showed a payable due to P of $550,000. However this disagreed to P's receivables balance of $750,000 due to cash in transit.

During the current year, P had sold $1,500,000 (selling price) of goods to S of which S still held one third in inventory at the year end.

It is group policy to record the NCI holding at fair value, which was deemed to be $2,500,000 at the date of acquisition. An impairment loss of $1,000,000 should be charged against goodwill at the reporting date.

Required:

Prepare the consolidated statement of financial position at 30 June 20X8.

11 PUPs on non-current assets

P and S may sell non-current assets to each other, resulting in a profit being recorded in the selling company's financial statements. If these non-current assets are still held by the purchasing company at the year-end, the profit is unrealised from the group's perspective and should be removed.

The profit on disposal should be removed from the seller's books (W2 if the sub is the seller, W5 if the parent is the seller).

In addition to the profit, there is depreciation to consider.

Prior to the transfer, the asset is depreciated based on the original cost. After the transfer depreciation is calculated on the transfer prices, i.e. a higher value. Therefore depreciation is higher after the transfer and this extra cost must be eliminated in the consolidated financial statements, i.e. profits need to be increased.

The extra depreciation that has been charged should be removed from the purchaser's books.

Adjust:

- Profit on disposal – reduce W2 Net assets at reporting date if S sells the asset or reduce W5 if P sells the asset;
- Extra depreciation – increase W5 if S sells the asset or increase W2 Net assets at reporting date if P sells the asset;
- Decrease the non-current asset in the CSFP with the net amount.

Illustration 2

If P transfers a non-current asset to its subsidiary

P acquired 80% of the share capital of S some years ago. P's reporting date is 31 August. P transfers an asset on 1 March 20X7 for $75,000 when its carrying value is $60,000. The remaining useful life at the date of sale is 2.5 years. The group depreciation policy is straight line on a monthly basis.

What adjustment is required in the consolidated financial statements of P for the year ended 31 August 20X8?

Profit recorded on the sale: $75,000 - $60,000 = $15,000

Extra depreciation: ($75,000 - $60,000) x 1.5/2.5 = $9,000

Adjustment required:

Dr Retained earnings (W5)	↓ $15,000
Cr Sub's net assets at reporting date (W2)	↑ $9,000
Cr NCA (CSFP)	↓ $6,000

If S transfers a non-current asset to its parent

Using the same example as above, but if S had sold the asset to P, the adjustment would be:

Adjustment required:

Dr Sub's net assets at reporting date (W2)	↓ $15,000
Cr Retained earnings (W5)	↑ $9,000
Cr NCA (CSFP)	↓ $6,000

Test your understanding 13

Rio purchased 75% of Salvador on 1 January 20X0. On 30 June 20X1 Salvador sold a lorry to Rio for $25,000. Its carrying value in Salvador's books was $20,000 and the remaining useful economic life at the date of transfer was 3 years.

Required:

What adjustment is required in the consolidated SFP of the Rio group as at 31 December 20X1?

12 Mid-year acquisitions

Mid year acquisitions are only relevant to the statement of financial position when completing W2 Net assets of the subsidiary. Reserves at acquisition are required and this figure may not be readily available if the acquisition took place part way through an accounting period.

It is assumed, unless otherwise stated in the question, that profits accrue evenly over the year and therefore profits for the year can be time apportioned. The reserves at acquisition can then be calculated by either:

- Subtracting the profits for the post acquisition portion of the year from the closing reserves balance; or
- Adding the profits for the pre-acquisition portion of the year to the opening reserves balance.

Illustration 3 - mid year acquisition

An entity is acquired on 1 March 20X9. Its profits for the year ended 31 December 20X9 are $12,000 and its retained earnings at the reporting date are $55,000.

Retained earnings at acquisition will be $55,000 – (10/12 x $12,000) = $45,000.

Test your understanding 14 - Aston and Martin

Aston and Martin

Aston acquired 80% of the share capital of Martin for $40,000 on 1 January 20X4 when the balance on the retained earnings of Martin stood at $9,000. The statements of financial position of the two companies are as follows at the 31 December 20X7:

		Aston		**Martin**
		$000		$000
Non-current assets				
Property, plant and equipment		88		39
Investment in Martin		40		
		128		39
Current assets				
Inventory	80		26	
Receivables	24		32	
Bank and cash	–		15	
		104		73
		232		112
Equity				
Share capital		100		24
Retained earnings		46		48
Current liabilities				
Overdraft	14		10	
Payables	72		30	
		86		40
		232		112

At the date of acquisition, the fair value of Martin's property, plant and equipment was $5,000 higher than its carrying value. It was estimated to have a remaining useful economic life of ten years at this date. A full year's depreciation charge is made in the year of acquisition. The fair value of all other net assets were equal to their carrying values.

Aston's payables balance includes $6,000 payable to Martin, and Martin's receivables balance includes $20,000 owing from Aston. At the year end, it was established that Martin had despatched goods to Aston with a selling price of $9,000 and that Aston did not receive delivery of these items until after the year end. At the same time, Aston had put a cheque in the post to Martin for $5,000 which also did not arrive until after the year end.

In addition to the goods in transit of $9,000, there were also some items included in Aston's inventory which had been purchased by Aston at the price of $21,000 from Martin. Martin had priced these goods at a mark-up of 20%.

It is group policy to value NCIs at fair value at acquisition. The fair value of the NCI holding in Martin as at 1 January 20X4 was $8,000. Goodwill is subject to an annual impairment review and it was determined that goodwill should be carried at 60% of its original value.

Required:

Prepare the consolidated statement of financial position as at 31 December 20X7 for the Aston Group.

Test your understanding 15 - K and S

On 1 May 20X7 K bought 60% of S paying $140,000 cash. The summarised statements of financial position for the two companies as at 30 November 20X7 are:

	K	S
	$	$
Non-current assets		
Property, plant and equipment	138,000	115,000
Investments	162,000	
	–––––––	–––––––
	300,000	115,000

Current assets				
Inventory	15,000		17,000	
Receivables	19,000		20,000	
Bank and cash	2,000		–	
		36,000		37,000
		336,000		152,000
Equity				
Share capital		114,000		40,000
Retained earnings		189,000		69,000
		303,000		109,000
Non-current liabilities				
8% Debentures		–		20,000
Current liabilities				
Payables		33,000		23,000
		336,000		152,000

The following information is relevant:

(1) The inventory of S includes $8,000 of goods purchased from K at cost plus 25%.

(2) On 1 May 20X7 a piece of S's plant with a carrying value of $30,000 had a fair value of $48,000. It had a remaining life of 10 years as at this date.

(3) S earned a profit after tax of $9,000 in the year ended 30 November 20X7 and did not pay any dividends during the year.

(4) The debenture in S's books represents monies borrowed from K on 1 May 20X7. P has recognised this loan as a non-current asset investment.

(5) Included in K's receivables is $4,000 relating to inventory sold to S since acquisition. S raised a cheque for $2,500 and sent it to K on 29 November 20X7. K did not receive this cheque until 4 December 20X7.

(6) It is group policy to value NCIs at acquisition using the proportion of net assets method. Goodwill is impaired by $5,100 at the reporting date.

Required:

Prepare the consolidated statement of financial position of the K group as at 30 November 20X7.

13 Chapter summary

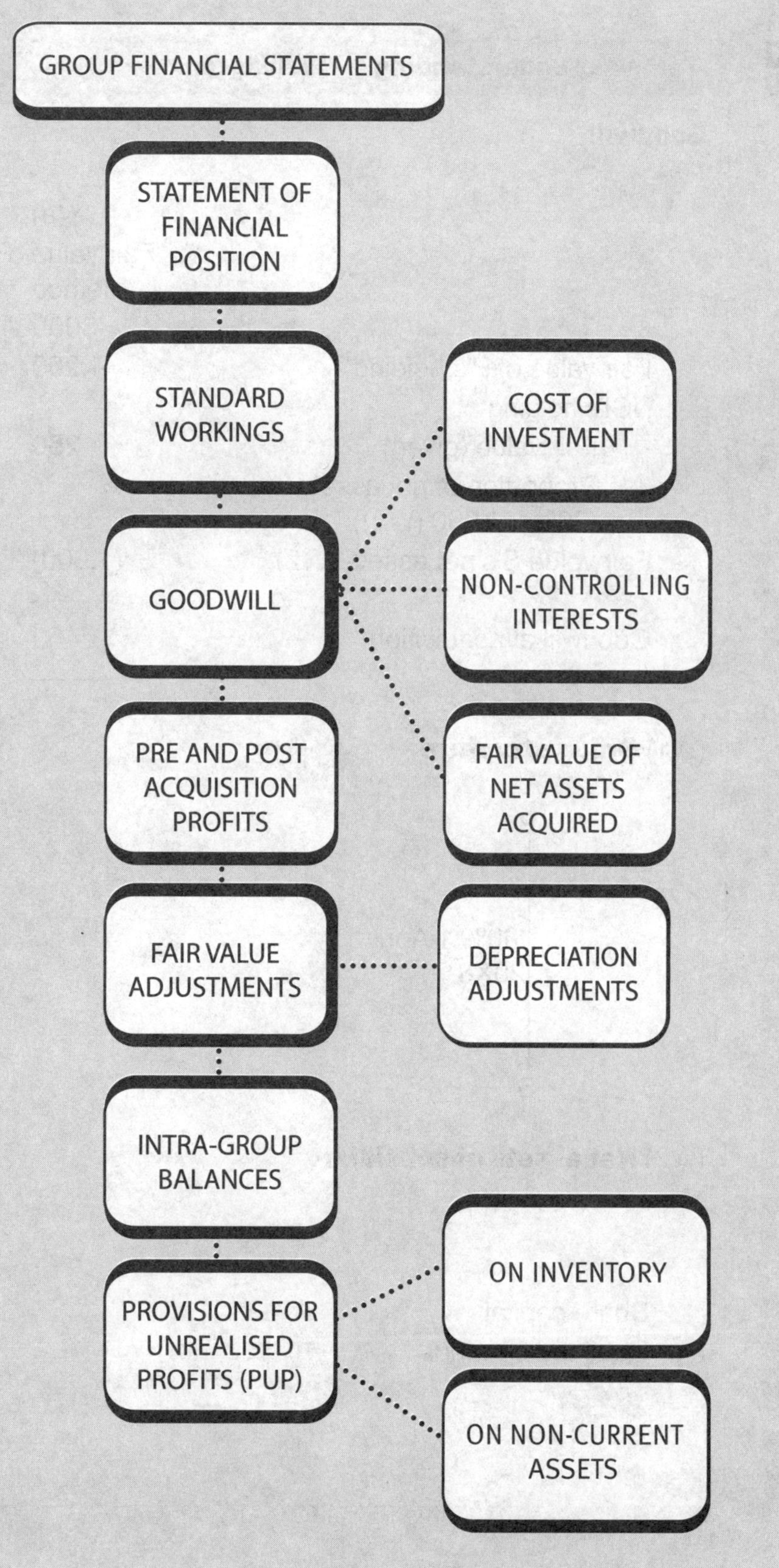

Test your understanding answers

Test your understanding 1 - Wellington

Goodwill

	(a) Fair value method	(b) Proportion of net assets method
	$000	$000
Fair value of P's holding	1,200	1,200
NCI's holding		
Fair value (given)	250	
Proportion of net assets (20% x 1,000 (W2))		200
Fair value S's net assets (W2)	(1,000)	(1,000)
Goodwill at acquisition	450	400

(W1) **Group structure**

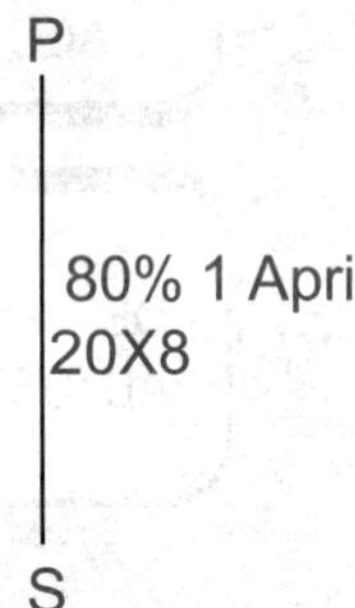

(W2) **Net assets of subsidiary**

	Acquisition
	$000
Share capital	200
Retained earnings	800
	1,000

Test your understanding 2 - Ruby

Goodwill

	(a) Fair value method	(b) Proportion of net assets method
	$000	$000
Fair value of P's holding	2,500	2,500
NCI's holding		
Fair value (25% x 500 x $6)	750	
Proportion of net assets (25% x 2,000 (W2))		500
Fair value S's net assets (W2)	(2,000)	(2,000)
Goodwill at acquisition	1,250	1,000

(W1) **Group structure**

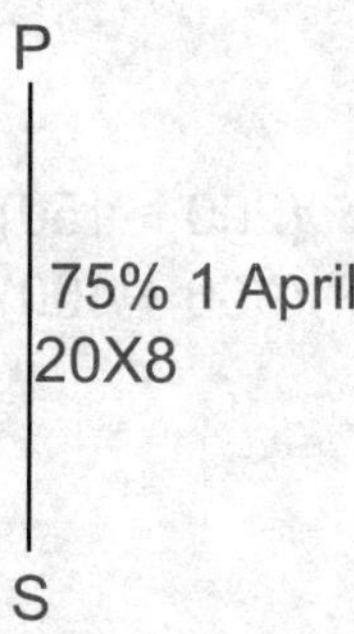

(W2) **Net assets of subsidiary**

	Acquisition
	$000
Share capital	500
Retained earnings	1,500
	2,000

Test your understanding 3

Consolidated statement of financial position as at 31 March 20X4

		$000
Non-current assets	(3,500 + 2,400)	5,900
Goodwill (W3)		1,000
Current assets	(1,000 + 600)	1,600
		8,500
Equity		
Share capital		4,000
Retained earnings (W5)		2,430
		6,430
Non-controlling interest (W4)		670
		7,100
Non-current liabilities	(200 + 150)	350
Current liabilities	(650 + 400)	1,050
		8,500

(W1) **Group structure**

P

80% 1 April 20X2 i.e. 2 years since acquisition

S

(W2) **Net assets of subsidiary**

	Acquisition	Reporting date
	$000	$000
Share capital	1,000	1,000
Retained earnings	950	1,450
	1,950	2,450

500 post acq'n profit

(W3) **Goodwill**

	$000
Fair value of P's holding (cost of investment)	2,500
NCI holding at fair value	600
Fair value of sub's net assets at acquisition (W2)	(1,950)
Goodwill at acquisition	1,150
Impairment	(150)
Goodwill at reporting date	1,000

(W4) **Non-controlling interest**

	$000
NCI holding at acquisition (W3)	600
NCI% x post acquisition reserves (20% x 500 (W2))	100
NCI% x impairment (20% x 150 (W3))	(30)
	670

(W5) **Reserves**

	Retained earnings
	$000
Parent's reserves	2,150
Sub (80% × 500 (W2))	400
Impairment (80% x 150 (W3))	(120)
	2,430

Test your understanding 4

Consolidated statement of financial position as at 31 March 20X8

	(a) Fair value method	(b) Proportion of net assets method
	$000	$000
Non-current assets (14,000 + 9,500)	23,500	23,500
Goodwill (W3)	800	700
Current assets (4,500 + 3,000)	7,500	7,500
	31,800	31,700
Equity		
Share capital	10,000	10,000
Retained earnings (W5)	12,150	12,125
	22,150	22,125
Non-controlling interest (W4)	2,450	2,375
	24,600	24,500
Non-current liabilities (750 + 600)	1,350	1,350
Current liabilities (3,450 + 2,400)	5,850	5,850
	31,800	31,700

(W1) **Group structure**

P

75% 1 April 20X5 i.e. 3 years since acquisition

S

(W2) **Net assets of subsidiary**

	Acquisition		Reporting date
	$000		$000
Share capital	5,000		5,000
Retained earnings	2,500		4,500
	7,500		9,500
		2,000 post acq'n profit	

(W3) **Goodwill**

	(a) Fair value method	(b) Proportion of net assets method
	$000	$000
Fair value of P's holding (cost of investment)	6,500	6,500
NCI holding		
- at fair value	2,000	
- at proportion of net assets (25% x 7,500 (W2))		1,875
Fair value of sub's net assets at acquisition (W2)	(7,500)	(7,500)
Goodwill at acquisition	1,000	875
Impairment (20% x goodwill at acquisition)	(200)	(175)
Goodwill at reporting date	800	700

(W4) **Non-controlling interest**

	(a) Fair value method	(b) Proportion of net assets method
	$000	$000
NCI holding at acquisition (W3)	2,000	1,875
NCI% x post acquisition reserves (25% x 2,000 (W2))	500	500
NCI% x impairment (25% x 200 (W3))	(50)	–
	2,450	2,375

(W5) **Reserves**

	(a) Fair value method	(b) Proportion of net assets method
	$000	$000
Parent's reserves	10,800	10,800
Sub (75% × 2,000 (W2))	1,500	1,500
Impairment loss		
- FV method (75% x 200 (W3))	(150)	
- Proportion of net assets method (W3)		(175)
	12,150	12,125

Test your understanding 5

Goodwill

	$
Fair value of P's holding (cost of investment)	
Cash	5,000
Shares (60% x 10,000 x 2/3 x $2.25)	9,000
Deferred consideration ($3,000 x 0.826)	2,478
Contingent consideration	700
	17,178
NCI holding at fair value or proportion of net assets	10,000
Fair value of sub's net assets at acquisition	(15,000)
Goodwill on acquisition	12,178
Impairment	–
Goodwill at reporting date (in CSFP)	12,178

Test your understanding 6 - King and Lear

Consolidated statement of financial position as at 31 December 20X7

		$000
Non-current assets	(2,000 + 1,000 + 150 – 90)	3,060
Goodwill	(W3)	850
Current assets	(200 + 450)	650
		4,560
Equity		
Share capital		2,000
Retained earnings	(W5)	1,286
		3,286
Non-controlling interest	(W4)	724
		4,010
Current liabilities	(150 + 400)	550
		4,560

(W1) **Group structure**

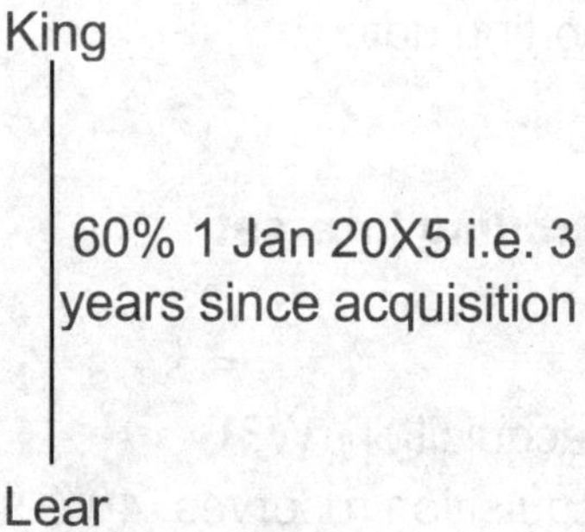

(W2) **Net assets of subsidiary**

	Acquisition		Reporting date
	$000		$000
Share capital	750		750
Retained earnings	100		300
Fair value adjustment (1,000 - 850)	150		150
Depreciation adj (150 x 3/5)	–		(90)
	1,000		1,110
		110 Post acquisition profit	

(W3) **Goodwill**

	$000
Fair value of P's holding (cost of investment)	1,200
NCI holding at fair value	700
Fair value of sub's net assets at acquisition (W2)	(1,000)
Goodwill at acquisition	900
Impairment	(50)
Goodwill at reporting date	850

(W4) **Non-controlling interest**

	$000
NCI holding at acquisition (W3)	700
NCI% x post acquisition reserves (40% x 110 (W2))	44
NCI% x impairment (40% x 50 (W3))	(20)
	724

(W5) **Reserves**

	Retained earnings
	$000
Parent's reserves	1,250
Sub (60% × 110 (W2))	66
Impairment (60% x 50 (W3))	(30)
	1,286

Test your understanding 7 - Romeo and Juliet

Consolidated statement of financial position as at 31 December 20X9

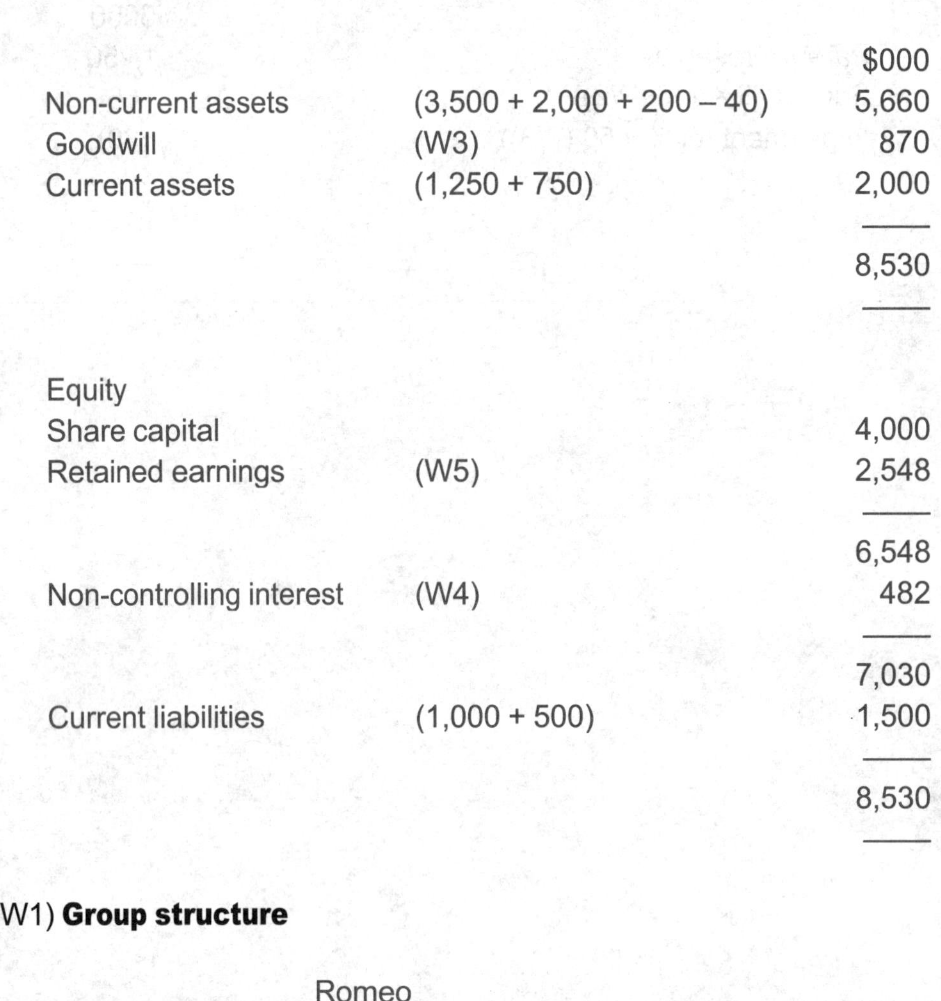

		$000
Non-current assets	(3,500 + 2,000 + 200 – 40)	5,660
Goodwill	(W3)	870
Current assets	(1,250 + 750)	2,000
		8,530
Equity		
Share capital		4,000
Retained earnings	(W5)	2,548
		6,548
Non-controlling interest	(W4)	482
		7,030
Current liabilities	(1,000 + 500)	1,500
		8,530

(W1) **Group structure**

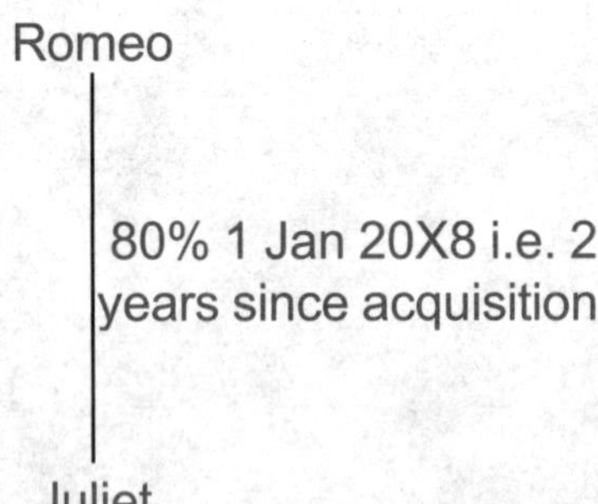

(W2) **Net assets of subsidiary**

	Acquisition		Reporting date
	$000		$000
Share capital	1,000		1,000
Retained earnings	800		1,250
Fair value adjustment	200		200
Depreciation adj (200 x 2/10)	–		(40)
	2,000		2,410
		410 Post acquisition profit	

(W3) **Goodwill**

	$000
Fair value of P's holding (cost of investment)	2,500
NCI holding at proportion of net assets (20% x 2,000 (W2))	400
Fair value of sub's net assets at acquisition (W2)	(2,000)
Goodwill at acquisition	900
Impairment	(30)
Goodwill at reporting date	870

(W4) **Non-controlling interest**

	$000
NCI holding at acquisition (W3)	400
NCI% x post acquisition reserves (20% x 410 (W2))	82
	482

(W5) **Reserves**

	Retained earnings
	$000
Parent's reserves	2,250
Sub (80% × 410 (W2))	328
Impairment (W3)	(30)
	2,548

Test your understanding 8

Consolidated statement of financial position as at 31 December 20X8

		$000
Non-current assets	(5,400 + 2,000 + 200 – 50)	7,550
Goodwill	(W3)	1,238
Current assets		
Inventory	(750 + 140)	890
Receivables	(650 + 95 – 30 (W6))	715
Cash	(400 + 85 + 5)	490
		10,883
Equity		
Share capital		7,000
Share premium		1,950
Retained earnings	(W5)	631
		9,581
Non-controlling interest	(W4)	227
		9,808
Current liabilities		
Payables	(900 + 200 – 25)	1,075
		10,883

(W1) **Group structure**

P

90% 5 years since acquisition

S

(W2) **Net assets of subsidiary**

	Acquisition		Reporting date
	$000		$000
Share capital	1,400		1,400
Share premium	280		280
Retained earnings	300		440
Fair value adjustment (1,200 – 1,000)	200		200
Depreciation adj (200 x 5/20)	–		(50)
	2,180		2,270
		90 Post acquisition profit	

(W3) **Goodwill**

	$000
Fair value of P's holding (cost of investment)	3,700
NCI holding at proportion of net assets (10% x 2,180 (W2))	218
Fair value of sub's net assets at acquisition (W2)	(2,180)
Goodwill at acquisition	1,738
Impairment	(500)
Goodwill at reporting date	1,238

(W4) **Non-controlling interest**

	$000
NCI holding at acquisition (W3)	218
NCI% x post acquisition reserves (10% x 90 (W2))	9
	227

(W5) **Reserves**

	Retained earnings
	$000
Parent's reserves	1,050
Sub (90% × 90 (W2))	81
Impairment (W3)	(500)
	631

(W6) **Intra-group balances**

The question states that P owes S $25,000 i.e. a payable. This is to be eliminated by reducing payables.

The question states that there is cash in transit at the reporting date of $5,000. This needs to be recorded by increasing cash.

The intercompany receivable that needs to be eliminated is therefore calculated as a balancing figure:

			$000
Dr	Payables	↓	25
Dr	Cash	↑	5
Cr	Receivables	↓	30

Tutorial note: Share premium

Share premium is just another reserve within equity. The share premium of the subsidiary is therefore recorded in W2 Net Assets since net assets = equity.

Share premium arises when shares are issued at a price above nominal value i.e. it is directly linked to share capital. Since it can be assumed that the share capital of the subsidiary is the same at both acquisition and reporting dates, it can be assumed that share premium is also the same at both dates.

In the CSFP, share capital is only the share capital of the parent. As share premium arises in connection with these shares, it is also the case that share premium in the CSFP is only that of the parent.

Test your understanding 9

The PUP will be:

Profit on the sale = 20% x $520 = $104

Profit still in inventory at y/e = 60% x $104 = $62.4

The parent is the seller and so deduct in W5 & from inventory by $62.4

Test your understanding 10

The PUP will be:

$$\left(360 \times \frac{33\frac{1}{3}}{133\frac{1}{3}}\right) = 90$$

The subsidiary is the seller and so reduce W2 NAs at reporting date & Inventory by $90.

Test your understanding 11

Consolidated statement of financial position as at 30 June 20X8

		$000
Non-current assets	(8,500 + 5,000)	13,500
Goodwill	(W3)	2,450
Current assets		
Inventory	(1,600 + 850 – 20 (W7))	2,430
Receivables	(1,350 + 950 – 60)	2,240
Cash	(850 + 400 + 10 (W6))	1,260
		21,880
Equity		
Share capital		10,000
Share premium		2,000
Retained earnings	(W5)	5,485
		17,485
Non-controlling interest	(W4)	1,395
		18,880
Current liabilities		
Payables	(1,750 + 1,300 – 50)	3,000
		21,880

(W1) **Group structure**

P

75% 2 years since acquisition

S

(W2) **Net assets of subsidiary**

	Acquisition		Reporting date
	$000		$000
Share capital	4,000		4,000
Share premium	500		500
Retained earnings	800		1,400
PUP (W7)	–		(20)
	5,300		5,880
		580 Post acquisition profit	

(W3) **Goodwill**

	$000
Fair value of P's holding (cost of investment)	6,500
NCI holding at fair value	1,250
Fair value of sub's net assets at acquisition (W2)	(5,300)
Goodwill at acquisition	2,450
Impairment	–
Goodwill at reporting date	2,450

(W4) **Non-controlling interest**

	$000
NCI holding at acquisition (W3)	1,250
NCI% x post acquisition reserves (25% x 580 (W2))	145
	1,395

(W5) **Reserves**

	Retained earnings
	$000
Parent's reserves	5,050
Sub (75% × 580 (W2))	435
	5,485

(W6) **Intra-group balances**

			$000
Dr	Payables	↓	50
Dr	Cash	↑	10
Cr	Receivables	↓	60

(W7) **PUP**

Profit in inventory = 20% x $100,000 = $20,000

Test your understanding 12

Consolidated statement of financial position as at 30 June 20X8

		$000
Non-current assets	(16,700 + 10,200 + 500 – 150)	27,250
Goodwill	(W3)	2,200
Current assets		
Inventory	(5,750 + 3,400 – 100 (W7))	9,050
Receivables	(4,250 + 2,950 – 750)	6,450
Cash	(2,500 + 1,450 + 200 (W6))	4,150
		49,100
Equity		
Share capital		20,000
Retained earnings	(W5)	13,260
		33,260
Non-controlling interest	(W4)	2,690
		35,950
Current liabilities		
Payables	(8,600 + 5,100 - 550)	13,150
		49,100

(W1) **Group structure**

P

80% 3 years since acquisition

S

(W2) **Net assets of subsidiary**

	Acquisition		Reporting date
	$000		$000
Share capital	5,000		5,000
Retained earnings	5,800		7,900
Fair value adjustment	500		500
Depreciation adj (500 x 3/10)	–		(150)
	11,300		13,250
		1,950 Post acquisition profit	

(W3) **Goodwill**

	$000
Fair value of P's holding (cost of investment)	12,000
NCI holding at fair value	2,500
Fair value of sub's net assets at acquisition (W2)	(11,300)
Goodwill at acquisition	3,200
Impairment	(1,000)
Goodwill at reporting date	2,200

(W4) **Non-controlling interest**

	$000
NCI holding at acquisition (W3)	2,500
NCI% x post acquisition reserves (20% x 1,950 (W2))	390
NCI% x impairment (20% x 1,000 (W3))	(200)
	2,690

(W5) **Reserves**

	Retained earnings
	$000
Parent's reserves	12,600
Sub (80% × 1,950 (W2))	1,560
Impairment (80% x 1,000 (W3))	(800)
PUP (W7)	(100)
	13,260

(W6) **Intra-group balances**

			$000
Dr	Payables	↓	550
Dr	Cash	↑	200
Cr	Receivables	↓	750

(W7) **PUP**

Profit on sale = 25/125 x $1,500,000 = $300,000

Profit in inventory = 1/3 x $300,000 = $100,000

Test your understanding 13

Salvador, the subsidiary, has sold the lorry to Rio, the parent, so the profit on disposal must be removed from W2 and the additional depreciation removed from W5.

Profit on disposal = $25,000 – $20,000 = $5,000

Extra depreciation = ($25,000 – $20,000) x 0.5/3 = $833

The adjustment will be:

Dr	Sub's net assets at reporting date (W2)	↓	$5,000
Cr	Retained earnings (W5)	↑	$833
Cr	NCA (CSFP)	↓	$4,167

Test your understanding 14 - Aston and Martin

Consolidated statement of financial position as at 31 December 20X7

		$000
Non-current assets		
Property, plant and equipment	(88 + 39 + 5 – 2 (W2))	130
Goodwill	(W3)	6
Current assets		
Inventory	(80 + 26 + 9 – 5 (W7))	110
Receivables	(24 + 32 – 20)	36
Cash	(15 + 5)	20
		302
Equity		
Share capital		100
Retained earnings	(W5)	68.4
		168.4
Non-controlling interest	(W4)	13.6
		182
Current liabilities		
Overdraft	(14 + 10)	24
Payables	(72 + 30 – 6)	96
		302

(W1) **Group structure**

Aston

80% 1 Jan X4 i.e. 4 years since acquisition

Martin

(W2) **Net assets of subsidiary**

	Acquisition		Reporting date
	$000		$000
Share capital	24		24
Retained earnings	9		48
Fair value adjustment	5		5
Depreciation adj (5 x 4/10)	–		(2)
PUP (W7)	–		(5)
	38		70
		32 Post acquisition profit	

(W3) **Goodwill**

	$000
Fair value of P's holding (cost of investment)	40
NCI holding at fair value	8
Fair value of sub's net assets at acquisition (W2)	(38)
Goodwill at acquisition	10
Impairment (40%)	(4)
Goodwill at reporting date	6

(W4) **Non-controlling interest**

	$000
NCI holding at acquisition (W3)	8
NCI% x post acquisition reserves (20% x 32 (W2))	6.4
NCI% x impairment (20% x 4 (W3))	(0.8)
	13.6

(W5) **Reserves**

	Retained earnings
	$000
Parent's reserves	46
Sub (80% × 32 (W2))	25.6
Impairment (80% x 4 (W3))	(3.2)
	68.4

(W6) **Intra-group balances**

			$000
Dr	Payables	↓	6
Cr	Receivables	↓	20
Dr	Inventory	↑	9
Dr	Cash	↑	5

(W7) **PUP**

Profit in inventory = 20/120 x ($9,000 + $21,000) = $5,000

Tutorial note – the goods in transit of $9,000 are included in inventory as a result of the intercompany adjustment in W6. Since these goods were purchased by Aston from Martin it is necessary to eliminate the profit in relation to these goods as well as from the $21,000 of goods already recognised in Aston's inventory.

Test your understanding 15 - K and S

Consolidated statement of financial position as at 30 November 20X7

		$
Non-current assets		
Property, plant and equipment	(138,000 + 115,000 + 18,000 – 1,050)	269,950
Investments	(162,000 – 140,000 (W3) – 20,000 (W6))	2,000
Goodwill	(W3)	61,850
		333,800
Current assets		
Inventory	(15,000 + 17,000 – 1,600 (W7))	30,400
Receivables	(19,000 + 20,000 – 4,000 (W6))	35,000
Cash	(2,000 + 0 + 2,500 (W6))	4,500
		403,700
Equity		
Share capital		114,000
Retained earnings	(W5)	184,820
		298,820
Non-controlling interest	(W4)	50,380
		349,200
Non-current liabilities		
8% Debentures	(0 + 20,000 – 20,000 (W6))	–
Current liabilities		
Payables	(33,000 + 23,000 – 1,500 (W6))	54,500
		403,700

(W1) **Group structure**

K

60% 1 May 20X7 i.e. 7 months since acquisition

S

(W2) **Net assets of subsidiary**

	Acquisition	Reporting date
	$	$
Share capital	40,000	40,000
Retained earnings (69,000 – (7/12 x 9,000))	63,750	69,000
Fair value adjustment (48,000 - 30,000)	18,000	18,000
Depreciation adj (18,000 x 1/10 x 7/12)	–	(1,050)
	121,750	125,950

4,200
Post acquisition profit

(W3) **Goodwill**

	$
Fair value of P's holding (cost of investment)	140,000
NCI holding at proportion of net assets (40% x 121,750 (W2))	48,700
Fair value of sub's net assets at acquisition (W2)	(121,750)
Goodwill at acquisition	66,950
Impairment	(5,100)
Goodwill at reporting date	61,850

(W4) **Non-controlling interest**

	$
NCI holding at acquisition (W3)	48,700
NCI% x post acquisition reserves (40% x 4,200 (W2))	1,680
	50,380

(W5) **Reserves**

	Retained earnings
	$
Parent's reserves	189,000
Sub (60% × 4,200 (W2))	2,520
Impairment (W3)	(5,100)
PUP (W7)	(1,600)
	184,820

(W6) **Intra-group balances**

Cr	Receivables	↓	$4,000
Dr	Cash	↑	$2,500
Dr	Payables	↓	$1,500
Dr	Debentures	↓	$20,000
Cr	Investments	↓	$20,000

(W7) **PUP**

Profit in inventory = 25/125 x $8,000 = $1,600

chapter

5

Consolidated statement of comprehensive income and statement of changes in equity

Chapter learning objectives

On completion of their studies students should be able to:

- Prepare consolidated financial statements (including the statement of changes in equity) for a group of companies;
- Explain the treatment in consolidated financial statements of pre and post-acquisition reserves, goodwill (including its impairment), fair value adjustments, intra-group transactions and dividends and mid-year acquisitions.

1 Session content

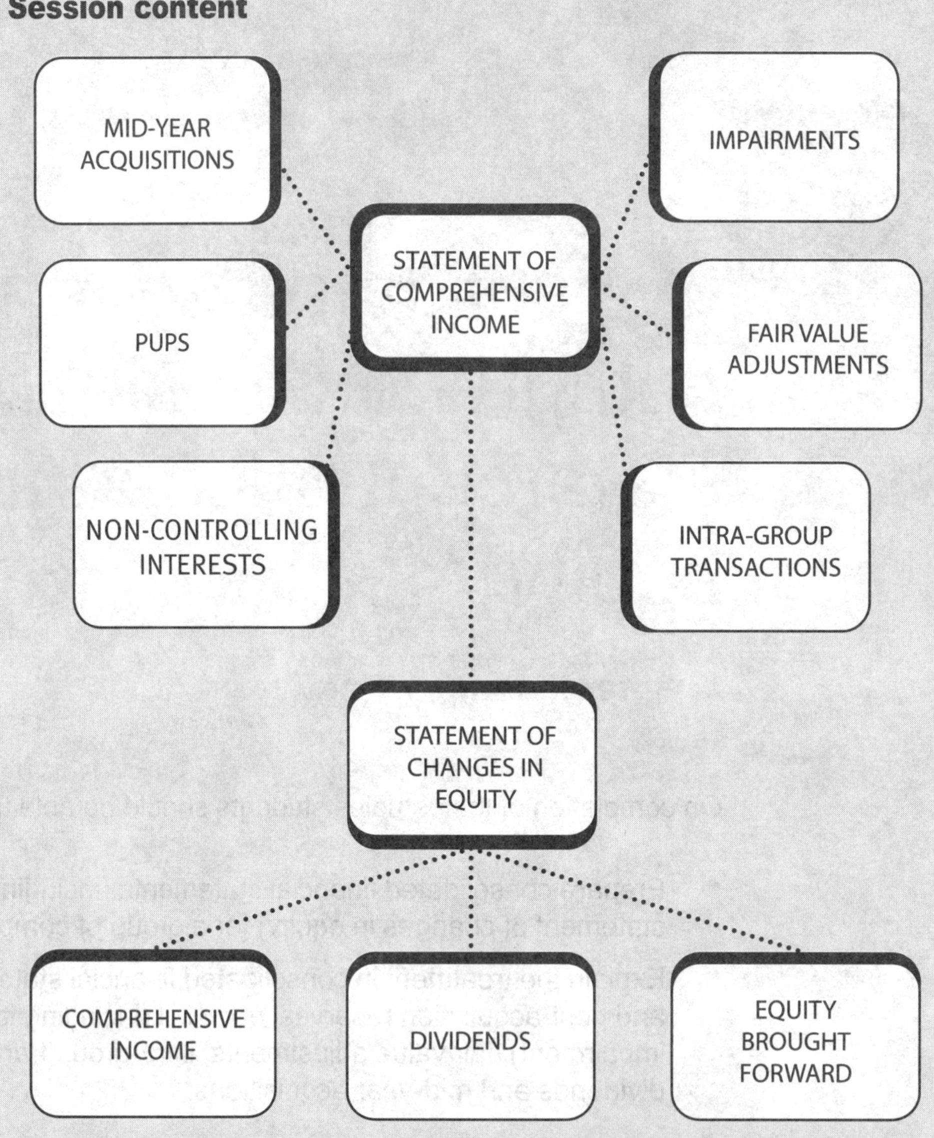

2 Consolidated statement of comprehensive income

The principles of consolidation are continued within the statement of comprehensive income (CSCI).

A statement of comprehensive income reflects the income and expenses generated by the net assets shown on the statement of financial position.

Since the group controls the net assets of the subsidiary, the income and expenses of the subsidiary should be fully included in the consolidated statement of comprehensive income i.e. add across 100% of the parent plus 100% of the subsidiary.

To reflect that the parent may not own 100% of the subsidiary, the profit for the year and the total comprehensive income for the year are split into how much is attributable to the parent shareholders and how much is attributable to the non-controlling interest shareholders.

3 CSCI adjustments

Adjustments will be necessary to the parent and subsidiary's individual SCIs when preparing the group SCI to reflect that the group is a single entity.

Consolidation adjustments should be dealt with as follows:

Impairments

Impairments of goodwill relating to the current accounting period will be charged as an expense (normally administration expenses) in the consolidated statement of comprehensive income.

Fair value adjustments

Fair value adjustments may be required as seen in Chapter 4 Consolidated Statement of Financial Position in order to reflect the fair value of the subsidiaries net assets at acquisition. This may then result in a change to the profits of the subsidiary for consolidation purposes. For example, an adjustment is required to increase the depreciation expense in the CSCI if a fair value uplift is made to a depreciable non-current asset in the CSFP.

Intra-group transactions

The group as a single entity cannot report transactions with itself and so intra-group transactions reported within the individual SCIs will need eliminating e.g. sales between parent and subsidiaries, dividends from subsidiary to parent and interest income/expenses between parent and subsidiary.

Provision for unrealised profit on inventory

An adjustment is required to increase the cost of the sales (and so reduce profit) of the selling company to remove the unrealised profit included within inventories at the reporting date.

Mid-year acquisitions

The income and expenses of the subsidiary should be time apportioned to reflect the period of control i.e. if a subsidiary is acquired on 1 September and the accounting period is the year to 31 December, only 4/12 of the subsidiary's income and expenses should be consolidated.

Non-controlling interests

The share of profit and total comprehensive income that belongs to the NCIs is to be calculated as follows:

		$	$
Sub's profit for the year per S's SCI (time apportioned if mid year acquisition)		X	
Depreciation adjustment		(X)	
PUP (if S is seller)		(X)	
Impairment expense (fair value method only)		(X)	
		___	
Adjusted profit		X	
NCI share of profits	x NCI%		X
Sub's other comprehensive income per S's SCI (time apportioned if mid year acquisition)		X	
		___	
Adjusted TCI		X	
NCI share of total comprehensive income	x NCI%		X

Example 1

On 1 January 20X7 Zebedee acquired 75% of the equity shares of Xavier.

The following statements of comprehensive income have been produced by Zebedee and Xavier for the year ended 31 December 20X9.

	Zebedee	Xavier
	$000	$000
Revenue	1,260	520
Cost of sales	(420)	(210)
	___	___
Gross profit	840	310
Distribution costs	(180)	(60)
Administration expenses	(120)	(90)
	___	___

Profit from operations	540	160
Investment income from Xavier	36	–
Profit before taxation	576	160
Taxation	(130)	(25)
Profit for the year	446	135
Other comprehensive income	100	50
Total comprehensive income	546	185

(1) During the year ended 31 December 20X9, Zebedee had sold $84,000 worth of goods to Xavier. These goods were sold at a mark up of 50% on cost. On 31 December 20X9, Xavier still had $36,000 worth of these goods in inventories.

(2) At acquisition, PPE of Xavier was increased in value by $50,000 to reflect its fair value at acquisition. These assets had a remaining useful economic life of 5 years at the date of acquisition. Depreciation is charged to cost of sales.

(3) At 31 December 20X9, goodwill arising on consolidation was reviewed for impairment. An impairment loss of $15,000 had arisen which should be charged to administrative expenses. NCI's had been valued using the fair value method at acquisition.

(4) During the year, Zavier paid a dividend of $48,000.

Required:

Prepare the consolidated statement of comprehensive income for the Zebedee group for the year ended 31 December 20X9.

Example 1 answer

Follow these steps to answer a CSCI question:

(1) Prepare W1 Group structure to determine the subsidiary status of each company and add dates to highlight mid year acquisitions and the number of months since control was acquired.

(2) Prepare the CSCI proforma adding across 100% of the income and expenses of the parent and subsidiary's line by line. If the subsidiary was acquired mid-year, apply time apportionment to the subsidiary's figures. It is recommended that you spread your answer out over a page so that you have room to record adjustments on the appropriate lines.

(3) Review the extra information in the question to determine any adjustments required. Calculate the adjustment needed in a separate working.

(4) Transfer the adjustments to the proforma, referencing your answer to the workings to ensure your answer is clear for a marker to follow.

(5) Calculate NCI's share of profits & total comprehensive income. Parent shareholders share of profits & total comprehensive income will be calculated as a balancing figure.

Zebedee

Consolidated statement of comprehensive income for the year ended 31 December 20X9

	$000
Revenue (1,260 + 520 - 84 (W2))	1,696
Cost of sales (420 + 210 – 84 (W2) + 12 (W2) + 10 (W3))	(568)
Gross profit	1,128
Distribution costs (180 + 60)	(240)
Administrative expenses (120 + 90 + 15 impairment)	(225)
Profit from operations	663
Investment income (36 – 36 (W4))	–
Profit before tax	663
Taxation (130 + 25)	(155)
Profit for the year	508
Other comprehensive income (100 + 50)	150
Total comprehensive income	658
Profit attributable to:	
Parent shareholders (balancing figure)	480.5
Non-controlling interests (W5)	27.5
	508
Total comprehensive income attributable to:	
Parent shareholders (balancing figure)	618
Non-controlling interests (W5)	40
	658

Workings

(W1) **Group structure**

Zebedee

75% — 1 January 20X7 i.e. 3 years since acquisition

Xavier

(W2) **Intercompany sales and PUP**

Intercompany sales of $84,000 to be eliminated by reducing both revenue and cost of sales

PUP adjustment to increase cost of sales:

$36,000 x 50/ 150 = $12,000

(W3) **Depreciation adjustment**

Fair value adjustment = $50,000

Depreciation adjustment = 1/5 x $50,000 = $10,000

(W4) **Intercompany dividend**

Sub paid $48,000

Parent received (75% x 48,000) $36,000

(W5) **NCI share of profit and total comprehensive income**

		$000	$000
Sub's profit for the year per S's SCI		135	
Depreciation adjustment (W3)		(10)	
Impairment expense (fair value method only)		(15)	
		110	
NCI share of profits	x 25%		27.5
Sub's other comprehensive income per S's SCI		50	
		160	
NCI share of total comprehensive income	x 25%		40

Nb. PUP adjustment is not deducted in the NCI working, as the parent made the profit.

Test your understanding 1 - Paris and London

Given below are the statements of comprehensive income for Paris and its subsidiary London for the year ended 31 December 20X5

	Paris	**London**
	$000	$000
Revenue	3,200	2,560
Cost of sales	(1,200)	(1,080)
Gross profit	2,000	1,480
Operating expenses	(560)	(400)
Profit from operations	1,440	1,080
Investment income	160	–
Profit before tax	1,600	1,080
Taxation	(400)	(480)
Profit for the year	1,200	600
Other comprehensive income	300	100
Total comprehensive income	1,500	700

Paris acquired 80% of London's equity shares several years ago.

(1) Goodwill was calculated valuing the NCI's holding at fair value. At 31 December 20X5, it was determined that goodwill was impaired by $30,000 in the year. Impairments are charged to operating expenses.

(2) A fair value adjustment of $400,000 was recorded at acquisition to increase the value of London's PPE. The assets had a remaining useful economic life of 10 years at acquisition. Depreciation is calculated on a straight line basis and charged to cost of sales.

(3) London made sales to Paris at a selling price of $600,000. At the year-end, half of these goods remain in Paris' inventory. London sold the goods at a 30% margin.

(4) London paid a dividend of $200,000 during the year.

Required:
Prepare a consolidated statement of comprehensive income for the year ended 31 December 20X5.

Test your understanding 2 - Rome and Madrid

Below are the statements of comprehensive income for Rome and its subsidiary Madrid for the year ended 30 June 20X9.

	Rome	**Madrid**
	$000	$000
Revenue	10,350	8,400
Cost of sales	(6,200)	(5,150)
Gross profit	4,150	3,250
Operating expenses	(2,350)	(1,550)
Profit from operations	1,800	1,700
Finance costs	(100)	(50)
Profit before tax	1,700	1,650
Taxation	(550)	(450)
Profit for the year	1,150	1,200
Other comprehensive income	850	300
Total comprehensive income	2,000	1,500

(1) Rome acquired 60% of Madrid's equity shares on 1 July 20X7 paying $6 million. At this date the fair value of Madrid's net assets was $5 million. It is Rome's group policy to value NCIs at acquisition using the proportion of net assets method. As at 30 June 20X9 it was determined that goodwill on acquisition had been impaired by 20%. No impairment loss had arisen previously.

(2) A fair value adjustment of $200,000 had been recorded at acquisition in relation to Madrid's depreciable non-current assets. The remaining life of these assets was 5 years as at the date of acquisition. Depreciation is calculated on a straight line basis and charged to cost of sales.

(3) During the year ended 30 June 20X9, Rome sold $1 million of goods to Madrid at a margin of 30%. Half of these goods remained in the inventory of Madrid at the reporting date.

Required:

Prepare a consolidated statement of comprehensive income for the Rome Group for the year ended 30 June 20X9.

Test your understanding 3 - P and S

P acquired 75% of the equity shares of S on 1 December 20X8. Below are their statements of comprehensive income for the year ended 31 March 20X9:

	P	**S**
	$	$
Revenue	300,000	216,000
Operating costs	(215,000)	(153,000)
Profit from operations	85,000	63,000
Finance costs	(16,000)	(9,000)
Profit before tax	69,000	54,000
Taxation	(21,600)	(16,200)
Profit for the year	47,400	37,800
Other comprehensive income	25,000	3,000
Total comprehensive income	72,400	40,800

(1) In the post acquisition period P sold $50,000 of goods to S at a margin of 20%. S held $10,000 of these goods in inventory at the year end.

(2) A fair value adjustment of $150,000 was recorded at acquisition to increase the value of S's property, plant & equipment. These assets have a remaining useful economic life of 5 years at acquisition. Depreciation is charged to operating costs.

(3) Goodwill was reviewed for impairment at the year end. It was determined that an impairment loss of $3,000 had arisen which is to be charged to operating costs. NCI's had been valued at acquisition using the proportion of net assets method.

Required:

Prepare the consolidated statement of comprehensive income for the year ended 31 March 20X9.

Test your understanding 4 - Tudor and Windsor

On 1 July 20X4 Tudor purchased 80% of the shares in Windsor. The summarised draft statement of comprehensive income for each company for the year ended 31 March 20X5 was as follows:

	Tudor	**Windsor**
	$000	$000
Revenue	60,000	24,000
Cost of sales	(42,000)	(20,000)
Gross profit	18,000	4,000
Operating costs	(6,000)	(200)
Profit from operations	12,000	3,800
Investment income	75	–
Finance costs	–	(200)
Profit before tax	12,075	3,600
Taxation	(3,000)	(600)
Profit for the year	9,075	3,000
Other comprehensive income	1,500	500
Total comprehensive income	10,575	3,500

(1) The fair values of Windsor's assets at the date of acquisition were mostly equal to their book values with the exception of plant, which was stated in the books at $2 million but had a fair value of $5.2 million. The remaining useful life of the plant in question was four years at the date of acquisition. Depreciation is charged to cost of sales and is time apportioned on a monthly basis.

(2) During the post acquisition period Tudor sold Windsor some goods for $12 million. The goods had originally cost $9 million. By the year end Windsor had sold $10 million of these goods (at cost to Windsor) to third parties for $13 million.

(3) Tudor invested $1 million in Windsor's 10% loan notes on 1 July 20X4.

(4) At 31 March 20X5 it was determined that an impairment loss of $100,000 had arisen in respect of goodwill. The NCI holding in Windsor was measured at fair value at acquisition. Impairment losses should be charged to operating costs.

Required:

Prepare the consolidated statement of comprehensive income for the Tudor Group for the year ended 31 March 20X5.

4 Consolidated statement of changes in equity

The statement of changes in equity explains the movement in the equity section of the statement of financial position from the previous reporting date to the current reporting date.

From a group perspective, the equity of the group belongs partly to the parent shareholders and partly to the NCI shareholders. A consolidated statement of changes in equity (CSOCIE) will therefore be made up of two columns reflecting:

- The changes in equity attributable to parent shareholders, made up of share capital, share premium, retained earnings and any other reserves
- The changes in equity attributable to NCI shareholders

The CSOCIE proforma is as follows:

	Parent shareholders	NCI shareholders
	$000	$000
Equity brought forward (b/f)	X	X
Comprehensive income	X	X
Dividends		
P's dividend	(X)	
NCI% x S's dividend		(X)
Equity carried forward (c/f)	X	X

Comprehensive income

These figures come from the foot of the consolidated statement of comprehensive income where the comprehensive income of the group is split between the parent and NCI shareholders.

Dividends

The CSOCIE reflects the dividends which are being paid outside of the group, i.e. the parent company's dividend and the share of the subsidiary's dividend paid to non-controlling interest shareholders.

Note that the share of the subsidiary's dividend that has been paid to the parent company will have been eliminated in the group accounts as it is an intra-group transaction.

Equity b/f

Parent shareholders

This is made up of the share capital, share premium, retained earnings and any other reserves as reported in last year's CSFP.

Share capital and share premium is that of the parent company only. Retained earnings and other reserves are calculated using W5. Therefore equity b/f can be calculated using the same format as W5 but starting with the parent's equity rather than just the parent's reserves. Also, only include the subsidiary's post acquisition reserves up to the b/f date.

NCI shareholders

This is the NCI figure as per W4 but again remembering to include only post acquisition reserves up to the b/f date.

Equity c/f

Parent shareholders

The equity c/f figures can be calculated using W5 but remembering to include the parent's share capital and share premium balances as well as their retained earnings / other reserves. In other words the working will start with the parent's equity c/f (rather than just its reserves).

When including the subsidiary, post acquisition reserves up to the c/f date (i.e. reporting date) will be included.

NCI shareholders

This is the NCI figure as calculated for a CSFP using W4.

Example 2

The following are the statements of changes in equity for Fulham and Putney for the year ended 31 March 20X7:

	Fulham	Putney
	$	$
Equity b/f	132,500	60,000
Comprehensive income	85,500	20,000
Dividends	(10,000)	(5,000)
Equity c/f	208,000	75,000

Fulham acquired 80% of Putney's equity shares on 1 April 20X4 when Putney's net assets had a fair value of $35,000. No fair value adjustments were required at acquisition. It is Fulham's group policy to record NCIs at fair value at acquisition. The NCI holding in Putney had a fair value of $7,500 at the date of acquisition.

Required

Prepare the consolidated statement of changes in equity for the year ended 31 March 20X7.

Example 2 answer

In order to complete the equity b/f and c/f figures in the CSOCIE, it is necessary to produce W4 NCIs and a working similar to W5 Reserves. In order to complete these workings it is necessary to know the post acquisition reserves of the subsidiary from W2 Net Assets of the subsidiary. The working should also contain a column as at the b/f date (as well as the acquisition and reporting date columns). This is so that the post acquisition reserves up to both the b/f and c/f dates can be calculated. It is also important to remember at this stage that net assets equals equity.

(W2) Net assets of subsidiary

	Acq	B/f	C/f (i.e. reporting date)
	$	$	$
Net assets = equity	35,000	60,000	75,000
		Post acquisition reserves = 25,000	Post acquisition reserves = 40,000

W4 NCIs share of equity as at the b/f and c/f dates can now be calculated:

	B/f	C/f (i.e. reporting date)
	$	$
NCI at acqn at fair value	7,500	7,500
NCI% x post acquisition reserves		
(20% x 25,000 (W2))	5,000	
(20% x 40,000 (W2))		8,000
	12,500	15,500

Equity b/f and c/f attributable to the parent shareholders can now be calculated. The format of the working is the same as that of W5 Reserves except that it starts with the parents equity rather than simply the parents reserves. This ensures that other elements of equity such as share capital and share premium are included:

	B/f	C/f (i.e. reporting date)
	$	$
Parent's equity	132,500	208,000
Sub: P% x post acquisition reserves		
(80% x 25,000 (W2))	20,000	
(80% x 40,000 (W2))		32,000
	152,500	240,000

The foot of the consolidated statement of comprehensive income should now be replicated in order to calculate the split of comprehensive income between the parent and NCI shareholders. It is important to remember that the total comprehensive income of the group will be 100% of the parent plus 100% of the subsidiary (subject to time apportionment) plus/minus any consolidation adjustments.

Since the subsidiary has paid a dividend, the intra-group element of this will have been eliminated on consolidation.

	$
P and S comprehensive income (85,500 + 20,000)	105,500
Less elimination of inter-co dividend (80% x 5,000)	(4,000)
	101,500
Total comprehensive income attributable to:	
Parent shareholders (balancing figure)	97,500
Non-controlling interests (20% x 20,000)	4,000
	101,500

Note that in this case the NCIs share of comprehensive income is simply NCI% x S's Comprehensive Income because there are no consolidation adjustments that affect the subsidiary's comprehensive income. If such adjustments exist it may be necessary to produce a working such as that shown in section 3 earlier.

Finally, the dividend figures can be calculated on the face of the CSOCIE proforma:

	Parent shareholders	NCI shareholders
	$	$
Equity b/f	152,500	12,500
Comprehensive income	97,500	4,000
Dividends		
P's dividend	(10,000)	
NCI% x S's dividend		(1,000)
Equity c/f	240,000	15,500

Test your understanding 5 - Islington and Southwark

The following are the statements of changes in equity for Islington and Southwark for the year ended 31 March 20X7:

	Islington	Southwark
	$	$
Equity b/f	210,000	125,000
Comprehensive income	50,000	35,000
Dividends	(15,000)	(10,000)
Equity c/f	245,000	150,000

Islington acquired 75% of Southwark's equity shares on 1 April 20X4 when Southwark's net assets had a fair value of $80,000. No fair value adjustments were required at acquisition. It is Islington's group policy to record NCIs at fair value at acquisition. The NCI holding in Southwark had a fair value of $25,000 at the date of acquisition.

Required

Prepare the consolidated statement of changes in equity for the year ended 31 March 20X7.

Test your understanding 6 - Pitcher and Straw

The following are the statements of changes in equity for Pitcher and Straw for the year ended 31 March 20X9:

	Pitcher	Straw
	$	$
Equity b/f	175,000	80,000
Comprehensive income	42,500	15,000
Dividends	(10,000)	(4,000)
Equity c/f	207,500	91,000

Pitcher acquired 80% of Straw's equity shares on 1 April 20X5 when Straw's net assets had a fair value of $55,000. No fair value adjustments were required at acquisition. It is Pitcher's group policy to record NCIs at their proportion of the subsidiary's net assets at acquisition.

Required

Prepare the consolidated statement of changes in equity for the year ended 31 March 20X9.

Test your understanding 7 - P and S

P bought 60% of S on 1 April 20X4 when S's net assets had a book value of $6,000. The following are the statements of comprehensive income of P and S for the year ended 31 March 20X7:

	P	S
	$	$
Revenue	31,200	10,400
Cost of sales	(17,800)	(5,600)
Gross profit	13,400	4,800
Operating expenses	(8,500)	(1,200)
Profit from operations	4,900	3,600
Investment income	2,000	–
Profit before tax	6,900	3,600
Taxation	(2,100)	(500)
Profit for the year	4,800	3,100
Other comprehensive income	1,200	400
Total comprehensive income	6,000	3,500

The following are the statements of changes in equity for the year ended 31 March 20X7:

	P	S
	$	$
Equity b/f	50,600	22,670
Comprehensive income	6,000	3,500
Dividends	(2,500)	(500)
Equity c/f	54,100	25,670

The following information is available:

(1) On 1 April 20X4 a property in the books of S had a fair value of $24,000 in excess of its carrying value. At this time, the plant had a remaining life of 10 years. Depreciation is charged to operating expenses.

(2) During the year S sold goods to P for $4,400. Of this amount $500 was included in the inventory of P at the year end. S earns a 35% margin on its sales.

(3) Goodwill amounting to $800 arose on the acquisition of S. Goodwill was impaired by 10% of the original value in the year ended 31 March 20X6 and a further 10% of the book value in the year ended 31 March 20X7. Impairment losses should be charged to operating expenses.

(4) It is P's group policy to value NCIs at fair value at acquisition. At 1 April 20X4, the fair value of the NCI holding in S was $2,500.

Required

Prepare the consolidated statement of comprehensive income and consolidated statement of changes in equity for the P group for the year ended 31 March 20X7.

Test your understanding 8 - Thunder and Lightning

On 1 January 20X5 Thunder acquired 80% of the equity share capital of Lightning when the net assets of Lightning were $65,000. Below are the statements of comprehensive income and statements of changes in equity for both companies for the year ended 31 December 20X6:

	Thunder	Lightning
	$	$
Revenue	85,000	42,000
Cost of sales	(32,500)	(12,500)
Gross profit	52,500	29,500
Operating expenses	(21,750)	(11,250)
Profit from operations	30,750	18,250
Investment income	800	–
Finance costs	(4,550)	(1,500)
Profit before tax	27,000	16,750
Taxation	(8,000)	(5,000)
Profit for the year	19,000	11,750
Other comprehensive income	5,000	2,000
Total comprehensive income	24,000	13,750

The following are the statements of changes in equity for the year ended 31 December 20X6:

	Thunder	Lightning
	$	$
Equity b/f	156,000	80,000
Comprehensive income	24,000	13,750
Dividends	(10,000)	(1,000)
Equity c/f	170,000	92,750

(1) On acquisition a fair value adjustment was recorded to increase the value of Lightning's plant and equipment by $20,000. The plant had a remaining life of 10 years at this time. Depreciation is charged to cost of sales.

(2) During the year Thunder sold $10,000 of goods to Lightning at a profit margin of 20%. A quarter of these goods remain in the inventory of Lightning at the reporting date.

(3) Thunder's group policy is to record the NCIs at fair value at acquisition. The fair value of the NCI holding in Lightning was $23,000 at acquisition.

(4) At 31 December 20X5, goodwill was reviewed for impairment but none had arisen. At 31 December 20X6, an impairment loss of $3,000 had arisen which is to be charged to operating expenses.

Required

Prepare the consolidated statement of comprehensive income and consolidated statement of changes in equity for the Thunder group for the year ended 31 December 20X6.

Test your understanding 9 - Papilla and Satago

Papilla acquired 70% of the Satago three years ago when Satago's retained earnings were $500,000. The financial statements of each company for the year ended 31 March 20X7 are as follows:

Statements of financial position as at 31 March 20X7

	Papilla $000	Satago $000
Non-current assets		
Property, plant and equipment	1,000	400
Investment in S	600	–
	1,600	400
Current assets	300	600
	1,900	1,000
Equity		
Share capital	250	150
Retained earnings	1,360	700
Non-current liabilities	100	90
Current liabilities	190	60
	1,900	1,000

Statements of changes in equity for the year ended 31 March 20X7

	Papilla	Satago
	$000	$000
Equity b/f	1,570	770
Comprehensive income	90	100
Dividends	(50)	(20)
Equity c/f	1,610	850

Statements of comprehensive income for the year ended 31 March 20X7

	Papilla	Satago
	$	$
Revenue	1,000	260
Cost of sales	(750)	(80)
Gross profit	250	180
Operating expenses	(60)	(35)
Profit from operations	190	145
Investment income	24	–
Finance costs	(25)	(15)
Profit before tax	189	130
Taxation	(109)	(30)
Profit for the year	80	100
Other comprehensive income	10	–
Total comprehensive income	90	100

You are provided with the following additional information:

(1) At the date of acquisition, land in the books of Satago with a carrying value of $100,000 had a fair value of $120,000.

(2) Papilla sold $40,000 of goods to Satago during the year at a mark up of 20%. 45% of the inventory remained unsold at the year-end. At the year-end Satago owes Papilla $6,000 which agrees with the receivable recorded in Papilla's books.

(3) Papilla's group policy is to value NCIs at fair value at acquisition. The NCI holding in Satago had a fair value of $250,000.

Required

Prepare the consolidated statement of financial position, consolidated statement of comprehensive income and consolidated statement of changes in equity for the Papilla group for the year ended 31 March 20X7.

Test your understanding 10 - Penguin and Smarties

The following are the statements of changes in equity for Penguin and Smarties for the year ended 31 March 20X9:

	Penguin	Smarties
	$	$
Equity b/f	275,000	180,000
Comprehensive income	100,000	50,000
Dividends	(20,000)	(10,000)
Equity c/f	355,000	220,000

Penguin acquired 80% of Smarties' equity shares on 1 April 20X7 when Smarties' net assets had a carrying value of $125,000. At this time property had a fair value of $40,000 in excess of its carrying value. The property had a remaining life of 20 years.

At 31 March 20X9, Smarties held inventory which had been purchased from Penguin for $20,000. Penguin had sold these goods at a margin of 25%.

It is Penguin's group policy to record NCIs at their fair value at acquisition. The fair value of the NCI holding in Smarties at 1 April 20X7 was $30,000.

Required

Prepare the consolidated statement of changes in equity for the year ended 31 March 20X9.

5 Chapter summary

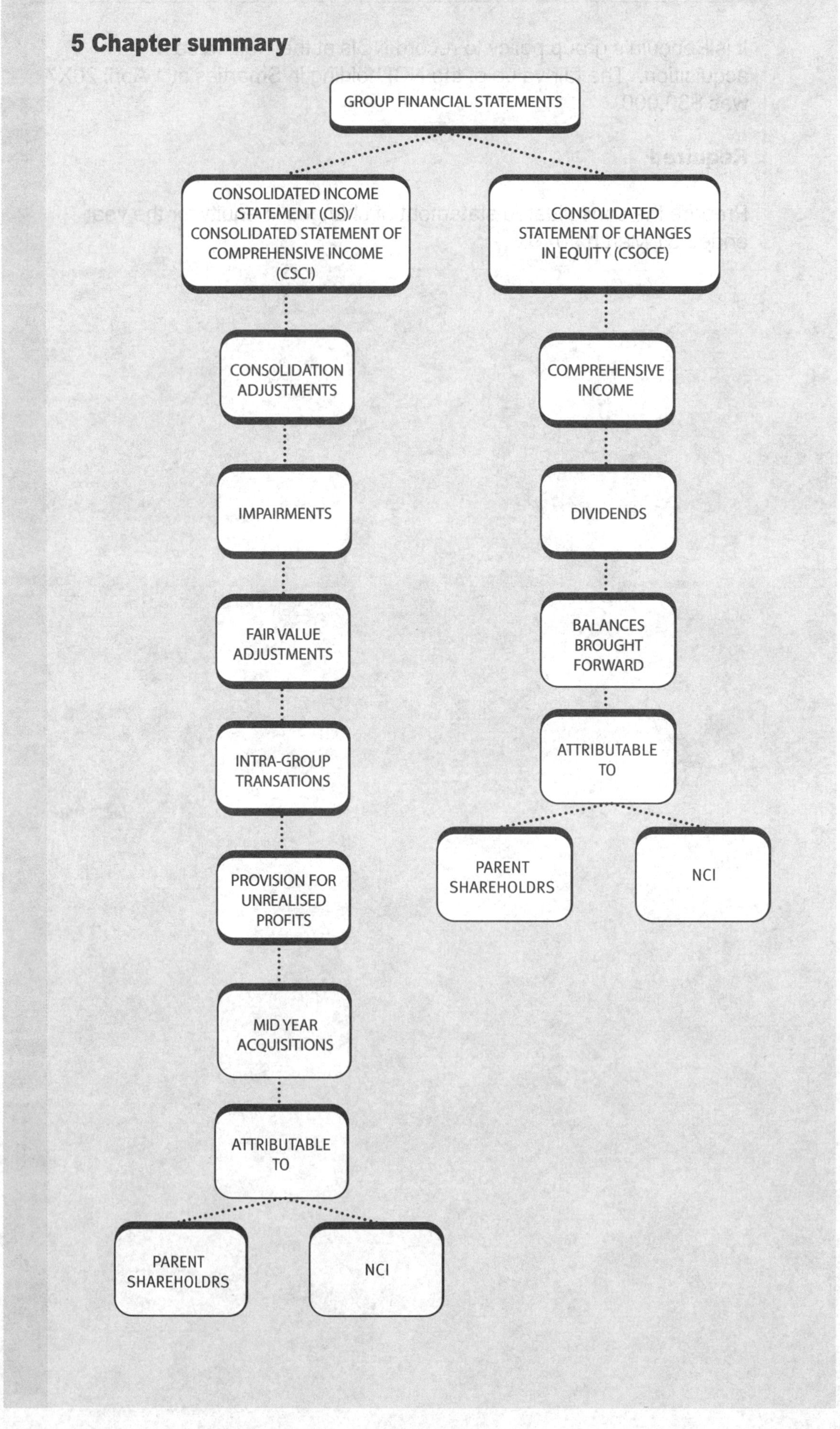

Test your understanding answers

Test your understanding 1 - Paris and London

Consolidated statement of comprehensive income

	$000
Revenue (3,200 + 2,560 - 600 (W2))	5,160
Cost of sales (1,200 + 1,080 - 600 (W2) + 90 (W2) + 40 (W3))	(1,810)
Gross profit	3,350
Operating expenses (560 + 400 + 30 imp)	(990)
Profit from operations	2,360
Investment income (160 - 160 (W4))	–
Profit before tax	2,360
Taxation (400 + 480)	(880)
Profit for the year	1,480
Other comprehensive income (300 + 100)	400
Total comprehensive income	1,880
Profit attributable to:	
Parent shareholders (balancing figure)	1,392
Non-controlling interests (W5)	88
	1,480
Total comprehensive income attributable to:	
Parent shareholders (balancing figure)	1,772
Non-controlling interests (W5)	108
	1,880

Workings

(W1) **Group structure**

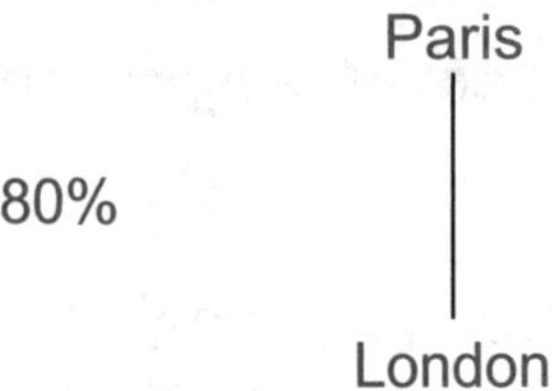

(W2) **Intercompany sales and PUP**

Intercompany sales of $600,000 to be eliminated by reducing both revenue and cost of sales

PUP adjustment to increase cost of sales:

Goods in inventory = 1/2 x $600,000 = $300,000

Profit in inventory = 30% x $300,000 = $90,000

(W3) **Depreciation adjustment**

Fair value adjustment = $400,000

Depreciation adjustment = 1/10 x $400,000 = $40,000

(W4) **Intercompany dividend**

Sub paid $200,000

Parent received (80% x $200,000) = $160,000

(W5) **NCI share of profit and total comprehensive income**

		$000	$000
Sub's profit for the year per S's SCI		600	
PUP (sub seller) (W2)		(90)	
Depreciation adjustment (W3)		(40)	
Impairment expense (fair value method only)		(30)	
		440	
NCI share of profits	x 20%		88
Sub's other comprehensive income per S's SCI		100	
		540	
NCI share of total comprehensive income	x 20%		108

Test your understanding 2 - Rome and Madrid

Consolidated statement of comprehensive income

	$000
Revenue (10,350 + 8,400 - 1,000 (W4))	17,750
Cost of sales (6,200 + 5,150 + 40 (W3) – 1,000 (W4) + 150 (W4))	(10,540)
Gross profit	7,210
Operating expenses (2,350 + 1,550 + 600 (W2))	(4,500)
Profit from operations	2,710
Finance costs (100 + 50)	(150)
Profit before tax	2,560
Taxation (550 + 450)	(1,000)
Profit for the year	1,560
Other comprehensive income (850 + 300)	1,150
Total comprehensive income	2,710

Profit attributable to:	
Parent shareholders (balancing figure)	1,096
Non-controlling interests (W5)	464
	1,560

Total comprehensive income attributable to:	
Parent shareholders (balancing figure)	2,126
Non-controlling interests (W5)	584
	2,710

Workings

(W1) **Group structure**

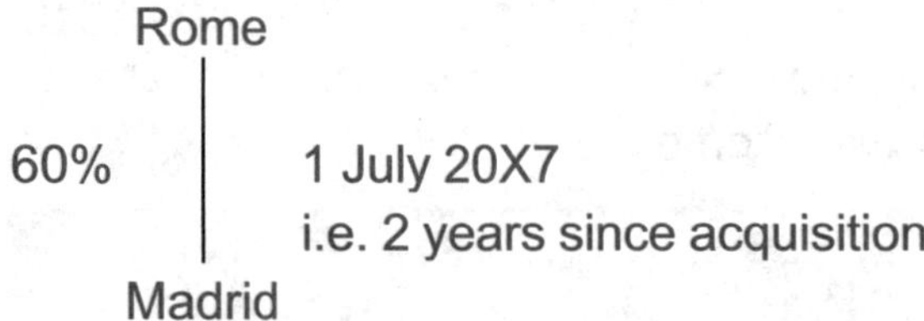

(W2) **Goodwill and impairment**

	$000
Fair value of P's holding (cost of investment)	6,000
NCI holding at proportion of net assets (40% x 5,000)	2,000
Fair value of sub's net assets at acquisition	(5,000)
Goodwill at acquisition	3,000
Therefore impairment (20% x 3,000)	600

(W3) **Depreciation adjustment**

Fair value adjustment = $200,000

Depreciation adjustment = 1/5 x $200,000 = $40,000

(W4) **Intercompany sales and PUP**

Intercompany sales of $1,000,000 to be eliminated by reducing both revenue and cost of sales

PUP adjustment to increase cost of sales:

Goods in inventory = 1/2 x $1,000,000 = $500,000

Profit in inventory = 30% x $500,000 = $150,000

(W5) **NCI share of profit and total comprehensive income**

		$000	$000
Sub's profit for the year per S's SCI		1,200	
Depreciation adjustment (W3)		(40)	
		1,160	
NCI share of profits	x 40%		464
Sub's other comprehensive income per S's SCI		300	
		1,460	
NCI share of total comprehensive income	x 40%		584

Nb. Impairment is not deducted in the NCI working as the NCI has been valued using the proportionate method. The PUP adjustment is also not deducted, as the parent made the profit.

Test your understanding 3 - P and S

Consolidated statement of comprehensive income for the year ended 31 March 20X9

	$
Revenue (300,000 + (4/12 x 216,000) – 50,000 (W2))	322,000
Operating costs (215,000 + (4/12 x 153,000) – 50,000 (W2) + 2,000 (W2) + 10,000 (W3) + 3,000 imp)	(231,000)
Profit from operations	91,000
Finance costs (16,000 + (4/12 x 9,000))	(19,000)
Profit before tax	72,000
Taxation (21,600 + (4/12 x 16,200))	(27,000)
Profit for the year	45,000
Other comprehensive income (25,000 + (4/12 x 3,000))	26,000
Total comprehensive income	71,000
Profit attributable to:	
Parent shareholders (balancing figure)	44,350
Non-controlling interests (W4)	650
	45,000
Total comprehensive income attributable to:	
Parent shareholders (balancing figure)	70,100
Non-controlling interests (W4)	900
	71,000

Workings

(W1) **Group structure**

P
75% | 1 December 20X8
i.e. 4 months since acquisition
S

(W2) **Intercompany sales and PUP**

Intercompany sales of $50,000 to be eliminated by reducing both revenue and cost of sales

PUP adjustment to increase cost of sales:

Profit in inventory = 20% x $10,000 = $2,000

(W3) **Depreciation adjustment**

Fair value adjustment = $150,000

Depreciation adjustment = 1/5 x 4/12 x $150,000 = $10,000

(W4) **NCI share of profit and total comprehensive income**

		$	$
Sub's profit for the year per S's SCI (4/12 x 37,800)		12,600	
Depreciation adjustment (W3)		(10,000)	
		2,600	
NCI share of profits	x 25%		650
Sub's other comprehensive income per S's SCI (4/12 x 3,000)		1,000	
		3,600	
NCI share of total comprehensive income	x 25%		900

Test your understanding 4 - Tudor and Windsor

Consolidated statement of comprehensive income for the year ended 31 March 20X5

	$000
Revenue (60,000 + (9/12 x 24,000) – 12,000 (W2))	66,000
Cost of sales (42,000 + (9/12 x 20,000) – 12,000 (W2) + 500 (W2) + 600 (W3))	(46,100)
Gross profit	19,900
Operating costs (6,000 + (9/12 x 200) + 100 imp)	(6,250)
Profit from operations	13,650
Investment income (75 – 75 (W4))	–
Finance costs ((9/12 x 200) – 75 (W4))	(75)
Profit before tax	13,575
Taxation (3,000 + (9/12 x 600))	(3,450)
Profit for the year	10,125
Other comprehensive income (1,500 + (9/12 x 500))	1,875
Total comprehensive income	12,000
Profit attributable to:	
Parent shareholders (balancing figure)	9,815
Non-controlling interests (W5)	310
	10,125
Total comprehensive income attributable to:	
Parent shareholders (balancing figure)	11,615
Non-controlling interests (W5)	385
	12,000

Workings

(W1) **Group structure**

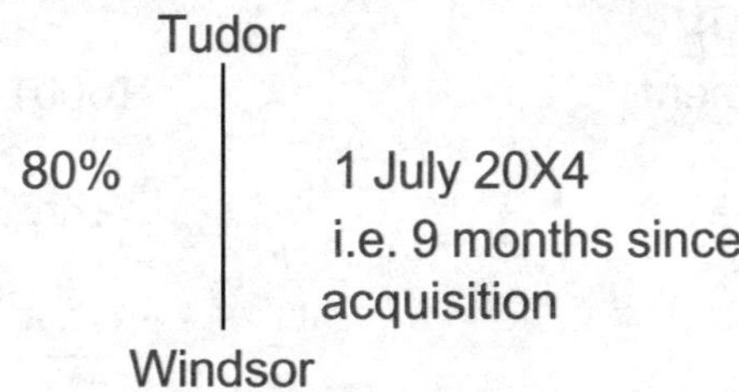

(W2) **Intercompany sales and PUP**

Intercompany sales of $12,000,000 to be eliminated by reducing both revenue and cost of sales

PUP adjustment to increase cost of sales:

Profit on sales: 12m – 9m = 3m/12m = 25% margin

Goods in inventory = 12m – 10m = $2,000,000

Profit in inventory = 25% x $2,000,000 = $500,000

(W3) **Depreciation adjustment**

Fair value adjustment = $5.2m – $2m = $3.2m

Depreciation adjustment = 1/4 x 9/12 x $3.2m = $600,000

(W4) **Intercompany interest**

Windsor paid interest to Tudor = 10% x $1m x 9/12 = $75,000

(W5) **NCI share of profit and total comprehensive income**

		$000	$000
Sub's profit for the year per S's SCI (9/12 x 3,000)		2,250	
Depreciation adjustment (W3)		(600)	
Impairment (fair value method)		(100)	
		1,550	
NCI share of profits	x 20%		310
Sub's other comprehensive income per S's SCI (9/12 x 500)		375	
		1,925	
NCI share of total comprehensive income	x 20%		385

Test your understanding 5 - Islington and Southwark

Consolidated statement of changes in equity for the year ended 31 March 20X7

	Parent shareholders	NCI shareholders
	$	$
Equity b/f (W4/ W3)	243,750	36,250
Comprehensive income (W5)	68,750	8,750
Dividends		
P's dividend	(15,000)	
NCI% x S's dividend (25% x 10,000)		(2,500)
Equity c/f (W4/ W3)	297,500	42,500

Workings

(W1) **Group structure**

Islington

75% | 1 April 20X4 i.e. 3 years since acquisition

Southwark

(W2) **Net assets of subsidiary**

	Acq	B/f	C/f (i.e. reporting date)
	$	$	$
Net assets = equity	80,000	125,000	150,000
		Post acquisition reserves = 45,000	Post acquisition reserves = 70,000

(W3) **NCI share of equity**

	B/f	C/f (i.e. reporting date)
	$	$
NCI at acqn at fair value	25,000	25,000
NCI% x post acquisition reserves		
(25% x 45,000 (W2))	11,250	
(25% x 70,000 (W2))		17,500
	36,250	42,500

(W4) **Parent's share of equity**

	B/f	C/f (i.e. reporting date)
	$	$
Parent's equity	210,000	245,000
Sub: P% x post acquisition reserves		
(75% x 45,000 (W2))	33,750	
(75% x 70,000 (W2))		52,500
	243,750	297,500

(W5) **Comprehensive income**

	$
P and S comprehensive income (50,000 + 35,000)	85,000
Less elimination of inter-co dividend (75% x 10,000)	(7,500)
	77,500
Total comprehensive income attributable to:	
Parent shareholders (balancing figure)	68,750
Non-controlling interests (25% x 35,000)	8,750
	77,500

Test your understanding 6 - Pitcher and Straw

Consolidated statement of changes in equity for the year ended 31 March 20X9

	Parent shareholders	NCI shareholders
	$	$
Equity b/f (W4/ W3)	195,000	16,000
Comprehensive income (W5)	51,300	3,000
Dividends		
P's dividend	(10,000)	
NCI% x S's dividend (20% x 4,000)		(800)
Equity c/f (W4/ W3)	236,300	18,200

Workings

(W1) **Group structure**

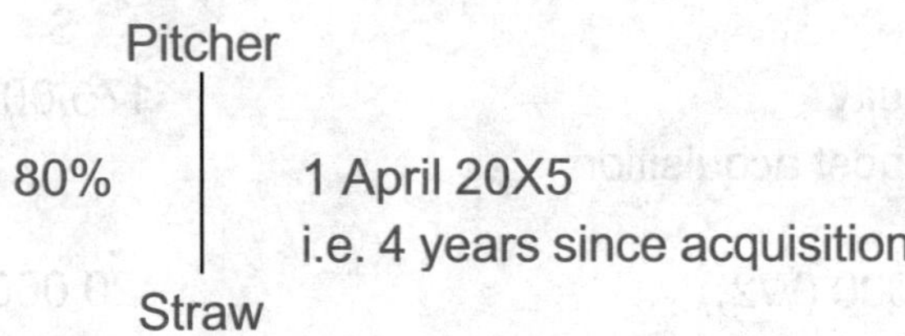

(W2) **Net assets of subsidiary**

	Acq	B/f	C/f (i.e. reporting date)
	$	$	$
Net assets = equity	55,000	80,000	91,000
		Post acquisition reserves = 25,000	Post acquisition reserves = 36,000

(W3) **NCI share of equity**

	B/f	C/f (i.e. reporting date)
	$	$
NCI at acqn at proportion of net assets (20% x 55,000)	11,000	11,000
NCI% x post acquisition reserves		
(20% x 25,000 (W2))	5,000	
(20% x 36,000 (W2))		7,200
	16,000	18,200

(W4) **Parent's share of equity**

	B/f	C/f (i.e. reporting date)
	$	$
Parent's equity	175,000	207,500
Sub: P% x post acquisition reserves		
(80% x 25,000 (W2))	20,000	
(80% x 36,000 (W2))		28,800
	195,000	236,300

(W5) **Comprehensive income**

	$
P and S comprehensive income (42,500 + 15,000)	57,500
Less elimination of inter-co dividend (80% x 4,000)	(3,200)
	54,300
Total comprehensive income attributable to:	
Parent shareholders (balancing figure)	51,300
Non-controlling interests (20% x 15,000)	3,000
	54,300

Test your understanding 7 - P and S

Consolidated statement of comprehensive income

	$000
Revenue (31,200 + 10,400 – 4,400 (W4))	37,200
Cost of sales (17,800 + 5,600 – 4,400 (W4) + 175 (W4))	(19,175)
Gross profit	18,025
Operating costs (8,500 + 1,200 + 2,400 (W3) + 72 (W5))	(12,172)
Profit from operations	5,853
Investment income (2,000 – (60% x 500))	1,700
Profit before tax	7,553
Taxation (2,100 + 500)	(2,600)
Profit for the year	4,953
Other comprehensive income (1,200 + 400)	1,600
Total comprehensive income	6,553
Profit attributable to:	
Parent shareholders (balancing figure)	4,771.8
Non-controlling interests (W6)	181.2
	4,953
Total comprehensive income attributable to:	
Parent shareholders (balancing figure)	6,211.8
Non-controlling interests (W6)	341.2
	6,553

Consolidated statement of changes in equity

	Parent shareholders	NCI shareholders
	$	$
Equity b/f (W7/ W8)	57,674	7,216
Comprehensive income per CSCI	6,211.8	341.2
Dividends		
P's dividend	(2,500)	
NCI% x S's dividend (40% x 500)		(200)
Equity c/f (W7/ W8)	61,385.8	7,357.2

Workings

(W1) **Group structure**

P

60% | 1 April 20X4
i.e. 3 years since acquisition

S

(W2) **Net assets of subsidiary**

	Acq	B/f	C/f (i.e. reporting date)
	$	$	$
Net assets = equity	6,000	22,670	25,670
Fair value adjustment	24,000	24,000	24,000
Depreciation adjustment (W3)		(4,800)	(7,200)
PUP (sub is seller) (W4)			(175)
	30,000	41,870	42,295
		Post acquisition reserves = 11,870	Post acquisition reserves = 12,295

(W3) **Depreciation adjustment**

Fair value adjustment = $24,000

Depreciation adjustment = 1/10 x $24,000 = $2,400 per annum

(W4) **Intercompany sales and PUP**

Intercompany sales of $4,400 to be eliminated by reducing both revenue and cost of sales

PUP adjustment to increase cost of sales:

Profit in inventory = 35% x $500 = $175

(W5) **Goodwill and impairment**

	$
Goodwill at acquisition	800
Impairment y/e 31 March 20X6 (10% x 800)	(80)
	720
Impairment y/e 31 March 20X7 (10% x 720)	(72)
Total impairment at 31 March 20X7 (80 + 72)	152

(W6) **NCI share of profit and total comprehensive income**

		$	$
Sub's profit for the year per S's SCI		3,100	
Depreciation adjustment (W3)		(2,400)	
PUP (sub is seller) (W4)		(175)	
Impairment (fair value method)		(72)	
		453	
NCI share of profits	x 40%		181.2
Sub's other comprehensive income per S's SCI		400	
		853	
NCI share of total comprehensive income	x 40%		341.2

(W7) **Parent's share of equity**

	B/f	C/f (i.e. reporting date)
	$	$
Parent's equity	50,600	54,100
Sub: P% x post acquisition reserves		
(60% x 11,870 (W2))	7,122	
(60% x 12,295 (W2))		7,377
Impairment loss (60% x 80)/ (60% x 152) (W5)	(48)	(91.2)
	57,674	61,385.8

(W8) **NCI share of equity**

	B/f	C/f (i.e. reporting date)
	$	$
NCI at acqn at fair value	2,500	2,500
NCI% x post acquisition reserves		
(40% x 11,870 (W2))	4,748	
(40% x 12,295 (W2))		4,918
NCI% x impairment loss (40% x 80)/ (40% x 152) (W5)	(32)	(60.8)
	7,216	7,357.2

Test your understanding 8 - Thunder and Lightning

Consolidated statement of comprehensive income for the year ended 31 December 20X6

	$
Revenue (85,000 + 42,000 – 10,000 (W4))	117,000
Cost of sales (32,500 + 12,500 + 2,000 (W3) – 10,000 (W4) + 500(W4))	(37,500)
Gross profit	79,500
Operating expenses (21,750 + 11,250 + 3,000 imp)	(36,000)
Profit from operations	43,500
Investment income (800 – (80% x 1,000))	–
Finance costs (4,550 + 1,500)	(6,050)
Profit before tax	37,450
Taxation (8,000 + 5,000)	(13,000)
Profit for the year	24,450
Other comprehensive income (5,000 + 2,000)	7,000
Total comprehensive income	31,450
Profit attributable to:	
Parent shareholders (balancing figure)	23,100
Non-controlling interests (W5)	1,350
	24,450
Total comprehensive income attributable to:	
Parent shareholders (balancing figure)	29,700
Non-controlling interests (W5)	1,750
	31,450

Consolidated statement of changes in equity for the year ended 31 December 20X6

	Parent shareholders	NCI shareholders
	$	$
Equity b/f (W6/ W7)	166,400	25,600
Comprehensive income per CSCI	29,700	1,750
Dividends		
P's dividend	(10,000)	
NCI% x S's dividend (20% x 1,000)		(200)
Equity c/f (W6/ W7)	186,100	27,150

Workings

(W1) **Group structure**

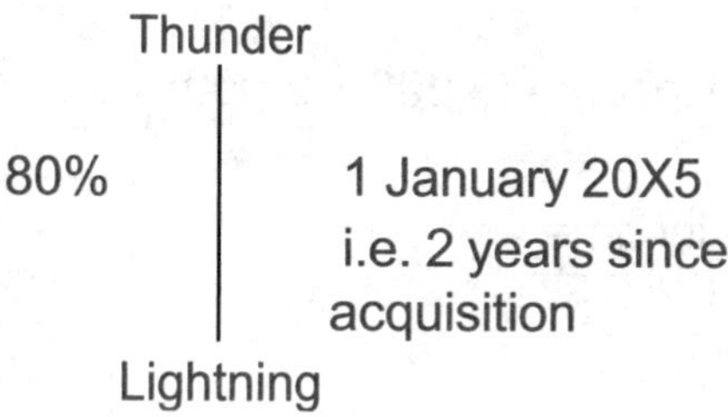

(W2) **Net assets of subsidiary**

	Acq	B/f	C/f (i.e. reporting date)
	$	$	$
Net assets = equity	65,000	80,000	92,750
Fair value adjustment	20,000	20,000	20,000
Depreciation adjustment (W3)		(2,000)	(4,000)
	85,000	98,000	108,750
		Post acquisition reserves = 13,000	Post acquisition reserves = 23,750

(W3) **Depreciation adjustment**

Fair value adjustment = $20,000

Depreciation adjustment = 1/10 x $20,000 = $2,000 per annum

(W4) **Intercompany sales and PUP**

Intercompany sales of $10,000 to be eliminated by reducing both revenue and cost of sales

PUP adjustment to increase cost of sales:

Goods in inventory = 1/4 x 10,000 = $2,500

Profit in inventory = 20% x $2,500 = $500

(W5) **NCI share of profit and total comprehensive income**

		$	$
Sub's profit for the year per S's SCI		11,750	
Depreciation adjustment (W3)		(2,000)	
Impairment (fair value method)		(3,000)	
		6,750	
NCI share of profits	x 20%		1,350
Sub's other comprehensive income per S's SCI		2,000	
		8,750	
NCI share of total comprehensive income	x 20%		1,750

(W6) **Parent's share of equity**

	B/f	C/f (i.e. reporting date)
	$	$
Parent's equity	156,000	170,000
PUP (P is seller) (W4)		(500)
Sub: P% x post acquisition reserves		
(80% x 13,000 (W2))	10,400	
(80% x 23,750 (W2))		19,000
Impairment loss (80% x 3,000)		(2,400)
	166,400	186,100

(W7) **NCI share of equity**

	B/f	C/f (i.e. reporting date)
	$	$
NCI at acqn at fair value	23,000	23,000
NCI% x post acquisition reserves		
(20% x 13,000 (W2))	2,600	
(20% x 23,750 (W2))		4,750
NCI% x impairment loss (20% x 3,000)		(600)
	25,600	27,150

Test your understanding 9 - Papilla and Satago

Consolidated statement of financial position at 31 March 20X7

		$000
Non-current assets		
Property, plant and equipment	(1,000 + 400 + 20 (W2))	1,420
Goodwill	(W3)	180
Current assets	(300 + 600 - 6 (W6) – 3 (W6))	891
		2,491
Equity		
Share capital		250
Retained earnings	(W5)	1,497
		1,747
Non-controlling interest	(W4)	310
		2,057
Non-current liabilities	(100 + 90)	190
Current liabilities	(190 + 60 – 6 (W6))	244
		2,491

Consolidated statement of comprehensive income for the year ended 31 March 20X7

	$000
Revenue (1,000 + 260 – 40 (W6))	1,220
Cost of sales (750 + 80 – 40 (W6) + 3 (W6))	(793)
Gross profit	427
Operating expenses (60 + 35)	(95)
Profit from operations	332
Investment income (24 – (70% x 20))	10
Finance costs (25 + 15)	(40)
Profit before tax	302
Taxation (109 + 30)	(139)
Profit for the year	163
Other comprehensive income	10
Total comprehensive income	173
Profit attributable to:	
Parent shareholders (balancing figure)	133
Non-controlling interests (W7)	30
	163
Total comprehensive income attributable to:	
Parent shareholders (balancing figure)	143
Non-controlling interests (W7)	30
	173

Consolidated statement of changes in equity for the year ended 31 March 20X7

	Parent shareholders	NCI shareholders
	$000	$000
Equity b/f (W8/ W4)	1,654	286
Comprehensive income per CSCI	143	30
Dividends		
P's dividend	(50)	
NCI% x S's dividend (30% x 20)		(6)
Equity c/f (CSFP/ W4)	1,747	310

Workings

(W1) **Group structure**

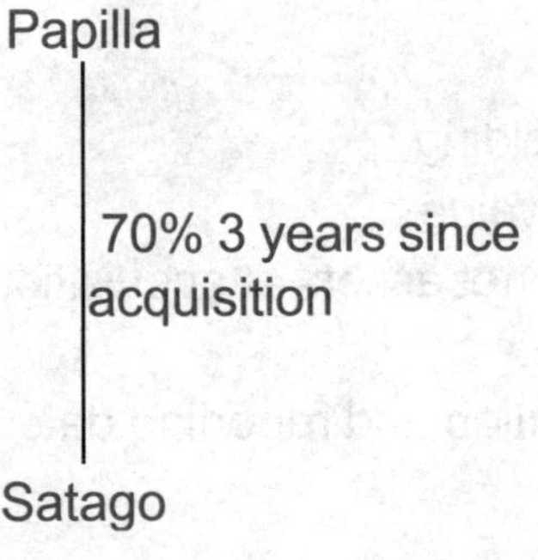

(W2) **Net assets of subsidiary**

	Acq	B/f	C/f (i.e. reporting date)
	$000	$000	$000
Share capital	150		150
Retained reserves	500		700
Equity	650	770	850
Fair value adjustment – land (120 – 100)	20	20	20
	670	790	870
		Post acquisition reserves = 120	Post acquisition reserves = 200

(W3) **Goodwill**

	$000
Fair value of P's holding	600
NCI holding at fair value	250
Fair value of sub's net assets at acquisition (W2)	(670)
Goodwill at acquisition and reporting date	180

(W4) **Non-controlling interest**

	B/f	C/f (i.e. reporting date)
	$000	$000
NCI at acqn at fair value	250	250
NCI% x post acquisition reserves		
(30% x 120 (W2))	36	
(30% x 200 (W2))		60
	286	310

(W5) **Retained earnings**

	$000
P's retained earnings	1,360
PUP (W6)	(3)
Sub: P% x post acquisition reserves	
(70% x 200 (W2))	140
	1,497

(W6) **Intercompany sales and PUP**

Intercompany sales of $40,000 to be eliminated by reducing both revenue and cost of sales.

Intercompany balance of $6,000 to be eliminated from current assets and current liabilities.

PUP adjustment to increase cost of sales:

Goods in inventory = 45% x 40,000 = $18,000

Profit in inventory = 20/120 x $18,000 = $3,000

Parent is the seller so eliminate from W5 and current assets and increase cost of sales.

(W7) **NCI share of profit and total comprehensive income**

		$	$
Sub's profit and total comprehensive income for the year per S's SCI		100	
NCI share of profits/TCI	x 30%		30

(W8) **Parent's share of equity b/f**

	$000
Parent's equity b/f	1,570
Sub: P% x post acquisition reserves	
(70% x 120 (W2))	84
	1,654

Test your understanding 10 - Penguin and Smarties

Consolidated statement of changes in equity for the year ended 31 March 20X9

	Parent shareholders	NCI shareholders
	$	$
Equity b/f (W4/ W3)	317,400	40,600
Comprehensive income (W5)	125,400	9,600
Dividends		
P's dividend	(20,000)	
NCI% x S's dividend (20% x 10,000)		(2,000)
Equity c/f (W4/ W3)	422,800	48,200

Workings

(W1) **Group structure**

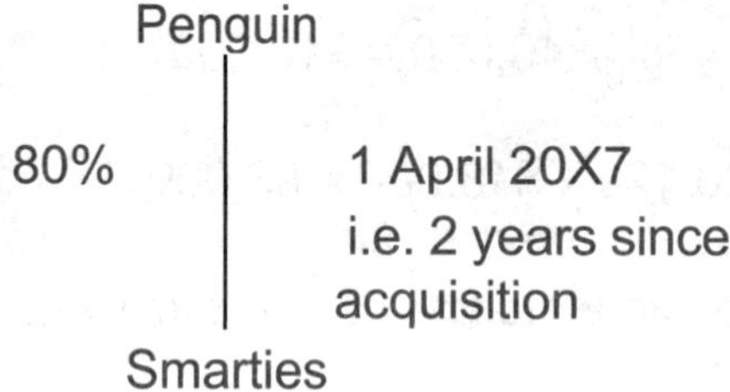

(W2) **Net assets of subsidiary**

	Acq	B/f	C/f (i.e. reporting date)
	$	$	$
Net assets = equity	125,000	180,000	220,000
Fair value adjustment	40,000	40,000	40,000
Depreciation adjustment			
(40,000 x 1/20)		(2,000)	
(40,000 x 2/20)			(4,000)
	165,000	218,000	256,000
		Post acquisition reserves = 53,000	Post acquisition reserves = 91,000

(W3) **NCI share of equity**

	B/f	C/f (i.e. reporting date)
	$	$
NCI at acqn at fair value	30,000	30,000
NCI% x post acquisition reserves		
(20% x 53,000 (W2))	10,600	
(20% x 91,000 (W2))		18,200
	40,600	48,200

(W4) **Parent's share of equity**

	B/f	C/f (i.e. reporting date)
	$	$
Parent's equity	275,000	355,000
PUP (P is seller) (W7)		(5,000)
Sub: P% x post acquisition reserves		
(80% x 53,000 (W2))	42,400	
(80% x 91,000 (W2))		72,800
	317,400	422,800

(W5) **Comprehensive income**

	$
P and S comprehensive income (100,000 + 50,000)	150,000
Consolidation adjustments:	
PUP (W7)	(5,000)
FV depreciation (W8)	(2,000)
Inter-company dividend (W9)	(8,000)
	135,000
Total comprehensive income attributable to:	
Parent shareholders (balancing figure)	125,400
Non-controlling interests (W6)	9,600
	135,000

(W6) **NCI share of total comprehensive income**

		$	$
Sub's total comprehensive income		50,000	
Depreciation adjustment (W8)		(2,000)	
		48,000	
NCI share of total comprehensive income	x 20%		9,600

(W7) **PUP**

Profit in inventory = 25% x $20,000 = $5,000

(W8) **Depreciation adjustment**

Fair value adjustment = $40,000

Depreciation adjustment = 1/20 x $40,000 = $2,000 per annum

(W9) **Intragroup dividend**

Sub paid dividend $10,000

Parent share (80% x 10,000) = $8,000

Will be eliminated from CSCI on consolidation.

chapter

6

Associates and joint ventures

Chapter learning objectives

On completion of their studies students should be able to:

- Prepare consolidated financial statements for a group of companies involving one or more subsidiaries and associates;
- Explain the accounting treatment of associates and joint ventures using the equity method.

1 Session Content

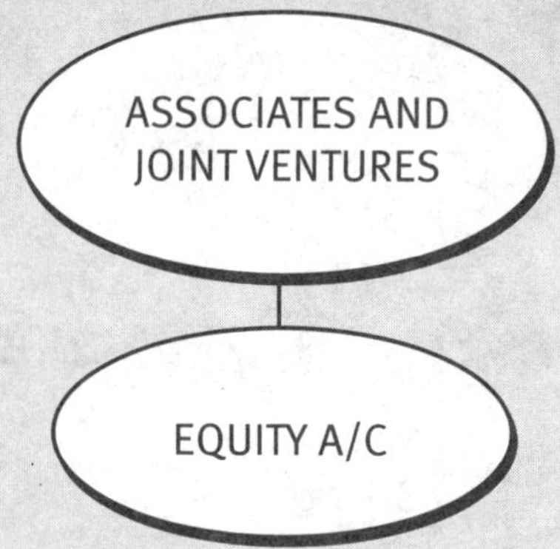

2 Associates

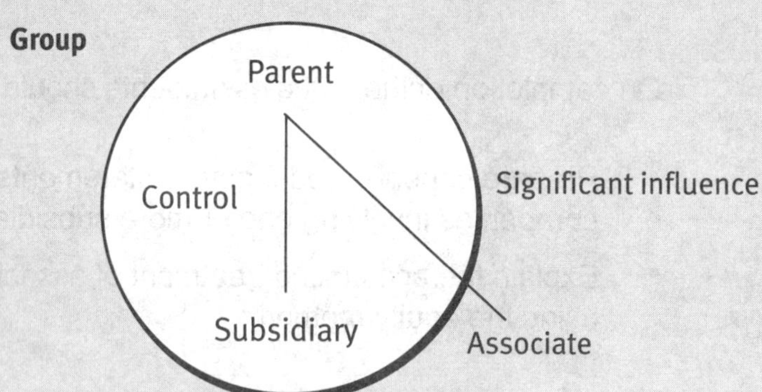

The following definitions relating to associates are included in IAS 28: *Investments in Associates and Joint Ventures (2011).*

Definition:

- An **associate** is an entity over which the investor has **significant influence** and which is neither a subsidiary nor a joint venture of the investor.

- **Significant influence** is the power to participate in the financial and operating policy decisions of the investee but not control or joint control of those policies.

  A holding of 20% or more of the voting power is presumed to give significant influence unless it can be clearly demonstrated that this is not the case. At the same time a holding of less than 20% is assumed not to give significant influence unless such influence can be clearly demonstrated.

IAS 28 explains that an investor probably has significant influence if:

- It is represented on the board of directors.
- It participates in policy-making processes, including decisions about dividends or other distributions.
- There are material transactions between the investor and investee.
- There is interchange of managerial personnel.
- There is provision of essential technical information.

IAS 28 was revised in 2011 to include both associates and joint ventures. The accounting treatment of associates has not changed, however joint ventures are now accounted for using the same method - equity accounting. Joint ventures are defined in IFRS 11 (see below) but are then accounted for in accordance with IAS 28 (revised).

3 IFRS 11 Joint Arrangements

IFRS 11 *Joint Arrangements* was issued in May 2011 and has changed the accounting treatment for joint ventures. Prior to the introduction of this standard, IAS 31 *Interests in Joint Ventures* (which has now been superseded) permitted two methods of accounting for joint ventures: equity method or proportionate consolidation. IFRS 11 requires that all joint ventures are accounted for using the equity method, in accordance with IAS 28 revised.

A **joint arrangement** is an arrangement of which two or more parties have joint control.

Joint control is the contractually agreed sharing of control of an arrangement, which exists only when decisions about the relevant activities require the unanimous consent of the parties sharing control.

A **joint venture** is a joint arrangement whereby the parties that have joint control of the arrangement have rights to the net assets of the arrangement.

Joint operations

A **joint operation** is a joint arrangement whereby the parties that have joint control of the arrangement have rights to the assets, and obligations for the liabilities, relating to the arrangement.

Under IFRS 11, a joint arrangement will either be a joint venture or a joint operation. A joint operation will exist where the arrangement is not structured through a separate vehicle.

A joint operator would account for its share of the assets, liabilities, revenues and expenses relating to its involvement with the joint operation in accordance with the relevant IFRSs

4 Accounting for associates and joint ventures

Associates and joint ventures are accounted for using **equity accounting**.

They are not consolidated as the parent does not have control.

Consolidated statement of financial position

The CSFP will include a single line within non-current assets called 'Investment in associate' or 'Investment in joint venture' calculated as:

Investment in associate / joint venture

	$
Cost of investment	X
Add: share of post acquisition reserves	X
Less: impairment losses	(X)
Less: PUP (if A/JV has inventory – see later)	(X)
	X

The above working would normally be set up as W6 within a consolidation question (W1 to W5 are as per Chapter 4).

The share of post acquisition reserves, impairment losses and PUP will also be recorded in W5 Retained earnings.

Consolidated statement of comprehensive income

The CSCI will include a single line before profit before tax called 'Income from associate' or 'Income from joint venture' calculated as:

Share of associate/joint venture's profit for the year	X
Less: impairment loss	(X)
Less: PUP (if A/JV is seller - see later)	(X)
	X

If the associate/joint venture has other comprehensive income, the investor's share will also be recorded in the other comprehensive income section of CSCI.

IAS 28 Investments in associates and joint ventures

The equity method of accounting is normally used to account for associates and joint ventures in the consolidated financial statements.

The equity method should not be used if:

- the investment is classified as held for sale in accordance with IFRS 5; or
- the parent is exempted from having to prepare consolidated accounts on the grounds that it is itself a wholly, or partially, owned subsidiary of another company (IFRS 10).

5 Adjustments with associates and joint ventures

Fair value & depreciation adjustments

When calculating the post-acquisition reserves for the associate/joint venture, the effect of fair value adjustments should be included. The fair value adjustment may then result in a depreciation adjustment after acquisition. If such adjustments are in an exam question, it would then be advisable to prepare a W2 Net assets table in order to calculate the post acquisition reserves.

Intercompany transactions & balances

Intercompany transactions between the group (whether with the parent or subsidiary) and the associate/joint venture are not eliminated within the CSCI or CSFP. This is because the associate/joint venture is outside of the group. Thus the transactions / balances are with a third party to the group and so may be reported within the group financial statements.

However, unrealised profit on transactions must be eliminated on consolidation.

Provisions for unrealised profit (PUP)

IAS 28 requires unrealised profits on transactions between the group and the associate/joint venture to be eliminated. Only the investor's share of the profit is removed since the group financial statements only reflect the investor's share of the associates/joint venture profits in the first place.

The PUP adjustment is calculated as:

PUP = **P%** × unrealised profit in inventory

Parent sells to associate / joint venture

In the CSFP:

- Reduce W5 retained earnings
- Reduce W6 investment in associate / joint venture

In the CSCI:

- Increase cost of sales

Associate / joint venture sells to parent

In the CSFP:

- Reduce W5 retained earnings
- Reduce inventory

In the CSCI:

- Reduce income from associate / joint venture

Illustration 1 - Parent sells to associate

P owns 40% of the equity shares of A.

P has sold $200,000 of goods to A at a mark up on cost of 25%.

At the reporting date 60% of these items remain in A's inventory.

The intercompany sale of $200,000 is not eliminated in the consolidated financial statements. However a PUP adjustment is calculated as:

Goods in inventory	60% × $200,000 = $120,000
Profit in inventory	25/125 × $120,000 = $24,000
PUP	40% × $24,000 = $9,600

The adjustment will be:

Dr Cost of sales	$9,600
Cr Investment in associate	$9,600

In the CSCI, cost of sales will increase.

In the CSFP, retained earnings will therefore be reduced. The investment in Associate will also be reduced.

The associate is holding the inventory, but the associate's inventory is not consolidated on the inventory line in the CSFP and so it is not appropriate to reduce inventory.

Illustration 2 - Associate sells to parent

Using the same information as illustration 1, the adjustment will now be:

Dr Income from associate	$9,600
Cr Inventory	$9,600

In the CSCI, income from associate will reduce.

In the CSFP, retained earnings will therefore be reduced. Inventory will also be reduced as it is the parent company holding the inventory.

Test your understanding 1

A parent company owns 25% of the equity shares of its associate. The parent made sales to the associate during the year amounting to $450,000. The sales price is cost plus 20%. At the reporting date, 30% of these items remain in the associate's inventory.

Required:

Identify the relevant adjustments to be made to the consolidated statement of financial position and consolidated statement of comprehensive income.

Example 1 - Tom, James and Emily

Below are the statements of financial position of three entities as at 31 December 20X9.

	Tom	James	Emily
	$000	$000	$000
Non-current assets			
Property, plant & equipment	959	980	840
Investments: 630,000 shares in James	805	–	–
168,000 shares in Emily	224	–	–
	1,988	980	840
Current assets			
Inventory	380	640	190
Receivables	190	310	100
Bank	35	58	46
TOTAL ASSETS	2,593	1,988	1,176
Equity			
Share capital ($1 shares)	1,120	840	560
Retained earnings	1,232	602	448
	2,352	1,442	1,008
Current liabilities			
Trade payables	150	480	136
Taxation	91	66	32
TOTAL EQUITY & LIABILITIES	2,593	1,988	1,176

Additional information:

(1) Tom acquired its shares in James on 1 January 20X9 when James had retained earnings of $160,000. NCIs are to be valued at their fair value at the date of acquisition. The fair value of the NCI holding in James at 1 January 20X9 was $250,000.

(2) Tom acquired its shares in Emily on 1 January 20X9 when Emily had retained earnings of $140,000.

(3) An impairment test at the year end shows that the goodwill for James remains unimpaired but that the investment in Emily is impaired by $2,000.

Required:

Prepare the consolidated statement of financial position for the year ended 31 December 20X9.

Example 1 answer

Consolidated statement of financial position as at 31 December 20X9

	$000
Non-current assets	
Goodwill (W3)	55
Property, plant & equipment (959 + 980)	1,939
Investment in associate (W6)	314.4
	2,308.4
Current assets	
Inventory (380 + 640)	1,020
Receivables (190 + 310)	500
Bank (35 + 58)	93
TOTAL ASSETS	3,921.4

Equity	
Share capital ($1 shares)	1,120
Retained earnings (W5)	1,653.9
	2,773.9
Non-controlling interest (W4)	360.5
	3,134.4
Current liabilities	
Trade payables (150 + 480)	630
Taxation (91 + 66)	157
TOTAL EQUITY & LIABILITIES	3,921.4

Workings

(W1) **Group structure**

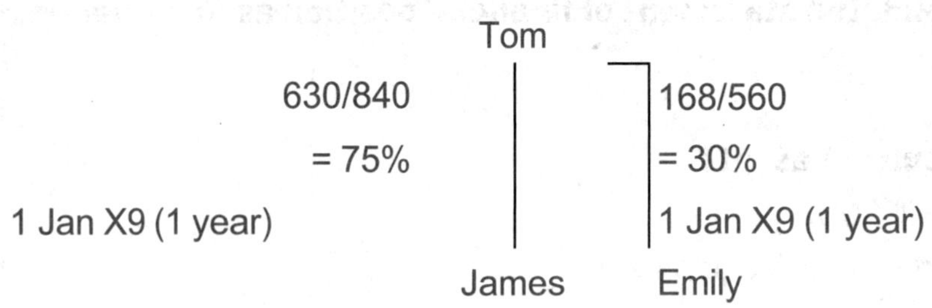

(W2) **Net assets of sub**

	Acquisition date	Reporting date
	$000	$000
Share capital ($1 shares)	840	840
Retained earnings	160	602
	1,000	1,442

Post acquisition profits = 442

(W3) **Goodwill**

	$000
Fair value of parent's holding	805
NCI holding at fair value	250
Fair value of sub's net assets at acquisition (W2)	(1,000)
Goodwill at acquisition/ reporting date	55

(W4) **Non-controlling interests**

	$000
NCI at acquisition at fair value (W3)	250
NCI% of post acquisition reserves (25% x 442 (W2))	110.5
	360.5

(W5) **Group retained earnings**

	$000
P's retained earnings	1,232
S: 75% of post acquisition profits (75% x 442 (W2))	331.5
A: 30% of post-acquisition profits (W6)	92.4
A: impairment (W6)	(2)
	1,653.9

(W6) **Investment in associate**

	$000
Cost of investment	224
P% x post acquisition profits (30% x (448 – 140))	92.4
Less: impairment	(2)
	314.4

In the question, the investment in Emily is included in Tom's SFP at its cost of $224,000. The investment was made at the start of the year.

This becomes the starting point for equity accounting i.e. the starting point for the calculation of investment in associate.

At acquisition the retained earnings of Emily were $140,000 and at the reporting date they are $448,000. Therefore the post acquisition reserves of Emily are $308,000 of which 30% belong to Tom i.e. $92,400. This increases both the value of investment in associate and retained earnings.

At the reporting date, the investment is impaired by $2,000. This is a reduction in the value of the Investment and is an expense and so also reduces retained earnings.

Test your understanding 2

Below are the Statements of Financial Position of three entities as at 30 September 20X8:

	P	S	A
	$000	$000	$000
Non-current assets			
Property, plant & equipment	6,000	1,500	1,000
Investments	1,800	–	–
	7,800	1,500	1,000
Current assets	1,70	1,000	500
TOTAL ASSETS	9,500	2,500	1,500
Equity			
Share capital ($1 shares)	5,000	1,000	500
Retained earnings	2,000	750	400
	7,000	1,750	900
Non-current liabilities	1,000	250	250
Current liabilities	1,500	500	350
TOTAL EQUITY & LIABILITIES	9,500	2,500	1,500

(1) P acquired 80% of the equity share capital of S several years ago, paying $1.5 million in cash. At this time the balance on S's retained earnings was $350,000.

(2) P's group policy is to value NCIs at fair value at acquisition. The fair value of the NCI holding in S at acquisition was $350,000.

(3) P acquired 30% of the equity share capital of A on 1 October 20X7, paying $300,000 in cash. At 1 October 20X7 the balance on A's retained earnings was $360,000.

(4) At the reporting date, it was determined that the investment in A was impaired by $5,000. No impairment losses had arisen in respect of the goodwill of S.

Required:

Prepare the consolidated statement of financial position of the P Group as at 30 September 20X8.

Test your understanding 3

Below are the statements of comprehensive income for P, S and A for the year ended 30 September 20X8:

	P	S	A
	$000	$000	$000
Revenue	4,000	500	200
Operating expenses	(1,800)	(320)	(130)
Operating profit	2,200	180	70
Finance costs	(1,000)	(30)	(25)
Profit before tax	1,200	150	45
Tax	(300)	(50)	(5)
Profit for the year	900	100	40
Other comprehensive income	100	–	10
Total comprehensive income	1,000	100	50

P acquired 80% of S several years ago.

P acquired 30% of the equity share capital of A on 1 October 20X7. At the reporting date, the investment in A was impaired by $2,000.

Required:

Prepare the consolidated statement of comprehensive income for the P Group for the year ended 30 September 20X8.

Test your understanding 4

Below are the Statements of Financial Position of three entities as at 30 September 20X8:

	P	S	J
	$000	$000	$000
Non-current assets			
Property, plant & equipment	14,000	7,500	3,000
Investments	10,000	–	–
	24,000	7,500	3,000
Current assets	6,000	3,000	1,500
TOTAL ASSETS	30,000	10,500	4,500
Equity			
Share capital ($1 shares)	10,000	1,000	500
Retained earnings	7,500	5,500	2,500
	17,500	6,500	3,000
Non-current liabilities	8,000	1,250	500
Current liabilities	4,500	2,750	1,000
TOTAL EQUITY & LIABILITIES	30,000	10,500	4,500

(1) P acquired 75% of the equity share capital of S several years ago, paying $5 million in cash. At this time the balance on S's retained earnings was $3 million. The NCI holding in S was measured at its fair value of $1 million at acquisition.

(2) P acquired 30% of the equity share capital of J on 1 October 20X6, paying $750,000 in cash. The shares were acquired as part of a contractual arrangement that will give P joint control over J and, consequently, J meets the IFRS 11 definition of a joint venture. At 1 October 20X6 the balance on J's retained earnings was $1.5 million.

(3) During the year, P sold goods to J for $800,000 at a margin of 25%. At the year-end, J still held one quarter of these goods in inventory.

(4) As a result of this trading, P was owed $250,000 by J at the reporting date. This agrees with the amount included within J's trade payables.

(5) At 30 September 20X8, it was determined that the investment in the joint venture was impaired by $35,000.

Required:

Prepare the consolidated statement of financial position of the P Group as at 30 September 20X8.

Test your understanding 5

Below are the statements of comprehensive income for P, S and J for the year ended 30 September 20X8:

	P	S	J
	$000	$000	$000
Revenue	8,000	4,500	3,000
Operating expenses	(4,750)	(2,700)	(2,050)
Operating profit	3,250	1,800	950
Finance costs	(750)	(100)	(50)
Profit before tax	2,500	1,700	900
Tax	(700)	(500)	(300)
Profit for the year	1,800	1,200	600
Other comprehensive income	200	–	250
Total comprehensive income	2,000	1,200	850

P acquired 80% of S several years ago.

P acquired 30% of the equity share capital of J on 1 October 20X6. The shares were acquired as part of a contractual arrangement that will give P joint control over J and, consequently, J meets the IFRS 11 definition of a joint venture.

During the year, J sold goods to P for $600,000 at a margin of 20%. At the year-end, P still held one quarter of these goods in inventory.

At 30 September 20X8, it was determined that an impairment loss of $20,000 had arisen in respect of the investment in J.

Required:

Prepare the consolidated statement of comprehensive income for the P Group for the year ended 30 September 20X8.

Test your understanding 6

The statements of f inancial position of three entities at 30 November 20X7 are as follows:

	Paul	Simon	Arthur
	$000	$000	$000
Non-current assets			
Property, plant & equipment	1,465	1,060	1,050
Investments	3,050	–	–
	4,515	1,060	1,050
Current assets			
Inventory	270	230	200
Receivables	100	340	400
Cash	160	50	140
TOTAL ASSETS	5,045	1,680	1,790
Equity			
Share capital ($1 shares)	1,900	500	250
Share premium	650	80	–
Retained earnings	1,145	400	1,200
	3,695	980	1,450
Non-current liabilities	500	300	–

Current liabilities			
Trade payables	520	330	250
Income tax	330	70	90
TOTAL EQUITY & LIABILITIES	5,045	1,680	1,790

(1) Paul acquired 85% of Simon on 1 December 20X4 paying $6 in cash per share. At this date the balance on Simon's retained earnings was $270,000.

(2) On 1 March 20X7 Paul acquired 30% of Arthur's equity shares. The consideration was settled by a share exchange of 4 new shares in Paul for every 3 shares acquired in Arthur. The share price of Paul at the date of acquisition was $5. Paul has accounted for the share exchange correctly in its individual financial statements. Arthur's profit after tax for the year ended 30 November 20X7 was $600,000.

(3) At 1 December 20X4, plant in the books of Simon was determined to have a fair value of $50,000 in excess of its carrying value. The plant had a remaining life of 5 years at this time.

(4) During the year, Simon sold goods to Paul for $400,000 at a mark-up of 25%. Paul had a quarter of these goods still in inventory at the reporting date.

(5) In September Arthur sold goods to Paul for $150,000. These goods had cost Arthur $100,000. Paul had $90,000 (at cost to Paul) in inventory at the reporting date.

(6) As a result of the above inter-company sales, Paul's books showed $50,000 and $20,000 as owing to Simon and Arthur respectively at the reporting date. These balances agreed with the amounts recorded in Simon's and Arthur's books.

(7) The NCI holding in Simon was valued at its fair value of $300,000 at acquisition. At the reporting date goodwill was determined to have suffered an impairment loss of $20,000.

(8) At the reporting date, the investment in associate was impaired by $15,000.

Required:

Prepare the consolidated statement of financial position as at 30 November 20X7.

6 Chapter summary

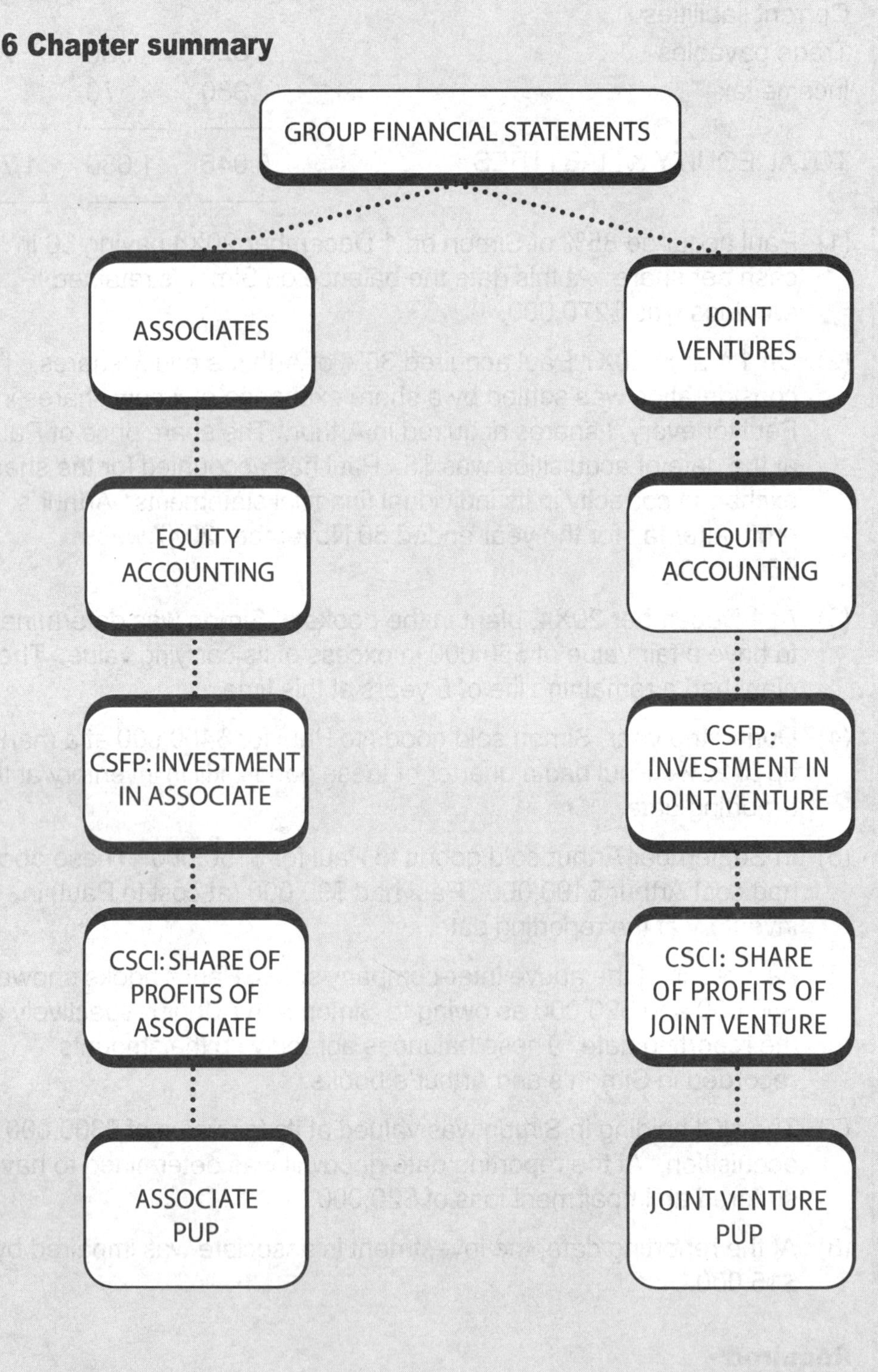

Test your understanding answers

Test your understanding 1

The PUP adjustment is $5,625.

In the CSFP:

Dr	Retained earnings (W5) – reduce
Cr	Investment in associate (W6) – reduce

In the CSCI:

Dr	Cost of sales (increase)
Cr	Investment in associate (W6)

(W1) **PUP**

Goods in inventory = 30% x $450,000 = $135,000

Profit in inventory = 20/120 x $135,000 = $22,500

PUP = 25% x $22,500 = $5,625

Test your understanding 2

Consolidated statement of financial position as at 30 September 20X8

	$000
Non-current assets	
Property, plant & equipment (6,000 + 1,500)	7,500
Goodwill (W3)	500
Investment in associate (W6)	307
	8,307
Current assets (1,700 + 1,000)	2,700
TOTAL ASSETS	11,007
Equity	
Share capital	5,000
Retained earnings (W5)	2,327
	7,327
Non-controlling interests (W4)	430
	7,757
Non-current liabilities (1,000 + 250)	1,250
Current liabilities (1,500 + 500)	2,000
TOTAL EQUITY & LIABILITIES	11,007

Workings

(W1) **Group structure**

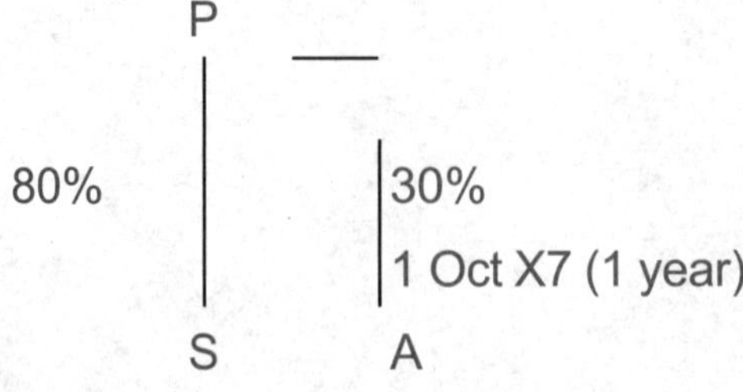

(W2) **Net assets of sub**

	Acquisition date	Reporting date
	$000	$000
Share capital ($1 shares)	1,000	1,000
Retained earnings	350	750
	1,350	1,750

Post acquisition profits = 400

(W3) **Goodwill**

	$000
Fair value of parent's holding	1,500
NCI holding at fair value	350
Fair value of sub's net assets at acquisition (W2)	(1,350)
Goodwill at acquisition/ reporting date	500

(W4) **Non-controlling interests**

	$000
NCI at acquisition at fair value (W3)	350
NCI% of post acquisition reserves (20% x 400 (W2))	80
	430

(W5) **Group retained earnings**

	$000
P's retained earnings	2,000
S: 80% of post acquisition profits (80% x 400 (W2))	320
A: 30% of post-acquisition profits (W6)	12
A: impairment (W6)	(5)
	2,327

(W6) **Investment in associate**

	$000
Cost of investment	300
P% x post acquisition profits (30% x (400 - 360))	12
Less: impairment	(5)
	307

Test your understanding 3

Consolidated statement of comprehensive income for the year ended 30 September 20X8

	$000
Revenue (4,000 + 500)	4,500
Operating expenses (1,800 + 320)	(2,120)
Operating profit	2,380
Finance costs (1,000 + 30)	(1,030)
Income from associate ((30% x 40) – 2 imp)	10
Profit before tax	1,360
Taxation (300 + 50)	(350)
Profit for the year	1,010
Other comprehensive income	100
Other comprehensive income from associate (30% x 10)	3
Total comprehensive income	1,113
Parent shareholders (balancing figure)	990
NCI shareholders (20% x 100)	20
	1,010
Total comprehensive income attributable to:	
Parent shareholders (balancing figure)	1,093
NCI shareholders (20% x 100)	20
	1,113

Test your understanding 4

Consolidated statement of financial position as at 30 September 20X8

	$000
Non-current assets	
Property, plant & equipment (14,000 + 7,500))	21,500
Goodwill (W3)	2,000
Investments (10,000 – 5,000 (W3) – 750 (W6))	4,250
Investment in joint venture (W6)	1,000
	28,750
Current assets (6,000 + 3,000)	9,000
TOTAL ASSETS	37,750
Equity	
Share capital ($1 shares)	10,000
Retained earnings (W5)	9,625
	19,625
Non-controlling interests (W4)	1,625
	21,250
Non-current liabilities (8,000 + 1,250)	9,250
Current liabilities (4,500 + 2,750)	7,250
TOTAL EQUITY & LIABILITIES	37,750

Workings

(W1) **Group structure**

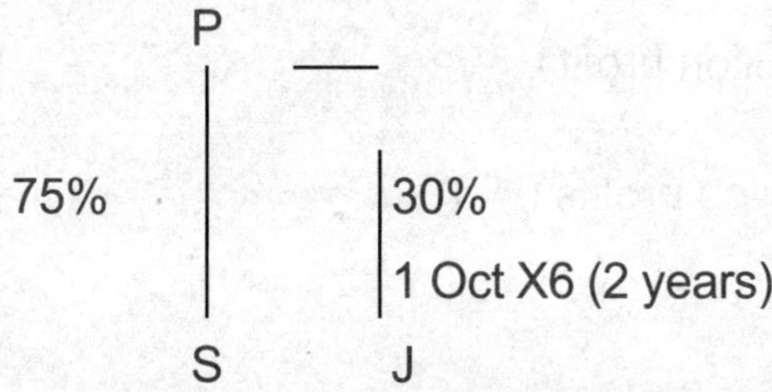

(W2) **Net assets of sub**

	Acquisition date	Reporting date
	$000	$000
Share capital ($1 shares)	1,000	1,000
Retained earnings	3,000	5,500
	4,000	6,500

Post acquisition profits = 2,500

(W3) **Goodwill**

	$000
Fair value of parent's holding	5,000
NCI holding at fair value	1,000
Fair value of sub's net assets at acquisition (W2)	(4,000)
Goodwill at acquisition/ reporting date	2,000

(W4) **Non-controlling interests**

	$000
NCI at acquisition at fair value (W3)	1,000
NCI% of post acquisition reserves (25% x 2,500 (W2))	625
	1,625

(W5) **Retained earnings**

	$000
P's retained earnings	7,500
S: 75% of post acquisition profits (75% x 2,500 (W2))	1,875
J: 30% of post-acquisition profits (W6)	300
J: PUP (W7)	(15)
J: impairment (W6)	(35)
	9,625

(W6) **Investment in joint venture**

	$000
Cost of investment	750
P% x post acquisition profits (30% x (2,500 – 1,500))	300
PUP (W7)	(15)
Impairment	(35)
	1,000

(W7) **Intercompany and PUP**

Intercompany balances between parent & joint venture are not eliminated as the joint venture is outside of the group. Therefore, no adjustment in respect of the balance of $250,000.

PUP = P% x profit in inventory

Goods in inventory = 1/4 x $800,000 = $200,000

Profit in inventory = 25% x $200,000 = $50,000

PUP = 30% x $50,000 = $15,000

PUP will reduce W5 and Investment in joint venture W6 since parent is the seller. The joint venture holds inventory at year end.

Test your understanding 5

Consolidated statement of comprehensive income

	$000
Revenue (8,000 + 4,500)	12,500
Operating expenses (4,750 + 2,700)	(7,450)
Operating profit	5,050
Finance costs (750 + 100)	(850)
Income from joint venture ((30% x 600) – 20 imp – 9 (W1))	151
Profit before tax	4,351
Taxation (700 + 500)	(1,200)
Profit for the year	3,151
Other comprehensive income	200
Other comprehensive income from joint venture (30% x 250)	75
Total comprehensive income	3,426
Profit attributable to:	
Parent shareholders (balancing figure)	2,911
NCI shareholders (20% x 1,200)	240
	3,151
Total comprehensive income attributable to:	
Parent shareholders (balancing figure)	3,186
NCI shareholders (20% x 1,200)	240
	3,426

(W1) **Intercompany and PUP**

Intercompany transactions between the parent and joint venture are not eliminated as the joint venture is outside of the group. Therefore, no adjustment in respect of the intercompany sales of $600,000.

PUP = P% x profit in inventory

Goods in inventory = 1/4 x $600,000 = $150,000

Profit in inventory = 20% x $150,000 = $30,000

PUP = 30% x $30,000 = $9,000

Joint venture is seller so reduce income from joint venture.

Test your understanding 6

Consolidated statement of financial position as at 30 November 20X7

	$000
Non-current assets	
Goodwill (W3)	1,930
Property, plant & equipment (1,465 + 1,060 + 50 (W2) – 30 (W2))	2,545
Investments (3,050 – 2,550 (W3) – 500 (W6))	–
Investment in associate (W6)	620
	5,095
Current assets	
Inventory (270 + 230 – 20 (W7) – 9 (W8))	471
Receivables (100 + 340 – 50 (W9))	390
Cash (160 + 50)	210
TOTAL ASSETS	6,166
Equity	
Share capital ($1 shares)	1,900
Share premium	650
Retained earnings (W5)	1,307
	3,857
Non-controlling interests (W4)	309
	4,166
Non-current liabilities (500 + 300)	800
Current liabilities	
Trade payables (520 + 330 - 50 (W9))	800
Income tax (330 + 70)	400
TOTAL EQUITY & LIABILITIES	6,166

Workings

(W1) **Group structure**

Paul

85%		30%
1 Dec X4 (3 years)		1 Mar X7 (9 months)
	Simon	Arthur

(W2) **Net assets of sub**

	Acquisition date	**Reporting date**
	$000	$000
Share capital ($1 shares)	500	500
Share premium	80	80
Retained earnings	270	400
Fair value adjustment	50	50
Depreciation adjustment (50 x 3/5)		(30)
PUP (W7)		(20)
	900	980

Post acquisition profits = 80

(W3) **Goodwill**

	$000
Fair value of parent's holding (85% x 500 x $6)	2,550
NCI holding at fair value	300
Fair value of sub's net assets at acquisition (W2)	(900)
Goodwill at acquisition	1,950
Impairment	(20)
Goodwill at reporting date	1,930

(W4) **Non-controlling interests**

	$000
NCI at acquisition at fair value (W3)	300
NCI% of post acquisition reserves (15% x 80 (W2))	12
NCI% x impairment (15% x 20 (W3))	(3)
	309

(W5) **Retained earnings**

	$000
P's retained earnings	1,145
S: 85% of post acquisition profits (85% x 80 (W2))	68
S: P% x impairment (85% x 20 (W3))	(17)
A: 30% of post-acquisition profits (W6)	135
A: PUP (W9)	(9)
A: impairment (W6)	(15)
	1,307

(W6) **Investment in associate**

	$000
Cost of investment	
Share consideration (30% x 250 x 4/3 x $5)	500
P% x post acquisition profits (30% x (9/12 x 600))	135
Impairment	(15)
	620

(W7) **PUP with subsidiary**

Goods in inventory = 1/4 x $400,000 = $100,000

Profit in inventory = 25/125 x $100,000 = $20,000

Sub is seller so reduce W2 and inventory.

(W8) **PUP with associate**

PUP = P% x profit in inventory

Profit in sale = $150,000 – $100,000 = $50,000

$50,000/ $150,000 = 33.3% margin

Goods in inventory = $90,000

Profit in inventory = 33.3% x $90,000 = $30,000

PUP = 30% x $30,000 = $9,000

PUP will reduce W5 and inventory since associate is the seller and parent holds inventory at year end.

(W9) **Intercompany**

The receivables balance with the subsidiary of $50,000 is eliminated from receivables and payables.

The intercompany balance with the associate of $20,000 is not eliminated.

chapter

7

Changes in group structure

Chapter learning objectives

On completion of their studies students should be able to:

- Prepare consolidated financial statements for a group of companies;
- Explain the treatment in consolidated financial statements of piece-meal and mid-year acquisitions and disposals;
- Explain the accounting for reorganisations and capital reconstruction schemes.

1 Session content

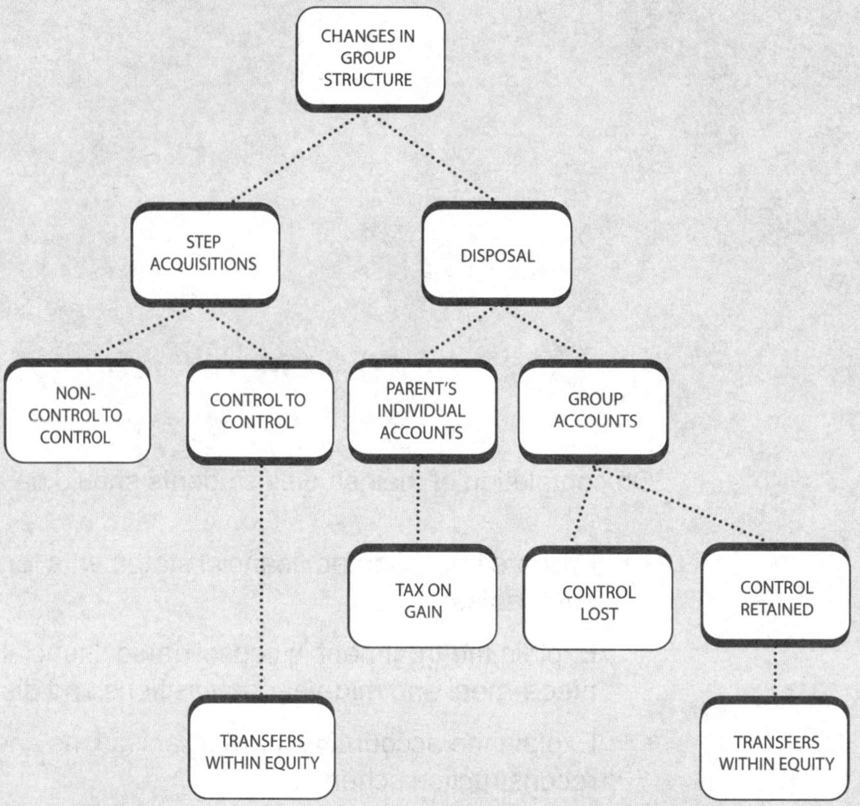

2 Step acquisitions

So far we have considered the situation of the parent company acquiring shares in a single transaction which has resulted in the investment either being classified as a subsidiary, associate or joint venture. If the purchase of shares does not result in any of these classifications, the investment is simply classified as a trade investment.

However, it is possible that having purchased shares, the parent subsequently purchases further shares. This is referred to as a step acquisition or a piecemeal acquisition.

There are three potential situations:

(1) **Non-control to non-control**

E.g. a company acquires 10% of the equity shares and then purchases a further 30% to bring the total shareholding up to 40%.

This situation is less examinable and is considered within the expandable text below.

(2) **Non-control to control**

E.g. a company acquires 40% of the equity shares and then purchases a further 20% to bring the total shareholding up to 60%.

(3) **Control to control**

E.g. a company acquires 60% of the equity shares and then purchases a further 15% to bring the total shareholding up to 75%.

These two situations are more examinable and are considered in further detail below.

Non-control to non-control

If a company acquires 10% of the equity shares of an entity it would be classified as a simple investment according to the rules of IAS 39 (see chapter 13). The investment would be recorded initially at cost in the investor's statement of financial position and any dividend income would be recorded within their income statement. This treatment would also apply within the consolidated accounts.

If subsequently the company purchases a further 30% of the equity shares, the total investment would now be 40%. This would result in the investment being classified as an associate. As a result, equity accounting would now be applied within the group accounts.

In the consolidated income statement, the income from associate would be 40% of the associate's post tax profits. If the step purchase of 30% had occurred mid-year, then the associate's profits would be time apportioned to reflect the period that the investor has been able to exercise significant influence.

In the consolidated statement of financial position, the investment in associate would be made up of the cost of the investment at the date that significant influence was achieved (i.e. the fair value of the original 10% acquired plus the cost of the additional 30% acquired) plus 40% of the associate's post acquisition change in net assets, i.e. profits or losses.

The original holding of 10% is remeasured to fair value in order to reflect the price that would have been paid if it had been acquired at the same time as the 30%. This is consistent with the treatment of other step acquisitions as we will see in the next section.

3 Non-control to control

This scenario is accounted for as if the previously held interest has been disposed of at its current fair value and the controlling shareholding is then subsequently acquired. Therefore, it is necessary to:

(1) Remeasure the previously held interest to fair value.

(2) Recognise any resulting gain or loss within the income statement (and so retained earnings).

The date on which control is achieved is considered to be the acquisition date. From this date, the investment is classified as a subsidiary and acquisition accounting is used. This means:

- consolidate income, expenses, assets and liabilities in full on a line by line basis;
- recognise goodwill;
- recognise non-controlling interests.

For the purposes of calculating goodwill, the cost of the investment is made up of:

Fair value of previously held interest	X
Fair value of consideration to acquire additional interest	X
	—
Fair value of P's controlling shareholding at acquisition date, i.e. cost of investment	X
	—

Example 1

Ayre holds a 10% investment in Byrne at $24,000 in accordance with IAS 39. On 1 June 20X7, it acquires a further 50% of Byrne's equity shares at a cost of $160,000.

On this date the fair values are as follows:

- Byrne's net assets – $200,000
- The non-controlling interest – $100,000
- The 10% investment – $26,000

Required:

Calculate the goodwill arising in Byrne.

Note: The non-controlling interest is to be valued using the fair value method.

Example 1 answer

(W1) **Group Structure**

Ayre

| 60% (10% + 50%)

Byrne

Due to the step acquisition, remeasure the original investment to fair value and take the gain or loss to income statement i.e. increase the carrying value from $24,000 cost to $26,000 fair value.

Dr Investment	2,000
Cr Profit on remeasurement	2,000

(W2) **Net assets**

	At date of acquisition 1 June 20X7
Net assets	200,000

(W3) **Goodwill**

	$
Fair value of P's holding (cost of investment)	
Fair value of previously held interest	26,000
Fair value of consideration for additional interest	160,000
	186,000
NCI holding at fair value	100,000
Fair value of sub's net assets at acquisition	(200,000)
Goodwill at acquisition	86,000

Test your understanding 1 - Major and Tom

The statements of financial position of two companies, Major and Tom as at 31 December 20X6 are as follows:

	Major	Tom
	$000	$000
Investment	160	
Other assets	350	250
	510	250
Equity share capital	200	100
Reserves	250	122
Liabilities	60	28
	510	250

Major acquired 40% of Tom on 31 December 20X1 for $90,000. At this time the reserves of Tom stood at $76,000. A further 20% of shares in Tom was acquired by Major three years later for $70,000. On this date, the fair value of the existing holding in Tom was $105,000. Tom's reserves were $100,000 on the second acquisition date.

Required:

Prepare the consolidated statement of financial position for the Major group as at 31 December 20X6, assuming that it is group policy to value the NCI using the proportion of net assets method.

Test your understanding 2 - Heat and Wave

The statements of financial position of two companies, Heat and Wave as at 30 June 20X5 are as follows:

	Heat	Wave
	$000	$000
Investment	142	–
Other assets	358	225
	500	225
Equity share capital	250	150
Reserves	200	55
Liabilities	50	20
	500	225

Heat acquired 35% of Wave on 1 July 20X3 for $62,000 when the reserves of Wave stood at $30,000. A further 40% of shares was acquired by Heat one year later for $80,000 when Wave's reserves were $45,000. On 1 July 20X4 the fair value of the existing holding in Wave was $70,000 and the fair value of the NCI share in Wave was $50,000.

It is group policy to measure NCI at fair value at the date of acquisition.

Required:

Prepare the consolidated statement of financial position for the Heat group as at 30 June 20X5.

Non-control to control: W5 alternative calculation

IFRS 3 views a step acquisition in which control is achieved as being a disposal of a previously held equity interest which is then replaced with the acquisition of a subsidiary.

The group is disposing of their previously held interest in the associate for "proceeds" equal to the fair value of the previous equity interest at the date of the step acquisition.

Therefore, strictly speaking, the consolidated income statement (CIS) should reflect the share of associate's profits under equity accounting for the appropriate period and then any gain/loss on disposal of the associate.

However, when calculating the retained profits in W5 for the consolidated statement of financial position (CSFP), the working can be approached in two ways:

(i) Reflect the gain on remeasurement that is recorded in the parent's books and then include the subsidiary from the date control is achieved;

(ii) Alternatively, the previous investment as an associate could be included for the period since acquisition together with any gain/loss on its disposal. This will result in the same profit or loss overall as (i).

The simplest method, and that which will be used in most test your understandings, is (i) above.

The alternative can be reviewed in TYU 3 Henderson below.

Test your understanding 3 - Henderson

Below are the income statements for the year ended 31 March 20X7 and statements of financial position as at 31 March 20X7 of Henderson and Springdale:

Statements of comprehensive income for the year ended 31 March 20X7

	Henderson	**Springdale**
	$000	$000
Revenue	23,700	15,900
Cost of sales	(7,510)	(6,800)
Gross profit	16,190	9,100
Operating expenses	(3,520)	(2,240)
Profit from operations	12,670	6,860
Finance cost	(1,000)	(540)
Profit before tax	11,670	6,320
Tax	(3,500)	(1,880)
Profit for the year	8,170	4,440
Other comprehensive income	–	–
Total comprehensive income	8,170	4,440

Statements of financial position as at 31 March 20X7

	Henderson		Springdale	
	$000	$000	$000	$000
Assets				
Non-current assets				
Property, plant and equipment		89,710		89,560
Investments		70,000		–
		159,710		89,560
Current assets				
Inventory	1,860		1,115	
Receivables	2,920		1,960	
Cash	4,390		1,870	
		9,170		4,945
		168,880		94,505
Equity and liabilities				
Issued share capital ($1 shares)		50,000		40,000
Retained earnings		89,430		36,930
		139,430		76,930
Non-current liabilities		25,000		14,000
Current liabilities				
Trade payables	1,240		1,675	
Taxation	3,210		1,900	
		4,450		3,575
		168,880		94,505

(1) Henderson acquired 40% of the equity share capital of Springdale on 1 April 20X2 at a cost of $27 million. At this date the balance on Springdale's retained earnings was $22.45 million. A fair value exercise was carried out but at this time it was determined that the carrying value of Springdale's net assets was a reasonable approximation of their fair value.

(2) Henderson acquired a further 35% shareholding in Springdale on 1 July 20X6 at a cost of $35 million. At this date, it was determined that the fair value of the original 40% holding in Springdale was $30 million.

(3) At 1 July 20X6 non-current assets held by Springdale were determined to have a fair value of $2 million in excess of their carrying value. These assets had a remaining life of 10 years at this date. Depreciation is charged to operating expenses.

(4) After 1 July 20X6, Henderson sold goods to Springdale for $2.4 million at a mark-up of 20% on cost. Springdale still held one fifth of these goods at the year-end. At the year-end Henderson's books showed a receivable of $800,000 in respect of the transaction. This disagreed to the corresponding balance in Springdale's books due to cash in transit at the year-end of $50,000.

(5) Henderson's policy is to value non-controlling interests at acquisition at their fair value. The fair value of the non-controlling interests at 1 July 20X6 was measured at $20 million.

(6) As at 31 March 20X7 goodwill was reviewed from impairment and it was determined that an impairment loss of $1 million should be recorded. The impairment loss should be charged to operating expenses.

Required:

Prepare the consolidated statement of comprehensive income for the year ended 31 March 20X7 and the consolidated statement of financial position as at 31 March 20X7 for the Henderson group.

NB. This is a tutorial exercise only. You would not be expected to deal with a scenario of this size in an exam question - although you may be asked to deal with certain aspects of the above.

4 Control to control

Where the parent already owns a controlling shareholding and subsequently purchases additional shares, they are simply purchasing the shares from the NCI shareholders. This means that the transaction is between the owners of the group, with the parent's share increasing and the NCI's share decreasing.

For example if the parent holds 80% of the shares in a subsidiary and buys 5% more the relationship remains one of a parent and subsidiary. As such, the subsidiary will be consolidated in the group accounts in the normal way but the NCI has decreased from 20% to 15%.

Where there is such a transaction:

- There is no change to the carrying value of goodwill
- The income, expenses, assets and liabilities continue to be consolidated line by line
- If the step acquisition happens mid-year, it will be necessary to time apportion profits when determining the NCI share of profits
- No gain or loss arises as this is a transaction within equity i.e. a transaction between owners
- A difference may arise that will be taken to other components of equity which can be determined using the following proforma.

	$
Transfer from NCI to reduce NCI	X
Cash paid	(X)
Difference to other components of equity	X/(X)

The transfer from NCI will represent the proportionate reduction in the NCI's equity figure (as calculated in W4) at the date of the step acquisition, which reflects the amount that the parent is effectively purchasing from the NCI.

Example 2

Earl has owned 60% of Grey for many years. At acquisition, the NCI's holding in Grey had a fair value of $100,000 and Grey's net assets had a fair value of $200,000.

On 1 July 20X8, Earl purchased a further 10% of Grey's shares for $30,000. At this time, the net assets of Grey had a carrying value of $225,000.

Required:

Calculate the adjustment required within equity as a result of this transaction.

Example 2 answer

At the date of the step acquisition, the NCI equity interest in Grey was:

	$
NCI holding at acquisition at fair value	100,000
NCI% x post acquisition reserves (40% x (225,000 – 200,000))	10,000
	110,000

As a result of the step acquisition, the NCI holding is reduced by 10% of 40% i.e. a quarter. Therefore, the difference to equity can be calculated as:

	$
Decrease in NCI (10/40 x 110,000)	27,500
Cash paid	(30,000)
Difference to other components of equity	(2,500)

To explain why the difference to equity is a decrease, it is possible to think of the above as Earl buying net assets valued at $27,500 for $30,000 and thus suffering a "loss" on the transaction. However, this is not strictly a loss as it arises on a transaction between owners.

The amount of $27,500 would be deducted from the carrying value of the NCI (i.e. in W4).

An alternative way to achieve the answer would be to consider:

	$
Cr Cash	30,000
Dr NCI (10/40 x 110,000)	27,500
Dr Other components of equity – balance	2,500

Test your understanding 4 - Gordon and Mandy

Gordon has owned 80% of Mandy for many years.

Gordon is considering acquiring more shares in Mandy.

At acquisition the fair value of the NCI in Mandy was $100,000. The net assets of Mandy at acquisition were $300,000 and are currently $400,000.

Gordon's options are to either:

(a) Buy 10% of Mandy's shares for $50,000; or

(b) Buy 15% of Mandy's shares for $95,000.

Required:

Calculate the difference arising that will be taken to other components of equity for each situation, together with the NCI's share of equity that will be reported after the purchase of shares.

5 Disposal scenarios

During the year, the parent may sell some or all of its shares in the subsidiary.

Possible situations are:

(1) the disposal of all the shares held in the subsidiary;

(2) the disposal of part of the shareholding, leaving a residual holding after the sale which is regarded as a trade investment;

(3) the disposal of part of the shareholding, leaving a residual holding after the sale which is regarded as an associate; or

(4) the disposal of part of the shareholding, leaving a controlling interest after the sale.

In situations (1), (2) and (3) the parent loses the ability to be able to control the investment i.e. there is no longer a subsidiary.

However, in situation (4) a subsidiary still exists as the parent company is still able to control the entity.

Consequently, these two situations – control is lost and control is maintained – are dealt with differently within the group financial statements. This will be discussed further in sections 8 and 12 below.

However, regardless of the above, the disposal of shares must also be recorded within the parent's individual financial statements.

6 Gain on disposal in parent's financial statements

In all of the above scenarios, the gain on disposal in the parent's accounts is calculated as follows:

	$
Sale proceeds	X
Carrying amount (usually cost) of shares sold	(X)
	X
Tax – amount or rate given in question	(X)
Net gain to parent	X

The tax arising as a result of the disposal is always calculated based on the gain in the parent's books. This is because the parent company and subsidiary company are distinct separate legal entities – the group does not legally exist. Tax can only be calculated in relation to a legal entity.

However, the link to the group accounts is that the tax arising on the gain forms part of the parent's tax charge and so forms part of the group's tax charge. The group's tax charge is simply arrived at by adding together the parent and subsidiary's tax charge, like all other expenses.

7 Disposals in group financial statements

In the group accounts, accounting for the sale of shares in a subsidiary will depend on whether the transaction causes control to be lost or whether after the sale, control is maintained.

The basic principles to be applied can be summarised as follows:

	Control lost	Control retained
Consolidated statement of comprehensive income (CSCI) gain or loss	Gain or loss to the group is calculated and included in the group CSCI for the year.	No gain or loss is recorded.
CSCI consolidation	Subsidiary's income and expenses will be consolidated up to the date of disposal i.e. they will be time apportioned in the case of a mid year disposal.	Subsidiary's income and expenses will be consolidated for the year.
Consolidated statement of financial position (CSFP) consolidation	Subsidiary's assets and liabilities are no longer added across.	Subsidiary's assets and liabilities are still added across at year end.
Goodwill	Goodwill is eliminated.	Goodwill remains the same.
NCI	NCI is eliminated.	NCI is increased to reflect the higher percentage of the subsidiary not owned by the parent entity.

8 Accounting for a disposal where control is lost

Where control **is lost** (i.e. the subsidiary is completely disposed of or becomes an associate or investment), the group:

- Recognises
  - the consideration received
  - any investment retained in the former subsidiary at fair value on the date of disposal

- Derecognises
  - the assets and liabilities of the subsidiary at the date of disposal
  - unimpaired goodwill in the subsidiary at the date of disposal
  - the non-controlling interest at the date of disposal (including any components of other comprehensive income attributable to them)
- Any difference between these amounts is recognised as an exceptional gain or loss on disposal in the group statement of comprehensive income.

The following is a proforma that can be used to calculate the exceptional gain or loss on disposal:

Proceeds		X
Fair value of retained interest		X
		X
Less: carrying value of subsidiary disposed of:		
Net assets of subsidiary at disposal date	X	
Unimpaired goodwill at disposal date	X	
Less: NCI at disposal date	(X)	
		(X)
Gain/loss to the group		X

The gain to the group is presented on the consolidated statement of comprehensive income after operating profit.

9 Group accounts – entire disposal

Example 3

Rock has held a 70% investment in Dog for two years. Rock is disposing of this investment in full. Goodwill has been calculated using the fair value method for measuring NCI. No goodwill has been impaired.

Tax is charged at 30%.

	$
Cost of investment	2,000
Dog – Fair value of net assets at acquisition	1,900
Dog – Fair value of the non-controlling interest at acquisition	800
Sale proceeds	3,000
Dog – Net assets at disposal	2,400

Required:

Calculate the profit/loss on disposal for:

(a) Rock's individual accounts
(b) the consolidated accounts

Example 3 answer

(a) **Gain to Rock**

	$
Sale proceeds	3,000
Cost of shares sold	(2,000)
Gain on disposal	1,000
Tax at 30%	(300)
Post-tax gain on disposal	700

All shares are sold so deduct 100% of the cost of the shares.

(b) **Consolidated accounts**

	$	$
Sale proceeds		3,000
Less: carrying value of subsidiary at disposal date		
Net assets at disposal	2,400	
Unimpaired goodwill (W1)	900	
Less: NCI at disposal (W2)	(950)	
		(2,350)
		650
Tax on gain as per Rock (part a)		(300)
Post-tax gain to group		350

(W1) **Goodwill**

	$
Fair value of P's holding (cost of investment)	2,000
NCI holding at fair value	800
Fair value of sub's net assets at acquisition	(1,900)
Goodwill at acquisition/ disposal	900

(W2) **NCI at disposal date**

	$
NCI holding at acquisition (W1)	800
NCI% x post acquisition reserves (30% x (2,400 – 1,900))	150
	950

Test your understanding 5 - Snooker

Snooker purchased 80% of the shares in Billiards for $100,000 when the net assets of Billiards had a fair value of $62,500. It is group policy to measure NCI at fair value at acquisition and the fair value of the NCI's holding at this date was $22,500. Goodwill has not suffered any impairment to date.

Snooker has just disposed of its entire shareholding in Billiards for $300,000 when the net assets were stated at $110,000. Tax is payable by Snooker at 30% on any gain on disposal of shares.

Required:

(a) Calculate the gain or loss arising to the parent company on the disposal of shares in Billiards.

(b) Calculate the gain or loss arising to the group on the disposal of the controlling interest in Billiards.

Test your understanding 6 - Padstow

Padstow purchased 80% of the shares in St Merryn four years ago for $100,000. On 30 June 20X6 it sold all of these shares for $250,000. The net assets of St Merryn at acquisition were $69,000 and at disposal were $88,000. Fifty per cent of the goodwill arising on acquisition has been written off.

Tax is charged at 30%. The Padstow Group values the non-controlling interest using the proportion of net assets method.

Required:

What profits/losses on disposal are reported in:

(a) Padstow's individual income statement

(b) the consolidated income statement.

10 Group accounts – disposal of subsidiary to become an associate

This situation is where the disposal results in the subsidiary becoming an associate, e.g. 90% holding is reduced to a 40% holding.

It is accounted for as if the group have disposed of the whole subsidiary and reacquired the remaining interest at the date of disposal. The remaining interest is therefore measured at fair value at the date of disposal and recorded by:

Dr Investment
Cr Gain on disposal

The fair value of the investment then becomes the "cost" of the investment for the purposes of subsequent equity accounting of the associate.

Consolidated statement of comprehensive income

- Pro rate the subsidiary's results for the year and :
  - consolidate the results line by line up to the date of disposal
  - equity account for the results after the date of disposal by including a single line representing the share of associate's profits
- Include the exceptional group gain or loss on disposal.

Consolidated statement of financial position

- Equity account for the associate at the year end, by including a single line representing the fair value of the investment retained plus the share of post acquisition profits.

Example 4

Thomas disposed of a 25% holding in Percy on 30 June 20X6 for $125,000. A 70% holding in Percy had been acquired five years prior to this when the net assets of Percy had a fair value of $150,000. Goodwill on the acquisition has been fully impaired.

Details of Percy are as follows:

	$
Net assets at 31 December 20X5	290,000
Profit for year ended 31 December 20X6 (assumed to accrue evenly)	100,000
Fair value of a 45% holding at 30 June 20X6	245,000

Ignore tax.

Required:

Assuming that the proportion of net assets method is used to value the NCI, what gain on disposal is reported in the Thomas Group accounts in the year ended 31 December 20X6?

Example 4 answer

Proportion of net assets method

(W1) **Group Structure**

Thomas	70%	Thomas
70%	(25%)	45%
	45%	
Percy		Percy
Subsidiary		Associate
x 6/12		x 6/12

(W2) **Net assets**

	Acquisition	**Disposal 30 June X6**
	$	$
Net assets at acquisition	150,000	
Net assets at 31 Dec 20X5		290,000
Profit to 30 June 20X6 (100,000 X 6/12)		50,000
	150,000	340,000

190,000
Post acquisition profits

(W3) **Gain on disposal**

		$
Proceeds		125,000
Fair value of retained interest		245,000
		370,000
Less carrying value of subsidiary disposed of:		
Net assets of subsidiary at disposal date (W2)	340,000	
Unimpaired goodwill at disposal date	0	
Less: NCI at disposal (W4)	(102,000)	
		(238,000)
Gain		132,000

(W4) **NCI**

	$
NCI holding at acquisition at proportion of net assets (30% x 150,000)	45,000
NCI% x post acquisition reserves (30% x 190,000 (W2))	57,000
NCI at disposal date	102,000

Test your understanding 7 - Hague

Hague has held a 60% investment in Maude for several years, using the fair value method to value the non-controlling interest. Half of the goodwill has been impaired. The group's year end is 31 December 20X5. A disposal of this investment has been made on 31 October 20X5. Details are:

	$
Cost of investment	6,000
Maude – Fair value of net assets at acquisition	2,000
Maude – Fair value of a 40% investment at acquisition date	1,000
Maude – Net assets at disposal	3,000
Maude – Fair value of a 30% investment at disposal	5,000
Maude – Profit for the year ended 31 December 20X5	2,200

Required:

(a) Assuming a full disposal of the holding and proceeds of $10,000, calculate the profit/loss arising:

(i) in Hague's individual accounts

(ii) in the consolidated accounts.

Tax is 25%.

(b) Assuming a disposal of half the holding and proceeds of $5,000:

(i) calculate the profit/loss arising in the consolidated accounts

(ii) explain how the residual holding will be accounted for and calculate the figures for inclusion in Hague's consolidated income statement for the year ended 31 December 20X5 and consolidated statement of financial position at 31 December 20X5.

Test your understanding 8 - Kathmandu

The statements of comprehensive income and statements of changes in equity for the year ended 31 December 20X9 are as follows:

Income statement

	Kathmandu	Nepal
	$	$
Revenue	553,000	450,000
Operating costs	(450,000)	(400,000)
Operating profits	103,000	50,000
Dividends receivable	8,000	–
Profit before tax	111,000	50,000
Tax	(40,000)	(14,000)
Profit after tax	71,000	36,000
Other comprehensive income	–	–
Total comprehensive income	71,000	36,000

Statement of changes in equity

	Kathmandu	Nepal
Equity b/f	200,000	130,000
Profit after tax	71,000	36,000
Dividend paid	(25,000)	(10,000)
Equity c/f	246,000	156,000

Additional information

- On 1 January 20X5 Kathmandu acquired 70% of the shares of Nepal for $100,000 when the fair value of Nepal's net assets was $90,000. At that date, the fair value of the non-controlling interest holding in Nepal was $35,000. It is group policy to measure the NCI at fair value at the date of acquisition.
- Nepal paid its 20X9 dividend in cash on 31 March 20X9.
- Goodwill has not been impaired.

Required:

(a) (i) Prepare the consolidated statement of comprehensive income for the year ended 31 December 20X9 for the Kathmandu group on the basis that Kathmandu sold its holding in Nepal on 1 July 20X9 for $200,000. This disposal is not yet recognised in any way in Kathmandu group's income statement.

(ii) Prepare the group statement of changes in equity for the year ended 31 December 20X9.

Ignore tax on the disposal.

(b) (i) Prepare the consolidated statement of comprehensive income for the year ended 31 December 20X9 for the Kathmandu group on the basis that Kathmandu sold half of its holding in Nepal on 1 July 20X9 for $100,000 This disposal is not yet recognised in any way in Kathmandu group's income statement. The residual holding of 35% has a fair value of $100,000 and leaves the Kathmandu group with significant influence.

(ii) Prepare the group statement of changes in equity for the year ended 31 December 20X9.

Ignore tax on the disposal.

11 Group accounts – disposal of a subsidiary to become a trade investment

This situation is where the subsidiary becomes a trade investment, e.g. 90% holding is reduced to a 10% holding.

It is again accounted for as if the group have disposed of the whole subsidiary and reacquired the remaining interest at the date of disposal. The remaining interest is therefore measured at fair value of the date of disposal and recorded by:

Dr Investment
Cr Gain on disposal

Consolidated statement of comprehensive income

- Pro rate the subsidiary's results up to the date of disposal and then:
  - consolidate the results up to the date of disposal;
  - only include dividend income after the date of disposal.
- Include the group gain on part disposal.

Consolidated statement of financial position

- Recognise the holding retained as an investment. This will initially be at 'cost' i.e. the fair value at the date of disposal, but may subsequently be remeasured to fair value at the reporting date under the rules of IAS 39: Financial Instruments (see chapter 13)

12 Accounting for a disposal where control is retained

From the perspective of the group accounts, where there is a sale of shares but the parent still retains control, there is simply a transaction between owners, with the parent's share decreasing and the NCI's share increasing.

For example if the parent holds 80% of the shares in a subsidiary and sells 5%, the relationship remains one of a parent and subsidiary and as such will remain consolidated in the group accounts in the normal way, but the NCI has risen from 20% to 25%.

Where there is such an increase in the non-controlling interest:

- No gain or loss on disposal is calculated
- No adjustment is made to the carrying value of goodwill
- The difference between the proceeds received and change in the non-controlling interest is accounted for in other components of equity as follows:

	$
Cash proceeds received	X
Transfer to NCI to increase NCI	(X)
Difference to other components of equity	X/(X)

The transfer to NCI will represent the share of the net assets and goodwill (fair value method only) of the subsidiary at the date of disposal which the parent has effectively sold to the NCI.

Consolidated statement of comprehensive income

- Consolidate the subsidiary's results for the whole year.
- Calculate the non-controlling interest relating to the periods before and after the disposal separately and then add together.

  For example, if the shares are sold on 1 November and year end is 31 December:

  (10 / 12 × profit × 20%) + (2 / 12 × profit × 25%)

Consolidated statement of financial position

- Consolidate as normal, with the non-controlling interest valued by reference to the year-end holding
- Take the difference between proceeds and the transfer to the NCI to other components of equity as previously discussed.

Example 5

Until 30 September 20X7, Juno held 90% of Hera. On that date it sold 15% for $100,000. At the date of disposal, the net assets of Hera were $650,000 and the goodwill was $150,000. It is group policy to measure the NCI at fair value at the date of acquisition.

Required:

How should the disposal transaction be accounted for in the Juno Group accounts?

Example 5 answer

	$
Dr Cash	100,000
Cr Non-controlling interest (15% x (650,000 + 150,000))	120,000
Dr Other components of equity (ß)	20,000

Alternatively:

	$
Cash proceeds received	100,000
Transfer to NCI (15% x (650,000 + 150,000))	(120,000)
Difference to other components of equity	(20,000)

To explain why the difference to equity is a decrease, it is possible to think of the above as Juno selling net assets valued at $120,000 for only $100,000 and thus they have suffered a "loss" on the transaction.

Test your understanding 9 - David and Goliath

David has owned 90% of Goliath for many years.

David is considering selling part of its holding, whilst retaining control of Goliath.

Goliath's net assets had a fair value of $200,000 at acquisition and the fair value of the NCI holding at acquisition was $35,000.

The net assets of Goliath are currently $350,000 and the goodwill is $175,000.

David's options are to either:

(a) Sell 5% of the Goliath shares for $60,000; or

(b) Sell 25% of the Goliath shares for $100,000.

Required:

Calculate the different arising that will be taken to other components of equity for each situation, together with the NCI's share of equity that will be reported after the sale of shares.

Test your understanding 10 - Pepsi

Statements of financial position for three entities at the reporting date are as follows:

	Pepsi	**Sprite**	**Tango**
	$000	$000	$000
Assets	1,000	800	500
Investment in Sprite	326	–	–
Investment in Tango	165	–	–
	1,491	800	500
Equity			
Equity shares $1	500	200	100
Retained earnings	391	100	200
	891	300	300
Liabilities	600	500	200
	1,491	800	500

Pepsi acquired 80% of Sprite when Sprite's retained earnings were $25,000, paying cash consideration of $300,000. It is group policy to measure NCI at fair value at the date of acquisition and the fair value of the NCI holding in Sprite at this date was $65,000.

At the reporting date, Pepsi purchased an additional 8% of Sprite's equity shares for cash consideration of $26,000. This amount has been debited to Pepsi's Investment in Sprite.

Pepsi acquired 75% of Tango when Tango's retained earnings were $60,000, paying cash consideration of $200,000. The fair value of the NCI holding in Tango at the date of acquisition was $50,000.

At the reporting date, Pepsi sold 10% of the equity shares of Tango for $35,000. The cash proceeds have been credited to Pepsi's Investment in Tango.

Required:

Prepare the consolidated statement of financial position of the Pepsi group.

Test your understanding 11 - Cagney and Lacey

The draft accounts of two companies at 31 March 20X1 were as follows.

Statements of financial position

	Cagney Group	Lacey
	$	$
Investment in Lacey at cost	3,440	–
Other assets	41,950	9,500
	45,390	9,500
Equity capital ($1 shares)	20,000	3,000
Retained earnings	11,000	3,500
Other liabilities	5,500	3,000
Sales proceeds of disposal (suspense account)	8,890	–
	45,390	9,500

Statements of comprehensive income

	Cagney Group	Lacey
	$	$
Revenue	31,590	11,870
Cost of sales	(15,290)	(5,820)
Gross profit	16,300	6,050
Distribution costs	(3,000)	(2,000)
Administrative expenses	(350)	(250)
Profit before tax	12,950	3,800
Tax	(5,400)	(2,150)
Profit after tax for the year	7,550	1,650
Other comprehensive income	–	–
Total comprehensive income	7,550	1,650

The equity of each company on 1 April 20X0 was as follows:

	Cagney	Lacey
	$	$
Equity brought forward	23,450	4,850

Cagney had acquired 90% of Lacey when the reserves of Lacey were $700. Goodwill was unimpaired. The Cagney group includes other fully owned subsidiaries.

On 31 December 20X0, Cagney sold 15% of the shares in Lacey .

It is group policy to measure the NCI at the proportion of the fair value of the net assets at acquisition.

Required:

Prepare the Cagney Group statement of financial position at 31 March 20X1 and statement of comprehensive income for the year ended 31 March 20X1. Also prepare the statement of changes in equity for the current year.

Test your understanding 12 - Howard

Howard, Sylvia and Sabrina are three entities preparing their financial statements under IFRSs. Their statements of financial position as at 30 September 20X5 are given below:

	Howard	Sylvia	Sabrina
	$000	$000	$000
Non-current assets			
Property, plant and equipment	160,000	60,000	64,000
Investments	80,000	–	–
	240,000	60,000	64,000
Current assets	65,000	50,000	36,000
	305,000	110,000	100,000
Equity and liabilities			
Equity shares ($1 shares)	50,000	20,000	15,000
Retained earnings	185,000	43,000	42,000
	235,000	63,000	57,000
Non-current liabilities	25,000	18,000	20,000
Current liabilities	45,000	29,000	23,000
	305,000	110,000	100,000

Note 1 – Investment by Howard in Sylvia

On 1 October 20X3, Howard acquired 70% of the equity share capital of Sylvia for $45 million in cash, when the balance on Sylvia's retained earnings was $28 million. It was determined that at this date, land with carrying value of $40 million had a fair value of $45 million.

On 30 September 20X5, Howard acquired a further 10% of the equity shares of Sylvia paying $10 million in cash.

Note 2 – Investment by Howard in Sabrina

On 1 January 20X2, Howard acquired 60% of the equity shares of Sabrina for $21 million in cash, when the balance on Sabrina's retained earnings was $15 million. It was determined that the book value of Sabrina's net assets on 1 January 20X2 were equal to their fair values.

On 30 September 20X5, Howard disposed of one quarter of its shareholding in Sabrina for $15 million cash. Howard's remaining 45% holding enabled Howard to exercise significant influence over the operating and financial policies of Sabrina. The fair value of the remaining 45% holding was £35 million at 30 September 20X5.

Howard have recorded the proceeds of $15 million by debiting cash and crediting investments, but no other entries have been made.

Note 3 – Intra-group trading

During the year ended 30 September 20X5, Howard sold goods to Sylvia for $8 million. These goods were sold at a profit margin of 25%. Half of these goods remain in Sylvia's inventory at the reporting date.

Note 4 – Valuation of NCI

Howard's policy is to value NCI at acquisition at fair value. The fair value of the non-controlling interests in Sylvia and Sabrina at the relevant dates of acquisition were:

- Sylvia: $17.4 million
- Sabrina: $13 million.

No impairment losses have arisen on goodwill.

Required:

Prepare the consolidated statement of financial position of the Howard group as at 30 September 20X5.

13 Business reorganisations

Reasons for reorganisation

There are a number of reasons why a group may wish to reorganise. These include the following.

- A group may wish to list on a public stock exchange. This is usually facilitated by creating a new holding company and keeping the business of the group in subsidiary entities.
- Reorganisation is forced by a group of stakeholders e.g. by lender where debt covenants are breached.
- The ownership of subsidiaries may be transferred from one group company to another. This is often the case if the group wishes to sell a subsidiary, but retain its trade.

- Part of a business is hived off into a separate group (a 'demerger' arrangement).
- An unlisted entity may arrange to be purchased by a listed entity with the aim of achieving a stock exchange listing itself. This is called a reverse acquisition.

Types of group reorganisations

There are a number of ways of effecting a group reorganisation. The type of reorganisation will depend on what the group is trying to achieve.

New holding company

A group might set up a new holding entity for an existing group in order to improve co-ordination within the group or as a vehicle for flotation.

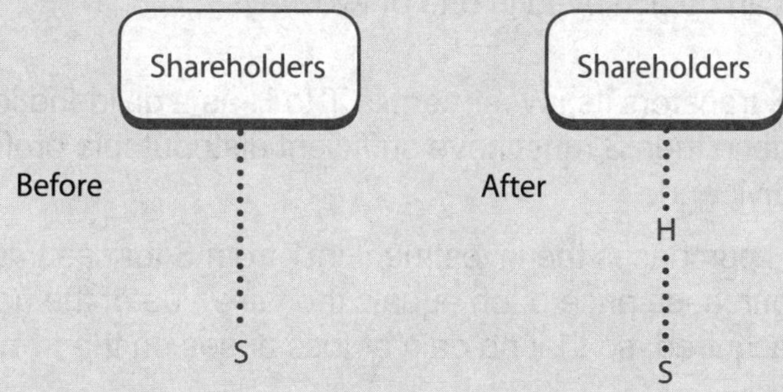

- H becomes the new holding entity of S.
- Usually, H issues shares to the shareholders of S in exchange for shares of S, but occasionally the shareholders of S may subscribe for shares in H and H may pay cash for S.

IFRS 3 excludes from its scope any business combination involving entities or businesses under 'common control', which is where the same parties control all of the combining entities/businesses both before and after the business combination.

As there is no mandatory guidance in accounting for these items, the acquisition method should certainly be used in examination questions.

Change of ownership of an entity within a group

This occurs when the internal structure of the group changes, for example, a parent may transfer the ownership of a subsidiary to another of its subsidiaries.

The key thing to remember is that the reorganisation of the entities within the group should not affect the group accounts, as shareholdings are transferred from one company to another and no assets will leave the group.

The individual accounts of the group companies will need to be adjusted for the effect of the transfer.

The following are types of reorganisation:

(a) **Subsidiary moved up**

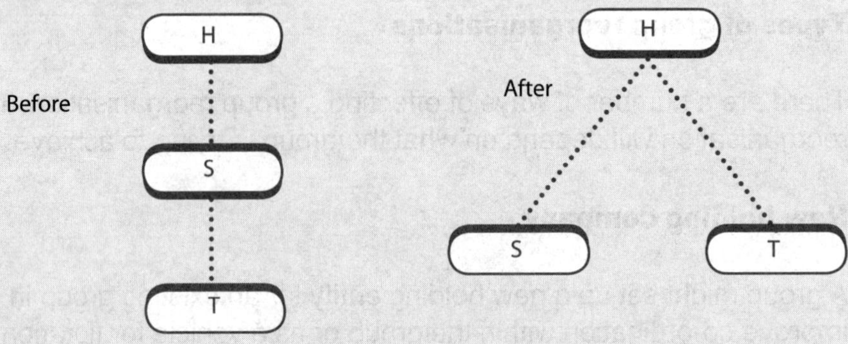

This can be achieved in one of two ways.

(i) S transfers its investment in T to H as a dividend in specie. If this is done then S must have sufficient distributable profits to pay the dividend.

(ii) H purchases the investment in T from S for cash. In practice the purchase price often equals the fair value of the net assets acquired, so that no gain or loss arises on the transaction.

Usually, it will be the carrying value of T that is used as the basis for the transfer of the investment, but there are no legal rules confirming this.

A share-for-share exchange cannot be used as in many jurisdictions it is illegal for a subsidiary to hold shares in the parent company.

(b) **Subsidiary moved down**

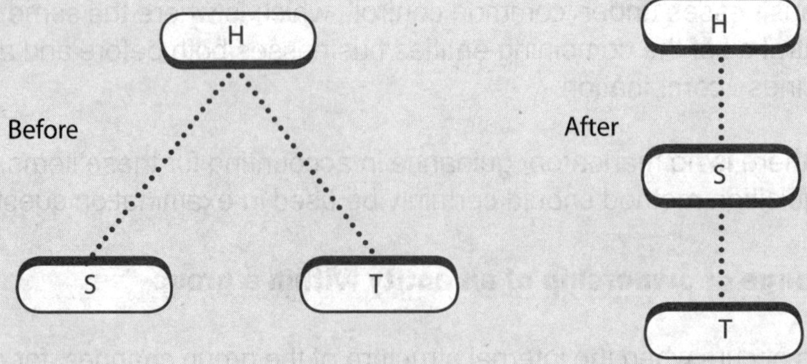

This reorganisation may be carried out where there are tax advantages in establishing a 'sub-group', or where two or more subsidiaries are linked geographically.

This can be carried out either by:

(i) a share-for-share exchange (S issues shares to H in return for the shares in T)

(ii) a cash transaction (S pays cash to H).

(c) **Subsidiary moved along**

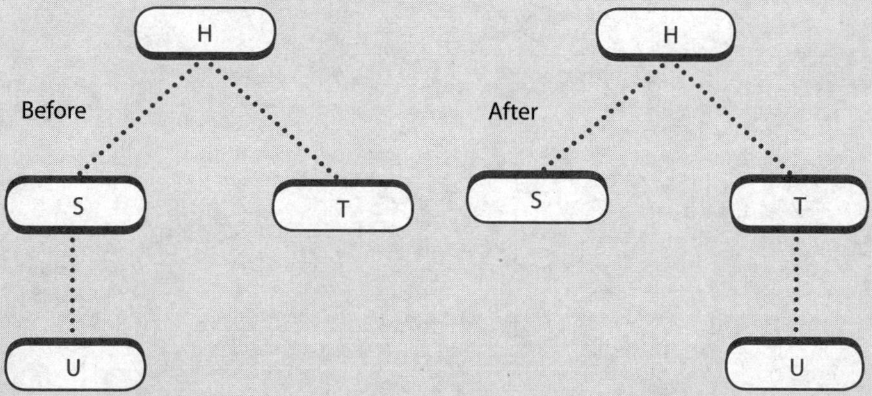

This is carried out by T paying cash (or other assets) to S. The consideration would not normally be in the form of shares because a typical reason for such a reconstruction would be to allow S to be managed as a separate part of the group or even disposed of completely. This could not be achieved effectively were S to have a shareholding in T.

If the purpose of the reorganisation is to allow S to leave the group, the purchase price paid by T should not be less than the fair value of the investment in U, otherwise S may be deemed to be receiving financial assistance for the purchase of its own shares, which is illegal in many jurisdictions.

Reverse acquisitions

Definition

A **reverse acquisition** occurs when an entity obtains ownership of the shares of another entity, which in turn issues sufficient shares so that the acquired entity has control of the combined entity.

Reverse acquisitions are a method of allowing unlisted companies to obtain a stock exchange quotation by taking over a smaller listed company.

For example, a private company arranges to be acquired by a listed company. This is affected by the public entity issuing shares to the private company so that the private company's shareholders end up controlling the listed entity. Legally, the public entity is the parent, but the substance of the transaction is that the private entity has acquired the listed entity.

14 Chapter summary

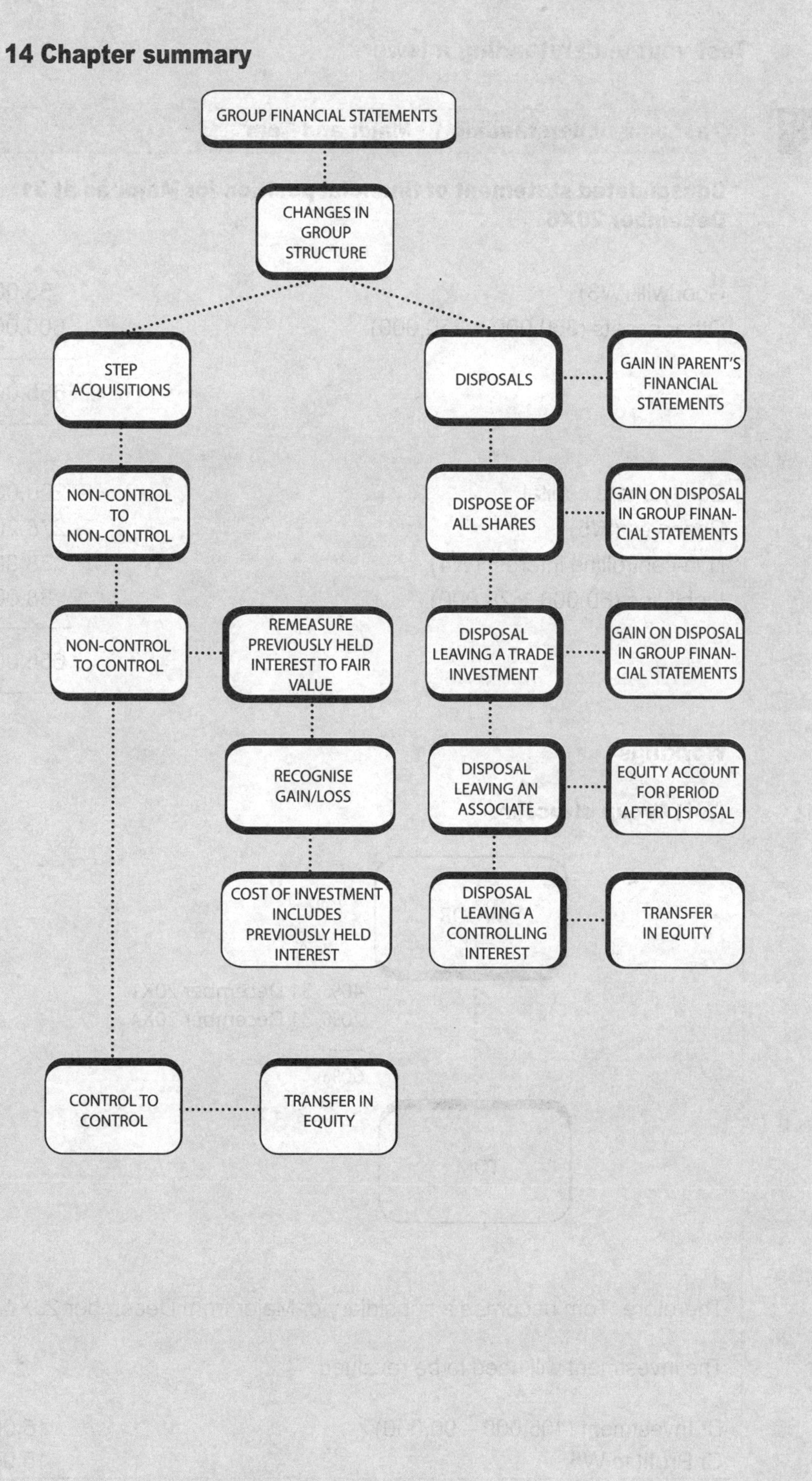

Test your understanding answers

Test your understanding 1 - Major and Tom

Consolidated statement of financial position for Major as at 31 December 20X6

	$
Goodwill (W3)	55,000
Other assets (350,000 + 250,000)	600,000
	655,000
Equity share capital	200,000
Reserves (W5)	278,200
Non-controlling interest (W4)	88,800
Liabilities (60,000 + 28,000)	88,000
	655,000

Workings

(W1) **Group structure**

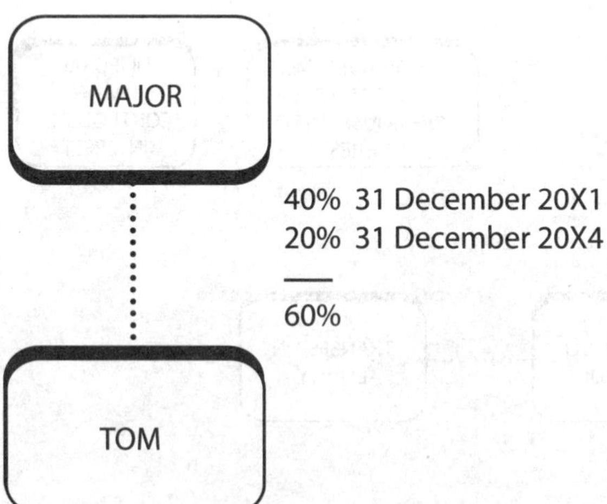

Therefore, Tom becomes a subsidiary of Major from December 20X4.

The investment will need to be revalued

Dr Investment (105,000 – 90,000)	15,000
Cr Profit to W5	15,000

(W2) **Net assets**

	At Acquisition 20X4	At Reporting date
	$	$
Share capital	100,000	100,000
Retained reserves	100,000	122,000
	200,000	222,000

(W3) **Goodwill**

	$
Fair value of P's holding (cost of investment)	
Fair value of previously held interest	105,000
Fair value of consideration for additional interest	70,000
	175,000
NCI holding at proportion of net assets (40% x 200,000 (W2))	80,000
Fair value of sub's net assets at acquisition (W2)	(200,000)
Goodwill at acquisition/ reporting date	55,000

(W4) **Non-controlling interest**

	$
NCI holding at acquisition (W3)	80,000
NCI% x post acquisition reserves (40% x 22,000 (W2))	8,800
	88,800

(W5) **Group Reserves**

	$
Major	250,000
Gain on revaluation of investment	15,000
Tom (60% x $22,000 (W2))	13,200
	278,200

Test your understanding 2 - Heat and Wave

Consolidated statement of financial position for Heat Group as at 30 June 20X5

	$
Goodwill (W3)	5,000
Other assets (358,000 + 225,000)	583,000
	588,000
Equity share capital	250,000
Reserves (W5)	215,500
Non-controlling interest (W4)	52,500
Liabilities (50,000 + 20,000)	70,000
	588,000

Workings

(W1) **Group structure**

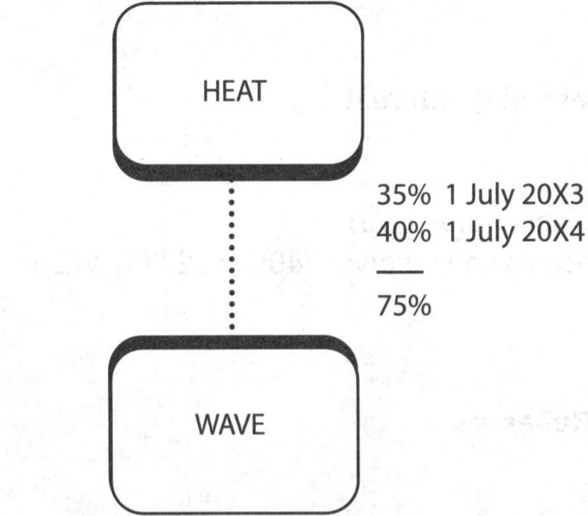

Therefore, Wave becomes a subsidiary of Heat from 1 July 20X4.

The investment will need to be revalued:

Dr Investment (70,000 – 62,000)	8,000
Cr Profit (to W5 as only SoFP being tested)	8,000

(W2) **Net assets**

	At Acquisition 20X4	At Reporting date
	$	$
Share capital	150,000	150,000
Retained earnings	45,000	55,000
	195,000	205,000

(W3) **Goodwill**

	$
Fair value of P's holding (cost of investment)	
Fair value of previously held interest	70,000
Fair value of consideration for additional interest	80,000
	150,000
NCI holding at fair value	50,000
Fair value of sub's net assets at acquisition (W2)	(195,000)
Goodwill at acquisition/ reporting date	5,000

(W4) **Non-controlling interest**

	$
NCI holding at acquisition (W3)	50,000
NCI% x post acquisition reserves (25% x 10,000 (W2))	2,500
	52,500

(W5) **Retained earnings**

	$
Heat	200,000
Gain on revaluation of investment	8,000
Wave (75% x $10,000 (W2))	7,500
	215,500

Test your understanding 3 - Henderson

Consolidated statement of comprehensive income for the year ended 31 March 20X7

	Henderson	Springdale 9/12	Adjustments	Consolidated
	$000	$000	$000	$000
Revenue	23,700	11,925	(2,400)	33,225
Cost of sales	(7,510)	(5,100)	2,400	(10,290)
– PUP	(80)			
Gross profit				22,935
Operating expenses	(3,520)	(1,680)		(6,350)
– Depreciation adjustment		(150)		
– Impairment loss		(1,000)		
Profit from operations				16,585
Finance cost	(1,000)	(405)		(1,405)
Income from associate (40% x 4,440 x 3/12)				444
Loss on disposal (W7)				(1,460)
Profit before tax				14,164
Tax	(3,500)	(1,410)		(4,910)
Profit for the period		2,180		9,254
Other comprehensive income	–	–		–
Total comprehensive income		2,180		9,254
Attributable to:				
Non-controlling interests		x 25%		545
Parent shareholders				8,709
				9,254

Consolidated statement of financial position as at 31 March 20X7

	$000	$000
Assets		
Non-current assets		
PPE (89,710 + 89,560 + 2,000 – 150 (W2))		181,120
Goodwill (W3)		8,400
Investments (70,000 + 3,000 – 65,000 (W3))		8,000
		197,520
Current assets		
Inventory (1,860 + 1,115 – 80 (W6))	2,895	
Receivables (2,920 + 1,960 – 800)	4,080	
Cash (4,390 + 1,870 + 50)	6,310	
		13,285
		210,805
Equity and liabilities		
Issued share capital ($1 shares)		50,000
Retained earnings (W5)		93,985
		143,985
Non-controlling interests (W4)		20,545
Non-current liabilities (25,000 + 14,000)		39,000
Current liabilities		
Trade payables (1,240 + 1,675 – 750)	2,165	
Taxation (3,210 + 1,900)	5,110	
		7,275
		210,805

Workings

(W1) **Group structure**

Henderson

40%	1.4.X2
35%	1.7.X6
75%	

Springdale

Springdale will be treated as a 40% associate in the consolidated income statement for 1 April 20X6 to 30 June 20X6 and as a 75% subsidiary for the period 1 July 20X6 to 31 March 20X7.

Springdale will be treated as a 75% subsidiary in the consolidated statement of financial position as at 31 March 20X7.

This is a step acquisition where Henderson achieves control on 1 July X6. Therefore, the previously held interest in Springdale is re-measured to fair value with any gain or loss recognised in reserves:

Dr	Investments (30m – 27m)	3m
Cr	Gain in retained earnings	3m

From the group's income statement point of view, the gain or loss is calculated by comparing the fair value with the carrying value of the associate at the deemed date of 'disposal'. See W7.

(W2) **Net assets of subsidiary**

	Acquisition date	**Reporting date**
	1.7.X6	31.3.X7
	$000	$000
Share capital	40,000	40,000
Retained earnings (W)	33,600	36,930
Fair value adjustment	2,000	2,000
Depreciation on fair value adjustment (2,000 x 1/10 x 9/12)	–	(150)
	75,600	78,780

Retained earnings at 1.7.X6 (bal. fig.)	33,600
Profit from 1.7.X6 to 31.3.X7 (9/12 x 4,440)	3,330
Retained earnings at 31.3.X7	36,930

(W3) **Goodwill**

	$000
Fair value of P's holding (cost of investment)	
Fair value of previously held interest	30,000
Fair value of consideration for additional interest	35,000
	65,000
NCI holding at fair value	20,000
Fair value of sub's net assets at acquisition (W2)	(75,600)
Goodwill at acquisition	9,400
Impairment	(1,000)
Goodwill at reporting date	8,400

(W4) **Non-controlling interests**

	$000
NCI holding at acquisition (W3)	20,000
NCI% x post acquisition reserves (25% x (78,780 - 75,600 (W2))	795
NCI% x impairment (25% x 1,000 (W3))	(250)
	20,545

(W5) **Retained earnings**

	$000
Henderson retained earnings	89,430
Gain on remeasurement (30m – 27m)	3,000
PUP (W6)	(80)
Springdale (75% x (78,780 – 75,600 (W2))	2,385
Impairment (75% x 1,000 (W3))	(750)
	93,985

(W6) **PUP**

Profit made on sale = 2,400 x 20/120 = 400

Profit in inventory = 400 x 1/5 = 80

(W7) **Gain/(loss) on disposal of associate**

	$000	$000
Fair value of 35% holding at 1.7.X6		30,000
Less: carrying value of associate		
Cost of investment	27,000	
Share of post acquisition profits 40% x (33,600 (W2) – 22,450)	4,460	
		(31,460)
Loss on disposal		(1,460)

Tutorial note: Step acquisition of non-control to control

IFRS 3 views a step acquisition in which control is achieved as being a disposal of a previously held equity interest which is then replaced with a subsidiary.

The group is disposing of their previously held interest in the associate for "proceeds" equal to the fair value of the previous equity interest at the date of the step acquisition.

The CIS should reflect the share of associate's profits under equity accounting for the appropriate period and then any gain/loss on disposal of the associate.

When calculating the retained earnings for the CSFP, the easiest thing to do is simply reflect the gain on remeasurement that is recorded in the parent's books and then to include the subsidiary from the date control is achieved.

In reality, this gain is made up of two elements:

	$000
Post acquisition profits of Springdale as an associate (40% x (33,600 – 22,450))	4,460
Loss on disposal (W7)	(1,460)
	3,000

Clearly, it is easier to use the quick method (as used in W5) in exam questions. If you are asked to produce a consolidated income statement however, the gain/(loss) should be calculated as in W7.

Test your understanding 4 - Gordon and Mandy

At the date of the purchase of additional shares, the NCI's share of equity is:

	$
NCI holding at acquisition at fair value	100,000
NCI% x post acquisition reserves (20% x (400,000 - 300,000))	20,000
Difference to equity (i.e. increase in equity)	120,000

(a) **Purchase of an additional 10% of the share capital**

	$
Decrease in NCI (10/20 x $120,000)	60,000
Cash paid	(50,000)
Difference to other components of equity – increase	10,000

NCI will become:

	$
NCI holding at acquisition at fair value	100,000
NCI% x post acquisition reserves (20% x (400,000 – 300,000))	20,000
	120,000
Decrease in NCI	(60,000)
NCI after purchase of shares by Gordon	60,000

(b) **Purchase of an additional 15% of the share capital**

	$
Decrease in NCI (15/20 x 120,000)	90,000
Cash paid	(95,000)
Difference to other components of equity – decrease	(5,000)

NCI will become:

	$
NCI holding at acquisition at fair value	100,000
NCI% x post acquisition reserves (20% x (400,000 – 300,000))	20,000
	120,000
Decrease in NCI	(90,000)
NCI after purchase of shares	30,000

Test your understanding 5 - Snooker

(a) **Gain to Snooker**

	$000
Sale proceeds	300
Carrying value of investment disposed (cost)	(100)
Gain on disposal	200
Tax at 30% (30% x 200)	60

(b) **Gain to group**

		$000
Proceeds		300
Fair value of retained interest		–
		300
Carrying value of investment disposed		
Net assets at disposal	110	
Goodwill at disposal (W1)	60	
NCI at disposal (W2)	(32)	
		(138)
Gain on disposal		162
Tax at 30% (per parent's individual FS)		60

Workings

(W1) **Goodwill**

	$000
Fair value of P's holding (cost of investment)	100
NCI holding at fair value	22.5
Fair value of sub's net assets at acquisition	(62.5)
Goodwill at acquisition/ disposal	60

(W2) **NCI**

	$000
NCI holding at acquisition (W1)	22.5
NCI% x post acquisition reserves (20% x (110,000 – 62,500))	9.5
	32

Test your understanding 6 - Padstow

(a) **Gain to Padstow**

	$
Sale proceeds	250,000
Cost of shares sold	(100,000)
Gain on disposal	150,000
Tax at 30%	(45,000)
Net gain on disposal	105,000

(b) **Consolidated accounts**

		$
Proceeds		250,000
Fair value of retained interest		–
		250,000
Carrying value of subsidiary		
Net assets at disposal	88,000	
Unimpaired goodwill at disposal (W1)	22,400	
NCI at disposal (W2)	(17,600)	
		(92,800)
		157,200
Tax on gain as per parent company (part a)		45,000

(W1) **Goodwill**

	$
Fair value of P's holding (cost of investment)	100,000
NCI holding at proportion of net assets (20% x 69,000)	13,800
Fair value of sub's net assets at acquisition	(69,000)
Goodwill at acquisition	44,800
Impairment (50% x 44,800)	(22,400)
Goodwill at disposal	22,400

(W2) **NCI**

	$
NCI holding at acquisition (W1)	13,800
NCI% x post acquisition reserves (20% x (88,000 – 69,000))	3,800
	17,600

Test your understanding 7 - Hague

(a) (i) **Gain in Hague's individual accounts**

	$
Sale proceeds	10,000
Less cost of shares sold	(6,000)
Gain to parent	4,000
Tax at 25%	(1,000)
Post tax gain	3,000

(a) (ii) **Gain in Hague Group accounts**

		$
Sale proceeds		10,000
Fair value of retained interest		–
Less carrying value of subsidiary disposed of:		
Net assets of subsidiary at disposal date	3,000	
Unimpaired goodwill at disposal date (W1)	2,500	
Less: NCI at disposal (W2)	(400)	
		(5,100)
Gain before tax		4,900
Tax on gain as per parent company – part (a)(i)		1,000

(W1) **Goodwill**

		$
Fair value of P's holding (cost of investment)		6,000
NCI holding at fair value		1,000
Fair value of sub's net assets at acquisition		(2,000)
Goodwill at acquisition		5,000
Impairment (50% x 5,000)		(2,500)
Goodwill at disposal		2,500

(W2) **NCI at disposal date**

		$
NCI holding at acquisition (W1)		1,000
NCI% x post acquisition reserves (40% x (3,000 – 2,000))		400
NCI% x impairment (40% x 2,500)		(1,000)
		400

(b) (i) **Group profit or loss**

		$
Sale proceeds		5,000
Fair value of retained interest		5,000
		10,000
Less carrying value of subsidiary disposed of:		
Net assets of subsidiary at disposal date	3,000	
Unimpaired goodwill at disposal date (W1)	2,500	
Less: NCI at disposal (W2)	(400)	
		(5,100)
Gain		4,900
Tax on gain as per parent company (5,000 – (6,000 / 2) x 25%)		500

(b) (ii)

After the date of disposal, the residual holding will be equity accounted, with a single amount in the income statement for the share of the post tax profits for the period after disposal and a single amount in the statement of financial position for the fair value at disposal date of the investment retained plus the share of post-acquisition retained profits.

Investment in associate for CSFP

	$
Cost (investment retained)	5,000
Share of post acquisition profits 30% x (2,200 x 2/12)	110
	5,110

Share of profit of associate for CSCI

Share of profits for the year 30% x (2,200 x 2/12)	110

Test your understanding 8 - Kathmandu

(a) (i) **Consolidated statement of comprehensive income for the year ended 31 December 20X9 – full disposal**

	$
Revenue (553,000 + (6/12 x 450,000))	778,000
Operating costs (450,000 + (6/12 x 400,000))	(650,000)
Operating profit	128,000
Dividend income (8,000 – (70% x 10,000))	1,000
Gain on disposal (W5)	66,400
Profit before tax	195,400
Tax (40,000 + (6/12 x 14,000))	(47,000)
Profit after tax	148,400
Other comprehensive income	–
Total comprehensive income	148,400
Profit/ TCI attributable to:	
Parent shareholders	143,000
NCI shareholders (W6)	5,400
	148,400

(ii) **Consolidated statement of changes in equity for the year ended 31 December 20X9 - full disposal**

	Parent shareholders	NCI shareholders
	$	$
Equity b/f (W8,W9)	228,000	47,000
Comprehensive income	143,000	5,400
Dividend paid	(25,000)	(3,000)
Disposal of sub (W4)	–	(49,400)
Equity c/f	346,000	–

(b) (i) **Consolidated statement of comprehensive income for the year ended 31 December 20X9 – part disposal**

	$
Revenue (553,000 + (6/12 x 450,000))	778,000
Operating costs (450,000 + (6/12 x 400,000))	(650,000)
Operating profit	128,000
Dividend income (8,000 – (70% x 10,000))	1,000
Gain on disposal (W5)	66,400
Income from associate (W7)	6,300
Profit before tax	201,700
Tax (40,000 + (6/12 x 14,000))	(47,000)
Profit after tax	154,700
Other comprehensive income	–
Total comprehensive income	154,700
Profit/ TCI attributable to:	
Parent shareholders	149,300
NCI shareholders (W6)	5,400
	154,700

(ii) **Consolidated statement of changes in equity for the year ended 31 December 20X9 - partial disposal**

	Parent shareholders	**NCI shareholders**
Equity b/f (W8,W9)	228,000	47,000
Comprehensive income	149,300	5,400
Dividend paid	(25,000)	(3,000)
Disposal of sub (W4)	–	(49,400)
Equity c/f	352,300	–

Workings

(W1) **Group structure**

Kathmandu			
	Full disposal		Partial disposal
	70%	1 Jan 20X5	70%
	(70%)	1 July 20X9	(35%)
	0%		35%
Nepal			

(W2) **Nepal net assets**

	Acquisition		**Disposal 1 July 20X9**
	$		$
Equity b/f			130,000
Profit to disposal (6/12 x 36,000)			18,000
Dividend (paid March)			(10,000)
	90,000		138,000
		48,000 Post acquisition profits	

(W3) **Goodwill**

	$
Fair value of P's holding (cost of investment)	100,000
NCI holding at fair value	35,000
Fair value of sub's net assets at acquisition (W2)	(90,000)
Goodwill at acquisition/ disposal	45,000

(W4) **NCI**

	$
NCI holding at acquisition (W3)	35,000
NCI% x post acquisition reserves (30% x 48,000 (W2))	14,400
NCI at disposal	49,400

(W5) **Gain on disposal**

	Full disposal		Partial disposal	
	$	$	$	$
Proceeds		200,000		100,000
Fair value of remaining interest		–		100,000
Net assets at disposal	138,000		138,000	
Goodwill at disposal	45,000		45,000	
NCI at disposal	(49,400)		(49,400)	
		(133,600)		(133,600)
Gain on disposal		66,400		66,400

(W6) **NCI share of profits for the year**

	$
NCI% x sub's profit for year (30% x 6/12 x 36,000)	5,400

(W7) **Income from associate**

	$
P% x A's profit for the year (35% x 6/12 x 36,000)	6,300

(W8) **Equity b/f for parent shareholders**

	$
Parent's equity b/f	200,000
Sub: P% x post acquisition reserves (70% x (130,000 - 90,000))	28,000
	228,000

(W9) **Equity b/f for NCI shareholders**

	$
NCI at acquisition at fair value	35,000
NCI% x post acquisition reserves (30% x (130,000 – 90,000))	12,000
	47,000

Test your understanding 9 - David and Goliath

(i) **Sell 5% of Goliath shares**

	$
Cash received	60,000
Increase in NCI (5% x (350,000 + 175,000))	(26,250)
Difference to other components of equity – increase	33,750

NCI will become:

	$
NCI holding at acquisition at fair value	35,000
NCI% x post acquisition reserves (10% x (350,000 – 200,000))	15,000
	50,000
Increase in NCI	26,250
NCI after sale of shares	76,250

(ii) **Sell 25% of Goliath shares**

	$
Cash received	100,000
Increase in NCI (25% x (350,000 + 175,000))	(131,250)
Difference to other components of equity – decrease	(31,250)

NCI will become:

	$
NCI holding at acquisition at fair value	35,000
NCI% x post acquisition reserves (10% x (350,000 – 200,000))	15,000
	50,000
Increase in NCI	131,250
NCI after sale of shares	181,250

Test your understanding 10 - Pepsi

Consolidated statement of financial position

	$000
Assets (1,000 + 800 + 500)	2,300
Goodwill (140 + 90) (W3)	230
	2,530
Equity	
Equity shares $1	500
Retained earnings (W5)	556
Other components of equity (6 – 4) (W6, W7)	2
	1,058
Non-controlling interests (48 + 124) (W4)	172
	1,230
Liabilities (600 + 500 + 200)	1,300
	2,530

Workings

(W1) **Group structure**

Pepsi

Sprite		Tango	
	80%		75%
Reporting date	8%	Reporting date	(10%)
	88%		65%

(W2) **Net assets of subsidiary**

Sprite	**Acquisition date**		**Reporting date**
	$000		$000
Share capital	200		200
Retained earnings	25		100
	225		300
		75	
		Post acquisition profit	

Tango	**Acquisition date**		**Reporting date**
	$000		$000
Share capital	100		100
Retained earnings	60		200
	160		300
		140	
		Post acquisition profits	

(W3) **Goodwill**

Sprite	$000
Fair value of P's holding (cost of investment)	300
NCI holding at fair value	65
Fair value of sub's net assets at acquisition (W2)	(225)
Goodwill at acquisition/reporting date	140

Tango	$000
Fair value of P's holding (cost of investment)	200
NCI holding at fair value	50
Fair value of sub's net assets at acquisition (W2)	(160)
Goodwill at acquisition/reporting date	90

(W4) **Non-controlling interests – Sprite**

	$000
NCI holding at acquisition (W3)	65
NCI% x post acquisition reserves (20% x 75 (W2))	15
NCI before control to control adjustment	80
Decrease in NCI (W6)	(32)
	48

Non-controllling interests – Tango

	$000
NCI holding at acquisition (W3)	50
NCI% x post acquisition reserves (25% x 140 (W2))	35
NCI before control to control adjustment	85
Increase in NCI (W7)	39
	124

(W5) **Group retained earnings**

	$000
P's reserves	391
Sub: P% x post acquisition reserves	
Sprite: 80% x 75 (W2)	60
Tango: 75% x 140 (W2)	105
	556

(W6) **Control to control adjustment – Sprite**

	$000	
Decrease in NCI (8/20 x 80 (W4))	32	Dr NCI
Cash paid	(26)	Cr Investments
Difference to other components of equity	6	Cr Equity

(W7) **Control to control adjustment – Tango**

	$000	
Cash received	35	Dr Investments
Increase in NCI (10% x (300 (W2) + 90 (W3))	(39)	Cr NCI (W4)
Difference to other components of equity	(4)	Dr Equity

Test your understanding 11 - Cagney and Lacey

Consolidated statement of comprehensive income for the year ended 31 March 20XI

	$
Revenue (31,590 + 11,870)	43,460
Cost of sales (15,290 + 5,820)	(21,110)
Gross profit	22,350
Distribution costs (3,000 + 2,000)	(5,000)
Admin expenses (350 + 250)	(600)
Profit before tax	16,750
Tax (5,400 + 2,150)	(7,550)
Profit after tax for the year	9,200
Other comprehensive income	–
Total comprehensive income	9,200
Attributable to:	
Parent shareholders (ß)	8,973
Non - controlling interest (W4)	227
	9,200

Statement of financial position at 31 March 20X1

	$
Goodwill (W3)	110
Other assets (41,950 + 9,500)	51,450
	51,560
Share capital	20,000
Retained earnings (W5)	13,458
Other components of equity (W8)	7,977
	41,435
Non-controlling interest (W4)	1,625
Other liabilities (5,500 + 3,000)	8,500
	51,560

Consolidated statement of changes in equity at 31 March 20X1

	Equity attributable to parent shareholders	**Non-controlling interest shareholders**
	$	$
B/f at 31 March 20X0 (W6, W7)	24,485	485
Comprehensive income	8,973	227
Disposal adjustment (W8)	7,977	913
31 March 20X1	41,435	1,625

(W1) **Group structure**

Cagney	Cagney
90%	75%
Lacey	Lacey
Subsidiary 9/12	Subsidiary 3/12

(W2) **Net assets of Lacey**

	Acqn date	B/f	Date of transfer	Reporting date
	$	$	$	$
Equity capital	3,000	3,000	3,000	3,000
Retained earnings (b/f = bal. fig.)	700	1,850	1,850	3,500
Earnings for the year (1,650 x 9/12)			1,238	
Net assets	3,700	4,850	6,088	6,500

(W3) **Goodwill**

	$
Fair value of P's holding (cost of investment)	3,440
NCI holding at proportion of net assets (10% x 3,700)	370
Fair value of sub's net assets at acquisition	(3,700)
Goodwill at acquisition / reporting date	110

(W4) **Non-controlling interests**

For CSCI

Lacey's profit after tax	$
1,650 x 9/12 x 10%	124
1,650 x 3/12 x 25%	103
	227

NCI for CSFP

	$
NCI holding at acquisition (W3)	370
NCI% x post acquisition reserves (W2):	
10% x (6,088 – 3,700)	239
25% x (6,500 – 6,088)	103
Increase in NCI (W8)	913
	1,625

(W5) **Retained earnings c/f**

	$
Cagney	11,000
Lacey share of profits to disposal	
90% x (6,088 – 3,700) (W2)	2,149
Lacey share of profits since disposal	
75% x (6,500 – 6,088) (W2)	309
Bal c/f	13,458

(W6) **Equity attributable to parent shareholders b/f**

	$
Cagney	23,450
Lacey (90% x (4,850 – 3,700) (W2)	1,035
	24,485

(W7) **NCI shareholders b/f**

	$
NCI holding at acquisition (W3)	370
NCI% x post acquisition reserves (10% x (4,850 - 3,700))	115
NCI at b/f date	485

(W8) **Disposal transaction**

		$
Dr Cash	Proceeds	8,890
Cr Non-controlling interests	Net assets disposed of 15% x 6,088 (W2)	(913)
Cr Shareholders' equity	Disposal adjustment (ß)	7,977

NB. As NCI is measured on the proportionate basis, the amount transferred from parent shareholders to NCI is based on the net assets only (with no transfer of goodwill). If the fair value method had been used, the amount transferred would have been 15% x (net assets plus goodwill).

Test your understanding 12 - Howard

Consolidated statement of financial position as at 30 September 20X5

	$000
Assets	
Property, plant and equipment (160,000 + 60,000 + 5,000 (W2))	225,000
Goodwill (W3)	9,400
Investments (80,000 – 45,000 (W3) – 10,000 (W7) – 21,000 (W3) + 15,000 (W8))	19,000
Investment in associate (F.V at the year end)	35,000
Current assets (65,000 + 50,000 - 1,000 (W6))	114,000
	402,400
Equity	
Equity shares	50,000
Retained earnings (W5)	223,500
Other components of equity (W7)	(2,700)
	270,800
Non-controlling interests (W4)	14,600
	285,400
Non-current liabilities (25,000 + 18,000)	43,000
Current liabilities (45,000 + 29,000)	74,000
	402,400

Workings

(W1) **Group structure**

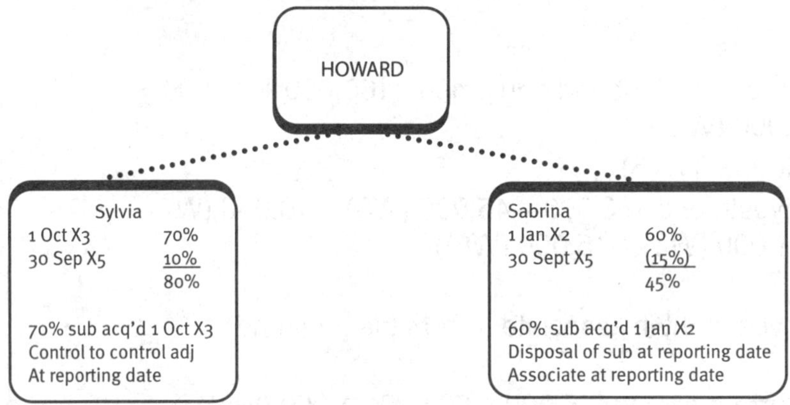

(W2) **Net assets of subsidiary**

Sylvia	**Acquisition date**		**Reporting date**
	1.10.X3		
	$000		$000
Share capital	20,000		20,000
Retained earnings	28,000		43,000
Fair value adjustment			
Land (45,000 - 40,000)	5,000		5,000
	53,000		68,000
		15,000 Post acquisition profit	

Sabrina	**Acquisition date**		**Disposal date**
			30 Sep X5
	$000		$000
Share capital	15,000		15,000
Retained earnings	15,000		42,000
	30,000		57,000
		27,000 Post acquisition profits	

(W3) **Goodwill**

Sylvia	$000
Fair value of P's holding (cost of investment)	45,000
NCI holding at fair value	17,400
Fair value of sub's net assets at acquisition (W2)	(53,000)
Goodwill at acquisition/ reporting date	9,400

Sabrina	$000
Fair value of P's holding (cost of investment)	21,000
NCI holding at fair value	13,000
Fair value of sub's net assets at acquisition (W2)	(30,000)
Goodwill at acquisition / disposal	4,000

(W4) **Non-controlling interests – Sylvia**

	$000
NCI holding at acquisition (W3)	17,400
NCI% x post acquisition reserves (30% x 15,000 (W2))	4,500
NCI before control to control adjustment	21,900
Decrease in NCI (W7)	(7,300)
	14,600

Non-controlllling interests - Sabrina

	$000
NCI holding at acquisition (W3)	13,000
NCI% x post acquisition reserves (40% x 27,000 (W2))	10,800
NCI at disposal	23,800

(W5) **Reserves**

	Retained earnings
	$000
P's reserves	185,000
PUP (P seller) (W6)	(1,000)
Sub: P% x post acquisition reserves	
Sylvia: 70% x 15,000 (W2)	10,500
Sabrina: 60% x 27,000 (W2)	16,200
Sabrina: gain on disposal (W8)	12,800
	223,500

(W6) **PUP**

	$000
Goods in inventory (1/2 x 8,000)	4,000
Profit in inventory (25% x 4,000)	1,000

Parent is seller so reduce W5 and reduce inventory (current assets).

(W7) **Control to control adjustment**

	$000	
Decrease in NCI (10/30 x 21,900 (W4))	7,300	Dr NCI (W4)
Cash paid	(10,000)	Cr Investments
Difference to other components of equity	(2,700)	Dr Equity

(W8) **Sabrina - gain on disposal**

	$000	$000
Proceeds		15,000
Plus: fair value of remaining interest		35,000
Less: carrying value of subsidiary		
Net assets at disposal (W2)	57,000	
Goodwill at disposal (W3)	4,000	
NCI at disposal (W4)	(23,800)	
		(37,200)
Gain on disposal taken to retained earnings W5		12,800

At the reporting date, the investment in Sabrina becomes an investment in associate at a deemed cost of $35 million.

The disposal proceeds have been credited to investments, but should have been credited to the gain on disposal calculation. Therefore the $15 million should be debited to investments.

chapter

8

Complex groups

Chapter learning objectives

On completion of their studies students should be able to:

- Prepare consolidated financial statements for a group of companies involving one or more subsidiaries, sub-subsidiaries and associates;
- Explain the treatment in consolidated financial statements of piece-meal and mid-year acquisitions to include sub-subsidiaries and mixed groups.

1 Session content

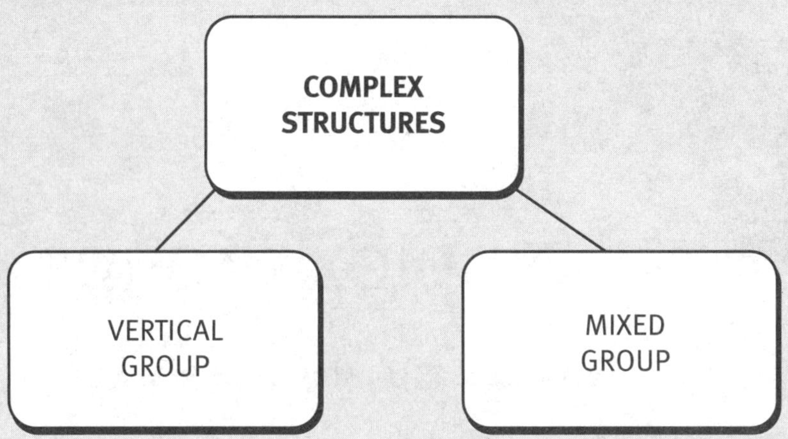

2 Complex group structures

Complex group structures exist where a subsidiary of a parent entity owns a shareholding in another entity which might make that other entity a subsidiary or associate of the parent entity of the group.

Complex structures can be classified under two headings:

- vertical groups
- mixed groups

3 Vertical groups

A vertical group exists where a subsidiary is **indirectly controlled** by the parent.

It is called a **sub-subsidiary**.

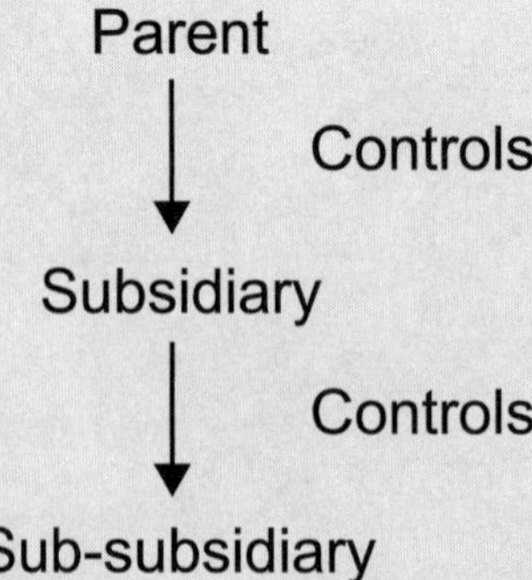

Where the parent owns a controlling interest in a subsidiary, which in turn owns a controlling interest in a sub-subsidiary, then the group accounts of the ultimate parent entity must include the underlying net assets and earnings of both the subsidiary and the sub-subsidiary.

Thus, both companies that are controlled by the parent are consolidated.

The basic techniques of consolidation are the same as seen previously, with some changes to the goodwill and NCI calculations.

Approach to a question

When establishing the group structure follow these steps:

- Control – which entities does the parent control directly or indirectly?
- Percentages – what are the effective ownership percentages for consolidation?
- Dates – when did the parent achieve control and so what is the date of acquisition?

Illustration 1

P
↓ 80% of ordinary shares on 31.12.X0
S
↓ 80% of ordinary shares on 31.12.X0
Q

Control

P controls S and S controls Q. Therefore P can indirectly control Q. Sub-subsidiaries are treated in almost exactly the same way as ordinary subsidiaries and will need parent ownership % and NCI ownership %.

Effective consolidation percentage

S will be consolidated with P owning 80% and NCI owning 20%.

Q will be consolidated with P owning 80% × 80% = **64%**

and NCI owning **36%**.

The effective ownership percentages will be used in standard workings (W3), (W4) and (W5).

Dates

S and Q will both be consolidated from 31 December 20X0.

Illustration 2

P
↓ 60% of ordinary shares on 31.5.X2
S
↓ 60% of ordinary shares on 31.5.X2
Q

Control

P controls S and S controls Q. Therefore P can indirectly control Q.

Effective consolidation percentage

S will be consolidated with P owning 60% and NCI owning 40%.

Q will be consolidated with P owning 60% × 60% = **36%**

and NCI owning **64%**.

Dates

S and Q will both be consolidated from 31.5.X2.

Illustration 3 - Effective date of control

P
↓ 80% of ordinary shares on 31.1.X2
S
↓ 70% of ordinary shares on 30.4.X1
Q

Control

P controls S and S controls Q. Therefore P can indirectly control Q.

Effective consolidation percentage

S will be consolidated with P owning 80% and NCI owning 20%.

Q will be consolidated with P owning 80% × 70% = **56%**

and NCI owning **44%**.

Dates

Consolidation is based upon the principle of control and Q will be controlled by P when P acquires its holding in S on 31.1.X2 since by this date S already controls Q.

S is consolidated from 31.1.X2.

Q is consolidated from 31.1.X2.

Illustration 4 - Effective date of control

P
↓ 60% of ordinary shares on 31.7.X2
S
↓ 70% of ordinary shares on 30.9.X2
Q

Control

P controls S and S controls Q. Therefore P can indirectly control Q.

Effective consolidation percentage

S will be consolidated with P owning 60% and NCI owning 40%.

Q will be consolidated with P owning 60% × 70% = **42%**

and NCI owning **58%**.

Dates

P controls S from 31.7.X2 but Q is not controlled by S until 30.9.X2. Therefore P cannot control Q until 30.9.X2.

S is consolidated from 31.7.X2.

Q is consolidated from 30.9.X2.

4 Accounting treatment of sub-subsidiary

The new adjustment required will be the **indirect holding adjustment** (IHA).

This will affect the calculation of the goodwill figure and the statement of financial position non-controlling interest figure i.e. W3 and W4.

Illustration 5

Consider this statement of financial position extract:

	A	B	C
	$000	$000	$000
Investments			
In B	500	–	–
In C	–	400	–

A owns 80% of B. B owns 75% of C.

The sub-subsidiary is controlled by the parent and so is consolidated in the normal way i.e. from the date of acquisition:

- consolidate income, expenses, assets and liabilities fully on a line by line basis
- recognise goodwill
- recognise non-controlling interests

However, since the sub-subsidiary is indirectly owned, it will be necessary to record an indirect holding adjustment (IHA). The IHA only effects (W3) Goodwill and (W4) NCI for CSFP.

In a vertical group, the consideration to acquire the sub-subsidiary is paid by the subsidiary and not the parent. The parent will only incur their share of this cost and the NCI in the subsidiary will incur the remainder.

Therefore in (W3) Goodwill, it is necessary to reduce the cost of the investment in the subsidiary's books to the parent's share. The amount of the reduction is the cost that is incurred by the NCI shareholders and so is charged to NCI by reducing (W4).

B had paid 400 to acquire C. A owns 80% of B and the NCI owns 20% of B. Therefore the cost of 400 is incurred (80% x 400) 320 by A and (20% x 400) 80 by the NCI.

- 320 is therefore the appropriate cost of the investment for the purposes of W3
- 80 will be the cost charged to the NCI shareholders in W4.

This would be reflected in the standard workings as follows:

(W3) **Goodwill of C**

	$000
Cost of investment (incurred by B)	400
Less: IHA (20% x 400)	(80)
Cost to A (80% x 400)	320
Value of NCI at acquisition	X
Less fair value of net assets of C at acquisition	(X)
Goodwill at acquisition	X

(W4) **NCI of B**

	$000
Value of B's NCI at acquisition (W3)	X
NCI% of B's post-acquisition reserves (W2)	X
Less: IHA (W3)	(80)
	X

The $80,000 represents the cost charged to the NCI shareholders and will be charged to the NCI calculation in W4.

Note that the IHA affects C's goodwill but that it should be deducted from B's NCI as it is B's NCI shareholders that have incurred part of the cost of the investment in C.

Example 1 - David, Colin and John

The draft statements of financial position of David, Colin and John at 31 December 20X4 are as follows:

	David	Colin	John
	$000	$000	$000
Investment in subsidiary	120	80	–
Other assets	280	180	130
	400	260	130
Share capital ($1 shares)	200	100	50
Retained earnings	100	60	30
Other liabilities	100	100	50
	400	260	130

You ascertain the following:

- David acquired 75,000 $1 shares in Colin on 1 January 20X4 when the retained earnings of Colin amounted to $40,000.
- Colin acquired 40,000 $1 shares in John on 30 June 20X4 when the retained earnings of John amounted to $25,000; they had been $20,000 on the date of David's acquisition of Colin.
- Goodwill has suffered no impairment.

Produce the consolidated statement of financial position of the David group at 31 December 20X4. It is group policy to value the non-controlling interest using the proportion of net assets method.

Example 1 answer

Step 1

Draw a diagram of the group structure noting the dates of acquisition.

David
| 75% acquired 1 January 20X4
Colin
| 80% acquired 30 June 20X4
John

Then work through the steps of control, ownership percentages and dates as this will influence the remaining workings.

Control

David controls Colin and Colin controls John. Therefore David can indirectly control John.

Effective consolidation percentages

Colin will be consolidated with David owning 75% and NCI owning 25%.

John will be consolidated with David owning 75% × 80% = **60%**

and NCI owning **40%**.

Dates

Colin is consolidated from 1 January 20X4.

John is consolidated from the date on which David acquired control i.e. 30 June 20X4.

Step 2

Start with the net assets consolidation working as normal.

Care must be taken to use the correct date of acquisition. The relevant date will be that on which David (the parent company) acquired control of each company as above. Therefore, the information given regarding John's reserves at 1 January 20X4 is irrelevant in this context.

(W2) **Net assets of subsidiaries**

	Colin		**John**	
	At acq'n	**At rep date**	**At acq'n**	**At rep date**
	1.1.X4	**31.12.X4**	**30.6.X4**	**31.12.X4**
	$000	$000	$000	$000
Share capital	100	100	50	50
Reserves	40	60	25	30
	140	160	75	80

Step 3

(W3) **Goodwill**

- Two calculations are required, one for each subsidiary.
- They are performed separately as positive goodwill/ negative goodwill is determined for each subsidiary.
- For the sub-subsidiary, the goodwill is calculated from the perspective of the ultimate parent company (David) rather than the immediate parent (Colin). Therefore, the cost of John is only David's share of the amount that Colin paid for John, i.e. $80,000 × 75% = $60,000. There is therefore an IHA of $20,000.
- Remember to use the effective share owned by David when deducting the share of net assets.

	Colin	**John**
	$000	$000
Sub's cost of investment in sub-sub		80
IHA (25% x 80)		(20)
Fair value of P's holding	120	60
NCI holding at proportion of net assets		
(25% x 140 (W2))	35	
(40% x 75 (W2))		30
Fair value of sub's net assets at acquisition (W2)	(140)	(75)
Goodwill on acquisition / at reporting date	15	15

Step 4

(W4) **Non-controlling interest**

When calculating NCI's ownership of Colin, it is necessary to deduct the IHA as calculated in W3.

This is to maintain double entry principles and to reflect that the NCI is charged with its share of the cost of investment in John. Again, be careful to use the NCI's effective percentage in John from W1.

	$000
Colin:	
NCI holding at acquisition (W3)	35
NCI% x post acquisition reserves (25% x (160 – 140 (W2)))	5
IHA (W3)	(20)
John:	
NCI holding at acquisition (W3)	30
NCI% x post acquisition reserves (40% x (80 – 75 (W2)))	2
	52

Step 5

(W5) **Group retained earnings**

	$000
David	100
Colin: 75% × (160 – 140) (W2)	15
John: 60% × (80 – 75) (W2)	3
	118

Note that again, only the parent or effective interest of 60% is taken of the post-acquisition profits in John.

Step 6

Summarised consolidated statement of financial position of the David group at 31 December 20X4

	$000
Goodwill (15 + 15) (Step 3)	30
Other assets (280 + 180 + 130)	590
	620
Equity and liabilities:	
Share capital	200
Retained earnings (Step 5)	118
	318
Non-controlling interest (Step 4)	52
Liabilities (100 + 100 +50)	250
Total equity	620

Test your understanding 1 - H, S & T

The following are the statements of financial position at 31 December 20X7 for H group companies:

	H	S	T
	$000	$000	$000
45,000 shares in S Ltd	65		
30,000 shares in T Ltd		55	
Sundry assets	280	133	100
	345	188	100
Equity share capital ($1 shares)	100	60	50
Retained earnings	45	28	25
Liabilities	200	100	25
	345	188	100

The inter-company shareholdings were acquired on 1 January 20X1 when the retained earnings of S were $10,000 and those of T were $8,000. At that date, the fair value of the non-controlling interest in S was $20,000. The fair value of the non-controlling interest in T based on effective shareholdings was $50,000.

Required:

Prepare the consolidated statement of financial position. It is group policy to value the non-controlling interest at acquisition at fair value. (Work to the nearest $)

Test your understanding 2 - Manchester

The following are all statements of financial position as at 31 December 20X6.

	Manchester	Leeds	Sheffield
	$000	$000	$000
Non-current assets	44	4	27
Investments			
In Leeds	41		
In Sheffield		40	
Current assets	29	31	43
	114	75	70
Share capital $1	40	10	20
Share premium reserve	4	10	–
Retained earnings	60	15	35
Current liabilities	10	40	15
	114	75	70

Manchester purchased 80% of the ordinary share capital of Leeds on 31.12.X1 when the balance on the retained earnings of Leeds stood at $5,000. The balance on the retained earnings of Sheffield at this date was $15,000.

Leeds had purchased 75% of the ordinary share capital of Sheffield on the 31.12.X0 when the balance on the retained earnings of Sheffield was $11,000.

Intra-group charges saw the following balances outstanding at the end of the year:

- Manchester was owed $4,000 by Leeds.
- Leeds owed Sheffield $2,000.
- Sheffield was owed $1,000 by Manchester.

All balances are agreed and entered in the respective books.

Leeds supplies Manchester with a component on a regular basis. Leeds also supplies Sheffield with raw materials. Both items are supplied on a mark-up of 25% and at the end of the year, $15,000 remained in Manchester's inventory from $26,250 worth of sales during the year and $5,000 remained in Sheffield's inventory from $8,750 worth of sales during the year.

Required:

Prepare the consolidated statement of financial position for the Manchester group at 31 December 20X6. It is group policy to use the proportionate share of net assets method to value the non-controlling interest.

Test your understanding 3 - Parsley

The summarised statements of financial position for three entities at 30 April 20X6 are provided below:

	Parsley	**Coriander**	**Thyme**
	$000	$000	$000
Non-current assets			
Property, plant and equipment	596,330	320,370	489,800
Investments	485,000	335,000	–
Current assets	87,320	56,550	54,800
	1,168, 650	711,920	544,600

Equity			
Share capital ($1 shares)	100,000	75,000	50,000
Retained earnings	875,400	525,500	435,750
	975,400	600,500	485,750
Non-current liabilities	150,000	80,000	30,000
Current liabilities	43,250	31,420	28,850
	1,168,650	711,920	544,600

(1) Parsley acquired 80% of the equity shares of Coriander on 1 May 20X3 at a cost of $350 million. At this time, the retained earnings of Coriander were $255 million and the fair value of the non-controlling interest was $80 million.

(2) At 1 May 20X3 it was determined that land in the books of Coriander with a carrying value of $100 million had a fair value of $135 million.

(3) Coriander acquired 70% of the equity shares of Thyme on 1 May 20X4 at a cost of $335 million. At this time, the retained earnings of Thyme were $285 million and the fair value of the non-controlling interest was $175 million.

(4) At 1 May 20X4 it was determined that plant in the books of Thyme had a fair value of $20 million in excess of its carrying value. The plant is being depreciated over its remaining life of 10 years.

(5) During the year ended 30 April 20X6, Parsley sold $35 million of goods to Coriander at a margin of 20%. Coriander still held one-fifth of these goods in inventory at the reporting date.

(6) It is group policy to measure NCIs at fair value at acquisition. At 30 April 20X6 it was determined that no impairment had arisen in respect of the goodwill of Coriander but that the goodwill of Thyme had suffered an impairment loss of $8 million.

Required:

Prepare the consolidated statement of financial position for the Parsley Group at 30 April 20X6.

5 Income statement preparation for vertical groups

Treat the sub-subsidiary in exactly the same way as a directly owned subsidiary but remember to use the effective percentages when calculating non-controlling interests' share of profit.

Test your understanding 4 - Alpha

Alpha purchased 80% of Bravo's equity share capital of $250m on 1 January 20X0 when the balance on Bravo's retained earnings was $20m. The fair value of the NCI's holding at acquisition was $54.3m.

Bravo purchased 60% of Charlie's equity share capital of $150m on 1 January 20X1 when Charlie's retained earnings stood at $30m. The fair value of the NCI's holding (both direct and indirect) at acquisition was $94.1m.

Goodwill in both Bravo and Charlie has been calculated measuring NCIs at fair value and both have remained unimpaired since acquisition.

Statements of changes in equity for the year ended 31 December 20X4:

	Alpha	**Bravo**	**Charlie**
	$m	$m	$m
Equity b/f	400	300	200
Comprehensive income for the year	134	121	111
Dividends	(30)	(15)	(5)
Equity c/f	504	406	306

The statements of comprehensive income for the year ended 31 December 20X4 are as follows:

	Alpha	**Bravo**	**Charlie**
	$m	$m	$m
Revenue	200	170	160
Cost of sales	(44)	(30)	(32)
Gross profit	156	140	128
Operating expenses	(10)	(7)	(7)
Investment income	12	3	
Profits before taxation	158	136	121
Income tax	(24)	(15)	(10)
Profit for the year	134	121	111
Other comprehensive income	–	–	–
Total comprehensive income	134	121	111

Required:

Prepare the consolidated income statement and consolidated statement of changes in equity for the year ended 31 December 20X4.

Note: Work in millions to 2 decimal places i.e. to the nearest $10,000.

6 Sub-associates

There may be the situation where P has control over S, but S only has significant influence over A.

P
↓ 75%
S
↓ 40%
A

A is referred to as a sub-associate i.e. an associate of the subsidiary S of P.

S has an investment in an associate which would be accounted for using equity accounting.

The investment in associate would be made up of the cost of the investment and 40% of the post acquisition profits (being S's share).

In the consolidated statement of financial position of the P group, this asset of S will be fully consolidated as it is under the control of P.

However, P only effectively owns 30% (75% x 40%) of A's post acquisition profits with S's NCI owning the remaining 10% (25% x 40%).

Therefore, the post acquisition profits of A will be split 30% : 10% within W4 : W5.

Similarly, in the consolidated statement of comprehensive income, income from the associate will be reported equal to 40% of A's profits after tax with 30% being attributable to P shareholders and 10% attributable to the NCI shareholders.

Example 2

P purchased 80% of the ordinary shares of S on 1 January 20X2 for $1.5m. On the same date S purchased 40% of the ordinary shares of A, paying $750,000 in cash. At the acquisition date, S had retained earnings of $200,000 and A had retained earnings of $1 million.

The statements of financial position for the three companies on 31 December 20X2 are as follows:

	P	S	A
	$000	$000	$000
Investment	1,500	750	–
Sundry assets	3,100	1,850	4,400
	4,600	2,600	4,400
Equity share capital	2,200	1,500	500
Retained earnings	2,100	1,000	3,500
Liabilities	300	100	400
	4,600	2,600	4,400

Required:

Prepare the consolidated statement of financial position for P group at 31 December 20X2. It is group policy to use the proportionate share of net assets method to value the non-controlling interest.

Example 2 answer

As with all questions, start by producing the group structure diagram.

Workings

(W1) **Group structure**

P
↓ 80% on 1.1.X2
S
↓ 40% on 1.1.X2
A

S will be consolidated as a subsidiary as normal, with P owning 80% and the NCI 20% from 1 January 20X2.

A is a sub-associate i.e. an associate of S. S's Investment in Associate will be fully consolidated as P controls S and so include 40% of A's post acquisition profits. The post acquisition profits of A are then effectively owned as follows:

Parent shareholders	(80% x 40%)	32%
NCI shareholders of S	(20% x 40%)	8%
		40%

Now, compile W2 as normal.

(W2) **Net assets – S**

	Acq'n (1.1.X2)	**Reporting date**
	$000	$000
Share capital	1,500	1,500
Retained earnings	200	1,000
	1,700	2,500

Post acquisition reserves = 800

(W3) **Goodwill in S**

	$000
Fair value of P's holding (cost of investment)	1,500
NCI holding at proportion of net assets (20% x 1,700 (W2))	340
Fair value of sub's net assets at acquisition (W2)	(1,700)
Goodwill at acquisition/ reporting date	140

(W4) **Non-controlling interests**

The NCI in S at the reporting date is made up of the value of the NCI holding at acquisition plus their share of post acquisition reserves in the normal way. Additionally the NCI of S own 8% (W1) of the sub-associate's post acquisition reserves.

	$000
NCI holding at acquisition (W3)	340
NCI% x post acquisition reserves of S (20% x 800 (W2))	160
NCI% x post acquisition reserves of A (8% x 2,500 (W6))	200
	700

(W5) **Retained earnings**

	$000
P's reserves	2,100
Sub: 80% × 800 (W2)	640
Sub-associate: 32% × 2,500 (W6)	800
	3,540

(W6) **Investment in associate**

	$000
Cost of investment	750
Share of post acquisition profits 40% x (3,500 – 1,000)	1,000
	1,750

The group's post acquisition reserves of the sub-associate of 2,500 are owned 32% by the parent shareholders and so included in W5 and 8% by the NCI shareholders and so included in W4.

Finally, prepare the consolidated statement of financial position remembering to only add the assets and liabilities of the parent and sub line by line:

Consolidated statement of financial position P group as at 31 December 20X2

		$000
Goodwill	(W3)	140
Investment in associate	(W6)	1,750
Sundry assets	(3,100 + 1,850)	4,950
		6,840
Share capital		2,200
Retained earnings	(W5)	3,540
Non-controlling interest	(W4)	700
Current liabilities	(300 + 100)	400
		6,840

7 Mixed groups

A mixed group exists where the parent company has a direct holding in the sub-subsidiary as well as the indirect holding via the subsidiary.

```
      P →   →
   %  ↓     ↓
      S     %
   %  ↓     ↓
      Q ←   ←
```

Accounting for a mixed group is similar to that of a vertical group but may also include a step acquisition.

Approach to a question

Follow the same steps as with a vertical group when establishing group structure:

- Control
- Percentages of ownership
- Dates

The IHA will need to be calculated on the indirect acquisition of the sub-subsidiary.

Illustration 6

		P →	→	
1 April 20X2	70%	↓	↓	
		S	30%	1 April 20X2
1 April 20X2	40%	↓	↓	
		Q ←	←	

Control

P controls S. Therefore S is a subsidiary.

P controls Q. P is able to direct 40% + 30% = 70% of the voting rights of Q. Therefore Q is a sub-subsidiary.

Effective consolidation percentage

S will be consolidated with P owning 70% and the NCI owning 30%.

Q will be consolidated with P owning 58% and the NCI owning 42%.

P's indirect ownership (70% × 40%)	28%
P's direct ownership	30%
	58%

Dates

The date of acquisition for S and Q is 1 April 20X2.

Example 3

The summarised draft statements of financial position of three companies at 31 December 20X5 are:

	P	S	Q
	$000	$000	$000
Property, plant and equipment	1,500	450	120
Investments			
In S	400		
In Q	200	80	
Current assets	250	125	35
	2,350	655	155
Share capital $1	300	150	50
Retained earnings	1,925	420	75
Current liabilities	125	85	30
	2,350	655	155

(1) On 1 January 20X3, P acquired 80% of the equity shares of S and 70% of the equity shares of Q. S's retained earnings at this date were $250,000 and Q's retained earnings were $20,000.

(2) On the same date, 1 January 20X3, S acquired 15% of the equity shares of Q.

(3) It is group policy to measure NCIs using the fair value method. The fair value of S's NCI at the date of acquisition was $70,000 and the fair value of Q's NCI (based on P's effective holding) was $50,000 .

Required:

Prepare the consolidated statement of financial positioon of the P Group as 31 December 20X5.

Example 3 answer

Step 1 - draw up W1 Group structure

(W1) **Group structure**

		P →	→		
1 Jan 20X3	80%	↓	↓		
		S		70%	1 Jan 20X3
1 Jan 20X3	15%	↓	↓		
		Q ←	←		

S will be consolidated as a 80% sub (NCI owning 20%) from 1 Jan 20X3.

Q will be consolidated as a 82% sub (NCI owning 18%) from 1 Jan 20X3.

P's direct ownership	70%
P's indirect ownership (80% × 15%)	12%
	82%

P achieves control of both S and Q on 1 January 20X3 - and on this date obtains both a direct and indirect holding. There is no step acquisition but both shareholdings must be taken into account (as above) when calculating goodwill and an IHA will need to be applied to the indirect element.

Step 2 - At the reporting date both S and Q are subsidiaries. Therefore you can now set up the proforma CSFP and add across the assets and liabilities of all three entities line by line.

Consolidated statement of financial position as at 31 December 20X5

		$000
Property, plant and equipment	(1,500 + 450 + 120)	2,070
Goodwill	(W3)	
Current assets	(250 + 125 + 35)	410

Equity		
Share capital		300
Retained earnings	(W5)	
Non-controlling interest	(W4)	
Current liabilities	(125 + 85 + 30)	240
		———
		———

Step 3 - now complete the workings for S and Q, remembering to bring in the IHA when dealing with Q. Deal with S first as it is the straightforward subsidiary.

(W2) **Net assets – S**

	Acq'n	**Reporting date**
	$000	$000
Share capital	150	150
Retained earnings	250	420
	———	———
	400	570
	———	———

Post acq'n profits = 170

Net assets – Q

	Acq'n	**Reporting date**
	$000	$000
Share capital	50	50
Retained earnings	20	75
	———	———
	70	125
	———	———

Post acq'n profits = 55

(W3) **Goodwill – S**

	$000
Fair value of P's holding (COI)	400
NCI holding at fair value	70
Fair value of sub's net assets at acquisition (W2)	(400)
Goodwill at acquisition/reporting date	70

Goodwill – Q

	$000	$000
Fair value of P's holding (COI) – Direct		200
Fair value of P's holding (COI) – Indirect:		
Sub's cost of investment	80	
Less: IHA (20% x 80)	(16)	
		64
NCI holding at fair value		50
Fair value of sub's net assets at acquisition (W2)		(70)
Goodwill at acquisition/reporting date		244

Non-controlling interests – S

	$000
NCI holding at acquisition (W3)	70
NCI% x post acquisition reserves (20% x 170 (W2))	34
Less IHA (W3)	(16)
	88

Non-controlling interests – Q

	$000
NCI holding at acquisition (W3)	50
NCI% x post acquisition reserves (18% x 55 (W2))	9.9
NCI at 31 Oct 20X3	59.9

(W5) **Retained earnings**

	$000
P's reserves	1,925
Sub: P% x post acquisition reserves	
S: 80% x 170 (W2)	136
Q: 82% x 55 (W2)	45.1
	2,106.1

Step 4 - Finally complete the proforma:

Consolidated statement of financial position as at 31 December 20X5

		$000
Property, plant and equipment	(1,500 + 450 + 120)	2,070
Goodwill	(70+ 244) (W3)	314
Current assets	(250 + 125 + 35)	410
		2,794
Equity		
Share capital		300
Retained earnings	(W5)	2,106.1
		2,406.1
Non-controlling interest	(88 + 59.9) (W4)	147.9
		2,554
Current liabilities	(125 + 85 + 30)	240
		2,794

Test your understanding 5 - Holdings

The summarised draft statements of financial position of three companies at 30 September 20X4 are:

	Holdings	Pepper	Salt
	$000	$000	$000
Property, plant and equipment	1,000	700	225
Investments			
In Pepper	350		
In Salt	175	50	
Current assets	370	300	75
	1,895	1,050	300
Share capital $1	500	300	100
Retained earnings	1,145	550	150
Current liabilities	250	200	50
	1,895	1,050	300

(1) On 1 October 20X1, Holdings acquired 70% of the equity shares of Pepper and 60% of the equity shares of Salt. Pepper's retained earnings at this date were $100,000 and Salt's retained earnings were $50,000.

(2) On the same date, 1 October 20X1, Pepper acquired 20% of the equity shares of Salt.

(3) It is group policy to measure NCIs using the proportion of fair value of net assets method.

Required:

Prepare the consolidated statement of financial position of the Holdings Group at 30 September 20X4.

Illustration 7 - Non-control to control

		P → →		
1 Jan 20X8	80%	↓	↓	
		S	30%	1 Jan 20X7
1 June 20X8	60%	↓	↓	
		Q ← ←		

Control

P controls S. Therefore S is a subsidiary.

P controls Q as P is able to direct 30% + 60% = 90% of the voting rights of Q. Therefore Q is a sub-subsidiary.

Effective consolidation percentage

S will be consolidated with P owning 80% and the NCI owning 20%.

Q will be consolidated with P owning 78% and the NCI owning 22%.

P's direct ownership	30%
P's indirect ownership (80% × 60%)	48%
	78%

Dates

S will be consolidated from 1 Jan 20X8.

Q will be consolidated as a sub-subsidiary from 1 June 20X8.

Since P owned only 30% prior to 1.6.X8, this is a step acquisition from non-control to control.

Example 4 - Red, Blue and Green

The following are the statements of financial position at 31 December 20X9 for the Red group companies:

	Red	Blue	Green
	$000	$000	$000
Investments	775	440	–
Other assets	725	460	1,200
	1,500	900	1,200
Equity share capital ($1 shares)	800	500	500
Retained earnings	500	200	350
Liabilities	200	200	350
	1,500	900	1,200

Red acquired 80% of the shares of Blue on 1 January 20X8 for $600,000. Blue's retained earnings were $150,000 at this date. The fair value of the NCI in Blue was $140,000.

Red acquired 30% of the shares of Green on 1 January 20X7 for $175,000 when Green's retained earnings were $100,000.

Blue acquired 60% of the shares of Green on 1 January 20X8 paying $440,000 when Green's retained earnings were $120,000. At this date, the fair value of a 30% holding in Green was $200,000 and the fair value of the NCI holding based on effective shareholdings was $145,000.

Required:

Prepare the consolidated statement of financial position as at 31 December 20X9.

Example 4 answer

Step 1 - draw up W1 Group structure

(W1) **Group structure**

```
                        Red    →  →
1 Jan 20X8   80%         ↓          ↓
                        Blue       30%   1 Jan 20X7
1 Jan 20X8   60%         ↓          ↓
                       Green   ←  ←
```

Blue will be consolidated as an 80% sub (NCI owning 20%) from 1 Jan 20X8.

Green will be consolidated as a 78% sub (NCI owning 22%) from 1 Jan 20X8.

X's direct ownership (1 Jan X7)	30%
X's indirect ownership (1 Jan X8) (80% × 60%)	48%
	78%

Red achieves control of Green at the later date of 1 Jan 20X8 when Blue achieves control of Green. Therefore this is a non-control to control step acquisition.

Step 2 - At the reporting date, both Blue and Green are subsidiaries. Therefore now start your proforma CSFP adding the assets and liabilities of all three entities line by line.

Consolidated statement of financial position as at 31 December 20X9

		$000
Goodwill	(W3)	
Investments	(775 + 440	
Other assets	(725 + 460 + 1,200)	2,385

Share capital		800
Retained earnings	(W5)	
Non-controlling interest	(W4)	
Liabilities	(200 + 200 + 350)	750

Step 3 - now complete the workings for Blue as it is the straightforward subsidiary.

(W2) **Net assets – Blue**

	Acq'n		**Reporting date**
	$000		$000
Share capital	500		500
Retained earnings	150		200
	650		700
		Post acq'n profits = 50	

(W3) **Goodwill**

	$000
Fair value of P's holding (cost of investment)	600
NCI holding at fair value	140
Fair value of sub's net assets at acquisition (W2)	(650)
Goodwill at acquisition/ reporting date	90

(W4) **Non-controlling interests**

	$000
NCI holding at acquisition	140
NCI% x post acquisition reserves (20% x 50 (W2))	10
IHA (20% x 440)	(88)
	62

(W5) **Reserves**

	$000
P's reserves	500
Sub: P% x post acquisition reserves	
Blue: 80% x 50 (W2)	40
Green:	

Step 3: Now complete the workings for Green, remembering to deal with the step acquisition adjustment i.e. remeasuring the existing holding to fair value at the date of acquisition and recording the subsequent gain in profits (retained earnings).

(W2) **Net assets – Green**

	Acq'n	**Reporting date**
	$000	$000
Share capital	500	500
Retained earnings	120	350
	620	850

Post acq'n profits
= 230

(W3) **Goodwill**

When calculating goodwill, the additional shareholding of 48% is an indirect acquisition and so the cost of the investment will be subject to an indirect holding adjustment.

	$000	$000
Fair value of P's holding (cost of investment)		
Fair value of previous 30%		200
Sub's COI in sub-sub	440	
IHA (20% x 440)	(88)	
		352
		552
NCI holding at fair value		145
Fair value of sub's net assets at acquisition (W2)		(620)
Goodwill at acquisition/ reporting date		77

(W4) **Non-controlling interests – Green**

	$000
NCI holding at acquisition (W3)	145
NCI% x post acquisition reserves (22% x 230 (W2))	50.6
	195.6

(W5) **Reserves**

	$000
P's reserves	500
Sub: P% x post acquisition reserves	
Blue: 80% x 50 (W2)	40
Green: 78% x 230 (W2)	179.4
Gain on step acquisition (W6)	25
	744.4

(W6) **Step acquisition adjustment**

	$000	
Fair value of previous 30%	200	Increase goodwill W3
Carrying value of previous 30% (cost)	(175)	Reduce investments
Gain to profit	25	Increase reserves W5

Step 4 – Finally complete the proforma:

Consolidated statement of financial position as at 31 December 20X9

		$000
Goodwill	(90 + 77) (W3)	167
Investments	(775 + 440 – 600 (W3) – 440 (W3) – 175 (W6))	-
Sundry assets	(725 + 460 + 1,200)	2,385
		2,552

Equity		
Share capital		800
Retained earnings	(W5)	744.4
		1,544.4
Non-controlling interest	(62 + 195.6 (W4))	257.6
		1,802
Liabilities	(200 + 200 + 350)	750
		2,552

Test your understanding 6 - Cavendish

The following are the statements of financial position at 31 December 20X2 for the Cavendish group of companies:

	Cavendish	Wiggins	Millar
	$000	$000	$000
Assets			
Property, plant and equipment	2,000	2,850	1,350
Investments	1,375	1,200	–
Current assets	225	350	950
	3,600	4,400	2,300
Equity share capital ($1 shares)	1,500	800	1,200
Retained earnings	880	400	450
	2,380	1,200	1,650
Non-current liabilities	700	2,000	350
Current liabilities	520	1,200	300
	3,600	4,400	2,300

(1) Cavendish acquired 70% of the shares of Wiggins and 25% of the shares of Millar on 1 January 20X1 paying $1,000,000 and $375,000 respectively. The balances on Wiggins' and Millar's retained earnings at this date were $320,000 and $250,000 respectively.

(2) The fair value of the NCI holding in Wiggins was $440,000 at 1 January 20X1.

(3) On 1 January 20X2, Wiggins acquired 60% of the shares of Millar paying $1,200,000 when Millar's retained earnings stood at $360,000. The fair value of Cavendish's 25% holding in Millar was $400,000 at this time and the fair value of the NCI holding in Millar was $525,000 (based on effective shareholdings).

Required:

Prepare the consolidated statement of financial position as at 31 December 20X2.

Illustration 8 - Control to control

		P →	→		
1 Jan 20X5	70%	↓	↓		
		S		60%	1 Jan 20X5
1 July 20X5	20%	↓	↓		
		Q ←	←		

Control

P controls S. Therefore S is a subsidiary.

P controls Q since it owns 60% of Q's shares directly. Therefore Q is a subsidiary.

Effective consolidation percentage

S will be consolidated with P owning 70% and the NCI owning 30%.

Q will be consolidated with P initially owning 60% and the NCI owning 40%. P then acquires an additional 14% (70% x 20%) and so P's shareholding increases to 74% and the NCI decreases to 26%.

Dates

The date of acquisition for S is 1 January 20X5.

The date of acquisition for Q is 1 January 20X5, with a control to control adjustment (decrease in the NCI) at 1 July 20X5.

Example 5 - Portmadhog

The following are the statements of financial position at 31 December 20X3 for Port group companies:

	Port	Mad	Hog
	$000	$000	$000
Investments	120	48	–
Other assets	280	132	100
	400	180	100
Equity share capital ($1 shares)	200	100	50
Retained earnings	55	20	25
Liabilities	145	60	25
	400	180	100

Port acquired 60% shareholdings in both Mad and Hog on 1 January 20X3, paying cash of $80,000 for Mad and $40,000 for Hog. The retained earnings of Mad and Hog at the time were $15,000 and $12,000 respectively. The fair value of the NCI in Mad and Hog on 1 January 20X3 were $53,000 and $26,000 respectively. Mad purchased a 40% share in Hog on 31 December 20X3 for $48,000.

Assume that profits accrue evenly over the year.

Required:

Prepare the consolidated statement of financial position at 31 December 20X3. It is group policy to value the non-controlling interest at acquisition at fair value.

Example 5 answer

Step 1

Complete W1

	Port → →	
1 January 20X3 60%	↓	↓
	Mad	60% 1 January 20X3
31 December 20X3 40%	↓	↓
	Hog ← ←	

Mad will be consolidated as a 60% sub (40% NCI) from 1 January 20X3.

Hog will be consolidated as a 60% sub (40% NCI) from 1 January 20X3.

At 31 December 20X3 Port increases their shareholding by 60% x 40% = 24% to 84%. So there is a decrease in the NCI of 24% at 31 December 20X3.

Step 2

Set up the SFP proforma

Consolidated statement of financial position as at 31 December 20X3

		$000
Goodwill	(W3)	
Sundry assets	(280 + 132 + 100)	512
Equity		
Share capital		200
Retained earnings	(W5)	
Non-controlling interest	(W4)	
Liabilities	(145 + 60 + 25)	230

Step 3

Complete the workings W2 through to W5 for Mad as it is a straightforward subsidiary:

(W2) **Net assets of Mad**

	Acq'n		**Reporting date**
	$000		$000
Share capital	100		100
Retained earnings	15		20
	115		120
		Post acq'n profit = 5	

(W3) **Goodwill**

	$000
Fair value of P's holding (cost of investment)	80
NCI holding at fair value	53
Fair value of sub's net assets at acquisition (W2)	(115)
Goodwill at acquisition/reporting date	18

(W4) **NCI**

	$000
NCI holding at acquisition (W3)	53
NCI% x post acquisition reserves (40% x 5 (W2))	2
	55

(W5) **Retained earnings**

	$000
P's reserves	55
Sub's: P% x post acquisition reserves	
Mad: 60% x 5 (W2)	3

Step 4

Now complete the workings for Hog, remembering to record the adjustment for the decrease in NCI at the reporting date.

(W2) **Net assets of Hog**

	Acq'n		**Reporting date**
	$000		$000
Share capital	50		50
Retained earnings	12		25
	62		75
		Post acq'n profit = 13	

(W3) **Goodwill**

	$000
Fair value of P's holding (cost of investment)	40
NCI holding at fair value	26
Fair value of sub's net assets at acquisition (W2)	(62)
Goodwill at acquisition/reporting date	4

(W4) **NCI**

	$000
NCI holding at acquisition (W3)	26
NCI% x post acquisition reserves (40% x 13(W2))	5.2
	31.2
Decrease in NCI (W6)	(18.72)
Less IHA (W6)	(19.2)
	(6.72)

(W5) **Retained earnings**

	$000
P's reserves	55
Sub's: P% x post acquisition reserves	
Mad: 60% x 5 (W2)	3
Hog: 60% x 13 (W2)	7.8
	65.8

(W6) **Decrease in NCI (control to control adjustment)**

		$000	
Decrease in NCI	(24/40) x 31.2 (W4))	18.72	Reduce W4
Cash paid		(48)	Reduce Investments
IHA on cash paid (40% x 48)		19.2	Reduce W4
Difference to other components of equity – decrease		(10.08)	

Note, the cash paid of $48,000 was by Mad therefore Port's share of this is only 60% x $48,000 = $28,800. To achieve this, an IHA is recorded and this will need to be deducted from NCI in W4.

Step 5 – Now complete the SFP proforma:

Consolidated statement of financial position as at 31 December 20X8

		$000
Goodwill	(18 + 4) (W3)	22
Other assets	(280 + 132 + 100)	512
		534

Equity		
Share capital		200
Retained earnings	(W5)	65.8
Other reserves	(W6)	(10.08)
		255.72
Non-controlling interest	(55 – 6.72) (W4)	48.28
		304
Liabilities	(145 + 60 + 25)	230
		534

Test your understanding 7 - Poppy

The following are the statements of financial position at 31 May 20X8 for the Poppy group of companies:

	Poppy	Sage	Thyme
	$000	$000	$000
Investments	450	50	–
Sundry assets	300	500	260
	750	550	260
Equity share capital ($1 shares)	400	300	100
Retained earnings	225	200	120
Liabilities	125	50	40
	750	550	260

(1) Poppy acquired 70% of the equity shares of Sage on 1 January 20X6 for $320,000 when Sage's retained earnings stood at $50,000. The fair value of the NCI holding in Sage was $125,000 at this time.

(2) Poppy acquired 60% of the equity shares of Thyme on 1 December 20X6 for $130,000 when Thyme's retained earnings stood at $50,000. The fair value of the NCI holding in Thyme was $85,000 at this time.

(3) Sage acquired 20% of Thyme on 31 May 20X8 for $50,000.

Required:

Prepare the consolidated statement of financial position as at 31 May 20X8.

Test your understanding 8 - ABC

The statements of financial position of three entities at 30 June 20X6 are given below:

	A	B	C
	$000	$000	$000
Non-current assets			
Property, plant and equipment	9,300	3,600	4,250
Investments	10,000	4,000	–
Current assets			
Inventory	1,750	700	400
Receivables	1,050	550	420
Cash	1,550	1,010	330
	23,650	9,860	5,400
Equity			
Share capital $1	15,000	7,000	4,000
Retained earnings	4,150	730	870
Non-current liabilities	2,000	750	250
Current liabilities	2,500	1,380	280
	23,650	9,860	5,400

On 1 July 20X5 A acquired 60% of the equity share capital of B for $6m cash. The retained earnings of B were $500,000 and the fair value of the NCI holding was $3.5m.

On the same date, B acquired 60% of the equity share capital of C for $4m cash. The retained earnings of C were $570,000 and the fair value of the NCI holding was $2.5m

On 30 June 20X6, A acquired 10% of the equity share capital of C for $1m cash.

At 1 July 20X5, property, plant and equipment in the books of B had a fair value of $250,000 in excess of its carrying value. The items had a remaining useful economic life of 5 years at this time.

At 30 June 20X6, B and C held goods in inventory which had been purchased from A for a total of $360,000. A had sold the goods at a 20% mark up.

At 30 June 20X6, goodwill arising on the acquisition of B had been impaired by $250,000. There was no impairment to goodwill arising on the acquisition of C. It is group policy to measure NCIs at fair value at acquisition.

Required:

Prepare the consolidated statement of financial position at 30 June 20X6.

Test your understanding 9 - Hitchcock

The summarised statements of comprehensive income for three entities for the year ended 30 April 20X3 are provided below:

	Hitchcock	Spencer	Spooner
	$m	$m	$m
Revenue	120	84	80
Operating costs	(83)	(67)	(55)
Profit before tax	37	17	25
Tax	(12)	(7)	(10)
Profit for the year	25	10	15
Other comprehensive income	10	6	–
Total comprehensive income	35	16	15

(1) Hitchcock acquired 80% of the equity shares of Spencer on 1 May 20X1 paying $70 million. The retained earnings of Spencer were $30 million at this time and the fair value of the NCI holding in Spencer was $15 million.

(2) Hitchcock acquired 15% of the equity shares of Spooner on 1 May 20X1 paying $13 million.

(3) On 1 May 20X2 Spencer acquired 60% of Spooner's equity shares paying $65 million. At this date the retained earnings of Spooner were $51 million. The fair value of Hitchcock's 15% holding in Spooner was $25 million and the fair value of the NCI holding (based on effective holdings) was $27 million.

(4) At 30 April 20X3 it was determined that the goodwill arising on the acquisition of Spencer had been impaired by 20%. The goodwill arising on the acquisition of Spooner remained unimpaired.

Required:

Prepare the consolidated statement of comprehensive income for the year ended 30 April 20X3 for the Hitchcock Group.

8 Chapter summary

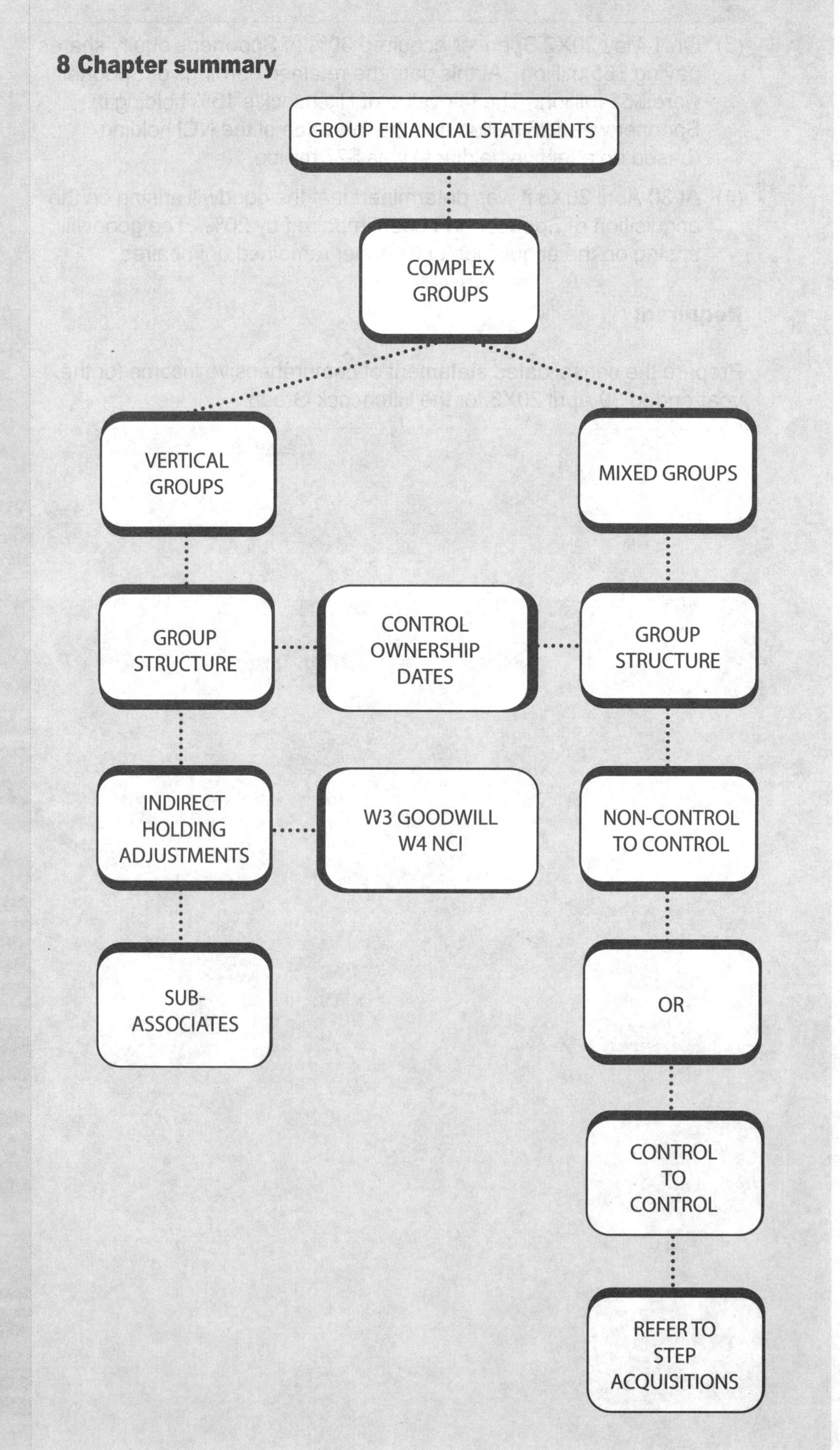

Test your understanding answers

Test your understanding 1 - H, S & T

Consolidated statement of financial position as at 31 December 20X7

	$
Goodwill (15,000 + 33,250) (W3)	48,250
Other net assets (280,000 + 133,000 + 100,000)	513,000
	561,250
Capital and reserves	
Equity share capital	100,000
Retained earnings (W5)	66,150
NCI (W4)	70,100
Liabilities (200,000 + 100,000 + 25,000)	325,000
	561,250

Workings

(W1) **Group structure**

H
↓ 45/60 = 75% on 1.1.X1
S
↓ 30/50 = 60% on 1.1.X1
T

Effective consolidation percentages:

	S	T
Group interest	75%	45% (75% × 60%)
Non controlling interest	25%	55%
	100%	100%

(W2) **Net assets**

	S		T	
	Acq'n date 1.1.X1	**Rep. date 31.12.X7**	**Acq'n date 1.1.X1**	**Rep. date 31.12.X7**
	$	$	$	$
Share capital	60,000	60,000	50,000	50,000
Retained earnings	10,000	28,000	8,000	25,000
	70,000	88,000	58,000	75,000

(W3) **Goodwill**

	S	T
	$	$
Sub's cost of investment in sub-sub		55,000
IHA (25% x 55,000)		(13,750)
Fair value of P's holding	65,000	41,250
NCI holding at fair value	20,000	50,000
Fair value of sub's net assets at acquisition (W2)	(70,000)	(58,000)
Goodwill on acquisition	15,000	33,250

(W4) **Non-controlling interest**

	$
S:	
NCI holding at acquisition (W3)	20,000
NCI% x post acquisition reserves (25% x (88,000 – 70,000) (W2))	4,500
IHA (W3)	(13,750)
T:	
NCI holding at acquisition (W3)	50,000
NCI% x post acquisition reserves (55% x (75,000 – 58,000) (W2))	9,350
	70,100

(W5) **Consolidated retained earnings**

	$
Retained earnings of H	45,000
Group share of post-acquisition profits	
S: 75% x (88,000 – 70,000) (W2)	13,500
T 45% x (75,000 – 58,000) (W2)	7,650
	66,150

Test your understanding 2 - Manchester

Consolidated statement of financial position of the Manchester group as at 31 December 20X6

		$000
PPE	(44 + 4 + 27)	75
Goodwill	(21 + 11) (W3)	32
Current assets	(29 + 31 + 43 – 4 PUP (W6) – 7 interco)	92
		199
Share capital		40
Share premium		4
Retained earnings	(W5)	76.8
Non-controlling interest	(W4)	20.2
Current liabilities	(10 + 40 + 15 – 7 interco)	58
		199

Workings

(W1) **Group structure**

Manchester
↓ 80% of ordinary shares on 31.12.X1
Leeds
↓ 75% of ordinary shares on 31.12.X0
Sheffield

Control

Manchester controls Leeds and Leeds controls Sheffield. Therefore Manchester can indirectly control Sheffield.

Effective consolidation percentages

	Leeds	**Sheffield**
Parent interest	80%	60% (80% × 75%)
Non controlling interest	20%	40%
	100%	100%

Dates

Leeds is consolidated from 31 December 20X1.

Sheffield is also consolidated on 31 December 20X1 i.e. the date on which Manchester acquired control.

(W2) **Net assets – Leeds**

	Acq'n (31.12.X1)	**Reporting date**
Share capital	10	10
Share premium	10	10
Retained earnings	5	15
PUP (W6)		(4)
	25	31

Net assets – Sheffield

	Acq'n (31.12.X1)	**Reporting date**
Share capital	20	20
Retained earnings	15	35
	35	55

(W3) **Goodwill**

	Leeds $000	**Sheffield** $000
Sub's cost of investment in sub-sub		40
IHA (20% x 40)		(8)
Fair value of P's holding	41	32
NCI holding at proportion of net assets		
(20% x 25 (W2))	5	
(40% x 35 (W2))		14
Fair value of sub's net assets at acquisition (W2)	(25)	(35)
Goodwill on acquisition/reporting date	21	11

(W4) **Non-controlling interests**

	$000
Leeds:	
NCI holding at acquisition (W3)	5
NCI% x post acquisition reserves (20% x (31 – 25) (W2))	1.2
IHA (W3)	(8)
Sheffield:	
NCI holding at acquisition (W3)	14
NCI% x post acquisition reserves (40% x (55 – 35) (W2))	8
	20.2

(W5) **Retained earnings**

Manchester	60
Leeds: 80% × (31 – 25) (W2)	4.8
Sheffield: 60% × (55 – 35) (W2)	12
	76.8

(W6) **PUP**

Leeds sells to Manchester and Sheffield, therefore adjust (W2) & inventory on CSFP

Amount left in inventories: $(15,000 + 5,000) = $20,000

PUP = 20,000 × $^{25}/_{125}$ = 4,000

Test your understanding 3 - Parsley

Consolidated statement of financial position as at 30 April 20X6

	$000
Goodwill (W3) (65,000 + 80,000)	145,000
Property, plant and equipment (596,330 + 320,370 + 489,800 + 35,000 (W2) + 20,000 (W2) – 4,000 (W2))	1,457,500
Investments (485,000 + 335,000 – 350,000 (W3) – 335,000 (W3))	135,000
Current assets (87,320 + 56,550 + 54,800 – 1,400 (W6))	197,270
	1,934,770
Equity	
Share capital	100,000
Retained earnings (W5)	1,168,100
	1,268,100
Non-controlling interests (W4) (67,100 + 236,050)	303,150
	1,571,250
Non-current liabilities (150,000 + 80,000 + 30,000)	260,000
Current liabilities (43,250 + 31,420 + 28,850)	103,520
	1,934,770

Workings

(W1) **Group structure**

Parsley
| 80% 1 May 20X3
Coriander
| 70% 1 May 20X4
Thyme

Coriander will be an 80% subsidiary from 1 May 20X3 (3 years) (NCI owning 20%).

Thyme will be a 56% (80% x 70%) subsidiary from 1 May 20X4 (2 years) (NCI owning 44%).

(W2) **Net assets – Coriander**

	Acq'n		**Reporting date**
	$000		$000
Share capital	75,000		75,000
Retained earnings	255,000		525,500
Fair value adjustment – land (135m –100m)	35,000		35,000
	365,000		635,500
		Post acq'n profits = 270,500	

Net assets – Thyme

	Acq'n		**Reporting date**
	$000		$000
Share capital	50,000		50,000
Retained earnings	285,000		435,750
Fair value adjustment – plant	20,000		20,000
Depreciation adjustment (20,000 x 2/10)			(4,000)
	355,000		501,750
		Post acq'n profits = 146,750	

(W3) **Goodwill – Coriander**

	$000
Fair value of P's holding (cost of investment)	350,000
NCI holding at fair value	80,000
Fair value of sub's net assets at acquisition (W2)	(365,000)
Goodwill at acquisition/reporting date	65,000

Goodwill – Thyme

	$000	$000
Sub's COI in sub-sub	335,000	
IHA (20% x 335,000)	(67,000)	
Fair value of P's holding (cost of investment)		268,000
NCI holding at fair value		175,000
Fair value of sub's net assets at acquisition (W2)		(355,000)
Goodwill at acquisition		88,000
Impairment		(8,000)
Goodwill at reporting date		80,000

(W4) **Non-controlling interests – Coriander**

	$000
NCI holding at acquisition (W3)	80,000
NCI% x post acquisition reserves (20% x 270,500 (W2))	54,100
IHA (W3)	(67,000)
	67,100

Non-controlling interests – Thyme

	$000
NCI holding at acquisition (W3)	175,000
NCI% x post acquisition reserves (44% x 146,750 (W2))	64,570
NCI% x impairment loss (44% x 8,000 (W3))	(3,520)
	236,050

(W5) **Retained earnings**

	$000
P's reserves	875,400
PUP (W6)	(1,400)
Sub: P% x post acquisition reserves	
Coriander: 80% x 270,500 (W2)	216,400
Thyme: 56% x 146,750 (W2)	82,180
Impairment: P% x impairment loss	
Thyme: 56% x 8,000 (W3)	(4,480)
	1,168,100

(W6) **PUP**

Goods in inventory = 35,000 x 1/5 = 7,000

Profit in inventory = 7,000 x 20% = 1,400

Test your understanding 4 - Alpha

Alpha consolidates 80% of Bravo from 1.1.X0

Charlie will be consolidated at 80% × 60% = 48% from 1.1.X1 with a non-controlling interest of 52%.

Consolidated statement of comprehensive income for the year ended 31 December 20X4

	$m
Revenue (200 + 170 + 160)	530
Cost of sales (44 + 30 + 32)	(106)
Gross profit	424
Operating expenses (10 + 7 + 7)	(24)
Investment income (12 + 3 – 12 – 3 (W2))	–
Profit before tax	400
Tax (24 + 15 + 10)	(49)
Profit for the year	351
Other comprehensive income	–
Total comprehensive income	351
Profit/ TCI attributable to:	
Parent shareholders (balance)	269.68
NCI shareholders (W3)	81.32
	351

Consolidated statement of changes in equity for the year ended 31 December 20X4

	Parent shareholders	NCI shareholders
	$m	$m
Equity b/f (W6, W5)	433.6	164.8
Comprehensive income	269.68	81.32
Dividends paid	(30)	
Bravo NCI (20% x 15)		(3)
Charlie NCI (40% x 5)		(2)
Equity c/f (W6, W5)	673.28	241.12

Workings

(W1) **Group structure**

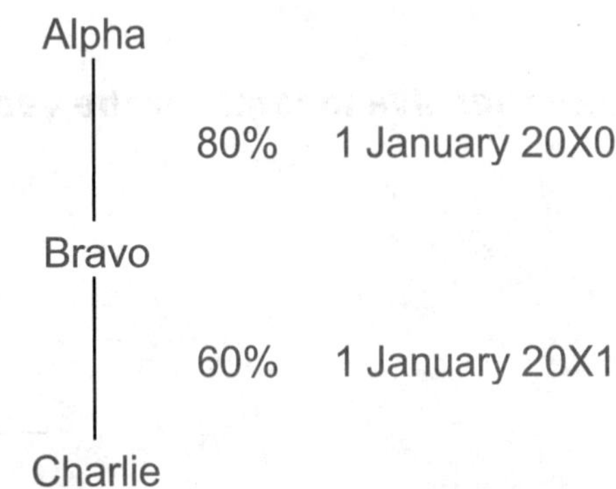

Charlie is a 48% sub from 1 January 20X1.

(W2) **Intra-group dividends**

Dividends will be paid to shareholders based on their actual shareholdings i.e. the effective shareholding percentages used for consolidation purposes are not relevant.

Bravo to Alpha	80% × 15 = \$12m
Charlie to Bravo	60% × 5 = \$3m

(W3) **NCI share of profit/ TCI**

		\$m	\$m
Bravo:			
Profit for year/ TCI		121	
Intra-group dividend eliminated (W2)		(3)	
		118	
NCI share	x 20%		23.6
Charlie:			
Profit for year/ TCI		111	
NCI share	x 52%		57.72
			81.32

(W4) **Net assets (equity) – Bravo**

	Acq'n	b/f	Rep date (c/f)
	$m	$m	$m
Share capital	250		
Retained earnings	20		
	270	300	406
		Post acq'n reserves = 30	Post acq'n reserves = 136

Net assets (equity) – Charlie

	Acq'n	b/f	Rep date (c/f)
	$m	$m	$m
Share capital	150		
Retained earnings	30		
	180	200	306
		Post acq'n reserves = 20	Post acq'n reserves = 126

(W5) **NCI equity**

	b/f	c/f
	$m	$m
Bravo:		
NCI at acquisition at fair value	54.3	54.3
NCI% x post acquisition reserves (W4)		
(20% x 30)	6	
(20% x 136)		27.2
Charlie:		
NCI at acquisition at fair value	94.1	94.1
NCI% x post acquisition reserves (W4)		
(52% x 20)	10.4	
(52% x 126)		65.52
	164.8	241.12

(W6) **Parent's equity**

	b/f	c/f
	$m	$m
Alpha	400	504
Sub: P% x post acquisition reserves (W4)		
Bravo:		
(80% x 30)	24	
(80% x 136)		108.8
Charlie:		
(48% x 20)	9.6	
(48% x 126)		60.48
	433.6	673.28

Test your understanding 5 - Holdings

Consolidated statement of financial position as at 30 September 20X4

		$000
Property, plant and equipment	(1,000 + 700 + 225)	1,925
Goodwill	(70 + 120) (W3)	190
Current assets	(370 + 300 + 75)	745
		2,860
Equity		
Share capital		500
Retained earnings	(W5)	1,534
		2,034
Non-controlling interest	(240+ 86) (W4)	326
		2,360
Liabilities	(250 + 200 + 50)	500
		2,860

Workings

(W1) **Group structure**

		Holdings → →		
1 Oct 20X1	70%	↓	↓	
		Pepper	60%	1 Oct 20X1
1 Oct 20X1	20%	↓	↓	
		Salt ← ←		

Pepper will be consolidated as a 70% sub (NCI owning 30%) from 1 Oct 20X1.

Salt will be consolidated as a 74% sub (NCI owning 26%) from 1 Oct 20X1.

Holdings' direct ownership	60%
Holdings' indirect ownership (70% × 20%)	14%
	74%

(W2) **Net assets – Pepper**

	Acq'n	**Reporting date**
	$000	$000
Share capital	300	300
Retained earnings	100	550
	400	850

Post acq'n profits = 450

Net assets – Salt

	Acq'n	**Reporting date**
	$000	$000
Share capital	100	100
Retained earnings	50	150
	150	250

Post acq'n profits = 100

(W3) **Goodwill – Pepper**

	$000
Fair value of P's holding (COI)	350
NCI holding at proportion of net assets (30% x 400 (W2))	120
Fair value of sub's net assets at acquisition (W2)	(400)
Goodwill at acquisition/reporting date	70

Goodwill – Salt

	$000	$000
Fair value of P's holding (COI) – Direct		175
Fair value of P's holding (COI) – Indirect:		
Sub's cost of investment	50	
Less: IHA (30% x 50)	(15)	
		35
NCI holding at proportion of net assets (40% x 150 (W2))		60
Fair value of sub's net assets at acquisition (W2)		(150)
Goodwill at acquisition/reporting date		120

(W4) **Non-controlling interests - Pepper**

	$000
NCI holding at acquisition (W3)	120
NCI% x post acquisition reserves (30% x 450 (W2))	135
Less IHA (W3)	(15)
	240

Non-controlling interests - Salt

	$000
NCI holding at acquisition (W3)	60
NCI% x post acquisition reserves (26% x 100 (W2))	26
NCI at 31 Oct 20X3	86

(W5) **Retained earnings**

	$000
P's reserves	1,145
Sub: P% x post acquisition reserves	
Pepper: 70% x 450 (W2)	315
Salt: 74% x 100 (W2)	74
	1,534

Test your understanding 6 - Cavendish

Consolidated statement of financial position as at 31 December 20X2

		$000
Goodwill	(320 + 205) (W3)	525
Property, plant and equipment	(2,000 + 2,850 + 1,350)	6,200
Investments	(1,375 + 1,200 – 1,000 (W3) – 1,200 (W3) – 375 (W6))	–
Current assets	(225 + 350 + 950)	1,525
		8,250
Equity		
Share capital		1,500
Retained earnings	(W5)	1,021.3
		2,521.3
Non-controlling interest	(104 + 554.7) (W4)	658.7
		3,180
Non-current liabilities	(700 + 2,000 +350)	3,050
Current liabilities	(520 + 1,200 + 300)	2,020
		8,250

Workings

(W1) **Group structure**

		Cavendish	→ →	
1 Jan 20X1	70%	↓	↓	
		Wiggins	25%	1 Jan 20X1
1 Jan 20X2	60%	↓	↓	
		Millar	← ←	

Wiggins will be consolidated as a 70% sub (NCI owning 30%) from 1 Jan 20X1.

Millar will be consolidated as a 67% sub (NCI owning 33%) from 1 Jan 20X2.

Cavendish's direct ownership – 1 Jan 20X1	25%
Cavendish's indirect ownership – 1 Jan 20X2 (70% × 60%)	42%
	67%

Cavendish achieves control of Millar at the later date of 1 Jan 20X2 when Wiggins achieves control of Millar. Therefore this is a non-control to control step acquisition.

(W2) **Net assets – Wiggins**

	Acq'n		Reporting date
	$000		$000
Share capital	800		800
Retained earnings	320		400
	1,120		1,200
		Post acq'n profits = 80	

Net assets – Millar

	Acq'n		Reporting date
	$000		$000
Share capital	1,200		1,200
Retained earnings	360		450
	1,560		1,650
		Post acq'n profits = 90	

(W3) **Goodwill – Wiggins**

	$000
Fair value of P's holding (cost of investment)	1,000
NCI holding at fair value	440
Fair value of sub's net assets at acquisition (W2)	(1,120)
Goodwill at acquisition/ reporting date	320

Goodwill – Millar

	$000	$000
Fair value of P's holding (cost of investment)		
FV of previous 25%		400
Sub's COI in sub-sub	1,200	
IHA (30% x 1,200)	(360)	
		840
		1,240
NCI holding at fair value		525
Fair value of sub's net assets at acquisition (W2)		(1,560)
Goodwill at acquisition/reporting date		205

(W4) **Non-controlling interests – Wiggins**

	$000
NCI holding at acquisition (W3)	440
NCI% x post acquisition reserves (30% x 80 (W2))	24
IHA (W3)	(360)
	104

Non-controlling interests – Millar

	$000
NCI holding at acquisition (W3)	525
NCI% x post acquisition reserves (33% x 90 (W2))	29.7
	554.7

(W5) **Retained earnings**

	$000
P's reserves	880
Sub: P% x post acquisition reserves	
Wiggins: 70% x 80 (W2)	56
Millar: 67% x 90 (W2)	60.3
Gain on step acquisition (W6)	25
	1,021.3

(W6) **Step acquisition adjustment**

	$000	
Fair value of previous 25%	400	Increase (Dr) goodwill W3
Carrying value of previous 25% (cost)	(375)	Reduce (Cr) investments
Gain to profit	25	Increase (Cr) reserves W5

Test your understanding 7 - Poppy

Consolidated statement of financial position as at 31 May 20X8

		$000
Goodwill	(95 + 65) (W3)	160
Investments	(450 + 50 – 320 (W3) – 130 (W3) – 50 (W6))	–
Sundry assets	(300 + 500 + 260)	1,060
		1,220
Equity		
Share capital		400
Retained earnings (W5)		372
Other components		5
		777
NCI	(W4)	228
		1,005
Liabilities	(125 + 50 + 40)	215
		1,220

Workings

(W1)

```
                              Poppy → →
1 January 20X6  70%             ↓        ↓
                               Sage     60%  1 December 20X6
   31 May 20X8  20%             ↓        ↓
                              Thyme ← ←
```

Sage will be consolidated as a 70% sub (NCI owning 30%) from 1 January 20X6.

Thyme will be consolidated as a 60% sub (NCI owning 40%) from 1 December 20X6 and as a 74% sub (NCI owning 26%) from 31 May 20X8 (reporting date).

Direct	60%
Indirect (70% × 20%)	14%
	74%

Since Thyme is owned 60% at 1 December 20X6 this is a step acquisition control to control.

(W2) **Net assets – Sage**

	Acq'n	Reporting date
	$000	$000
Share capital	300	300
Retained earnings	50	200
	350	500

Post acq'n profits
= 150

Net assets – Thyme

	Acq'n		Reporting date
	$000		$000
Share capital	100		100
Retained earnings	50		120
	150		220
		Post acq'n profits = 70	

(W3) **Goodwill – Sage**

	$000
Fair value of P's holding (cost of investment)	320
NCI holding at fair value	125
Fair value of sub's net assets at acquisition (W2)	(350)
Goodwill at acquisition/reporting date	95

Goodwill – Thyme

	$000
Fair value of P's holding (cost of investment)	130
NCI holding at fair value	85
Fair value of sub's net assets at acquisition (W2)	(150)
Goodwill at acquisition/reporting date	65

(W4) **Non-controlling interests**

		$000
Sage	NCI holding at acquisition (W3)	125
	NCI% x post acquisition reserves (30% x 150 (W2))	45
	Less IHA (W6)	(15)
Thyme	NCI holding at acquisition (W3)	85
	NCI% x post acquisition reserves (40% x 70 (W2))	28
	Decrease in NCI (W6)	(40)
		228

(W5) **Retained earnings**

	$000
P's reserves	225
Sub: P% x post acquisition reserves	
Sage: 70% x 150 (W2)	105
Thyme: 60% x 70 (W2)	42
	372

(W6) **Decrease in NCI (control to control adjustment)**

		$000	
Decrease in NCI	((85 + 28) x 14/40)	40	Reduce W4
Cash paid		(50)	Reduce investments
IHA on cash paid	(30% x 50)	15	Reduce W4
Difference to other components of equity		5	Increase equity

Test your understanding 8 - ABC

Consolidated statement of financial position as at 30 June 20X6

	$000
Property, plant and equipment (9,300 + 3,600 + 4,250 + 250 (W2) – 50 (W2))	17,350
Goodwill (W3) (1,500 + 330)	1,830
Investments (10,000 + 4,000 – 6,000 (W3) – 4,000 (W3) – 1,000 (W6))	3,000
Current assets	
Inventory (1,750 + 700 + 400 – 60 (W7))	2,790
Receivables (1,050 + 550 + 420)	2,020
Cash (1,550 + 1,010 + 330)	2,890
	29,880
Equity	
Share capital	15,000
Retained earnings (W5)	4,156
Other components (W6)	(579.4)
	18,576.6
Non-controlling interest (1,872 + 2,271.4) (W4)	4,143.4
	22,720
Non-current liabilities (2,000 + 750 + 250)	3,000
Current liabilities (2,500 + 1,380 + 280)	4,160
	29,880

Workings

(W1) **Group structure**

```
                     A →   →
1 July 20X5   60%    ↓     ↓
                     B    10%   30 June 20X6
1 July 20X5   60%    ↓     ↓
                     C ←   ←
```

B will be consolidated as a 60% sub (NCI owning 40%) from 1 July 20X5.

C will be consolidated as a 36% sub (NCI owning 64%) from 1 July 20X5 and as a 46% sub (NCI owning 54%) from 30 June 20X6.

A's indirect ownership – 1 July 20X5 (60% x 60%)	36%
A's direct ownership – 30 June 20X6	10%
	46%

A achieves control of C at the earlier date of 1 July 20X5 when B achieves control of C. Therefore the additional 10% shares acquired at the reporting date represent a control to control acquisition, i.e. decrease in the NCI.

(W2) **Net assets – B**

	Acq'n	**Reporting date**
	$000	$000
Share capital	7,000	7,000
Retained earnings	500	730
Fair value adjustment	250	250
Depreciation adjustment (250 x 1/5)		(50)
	7,750	7,930

Post acq'n profits = 180

Net assets – C

	Acq'n	**Reporting date**
	$000	$000
Share capital	4,000	4,000
Retained earnings	570	870
	4,570	4,870

Post acq'n profits = 300

(W3) **Goodwill – B**

	$000
Fair value of P's holding (cost of investment)	6,000
NCI holding at fair value	3,500
Fair value of sub's net assets at acquisition (W2)	(7,750)
Goodwill at acquisition	1,750
Impairment	(250)
Goodwill at reporting date	1,500

Goodwill – C

	$000	$000
Sub's COI in sub-sub	4,000	
IHA (40% x 4,000)	(1,600)	
Fair value of P's holding (cost of investment)		2,400
NCI holding at fair value		2,500
Fair value of sub's net assets at acquisition (W2)		(4,570)
Goodwill at acquisition / reporting date		330

(W4) **Non-controlling interests – B**

	$000
NCI holding at acquisition (W3)	3,500
NCI% x post acquisition reserves (40% x 180 (W2))	72
NCI% x impairment loss (40% x 250 (W3))	(100)
IHA (W3)	(1,600)
	1,872

Non-controlling interests – C

	$000
NCI holding at acquisition (W3)	2,500
NCI% x post acquisition reserves (64% x 300 (W2))	192
	2,692
Decrease in NCI (W6)	(420.6)
	2,271.4

(W5) **Retained earnings**

	$000
P's reserves	4,150
PUP (W7)	(60)
Sub: P% x post acquisition reserves	
B: 60% x 180 (W2)	108
C: 36% x 300 (W2)	108
Impairment: P% x impairment loss	
B: 60% x 250 (W3)	(150)
	4,156

(W6) **Decrease in NCI (control to control adjustment)**

	$000	
Decrease in NCI (10/64 x 2,692 (W4))	420.6	Reduce W4
Cash paid	(1,000)	Reduce investments
Difference to other components of equity - decrease	(579.4)	

(W7) **PUP**

	$000
Profit in inventory (20/120 x 360)	60

Test your understanding 9 - Hitchcock

Consolidated statement of comprehensive income for the year ended 30 April 20X3

	$m
Revenue (120 + 84 + 80)	284
Operating costs (83 + 67 + 55 + 5 (W3))	(210)
Gain on step acquisition (W5)	12
Profit before tax	86
Tax (12 + 7 + 10)	(29)
Profit for the year	57
Other comprehensive income (10 + 6 + 0)	16
Total comprehensive income	73
Profit attributable to:	
Parent shareholders	50.45
NCI shareholders (W4) (1 + 5.55)	6.55
	57
Profit attributable to:	
Parent shareholders	65.25
NCI shareholders (W4) (2.2 + 5.55)	7.75
	73

Workings

(W1) Group structure

	Hitchcock	→ →	
1 May 20X1 80%	↓	↓	
	Spencer	15%	1 May 20X1
1 May 20X2 60%	↓	↓	
	Spooner	← ←	

Spencer will be an 80% sub (NCI owning 20%) from 1 May 20X1.

Spooner will be a 63% sub (NCI owning 37%) from 1 May 20X2.

Hitchcock's direct ownership – 1 May 20X1	15%
Hitchcock's indirect ownership – 1 May 20X2 (80% × 60%)	48%
	63%

Hitchcock acquires control of Spooner on 1 May 20X2. This is therefore a step acquisition of non-control to control and a gain is recognised in the income statement.

(W2) **Net assets – Spencer**

	Acq'n
	$000
Share capital	30
Retained earnings	30
	60

(W3) **Goodwill impairment – Spencer**

	$000
Fair value of P's holding (cost of investment)	70
NCI holding at fair value	15
Fair value of sub's net assets at acquisition (W2)	(60)
Goodwill at acquisition	25
Impairment (20% x 25)	5

(W4) **NCI share of profits/ TCI**

		$m	$m
Spencer			
Profit for the year		10	
Impairment (W3)		(5)	
		5	
NCI%	x 20%		1
OCI		6	
		11	
NCI%	x 20%		2.2
		$m	$m
Spooner			
Profit for the year/ TCI		15	
NCI%	x 37%		5.55

(W5) **Step acquisition adjustment**

Fair value of previous 15%	25	Increase goodwill W3
Carrying value of previous 15% (cost)	(13)	Reduce investments
Gain to profit	12	Increase reserves W5

chapter

9

Foreign currency translation

Chapter learning objectives

On completion of their studies students should be able to:

- Explain foreign currency translation principles, including the difference between the closing rate/net investment method and the historical rate method;
- Apply foreign currency translation to overseas transactions and investments in overseas subsidiaries.

1 Session content

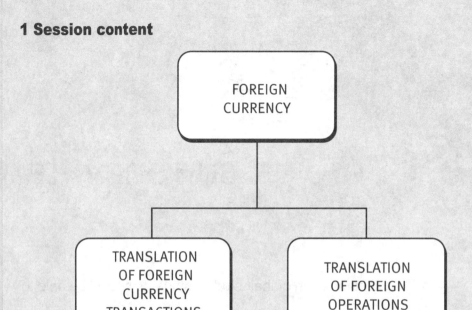

2 IAS 21 The effects of changes in exchange rates

IAS 21 deals with:

- the definition of functional and presentation currencies
- accounting for individual transactions in a foreign currency
- translating the financial statements of a foreign operation

3 Functional and presentation currencies

The **functional currency** is the currency of the primary economic environment in which the entity operates. In most cases this will be the local currency.

An entity should consider the following when determining its functional currency:

- The currency that mainly influences sales prices for goods and services
- The currency of the country whose competitive forces and regulations mainly determine the sales prices of goods and services
- The currency that mainly influences labour, material and other costs of providing goods and services

The following factors may also be considered:

- The currency in which funding from issuing debt and equity is generated
- The currency in which receipts from operating activities are usually retained

The entity maintains its day-to-day financial records in its functional currency.

The **presentation currency** is the currency in which the entity presents its financial statements. This can be different from the functional currency, particularly if the entity in question is a foreign owned subsidiary. It may have to present its financial statements in the currency of its parent, even though that is different to its own functional currency.

4 Translation of foreign currency transactions

Where an entity enters into a transaction denominated in a currency other than its functional currency, that transaction must be translated into the functional currency before it is recorded.

Examples of foreign currency transactions

Whenever a business enters into a contract where the consideration is expressed in a foreign currency, it is necessary to translate that foreign currency amount into the functional currency for inclusion in its own accounts. Examples include:

- imports of raw materials;
- exports of finished goods;
- importation of foreign manufactured non-current assets;
- investments in foreign securities;
- raising an overseas loan.

Initial recognition

- The transaction will initially be recorded by applying the spot exchange rate, i.e. the exchange rate at the date of the transaction.

Subsequent measurement – settled transactions

When cash settlement occurs, for example payment by a receivable, the settled amount should be translated using the spot exchange rate on the settlement date.

If this amount differs from that recorded when the transaction occurred, there will be an exchange difference which is taken to the income statement in the period in which it arises.

Example 1

A company based in the US sells goods to the UK for £200,000 on 28 February 20X3 when the exchange rate was £0.55: $1.

The customer pays in April 20X3 when the rate was £0.60:$1.

Required:

How does the US company account for the transaction in its financial statements for the year ended 31 July 20X3?

Example 1 answer

On the sale:

Translate the sale at the spot rate prevailing on the transaction date.

£200,000/ 0.55 = $363,636

		$
Dr	Receivables	363,636
Cr	Sales	363,636

When the cash is received:

Dollar value of cash received = £200,000/ 0.60 = $333,333

Loss on transaction = 363,636 – 333,333= 30,303

		$
Dr	Bank	333,333
Cr	Receivables	363,636
Dr	Income statement (loss)	30,303

Test your understanding 1

Butler, whose functional currency is the $, has a year end of 31 December. On 27 November 20X6 Butler buys goods from a Swedish supplier for SwK 324,000.

On 19 December 20X6 Butler pays the Swedish supplier in full.

Exchange rates are as follows:

27 November 20X6 $1 = SwK 11.15

19 December 20X6 $1 = SwK 10.93

Required:

Show the accounting entries for these transactions for the year ended 31 December 20X6.

Subsequent measurement – unsettled transactions

The treatment of any 'foreign' items remaining in the statement of financial position at the year end will depend on whether they are classified as monetary or non-monetary.

Monetary items	**Non-monetary items**
Currency held and assets or liabilities to be received or paid in currency.	Other items in the statement of financial position.
E.g. cash, receivables, payables, loans	E.g. non-current assets, inventory, investments
Treatment: Retranslate using the closing rate (year end exchange rate)	*Treatment:* Do not translate i.e. leave at historic rate

Any exchange difference arising on the retranslation of monetary items must be taken to the income statement in the period in which it arises.

Example 2

A US company sells apples to a company based in Moldovia where the currency is the Moldovian pound (Mol). The apples were sold on 1 October 20X1 for Mol 200,000 and were paid for in February 20X2.

The rate on 1 October 20X1 is US $1: Mol 1.55.

The rate on 31 December 20X1 (the reporting date) is US $1: Mol 1.34.

Required:

How does the US company account for the transaction in its financial statements for the year ended 31 December 20X1?

Example 2 answer

On the sale:

Translate the sale at the spot rate prevailing on the transaction date.

Mol 200,000/ 1.55 = $129,032

		$
Dr	Receivables	129,032
Cr	Sales	129,032

At the reporting date:

The receivables balance is a monetary item and so must be retranslated using the closing rate.

Mol 200,000/ 1.34 = $149,254

Gain = 149,254 – 129,032 = 20,222

		$
Dr	Receivables	20,222
Cr	Income statement (gain)	20,222

Test your understanding 2

On 15 March 20X1 an entity, whose functional currency is the $, purchases a non-current asset on one month's credit for KR20,000.

Exchange rates

15 March 20X1	KR5 : $1
31 March 20X1	KR4 : $1

Required:

(a) Explain and illustrate how the transaction is recorded and dealt with given a financial year end of 31 March 20X1.

The following transactions were undertaken by Jeyes, whose functional currency is the $, in the accounting year ended 31 December 20X1.

Date	**Narrative**	**Amount KR**
1 January 20X1	Purchase of a non-current asset on credit	100,000
31 March 20X1	Payment for the non-current asset	100,000
	Purchases on credit	50,000
30 June 20X1	Sales on credit	95,000
30 September 20X1	Payment for purchases	50,000
30 November 20X1	Long-term loan taken out	200,000

Exchange rates	**KR : $**
1 January 20X1	2.0 : 1
31 March 20X1	2.3 : 1
30 June 20X1	2.1 : 1
30 September 20X1	2.0 : 1
30 November 20X1	1.8 : 1
31 December 20X1	1.9 : 1

Required:

(b) Prepare journal entries to record the above transactions for the year ended 31 December 20X1.

5 Translating the financial statements of a foreign operation

If the functional currency of a subsidiary is different to the presentation currency of the parent company, it will be necessary to translate the subsidiary's financial statements into the parent's presentation currency prior to consolidation.

This is done using the 'closing rate' or 'net investment' method and the following exchange rates should be used in the translation:

Income statement/ statement of comprehensive income

- Income and expenses – average rate for the year

Statement of financial position

- Assets and liabilities – closing rate i.e. the rate at the reporting date
- Goodwill of subsidiary – closing rate

Exchange gains or losses on translation

There will be exchange gains or losses on the translation of the subsidiary's financial statements from its functional currency to the parent's presentation currency. This is because balances are translated at different rates at different times.

For example, an asset such as land in last year's statement of financial position was translated at last year's closing rate, i.e. this year's opening rate. However, the same asset in this year's statement of financial position will be translated at this year's closing rate. An exchange gain or loss therefore arises. This principle would continue to all of the subsidiary's net assets in last year's statement of financial position, i.e. this year's opening net assets. Further discussion of the other exchange gains or losses arising is below.

The foreign exchange gains/losses arising are recorded in equity. They are unrealised gains/losses and would only be recycled through profit or loss upon disposal of the subsidiary (i.e. when they become realised).

Most of the exchange gains/losses are captured automatically by following the standard workings and the approach outlined above. If preparing a consolidated statement of financial position however, it will be necessary to calculate the exchange gain/loss arising on the cost of the investment in W3 and carry this through to W5. Note that this is a consequence of using the standard working approach. The examiner's method is slightly different (as mentioned in chapter 4) and when reviewing the examiner solutions you will therefore find that this cost of investment adjustment is not reflected in the reserves working.

Exchange differences generated in the current year only will need reporting in the other comprehensive section of the consolidated statement of comprehensive income (CSCI). This is because they are gains/losses that have been recorded directly within equity. You will therefore need to be familiar with the full calculation of exchange gains/losses for the year for the purposes of a CSCI question or if you are asked to prepare a consolidated statement of changes in equity.

Exchange differences in reserves

Exchange differences that have arisen since acquisition can be summarised into three categories:

1	Net assets at acquisition	acquisition rate to closing rate
2	Post-acquisition profits	average rates to closing rate
3	Goodwill	acquisition rate to closing rate

Differences on net assets at acquisition and post-acquisition profits are shared by non-controlling interests and the parent. Differences on goodwill are borne by the parent only if the proportionate goodwill method is used or by both parent and NCI if the full goodwill method is applied.

In the above approach, because all of the financial position items are translated at closing rate, some of the above exchange differences are automatically included in W5. The only exchange difference that will not be included will be the gain or loss arising on the cost of the investment (part of the goodwill exchange difference). It is therefore necessary for you to include this within W5.

The following test your understandings illustrate this point.

Foreign exchange gains/losses included within other comprehensive income

A question may require you to produce a consolidated statement of comprehensive income or consolidated statement of changes in equity and to therefore show the foreign exchange gain/ loss arising during the year.

The exchange gain/loss will be made up of:

Opening net assets	Opening rate v Closing rate
Profit for the year	Average rate v. Closing rate
Opening goodwill	Opening rate v Closing rate

In order to calculate the exchange differences for the year, calculate the following:

Illustration 1 - Foreign exchange differences for the year

			Parent s/h	NCI s/h
		$	$	$
Opening net assets of subsidiary (= equity brought forward)	@ closing rate	X		
	@ opening rate	(X)		
Gain/(loss)		X/(X)	X/(X)	X/(X)
Profit for year of subsidiary	@ closing rate	X		
	@ average rate	(X)		
Gain/(loss)		X/(X)	X/(X)	X/(X)
Opening goodwill	@ closing rate	X		
	@ opening rate	(X)		
Gain/(loss)		X/(X)		
Proportion of net assets method: P s/h only			X/(X)	
Fair value method: P s/h and NCI s/h (see below)			X/(X)	X/(X)
Total gains/losses for year			X/(X)	X/(X)

Exchange gain/loss on goodwill:

Under the proportion of net assets method, the gain/loss is borne entirely by the parent shareholders.

Under the fair value method, the gain/loss is borne by both the parent and NCI shareholders. However it is not necessarily shared in the same ratio that they own the subsidiary. To calculate the ratio in which the gain/loss should be allocated, it is necessary to consider the following:

Difference between FV method and proportionate method of goodwill:

NCI at acquisition at fair value	X
NCI at acquisition at proportion of net assets	(X)
NCI s/h element of goodwill	X
Parent s/h element of goodwill (balance)	X
Total goodwill at acquisition	X

6 Approach to a question

In a question it is recommended that you take the following approach:

Consolidated income statement (down to profit for the year)

(1) Translate the subsidiary's income and expenses at the *average rate* for the year.

(2) Record any adjustments translated at the *average rate,* e.g. impairments, PUPs, fair value adjustments.

(3) Add across the parent and subsidiary's figures in dollars to calculate the consolidated totals.

(4) Calculate profit for the year attributable to NCI in the same way as usual, i.e. NCI% multiplied by the subsidiary's translated and adjusted profit for the year.

Consolidated statement of financial position (CSFP)

(1) Prepare W1 Group structure.

(2) Translate the subsidiary's assets and liabilities on the face of the CSFP, e.g. Current assets (P + (S translated at *closing rate*) + (fair value adjustments at *closing rate*)).

(3) Add the parent's share capital only.

(4) Prepare **W2** Net assets of the subsidiary in the subsidiary's **functional currency**, reflecting any fair value adjustments or PUPs if the subsidiary is the seller.

(5) Prepare **W3** Goodwill in the **functional currency and then translate** to dollars using the *closing rate*. Also calculate the exchange gain or loss on the cost of investment as the difference between the cost of investment at the acquisition rate compared to the cost of investment at the closing rate. This exchange difference is taken to W5.

(6) Prepare **W4** Non-controlling interests in the **functional currency and then translate** to dollars at the *closing rate*.

(7) Prepare **W5** Group reserves in the **presentation currency** (dollars) as follows:

	$
Parent reserves	X
Share of subsidiary's post acquisition reserves (P's % x ((net assets at reporting date (W2) – net assets at acquisition (W2)) translated at closing rate))	X
Less: impairments (translated at closing rate)	(X)
Exchange gain/loss on cost of investment (W3)	X/(X)
	X

Note that W5 above is entitled group reserves (rather than group retained earnings). In practice, the unrealised exchange gain/loss arising each year would be recorded in a separate reserve - and would contain more than just the re-translation of the cost of investment, as reflected in illustration 1. The above is an acceptable exam adapted approach to answering questions.

Foreign exchange gains/losses (other comprehensive income)

(1) Use the proforma in illustration 1 above to calculate the exchange gains/losses for the year and split them between parent and NCI shareholders accordingly.

(2) The total exchange gain/loss arising will be reported in "other comprehensive income".

(3) Total comprehensive income is then split as being attributable to parent shareholders and NCI shareholders. The amount attributable to NCI shareholders will be the profit for the year attributable to the NCI (already calculated) plus/minus the NCI share of the total exchange gain/loss. Total comprehensive income attributable to parent shareholders can be calculated as a balancing figure.

Consolidated statement of changes in equity

(1) Add the comprehensive income from the statement of comprehensive income split between parent and NCI shareholders.

(2) Deduct any dividends paid by the parent and the NCI share of any subsidiary dividends.

(3) Calculate NCI brought forward in a similar way to CSFP W4, i.e. in the functional currency and then translating at the *opening rate*.

(4) Calculate equity attributable to parent shareholders brought forward in a similar way to CSFP W5 adding the parent's share capital. Remember to translate the subsidiary's post acquisition profits (up to the brought forward date) at the opening rate. You will need to recalculate the foreign exchange gain/loss on the cost of investment by comparing it at the acquisition rate to the *opening rate*.

Example 3

P acquired 75% of the share capital of S on 1 January 20X5 for 500,000Fr, when the retained earnings of S were 120,000Fr.

Statements of financial position at 31 December 20X6

	P	S
	$000	Fr000
Non-current assets	1,250	850
Investment in S	100	–
Current assets	325	150
	1,675	1,000
Share capital	700	250
Reserves	675	350
Liabilities	300	400
	1,675	1,000

Statements of comprehensive income for the year ended 31 December 20X6 (summarised)

	P	S
	$000	Fr000
Revenue	600	150
Expenses	(475)	(90)
Profit after tax	125	60
Other comprehensive income	–	–
Total comprehensive income	125	60

Statement of changes in equity for the year ended 31 December 20X6

	P	S
	$000	Fr000
Balance brought forward	1,300	540
Comprehensive income	125	60
Dividends	(50)	–
Balance carried forward	1,375	600

Exchange rates:

1 January 2005	$1 = 5Fr
31 December 2005	$1 = 4.2Fr
31 December 2006	$1 = 4.5Fr
Average for the year ended 31 December 2005	$1 = 4.6Fr
Average for the year ended 31 December 2006	$1 = 4.4Fr

P has a policy of measuring NCI at acquisition at fair value. The fair value of the NCI holding in S at acquisition was 160,000Fr. The goodwill has been impaired by 10% in the year ended 31 December 20X5 and a further 10% of its book value in the current year.

Required:

(a) Prepare the consolidated statement of financial position and consolidated statement of comprehensive income for the year ended 31 December 20X6.

(b) Prepare the consolidated statement of changes in equity for the year ended 31 December 20X6.

Note: Work to the nearest $100.

Example 3 answer

Prepare the consolidated statement of financial position first and follow the steps provided in section 6.

(1) Prepare W1 Group structure

Workings

(W1) **Group structure**

P
|
75%
|
S

(2) Translate the subsidiary's assets and liabilities on the face of the CSFP using the closing rate of 4.5. This applies to non-current assets, current assets and liabilities.

(3) Add in P's share capital of $700,000.

P Group consolidated statement of financial position at 31 December 20X6

	$000
Goodwill (W3)	
Non-current assets	
(1,250 + (850/ 4.5))	1,438.9
Current assets	
(325 + (150/ 4.5))	358.3
	–––––
	–––––
Share capital	700
Reserves (W5)	
Non-controlling interests (W4)	
Liabilities	
(300 + (400/ 4.5))	388.9
	–––––
	–––––

(4) Prepare **W2** Net assets of the subsidiary in the subsidiary's **functional currency**. There are no adjustments to deal with in this question.

(5) Prepare **W3** Goodwill in the **functional currency and then translate** to dollars using the *closing rate of 4.5.*

Also calculate the exchange gain or loss on the cost of investment as the difference between the cost of investment at the acquisition rate (5) compared to the cost of investment at the closing rate (4.5). This exchange gain of 11.1 is taken to W5.

(W2) **Net assets of subsidiary**

	Acquisition date	**Reporting date**
	Fr000	Fr000
Share capital	250	250
Reserves	120	350
	370	600

(W3) **Goodwill**

	Fr000
Fair value of Ps holding (cost of investment)	500
NCI holding at fair value	160
Fair value of sub's net assets at acquisition (W2)	(370)
Goodwill at acquisition	290
Impairment year ended 31 Dec 20X5 (10% x 290)	(29)
Gross goodwill at 31 December 20X5	261
Impairment year ended 31 Dec 20X6 (10% x 261)	(26.1)
Goodwill at reporting date	234.9
Translate at closing rate of 4.5	$52.2

Foreign exchange gain/ loss on cost of investment (COI)

	$
COI at closing rate (Fr 500,000 / 4.5)	111.1
COI at acquisition rate (Fr 500,000 / 5)	100
Exchange gain to W5	11.1

(6) Prepare **W4** Non-controlling interests in the **functional currency (Fr)and then translate** to dollars at the *closing rate of 4.5.*

(7) Prepare **W5** Retained earnings in the **presentation currency** (dollars).

(W4) **Non-controlling interests**

	Fr000
NCI at acquisition (W3)	160
NCI% x post acquisition reserves (25% x (600 – 370 (W2)))	57.5
NCI% x impairment loss (25% x (29 + 26.1 (W3)))	(13.8)
	203.7
Translate at closing rate of 4.5	$45.3

(W5) **Reserves**

	$000
P	675
S: (75% x (600 – 370 (W2) / 4.5)	38.3
Impairment (75% x ((29 + 26.1)/ 4.5))	(9.2)
Gain on COI (W3)	11.1
	715.2

Complete the consolidated statement of financial position with the figures from W3, W4 and W5.

P Group consolidated statement of financial position at 31 December 20X6

	$000
Goodwill (W3)	52.2
Non-current assets (1,250 + (850/ 4.5))	1,438.9
Current assets (325 + (150/ 4.5))	358.3
	1,849.4

Share capital	700
Reserves (W5)	715.2
Non-controlling interests (W4)	45.3
Payables	
(300 + (400/4.5))	388.9
	1,849.4

Now complete the consolidated statement of comprehensive income down to profit for the year split between parent and NCI shareholders.

P Group consolidated statement of comprehensive income for the year ended 31 December 20X6

	$000
Revenue (600 + (150/4.4))	634.1
Expenses (475 + (90 + 26.1 (W3)) /4.4)	(501.4)
Profit for the year	132.7
Other comprehensive income	
Items that may be reclassified subsequently to profit or loss:	
Foreign exchange gains	
Total comprehensive income	
Profit for the year attributable to:	
Non-controlling interest (25% x (60 – 26.1 (W3)) /4.4))	1.9
Parent shareholders (balance)	130.8
	132.7
Total comprehensive income attributable to:	
Non-controlling interest	
Parent shareholders (balance)	

You can also prepare the proforma for the consolidated statement of changes in equity and then we can complete the CSOCE workings and the calculation of the exchange gain or loss for the current year.

P Group consolidated statement of changes in equity for the year ended 31 December 20X6

	Parent shareholders	NCI shareholders
	$000	$000
Balance brought forward (W7, W6)		
Comprehensive income		
Dividends paid (parent only)	(50)	–
Balance carried forward per CSFP	1,415.2	45.3

Follow the approach given in section 6 for the CSOCE workings.

- Calculate NCI brought forward in a similar way to CSFP W4, i.e. in the functional currency and then translating at the *opening rate of 4.2.*
- Calculate equity attributable to parent shareholders brought forward in a similar way to CSFP W5. Start with P's equity b/f per its individual SOCE which includes P's share capital plus retained earnings b/f. The impairment is in Francs so must be translated at the opening rate.

(W6) **NCI equity b/f**

	Fr000
NCI holding at acquisition (W3)	160
NCI% x post acquisition reserves (25% x (540 – 370 (W2)))	42.5
NCI% x impairment loss (25% x 29 (W3))	(7.3)
	195.2
Translate at opening rate of 4.2	$46.5

(W7) **Parent shareholders equity b/f**

	$000
P	1,300
S: (75% x (540 – 370) (W2) / 4.2)	30.4
Impairment b/f (75% x (29/ 4.2))	(5.2)
Gain on COI to b/f date (W8)	19
	1,344.2

(W8) **Foreign exchange gain/ loss on COI brought forward**

	$
COI @ b/f rate (Fr 500,000 / 4.2)	119
COI @ acq rate (Fr 500,000 / 5)	100
Gain for W7	19

P Group consolidated statement of changes in equity for the year ended 31 December 2005

	Parent shareholders $000	NCI shareholders $000
Balance brought forward (W7, W6)	1,344.2	46.5
Comprehensive income		
Dividends paid (parent only)	(50)	–
Balance carried forward	1,415.2	45.3

The final working is to calculate the foreign exchange gain/loss for the current year to be included in the statement of comprehensive income and therefore flow through to the CSOCE.

(W9) **Foreign exchange gains**

		$000		**P s/h**	**NCI s/h**
				75%	**25%**
				$000	$000
Opening net assets (=equity b/f)	540				
@ cl. rate	4.5	120			
@ op. rate	4.2	(128.6)			
Loss		(8.6)		(6.45)	(2.15)
Profit for the year (60 – 26.1 impairment)	33.9				
@ cl. rate	4.5	7.5			
@ av. rate	4.4	7.7			
Loss		(0.2)		(0.15)	(0.05)
Opening goodwill	261 (W3)				
@ cl. rate	4.5	58			
@ op. rate	4.2	(62.1)			
Loss		(4.1)			
Split 222.5:67.5 (see below)				(3.15)	(0.95)
Total losses		(12.9)		(9.8)	(3.1)

Difference between fair value method and proportion of net assets method of goodwill:

	Fr000
NCI at acquisition at fair value	160
NCI at acquisition at proportion of net assets (25% x 370 (W2))	(92.5)
NCI s/h element of goodwill	67.5
Parent s/h element of goodwill (balance)	222.5
Total goodwill at acquisition (W3)	290

Goodwill is therefore split in a ratio of 222.5 : 67.5 to P shareholders and NCI shareholders and so this is the ratio in which they share the foreign exchange loss on goodwill.

P Group consolidated statement of comprehensive income for the year ended 31 December 20X6

	$000
Revenue (600 + (150 / 4.4))	634.1
Expenses (475 + (90 + 26.1 (W3)) / 4.4))	(501.4)
Profit for the year	132.7
Other comprehensive income	
Items that may be reclassified subsequently to profit or loss:	
Foreign exchange losses (W9)	(12.9)
Total comprehensive income	119.8
Profit for the year attributable to:	
Non-controlling interest (25% x (60 – 26.1 (W3)) / 4.4))	1.9
Parent shareholders (balance)	130.8
	132.7
Total comprehensive income attributable to:	
Non-controlling interest (1.9 – 3.1 (W9))	(1.2)
Parent shareholders (balance)	121.0
	119.8

P Group consolidated statement of changes in equity for the year ended 31 December 2005

	Parent shareholders	NCI shareholders
	$000	$000
Balance brought forward (W7, W6)	1,344.2	46.5
Comprehensive income	121.0	(1.2)
Dividends paid (parent only)	(50)	–
Balance carried forward	1,415.2	45.3

Test your understanding 3 - Paul and Simon

Paul is an entity whose functional and presentational currency is the dollar ($). On 1 January 20X7, Paul acquired 80% of the share capital of Simon, an entity whose functional currency is the Franc. Simon's reserves at this date showed a balance of Fr4,000. Paul paid Fr21,000 for the investment in Simon.

Below are the financial statements of Paul and Simon for the year ended 31 December 20X8.

Statements of financial position at 31 December 20X8

	Paul	Simon
	$	Fr
Non-current assets	60,000	25,000
Investment in Simon	4,200	
Current assets	35,800	15,000
	100,000	40,000
Equity		
Share capital	50,000	15,000
Reserves	20,000	14,000
	70,000	29,000
Current liabilities	30,000	11,000
	100,000	40,000

Statements of comprehensive income for the year ended 31 December 20X8

	Paul	Simon
	$	Fr
Revenue	25,000	10,000
Operating expenses	(10,000)	(4,000)
Operating profit	15,000	6,000
Finance costs	(5,000)	(1,500)
Profit before tax	10,000	4,500
Tax	(3,000)	(1,000)
Profit for the year	7,000	3,500
Other comprehensive income	–	–
Total comprehensive income	7,000	3,500

Statements of changes in equity for the year ended 31 December 20X8

	Paul	Simon
	$	Fr
Equity brought forward	64,000	25,500
Comprehensive income	7,000	3,500
Dividends paid	(1,000)	–
Equity carried forward	70,000	29,000

Exchanges rates have been as follows:

	Fr: $1
1 January 20X7	5
31 December 20X7	3
31 December 20X8	2
Average for the year ended 31 December 20X8	2.5

It is Paul's policy to measure NCI at fair value at the date of acquisition and the fair value of the non-controlling interest in Simon was deemed to be Fr4,500 at this date. Goodwill had been reviewed for impairment as at 31 December 20X7 but none had arisen. At 31 December 20X8, it was determined that goodwill should be impaired by Fr1,000.

Required:

Prepare the consolidated statement of financial position, consolidated statement of comprehensive income and consolidated statement of changes in equity for the year ended 31 December 20X8.

Test your understanding 4 - North

North is an entity incorporated in Asia. North has a subsidiary, South, that is located in Africa and prepares its financial statements under local accounting standards. South prepares its financial statements in African Francs (Afr). Financial information relating to the two entities for the financial year ended 30 September 20X4 is given below:

Statements of financial position at 30 September 20X4

	North		**South**	
	$m	$m	Afrm	Afrm
Non-current assets				
Property, plant and equipment	107		164	
Investments	60		–	
		167		164
Current assets				
Inventories	70		50	
Receivables	65		60	
Cash and bank balances	25		12	
		160		122
		327		286

Equity				
Share capital ($1/Afr1 shares)	100		60	
Reserves	127		89	
		227		149
Non-current liabilities		65		72
Current liabilities		35		65
		327		286

Statements of comprehensive income for the year ended 30 September 20X4

	North	South
	$m	Afrm
Revenue	200	240
Cost of sales	(120)	(145)
Gross profit	80	95
Other operating expenses	(35)	(40)
Profit from operations	45	55
Intra-group investment income	4.5	–
Finance cost	(7.5)	(10)
Profit before tax	42	45
Income tax expense	(10)	(15)
Profit for the year	32	30
Other comprehensive income	–	–
Total comprehensive income	32	30

Statements of changes in equity for the year ended 30 September 20X4

	North	South
	$m	Afrm
Balance at 1 October 20X3	211	134
Comprehensive income	32	30
Dividends paid	(16)	(15)
Balance at 30 September 20X4	227	149

Notes to the financial statements

Note 1 On 1 October 20X1, when the retained earnings of South were Afr38 million, North purchased 45 million shares in South for Afr4.00 each. At this date a non-current asset in the books of South with a carrying value of Afr50 million was deemed to have a fair value of Afr80 million. This asset had a remaining life of 10 years at this time and depreciation is charged to cost of sales. It is the North group's policy to measure NCI at acquisition at their proportionate share of the fair value of net assets.

Note 2 South paid its dividend on 30 June 20X4.

Note 3 Exchange rates on relevant dates were:

Date	Exchange rate Afr to $1
1 October 20X1	3.00
30 September 20X3	2.70
30 June 20X4	2.50
30 September 20X4	2.40

The weighted average exchange rate for the year ended 30 September 20X4 was Afr2.5 = $1.

Required:

(a) Prepare the consolidated statement of financial position of North at 30 September 20X4.

(b) Prepare the consolidated statement of comprehensive income of North for the year ended 30 September 20X4.

(c) Prepare a consolidated statement of changes in equity for the year ended 30 September 20X4.

You should prepare all computations to the nearest $100,000.

7 Chapter summary

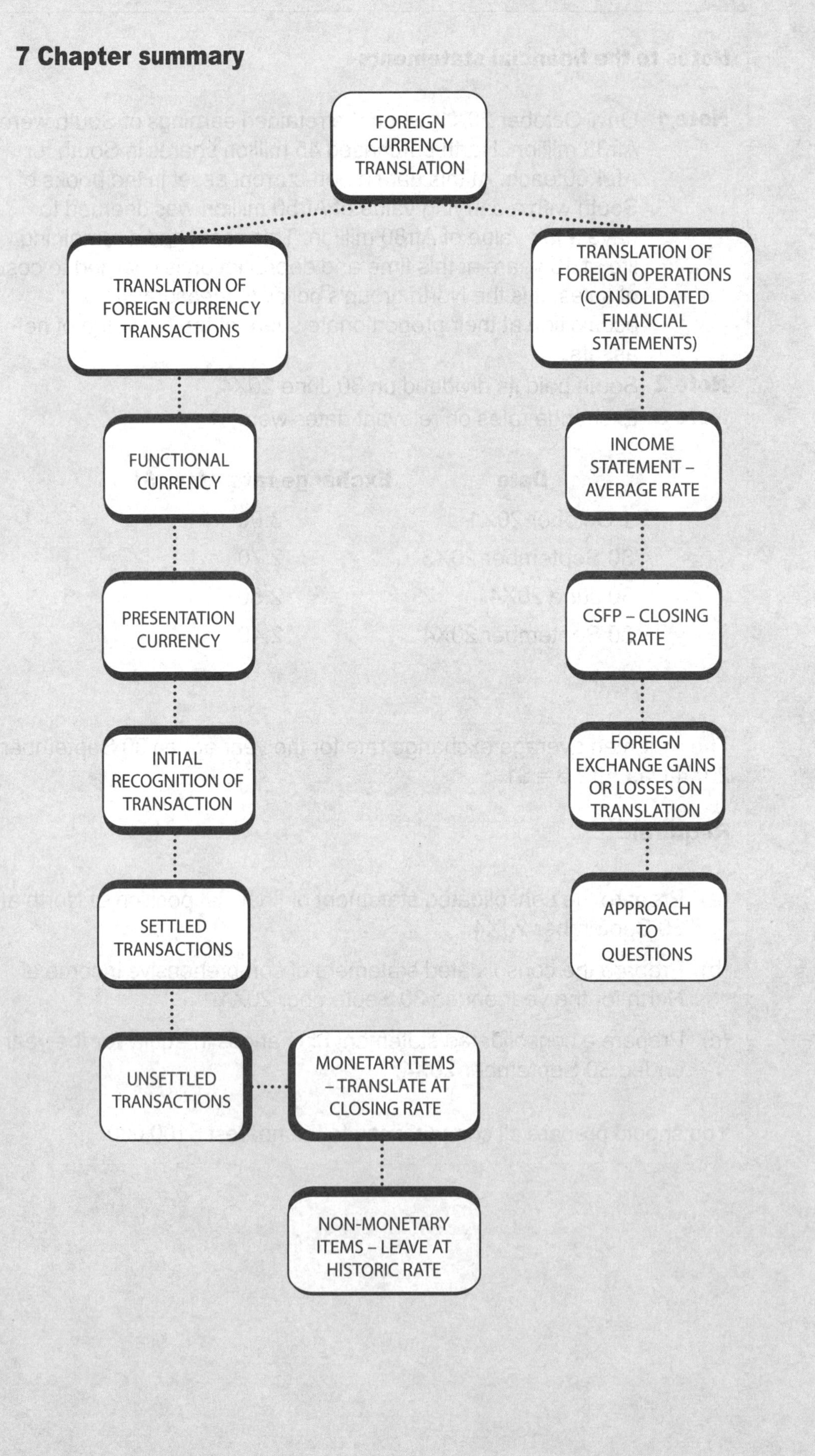
FOREIGN CURRENCY TRANSLATION
TRANSLATION OF FOREIGN CURRENCY TRANSACTIONS
TRANSLATION OF FOREIGN OPERATIONS (CONSOLIDATED FINANCIAL STATEMENTS)
FUNCTIONAL CURRENCY
PRESENTATION CURRENCY
INTIAL RECOGNITION OF TRANSACTION
SETTLED TRANSACTIONS
UNSETTLED TRANSACTIONS
MONETARY ITEMS – TRANSLATE AT CLOSING RATE
NON-MONETARY ITEMS – LEAVE AT HISTORIC RATE
INCOME STATEMENT – AVERAGE RATE
CSFP – CLOSING RATE
FOREIGN EXCHANGE GAINS OR LOSSES ON TRANSLATION
APPROACH TO QUESTIONS

Test your understanding answers

Test your understanding 1

Translate transaction at the spot rate prior to recording:
324,000 / 11.15 = $29,058

27 November 20X6

Dr Purchases	$29,058
Cr Payables	$29,058

19 December 20X6

SwK 324,000 is paid.
At 19 December rate this is:
324,000 / 10.93 = $29,643

Dr Payables	$29,058 (being the payable created on 27 November)
Dr Income statement	$585
Cr Cash	$29,643

$585 is an exchange loss arising because the functional currency ($) has weakened against the transaction currency (SwK) since the transaction occurred.

Test your understanding 2

Part (a)

On 15 March the purchase is recorded using the exchange rate on that date.

Dr Non-current asset	(KR20,000/5)	$4,000
Cr Payable		$4,000

- At the year end the non-current asset, being a non-monetary item, is not retranslated but remains measured at $4,000.
- The payable remains outstanding at the year-end. This is a monetary item and must be retranslated using the closing rate: KR20,000 / 4 = $5,000
- The payable must be increased by $1,000, giving rise to an unrealised exchange loss:

Dr Income statement (exchange loss)	$1,000
Cr Payable	$1,000

Part (b)

1 Jan 20X1	KR100,000 / 2.0	= $50,000	Dr Non-current assets	$50,000
			Cr Payable	$50,000
31 Mar 20X1	KR100,000 / 2.3	= $43,478	Dr Payable	$50,000
			Cr Cash	$43,478
			Cr Income statement	$6,522
	KR 50,000 / 2.3	= $21,739	Dr Purchases	$21,739
			Cr Payables	$21,739
30 Jun 20X1	KR 95,000 / 2.1	= $45,238	Dr Receivables	$45,238
			Cr Sales revenue	$45,238

30 Sep 20X1	KR50,000 / 2.0	= $25,000	Dr Payables	$21,739
			Dr Income statement	$3,261
			Cr Cash	$25,000
30 Nov 20X1	KR200,000 / 1.8	= $111,111	Dr Cash	$111,111
			Cr Loan	$111,111
31 Dec 20X1	KR95,000 / 1.9	= $50,000	Dr Receivables	$4,762
			Cr Income statement	$4,762
	KR200,000 / 1.9	= $105,263	Dr Loan	$5,848
			Cr Income statement	$5,848

Test your understanding 3 - Paul and Simon

Consolidated statement of financial position at 31 December 20X8

	$
Goodwill (W3)	2,750
Non-current assets (60,000 + (25,000/ 2))	72,500
Current assets (35,800 + (15,000/ 2))	43,300
	118,550
Equity	
Share capital	50,000
Reserves (W5)	29,900
	79,900
Non-controlling interests (W4)	3,150
Current liabilities (30,000 + (11,000/ 2))	35,500
	118,550

Consolidated statement of comprehensive income for the year ended 31 December 20X8

	$
Revenue (25,000 + (10,000 /2.5))	29,000
Operating expenses (10,000 + (4,000 + 1,000 (W3)) /2.5))	(12,000)
Operating profit	17,000
Finance costs (5,000 + (1,500 / 2.5))	(5,600)
Profit before tax	11,400
Tax (3,000 + (1,000 / 2.5))	(3,400)
Profit for the year	8,000

Other comprehensive income	
Items that may be reclassified subsequently to profit or loss:	
Foreign exchange gains (W10)	5,584
Total comprehensive income	13,584
Profit attributable to:	
NCI shareholders (W6)	200
Parent shareholders (balance)	7,800
	8,000
Total comprehensive income attributable to:	
NCI shareholders (200 + 1,017 (W10))	1,217
Parent shareholders (balance)	12,367
	13,584

Consolidated statement of changes in equity for the year ended 31 December 20X8

	Parent	**NCI**
Equity brought forward (W8, W7)	68,533	1,933
Comprehensive income	12,367	1,217
Dividends	(1,000)	–
Equity carried forward	79,900	3,150

Workings

(W1) **Group structure**

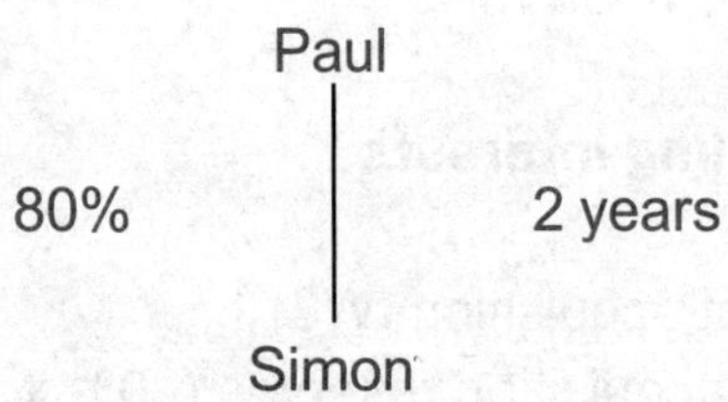

(W2) **Net assets of subsidiary**

	Acquisition date	B/f	Reporting date
	Fr	Fr	Fr
Share capital	15,000		15,000
Retained earnings	4,000		14,000
	19,000	25,500	29,000
		Post acquisition reserves = 6,500	Post acquisition reserves = 10,000

(W3) **Goodwill**

	Fr
Fair value of P's holding (cost of investment)	21,000
NCI holding at fair value	4,500
Fair value of sub's net assets at acquisition (W2)	(19,000)
Goodwill at acquisition/start of the year	6,500
Impairment	(1,000)
Goodwill at reporting date	5,500
Translate at closing rate of 2	$2,750

Foreign exchange gain/ loss on cost of investment (COI)

	$
COI at closing rate (Fr 21,000 / 2)	10,500
COI at acquisition rate (Fr 21,000 / 5)	(4,200)
Exchange gain to W5	6,300

(W4) **Non-controlling interests**

	Fr
NCI holding at acquisition (W3)	4,500
NCI% x post acquisition reserves (20% x 10,000 (W2))	2,000
NCI% x impairment (20% x 1,000)	(200)
	6,300
Translate at closing rate of 2	$3,150

(W5) **Reserves**

	$
Paul	20,000
Simon: (80% x 10,000 (W2) / 2)	4,000
Impairment (80% x (1,000 / 2))	(400)
Gain on COI (W3)	6,300
	29,900

(W6) **NCI share of profits**

	Fr
S's profit for the year	3,500
Impairment (fair value method)	(1,000)
Equity b/f per individual SOCE	2,500
x 20%	500
Translated at average rate (500 @ 2.5)	$200

(W7) **NCI equity b/f**

	Fr
NCI holding at acquisition (W3)	4,500
NCI% x post acquisition profits (20% x 6,500 (W2))	1,300
NCI% x impairment	–
	5,800
Translate at opening rate of 3	$1,933

(W8) **Parent shareholders equity b/f**

	$
Paul	64,000
Simon: (80% x 6,500 (W2) / 3)	1,733
Impairment b/f	–
Gain on COI to b/f date (W9)	2,800
	68,533

(W9) **Foreign exchange gain/ loss on COI brought forward**

	$
COI @ b/f rate (Fr 21,000 / 3)	7,000
COI @ acq rate (Fr 21,000 / 5)	4,200
Gain for W8	2,800

(W10) **Foreign exchange gains**

			P s/h	NCI s/h
			80%	20%
		$	$	$
Opening net assets (=equity b/f)	25,500			
@ cl. rate	2	12,750		
@ op. rate	3	8,500		
Gain		4,250	3,400	850
Profit for the year (3,500 – 1,000 impairment)	2,500			
@ cl. rate	2	1,250		
@ av. rate	2.5	1,000		
Gain		250	200	50
Opening goodwill	6,500 (W3)			
@ cl. rate	2	3,250		
@ op. rate	3	2,166		
Gain		1,084		
Split 5,800: 700			967	117
Total gains		5,584	4,567	1,017

Difference between fair value method and proportionate method of goodwill:

	Fr
NCI at acquisition at fair value	4,500
NCI at acquisition at proportion of net assets (20% x 19,000 (W2))	(3,800)
NCI s/h element of goodwill	700
Parent s/h element of goodwill (balance)	5,800
Total goodwill at acquisition	6,500

Test your understanding 4 - North

Part (a)

Consolidated statement of financial position at 30 September 20X4

	$m
Non-current assets	
Goodwill (W3)	35
Property, plant and equipment (107 + (164/ 2.4) + (30/ 2.4) – (9/2.4))	184.1
Current assets	
Inventories (70 + (50/ 2.4))	90.8
Receivables (65 + (60/2.4))	90.0
Bank (25 + (12/ 2.4))	30
	429.9
Share capital	100
Reserves (W5)	155.1
Non-controlling interests (W4)	17.7
Non-current liabilities (65 + (72/ 2.4))	95
Current liabilities (35 + (65/ 2.4))	62.1
	429.9

Part (b)

Consolidated statement of comprehensive income for year ended 30 September 20X4

	$m
Revenue (200 + (240 / 2.5)	296
Cost of sales (120 + (145 + 3 (W2) / 2.5)	(179.2)
Gross profit	116.8
Operating expenses (35 + (40 / 2.5))	(51)
Profit from operations	65.8
Investment income (4.5 - (75% x (15 / 2.5))	–
Finance cost (7.5 + (10 / 2.5))	(11.5)
Profit before tax	54.3
Tax (10 + (15 / 2.5))	(16)
Profit for the year	38.3
Other comprehensive income	
Items that may be reclassified subsequently to profit or loss:	
Foreign exchange gains (W10)	11.6
Total comprehensive income	49.9
Profit for the year attributable to:	
NCI shareholders (W6)	2.7
Parent shareholders (balance)	35.6
	38.3
Total comprehensive income attributable to:	
NCI shareholders (2.7 + 1.9 (W10))	4.6
Parent shareholders (35.6 + 9.7 (W10))	45.3
	49.9

Part (c)

Consolidated statement of changes in equity for year ended 30 September 20X4

	Parent shareholders	NCI shareholders
	$m	$m
Equity brought forward (W8, W7)	226	14.6
Comprehensive income	45.3	4.6
Dividends paid	(16)	
to NCI = 25% x 15 / 2.5		(1.5)
Equity carried forward	255.3*	17.7

* There is a rounding error of 0.2 compared to the CSFP.

(W1) **Group structure**

North

45m/60m = 75% | 3 years ago

South

(W2) **Net assets of South**

	Acquisition date	**B/f date**	**Reporting date**
	AFrm	AFrm	AFrm
Share capital	60		60
Reserves	38		89
	98	134	149
Fair Value Adj (80 – 50)	30	30	30
Depreciation adjustment (30 x 1/10 per annum)	–	(6)	(9)
	128	158	170
		Post acquisition reserves = 30	Post acquisition reserves = 42

(W3) **Goodwill**

	AFrm
Fair value of P's holding (cost of investment) (45m × Afr 4)	180
NCI holding at proportion of net assets (25% x 128 (W2))	32
Fair value of sub's net assets at acquisition (W2)	(128)
Goodwill at acquisition/ reporting date	84
Translated at closing rate 2.4	$35 m
Foreign exchange gain/ loss on cost of investment (COI)	
COI at closing rate (AFr 180/ 2.4)	75
COI at acquisition rate (AFr 180/ 3)	60
Exchange gain to W5	15

(W4) **Non-controlling interests**

	AFrm
NCI holding at acquisition (W3)	32
NCI% x post acquisition reserves (25% x 42 (W2))	10.5
	42.5
Translated at closing rate 2.4	$17.7m

(W5) **Reserves**

	$m
North	127
South (75% × (42 (W2) / 2.4))	13.1
Exchange gain on cost of investment (W3)	15
	155.1

(W6) **NCI share of profits**

	AFrm
S's profit for the year	30
Depreciation adjustment (W2)	(3)
	27
x 25%	6.75
Translated at average rate @ 2.5	$2.7

(W7) **NCI equity b/f**

	AFrm
NCI holding at acquisition (W3)	32
NCI% x post acquisition reserves (25% x 30 (W2))	7.5
	39.5
Translate at opening rate of 2.7	$14.6m

(W8) Parent shareholders equity brought forward

	$
North	211
South: (75% x (30 (W2) / 2.7))	8.3
Gain on cost of investment to b/f date (W9)	6.7
	226

(W9) Foreign exchange gain/ loss on COI brought forward

	$
COI @ b/f rate (AFr 180/ 2.7)	66.7
COI @ acq rate (AFr 180/ 3)	60
Gain for W9	6.7

(W10) Foreign exchange gains

			P s/h 75%	**NCI s/h 25%**
		$m	$m	$m
Opening net assets	158 (W2)			
@ cl. rate	2.4	65.8		
@ op. rate	2.7	58.5		
Gain		7.3	5.5	1.8
Profit for the year (30 – 3 depreciation)	27			
@ cl. rate	2.4	11.2		
@ av. rate	2.5	10.8		
Gain		0.4	0.3	0.1
Opening goodwill (W3)	84 (W3)			
@ cl. rate	2.4	35		
@ op. rate	2.7	31.1		
Gain		3.9	3.9	–
Total gains		11.6	9.7	1.9

chapter

10

Group statement of cash flows

Chapter learning objectives

On completion of their studies students should be able to:

- Prepare consolidated financial statements (including the group cash flow statement) for a group of companies.

1 Session content

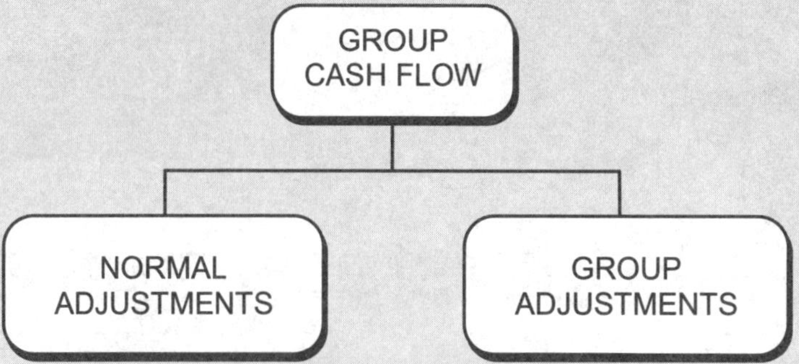

- Cash flow from operations reconciliation
- Interest paid
- Tax
- Non-current assets
- Loans/shares

- Acquisition/disposal of subsidiary
- Associates
- Non-controlling interests
- Foreign exchange

2 Objective of statements of cash flows

- IAS 7 **Statement of cash flows** provides guidance on the preparation of a statement of cash flow.
- The objective of a statement of cash flows is to provide information on an entity's changes in cash and cash equivalents during the period.
- The statement of financial position and income statement or statement of comprehensive income (SCI) are prepared on an accruals basis and do not show how the business has generated and used cash in the accounting period.
- The income statement (SCI) may show profits on an accruals basis even if the company is suffering severe cash flow problems.
- Statements of cash flows enable users of the financial statements to assess the **liquidity, solvency** and **financial adaptability** of a business.

Definitions:

- **Cash** consists of cash in hand and deposits repayable upon demand, less overdrafts. This includes cash held in a foreign currency.
- **Cash equivalents** are short-term, highly liquid investments that are readily convertible into known amounts of cash and are subject to an insignificant risk of changes in value.
- **Cash flows** are inflows and outflows of cash and cash equivalents.

3 Classification of cash flows

IAS 7 does not prescribe a specific format for the statement of cash flows, although it requires that cash flows are classified under three headings:

- cash flows from operating activities, defined as the entity's principal revenue earning activities and other activities that do not fall under the next two headings
- cash flows from investing activities, defined as the acquisition and disposal of long-term assets and other investments (excluding cash equivalents)
- cash flows from financing activities, defined as activities that change the size and composition of the entity's equity and borrowings

Classification of cash flows

Cash flows from operating activities

There are two methods of calculating the cash from operations.

- The **direct method** shows operating cash receipts and payments. This includes cash receipts from customers, cash payments to suppliers and cash payments to and on behalf of employees. The Examiner has indicated that the direct method will not be examined and is not considered further within this text.
- The **indirect method** starts with profit before tax and adjusts it for non-cash charges and credits, to reconcile it to the net cash flow from operating activities.

IAS 7 permits either method.

Under the **indirect method** adjustments are needed for a number of items, the most frequently occurring of which are:

- depreciation, amortisation and impairment
- profit or loss on disposal of non current assets
- change in inventory
- change in receivables
- change in payables

Cash flows from investing activities

Cash flows to appear under this heading include:

- cash paid for property, plant and equipment and other non-current assets
- cash received on the sale of property, plant and equipment and other non-current assets
- cash paid for investments in or loans to other entities (excluding movements on loans from financial institutions, which are shown under financing)
- cash received for the sale of investments or the repayment of loans to other entities (again excluding loans from financial institutions).

Cash flows from financing activities

Financing cash flows mainly comprise receipts or repayments of principal from or to external providers of finance.

Financing **cash inflows** include:

- receipts from issuing shares or other equity instruments
- receipts from issuing debentures, loan notes and bonds and from other long-term and short-term borrowings (other than overdrafts, which are normally included in cash and cash equivalents).

Financing **cash outflows** include:

- repayments of amounts borrowed (other than overdrafts)
- the capital element of finance lease rental payments
- payments to reacquire or redeem the entity's shares.

Interest and dividends

There are divergent and strongly held views about how interest and dividends cash flows should be classified. Some regard them as part of operating activities, because they are as much part of the day to day activities as receipts from customers, payments to suppliers and payments to staff. Others regard them as part of financing activities, the heading under which the instruments giving rise to the payments and receipts are classified. Still others believe they are part of investing activities, because this is what the long-term finance raised in this way is used for.

IAS 7 allows interest and dividends, whether received or paid, to be classified under any of the three headings, provided the classification is consistent from period to period.

The practice adopted in this workbook is to classify:

- interest received as a cash flow from investing activities
- interest paid as a cash flow from operating activities
- dividends received as a cash flow from investing activities
- dividends paid as a cash flow from financing activities.

4 Proforma statement of cash flows

Group statement of cash flows

Cash flows from operating activities	$	$
Group profit before tax	X	
Adjustments for:		
Finance costs	X	
Investment income	(X)	
Share of associate's profit	(X)	
Depreciation	X	
Amortisation	X	
Impairments	X	
Profit/loss on sale of property, plant and equipment	(X)/X	
	X	
Change in inventory	(X)/X	
Change in receivables	(X)/X	
Change in payables	X/(X)	
Cash generated from operations	X	
Interest paid	(X)	
Tax paid	(X)	
Net cash from operating activities		X
Cash flows from investing activities		
Sale proceeds on disposal of property, plant and equipment	X	
Purchases of property, plant and equipment	(X)	
Investment income received	X	
Dividends received from associate	X	
Acquisition/ sale of subsidiary, net of cash balances	(X)/X	
Net cash used in investing activities		X

Cash flows from financing activities

Loans – issue/repayment	X/(X)	
Share issues	X	
Dividends paid to NCI	(X)	
Dividends paid to parent shareholders	(X)	
Net cash used in financing activities		X
Increase decrease in cash and cash equivalents		X/(X)
Opening cash and cash equivalents		X
Closing cash and cash equivalents		X

5 Approach for a single company statement of cash flows

(1) Calculate cash and cash equivalents carried forward and brought forward, taking into account any overdraft. These figures can go directly to the bottom of the statement of cash flows.

(2) Reconcile accounting profit before tax back to cash from operations using the proforma provided in the statement of cash flows. Remember an increase in inventory or receivables means a deduction in the reconciliation.

(3) Complete the cash flows from operating activities section by calculating tax paid and interest paid.

(4) Within the cash flows from investing activities, it may be necessary to prepare a T account or similar working for property, plant and equipment (PPE) to calculate missing figures e.g. additions, depreciation or the book value of disposals to then calculate sale proceeds or profit/ loss on disposal.

(5) Cash flows from financing activities reflects movements in share capital, loans and dividends paid. Remember to look at share capital and share premium together to ascertain cash received from a share issue.

(6) Ensure that any foreign exchange gains/losses are eliminated from the calculations as they are not cash movements.

NB: In the exercises in this chapter, the workings have been shown using both column format and T account format, both of which are acceptable in the exam.

Test your understanding 1 - Finance cost and tax paid

Y's income statement for the year shows the following:

	$000
Finance costs	(240)
Tax	(180)

Y's opening and closing statements of financial position show the following:

	Closing	Opening
	$000	$000
Accrued interest	130	80
Income tax payable	120	100
Deferred tax	100	50

Required:

(a) How much were finance costs paid in the year?

(b) How much tax was paid in the year?

Test your understanding 2 - Non-current assets

Z's opening and closing statements of financial position show the following:

	Closing	Opening
	$000	$000
Non-current assets (NBV)	250	100

During the year depreciation of $20,000 was charged and a revaluation surplus of $60,000 was recorded. Assets with a net book value of $15,000 were disposed and non-current assets acquired under finance leases totalled $30,000.

Required:

How much cash was spent on non-current assets in the year?

6 Approach to consolidated statement of cash flows

The approach is similar to that of a single company statement of cash flows.

There are four further issues to deal with:

- Dividends paid to non-controlling interests (financing cash outflow)
- Dividends received from the associate (investing cash inflow)
- Cash flows related to the acquisition or disposal of a subsidiary during the year (cash received/ paid net of the sub's cash balance)
- If there has been an acquisition or disposal during the year, the impact of it will need to be considered in your workings when calculating cash flows.

Dividends paid to non-controlling interests

- When a subsidiary that is not wholly owned pays a dividend, some of that dividend is paid outside of the group to the non-controlling interest.
- Such dividends paid to non-controlling interests should be disclosed separately in the statement of cash flows.
- To calculate the amount paid, reconcile the non-controlling interest in the statement of financial position from the opening to the closing balance.

Example 1

The following information has been extracted from the consolidated financial statements of WG for the years ended 31 December:

	20X7	**20X6**
	$000	$000
NCI in consolidated SFP	780	690
NCI in consolidated SCI	120	230

Required:

What is the dividend paid to non-controlling interests in the year 20X7?

Example 1 answer

Steps:

(1) Set up a working (column or T account style).

(2) Insert the opening and closing balances and the NCI share of profit after tax.

(3) The balancing figure is the cash paid to the NCI.

Non-controlling interests

	$000
Bal b/f	690
Profit attributable to the NCI	120
	810
Dividends paid (balance)	(30)
Bal c/f	780

or

Non-controlling interests

	$000		$000
Dividends paid (bal fig)	30	Balance b/f	690
Balance c/f	780	Share of profits in year	120
	810		810

Watch out for an acquisition or disposal of a subsidiary in the year. This will affect the NCI and will need to be taken account of in the working, showing the NCI that has been acquired or disposed of in the period.

Test your understanding 3

Group A's income statement shows the profit attributable to parent shareholders of $3,200,000 and to non-controlling interests of $500,000.

The opening and closing statements of financial position show the following:

	Closing	**Opening**
	$000	$000
Retained earnings	4,325	1,625
Non-controlling interests	580	440

Required:

(a) Calculate the dividends paid to non-controlling interests.

(b) Calculate the dividends paid to shareholders of the parent.

Dividends received from associates

- Associates generate cash flows into the group to the extent that dividends are received out of the profits of the associate.
- Such dividends received from associates should be disclosed separately in the statement of cash flows.
- To calculate the amount received, reconcile the investment in associate in the statement of financial position from the opening to the closing balance.
- The share of profit/loss of the associate is a non-cash item included within profit and therefore will be an adjustment in the operating activities section of the statement of cash flows.

Example 2

The following information has been extracted from the consolidated financial statements of H for the year ended 31 December 20X1:

Group income statement

	$000
Operating profit	734
Income from associate	48
Profit before tax	782
Tax	(304)
Profit after tax	478

Group statement of financial position

	20X1	20X0
	$000	$000
Investment in associate	466	456

Required:

Show the figures relevant to the associate to be included in the group statement of cash flows for the year ended 31 December 20X1.

Example 2 answer

When dealing with the dividend from the associate, the process is the same as we have already seen with the non-controlling interest.

Set up a working (column or T-account format) and bring in all the balances that relate to the associate. When you balance the account, the balancing figure will be the cash received from the associate.

(W1) **Dividend received from associate**

	$000
Bal b/f	456
Income from associate	48
	504
Less Bal c/f	(466)
Dividend received from associate	38

or

Associate

	$000		$000
		Dividend received	
Balance b/f	456	(bal fig)	38
Income from associate	48	Balance c/f	466
	504		504

Extracts from statement of cash flows for the year ended 31 December 20X1

	$000
Cash flows from operating activities	
Profit before tax	782
Adjustment for:	
Income from associate	(48)
Investing activities	
Dividend received from associate (W1)	38

Test your understanding 4

Group B's income statement reports 'Share of associate's profits' of $750,000. The opening and closing statements of financial position show:

	Closing	Opening
	$000	$000
Investment in associate	500	200

Required:

How much cash was received by the group from the associates in the year?

Acquisition and disposal of subsidiaries

Standard accounting practice

- If a subsidiary joins or leaves a group during a financial year, the cash flows of the group should include the cash flows of that subsidiary for the same period that the results of the subsidiary are included in the income statement/SCI.
- Cash payments to acquire subsidiaries and receipts from disposals of subsidiaries must be reported separately in the statement of cash flows under investing activities.

Acquisitions

- In the statement of cash flows we must record the actual cash flow for the purchase, not the net assets acquired. The cash outflow is net of any cash balances purchased with the subsidiary.
- All assets and liabilities acquired must be included in any workings to calculate the cash movement for an item during the year. If they are not included in deriving the balancing figure, the incorrect cash flow figure will be calculated. This applies to all assets and liabilities acquired and also to the NCI reconciliation (to calculated dividends paid to NCI).

Disposals

- The statement of cash flows will show the cash received from the sale of the subsidiary, net of any cash balances that were transferred out with the sale.
- When calculating the movement between the opening and closing balance of an item, the assets and liabilities that have been disposed of must be taken into account in order to calculate the correct cash figure. As with acquisitions, this applies to all asset and liability reconciliations and also to the NCI reconciliation (to calculated dividends paid to NCI).

Example 3

The extracts of a company's statement of financial position is shown below:

	20X8	**20X7**
	$	$
Inventory	74,666	53,019

During the year, a subsidiary was acquired. At the date of acquisition, the subsidiary had an inventory balance of $9,384.

Required:

Calculate the movement on inventory for the statement of cash flows.

Example 3 answer

At the beginning of the year, the inventory balance of $53,019 **does not** include the inventory of the subsidiary.

At the end of the year, the inventory balance of $74,666 **does** include the inventory of the newly acquired subsidiary.

In order to calculate the correct cash movement, the acquired inventory must be excluded as it is dealt with in the cash paid to acquire the subsidiary. The comparison of the opening and closing inventory figures is then calculated on the same basis.

The movement on inventory is: (74,666 – 9,384) – 53,019 = $12,263 increase. This is shown as a negative adjustment in cash flows from operating activities.

Example 4

The same principle applies if there is a disposal in the period.

For example, the year end receivables balance was as follows:

	20X8	20X7
	$	$
Receivables	52,335	48,911

During the year, a subsidiary was disposed of. At the date of disposal the subsidiary had a receivables balance of $6,543.

Required:

Calculate the movement on receivables for the statement of cash flows.

Example 4 answer

At the beginning of the year, the receivables balance of $48,911 **does** include the receivables of the subsidiary.

At the end of the year, the receivables balance of $52,335 **does not** include the receivables of the disposed subsidiary.

In order to calculate the correct cash movement, the receivables of the disposed subsidiary must be excluded.

The movement on receivables is:

52,335 – (48,911 – 6,543) = $9,967 increase, which is shown as a negative adjustment in cash flows from operating activities.

Test your understanding 5

Group P's opening and closing statements of financial position show the following:

	Closing	Opening
	$000	$000
Non-current assets (NBV)	500	150

During the year depreciation of $50,000 was charged. During the year, the group acquired a 75% shareholding in a subsidiary which held non-current assets of $200,000 and disposed of a 60% shareholding in a subsidiary which held non-current assets of $180,000 at the date of disposal.

Required:

How much cash was spent on non-current assets in the year?

Foreign currency transactions

Individual entity stage

- Exchange differences arising at the individual entity stage are in most instances reported as part of operating profit. If the foreign currency transaction has been settled in the year, the cash flows will reflect the reporting currency cash receipt or payment and thus no problem arises.
- An unsettled foreign currency transaction will, however, give rise to an exchange difference for which there is no cash flow effect in the current year. Such exchange differences therefore need to be eliminated in computing net cash flows from operating activities.
- Fortunately this will not require much work if the unsettled foreign currency transaction is in working capital. Adjusting profit by movements in working capital will automatically adjust correctly for the non-cash flow exchange gains and losses.

Group financial statements

- Exchange differences arising on the retranslation of a foreign operation have no impact on profit, they are recorded instead within other comprehensive income. Therefore no adjustment is required within the operating activities section.

- However, their impact on the SFP balances should be taken into account when reconciling opening to closing balances in your cash flow workings.

Example 5

The following are excerpts from a group's financial statements

	Closing balance	Opening balance
	$000	$000
Group statement of financial position extracts		
Non-current assets	500	400
Loans	300	600
Tax	200	300
Income statement extracts		
	$000	
Depreciation	50	
Loss on disposal of non-current asset (sold for 30)	10	
Tax charge	200	

During the accounting period, a subsidiary was sold, and another acquired. Extracts from the statements of financial position are as follows:

	Sold	Acquired
	$000	$000
Non-current assets	60	70
Loans	110	80
Tax	45	65

During the accounting period, the following exchange gains/losses arose in respect of overseas net assets:

	$000
Non-current assets – forex gain	40
Loans – forex loss	(5)
Tax – forex loss	(5)

Required:

Calculate the group cash flows for non-current assets, loans and tax.

Example 5 answer

Non-current assets

	$000
Opening balance	400
Depreciation	(50)
Disposal (30 + 10)	(40)
Disposal of subsidiary	(60)
Acquisition of subsidiary	70
Exchange gain	40
	360
Therefore acquisitions / cash paid (bal figure)	140
Closing balance	500

Loans

	$000
Opening balance	600
Disposal of subsidiary	(110)
Acquisition of subsidiary	80
Exchange loss	5
	575
Therefore redemption / cash paid (bal figure)	(275)
Closing balance	300

Tax

	$000
Opening balance	300
Charge for the year	200
Disposal of subsidiary	(45)
Acquisition of subsidiary	65
Exchange loss	5
	525
Therefore cash paid (bal figure)	(325)
Closing balance	200

Test your understanding 6

Group R's opening and closing statements of financial position show the following:

	Closing	**Opening**
	$000	$000
Inventory	100	200
Receivables	300	200
Payables	500	200

During the period the group acquired a subsidiary with the following working capital:

	$000
Inventory	50
Receivables	200
Payables	40

During the period the group disposed of a subsidiary with the following working capital:

	$000
Inventory	25
Receivables	45
Payables	20

During the period the group experienced the following exchange rate gains/losses:

	$000	
Inventory	11	Gain
Receivables	21	Gain
Payables	31	Loss

Required:

What are the adjustments required in respect of movements in working capital that should be shown in the operating activities section of the statement of cash flows?

Example 6

Extracts from the consolidated financial statements of the Kelly Group are given below:

Consolidated statements of financial position as at 31 March

	20X5		20X4	
	$000	$000	$000	$000
Non-current assets				
Property, plant and equipment	5,900		4,400	
Goodwill	85		130	
Investment in associate	170		140	
		6,155		4,670
Current assets				
Inventories	1,000		930	
Receivables	1,340		1,140	
Short-term deposits	35		20	
Cash at bank	180		120	
		2,555		2,210
		8,710		6,880
Share capital	2,000		1,500	
Share premium	300		–	
Revaluation reserve	50		–	
Retained earnings	3,400		3,320	
		5,750		4,820
Non-controlling interests		75		175
Equity		5,825		4,995

Non-current liabilities				
Interest-bearing borrowings	1,400		1,000	
Obligations under finance leases	210		45	
Deferred tax	340		305	
		1,950		1,350
Current liabilities				
Trade payables	885		495	
Accrued interest	7		9	
Income tax	28		21	
Obligations under finance leases	15		10	
		935		535
		8,710		6,880

Consolidated statement of comprehensive income for the year ended 31 March 20X5

	$000
Revenue	875
Cost of sales	(440)
Gross profit	435
Other operating expenses	(210)
Profit from operations	225
Finance cost	(100)
Gain on sale of subsidiary	30
Share of associate's profit	38
Profit before tax	193
Tax	(48)
Profit for the year	145

Other comprehensive income	
Gains on land revaluation	50
Total comprehensive income for the year	195
Profit attributable to:	
Equity holders of the parent	120
Non-controlling interests	25
	145
Total comprehensive income attributable to:	
Equity holders of the parent	170
Non-controlling interests	25
	195

Notes:

Dividends

Kelly, the parent company, paid a dividend of $40,000 during the year.

Property, plant and equipment

The following transactions took place during the year:

- Land was revalued upwards by $50,000 on 1st April 20X4.
- During the year, depreciation of $80,000 was charged in the income statement.
- Additions include $300,000 acquired under finance leases.
- A property was disposed of during the year for $250,000 cash. Its carrying amount was $295,000 at the date of disposal. The loss on disposal has been included within cost of sales.

Gain on sale of subsidiary

- On 1 January 20X5, Kelly disposed of an 80% owned subsidiary for $390,000 in cash. The subsidiary had the following net assets at the date of disposal:

	$000
Property, plant and equipment	635
Inventory	20
Receivables	45
Cash	35
Payables	(130)
Income tax	(5)
Interest-bearing borrowings	(200)
	400

This subsidiary had been acquired on 1 January 20X1 for a cash payment of $220,000 when its net assets had a fair value of $225,000 and the non-controlling interest had a fair value of $50,000.

Goodwill

The Kelly Group uses the fair value method for measuring NCI at the date of acquisition.

Required:

Prepare the consolidated statement of cash flows of the Kelly group for the year ended 31 March 20X5 in the form required by IAS 7 Statement of cash flows. Show your workings clearly.

Example 6 answer

Ensure that you read the notes accompanying the question thoroughly and annotate the question before you begin. The sale of the subsidiary will affect numerous balances because the opening balances include the subsidiary and the closing balances do not so the subsidiary's balances at disposal must be deducted from the opening balance (or added to the closing balance for the same result).

Follow these steps to prepare the consolidated statement of cash flows:

(1) Start with cash generated from operations and work back from profit before tax to profit from operations i.e. deduct share of associate's profit, deduct gain on sale of subsidiary etc.

(2) Eliminate the effect of any non-cash items e.g. depreciation and the loss on the sale of property during the year.

(3) Then deal with working capital changes i.e. the movement in inventory, receivables and payables. Remember the sale of the subsidiary and the need to include its balances in the workings.

(4) Complete the cash flows from operating activities section by calculating interest and tax paid (W2, W3).

(5) Think about movements in non-current assets for the cash flows from investing activities section e.g. additions of property, plant and equipment. Sometimes you may need to prepare a working to see whether there is an unexplained balance which is cash paid or received.

(6) The disposal proceeds are given to you in the question of $250,000.

(7) A working is required to check whether there are any additions (W4). Remember the disposal of the subsidiary and note the additions under finance leases. Finance leased assets are included on the statement of financial position as non-current assets and are not paid for immediately.

(8) The disposal of the subsidiary requires a line for disposal proceeds, net of cash in the subsidiary given up. This line is straightforward.

(9) Finally, prepare a working for the investment in associate to see whether any dividends were received (W5).

(10) The final section is cash flows from financing activities and movements may be cash flows from issuing or redeeming debt or dividends paid.

(11) Check interest bearing borrowings for any movement in a working (W7).

(12) Similarly if there are any finance leases there may have been repayments (W6).

(13) Cash inflows from issuing shares can be calculated directly from the statement of financial position as the cumulative increase in share capital and share premium.

(14) You are given the dividend paid by the parent in the question ($40,000).

(15) Dividends paid to NCI require a working (W8). NCI brought and carried forward is taken from the CSFP and share of profits from the CSCI. The NCI related to the subsidiary which has been disposed of needs removing. Because the fair value method is used, the value of its NCI at disposal is:

	$000
NCI holding at acquisition	50
NCI% x post acquisition reserves (20% x (400 - 225))	35
NCI at disposal date	85

(16) There is a working for goodwill (W1) to check whether there is any impairment in the goodwill of any subsidiary which would need to be added back to cash generated from operations. The goodwill on the sold subsidiary is eliminated. In this case there are no impairments.

Consolidated statement of cash flows for the year ended 31 March 20X5

	$000	$000
Cash flows from operating activities		
Profit before tax	193	
Adjustments for:		
Share of associate's profit	(38)	
Gain on sale of subsidiary	(30)	
Finance cost	100	
Depreciation	80	
Loss on disposal of property (250 – 295)	45	
Increase in inventory (1,000 – (930 – 20))	(90)	
Increase in receivables (1,340 – (1,140 – 45))	(245)	
Increase in payables (885 – (495 – 130))	520	
	535	
Interest paid (W2)	(102)	
Tax paid (W3)	(1)	
		432

Cash flows from investing activities		
Sale of property	250	
Purchases of property, plant and equipment (W4)	(2,160)	
Dividends received from associate (W5)	8	
Proceeds from sale of subsidiary, net of cash balances (390 – 35)	355	
		(1,547)
Cash flows from financing activities		
Repayments of finance leases (W6)	(130)	
Cash raised from interest-bearing borrowings (W7)	600	
Issue of shares (2,000 + 300 – 1,500)	800	
Dividends paid to equity shareholders of parent	(40)	
Dividends paid to non-controlling interests (W8)	(40)	
		1,190
Increase in cash and cash equivalents		75
Opening cash and cash equivalents (120 + 20)		140
Closing cash and cash equivalents (180 + 35)		215

(W1) **Goodwill**

	$000
Bal b/f	130
Disposal of subsidiary (see below)	(45)
	85
Impairment (balance)	-
Bal c/f	85

or

Goodwill

	$000		$000
Bal b/f	130	Disposal of sub (below)	45
		Bal c/f	85
	130		130

Goodwill of disposed sub:

	$000
Fair value of P's holding (cost of investment)	220
NCI holding at fair value	50
Fair value of sub's net assets at acquisition	(225)
Goodwill at acquisition/ disposal	45

(W2) **Finance costs**

	$000
Bal b/f	9
Charge in CSCI	100
Bal c/f	(7)
Cash paid	102

or

Finance costs

	$000		$000
Cash (bal fig)	102	Bal b/f	9
Bal c/f	7	SCI	100
	109		109

(W3) **Tax payable**

	$000
Bal b/f (21 + 305)	326
Disposal of subsidiary	(5)
Income statement charge	48
	369
Cash paid (balance)	(1)
Bal c/f (28 + 340)	368

or

Tax

		Bal b/f – income tax	21
		Bal b/f – deferred tax	305
Disposal of sub	5		
		SCI – group	48
Tax paid (bal fig)	1		
Bal c/f – income tax	28		
Bal c/f – deferred tax	340		
	374		374

(W4) **Property, plant and equipment**

	$000
Bal b/f	4,400
Revaluation	50
Depreciation	(80)
Finance leases	300
Disposal of property	(295)
Disposal of subsidiary	(635)
	3,740
Cash (balance)	2,160
Bal c/f	5,900

or

PPE

Bal b/f	4,400		
Revaluation	50	Depreciation	80
Finance leases	300	Disposal –property	295
Cash (bal fig)	2,160	Disposal – sub	635
		Bal c/f	5,900
	6,910		6,910

(W5) **Investment in associates**

	$000
Bal b/f	140
Share of profit of associate	38
	178
Bal c/f	(170)
Dividend (cash) received	8

or

Investments in associates

Bal b/f	140		
Share of profits before tax	38	Dividend received (bal fig)	8
		Bal c/f	170
	178		178

(W6) **Finance leases**

	$000
Bal b/f (10 + 45)	55
New leases	300
	355
Repayments (cash) (balance)	(130)
Bal c/f (15 + 210)	225

or

Finance leases

		Bal b/d (10 + 45)	55
		New leases	300
Repayments (bal fig)	130		
Bal c/d (15 + 210)	225		
	355		355

(W7) **Interest-bearing borrowings**

	$000
Bal b/f	1,000
Disposal of sub	(200)
	800
New loans / cash (balance)	600
Bal c/f	1,400

or

Interest-bearing borrowings

		Bal b/d	1,000
Disposal of sub	200		
		Cash (bal fig)	600
Bal b/d	1,400		
	1,600		1,600

(W8) **Non-controlling interests**

	$000
Bal b/f	175
Comprehensive income per CSCI	25
Disposal of sub (below)	(85)
	115
Cash paid (balance)	(40)
Bal c/f	75

or

Non-controlling interests

		Bal b/f	175
Disposal of sub (below)	85	Comprehensive income per CSCI	25
Dividends paid (bal fig)	40		
Bal c/f	75		
	200		200

NCI of disposed sub:

	$000
NCI at acquisition at fair value	50
NCI% x post acquisition reserves (20% x (400 – 225))	35
NCI at disposal	85

Test your understanding 7 - Linford

The group financial statements of Linford are given below:

Consolidated income statement for the year ended

	30 September 20X9
	$m
Revenue	600
Cost of sales	(300)
Gross profit	300
Operating expenses	(150)
Investment income	6
Finance costs	(50)
Share of associate profit	17
Profit before tax	123
Taxation	(35)
Profit after tax	88
Attributable to:	
Non-controlling interests	10
Parent shareholders	78
	88

Consolidated statements of financial position as at

	30 Sept 20X9		30 Sept 20X8	
	$m	$m	$m	$m
Non-current assets				
Goodwill	25		19	
Property, plant and equipment	240		280	
Investments in associates	80	345	70	369
Current assets				
Inventory	105		90	
Receivables	120		100	
Cash and cash equivalents	30		75	
		255		265
		600		634
Share capital		100		100
Retained earnings		194		142
Non controlling interest		70		40
		364		282
Non-current liabilities				
Obligations under finance leases	80		70	
12% loan stock	–		90	
Deferred taxation	30		24	
		110		184
Current liabilities				
Trade payables	65		55	
Taxation	10		8	
Obligations under finance leases	25		20	
Overdraft	26		85	
		126		168
		600		634

Notes to the accounts

(1) **Acquisition of subsidiary**

During the year ended 30 September 20X9, Linford purchased 80% of the issued equity share capital of Christie for $100m, payable in cash. The net assets of Christie at the date of acquisition were assessed as having fair values as follows:

	$m
PPE	60
Inventory	30
Receivables	25
Bank and cash	10
Trade payables	(15)
Taxation	(5)
	105

It is group policy to measure NCI at the proportionate share of the fair value of net assets at acquisition.

(2) **Goodwill**

Goodwill suffered an impairment during the year.

(3) **Property, plant and equipment**

The only disposal in the year was of land with a carrying value of $90m. The profit on disposal of $10m is included within operating expenses. During the year the group entered into new finance leases in respect of some items of plant and the amount debited to PPE in respect of these leases was $40m. Depreciation of $58m was charged on PPE in the year.

(4) **Dividends**

Dividends paid to parent shareholders of Linford in the current year amounted to $26m.

Required:

Prepare the consolidated statement of cash flows for Linford group for the year ended 30 September 20X9.

Test your understanding 8 - Pearl

Below are the consolidated financial statements of the Pearl Group for the year ended 30 September 20X2:

Consolidated statements of financial position

	20X2	20X1
	$000	$000
Non-current assets		
Goodwill	1,930	1,850
Property, plant and equipment	2,545	1,625
Investment in associate	620	540
	5,095	4,015
Current assets		
Inventories	470	435
Receivables	390	330
Cash and cash equivalents	210	140
Total assets	6,165	4,920
Equity		
Share capital ($1 shares)	1,500	1,500
Retained earnings	1,755	1,085
Other reserves	750	525
	4,005	3,110
Non-controlling interests	310	320
	4,315	3,430
Non-current liabilities		
Loans	500	300
Deferred tax	150	105

Current liabilities		
Trade payables	800	725
Income tax	400	360
	6,165	4,920

Consolidated income statement for the year ended 31 March 20X5

	$000
Revenue	2,090
Operating expenses	(1,155)
Profit from operations	935
Gain on disposal of subsidiary	100
Finance cost	(35)
Income from associate	115
Profit before tax	1,115
Tax	(225)
Profit for the year	890
Other comprehensive income	200
Other comprehensive income from associate	50
Total comprehensive income	1,140
Profit attributable to:	
Parent shareholders	795
NCI shareholders	95
	890
Total comprehensive income attributable to:	
Parent shareholders	1,020
NCI shareholders	120
	1,140

Consolidated statement of changes in equity

	Parent shareholders	NCI shareholders
	$000	$000
Equity brought forward	3,110	320
Comprehensive income	1,020	120
Acquisition of subsidiary		340
Disposal of subsidiary		(420)
Dividends	(125)	(50)
Equity carried forward	4,005	310

(1) Depreciation totalling $385,000 was charged during the year. Plant with a carrying value of $250,000 was sold for $275,000. The gain on disposal was recognised in operating costs. Certain properties were revalued during the year resulting in a revaluation gain of $200,000 being recognised.

(2) During the year, Pearl acquired 80% of the equity share capital of Gem paying cash consideration of $1.5 million. The NCI holding was measured at its fair value of $340,000 at the date of acquisition. The fair value of Gem's net assets at acquisition was made up as follows:

	$000
Property, plant and equipment	1,280
Inventory	150
Receivables	240
Cash and cash equivalents	80
Trade payables	(220)
Taxation	(40)
	1,490

(3) During the year, Pearl also disposed of its 60% equity shareholding in Stone for cash proceeds of $850,000. The subsidiary had been acquired several years ago for cash consideration of $600,000. The NCI holding was measured at its fair value of $320,000 at acquisition and the fair value of Stone's net assets were $730,000. Goodwill had not suffered any impairment. At the date of disposal, the net assets of Stone had carrying values in the consolidated statement of financial position as follows:

	$000
Property, Plant and Equipment	725
Inventory	165
Receivables	120
Cash and cash equivalents	50
Trade payables	(80)
	980

Required:

Prepare the consolidated statement of cash flows for the Pearl group for the year ended 30 September 20X2.

7 Chapter summary

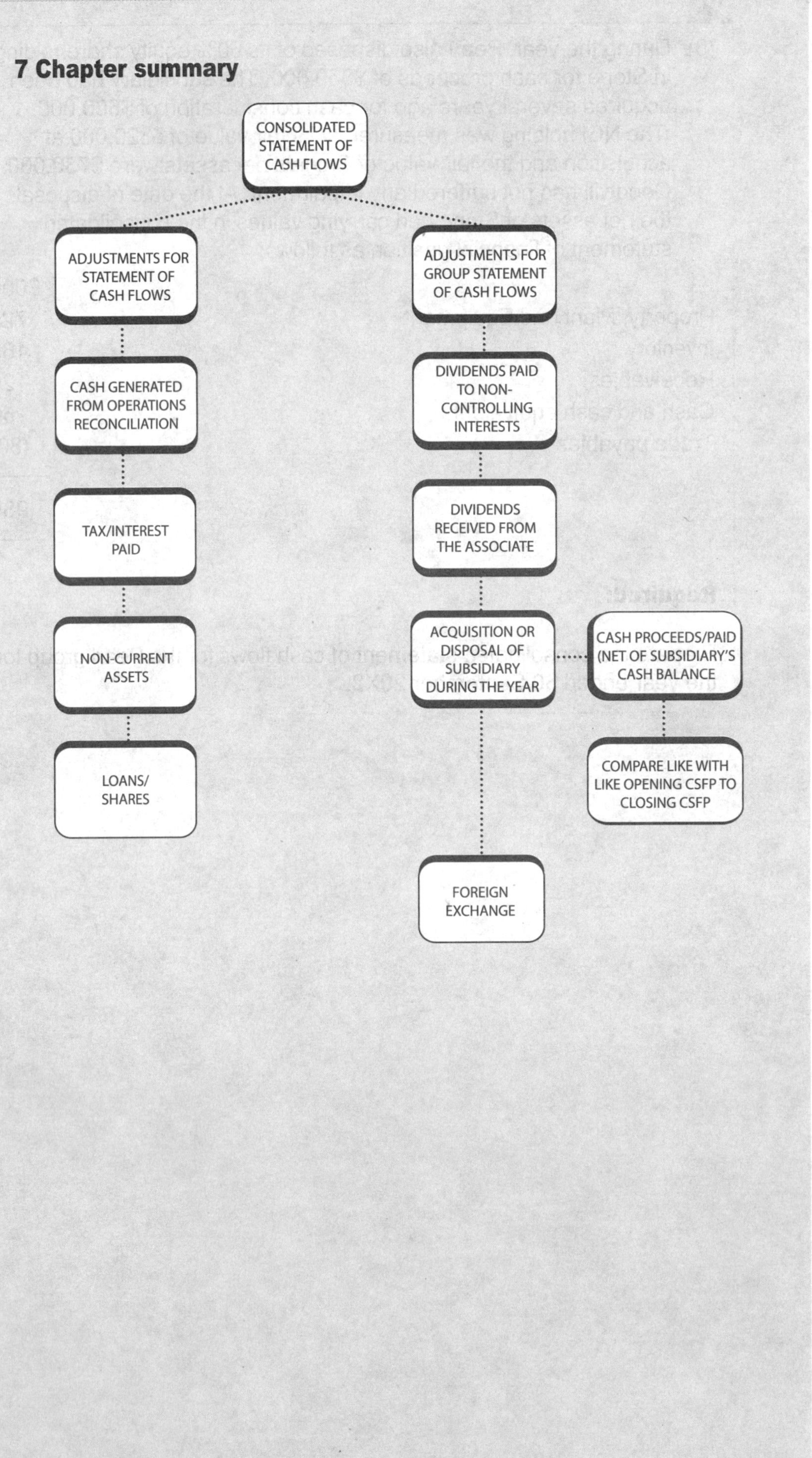

Test your understanding answers

Test your understanding 1 - Finance cost and tax paid

	$000
Opening accrual	80
Finance costs per IS	240
Closing accrual	(130)
Finance costs (cash) paid	190

Finance costs

		Bal b/f	80
Cash paid	190	Finance costs – IS	240
Bal c/f	130		
	320		320

	$000
Opening income tax	100
Opening deferred tax	50
Tax per IS	180
Closing income tax	(120)
Closing deferred tax	(100)
Tax (cash) paid	110

Tax

		Bal b/f – income tax	100
		Bal b/f – deferred tax	50
Cash paid	110	Tax – IS	180
Bal c/f – income tax	120		
Bal c/f – deferred tax	100		
	330		330

Test your understanding 2 - Non-current assets

	$000
Opening NBV	100
Depreciation	(20)
Revaluation surplus	60
Disposal	(15)
Additions under leases	30
Additions – cash paid (β)	95
Closing NBV	250

Non-current assets

Bal b/f	100	Depreciation	20
Revaluation	60	Disposal	15
Additions – leases	30		
Additions – cash paid (β)	95		
		Bal c/f	250
	285		285

Test your understanding 3

	$000
Opening NCI	440
NCI share of profit per IS	500
Divi paid (bal)	(360)
Closing NCI	580

Non-controlling interests

		Bal b/f	440
Divs paid (β)	360	NCI share of profit per IS	500
Bal c/f	580		
	940		940

Retained earnings	$000
Op. bal	1,625
Parent profit	3,200
Divi paid (bal)	(500)
Cl. bal	4,325

Retained earnings

		Bal b/f	1,625
Divs paid (β)	500	Parent profit	3,200
Bal c/f	4,325		
	4,825		4,825

Test your understanding 4

	$000
Opening investment in associate	200
Share of profits	750
Closing investment in associate	(500)
Cash received	450

Investment in Associate

Bal b/f	200		
Share of profits	750	Cash received (β)	450
		Bal c/f	500
	950		950

Test your understanding 5

	$000
Opening NBV	150
Depreciation	(50)
Disposal of sub	(180)
New sub	200
Additions – cash (β)	380
Closing NBV	500

Non-current assets

Bal b/f	150	Depreciation	50
New sub	200	Disposal of sub	180
Additions – cash (β)	380		
		Bal c/f	500
	730		730

Test your understanding 6

	$000
Opening inventory	200
New sub	50
Disposal sub	(25)
Forex gain	11
Decrease (β)	(136)
Closing Inventory	100

Inventory

Bal b/f	200		
New sub	50	Disposal – sub	25
Forex gain	11	Decrease (β)	136
		Bal c/f	100
	261		261

	$000
Opening rec'bles	200
New sub	200
Disposal sub	(45)
Forex gain	21
Decrease (β)	(76)
Closing rec'bles	300

Receivables

Bal b/f	200		
New sub	200	Disposal – sub	45
Forex gain	21	Decrease (β)	76
		Bal c/f	300
	421		421

	$000
Opening payables	200
New sub	40
Disposal sub	(20)
Forex loss	31
Increase (β)	249
Closing payables	500

Payables

		Bal b/f	200
Disposal – sub	20	New sub	40
		Forex loss	31
Bal c/f	500	Increase (β)	249
	520		520

Test your understanding 7 - Linford

Group statement of cash flows for Linford for year ending 30 September 20X9

Cash flows from operating activities	$m	$m
Group profit before tax	123	
Adjustments for:		
Depreciation	58	
Goodwill impairment (W1)	10	
Profit on sale of property	(10)	
Share of associate's profit	(17)	
Investment income	(6)	
Finance costs	50	
	208	
Decrease in inventory ((105 – 90) – 30)	15	
Decrease in receivables ((120 – 100) – 25)	5	
Decrease in payables ((65 – 55) – 15)	(5)	
Cash generated from operations	223	
Interest paid	(50)	
Tax paid (W3)	(32)	
Net cash from operating activities		141
Cash flows from investing activities		
Proceeds on disposal of property (90 + 10)	100	
Purchase of property, plant and equipment (W2)	(8)	
Investment income received	6	
Dividends received from associate (W6)	7	
Acquisition of sub, net of cash balances (100 – 10)	(90)	
Net cash used in investing activities		15

Cash flows from financing activities

Repayment of loan – 12% loan stock	(90)	
Repayment of capital element of finance leases (W4)	(25)	
Dividends paid to NCI (W5)	(1)	
Dividends paid to parent shareholders	(26)	(142)
Increase in cash and cash equivalents		14
Brought forward cash and cash equivalents (75 – 85)		(10)
Carried forward cash and cash equivalents (30 – 26)		4

Workings

(W1) **Goodwill**

	$m
Bal b/f	19
Acquisition of sub (below)	16
	35
Impairment (balance)	(10)
Bal c/f	25

Or

Goodwill

B/f	19	**Impairment (balance)**	10
Acquisition of subsidiary (below)	16	C/f	25
	35		35

Goodwill of acquired sub:

	$m
Fair value of P's holding (cost of investment)	100
NCI holding at proportion of net assets (20% x 105)	21
Fair value of sub's net assets at acquisition	(105)
Goodwill at acquisition	16

(W2) **Non-current assets**

	$m
Bal b/f	280
Finance lease	40
New subsidiary	60
Depreciation	(58)
Disposal	(90)
	232
Cash paid for new assets (balance)	8
Bal c/f	240

Or

Non-current assets

B/f	280	Depreciation	58
Finance lease	40	Disposal	90
New sub	60	C/f	240
Bank (balance)	**8**		
	388		388

(W3) **Taxation**

	$m
Bal b/f (8 + 24)	32
Income statement charge	35
New subsidiary	5
	72
Cash paid (balance)	(32)
Bal c/f (10 + 30)	40

Or

Taxation

Bal c/f (10 + 30)	40	Bal b/f (8 + 24)	32
		Income statement charge	35
		New sub	5
Bank (balance)	**32**		
	72		72

(W4) **Finance leases**

	$m
Bal b/f (20 + 70)	90
New leases	40
	130
Cash paid (balance)	(25)
Bal c/f (25 + 80)	105

Or

Finance leases

C/f < 1 yr	25	B/f < 1 yr	20
C/f > 1 yr	80	B/f > 1 yr	70
		New leases	40
Bank (balance)	**25**		
	130		130

(W5) **Non-controlling interests**

	$m
Bal b/f	40
Comprehensive income per CSCI	10
New subsidiary (105 x 20%)	21
	71
Dividends paid (balance)	(1)
Bal c/f	70

Or

Non-controlling interests

C/f	70	B/f	40
		Comp income	10
		New sub	21
Bank (balance)	**1**	(105 x 20%)	
	71		71

(W6) **Investment in associate**

	$m
Bal b/f	70
Share of profits	17
	87
Cash received (balance)	(7)
Bal c/f	80

Or

Investment in associate

B/f	70	C/f	80
Share of profit	17	**Bank (balance)**	**7**
	87		87

Test your understanding 8 - Pearl

Consolidated statement of cash flows

	$000	$000
Cash flows from operating activities		
Profit before tax	1,115	
Adjustments for:		
Finance costs	35	
Gain of sale of subsidiary	(100)	
Income from associate	(115)	
Depreciation	385	
Impairment (W1)	80	
Gain on disposal of PPE (275 – 250)	(25)	
Increase in inventory (W2)	(50)	
Decrease in receivables (W2)	60	
Decrease in payables (W2)	(65)	
		1,320
Finance costs paid		(35)
Tax paid (W3)		(180)
		1,105
Cash flows from investing activities		
Sale proceeds of PPE	275	
Purchases of PPE (W4)	(800)	
Dividends received from associate (W5)	85	
Acquisition of subsidiary (1,500 – 80)	(1,420)	
Sale of subsidiary (850 – 50)	800	
		(1,060)
Cash flows from financing activities		
Increase in loans (500 – 300)	200	
Dividends paid to parent shareholders (per CSOCE)	(125)	
Dividends paid to NCI shareholders (per CSOCE)	(50)	
		25
Increase in cash and cash equivalents		70
Opening cash and cash equivalents		140
Closing cash and cash equivalents		210

Workings

(W1) **Goodwill**

	$000
Bal b/f	1,850
Acquisition of sub (below)	350
Disposal of sub (below)	(190)
	2,010
Impairment (balance)	(80)
Bal c/f	1,930

Or

Goodwill

Bal b/f	1,850		
Acq'n of sub (below)	350	Disposal of sub (below)	190
		Impairment – balance	80
		Bal c/f	1,930
	2,200		2,200

Goodwill of acquired sub:

	$000
Fair value of P's holding (cost of investment)	1,500
NCI holding at fair value	340
Fair value of sub's net assets at acquisition	(1,490)
Goodwill at acquisition/ disposal	350

Goodwill of disposed sub:

	$000
Fair value of P's holding (cost of investment)	600
NCI holding at fair value	320
Fair value of sub's net assets at acquisition	(730)
Goodwill at acquisition/ disposal	190

(W2) **Working capital**

	Inventory	Receivables	Payables
	$000	$000	$000
Bal b/f	435	330	725
Acquisition of subsidiary	150	240	220
Disposal of subsidiary	(165)	(120)	(80)
	420	450	865
Increase/ (decrease) (balance)	50	(60)	(65)
Bal c/f	470	390	800

(W3) **Tax**

	$000
Bal b/f (360 + 105))	465
Acquisition of subsidiary	40
Disposal of subsidiary	(–)
Income statement charge	225
	730
Tax paid (balance)	(180)
Bal c/f (400 + 150)	550

Or

Tax

		Bal b/f (360 + 105)	465
		Acquisition of subsidiary	40
		Income statement	225
Tax paid (balance)	180		
Bal c/f (400 + 150)	550		
	730		730

(W4) **PPE**

	$000
Bal b/f	1,625
Depreciation	(385)
Revaluation gain	200
Disposal of plant	(250)
Acquisition of subsidiary	1,280
Disposal of subsidiary	(725)
	1,745
Cash paid (balance)	800
Bal c/f	2,545

Or

Property, Plant and Equipment

Bal b/f	1,625		
Revaluation	200	Depreciation	385
Acquisition of sub	1,280	Disposal of plant	250
		Disposal of sub	725
Cash paid – balance	800		
		Bal c/f	2,545
	3,905		3,905

(W5) **Dividend from associate**

	$000
Bal b/f	540
Income from associate	115
OCI from associate	50
	705
Dividends received (balance)	(85)
Bal c/f	620

Or

Associate

Bal b/f	540		
Income from associate	115		
OCI from associate	50	**Dividends received – balance**	85
		Bal c/f	620
	705		705

chapter

11

Developments in external reporting

Chapter learning objectives

On completion of their studies students should be able to:

- Discuss pressures for extending the scope and quality of external reports to include prospective and non-financial matters, and narrative reporting generally;
- Explain how information concerning the interaction of a business with society and the natural environment can be communicated in the published accounts;
- Discuss social and environmental issues which are likely to be most important to the stakeholders in an organisation;
- Explain the process of measuring, recording and disclosing the effect of exchanges between a business and society - human resource accounting;
- Discuss major differences between IFRS and US GAAP, and the measures designed to contribute towards their convergence.

1 Session Content

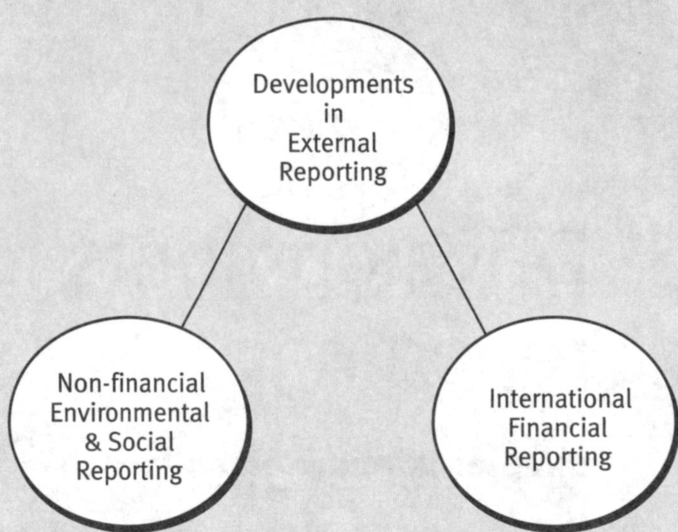

2 Non-financial reporting

According to the IASB's conceptual framework, the objective of financial reporting is to 'provide information about the reporting entity that is useful to existing and potential investors, lenders and other creditors in making decisions about providing resources to the entity'.

Financial statements provide historic information. To help users make decisions, it may be helpful to provide information relating to other aspects of an entity's performance.

For example:

- how the business is managed;
- its future prospects;
- the entity's policy on the environment;
- its attitude towards social responsibility etc.

There has been increasing pressure for entities to provide more information in their annual reports beyond just the financial statements since non-financial information can also be important to users' decisions.

Entities have also begun to accept over recent years that they have responsibilities to stakeholders other than just shareholders:

- customers and suppliers;
- local communities;
- society as a whole and the environment.

This additional non-financial reporting can be reported in a number of ways:

- A management commentary (operating and financial review) will assess the results of the period and discuss future prospects of the business.
- An environmental report will discuss responsibilities towards the environment and a social report will discuss responsibilities towards society. Both these issues could be combined in a report on sustainability which will also encompass economic issues.

3 IFRS Practice Statement – Management Commentary

Purpose of the Management Commentary (MC)

The IFRS Practice Statement on Management Commentary provides a broad, non-binding framework for the presentation of management commentary that accompanies financial statements that have been prepared in accordance with International Financial Reporting Standards (IFRSs).

It sets out the principles, qualitative characteristics and elements that are necessary to provide users of financial statements with useful information. As the guidance is in the form of a practice statement (rather than an IFRS) compliance with it is voluntary, however where an entity chooses to apply the practice statement it should explain the extent to which it has been applied.

Management commentary is a narrative report that provides a context within which to interpret the financial position, financial performance and cash flows of an entity. Management are able to explain their objectives and strategies for achieving those objectives. Users routinely use the type of information provided in management commentary to help them evaluate an entity's prospects and its general risks, as well as the success of management's strategies for achieving the entity's stated objectives. For many entities, management commentary is already an important element of their communication with the capital markets, supplementing as well as complementing the financial statements.

The practice statement helps management to produce the management commentary that will be reported alongside the financial statements prepared in accordance with IFRS. The users are identified as existing and potential members, together with lenders and creditors.

Framework for presentation

The following principles should be applied when considering the content of the management commentary:

(a) it should provide management's perspective of the entity's performance, position and progress;

(b) it should supplement and complement information presented in the financial statements;

(c) it should have an orientation to the future;

(d) it should possess the qualitative characteristics of relevance and faithful representation as described in the IASB's *Conceptual Framework for Financial Reporting*.

The management commentary should provide information to help users of the financial reports to assess the performance of the entity and the actions of its management relative to stated strategies and plans for progress. That type of commentary will help users of the financial reports to understand risk exposures and strategies of the entity, relevant non-financial factors and other issues not otherwise included within the financial statements.

Management commentary should provide management's perspective of the entity's performance, position and progress and therefore should derive from the information that is important to management in managing the business.

Elements of Management Commentary

Although the particular focus of management commentary will depend on the facts and circumstances of the entity, the commentary should include information that is essential to an understanding of:

(a) the nature of the business;

(b) management's objectives and its strategies for meeting those objectives;

(c) the entity's most significant financial and non-financial resources, risks and relationships;

(d) the results of operations and management's assessment of the entity's prospects; and

(e) the critical performance measures and indicators that management uses to evaluate the entity's performance against stated objectives.

It can be adopted by entities, where applicable, any time from the date of issue in December 2010.

Advantages and disadvantages of Management Commentary (MC)

Advantages of preparing MC:

- It helps companies appear transparent and willing to communicate.
- It may enhance a company's reputation to produce such documents voluntarily.
- It can be used to explain the background behind certain numbers in the financial statements, especially if they may otherwise be perceived in a negative light.
- It can compare the actual results against expected results and explain the reasons why performance differed.
- It is a useful summary of information found in a more complex form elsewhere in the financial statements.
- It may provide genuinely useful statements of management's intended business strategy, and sufficient information to be able to assess the relative success of business strategies to date.
- It may be more likely to be read and absorbed than some other parts of the annual report.

Disadvantages of preparing MC:

- Costly and time-consuming since it is likely to require significant time of senior management.
- Lack of requirements in terms of content will reduce the comparability of reports across entities.
- Companies may be selective and biased in the information they choose to discuss which will reduce its reliability for users.
- Users may rely too heavily on the commentary, and may read it in preference to a thorough examination of the detailed figures.
- Management commentary currently has the status of voluntary disclosure and so it suffers from all the general drawbacks of voluntary disclosure (e.g. it may not be prepared on an entirely consistent basis, bad news may be underplayed and so on).

UK – The Operating and Financial Review (OFR)

The UK Companies Act 2006 requires quoted companies to produce a Business Review, informing the shareholders and helping them assess how the directors have performed their duties to promote the success of the company.

Specific requirements include the provision of disclosures to the extent necessary for an understanding of the development, performance and position of the business. These disclosures include:

- The main trends and factors likely to affect future developments and activities;
- Information about employees, environmental matters and social and community issues;
- Information about contractual arrangements that are central to the company's activities.

To comply with these regulations, quoted companies are encouraged to follow the UK Accounting Standard Board's Reporting Statement on Operating and Financial Review (OFR).

This statement is the UK equivalent of the IASB's practice statement and sets out a framework for an OFR as follows:

(a) the nature, objectives and strategies of the business;

(b) the development and performance of the business, both in the period under review and in the future;

(c) the resources, risks and uncertainties and relationships that may affect the entity's long-term value; and

(d) the position of the business including a description of the capital structure, treasury policies and objectives and liquidity of the entity, both in the period under review and in the future.

OFR: The ASB's statement of best practice

The ASB specifies that an OFR should be a balanced and comprehensive analysis, consistent with the size and complexity of the business, of:

(a) the development and performance of the entity during the financial year;

(b) the position of the entity at the end of the year;

(c) the main trends and factors underlying the development, performance and position of the business of the entity during the financial year; and

(d) the main trends and factors which are likely to affect the entity's future development, performance and position.

The OFR should be prepared so as to assist members (i.e., shareholders) to assess the strategies adopted by the entity and the potential for those strategies to succeed. It is thus capable, potentially, of addressing some of the traditional limitations of financial statements, in that it specifically examines future business developments.

The ASB sets out the following principles for the preparation of an OFR:

The OFR shall:

(a) set out an analysis of the business through the eyes of the board of directors;

(b) focus on matters that are relevant to the interests of members (i.e., shareholders);

(c) have a forward-looking orientation, identifying those trends and factors relevant to the members' assessment of the current and future performance of the business and the progress towards the achievement of long-term business objectives;

(d) complement, as well as supplement, the financial statements in order to enhance the overall corporate disclosure;

(e) be comprehensive and understandable;

(f) be balanced and neutral, dealing even-handedly both with good and bad aspects;

(g) be comparable over time.

The principal disclosure requirements are as follows:

(a) the nature of the business, including a description of the market, competitive and regulatory environment in which the entity operates, and the entity's objectives and strategies;

(b) the development and performance of the business, both in the financial year under review and in the future;

(c) the resources, principal risks and uncertainties, and relationships that may affect the entity's long-term value;

(d) the position of the business including a description of the capital structure, treasury policies and objectives and liquidity of the entity, both in the financial year under review and the future.

Some more specific requirements relating to particular matters are added to this broad, general description of disclosures. The statement specifies that information should be included about:

(a) environmental matters (including the impact of the business on the environment);

(b) the entity's employees;

(c) social and community issues;

(d) persons with whom the entity has contractual or other arrangements which are essential to the business of the entity;

(e) receipts from, and returns to, members of the entity in respect of shares held by them; and

(f) all other matters directors consider to be relevant.

Test your understanding 1

Many entities produce a "Management Commentary" (known in the UK as the Operating and Financial Review).

Required:

(a) Explain why entities produce such a commentary together with a brief description of the typical information that it might contain.

(b) From the perspective of a user of financial statements, explain the advantages and disadvantages of such a report.

4 Sustainability

Definition

Sustainability is the process of conducting business in such a way that it enables an entity to meet its present needs without compromising the ability of future generations to meet their needs.

Introduction

In a corporate context, sustainability means that a business entity must attempt to reduce its environmental impact through more efficient use of natural resources and improving environmental practices.

More and more business entities are reporting their approach to sustainability in addition to the financial information reported in the annual report. There are increased public expectations for business entities and industries to take responsibility for the impact their activities have on the environment and society.

Reporting sustainability

- Currently, sustainability reporting is voluntary, although its use is increasing.
- Reports include highlights of non-financial performance such as environmental, social and economic reports during the accounting period.
- The report may be included in the annual report or published as a stand alone document, possibly on the entity's website.
- The increase in popularity of such reports highlights the growing trend that business entities are taking sustainability seriously and are attempting to be open about the impact of their activities.
- Reporting sustainability is sometimes called reporting the 'triple bottom line' covering environmental, social and economic reporting.

Framework for sustainability reporting

- There is no framework for sustainability reporting in IFRS, so this reporting is voluntary.
- This lack of regulation leads to several potential problems:
  - Because disclosure is largely voluntary, not all businesses disclose information. Those that do tend to do so either because they are under particular pressure to prove their 'green' credentials (for example, large public utility companies whose operations directly affect the environment), or because they have deliberately built their reputation on environmental friendliness or social responsibility.
  - The information disclosed may not be complete or reliable. Many businesses see environmental reporting largely as a public relations exercise and therefore only provide information that shows them in a positive light.
  - The information may not be disclosed consistently from year to year.
  - Some businesses, particularly small and medium sized entities, may believe that the costs of preparing and circulating additional information outweigh the benefits of doing so.

Global reporting initiative

- The most accepted framework for reporting sustainability is the Global Reporting Initiative's (GRI's) Sustainability Reporting Guidelines, the latest of which 'G3' – the third version of the guidelines – was issued in October 2006. It has recently been expanded with the launch of 'G3.1' in March 2011.
- The G3 Guidelines provide universal guidance for reporting on sustainability performance. They are applicable to all entities including SMEs and not-for-profit entities worldwide.
- The G3 consist of principles and disclosure items.The principles help to define report content, quality of the report, and give guidance on how to set the report boundary. Disclosure items include disclosures on management of issues, as well as performance indicators themselves.
- Applying these guidelines is voluntary.

The GRI suggests that entities report performance indicators so that users can monitor their performance from economic, environmental and social perspectives. Examples of such performance indicators may be:

- *Economic*

  E.g. proportion of spending with local suppliers; proportion of local workforce employed by the entity and their wages, pensions and other benefits; levels of taxes paid and subsidies received.

- *Environmental*

  E.g. percentage of recycled material used in production, levels of gas emissions, levels of organic ingredients used in products.

- *Social*

  E.g. human rights, breakdown of workforce by ethnic background, policies in respect of working hours and labour practices, benefits provided to employees such as healthcare, gym membership.

The best way to understand sustainability is to look at some examples of sustainability reports in financial statements.

You can also look at the Global Reporting Initiative website: www.globalreporting.org

The financial statements of companies that have applied the GRI guidelines are listed with a link to their reports.

The Global Reporting Initiative

Principles and guidance

This section of the G3 provides:

- Guidance for **defining report content**, by applying the principles of materiality, stakeholder inclusiveness, sustainability context and completeness:

  Materiality

  The information in the report should cover topics which reflect the entity's significant economic, environmental and social impacts.

  Stakeholder inclusiveness

  The reporting entity should identify its stakeholders and explain in the report how it has responded to their expectations and interests.

  Sustainability context

  The report should present the entity's performance in the wider context of sustainability.

  Completeness

  Coverage of the material topics and indicators and definition of the report boundary should be enough to reflect significant impacts and allow stakeholders to assess the reporting entity's performance.

- Principles for **ensuring report quality**, these being balance, comparability, accuracy, timeliness, clarity and reliability:

  Balance

  The report should reflect both positive and negative aspects of an entity's performance to enable a reasoned overall assessment.

  Comparability

  Issues and information should be reported consistently. Reported information should be presented in a way which allows stakeholders to assess trends over time and compare the entity to other organisations.

Accuracy

The reported information should be substantially accurate.

Timeliness

Reporting should occur regularly and in time for stakeholders to make informed decisions.

Clarity

Information should be understandable and accessible.

Reliability

Information and processes used to prepare a report should be compiled and disclosed in a way which establishes the quality of the information.

- Guidance for **report boundary setting** in terms of determining the range of entities to be included in the report.

Standard disclosures

There are three different types of measures that can be used:

- strategic approach;
- management goals;
- performance results.

Strategy and analysis (strategic approach)

Statement from CEO explaining the relevance of sustainability to organisational strategy in the short, medium and long terms.

Description of organisation's key impacts on sustainability and impact of sustainability trends, risks and opportunities on the organisation.

Organisational profile

Overview of the reporting entity in terms of products, organisational structure, location of operations and markets etc.

Report parameters

- Boundary of report
- Specific exclusions
- Basis for reporting on subsidiaries etc
- Location of standard disclosures in the report

Governance

- Committees and responsibilities
- Mechanisms for stakeholders to provide recommendations to governance bodies
- Internal codes of conduct and their application

Commitments to external initiatives

- External initiatives to which the entity subscribes
- Strategic memberships, funding and participation in industry associations

Stakeholder engagement

- List of stakeholder groups engaged by entity
- Approach to stakeholder engagement
- Key topics and concerns of stakeholders

Management approach (management goals)

Disclosures are intended to address the entity's approach to managing the sustainability topics associated with risks and opportunities.

Disclosures may include:

- Goals and performance;
- Policy;
- Organisational responsibility;
- Training and awareness;
- Monitoring and follow up;
- Additional contextual information.

Performance results

Elicit comparable information on a number of areas, including:

- Environmental, for example, level of materials; energy and water used; biodiversity; level of emissions and waste; impact of products and services; and transport.
- Human rights, for example number of suppliers who have undergone human rights screening; number of discrimination actions; measures taken to contribute to the elimination of child and forced and compulsory labour.
- Labour practices, for example employment turnover; percentage of employees covered by collective bargaining agreements; rates of injury and occupational diseases; average hours training per employee per year; indicators of diversity.
- Society, for example impact of operations on communities; number of corruption investigations; number of legal actions for anti-competitive behaviour; level of fines for non-compliance with legal requirements.
- Product responsibility, for example results of customer satisfaction surveys; number of breaches of customer confidentiality and losses of personal data.
- Economic, for example level of spending on local suppliers; number of senior management hired from local community.

5 Environmental reporting

Definition

Environmental reporting is the disclosure of information in the published annual report or elsewhere, of the effect that the operations of the business have on the natural environment.

As detailed in the section above, the sustainability report combines environmental, social and economic reporting in one report. Environmental reports were the first step in reporting an entity's impact on its environment.

This section details the contents of an environment report together with any accounting issues.

Environmental reporting in practice

There are two main vehicles that companies use to publish information about the ways in which they interact with the natural environment:

- The published annual report (which includes the financial statements)
- A separate environment report (either as a paper document or simply posted on the company website).

The IASB encourages the presentation of environmental reports if management believe that they will assist users in making economic decisions, but they are not mandatory.

IAS 1 points out that any statement or report presented outside financial statements is outside the scope of IFRSs, so there are no mandatory IFRS requirements on separate environmental reports.

Reasons for environmental reporting

An entity may publish an environmental report:

- to differentiate itself from its competitors;
- to acknowledge responsibility for the environment;
- to demonstrate compliance with regulations;
- to obtain social approval for its activities.

The first environmental reports were largely a public relations exercise and the aim was to demonstrate a company's commitment to the environment. Some entities continue to view them in this light. However, many others now view the environmental report as a vehicle for communicating an entity's performance in safeguarding the natural environment.

Separate environmental reports

Many large public companies publish environmental reports that are completely separate from the annual report and financial statements. The environmental report is often combined in a sustainability report.

Most environmental reports take the form of a combined statement of policy and review of activity. They cover issues such as:

- waste management;
- pollution;
- intrusion into the landscape;
- the effect of an entity's activities upon wildlife;

- use of energy;
- the benefits to the environment of the entity's products and services.

Generally, the reports disclose the entity's targets and/or achievements, with direct comparison between the two in some cases. They may also disclose financial information, such as the amount invested in preserving the environment.

Public and media interest has tended to focus on the environmental report rather than on the disclosures in the published annual report and financial statements. This separation reflects the fact that the two reports are aimed at different audiences.

Shareholders are the main users of the annual report, while the environmental report is designed to be read by the general public. Many companies publish their environmental and social reports on their websites, which encourages access to a wide audience.

The content of environment reports

The content of an environment report may cover the following areas.

(a) **Environmental issues pertinent to the entity and industry**

- The entity's policy towards the environment and any improvements made since first adopting the policy.
- Whether the entity has a formal system for managing environmental risks.
- The identity of the director(s) responsible for environmental issues.
- The entity's perception of the risks to the environment from its operations.
- The extent to which the entity would be capable of responding to a major environmental disaster and an estimate of the full economic consequences of such a future major disaster.
- The effects of, and the entity's response to, any government legislation on environmental matters.
- Details of any significant infringement of environmental legislation or regulations.
- Material environmental legal issues in which the entity is involved.
- Details of any significant initiatives taken, if possible linked to amounts in financial statements.
- Details of key indicators (if any) used by the entity to measure environmental performance. Actual performance should be compared with targets and with performance in prior periods.

(b) **Financial information**

- The entity's accounting policies relating to environmental costs, provisions and contingencies.
- The amount charged to the income statement or statement of comprehensive income during the accounting period in respect of expenditure to prevent or rectify damage to the environment caused by the entity's operations. This could be analysed between expenditure that the entity was legally obliged to incur and other expenditure.
- The amount charged to the income statement or statement of comprehensive income during the accounting period in respect of expenditure to protect employees and society in general from the consequences of damage to the environment caused by the entity's operations. Again, this could be analysed between compulsory and voluntary expenditure.
- Details (including amounts) of any provisions or contingent liabilities relating to environmental matters.
- The amount of environmental expenditure capitalised during the year.
- Details of fines, penalties and compensation paid during the accounting period in respect of non-compliance with environmental regulations.

Accounting for environment costs

Definitions

Environmental costs	include environmental measures and environmental losses.
Environmental measures	are the costs of preventing, reducing or repairing damage to the environment and the costs of conserving resources.
Environmental losses	are costs that bring no benefit to the business.

Environmental measures can include:

- capital expenditure;
- closure or decommissioning costs;
- clean-up costs;
- development expenditure;
- costs of recycling or conserving energy.

Environmental losses can include:

- fines, penalties and compensation;
- impairment or disposal losses relating to assets that have to be scrapped or abandoned because they damage the environment.

Accounting treatment

Environmental costs are treated in accordance with the requirements of current accounting standards.

(i) Most expenditure is charged in the income statement or statement of comprehensive income in the period in which it is incurred. Material items may need to be disclosed separately in the notes to the accounts or on the face of the income statement/statement of comprehensive income as required by IAS 1.

(ii) Entities may have to undertake fundamental reorganisations or restructuring or to discontinue particular activities in order to protect the environment. If a sale or termination meets the definition of a discontinued operation, its results must be separately disclosed in accordance with the requirements of IFRS 5. Material restructuring costs may need to be separately disclosed on the face of the income statement/statement of comprehensive income.

(iii) Fines and penalties for non-compliance with regulations are charged to the income statement or statement of comprehensive income in the period in which they are incurred. This applies even if the activities that resulted in the penalties took place in an earlier accounting period, as they cannot be treated retrospectively as prior period adjustments.

(iv) Expenditure on non-current assets is capitalised and depreciated in the usual way as per IAS 16 **Property, plant and equipment**.

(v) Non-current assets (including goodwill) may become impaired as a result of environmental legislation or new regulations. IAS 36 **Impairment of assets** lists events that could trigger an impairment review, one of which is a significant adverse change in the legal environment in which the business operates.

(vi) Research and development expenditure in respect of environmentally friendly products, processes or services is covered by IAS 38 **Intangible assets**.

Provisions for environmental liabilities

IAS 37 **Provisions, contingent liabilities and contingent assets** states that three conditions must be met before a provision may be recognised:

- the entity has a present **obligation** as a result of a past event;
- it is **probable** that a transfer of economic benefits will be required to settle the obligation;
- a **reliable estimate** can be made of the amount of the obligation.

IAS 37 is covered in detail in the F1 syllabus, but some points are particularly relevant to provisions for environmental costs:

- The fact that the entity's activities have caused environmental contamination does not in itself give rise to an obligation to rectify the damage. However, even if there is no legal obligation, there may be a constructive obligation. An entity almost certainly has a constructive obligation to rectify environmental damage if it has a policy of acting in an environmentally responsible way and this policy is well publicised.
- The obligation must arise from a past event. This means that a provision can only be set up to rectify environmental damage that has already happened. If an entity needs to incur expenditure to reduce pollution in the future, it should not set up a provision. This is because in theory it can avoid the expenditure by its future actions, for example by discontinuing the particular activity that causes the pollution.

Capitalisation of environmental expenditure

If environmental expenditure provides access to future economic benefits, it meets the IASB's definition of an asset. It would normally be capitalised and depreciated over the useful life of the asset.

An asset may also arise as the result of recognising a provision. In principle, when a provision or change in a provision is recognised, an asset should also be recognised when, and only when, the incurring of the present obligation gives access to future economic benefits. Otherwise the setting up of the provision should be charged immediately to the income statement or statement of comprehensive income.

Illustration 1 - Redco

Redco has just purchased a licence that will allow it to drill for oil in an area of Alaska. The purchase cost of this licence is $20m.

In addition Redco has agreed to pay $6.5m to restore the landscape once it has finished. This payment will be made at the end of year 5 when the licence expires.

The pre-tax discount rate that reflects current market risks is 8%.

Required:

Explain the accounting treatment of the licence and associated restoration costs.

Solution

There is an obligation to pay the $6.5m to restore the landscape at the end of the five years and so the present value of the obligation should be capitalised to the cost of the non-current asset and subsequently depreciated. The corresponding provision will need to be increased every year to represent the unwinding of the discount and this is charged to the income statement.

The present value of $6.5m discounted at 8% over 5 years is:

$6.5m x 0.681 = $4,426,500.

This amount will be recorded as follows at the start of year 1:

Dr Non-current assets

Cr Provision

The provision is 'unwound' at 8% each year with the cost of unwinding reflected as a finance cost in the income statement. In year 1, a finance cost of $354,120 (8% x $4,426,500) would be charged and the closing provision at the end of year 1 would be $4,780,620 ($4,426, 500 + $354,120).

Test your understanding 2

You are the chief accountant of Redstart and you are currently finalising the financial statements for the year ended 31 December 20X1. Your assistant (who has prepared the draft accounts) is unsure about the treatment of two transactions that have taken place during the year. She has written you a memorandum that explains the key principles of each transaction and also the treatment adopted in the draft accounts.

Transaction one

One of the corporate objectives of the enterprise is to ensure that its activities are conducted in such a way as to minimise any damage to the natural environment. It is committed in principle to spending extra money in pursuit of this objective but has not yet made any firm proposals. The directors believe that this objective will prove very popular with customers and are anxious to emphasise their environmentally friendly policies in the annual report.

Your assistant suggests that a sum should be set aside from profits each year to create a provision in the financial statements against the possible future costs of environmental protection. Accordingly, she has charged the income statement for the year ended 31 December 20X1 with a sum of $100,000 and proposes to disclose this fact in a note to the accounts.

Transaction two

A new law has recently been enacted that will require Redstart to change one of its production processes in order to reduce the amount of carbon dioxide that is emitted. This will involve purchasing and installing some new plant that is more efficient than the equipment currently in use. To comply with the law, the new plant must be operational by 31 December 20X2. The new plant has not yet been purchased.

In the draft financial statements for the year ended 31 December 20X1, your assistant has recognised a provision for $5 million (the cost of the new plant). This has been disclosed as a separate item in the notes to the income statement.

The memorandum from your assistant also expresses concern about the fact that there was no reference to environmental matters anywhere in the published financial statements for the year ended 31 December 20X0. As a result, she believes that the financial statements did not comply with the requirements of International Financial Reporting Standards and therefore must have been wrong.

Required:

Draft a reply to your assistant that:

(a) reviews the treatment suggested by your assistant and recommends changes where relevant. In each case your reply should refer to relevant International Accounting Standards

(b) replies to her suggestion that the financial statements for the year ended 31 December 20X0 were wrong because they made no reference to environmental matters.

Background to environmental reporting

Introduction

During the late 1980s and early 1990s there were several well publicised environmental disasters, including the Exxon Valdez oil spill and the explosion at the Bhopal chemical factory. In addition, the 1992 Rio Earth Summit and the activities of organisations such as Greenpeace and Friends of the Earth drew the general public's attention to issues such as global warming.

There are now considerable incentives for businesses to take action to preserve the environment, such as controlling pollution, using recyclable materials, choosing renewable materials and developing environmentally friendly products. Public interest in safeguarding the environment affects businesses in two main ways.

- They may suffer direct losses as a result of their actions, for example, they may be legally or constructively obliged to incur the expense of rectifying environmental damage, or they may have to pay additional taxes or suffer financial penalties if they cause pollution.
- If a business is believed to cause damage to the environment or to otherwise act in an unethical way, it may attract considerable adverse publicity. This leads to loss of customers. Environmental disasters can harm businesses as well as society in general. For example, the Exxon Valdez oil spillage reduced the company's profits by almost 90% in one quarter alone.

There is a positive side: a business can attract customers if it has a 'green' image. One example of this is The Body Shop, a chain of retail cosmetic shops.

As a result of these factors, the number of companies disclosing information about the effect of their operations on the environment is steadily increasing.

Test your understanding 3

Company B owns a chemical plant, producing paint.

The plant uses a great deal of energy and releases emissions into the environment. Its by-product is harmful and is treated before being safely disposed of. The company has been fined for damaging the environment following a spillage of the toxic waste product. Due to stricter monitoring routines set up by the company, the fines have reduced and in the current year they have not been in breach of any local environment laws.

The company is aware that emissions are high and has been steadily reducing them. They purchase electricity from renewable sources and in the current year have employed a temporary consultant to calculate their carbon footprint so they can take steps to reduce it.

Required:

(a) Explain why companies may wish to make social and environmental disclosures in their annual report. Discuss how this content should be determined.

(b) Discuss the information that could be included in Company B's environmental report.

6 Social reporting

Definition

Corporate social reporting is the process of communicating the social and environmental effects of organisations' economic actions to particular interest groups within society and to society at large.

It involves extending the accountability of organisations (particularly companies) beyond the traditional role of providing a financial account to the owners of capital. Social and ethical reporting would seem to be at variance with the prevailing business. However, there are a number of reasons why entities publish social reports:

- They may have deliberately built their reputation on social responsibility (e.g. Body Shop, Traidcraft) in order to attract a particular customer base.

- They may perceive themselves as being under particular pressure to prove that their activities do not exploit society as a whole or certain sections of it (e.g. Shell International and large utility companies).
- They may be genuinely convinced that it is in their long-term interests to balance the needs of the various stakeholder groups.
- They may fear that the government will eventually require them to publish socially oriented information if they do not do so voluntarily.

Social responsibility

A business interacts with society in several different ways as follows:

- It employs human resources in the form of management and other employees.
- Its activities affect society as a whole, for example, it may:
  - be the reason for a particular community's existence;
  - produce goods that are helpful or harmful to particular members of society;
  - damage the environment in ways that harm society as a whole;
  - undertake charitable works in the community or promote particular values.

If a business interacts with society in a responsible manner, the needs of other stakeholders should be taken into account and performance may encompass:

- providing fair remuneration and an acceptable working environment;
- paying suppliers promptly;
- minimising the damage to the environment caused by the entity's activities;
- contributing to the community by providing employment or by other means.

Social reporting in practice

Social reporting in the financial statements

- Disclosures of social reporting matters in financial statements tend to be required by national legislation and by the stock exchange on which an entity is quoted. There is little mention of social matters in international accounting standards.

- IAS 1 requires disclosure of the total cost of employee benefits for the period. If the 'nature of expense' method is chosen for the income statement/statement of comprehensive income, then the total charge for employee costs will be shown on the face of the income statement/statement of comprehensive income. If the 'function of expense' method is chosen, then IAS 1 requires disclosure of the total employee costs in a note to the financial statements.
- IAS 24 **Related party disclosures** requires the benefits paid to key management personnel to be disclosed in total and analysed into the categories of benefits.
- Other possible disclosures (e.g. details of directors and corporate governance matters, employee policies, supplier payment policies, charitable contributions, etc.) are normally dealt with by local legislation and would only be required by IFRSs when such disclosure is necessary to present fairly the entity's financial performance.

Separate social reports

- Stand alone social and ethical reports do not have to be audited and there are no international regulations prescribing their content.
- There are some sets of non-mandatory guidelines and codes of best practice, for example, the standard AA1000, which has been issued by the Institute of Social and Ethical Accountability (ISEA).
- Some organisations have the data in their reports independently verified and include the auditor's report in their published document. The social report may or may not be combined with the environmental report.

It has been suggested that there should be three main types of information in the social report.

(a) **Information about relationships with stakeholders**, e.g. employee numbers, wages and salaries, provision of facilities for customers and information about involvement with local charities.

(b) **Information about the accountability of the entity**, e.g. sickness leave, accident rates, noise levels, numbers of disabled employees, compliance with current legal, ethical and industry standards.

(c) **Information about dialogue with stakeholders**, e.g. the way in which the entity consults with all stakeholders and provides public feedback on the stakeholders' perceptions of the entity's responsibilities to the community and its performance in meeting stakeholder needs.

7 Human resource accounting

Definition

Human resource accounting is the process of measuring and disclosing the value of an entity's human resources: its employees. It is one aspect of social accounting.

One of the criticisms of conventional accounting is that the statement of financial position does not represent the true value of a business because it fails to recognise its intellectual capital i.e. skills, knowledge and experience of employees.

Traditional businesses normally have a capital base largely made up of tangible assets such as property, plant and equipment and inventories. However, an increasing number of businesses develop information technology or provide services. These businesses generate revenue by means of their intellectual capital.

Businesses that rely on intellectual capital often have relatively few 'traditional' assets. As a result, there is often a large gap between the market capitalisation of businesses and the carrying value of their net assets. The existence of this 'gap' suggests that the market recognises that intellectual capital is an asset.

This can distort interpretation of their results since a ratio such as return on capital employed (ROCE) will be high due to the low level of capital employed on the statement of financial position.

Some argue that it would be logical to recognise this asset and that the fact that it is 'missing' from the statement of financial position undermines the credibility of the financial statements. Users of the financial statements do not have sufficient information about the full extent of the resources available to the business.

Advantages of recognising human resources as assets

By recording the asset on the statement of financial position, management of an entity are perhaps more likely to consider their value to the business and therefore take more responsibility for looking after their well-being.

Limitations to capitalising human resources

An asset is a resource controlled by an entity as a result of past events from which future economic benefits are expected to flow to the entity (IASB conceptual framework).

One of the main arguments against capitalising intellectual capital is that it does not meet the definition of an asset per the IASB conceptual framework. This is because the entity cannot "control" human resources.

It will also be very difficult to reliably measure the value of intellectual capital. The problems associated with this area may result in manipulation of financial statements and also lack of comparability between the financial statements of different entities.

Capitalising human resources

An asset is a resource controlled by an entity as a result of past events from which future economic benefits are expected to flow to the entity (IASB Framework).

The employer has the ability to earn future profits and obtain future inflows of cash as a result of an employee's services to the entity. The asset is not the actual person, but this right to future economic benefit, which does not have to be certain.

The main difficulty in treating human resources as assets is uncertainty as to whether the employer can control the benefits. Control implies the ability to obtain any economic benefits that arise or to restrict the access of others to those benefits. Whether an employer can exercise control may depend on the terms of the employee's contract and on what happens in practice. For example, employees are normally required to work a minimum number of hours and there is usually an expectation that an employee will not provide services to anybody other than the employer.

However, one of the main arguments against recognising human resources in the statement of financial position is that employees are free to leave the employer if they wish to do so. This implies that the employer does not control the rights to future benefits from the employee's services and that human resources do not meet the IAS 38 definition of an asset. IAS 38 now specifically prohibits the recognition of either a team of skilled staff or specific management or technical talent as an intangible asset, unless it is protected by legal rights to use it and to obtain the future economic benefits expected from it.

Even if it could be argued that a human resource did meet the definition of an intangible asset, it can only be recognised in the financial statements if:

(a) it is probable that the expected future economic benefits that are attributable to the asset will flow to the entity; and
(b) the cost of the asset can be measured reliably.

The second of these two criteria is likely to cause problems in practice. In theory, a human resource asset could be valued at historic cost, at current value (value to the business) or at fair value.

- **Historical cost** – This is the actual cost of recruiting, employing and training an employee.
- **Value to the business** – This is the lower of replacement cost and recoverable amount. Replacement cost would be the cost of recruiting and developing another employee to the same level of competence as present staff. Recoverable amount would be value in use: the present value of the cash flows that the employee's services would generate in future periods. There is unlikely to be a net realisable value for an employee's services.
- **Fair value** – This is an employee's 'market value' (in practice, probably the cost of recruiting and developing another employee to the same level of competence).

In practice, human resources would almost certainly have to be valued at historical cost as it is doubtful whether any other basis would be sufficiently reliable. There would then remain the problem of deciding which costs to capitalise and of selecting an amortisation period.

There is an argument for capitalising and amortising recruitment and training costs, because these are incurred specifically in order to obtain future economic benefits. Wages and salaries are the expense of obtaining an employee's services for a specific period and therefore it is logical to charge them to the income statement as they are incurred.

The amortisation period could be the average period of service of employees as a whole, or of the relevant category of employees.

Test your understanding 4

Intellectual capital can be defined as "knowledge which can be used to create value".

Currently, IFRS permit the recognition of only a limited range of internally generated intellectual assets including, for example, copyrights.

Required:

(a) Explain the advantages that could be gained by entities and their stakeholders if the scope of IFRS were expanded to permit the recognition in the statement of financial position of a wider range of intellectual assets, such as know-how, the value of the workforce, and employee skills.

(b) Explain the principal reasons why IFRS do not currently permit the recognition in the statement of financial position of intellectual assets such as know-how, the value of the workforce, and employee skills.

8 Impact of non-financial reporting

The sections above have highlighted the developments in non-financial reporting. Due to the voluntary nature of these disclosures their impact and effectiveness will depend on various factors:

- **Relevance**: how much weight do/will investors, employees and consumers give to these factors, compared with that given to financial factors (so return on investment, employee benefits and price, respectively)?
- **Reliability**: how much can the performance measured in these areas be relied on? How sure can users of this information be that it is a faithful representation of what has occurred, as opposed to a selective view focusing on the successes? Are there external assurance processes that can validate the information, perhaps using the GRI guidelines?
- **Comparability**: is the information produced by different entities pulled together on a comparable basis, using similar measurement policies, so that the users can make informed choices between entities? If not, all that can be measured is an entity's performance compared with its own performance in previous periods.

Even if the information is reliable and comparable, is it useful, i.e. will it change the behaviour of investors, employees and consumers?

The answers to these questions will determine whether entities take such reporting seriously or merely treat it as part of their promotional activities. The answers in ten years' time will almost certainly be different from those of today.

9 International financial reporting

As more and more companies operate globally, there has been an increasing need for accounting practices to become more harmonised. Businesses operate on a global scale and investors make investment decisions on a worldwide basis. There is therefore a need for financial information to be presented on a consistent basis.

Advantages	Disadvantages
• Increased efficiency and decreased costs for global companies	• Costs for non-global companies
• Increased comparability	• Differences in attitudes and traditions
• Increased competition in world markets	
• Easier access to international finance.	

The EU issue directives which member states are required to adopt within their national legislation.

One of these directives required EU listed entities to prepare consolidated financial statements in accordance with International Accounting Standards from 1 January 2005.

The UK's ASB are also in the process of harmonising UK accounting standards with International Standards.

10 Convergence project between IASB & FASB

2002 Norwalk Agreement

In September 2002, the IASB and US Financial Accounting Standards Board (FASB) signed the Norwalk agreement to start convergence of IFRS and US GAAP.

Both Boards committed to the development of high quality, compatible accounting standards that are suitable for both domestic and cross border financial reporting.

Objectives set in agreement:

- Make existing accounting standards compatible as soon as practicable;
- Once compatibility is achieved, to work together in the future to ensure compatibility is maintained.

Roadmap to convergence

In February 2006, the IASB and FASB released a Memorandum of Understanding, also called the Roadmap, identifying short-term and long-term convergence projects and this was further updated in 2008. The most recent progress report, issue in April 2012, reported that most of the short-term projects are completed or close to completion and, of the longer term projects, three remain outstanding:

- leases - current proposal is for all leasing arrangements to result in the recognition of an asset (the right to use the leased asset) and a liability (to pay the lease rentals);
- revenue recognition - a comprehensive standard that can be applied to all revenue transactions, regardless of industry; and
- financial instruments (part complete - see IFRS 9 below).

Recent changes

IAS 1 *Presentation of Financial Statements*

The IASB published their most recent amendments to IAS 1 in June 2011. The main amendment was to require entities to group items presented in other comprehensive income based on whether they are potentially reclassifiable to profit or loss or not.

IAS 19 *Employee Benefits (2011)*

These amendments have simplifed the accounting treatment for defined benefit pension schemes and removed options that previously existed for accounting for actuarial gains and losses. This will improve consistency and comparability across entities. See chapter 15 for the new rules.

IFRS 13 *Fair Value Measurement*

Published in May 2011, the objective of IFRS 13 is to establish a single framework for measuring fair values. See chapter 13 for more detail.

'Pack of five' reporting standards

The issue of the 'pack of five' new or revised standards in May 2011, particularly IFRS 10 *Consolidated Financial Statements*, brings the accounting treatment of off-balance sheet finance activities in IFRS broadly into alignment with US GAAP. The 2006 Memorandum of Understanding between the IASB and US FASB included agreement to undertake a joint project on consolidation. It also represented a significant element of the IASB response to the global financial crisis.

The 'pack of five' reporting standards are:

- IFRS 10 *Consolidated Financial Statements*
- IFRS 11 *Joint Arrangements*
- IFRS 12 *Disclosure of Interests in Other Entities*
- IAS 27 (revised) *Separate Financial Statements*
- IAS 28 (revised) *Investments in Associates and Joint Ventures*

See chapters 4 and 6 for more detail.**IFRS 9 *Financial Instruments***

This is part of a project to replace IAS 39 Financial Instruments – Recognition and Measurement. It was published in November 2009, dealing with recognition and measurements of financial assets, and was then updated in October 2010 to include recognition and measurement of financial liabilities.

Accounting for financial assets

The four categories of financial assets as defined by IAS 39 have now been replaced by three categories as follows in IFRS 9:

(1) Financial assets at fair value through profit or loss – this is the default category which will apply unless an entity adopts an alternative designation.

(2) Financial assets at fair value through other comprehensive income - This designation must be made upon initial recognition and is irrevocable. It applies to equity instruments only, with any movement in fair value taken to other comprehensive income. Upon derecognition, there is no recycling of gains or losses already recognised in equity.

(3) Financial assets at amortised cost – This designation must be made upon initial recognition and is irrevocable. To apply this designation, two tests must be passed; if either or both test are failed, the debt instrument must be measured at fair value through profit or loss. The tests are:

   (a) The business model test – the primary reason for holding the financial assets must be to collect the contractual cash flows associated with the asset (as opposed to managing them to take advantage of changes in fair value); and

   (b) The contractual cashflows characteristics test - the cash flows collected must consist solely of repayment of interest and principal. Convertible debt would not pass this test as there is also the option or right to convert the debt into shares at a later date.

This has simplified accounting for financial assets as the Available For Sale category included within IAS 39 has been removed. The need to recycle some gains and losses taken to equity upon subsequent derecognition has also been removed.

Accounting for financial liabilities

The categorisation and accounting treatment for financial liabilities within IAS 39 has essentially been retained within IFRS 9. Financial liabilities are accounted for as:

(1) Financial liabilities at fair value through profit or loss, or

(2) Other financial liabilities at amortised cost.

The overall impact of IFRS 9 is that there is likely to be increased emphasis on fair value accounting, rather than the use of other forms of measurement such as amortised cost or historical cost.

IFRS 9 is effective for accounting periods commencing on or after 1 January 2015, with earlier application possible. Note that further developments are in the pipeline dealing with impairment, derivatives and hedging. To the extent that IFRS 9 does not yet deal with a particular issue, the provisions of IAS 39 continue to apply.

Conceptual Framework for Financial Reporting 2010

This is a long-term joint project between the IASB and US FASB, which was first agreed in 2004. The end point of the eight-stage project will be approval of a single, self-contained document which will create a foundation for the development of future accounting standards that are principles based, internally consistent and internationally converged. Ultimately, it will replace the IASB's *Framework for Preparation and Presentation of Financial Statements* which was first published in 1989. As this project progresses and individual chapters are approved, the new Conceptual Framework will be updated and the superseded provisions of the original Framework document will be deleted.

The Conceptual Framework for Financial Reporting 2010 project has the following phases:

Phase A – objectives and qualitative characteristics

In September 2010, the IASB and FASB approved chapters 1 and 3 of the updated 2010 Conceptual Framework. There is no significant change to the underlying purpose and objectives of the Framework as established in the 1989 document. The underlying assumptions of accruals and going concern are currently retained within the 2010 document.

However, there is a change dealing with qualitative characteristics of useful financial information. There are two fundamental qualitative characteristics of relevance and faithful representation, together with four enhancing qualitative characteristics of:

- Comparability
- Verifiability
- Timeliness
- Understandability

Phase B – elements and recognition

The objectives of this phase of the project are to refine and converge the IASB and FASB frameworks including draft revised definitions as follows:

An asset of an entity is a present economic resource to which the entity has either a right or other access that others do not have.

A liability of an entity is a present economic obligation for which the entity is the obligor.

Remaining phases

There has been little or no development or progress on the remaining phases of the project:

- Phase C – measurement
- Phase D – the reporting entity
- Phase E – presentation and disclosure
- Phase F – purpose and status
- Phase G – application to not-for-profit entities
- Phase H – remaining issues

IFRS 3 *Business Combinations (2008)*

In January 2008, the IASB issued amendments to IFRS 3 (and IAS 27). The new standards changed the calculation of goodwill by introducing the fair value method as an option for measuring non-controlling interests. The treatment of piecemeal acquisitions was also amended to reflect the control based approach.

Borrowing costs

IAS 23 permitted borrowing costs on the construction of an asset to be either capitalised or written off, whereas US GAAP required such costs to be capitalised. IAS 23 was amended in March 2007 and is now in line with US GAAP, requiring the capitalisation of such costs.

Other standards

- IFRS 8 Operating segments;
- IFRS 5 Non-current assets held for sale and discontinued operations.

SEC reconciliations

Until recently, entities that prepare financial statements under International GAAP but who are listed on the US markets had to prepare a reconciliation of their financial statements to US GAAP. In November 2007, the SEC released companies from this requirement. This was seen as one of the most significant step towards full convergence.

Some further remaining differences between IASs and US GAAP

Topic	IAS/ IFRS	US GAAP
Inventory valuation	LIFO not allowed as a method of measuring cost	LIFO allowed
Development costs	Capitalise when criteria are met	Expense
Non-current assets	Historic cost or valuation	Historic cost
Extraordinary items	Prohibited	Permitted although rare

Test your understanding 5

An important development in international accounting in recent years has been the convergence project between the IASB and the US standard setter, the Financial Accounting Standards Board (FASB).

Required:

(a) Describe the objectives, and progress to date, of the convergence project, illustrating your response with examples of the work that has been successfully undertaken.

(b) Identify and briefly explain the three remaining long-term projects that the IASB and FASB are currently working on.

(c) List three examples of other remaining differences between IFRS and US GAAP.

11 Further guidance

A number of useful articles have been published by Jayne Howson, a member of the F2 marking team. They are specifically designed to assist students in answering exam question on developments in external reporting, as this is a topic that is often poorly attempted.

You can access these articles at http://www.cimaglobal.com/Students/2010-professional-qualification/Management-level/F2-study-resources/Useful-articles/ and they include:

- Environmental reporting, May 2012
- IFRS and US GAAP convergence – are we there yet?, February 2012
- Human asset accounting, April 2011

12 Chapter summary

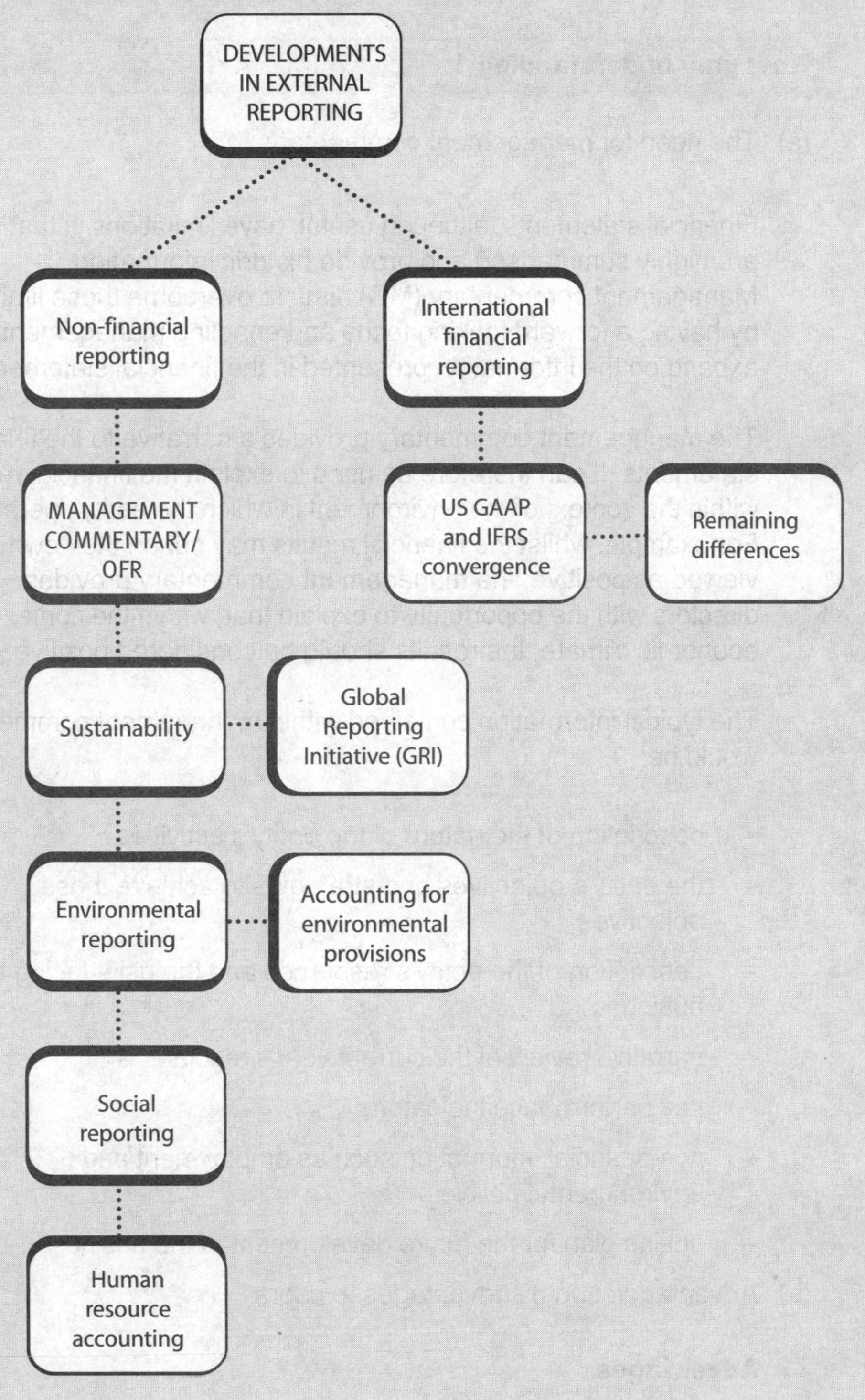

Test your understanding answers

Test your understanding 1

(a) The need for management commentary

Financial statements, although useful, have limitations in that they are highly summarised and provide historic information. Management commentary (MC) aims to overcome these limitations by having a forward looking focus and enabling management to expand on the information presented in the financial statements.

The management commentary provides a narrative to the financial statements. It can therefore be used to explain the financial results within the context of the environment in which the entity operates. For example, whilst the financial results may not on their own be viewed as positive, the management commentary provides directors with the opportunity to explain that, within the context of the economic climate, the results should be considered positive.

The typical information contained within management commentary would be:

- description of the nature of the entity's activities
- the entity's objectives and strategies to achieve those objectives
- description of the entity's resources and the risks facing the business
- narrative review of the current year's results
- key performance indicators
- non-financial information such as employment and environmental policies
- outline plan for the future development of the business

(b) Advantages and disadvantages to users

Advantages

The MC will provide information regarding the future prospects of an entity. This should enhance the users' ability to make more appropriate investment decisions.

The narrative information should give users a better understanding of the performance and position of the entity.

Producing an MC voluntarily shows the entity as being transparent and willing to communicate. Users may wish to consider such factors, as well as financial information, when making investment decisions.

Users can gain information on non-financial factors addressed by the entity such as how the skills of the workforce contribute to the performance of the entity and whether the entity have a responsible attitude to the environment.

Disadvantages

Since the MC is voluntarily produced, it is unlikely to be prepared in a consistent manner between entities. Therefore users may not be able to perform any meaningful comparison between different entities.

Disclosing information regarding future prospects of an entity may raise the expectations of users. Users may be disadvantaged in the future if the performance does not meet these expectations.

The content of an MC is at the discretion of the directors. They may therefore choose to only disclose positive information. This reduces the reliability of the document for the users.

The content of the MC is not audited. Again, this reduces the level of reliance that users may be willing to place on the information.

Test your understanding 2

MEMORANDUM

To: Assistant Accountant

From: Chief Accountant

Subject: Accounting treatment of two transactions and disclosure of environmental matters in the financial statements

(a) **Accounting treatment of two transactions**

Transaction one

IAS 37 **Provisions, contingent liabilities and contingent assets** states that provisions should only be recognised in the financial statements if:

- there is a present obligation as a result of a past event
- it is probable that a transfer of economic benefits will be required to settle the obligation
- a reliable estimate can be made of the amount of the obligation.

In this case, there is no obligation to incur expenditure. There may be a constructive obligation to do so in future, if the board creates a valid expectation that it will protect the environment, but a board decision alone does not create an obligation.

The sum of $100,000 could be appropriated from retained earnings and transferred to an environmental protection reserve within other components of equity, subject to formal approval by the board. A note to the financial statements should explain the transfer.

Transaction two

Again, IAS 37 states that a provision cannot be recognised if there is no obligation to incur expenditure. At first sight it appears that there is an obligation to purchase the new equipment, because the new law has been enacted. However, the obligation must arise as the result of a past event. At 31 December 20X1, no such event had occurred as the new plant had not yet been purchased and the new law had not yet come into effect. In theory, the company does not have to purchase the new plant. It could completely discontinue the activities that cause pollution or it could continue to operate the old equipment and risk prosecution under the new law. Therefore no provision can be recognised for the cost of new equipment.

It is likely that another effect of the new law is that the company will have to dispose of the old plant before it would normally have expected to do so. IAS 36 **Impairment of assets** requires that the old plant must be reviewed for impairment. If its carrying value is greater than its recoverable amount, it must be written down and an impairment loss must be charged against profits. This should be disclosed separately in the notes to the income statement/statement of comprehensive income if it is material.

(b) **Reference to environmental matters in the financial statements**

At present, companies are not obliged to make any reference to environmental matters within their financial statements. Current international financial reporting practice is more designed to meet the needs of investors and potential investors, rather than the general public. Some companies choose to disclose information about the ways in which they attempt to safeguard the environment, something that is often carried out as a public relations exercise. Disclosures are often framed in very general terms and appear outside the financial statements proper. This means that they do not have to be audited.

Several companies publish fairly detailed 'environmental reports'. It could be argued that as Redstart's operations affect the wider community, it has a moral responsibility to disclose details of its activities and its environmental policies. However, at present it is not required to do so by IFRSs.

If a company has, or may have, an obligation to make good any environmental damage that it has caused, it is obliged to disclose information about this commitment in its financial statements (unless the likelihood of this is remote).

If it is probable (more likely than not) that the company will have to incur expenditure to meet its obligation, then it is also required to set up a provision in the financial statements.

In practice, these requirements are unlikely to apply unless a company is actually obliged by law to rectify environmental damage or unless it has made a firm commitment to the public to do so (for example, by promoting itself as an organisation that cares for the environment, as the directors propose that Redstart should do in future).

Test your understanding 3

(a) The way in which companies manage their social and environmental responsibilities is a high level strategic issue for management. Companies that actively manage these responsibilities can help create long-term sustainable performance in an increasingly competitive business environment.

Reports that disclose transparent information will benefit organisations and their stakeholders. These stakeholders will have an interest in knowing that the company is attempting to adopt best practice in the area. Institutional investors will see value in the 'responsible ownership' principle adopted by the company.

Although there is no universal 'best practice', there seems to be growing consensus that high performance is linked with high quality practice in such areas as recruitment, organisational culture, training and reduction of environmental risks and impact. Companies that actively reduce environmental risks and promote social disclosures could be considered to be potentially more sustainable, profitable, valuable and competitive. Many companies build their reputation on the basis of social and environmental responsibility and go to substantial lengths to prove that their activities do not exploit their workforce or any other section of society.

Governments are encouraging disclosure by passing legislation, for example in the area of anti-discrimination and by their own example in terms of the depth and breadth of reporting (also by requiring companies who provide services to the government to disclose such information). External awards and endorsements, such as environmental league tables and employer awards, encourage companies to adopt a more strategic approach to these issues. Finally, local cultural and social pressures are causing greater demands for transparency of reporting.

There is no IFRS that determines the content of an environmental and social report. While companies are allowed to include the information they wish to disclose, there is a lack of comparability and the potential that only the positive actions will be shown.

A common framework that provides guidelines on sustainability reporting would be useful for both companies and stakeholders.

The Global Reporting Initiative (GRI) provides guidelines on the content of a sustainability report, but these are not mandatory. However, a number of companies prepare their reports in accordance with the guidelines and the GRI is becoming the unofficial best practice guide in this area.

(b) Company B's environmental report should include the following information.

(i) A statement of the environmental policy covering all aspects of business activity. This can include their aim of using renewable electricity and reducing their carbon footprint – the amount of carbon dioxide released into the environment as a result of their activities.

(ii) The management systems that reduce and minimise environmental risks.

(iii) Details of environmental training and expertise.

(iv) A report on their environmental performance including verified emissions to air/land and water, and how they are seeking to reduce these and other environmental impacts. Company B's activities have a significant impact so it is important to show how this is dealt with. The emissions data could be graphed to show it is reducing. If they have the data, they could compare their carbon dioxide emissions or their electricity usage over previous periods. Presenting this information graphically helps stakeholders see how the business is performing in the areas it is targeting.

(v) Details of any environmental offence that resulted in enforcement action, fine, etc. and any serious pollution incident. They can disclose how fines have been reducing and state that there have not been any pollution incidents in the current period.

(vi) A report on historical trends for key indicators and a comparison with the corporate targets.

Test your understanding 4

(a) Advantages to entities and stakeholders

The recognition of intangible assets, and of intellectual capital assets in particular, has been much discussed in recent years. The traditional business model involving exploitation of physical assets in the form of tangible non-current assets and inventory is no longer so prevalent. For many service businesses, the most significant category of "asset" relates to the skills and talents of the people who work for them. If accounting regulation and practice permitted the recognition of such assets as part of the business statement of financial position, there could be some positive effects.

Under current accounting practice, the statements of financial position of many types of business recognise few intangible assets. Recognition of a wider range of assets would provide a more realistic view of the productive capacity of the business, which could be helpful to many categories of stakeholder. For example, existing and potential investors would find it easier to relate the flow of revenue to the "assets" that had produced it, thus improving understanding of the nature of the business and its ability to generate positive income streams.

A related point is that realistic analysis of financial statements would be much easier where a greater range of assets was recognised. Under current IFRS many of the standard accounting ratios make little sense because the recognised asset base is so low. Accounting ratios such as asset turnover, return on assets and return on capital employed are essentially meaningless in businesses that rely principally on intellectual capital assets. With full recognition of intellectual assets, comparisons between the productivity of different types of business would become more realistic.

From the point of view of the employee stakeholder group, recognition of intellectual assets would increase the prominence of the value they add to the organisation. Instead of being viewed as a cost to be borne by the business, the amounts incurred in remunerating and training employees could be seen as an investment by the business. If a formal valuation process were adopted in respect of individuals their status and prospects could be improved.

(b) Reasons why IFRS do not permit recognition

The principal problems relating to the recognition of intellectual assets are as follows:

- Intellectual assets such as know-how and skills do not usually fall into the *Framework* definition of an asset ("a resource controlled by the entity as a result of past events and from which future economic benefits are expected to flow to the entity").
- The problem is one of control: skills are in the possession of the individual employee who has the option to cease working for the entity and to take his or her skills elsewhere. Where resources cannot be controlled their value to the entity is questionable.
- Realistic measurement of intellectual assets presents a challenge that may well be insuperable in practice. Although some guidance is provided by market salary rates from which a capital value could in theory be extrapolated, any such values would necessarily be vague and imprecise. The difficulties in reaching realistic values would rule out inter-firm comparability.
- Finally, because of the problems of arriving at consistent and robust measurement techniques, there would be scope for creative accounting by the unscrupulous.

Test your understanding 5

(a) Objectives and progress to date

In September 2002, FASB and IASB agreed to undertake a project with the objective of converging international standards and US GAAP, thus reducing the number of differences between the two sets of conventions. The 2002 agreement (the "Norwalk agreement") committed the two parties to making their existing standards fully compatible as soon as practicable, and to co-ordinating their future work programs. To date, the Boards have undertaken a short-term project to address, and where possible, remove some of the differences between standards. The longer term issues have been tackled by undertaking work jointly on the development of new standards.

A memorandum of understanding between the FASB and IASB set out a "Roadmap" of convergence between IFRS and US GAAP. This was aimed at removing the need for entities having prepared their financial statements using IFRS to prepare reconciliation to US GAAP in order to be listed on a US exchange. The requirement for the reconciliation was removed in late 2007, ahead of schedule.

The convergence project has produced a number of tangible results, most recently including the following:

- IFRS 8 *Operating Segments*
- IFRS 9 *Financial Instruments*
- IFRS 10 *Consolidated Financial Statements*
- IFRS 11 *Joint Arrangements*
- IFRS 12 *Disclosure of Interests in Other Entities*
- IFRS 13 *Fair Value Measurement*
- Conceptual Framework for Financial Reporting 2010 (in progress)

(b) Three remaining long-term projects

Leasing

The aim is to remove the distinction between operating and finance leases and reflect that all leases give rise to an asset (the right to use the leased asset) and a liability (to pay the lease rentals).

Revenue recognition

The aim is to produce a comprehensive standard that clarifies the principles for recognising revenue and that can be applied across various transactions, industries and capital markets.

Financial instruments

The last part of a 3 stage project that will result in IAS 39 being superseded. The remaining stage will deal in particular with impairment, derivatives and hedging.

(c) Other remaining differences

- Inventory valuation - LIFO allowed under US GAAP, not under IFRS
- Development costs - expensed under US GAAP, capitalised (when criteria satisfied) under IFRS
- Non-current assets - revaluation model permitted under IFRS, only historic cost model under US GAAP

chapter

12

Changing price levels

Chapter learning objectives

On completion of their studies students should be able to:

- Discuss the problems of profit measurement and alternative approaches to asset valuations;
- Discuss measures to reduce distortion in financial statements when price levels change.

1 Session content

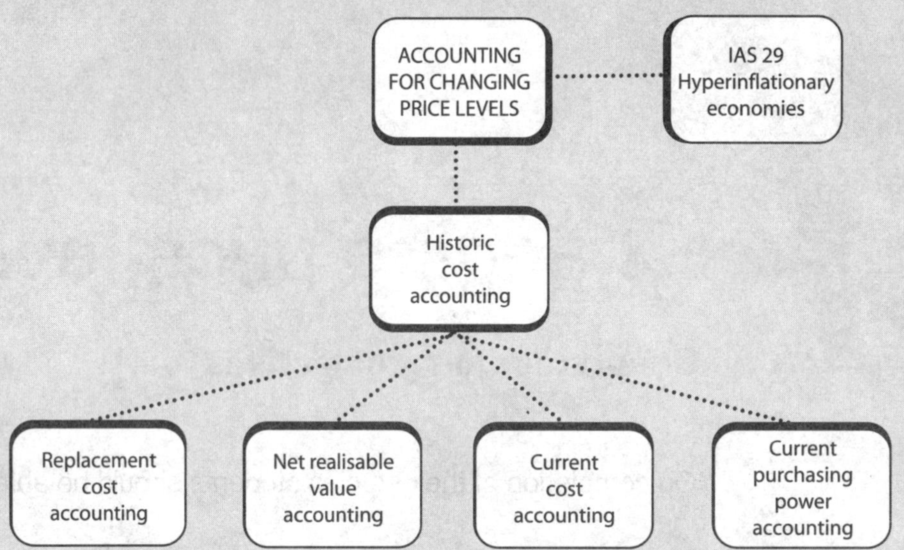

The F2 syllabus does not include applying knowledge of accounting for changing price levels to a numerical examination question.

However, it is an important area of accounting and students are required to describe or explain the different methods of accounting that can be applied in this area.

2 Historical cost accounting

Definition

Historic cost accounting is the accounting method in which transactions are recorded at their monetary amount at the date of the transaction with no further amendment.

This is the system of accounting used traditionally in the preparation of financial statements.

Advantages of historic cost accounting

- Objective, i.e. financial statements are based on verifiable fact rather than subjective opinions;
- Easy (and therefore relatively cheap) to apply;
- Easy to understand

Disadvantages of historic cost accounting

- The failure to take inflation into account, leading to unreliable information being provided in financial statements;
- Income at current value matched against costs recorded in an earlier period leading to a distortion in profit;
- Carrying value of assets bearing little relationship to current values;
- Ratio and performance analysis are distorted as a result of above, particularly when comparing performance over a number of accounting periods. This is due to overstating profits and understating assets.

Due to the limitations of historic cost accounting in times of changing prices, alternative systems may be adopted. These alternatives include:

- replacement cost accounting;
- net realisable value accounting;
- current cost accounting;
- current purchasing power accounting; and
- 'real terms' system of accounting.

To understand the effects of these alternative systems we will first look at the different methods of ascertaining capital maintenance.

3 Capital maintenance

Capital represents the amount of money invested and retained in the business by its owners.

Under historic cost accounting, an entity would be required to break even in order to maintain the level of capital.

However, if price levels are rising, break even would not be enough to maintain the level of capital, a profit would need to be generated.

Illustration 1

An entity is set up at the beginning of the financial period and capital of $10,000 is invested.

In the first accounting period the entity generates a profit of $250. However, price levels increase by 7%.

To maintain the value of the initial investment in the business, capital would need to increase by 7% x $10,000 = $700 by the end of the accounting period.

		$
Required capital	(10,000 + 700)	10,700
Historic cost capital	(10,000 + 250)	10,250
Shortfall		450

Therefore, although the entity has made an accounting profit, in real terms a loss of $450 has been incurred.

Capital maintenance - further detail

Profit for a period is measured by comparing closing net assets with opening net assets. This is the basis of the accounting equation:

ASSETS less LIABILITIES = CAPITAL

OPENING NET ASSETS + PROFIT – DISTRIBUTIONS = CLOSING NET ASSETS

Under historic cost accounting, as long as closing shareholders' funds (equity capital and reserves) are equal to or greater than opening shareholders' funds in absolute terms the entity has maintained its capital.

As we have seen, this is not always a relevant way of measuring profit in times of inflation.

Two types of capital maintenance are defined:

Physical capital maintenance

- The concept that profit is earned only if the physical productive capacity/operating capability of the entity at the end of the accounting period exceeds that at the beginning of the period, after excluding distributions to and contributions from the owners.

Financial capital maintenance

- The concept that profit is earned only if the financial amount of net assets at the end of the accounting period exceeds that at the beginning of the period, after excluding distributions to and contributions from the owners (as shown in illustration above).

4 Replacement cost accounting

Definition

Replacement cost is the price at which identical goods or capital equipment could be purchased at the date of valuation.

Accounting

- Record assets at replacement cost (therefore, increasing statement of financial position values).
- For non-current assets, adjust current replacement cost to reflect proportion of useful economic life consumed, i.e. depreciate it.
- Changes in values incorporated into the profit or loss for the period, disclosed separately as 'holding gains/losses'.

Note: Operating profit will be lower than under historic cost accounting.

Advantages

- Application of physical capital maintenance.
- Statement of financial position aims to reflect true value of assets.

Disadvantages

- Asset valuation is subjective.
- Replacement cost information may not be available.
- Higher cost of accounts preparation.
- Does not reflect financial capital maintenance.

5 Net realisable value accounting

Definition

Similar to replacement cost accounting but **net realisable value accounting** uses net selling prices instead of replacement cost.

Similar advantages and disadvantages to replacement cost accounting.

Main benefit of this method over replacement cost is that the statement of financial position is more likely to reflect the true value of assets.

Additional disadvantages

- Effectively values statement of financial position on a break-up basis which conflicts with the going concern assumption.
- Does not take value in use into account, however an asset with scrap value may have continuing use within the business.

6 Current cost accounting

Definition

Current cost accounting (CCA) adopts the principle of valuing assets at their 'value to the business', also known as deprival value.

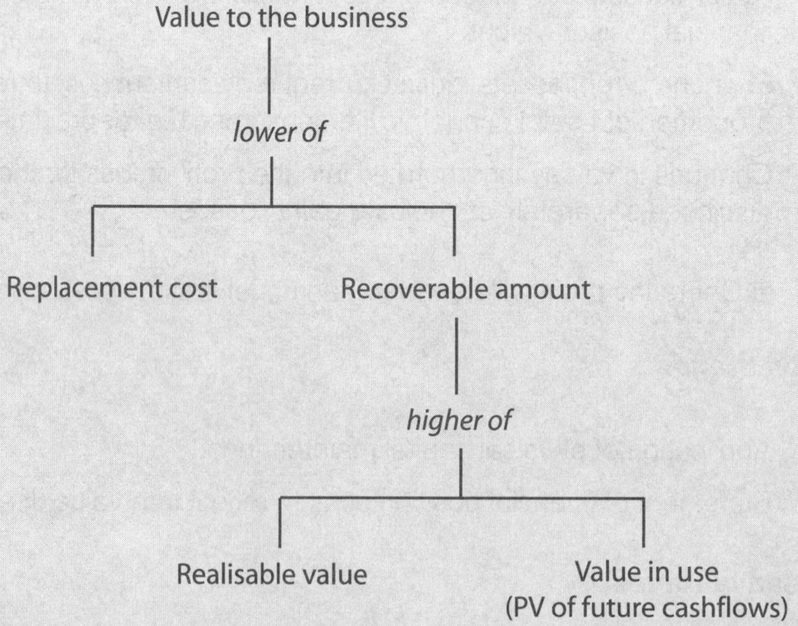

Requirements of CCA system

- Identify each individual asset and calculate value to business.
- In income statement, need to disclose historic cost profit plus:
  - *Cost of sales adjustment (COSA)*

    shows value to business of inventories consumed during the year by updating cost of sales

  - *Depreciation adjustment*

    shows value to business of non-current assets consumed in the year

    = difference between CCA charge and historic cost charge

  - *Monetary working capital adjustment (MWCA)*

    takes account of additional investment required to maintain monetary working capital of the business – taking into account concept of financial capital maintenance

  - *Gearing adjustment*

    apportions total of COSA, depreciation adjustment and MWCA between equity holders and lenders in proportion to their holdings

Advantages of CCA

- Valuable information for users to make informed economic decisions.
- Application of physical capital maintenance concept.
- Provides prudent estimate of profit in times of rising prices.

Disadvantages of CCA

- Unpopular with preparers.
- Time-consuming and costly.
- Difficult to assess whether benefits outweigh costs.
- Inappropriate for service industry entities.
- Subjectivity involved.
- Difficult to understand, therefore may not be as useful.

7 Current purchasing power accounting

Definition

Current purchasing power (CPP) is a method of accounting for inflation in which the values of the non-monetary items in the accounts are adjusted using a general price index (RPI) to show the change in the general purchasing power of money.

Advantages of CPP

- Easier to prepare than CCA with mechanistic calculations. Therefore less time consuming and costly than CCA.
- RPI easily obtainable and objective.
- Easier to understand than CCA.
- Reflects concept of real/financial capital maintenance.

Disadvantages of CPP

- RPI based on general inflation, may not reflect actual inflation in specific industry.
- Measures value of money rather than true value of assets.

8 'Real terms' system of accounting

The 'real terms' accounting system is a hybrid system that combines the best features of current cost accounting and current purchasing power accounting.

It retains current cost accounting valuation for assets.

This system requires calculation and disclosure of shareholders funds using the current purchasing power method.

9 IAS 29: Financial reporting in hyperinflationary economies

The characteristics of an economic environment of a country that would indicate hyperinflation are:

- Inhabitants keep their wealth in non-monetary assets or in a relatively stable foreign currency;
- Amounts of local currency are immediately invested to maintain purchasing power;
- Prices are quoted in a relatively stable foreign currency rather than in local currency;

- Transactions on credit take place at prices that compensate for the expected loss in purchasing power during the credit period, even if period is short;
- Interest rates, wages and prices are linked to a price index;
- Cumulative inflation rate over 3 years approaches, or exceeds, 100%.

Requirement of accounting standard

For entities reporting in currency of hyperinflationary economy:

- Restate accounts in current terms at reporting date.
- Restate comparatives so all figures are expressed in common terms.
- Requires application of general price index to non-monetary items (very similar to CPP).

Test your understanding 1

(i) Explain, in a maximum of 50 words, what is meant by current (constant) purchasing power accounting (CPP).

(ii) Current cost accounting adopts the principle of value to the business.

State what the missing words are in the following sentences.

Value to the business is the ____________ of replacement cost and recoverable amount.

Recoverable amount is the ____________ of realisable value and value in use.

Test your understanding 2

Holly Co is a manufacturing and trading entity. It operates in a country with relatively high rates of inflation. Most entities operating in that country voluntarily present two versions of their financial statements: one at historical cost, and the other incorporating current cost adjustments. Holly Co complies with this accepted practice.

Extracts from the income statement adjusted for current costs for the year ended 30 September 20X1 are as follows:

		Crowns 000	Crowns 000
Historical cost operating profit			750
Current cost adjustments:			
	Cost of sales adjustment	65	
	Depreciation adjustment	43	
	Loss on net monetary position	16	
			(124)
			626

Required:

(a) Explain the defects of historical cost accounting in times of increasing prices.

(b) Explain how EACH of the three current cost accounting adjustments in Holly's financial statements contributes to the maintenance of capital.

10 Chapter summary

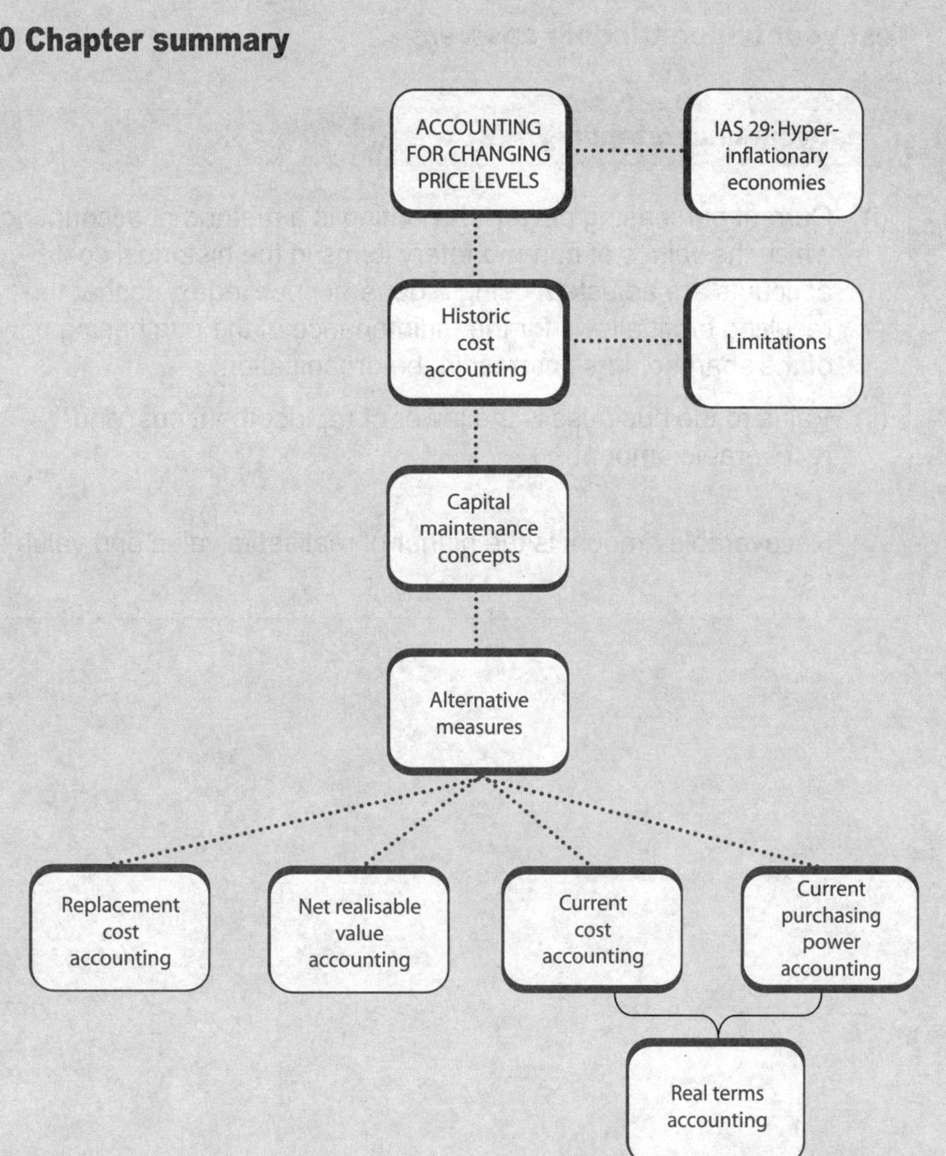

Test your understanding answers

Test your understanding 1

(i) Current purchasing power accounting is a method of accounting in which the values of non-monetary items in the historical cost accounts are adjusted, using a general price index, so that the resulting profit allows for the maintenance of the purchasing power of the shareholders' interest in the organisation.

(ii) Value to the business is the lower of replacement cost and recoverable amount.

Recoverable amount is the higher of realisable value and value in use.

Test your understanding 2

Defects of historic cost accounting

There are many problems associated with traditional historic cost accounting.

- The amounts at which non-monetary assets (such as property, plant and equipment and inventories) are stated bears no relation to their current value and therefore provides a poor guide to the resources available to the business. Holding gains are not shown in the financial statements until assets are sold, even though many believe that these make an important contribution to an entity's overall financial performance.
- In a company's income statement, out of date costs are matched against current revenues. This produces an overstated and misleading profit figure.
- The income statement fails to show gains or losses made by owing money or holding monetary assets such as trade receivables and trade payables. When prices are rising, holding a cash balance results in a loss of purchasing power, while borrowing money may result in a gain in purchasing power.
- Because profits are overstated and assets are understated, return on capital employed and similar measures may be extremely misleading.
- Trend information, such as that provided by comparative figures or in a five-year summary, is distorted because it fails to take into account the changing value of money over time.

As a result of the above, users of financial statements find it extremely difficult to assess a company's progress from year to year or to compare the results of different operations.

How current cost accounting adjustments contribute to the maintenance of capital

Under the traditional approach to capital maintenance associated with historic cost accounting, a company has made a profit for an accounting period if its capital (its net assets) at the end of the period is greater than its capital at the beginning of the period. Under current cost accounting, a company only makes a profit if its operating capital at the end of the period is greater than its operating capital at the beginning of the period.

A company's operating capital is its ability to produce a certain volume of goods and services.

- The cost of sales adjustment is the difference between the current cost of sales and the historic cost of sales. It uplifts the cost of the inventories sold to their current value to the business rather than their cost. In this way the company only records a profit if they generate sufficient revenue to replace that quantity of inventory at current prices and retain some of the earnings in the business. This is not achieved in historic cost accounting, where profits are recorded if the business generates more revenue than the historic cost of inventory sold. This may not be sufficient to purchase replacement inventories in times of rising prices.
- The depreciation adjustment is the difference between depreciation based on the historic cost of property, plant and equipment and depreciation based on current cost (value to the business or deprival value). The company only makes a profit if revenues are sufficient to cover depreciation at current cost levels. This ensures that sufficient earnings are made to replace all its operating assets and to continue production at the same level as before. (Imagine depreciating some plant with a value of $100,000 over ten years. As long as the business generates profits before depreciation of $10,001 a year it wil generate a net profit. However, if it costs the business $150,000 to replace the asset it will not have generated sufficient revenue internally to be able to afford the replacement without additional finance.)
- The loss on net monetary position (sometimes called the monetary working capital adjustment) is the increase in the real value of monetary working capital (trade receivables and trade payables) that has occurred during the year. When trade receivables are realised in cash the company makes a loss because the cash is based on the historic amount of the debt rather than the current amount. (Imagine if the business had received the cash instantly; they could place it in a bank and earn interest. By offering 60 days credit they lose earnings!). The adjustment recognises this loss in the income statement and ensures that enough earnings are retained in the business to maintain the current level of monetary working capital.

chapter

13

Financial instruments

Chapter learning objectives

On completion of their studies students should be able to:

- Discuss the principle of substance over form applied to the treatment of financial instruments;
- Discuss the possible treatments of financial instruments in the issuer's accounts (i.e. liabilities versus equity, and the implications for finance costs);
- Identify and discuss circumstances in which amortised cost, fair value and hedge accounting are appropriate for financial instruments, explain the principles of these accounting methods and discuss considerations in the determination of fair value;
- Explain the correct treatment for foreign loans financing foreign equity investments.

1 Session content

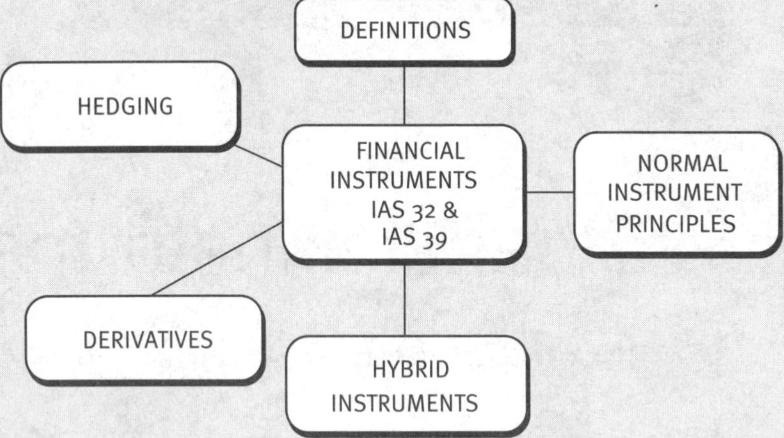

2 Introduction

Definitions

A **financial instrument** is any contract that gives rise to a financial asset of one entity and a financial liability or equity instrument of another entity.

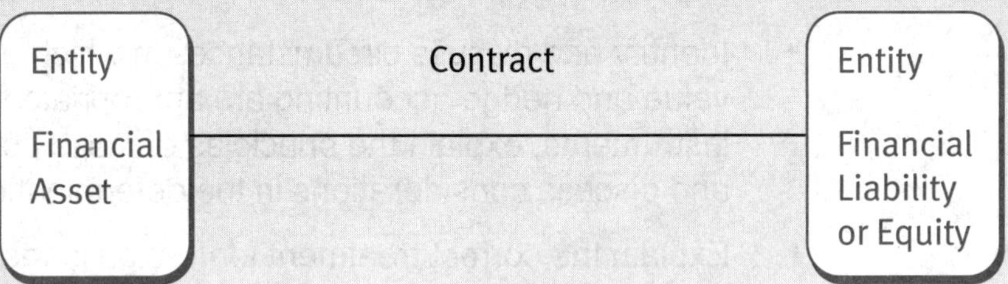

A **financial asset** is any asset that is:

- cash
- an equity instrument of another entity
- a contractual right to receive cash or another financial asset from another entity
- a contractual right to exchange financial instruments with another entity under conditions that are potentially favourable

Examples of financial assets are:

- Investments in ordinary shares of another entity
- Investments in debentures/ loan stock/ loan notes/ bonds i.e. lending money to another entity

A **financial liability** is any liability that is a contractual obligation:

- to deliver cash or another financial asset to another entity
- to exchange financial instruments with another entity under conditions that are potentially unfavourable

Examples of financial liabilities are:

- Issue of debentures/ loan stock/ loan notes/ bonds i.e. borrowing money from another entity

An **equity instrument** is any contract that evidences a residual interest in the assets of an entity after deducting all of its liabilities.

An example of an equity instrument is:

- Issue of ordinary shares

Accounting standards

There are four accounting standards that deal with financial instruments:

- IAS 32 **Financial instruments: presentation**
- IAS 39 **Financial instruments: recognition and measurement**
- IFRS 7 **Financial instruments: disclosures**
- IFRS 9 **Financial instruments**

IAS 32 deals with the classification of financial instruments and their presentation in financial statements.

IAS 39 deals with how financial instruments are measured and when they should be recognised in financial statements.

IFRS 7 deals with the disclosure of financial instruments in financial statements.

IFRS 9 will eventually supersede IAS 39. Its effective date for application is 1 January 2015 and therefore is only examinable as a current issue - see chapter 11 for more detail.

3 Classification of financial instruments

IAS 32 **Financial instruments: presentation** provides the rules on classifying financial instruments as liabilities or equity. These are detailed below.

Presentation of liabilities and equity

The issuer of a financial instrument must classify it as a financial liability or equity instrument on initial recognition according to its substance.

Financial liabilities

The instrument will be classified as a liability if the issuer has a contractual **obligation**:

- to deliver cash (or another financial asset) to the holder
- to exchange financial instruments on potentially unfavourable terms.

A redeemable preference share will be classified as a liability, because the issuer has the contractual obligation to deliver cash to the holders on the redemption date.

Equity instruments

A financial instrument is only an equity instrument if there is no such contractual obligation.

Interest, dividends, losses and gains

- The accounting treatment of interest, dividends, losses and gains relating to a financial instrument follows the treatment of the instrument itself.
- For example, dividends paid in respect of preference shares classified as a liability will be charged as a finance expense through profit or loss.
- Dividends paid on shares classified as equity will be reported in the statement of changes in equity.

Offsetting a financial asset and a financial liability

IAS 32 states that a financial asset and a financial liability may only be offset in very limited circumstances. The net amount may only be reported when the entity:

- has a legally enforceable right to set off the amounts
- intends either to settle on a net basis, or to realise the asset and settle the liability simultaneously.

4 Recognition and measurement of financial instruments

IAS 39 **Financial instruments: recognition and measurement** provides guidance as to when financial instruments should be recognised in the financial statements and how they should be measured.

Initial recognition of financial instruments

An entity should recognise a financial asset or a financial liability in its statement of financial position when, and only when, it becomes a party to the contractual provisions of the instrument.

Initial measurement of financial instruments

A financial asset or liability should be initially recognised at its **fair value**. Except in the case of assets or liabilities at fair value through profit or loss (see next section), directly attributable transaction costs are added to an asset and deducted from a liability.

Subsequent measurement of financial instruments

Equity instruments are not re-measured after initial recognition.

Subsequent measurement of other financial instruments depends on how that particular financial instrument is classified.

IAS 39 deals separately with **four types of financial asset** and **two types of financial liability**.

Financial liabilities are dealt with first below.

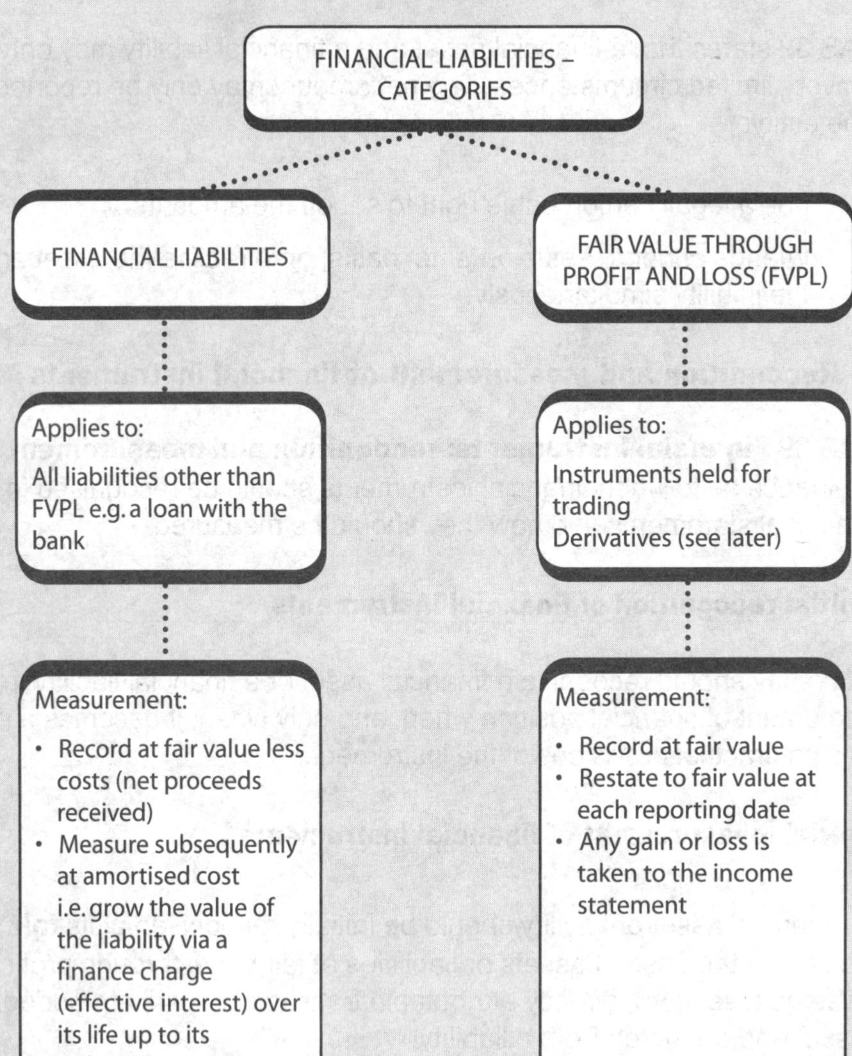

Amortised cost

- One common form of financial instrument for many entities will be loans payable. These will be measured at amortised cost. The amortised cost of a liability equals: initial cost plus interest less repayments.
- The interest will be charged on the outstanding balance at the effective rate. This is the internal rate of return of the instrument.

The simplest way to prepare a working for amortised cost is to use the following table.

Year	Opening balance	Effective interest % (IS)	Coupon paid %	Closing balance (SFP)
	$	$	$	$
1	X	X	(X)	X
2	X	X	(X)	X
3	X	X	(X)	X

The opening balance in year 1 is the net proceeds (i.e. after deduction of any discounts and issue costs):

- Dr Cash
- Cr Liability

Effective interest is charged to the income statement (IS):

- Dr Finance costs (IS)
- Cr Liability

The coupon paid is the coupon percentage multiplied by the face/nominal value of the debt:

- Dr Liability
- Cr Cash

The closing balance is the figure for the statement of financial position (SFP) at the reporting date.

Example 1

A company issues 5% loan notes at their nominal value of $20,000. The loan notes are repayable at par after 4 years.

Required:

(a) What amount will be recorded as a financial liability when the loan notes are issued?

(b) What amounts will be shown in the income statement and statement of financial position for years 1-4?

Example 1 answer

(a) When the loan notes are issued:

Dr Bank	$20,000
Cr Loan notes	$20,000

(b) Financial statement extracts

Note: Because the loan is repayable at par i.e. face (nominal) value of $20,000, the coupon rate is equal to the effective rate.

Use the amortised cost table provided in (W1) to answer this style of question.

Income statement (IS)

Year	1	2	3	4
	$	$	$	$
Finance costs (W1)	(1,000)	(1,000)	(1,000)	(1,000)

Statement of financial position (SFP)

Year	1	2	3	4
	$	$	$	$
Non-current liabilities	20,000	20,000		
Current liabilities			20,000	0

(W1) **Amortised cost table**

Year	Opening balance	Effective interest 5% (IS)	Coupon paid 5%	Closing balance (SFP)
	$	$	$	$
1	20,000	1,000	(1,000)	20,000
2	20,000	1,000	(1,000)	20,000
3	20,000	1,000	(1,000)	20,000
4	20,000	1,000	(1,000)	
			(20,000)*	0

* The loan notes are repaid at par i.e. $20,000 at the end of year 4.

Test your understanding 1 - Daytona

Daytona issues a $10m zero coupon bond which requires one single payment of $12.95m in three years' time. The effective rate of interest is 9% per annum.

Required:

Show the effect of the transaction on the statement of financial position and income statement for the three year term of the bond.

Test your understanding 2

A company issues 0% loan notes at their nominal value of $40,000. The loan notes are repayable at a premium of $11,800 after 3 years. The effective rate of interest is 9%.

Required:

(a) What amount will be recorded as a financial liability when the loan notes are issued?

(b) What amounts will be shown in the income statement and statement of financial position for years 1–3?

Test your understanding 3

A company issues 5% redeemable preference shares at their nominal value of $10,000. The loan notes are repayable at a premium of $1,760 after 5 years. The effective rate of interest is 8%.

Required:

What amounts will be shown in the income statement and statement of financial position for years 1–5?

Test your understanding 4 - Fratton

Fratton issues $360,000 of redeemable 2% debentures at a discount of 14% on 1 January 20X5. Issue costs were $5,265. The debenture will be redeemed on 31 December 20X7 at par. Interest is paid annually in arrears and the effective interest rate is 8%.

Required:

Show the effect of the transaction on the statement of financial position and income statement for the three year term of the debenture.

Test your understanding 5

A company issues 4% loan notes with a nominal value of $20,000.

The loan notes are issued at a discount of 2.5% and $534 of issue costs are incurred.

The loan notes will be repayable at a premium of 10% after 5 years. The effective rate of interest is 7%.

Required:

(a) What amount will be recorded as a financial liability when the loan notes are issued?

(b) What amounts will be shown in the income statement and statement of financial position for years 1–5?

Test your understanding 6

A company issues 3% bonds with a nominal value of $150,000.

The bonds are issued at a discount of 10% and issue costs of $11,455 are incurred.

The bonds will be repayable at a premium of $10,000 after 4 years. The effective rate of interest is 10%.

Required:

(a) What amount will be recorded as a financial liability when the bonds are issued?

(b) What amounts will be shown in the income statement and statement of financial position for years 1-4?

(c) In year 1, the discounted proceeds of $135,000 have been credited to non-current liabilities and debited to bank. The issue costs were expensed to the income statement as a finance cost, along with the 3% interest paid in the year. Prepare the journal entries required to correct the accounting treatment of the bonds in year 1.

5 Presentation of compound instruments

- A **compound instrument** is a financial instrument that has characteristics of both equity and liabilities, for example debt that can be converted into shares (convertible bonds).
- The bondholder has the prospect of acquiring cheap shares in an entity, because the terms of conversion are normally quite generous. Even if the bondholder wants cash rather than shares, the deal may still be good. On maturity the cash hungry bondholder will accept the conversion, and then sell the shares on the market for a tidy profit.
- In exchange though, the bondholders normally have to accept a below-market rate of interest, and will have to wait some time before they get the shares that form a large part of their return. There is also the risk that the entity's shares will under-perform, making the conversion unattractive.

- IAS 32 requires compound financial instruments be split into their component parts:
  - a financial liability (the debt) – measured as the present value of the future cashflows, including redemption, using a discount rate that equates to the interest rate on similar instruments without conversion rights
  - an equity instrument (the option to convert into shares) – calculated as the balancing figure.
- These must be shown separately in the financial statements.
- Subsequently, the liability component is measured at amortised cost and the equity component remains unchanged.

Example 2

On 1 January 20X1 Daniels issued a $50m three year convertible bond at par.

- There were no issue costs.
- The coupon rate is 10%, payable annually in arrears on 31 December.
- The bond is redeemable at par on 1 January 20X4.
- Bondholders may opt for conversion. The terms of conversion are two 25 cent shares for every $1 owed to each bondholder on 1 January 20X4.
- Bonds issued by similar companies without any conversion rights currently bear interest at 15%.
- Assume that all bondholders opt for conversion in full.

Required:

How will this be accounted for by Daniels?

Example 2 answer

On initial recognition, the method of splitting the bond between equity and liabilities is as follows.

- Calculate the present value of the debt component by discounting the cash flows at the market rate of interest for an instrument similar in all respects, except that it does not have conversion rights.
- Deduct the present value of the debt from the proceeds of the issue. The difference is the equity component.

(1) **Splitting the proceeds**

The cash payments on the bond should be discounted to their present value using the interest rate for a bond without the conversion rights i.e. 15%.

Date		**Cash flow**	**Discount factor @ 15%**	**Present value**
		$000		$000
31/12/X1	Interest	5,000	0.870	4,350
31/12/X2	Interest	5,000	0.756	3,780
31/12/X3	Interest	5,000	0.658	3,290
01/01/X4	Redemption	50,000	0.658	32,900
Present value = the liability component				44,320
Equity (balancing figure)				5,680
Net proceeds of issue				50,000

The journal entry required to record the issue is:

Dr Bank	$50m
Cr Financial Liability	$44.32m
Cr Equity (bal fig)	$5.68m

(2) **The annual finance costs and year end carrying amounts**

	Opening balance	**Effective interest rate 15%**	**Payments**	**Closing balance**
	$000	$000	$000	$000
20X1	44,320	6,648	(5,000)	45,968
20X2	45,968	6,895	(5,000)	47,863
20X3	47,863	7,137*	(5,000)	50,000

* Note that the effective interest in 20X3 is rounded (due to the discount factors having only been applied to 3 decimal places) to ensure that the closing balance equals the redemption amount of $50 million.

(3) The conversion of the bond

The carrying amounts at 1 January 20X4 are:

	$000
Equity (as initially recognised)	5,680
Liability – bond	50,000
	55,680

The conversion terms are two 25c shares for every $1, so $50m × 2 = 100m shares, which have a nominal value of $25m. The remaining $30.68 million should be classified as the share premium, also within equity. There is no remaining liability, because conversion has extinguished it.

Note: This third step is rarely required in F2 but has been included for illustration purposes.

Test your understanding 7 - Hybrid

An entity issues 3,000 convertible bonds at the start of year 1 at par. They have a three year term and a face value of $1,000 per bond. Interest is payable annually in arrears at 7% per annum. Each bond is convertible at any time up to maturity into 250 common shares. When the bonds are issued, the prevailing market interest rate for similar debt without conversion options is 9%.

Required:

(a) How is this initially recorded?

(b) What will be shown in the statement of financial position and income statement for year 1?

Test your understanding 8

A company issues 2% convertible bonds at their nominal value of $36,000.

The bonds are convertible at any time up to maturity into 120 ordinary shares for each $100 of bond. Alternatively the bonds will be redeemed at par after 3 years.

Similar non-convertible bonds would carry an interest rate of 9%.

Required:

(a) What amounts will be shown as a financial liability and as equity when the convertible bonds are issued?

(b) What amounts will be shown in the income statement and statement of financial position for year 1?

Test your understanding 9

A company issues 4% convertible bonds at their nominal value of $5 million on 1 January 20X3.

Each bond is convertible at any time up to maturity into 400 ordinary shares. Alternatively the bonds will be redeemed at par after 3 years.

The market rate applicable to non-convertible bonds is 6%.

The company are preparing their financial statements for the year ended 31 December 20X3. They are not sure how to record the convertible debt and therefore, so far, have credited the $5 million cash received to non-current liabilities and have recognised the interest paid in the year as a finance cost.

Required:

(a) What amounts should be shown as a financial liability and as equity when the convertible bonds are issued?

(b) What amounts should be shown in the income statement and statement of financial position for the years ended 31 December 20X3 and 20X4?

(c) What are the journal entries required to correct the accounting records for the year ended 31 December 20X3?

6 Measurement of financial assets

Subsequent measurement of financial instruments depends on how that particular financial instrument is classified.

IAS 39 deals separately with **four types of financial asset** as follows.

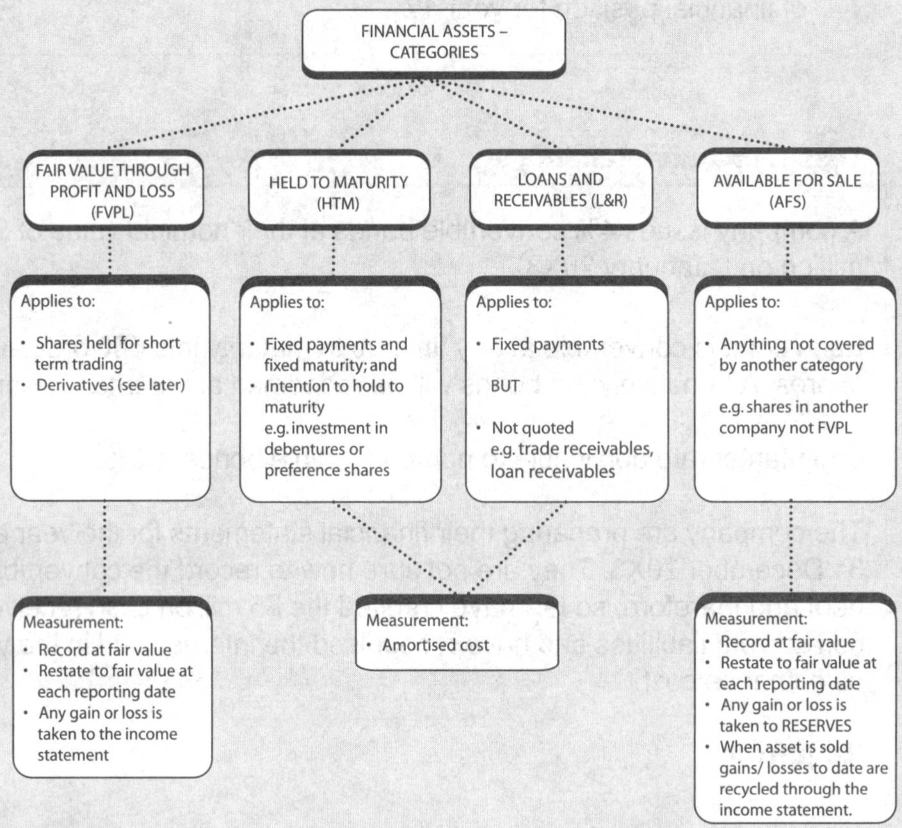

A financial asset can be classified in one or more categories. For example, an investment in the loan stock of another entity could be classified as:

- FVPL – if the loan was to be traded;
- HTM – if the loan was quoted and there was an ability and intention to hold to maturity; or
- L&R – if the loan was unquoted.

Similarly an investment in another entity's ordinary shares could be classified as:

- FVPL – if the shares are held for trading; or
- AFS – otherwise.

Amortised cost

- Assets classified as loans and receivables or held to maturity will be measured at amortised cost. The amortised cost of an asset equals: initial cost plus interest less cash received.
- The interest will be charged at the effective rate. This is the internal rate of return of the instrument.

The simplest way to prepare a working for amortised cost is to use the following table.

Year	Opening balance	Effective interest % (IS)	Cash received (coupon) %	Closing balance (SFP)
	$	$	$	$
1	X	X	(X)	X
2	X	X	(X)	X
3	X	X	(X)	X

The opening balance in year 1 is the total investment (cash invested plus transaction costs):

- Dr Asset
- Cr Cash

Effective interest is credited to the income statement (IS) as finance income:

- Dr Asset
- Cr Finance income (IS)

The coupon received is the coupon percentage multiplied by the face value of the instrument:

- Dr Cash
- Cr Asset

The closing balance is the figure for the statement of financial position (SFP) at the reporting date.

Test your understanding 10

Ashes has the following financial assets:

(1) Investments held for trading purposes.

(2) Interest-bearing debt instruments that will be redeemed in five years; Ashes fully intends to hold them until redemption.

(3) A trade receivable.

(4) Derivatives held for speculation purposes.

(5) Equity shares that Ashes has no intention of selling.

Required:

How should Ashes classify its financial assets?

Test your understanding 11

A company invests $5,000 in 10% debentures. The debentures are repayable at a premium after 3 years and A intends to hold the debentures until this time. The effective rate of interest is 12%.

Required:

What amounts will be shown in the income statement and statement of financial position for years 1-3?

Test your understanding 12

A company invested in 10,000 shares of a listed company in November 20X7 at a cost of $4.20 per share. At 31 December 20X7 the shares have a market value of $4.90. The company are planning on selling these shares in April 20X8.

Required:

(a) Prepare extracts from the income statement for the year ended 31 December 20X7 and a statement of financial position as at that date.

(b) Explain how the treatment would differ if there was no plan to sell the shares.

7 Impairment of financial assets

Impairments apply only to assets categorised as held to maturity or loans and receivables i.e. those that are measured at amortised cost.

Other financial assets are already recorded at fair value and any impairment would have been taken into account when measuring the fair value.

Impairment rules per IAS 39 are as follows:

- Assess at each reporting date whether there is any evidence of impairment.
- If there is evidence, a detailed impairment review must be undertaken.
- The impairment loss (if not given in the question) is the difference between the carrying amount and the present value of the cash flows estimated to arise from the asset, discounted at the asset's original effective interest rate.
- Impairment losses are recognised through the income statement.

Example 3

On 1 January 20X6, Eve makes a four year loan of $100,000 to Fern. The coupon and effective rate on the loan is 6%. Interest is received at the end of each year.

At the end of December 20X8 it becomes clear that Fern is in financial difficulties. This is the necessary objective evidence of impairment.

It is estimated that the future remaining cash flows from the loan will be only $6,000 instead of $10,600 (the $10,000 principal plus interest for the fourth year of $600).

Example 3 answer

The carrying amount of the principal prior to the impairment will be $10,000 (as the coupon and effective rate are the same).

On 31 December 20X8, the carrying amount should be restated to the present value of the estimated cash flows of $6,000, discounted at the original effective interest rate of 6% for one year.

Present value = $6,000 x 1/1.06 = $5,660

The result is an impairment loss of $4,340 (10,000 – 5,660)

The impairment loss is recognised as an expense in the income statement.

The asset will then continue to be accounted for using amortised cost, based on the revised carrying amount of the loan. In the last year, interest income of $340 (6% x 5,660) will be recognised in profit or loss.

The movement on the loan in the final year will be:

Opening balance ($)	Effective interest 6%	Cash received	Closing balance ($)
5,660	340	(6,000)	0

8 Derivative financial instruments

Definition of derivatives

A derivative is a financial instrument that **derives its value from the value of an underlying asset, price, rate or index**.

- Underlying items include equities, bonds, commodities, interest rates, exchange rates and stock market and other indices.
- Derivative financial instruments include futures, options, forward contracts, interest rate and currency swaps.

Characteristics of a derivative

A derivative has all of the following characteristics:

- Its value changes in response to changes in the underlying item.
- It requires little or no initial investment.
- It is settled at a future date.

The risks associated with derivatives

- Derivatives were originally designed to hedge against fluctuations in agricultural commodity prices on the Chicago Stock Exchange. A speculator would pay a small amount (say $100) now for the contractual obligation to buy a thousand units of wheat in three months' time for $10,000. If in three months time one thousand units of wheat costs $11,000, then the speculator would make a profit of $900 (11,000 – 100 – 10,000). This would be a 900% return on the original investment over 3 months, which is one of the attractions of derivatives to speculators. But if the price had dropped to $9,000, then the trader would have made a loss of $1,100 (100 + 1,000) despite the initial investment only having been $100.
- This shows that losses on derivatives can be far greater than the historical cost carrying amount of the related asset. Therefore, shareholders need to be given additional information about derivatives in order to assess the entity's exposure to loss.
- In most cases, entering into a derivative is at a low or no cost. Therefore it is important that derivatives are recognised and disclosed in the financial statements as they have very little initial outlay but can expose the entity to significant gains and losses.

Recognition and measurement

All derivatives are categorised as fair value through the profit and loss (FVPL).

On initial recognition they are recorded at fair value which is usually zero as the derivative gains value as the underlying item's price moves.

At each reporting date, the derivative is restated to fair value and recorded as a financial asset or financial liability on the statement of financial position. Any gains/losses are taken to the income statement.

There is an exception to this rule if the derivative is being used as a cash flow hedge (see later notes).

Types of derivative

- **Forward** – the obligation to buy or sell a defined amount of a specific underlying asset, at a specified price at a specified future date.
- **Forward rate agreements** – a contract to fix the interest charge on a floating rate loan.
- **Futures contracts** – the obligation to buy or sell a standard quantity of a specific underlying item at a specified future date.
- **Swaps** – an agreement to exchange periodic payments at specified intervals over a specified time period.
- **Options** – the right, but not the obligation, to buy or sell a specific underlying asset on or before a specified future date.

Types of derivatives - further detail

Forward contracts

The holder of a forward contract is obliged to buy or sell a defined amount of a specific underlying asset, at a specified price at a specified future date. For example, a forward contract for foreign currency might require £100,000 to be exchanged for $150,000 in three months' time. Both parties to the contract have both a financial asset and a financial liability. For example, one party has the right to receive $150,000 and the obligation to pay £100,000.

Forward currency contracts may be used to minimise the risk on amounts receivable or payable in foreign currencies.

Example

On 1 January 20X9 a dollar based company buys goods from an overseas company. This results in a liability for €8 million which must be settled on 31 March 20X9. The exchange rate on 1 January is €8 = $1. The company takes out a forward exchange contract to buy €8 million for $1 million on 31 March 20X9. This is at the exchange rate ruling at 1 January (i.e. €8 = $1).

At 31 March the exchange rate is actually €8.5 = $1. If the company had not taken out the forward exchange contract it would have made an exchange gain of $58,824 (1,000,000 – 941,176). By taking out the forward exchange contract it has given up the chance to make this gain, but has also protected itself against the possibility of making a loss. In other words, it has used the forward exchange contract to eliminate exchange rate risk.

Forward rate agreements

Forward rate agreements can be used to fix the interest charge on a floating rate loan. For example, a company has a $1m dollar floating rate loan, and the current rate of interest is 7%. The rates are reset to the market rate every six months, and the company cannot afford to pay more than 9% interest. The company enters into a six month forward rate agreement (with, say, a bank) at 9% on $1m. If the market rates go up to 10%, then the bank will pay them $5,000 (1% of $1m for 6 months) which in effect reduces their finance cost to 9%. If the rates only go up to 8% then the company pays the bank $5,000.

Futures contracts

Futures contracts oblige the holder to buy or sell a standard quantity of a specific underlying item at a specified future date. Futures contracts are very similar to forward contracts. The difference is that futures contracts have standard terms and are traded on a financial exchange, whereas forward contracts are tailor made and are not traded on a financial exchange.

Swaps

Two parties agree to exchange periodic payments at specified intervals over a specified time period. For example, in an interest rate swap, the parties may agree to exchange fixed and floating rate interest payments calculated by reference to a notional principal amount. This enables companies to keep a balance between their fixed and floating rate interest payments without having to change the underlying loans.

Options

These give the holder the right, but not the obligation, to buy or sell a specific underlying asset on or before a specified future date.

Example 4

Entity A enters into a call option on 1 June 20X5, to purchase 10,000 shares in another entity on 1 November 20X5 at a price of $10 per share. The cost of each option is $1. A has a year end of 30 September.

By 30 September the fair value of each option has increased to $1.30. A exercises the option on 1 November and the shares are classified as at fair value through profit or loss. The share price at this date is $12.

Required:

Prepare the journal entries required to record the transaction.

Example 4 answer

On 1 June 20X5 the cost of the option is recognised:

Debit	Call option (10,000 × $1)	$10,000
Credit	Cash	$10,000

On 30 September the increase in fair value is recorded:

Debit	Call option (10,000 × ($1.30 – 1))	$3,000
Credit	Profit or loss - gain on option	$3,000

On 1 November the option is exercised, the shares recognised and the call option derecognised. As the shares are financial assets at fair value through profit or loss, they are recognised at $120,000 (10,000 × the current market price of $12).

Debit	Investment in shares at fair value	$120,000
Credit	Cash (10,000 x $10)	$100,000
Credit	Call option (10,000 + 3,000 carrying amount)	$13,000
Credit	Profit or loss – further gain (bal fig)	$7,000

The total gain recognised is $10,000 which equates to $1 per share, being the difference between the share price of $12 and the price paid of $11 ($1 for the option and $10 upon exercise). As $3,000 has already been recognised in the year ended 30 September 20X5, the remaining $7,000 is recognised upon exercise.

Test your understanding 13

B entered into a forward contract on 30 November 20X1 to buy platinum for $435m on 31 March 20X2. The contract was entered into on 30 November 20X1 at nil cost.

B does not plan to take delivery of the platinum but to settle the contract net in cash, i.e. B hopes to generate a profit from short term price fluctuations.

The year end is 31 December 20X1 and the price of platinum has moved so that making the equivalent purchase on 31 December 20X1 would require B to spend $455m.

On 31 March 20X2, the value of the underlying item has changed such that the equivalent purchase of platinum would now cost $442m.

Required:

Prepare journal entries to record the above transaction.

Test your understanding 14

On 1 March 20X1, ABC decided to enter into a forward foreign exchange contract to buy 5 million florins for $1 million on 31 January 20X3. ABC's reporting date is 30 June.

Relevant exchange rates were as follows:

1 March 20X1	$1 = 5 florins
30 June 20X1	$1 = 4.7 florins
30 June 20X2	$1 = 4.2 florins

Required:

(a) Prepare relevant extracts from ABC's statement of comprehensive income and statement of financial position to reflect the forward foreign exchange contract at 30 June 20X2, with comparatives.

(b) At 31 January 20X3, the settlement date, the exchange rate is $1 = 4.5 florins. What gain or loss would be recorded in the income statement in the year ended 30 June 20X3?

9 Hedge accounting

Definitions

Hedging is a method of managing risk by designating one or more hedging instruments so that their change in fair value is offset, in whole or in part, to the change in fair value or cash flows of a hedged item.

A **hedged item** is an asset or liability that exposes the entity to risks of changes in fair value or future cash flows (and is designated as being hedged).

A **hedging instrument** is a designated derivative whose fair value or cash flows are expected to offset changes in fair value or future cash flows of the hedged item.

Special hedge accounting rules apply to reflect the substance of the arrangement, i.e. to ensure that the gains and losses are off-set.

Conditions for hedge accounting

Hedge accounting may only be used if certain conditions are met:

- Arrangement must be designated as a hedge at the inception. There must be formal documentation which identifies:
  - hedged item;
  - hedge instrument;
  - nature of risk that is to be hedged;
  - how the entity will assess the hedging instrument's effectiveness.
- Hedge is expected to be highly effective (80% - 125%).
- Effectiveness is capable of reliable measurement.
- Assessment of effectiveness takes place on an ongoing basis.

Types of hedge

There are three types of hedging arrangement:

- fair value hedge;
- cash-flow hedge;
- net investment in a foreign operation.

Fair value hedge

The risk being hedged is the change in the fair value of an asset or liability, which is already recognised in the financial statements.

Hedge accounting requires both the hedged item and the hedging instrument to be measured at fair value at each year end.

The changes in fair value of both the hedged item and the hedging instrument are recognised in the income statement and will off-set each other.

Illustration 1

An entity owns inventories of 10,000 tons of steel which cost $100,000 on 1 December 20X5.

If the price of steel falls, the entity will suffer a loss when they sell the steel. To minimise this risk, it enters into a futures contract to sell 10,000 tons of steel for $120,000 on 1 February 20X6 i.e. at a price of $12 per ton.

At the year end of 31 December 20X5, the market value of the steel is $9 per ton and the futures price for delivery on 1 February 20X6 is $11 per ton.

Required:

What is the impact of the fair value hedge on the financial statements of the entity at 31 December 20X5?

Solution

The hedged item is the steel. The hedging instrument is the futures contract (a derivative).

At the year end both the hedged item and hedging instrument will be measured at fair value and gains or losses recorded in the income statement.

Hedged item (steel)	
10,000 tons x £9 per ton	$90,000
Cr Inventory	$10,000
Dr Income statement (loss)	$10,000

Hedging instrument (futures contract)	
10,000 x (12–11)	$10,000
Dr Derivative (financial asset)	$10,000
Cr Income statement (gain)	$10,000

The overall effect on the income statement is nil (gain of $10,000 on derivative less loss of $10,000 on inventory).

Test your understanding 15

ST acquired 10,000 shares in another entity, WX, in October 20X1 for $1.35 per share. The investment was classified as available for sale on initial recognition. The shares were trading at $1.58 per share on 31 December 20X1.

Required:

(a) Prepare financial statement extracts for the year ended 31 December 20X1.

(b) Explain how the accounting treatment would differ if ST were to enter into a derivative contract to hedge against the risk of a fall in value of the shares.

Cash-flow hedge

The risk being hedged is the change in future cash flows.

The cash flows will not impact on profits until they occur (i.e. in the future). To achieve the offset, the gain or loss on the hedging instrument should also not impact on profits until the cash flow occurs.

The gain or loss on the hedging instrument is therefore recorded in reserves and then transferred back to the income statement ("recycled") when the hedged item (the cash flow) affects the income statement.

Illustration 2

An entity based in the US expects sales of €300m in September 20X2. There is a risk that the euro dollar exchange rate will rise, reducing the dollar value of the sales.

Before the year-end on 30 June 20X2, the entity takes out a forward contract to sell €300m on 30 September 20X2 at an agreed exchange rate of €2:$1.

At 30 June 20X2, the exchange rate is €2.5 = $1.

At 30 September 20X2, the exchange rate is €3 = $1.

Required:

What is the impact of the cash flow hedge on the financial statements of the entity at 30 June 20X2 and 30 June 20X3?

Solution

Year ended 30 June 20X2

At 30 June 20X2, the hedging instrument i.e. the forward contract will be measured at fair value with the gain or loss being recognised in equity i.e. reserves:

Dr	Forward contract	$30m
Cr	Equity – gain (€300m ÷ 2) – (€300m ÷ 2.5)	$30m

Year ended 30 June 20X3

Gain on the forward contract at 30 September 20X2:

(€300m ÷ 2) – (€300m ÷ 3) = £50m gain in total

A $30m gain has already been recognised at 30 June 20X2 therefore an additional £20m gain needs to be recognised in reserves.

Dr	Forward contract	$20m
Cr	Equity – gain	$20m

Once the sales (the hedged item) are recognised all gains or losses previously recognised in equity are recycled through the income statement.

Cr	Revenue (€300m / 3)	$100m
Cr	Forward contract (to derecognise)	$50m
Dr	Cash ((€300m / 2)	$150m
Dr	Equity (£30m + $20m)	$50m
Cr	Income Statement	$50m

The overall effect on the income statement is a credit (gain) of $150m which reflects sales made of €300m at the contracted exchange rate of €2:$1.

Test your understanding 16

AB entered into a forward contract on 31 January 20X1 to purchase B$1 million at a contracted rate of A$1:B$0.75 on 31 May 20X1. The contract cost was $nil. AB prepares its financial statements to 31 March each year.

At 31 March 20X1 an equivalent contract for the purchase of B$1 million could be acquired at a rate of A$1:B$0.80.

Required:

(a) Prepare journal entries to show how this derivative contract would be recorded in the financial statements of AB in the year ended 31 March 20X1.

(b) Assume now that the instrument described above was designated as a hedging instrument in a cash flow hedge, and that the hedge was 100% effective. Explain how the gain or loss on the instrument for the year ended 31 March 20X1 should now be recorded and why different treatment is necessary.

Net investment in a foreign operation

The hedged item is the investment in a foreign operation and the risk being hedged is the change in the value of the investment due to movements in exchange rates.

The hedging instrument is a foreign currency loan (a non-derivative financial instrument).

Under IAS 21 the investment would be a non-monetary asset and so would be translated at historic rate and not retranslated at each year end.

But the loan is a monetary item and so would be translated at the closing rate at each reporting date and the gain or loss recorded in profit or loss.

This treatment does not reflect the substance of the arrangement i.e. that the gains or losses should be off-set against each other.

Under hedge accounting, both the investment and the loan will be translated at closing rate at each year end and gains or losses on both items should be offset in equity.

Any remaining gain or loss from the ineffective part of the hedge should be recognised in profit or loss.

Illustration 3

Perry, whose functional currency is the dollar ($), had partly financed an investment of 750m crowns (Cr) in a foreign company via the use of a loan of 700m crowns (Cr) taken out on the 1 January 20X1.

Exchange rates were as follows:

01.01.X1	$1 = Cr 0.90
31.12.X1	$1 = Cr 0.80

The above hedging arrangement satisfies the requirements for off-set per IAS 39.

Required:

What is the impact of the net investment hedge on the financial statements of the entity at 31 December 20X1?

Solution

Both the investment and the loan will initially be translated at historic rate and re-translated at closing rate at the year end:

Investment			*Loan*		
Historic rate	Cr750m / 0.9	$833m	Historic rate	Cr700m / 0.9	$778m
Closing rate	Cr750m / 0.8	$937.5m	Closing rate	Cr700m / 0.8	$875m
Gain		$104.5m	Loss		$97m

The gain and loss is off-set against each other in equity. The remaining $7.5m gain is recognised in profit and loss as it represents the ineffective part of the hedge.

(**Nb.** The hedge would be considered 93% (700/750) effective)

10 Disclosure of financial instruments

IFRS 7 **Financial instruments: disclosures** provides the disclosure requirements for financial instruments. A summary of the requirements is detailed below.

The two main categories of disclosures required are:

(1) Information about the significance of financial instruments.

(2) Information about the nature and extent of risks arising from financial instruments.

The disclosures should be made by each class of financial instrument.

IFRS 7 Disclosures

Information about the significance of financial instruments

(a) **Statement of financial position**

An entity must disclose the **significance** of financial instruments for their financial position and performance. The disclosures must be made for each class of financial instruments.

Additionally, IFRS 7 requires additional disclosures for items such as reclassifications or derecognition of financial instruments, information about financial instruments to be measured at fair value through profit and loss, reconciliation of the allowance for credit losses (irrecoverable debts) and breaches of loan agreements.

(b) **Statement of comprehensive income / income statement**

An entity must disclose items of income, expense, gains and losses, with separate disclosure of gains and losses from each class of financial instrument.

For financial instruments that are not measured at fair value through profit and loss, the interest income and interest expense must be disclosed.

The amount of impairment losses on financial assets and interest income on impaired financial assets must also be disclosed.

(c) **Other Disclosures**

Additionally, the following must be disclosed:

- Accounting policies for financial instruments.
- Detailed information about hedge accounting, including a description of each hedge, hedging instrument, and fair values of those instruments, and nature of risks being hedged.
- For cash flow hedges, the periods in which the cash flows are expected to occur, when they are expected to enter into the determination of profit or loss, and a description of any forecast transaction for which hedge accounting had previously been used but which is no longer expected to occur.
- For cash flow hedges, the amounts recognised in other comprehensive income or reclassified from equity into profit or loss, or transfers into the carrying value of a non-financial asset or non-financial liability.
- For fair value hedges, information about the fair value changes of the hedging instrument and the hedged item. Cash flow hedge ineffectiveness recognised in profit and loss.
- Information about the fair values of each class of financial asset and financial liability, along with the comparable carrying amounts, a description of how fair value was determined and detailed information if fair value cannot be reliably measured.

Nature and extent of exposure to risks arising from financial instruments

(a) **Qualitative disclosures**

The qualitative disclosures describe:

- Risk exposures for each type of financial instrument.
- Management's objectives, policies, and processes for managing those risks.
- Changes from the prior period.

(b) **Quantitative disclosures**

The quantitative disclosures provide information about the extent to which the entity is exposed to risk, based on information provided internally to the entity's key management personnel. These disclosures include:

- Summary quantitative data about exposure to each risk at the reporting date.
- Disclosures about credit risk, liquidity risk, and market risk as further described below.
- Concentrations of risk.

(c) **Credit risk**

Disclosures about credit risk include.

- Maximum amount of exposure (before deducting the value of collateral), description of collateral, information about credit quality of financial assets that are neither past due nor impaired, and information about credit quality of financial assets whose terms have been renegotiated.
- For financial assets that are past due or impaired, analytical disclosures are required.
- Information about collateral or other credit enhancements obtained or called.

(d) **Liquidity risk**

Disclosures:

- a maturity analysis of financial liabilities
- description of approach to risk management.

(e) **Market Risk**

Market risk is the risk that the fair value or cash flows of a financial instrument will fluctuate due to changes in market prices. Market risk reflects interest rate risk, currency risk, and other price risks.

Disclosures about market risk include:

– A sensitivity analysis of each type of market risk to which the entity is exposed.

IFRS 7 provides that if an entity prepares a sensitivity analysis for management purposes that reflects interdependencies of more than one component of market risk (for instance, interest risk and foreign currency risk combined), it may disclose that analysis instead of a separate sensitivity analysis for each type of market risk.

11 IFRS 13 Fair Value Measurement

IFRS 13 *Fair Value Measurement*, published in May 2011 and applicable for accounting periods commencing from 1 January 2013, sets out a single framework for measuring fair value. It does not extend the use of fair values but provides guidance on how to measure fair value when it is required by a reporting standard (with some exceptions, see expandable text below).

IFRS 13 defines fair value as the price that would be received to sell an asset or paid to transfer a liability in an orderly transaction between market participants at the measurement date.

It requires an entity to determine the following when establishing fair values:

- the particular asset or liability that is subject to the measurement
- the principal (or most advantageous) market for the asset or liability
- the valuation technique(s) appropriate for the measurement

An entity is required to use a valuation technique appropriate in the circumstances and for which sufficient data are available to measure fair value, maximising the use of relevant observable inputs and minimising the use of unobservable inputs.

Three widely used valuation techniques specifically mentioned in IFRS 13 are:

- **market approach** - uses prices and other relevant information generated by market transactions involving identical or comparable (similar) assets or liabilities
- **cost approach** - reflects the amounts that would be required currently to replace the service capacity of an asset
- **income approach** - converts future amounts (cash flows or income and expenses) to a single current (discounted) amount, reflecting current market expectations about those future amounts

The market approach would be considered the most appropriate approach for the majority of financial instruments.

The fair value hierarchy

IFRS 13 establishes a hierarchy that categorises the inputs used in valuation techniques. The hierarchy gives the highest priority to market prices and the lowest priority to unobservable inputs. An asset or liability is then regarded as having been measured using the lowest level of inputs significant to its valuation.

Level 1 inputs

These are quoted prices in active markets for identical assets or liabilities that the entity can access at the measurement date. Such inputs are considered to be the most reliable evidence of fair value and should be used without adjustment whenever possible.

Level 2 inputs

These are inputs other than quoted market prices included within Level 1 that are observable for the asset or liability, either directly or indirectly.

They would include:

- quoted prices for similar (not identical) assets or liabilities in active markets
- quoted prices for identical or similar assets or liabilities in markets that are not active
- inputs other than quoted prices that are observable for the asset or liability, i.e. interest rates, credit spreads
- inputs that are derived principally from or corroborated by observable market data

They will typically require some adjustment to arrive at fair value.

Level 3 inputs

These are unobservable inputs for the asset or liability, based on the best information available.

An example would be the use of own data to make an estimate of expected future cash outflows to fulfil an obligation (this would typically then be discounted to present value).

Example 5 - fair value of an equity instrument

If an equity investment is held in a listed entity then the fair value will typically be determined by reference to the quoted price at the measurement date. This is a level 1 input.

If the equity investment is in an unlisted entity then the fair value will either be level 2 or level 3. A quoted price of equity shares in a similar company/investment can be used as a basis for fair value (this would be observable data) but the price would then need to be adjusted. The basis and significance of the adjustment would determine whether the valuation would be categorised as level 2 (where other observable data is used) or level 3 (where unobservable data is used). If any element of the valuation is based on unobservable data then the fair value measurement should be classed as level 3.

12 Chapter summary

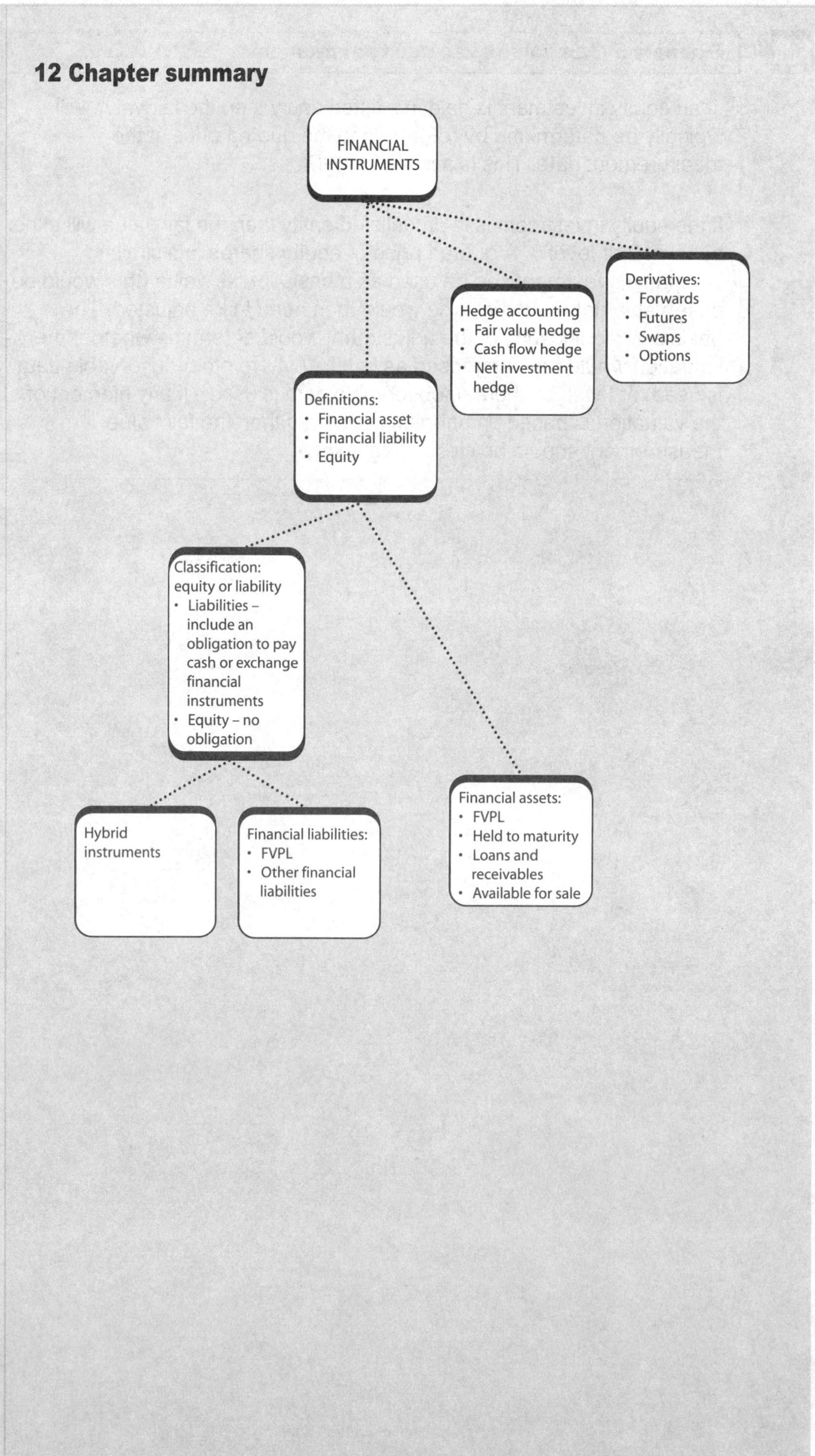

Test your understanding answers

Test your understanding 1 - Daytona

Income statement (IS)

Year	1	2	3
	$000	$000	$000
Finance costs (W1)	(900)	(981)	(1,069)

Statement of financial position (SFP)

Year	1	2	3
	$000	$000	$000
Non-current liabilities	10,900		
Current liabilities		11,881	0

(W1) **Amortised cost table**

Year	Opening balance	Effective interest 9% (IS)	Payments	Closing balance (SFP)
	$000	$000	$000	$000
1	10,000	900	–	10,900
2	10,900	981	–	11,881
3	11,881	1,069	(12,950)	–
		2,950		

The total finance cost is found by taking the difference between the amount to be repaid and the amount borrowed.

12,950 – 10,000 = 2,950

Test your understanding 2

(a) When the loan notes are issued:

Dr Bank	$40,000
Cr Loan notes	$40,000

(b) Financial statement extracts

Income statement (IS)

Year	1	2	3
	$	$	$
Finance costs (W1)	(3,600)	(3,924)	(4,276)

Statement of financial position (SFP)

Year	1	2	3
	$	$	$
Non-current liabilities	43,600		
Current liabilities		47,524	0

(W1) **Amortised cost table**

Year	Opening balance	Effective interest 9% (IS)	Coupon paid 0%	Closing balance (SFP)
	$	$	$	$
1	40,000	3,600	–	43,600
2	43,600	3,924	–	47,524
3	47,524	4,276	–	
			(51,800)	0

The loan notes are repaid at par i.e. $40,000, plus a premium of $11,800 at the end of year 3.

Test your understanding 3

Income statement (IS)

Year	1	2	3	4	5
	$	$	$	$	$
Finance costs (W1)	(800)	(824)	(850)	(878)	(908)

Statement of financial position (SFP)

Year	1	2	3	4	5
	$	$	$	$	$
Non-current liabilities	10,300	10,624	10,974		
Current liabilities				11,352	0

(W1) **Amortised cost table**

Year	**Opening balance**	**Effective interest 8% (IS)**	**Coupon paid 5%**	**Closing balance (SFP)**
	$	$	$	$
1	10,000	800	(500)	10,300
2	10,300	824	(500)	10,624
3	10,624	850	(500)	10,974
4	10,974	878	(500)	11,352
5	11,352	908	(500)	
			(11,760)	0

Note: Effective interest rate is multiplied by opening balance.

Note: Coupon rate is multiplied by face value of debt i.e. $10,000.

Test your understanding 4 - Fratton

Amortised cost table

Year	Opening balance	Effective interest 8% (IS)	Coupon paid 2%	Closing balance (SFP)
	$	$	$	$
1	(W1) 304,335	24,347	(7,200)	321,482
2	321,482	25,718	(7,200)	340,000
3	340,000	27,200	(7,200)	
			(360,000)	0
		77,265		

Note: Effective interest rate is multiplied by opening balance.

Note: Coupon rate is multiplied by face value of debt.

Tutorial note

The total finance cost will be as follows:

		$
Redemption value	At par	360,000
Payments	2% × 360,000 x 3 years	21,600
		381,600
Net proceeds (W1)		(304,335)
Total finance cost		77,265

The total finance cost will be allocated at a constant rate based upon carrying value over the life of the instrument. This is performed by applying the 8% effective interest rate.

(W1) **Net proceeds = opening balance**

	$
Nominal value	360,000
Discount 14%	(50,400)
Issue costs	(5,265)
	304,335

Test your understanding 5

(a) When the loan notes are issued:

Dr Bank	$18,966
Cr Loan notes	$18,966

Working

	$
Nominal value	20,000
Discount 2.5%	(500)
Issue costs	(534)
	18,966

(b) **Income statement (IS)**

Year	1	2	3	4	5
	$	$	$	$	$
Finance costs (W1)	(1,328)	(1,365)	(1,404)	(1,446)	(1,491)

Statement of financial position (SFP)

Year	1	2	3	4	5
	$	$	$	$	$
Non-current liabilities	19,494	20,059	20,663		
Current liabilities				21,309	0

(W1) **Amortised cost table**

Year	**Opening balance**	**Effective interest 7% (IS)**	**Coupon paid 4%**	**Closing balance (SFP)**
1	18,966	1,328	(800)	19,494
2	19,494	1,365	(800)	20,059
3	20,059	1,404	(800)	20,663
4	20,663	1,446	(800)	21,309
5	21,309	1,491	(800)	
			(22,000)	0

Note: Effective interest rate is multiplied by opening balance.

Note: Coupon rate is multiplied by face value of debt.

Test your understanding 6

(a) When the bonds are issued:

Dr Bank	$123,545
Cr Bonds	$123,545

Working

	$
Nominal value	150,000
Discount 10%	(15,000)
Issue costs	(11,455)
	123,545

(b) Financial statement extracts

Income statement (IS)

Year	1	2	3	4
	$	$	$	$
Finance costs	(12,355)	(13,140)	(14,004)	(14,956)

Statement of financial position

Year	1	2	3	4
	$	$	$	$
Non-current liabilities	131,400	140,040		
Current liabilities			149,544	0

(W1) **Amortised cost table**

Year	**Opening balance ($)**	**Effective interest 10% (IS)**	**Coupon paid 3%**	**Closing balance (SFP) ($)**
1	123,545	12,355	(4,500)	131,400
2	131,400	13,140	(4,500)	140,040
3	140,040	14,004	(4,500)	149,544
4	149,544	14,956	(4,500)	
			(160,000)	0

Note: Effective interest rate is multiplied by opening balance.

Note: Coupon rate is multiplied by face value of debt.

(c) Journal entries required

Dr Non-current liabilities	$11,455
Cr Finance costs	$11,455

being the required correction to show the issue costs as a deduction from the liability rather than an expense in the income statement

Dr Finance costs (12,355 – 4,500)	$7,855
Cr Non-current liabilities	$7,855

being the correct treatment of finance costs, which should be based on the effective rate of 10% rather than the coupon rate of 3%

Test your understanding 7 - Hybrid

(a) The cash proceeds are 3,000 × $1,000 = $3m

The present value of future cash flows i.e. the liability component will be calculated as:

Year	Cash flow	Discount factors @ 9%	Present value ($)
1	7% × $3m = $210,000	0.917	192,570
2	$210,000	0.842	176,820
3	$3,210,000	0.772	2,478,120
			2,847,510

Thus:

– The debt will be recorded at $2,847,510.

– The equity will be recorded at (3,000,000 – 2,847,510) $152,490

The equity will remain unchanged at $152,490 at subsequent reporting dates.

The debt will be amortised.

(b) **Income statement**

Year 1	$
Finance costs (W1)	(256,276)

Statement of financial position

Year 1	$
Equity	
Equity option	152,490
Non-current liabilities (W1)	2,893,786

(W1) **Amortised cost table**

Year	Opening balance ($)	Effective interest 9% (IS)	Coupon paid 7%	Closing balance (SFP) ($)
1	2,847,510	256,276	(210,000)	2,893,786

Note: Effective interest rate is multiplied by opening balance.

Note: Coupon rate is multiplied by face value of debt.

Test your understanding 8

(a) When the convertible bonds are issued:

Dr Bank	$36,000
Cr Financial Liability	$29,614
Cr Equity (bal fig)	$6,386

Year	Cash flow (W) ($)	Discount factor 9%	Present value ($)
1	720	0.917	660
2	720	0.842	606
3	36,720	0.772	28,348
			29,614

(W) Cash flow = 2% × 36,000 = $720

(b) **Income statement**

Year 1	$
Finance costs (W1)	(2,665)

Statement of financial position

Year 1	$
Equity	
Equity option	6,386
Non-current liabilities (W1)	31,559

(W1) **Amortised cost table**

Year	Opening balance ($)	Effective interest 9% (IS)	Coupon paid 2%	Closing balance (SFP) ($)
1	29,614	2,665	(720)	31,559

Note: Effective interest rate is multiplied by opening balance.

Note: Coupon rate is multiplied by face value of debt.

Test your understanding 9

(a) When the convertible bonds are issued, the following should be recorded:

Dr Bank	$5,000,000
Cr Financial Liability	$4,734,600
Cr Equity (bal fig)	$265,400

Year	Cash flow (W) ($)	Discount factor 6%	Present value ($)
1	200,000	0.943	188,600
2	200,000	0.890	178,000
3	5,200,000	0.840	4,368,000
			4,734,600

(W) Cash flow = 4% × 5,000,000 = $200,000

(b) **Income statement for the year ended 31 December**

	20X3 $	20X4 $
Finance costs (W1)	(284,076)	(289,121)

Statement of financial position at 31 December

	20X3 $	20X4 $
Equity		
Equity option	265,400	265,400
Non-current liabilities (W1)	4,818,676	
Current liabilities (W1)		4,907,797

(W1) **Amortised cost table**

Year	Opening balance ($)	Effective interest 6% (IS)	Coupon paid 4%	Closing balance (SFP) ($)
1	4,734,600	284,076	(200,000)	4,818,676
2	4,818,676	289,121	(200,000)	4,907,797

Note: Effective interest rate is multiplied by opening balance.

Note: Coupon rate is multiplied by face value of debt.

(c) Journal entries required

Dr Non-current liabilities	$265,400
Cr Equity reserve	$265,400

being the correct treatment of the initial recognition, after splitting the liability and equity components

Dr Finance costs (284,076 – 200,000)	$84,076
Cr Non-current liabilities	$84,076

being the correct treatment of finance costs, based on effective rate applied to the liability component

Test your understanding 10

Financial asset	Classification
1. Investments held for trading purposes	Financial assets at fair value through profit or loss
2. Interest-bearing debt instruments that will be redeemed in five years and held to redemption	Held-to-maturity investments
3. A trade receivable	Loans and receivables
4. Derivatives held for speculation purposes	Financial assets at fair value through profit or loss
5. Equity shares that Ashes has no intention of selling	Available-for-sale financial assets (because they do not fit under any other heading)

Test your understanding 11

Income statement (IS)

Year	1	2	3
	$	$	$
Finance income	600	612	625

Statement of financial position (SFP)

Year	1	2	3
	$	$	$
Non-current assets			
Financial assets	5,100	5,212	0

(W1) **Amortised cost table**

Year	**Opening balance ($)**	**Effective interest 12% (IS)**	**Coupon received 10%**	**Closing balance (SFP) ($)**
1	5,000	600	(500)	5,100
2	5,100	612	(500)	5,212
3	5,212	625	(500)	
			(5,337)	0

Note: Effective interest rate is multiplied by opening balance.

Note: Coupon rate is multiplied by face value of debt.

Test your understanding 12

(a) The financial assets are classified as fair value through profit and loss as the shares will be sold shortly after the reporting date and are therefore held for trading.

Income statement

Finance income (10,000 × (4.90 – 4.20))	$7,000

Statement of financial position

Current assets	
Investments (10,000 × 4.90)	$49,000

(b) The financial assets would instead be classified as available for sale. They would be recognised as non-current assets on the statement of financial position and the gain of $7,000 would be taken to reserves and shown as other comprehensive income in the statement of comprehensive income. It would be presented as an item that may be reclassified subsequently to profit or loss.

Test your understanding 13

On 30 November 20X1 (contract date):

Derivative has no value.

On 31 December 20X1 (reporting date):

Dr	Derivative (financial asset)	$20m
Cr	Income statement (gain)	$20m

On 31 March 20X2 (settlement):

Dr	Income statement (loss)	$13m
Cr	Derivative (financial asset)	$13m

To record the further change in fair value

Dr	Bank	$7m
Cr	Derivative (to derecognise)	$7m

To record the settlement of the contract

Test your understanding 14

(a) Extracts from financial statements

Statement of comprehensive income for year ended 30 June 20X2

	20X2	20X1
	$	$
Gain on derivative (W2)	126,646	63,830

Statement of financial position at 30 June 20X2

	20X2	20X1
	$	$
Derivative asset (W1)	190,476	63,830

Workings

(W1) **Value of derivative**

	$
Value of forward contract at 1 March 20X1	Nil
(Fl 5m / 5) – $1m	
Value of forward contract at 30 June 20X1	
(Fl 5m / 4.7) – $1m	63,830
Value of forward contract at 30 June 20X2	
(Fl 5m / 4.2) – $1m	190,476

(W2) **Gain**

	$
Gain for year ended 30 June 20X1	63,830
Gain for year ended 30 June 20X2	126,646
(190,476 – 63,830)	

(b) **Gain or loss in year ended 30 June 20X3**

Value of forward contract at 31 January 20X3	
(Fl 5m / 4.5) – $1m	$111,111
Therefore loss would be recognised (190,476 – 111,111)	$79,365

Test your understanding 15

(a) The financial asset is classified as available for sale and would therefore be remeasured at fair value at the reporting date, with the gain being shown as other comprehensive income.

Other comprehensive income

Items that may be reclassified subsequently to profit or loss:

Gain on AFS assets (10,000 × (1.58 – 1.35))	$2,300

Statement of financial position

Non-current assets	
AFS assets (10,000 × 1.58)	$15,800

(b) In accordance with IAS 39, all derivative contracts are classified as fair value through profit and loss, therefore any gain or loss in the value of the derivative contract would be taken directly to the income statement. Gains or losses on available for sale investments are normally recorded through other comprehensive income. However, assuming that hedge accounting could be applied (certain criteria must be satisfied for this to be the case) then the gain on the available for sale investment (the hedged item) would instead be recognised in the income statement where it would be offset against the gain/loss on the derivative contract (the hedging instrument). This is an example of a fair value hedge.

Test your understanding 16

(a) Derivative contracts should be accounted for as financial instruments held at fair value through profit or loss.

The value of the derivative will be the difference between the value of the contract when settled compared with the cost of B$1 million being purchased at the spot rate at the year-end date.

Cost of B$1 million at the contracted rate of B$0.75 = 1m / 0.75 = A$1,333,333

Cost of B$1 million at the year end rate of B$0.80 = 1m/0.8 = A$1,250,000

Therefore , the derivative results in a liability at the year-end date of A$83,333 (1,333,333 - 1,250,000) as the contract has unfavourable terms when compared to the year end rate. The loss on the derivative would be charged to the income statement in the year to 31 March 20X1.

The journal entry to record the derivative would be:

Dr Income statement (loss) A$83,333

Cr Derivative liability A$83,333

(b) If the derivative was designated as a hedging instrument in a cash flow hedge then the loss of A$83,333 would be recognised in other comprehensive income until the related cash flow (the hedged item) occurred. This ensures that the movements in the hedged item and the hedging instrument can be offset in the same accounting period.

chapter

14

Share-based payments

Chapter learning objectives

On completion of their studies students should be able to:

- Discuss the recognition and valuation issues concerned with share-based payments.

1 Session content

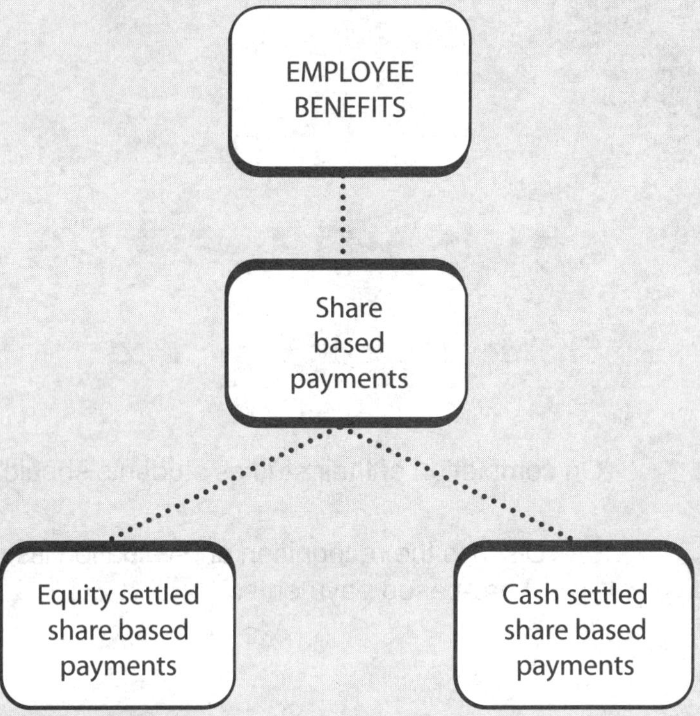

2 Share-based payment

Introduction

Share-based payment has become increasingly common. Part of the remuneration of directors is often in the form of shares or options. Employees may also be granted share options.

Many new 'e-businesses' do not expect to be profitable in their early years, so try to attract quality staff by offering them share options rather than high cash salaries.

Share-based payment also occurs when an entity buys goods or services from other parties (such as employees or suppliers), and settles the amounts payable by issuing shares or share options to them.

The problem

If a company pays remuneration in cash, an expense is recognised in profit or loss. If a company 'pays' for employee services in share options, there is no cash outflow and under traditional accounting, no expense would be recognised.

However, when a company issues shares to employees, a transaction has occurred; the employees have provided a valuable service to the entity, in exchange for the shares/options. It is illogical not to recognise this transaction in the financial statements.

IFRS 2 **Share-based payment** was issued to deal with this accounting anomaly. IFRS 2 requires that all share-based payment transactions must be recognised in the financial statements.

Types of transaction

IFRS 2 applies to all types of share-based payment transaction. There are two main types:

- in an **equity-settled share-based payment transaction**, the entity rewards staff with equity instruments (e.g. shares or share options)
- in a **cash-settled share-based payment transaction**, the entity rewards staff with amounts of cash measured by reference to the entity's share price.

The most common type of share-based payment transaction is where share options are granted to employees or directors as part of their remuneration.

The basic principles

When an entity receives employee services or goods as a result of a share-based payment transaction, it recognises either an expense or an asset.

- If the goods or services are received in exchange for equity (e.g. for share options), the entity recognises an increase in equity.
  - The double entry is:
    - Dr Expense/Asset
    - Cr Equity (normally a special reserve).
- If the goods or services are received or acquired in a cash-settled share-based payment transaction, the entity recognises a liability.
  - The double entry is:
    - Dr Expense/Asset
    - Cr Liability.

All share-based payment transactions are measured at fair value.

3 Equity-settled share-based payments

Illustration 1 - How options work

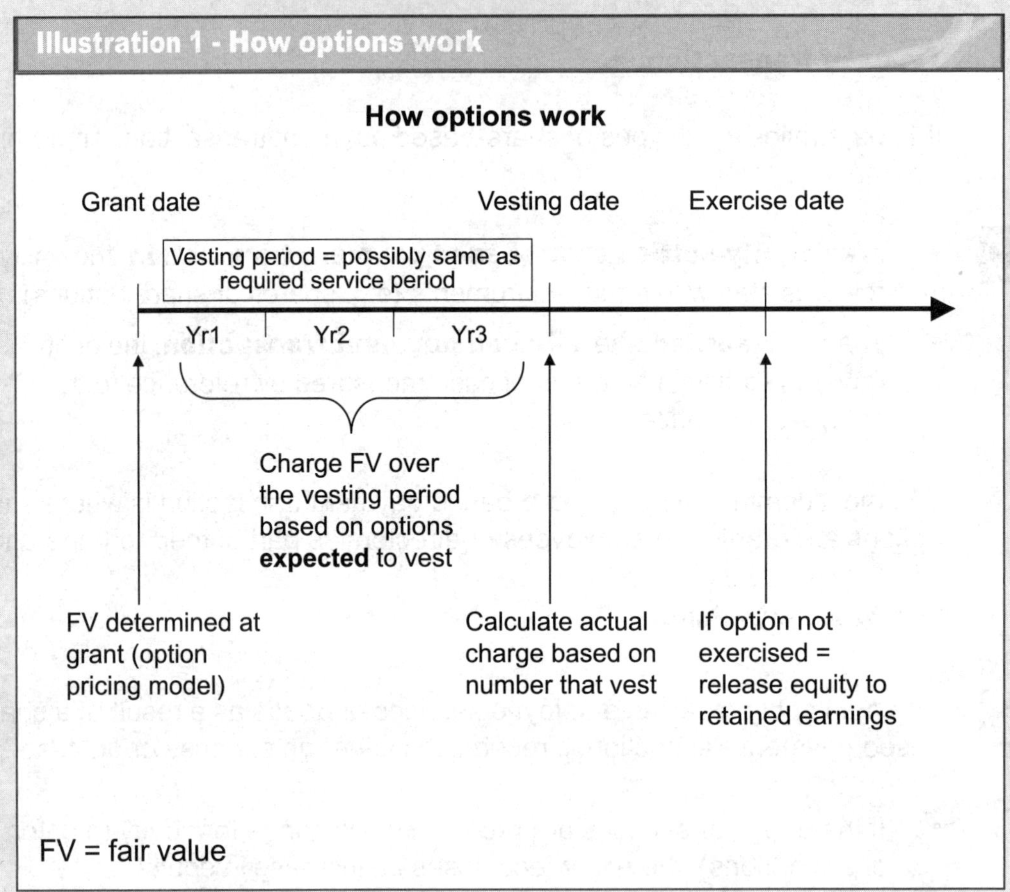
How options work
Grant date
Vesting date
Exercise date
Vesting period = possibly same as required service period
Yr1
Yr2
Yr3
Charge FV over the vesting period based on options expected to vest
FV determined at grant (option pricing model)
Calculate actual charge based on number that vest
If option not exercised = release equity to retained earnings
FV = fair value

Measurement

The basic principle is that all transactions are measured at fair value at the grant date i.e. the date at which the entity and another party agree to the arrangement.

For equity-settled transactions the fair value is typically the option price at the grant date (rather than the fair value of the goods or services received).

If the options vest immediately i.e. employees are entitled to the shares immediately, it is presumed that the entity has received the benefit of the services and the full amount is recognised on the grant date.

If the options do not vest immediately, as is usually the case, the company should spread the cost of the options over the vesting period, the period during which the specific vesting conditions are satisfied e.g. length of service with the company.

To record the cost on an annual basis:

Dr Income statement

Cr Equity (other reserves)

The amount is: total number of options issued and *expected* to vest multiplied by the fair value of an option at grant date, spread over the vesting period.

Example 1

On 1 January 20X1 an entity grants 100 share options to each of its 500 employees. Each grant is conditional upon the employee working for the entity until 31 December 20X3. At the grant date the fair value of each share option is $15.

During 20X1, 20 employees leave and the entity estimates that a total of 20% of the 500 employees will leave during the three- year period.

During 20X2, a further 20 employees leave and the entity now estimates that only a total of 15% of its 500 employees will leave during the three-year period.

During 20X3, a further 10 employees leave.

Required:

Calculate the remuneration expense that will be recognised in respect of the share-based payment transaction for each of the three years ended 31 December 20X3.

Example 1 answer

The entity recognises the remuneration expense as the employees' services are received over the three year vesting period. The amount recognised is based on the fair value of the share options granted at the grant date (1 January 20X1).

Assuming that no employees left, the total expense would be $750,000 (100 × 500 × 15) and the expense charged to profit or loss for each of the three years would be $250,000 (750,000/3).

In practice, the entity estimates the number of options expected to vest by estimating the number of employees likely to leave. This estimate is revised at each year end. The expense recognised for the year is based on this re-estimate. On the vesting date (31 December 20X3), it recognises an amount based on the number of options that actually vest.

A total of 50 employees left during the three year period and therefore 45,000 options ((500 – 50) × 100) vested.

The amount recognised as an expense for each of the three years is calculated as follows:

	Cumulative expense at year-end	**Expense for the year (change in cumulative)**
	$	$
20X1 100 × (500 × 80%) × 15 × 1/3	200,000	200,000
20X2 100 × (500 × 85%) × 15 × 2/3	425,000	225,000
20X3 45,000 × 15	675,000	250,000

The financial statements will include the following amounts:

Income statement	**20X1**	**20X2**	**20X3**
	$	$	$
Staff costs	200,000	225,000	250,000

Statement of financial position	**20X1**	**20X2**	**20X3**
	$	$	$
Included with equity	200,000	425,000	675,000

Test your understanding 1

On the 1 January 20X5, 400 staff receive 100 share options each. They must work for the company for the next three years and the options become exercisable on 31 December 20X7. The fair value at the time of granting is $20 per option.

In the year ending 31 December 20X5, 10 staff leave and it is thought that during the three year vesting period, the total amount leaving will be 15%.

In 20X6, a further 15 leave but the estimate of total leaving is now reduced to 10%. In the final year 12 staff leave.

Required:

Show how this will impact on the financial statements of the years 20X5, 20X6 and 20X7.

Test your understanding 2

Asif has set up an employee option scheme to motivate its sales team of ten key sales people. Each sales person was offered 1 million options exercisable at 10c, conditional upon the employee remaining with the company during the vesting period of 5 years. The options are then exercisable three weeks after the end of the vesting period.

This is year two of the scheme. At the end of year one, two sales people had suggested that they would be leaving the company during the second year. However, although one did leave, the other recommitted to the company and the scheme during year two. The other employees have always been committed to the scheme and stated their intention to stay with the company during the 5 years. Relevant market values are as follows:

Date	**Share price**	**Option price**
Grant date	10c	20c
End of Year One	24c	38c
End of Year Two	21c	33c

The option price is the market price of an equivalent marketable option on the relevant date.

Required:

Show the effect of the scheme on the financial statements of Asif for Year Two.

4 Cash-settled share-based payments

An example of a cash-settled share-based payment transaction is the payment of a bonus to an employee based on the entity's share price.

The basic principle is that the entity measures the goods or services acquired and the liability incurred at the **fair value of the liability**.

- Until the liability is settled, the entity remeasures the fair value of the liability at each reporting date and then at the date of settlement. (Notice that this is different from accounting for equity share-based payments, where the fair value is fixed at the grant date.)
- Changes in fair value are recognised in profit or loss for the period.
- Where services are received, these are recognised over the period that the employees render the services. (This is the same principle as for equity-settled transactions).
- The expense recognised in each accounting period has a double entry to a provision/liability account.
  - Dr Income statement
  - Cr Liability/ provision
- On the vesting date, the amount of the provision/liability should equal the cash to be paid.

Example 2

On 1 January 20X1 an entity grants 100 cash share appreciation rights (SAR) to each of its 300 employees, on condition that they continue to work for the entity until 31 December 20X3.

During 20X1 20 employees leave. The entity estimates that a further 40 will leave during 20X2 and 20X3.

During 20X2 10 employees leave. The entity estimates that a further 20 will leave during 20X3.

During 20X3 10 employees leave.

The fair values of one SAR at each year end are shown below.

	Fair value
	$
20X1	10.00
20X2	12.00
20X3	15.00

Required:

Calculate the amount to be recognised as an expense for each of the three years ended 31 December 20X3 and the liability to be recognised in the statement of financial position at 31 December for each of the three years.

Example 2 answer

Year	Liability at year-end	Expense for year
	$000	$000
20X1 ((300 – 20 – 40) × 100 × $10 × 1/3)	80	80
20X2 ((300 – 20 – 10 – 20) × 100 × $12 × 2/3)	200	120
20X3 ((300 – 20 – 10 – 10) × 100 × $15)	390	190

You need to measure the fair value of the liability at each reporting date based on the number of employees who have left and those that are expected to leave before 31 December 20X3.

Also remeasure the change in the fair value of the liability based on the fair value of the SAR at the reporting date.

Test your understanding 3

On 1 January 20X1 Kindly sets up a cash based payment to each of its 100 employees, on condition that they continue to work for the entity until 31 December 20X3. Each employee has been allocated 100 shares and will receive a payment in cash if the share price exceeds $10 on 31 December 20X3, of the amount by which it exceeds $10.

During 20X1, 5 employees leave. The entity estimates that a further 12 will leave during 20X2 and 20X3.

During 20X2, 10 employees leave. The entity estimates that a further 15 will leave during 20X3.

During 20X3, 18 employees leave.

The share prices at the reporting date in each year are shown below.

	$
20X1	11.00
20X2	12.00
20X3	14.00

Required:

Calculate the amount to be recognised as an expense for each of the three years ended 31 December 20X3 and the liability to be recognised in the statement of financial position at 31 December for each of the three years.

Test your understanding 4

G grants 100 share appreciation rights (SARs) to its 500 employees on 1 January 20X7 on the condition that the employees stay with the entity for the next two years. The SARs must be exercised at the start of 20X9.

During 20X7 15 staff leave and another 20 are expected to leave in 20X8.

During 20X8 25 staff leave.

The fair value of the SARs is $10 at 31 December 20X7 and $13 at 31 December 20X8.

Required:

Calculate the amount to be recognised as an expense for the two years ended 31 December 20X7 and 20X8 and the liability to be recognised in the statement of financial position at 31 December for both years.

Test your understanding 5

The following information relates to two share-based transactions that LM entered into in 20X6.

(1) LM granted share options to its 200 employees on 1 January 20X6. Each employee will receive 500 share options if they continue to work for LM for the next three years. The fair value of the options at the grant date was $2.00 each.

(2) LM grants 8,000 share appreciation rights (SARs) to each of its employees on 1 January 20X6. Payment will be made on 31 March 20X9. Again the scheme is only open to those who remain employed with LM for the three year period up to 31 December 20X8. The fair value per SAR at the end of each of the three years is:

– 20X6 – $1.60

– 20X7 – $1.80

– 20X8 – $2.10

During 20X6 20 employees left and another 45 were expected to leave over the next two years.

During 20X7 15 employees left and another 20 were expected to leave in 20X8.

During 20X8 10 employees left.

Required:

Briefly describe the accounting treatment to be adopted for these transactions, in accordance with *IFRS 2 Share-based payments* and calculate the amount to be recorded in the income statement for staff costs in respect of each of the three years.

5 Chapter summary

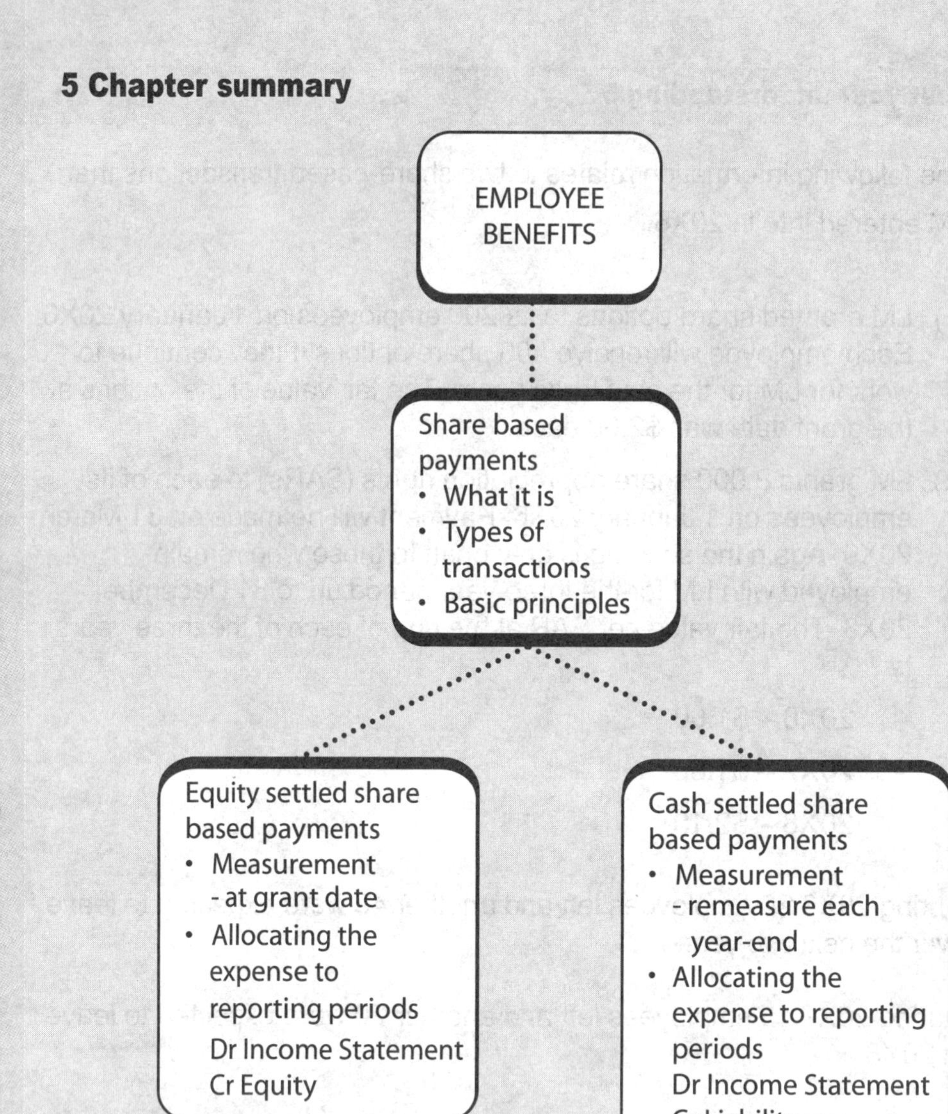
EMPLOYEE BENEFITS
Share based payments
• What it is
• Types of transactions
• Basic principles
Equity settled share based payments
• Measurement - at grant date
• Allocating the expense to reporting periods
Dr Income Statement
Cr Equity
Cash settled share based payments
• Measurement - remeasure each year-end
• Allocating the expense to reporting periods
Dr Income Statement
Cr Liability

Test your understanding answers

Test your understanding 1

	20X5	20X6	20X7
Share options	40,000	40,000	40,000
Expected to vest	85%	90%	(3,700)*
	34,000	36,000	36,300
Fair value at grant date	$20	$20	$20
Total cost	$680,000	$720,000	$726,000
Proportion of vesting period passed	1/3	2/3	3/3
Equity	$226,667	$480,000	$726,000
Cost charged to income statement (= equity c/f - equity b/f)	$226,667	$253,333	$246,000

* of the 400 staff 37 have left by the end of the 3 year period. Each staff member had the right to exercise 100 share options, which would have amounted to 3,700 in total. This leaves 36,300 remaining legitimate options.

Test your understanding 2

The expense is measured using the fair value of the option at the grant date, i.e. 20c.

At the end of year two the amount recognised in equity should be $720,000 (1m × (10 – 1) × 20c × 2/5).

At the beginning of year two the amount recognised in equity would have been $320,000 (1m × 8 × 20c × 1/5).

The charge to profit for Year Two is the difference between the two: $400,000 (720,000 – 320,000).

Test your understanding 3

Year		Liability at year-end	Expense for year
		$	$
20X1	((100 – 5 – 12) × 100 × (11-10) × 1/3)	2,767	2,767
20X2	((100 – 5 – 10 – 15) × 100 × (12-10) × 2/3)	9,333	6,566
20X3	((100 – 5 – 10 – 18) × 100 × (14-10))	26,800	17,467

Test your understanding 4

Year		Liability at year-end	Expense for year
		$	$
20X7	((500 – 15 – 20) × 100 × $10 × 1/2)	232,500	232,500
20X8	((500 – 15 – 25) × 100 × $13)	598,000	365,500

Test your understanding 5

Transaction (1)

This is an equity-settled share-based payment and under IFRS 2 the fair value of the options will be used to estimate the fair value of the services provided by employees. The total fair value will be allocated over the vesting period of three years and will be based on the fair value at the grant date and will not be remeasured for subsequent changes in the value of the options. The income statement will be charged and equity will be credited in each of the three years of the vesting period.

20X6 500 options x $2 per share x (200 – 20 – 45) = $135,000
Charge for 20X6 = $135,000/3 = $45,000

20X7 500 options x $2 per share x (200 – 20 – 15 – 20) = $145,000
Amount to be recognised to date = 145,000 x 2/3 = $96,667
Charge for 20X7 = (96,667 – 45,000) = $51,667

20X8 500 options x $2 per share x (200 – 20 – 15 – 10) = $155,000
Charge for 20X8 = (155,000 – 96,667) = $58,333

Transaction (2)

This is a cash-settled equity-based transaction. The cost to the income statement will be calculated in a similar way but will take account of the change in the fair value of the SARs. The income statement will be charged with the equivalent expense but as this is cash settled, the credit will be to liability in the statement of financial position.

20X6 8,000 x \$1.60 x (200 – 20 – 45) = \$1,728,000
Charge for 20X6 = \$1,728,000/3 = \$576,000

20X7 8,000 x \$1.80 x (200 – 20 – 15 – 20) = \$2,088,000
Amount to be recognised to date = 2,088,000 x 2/3 = \$1,392,000
Charge for 20X7 = (1,392,000 – 576,000) = \$816,000

20X8 8,000 x \$2.10 x (200 – 20 – 15 – 10) = \$2,604,000
Charge for 20X8 = (2,604,000 – 1,392,000) = \$1,212,000

chapter

15

Pension benefits

Chapter learning objectives

On completion of their studies students should be able to:

- Discuss the recognition and valuation issues concerned with pension schemes and the treatment of actuarial deficits and surpluses.

1 Session content

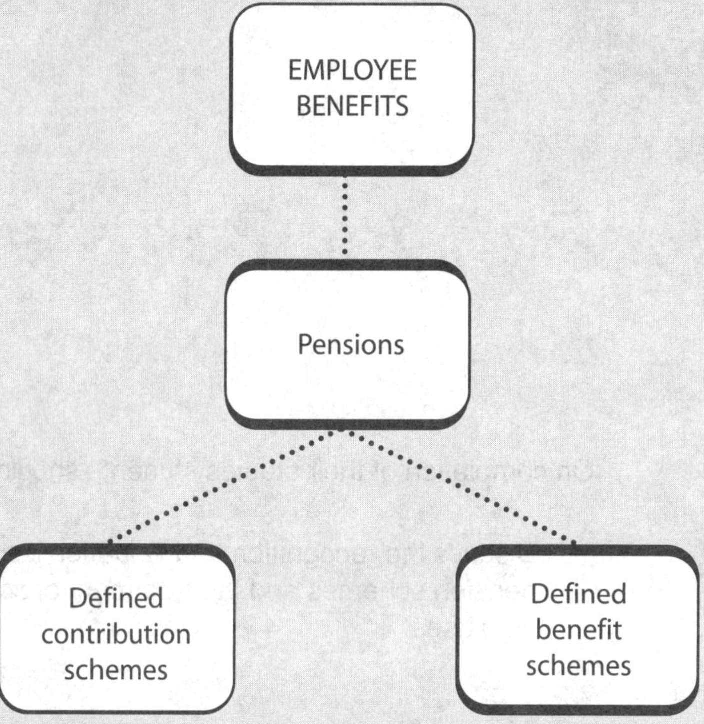

2 Types of pension plan

Introduction

A pension plan (sometimes called a post-employment benefit scheme) consists of a pool of assets and a liability for pensions owed to employees. Pension plan assets normally consist of investments, cash and (sometimes) properties. The return earned on the assets is used to pay pensions.

There are two main types of pension plan:

- defined contribution plans
- defined benefit plans.

Defined contribution plans

The pension payable on retirement depends on the contributions paid into the plan by the employee and the employer.

- The employer's contribution is usually a fixed percentage of the employee's salary. The employer has no further obligation after this amount is paid.
- Therefore, the annual cost to the employer is reasonably predictable.
- Defined contribution plans present few accounting problems.

Defined benefit plans

The pension payable on retirement normally depends on either the final salary or the average salary of the employee during their career.

- The employer undertakes to finance a pension income of a certain amount, e.g.

  2/3 × final salary × (years of service / 40 years)

- The employer has an ongoing obligation to make sufficient contributions to the plan to fund the pensions.
- An actuary calculates the amount that must be paid into the plan each year in order to provide the promised pension. The calculation is based on various estimates and assumptions including:
  - life expectancy
  - expected length of service to retirement / employee turnover
  - investment returns
  - wage inflation.
- Therefore, the cost of providing pensions is not certain and varies from year to year.

The actual contribution paid in a period does not usually represent the true cost to the employer of providing pensions in that period. The financial statements must reflect the true cost of providing pensions.

3 Accounting for pension plans (IAS 19)

Defined contribution plans

The expense of providing pensions in the period is normally the same as the amount of contributions paid.

- The entity should charge the agreed pension contribution to profit or loss as an employment expense in each period.
- An asset (prepayment) or liability (accrual) for pensions only arises if the cash paid does not equal the amount of contributions due.
- IAS 19 requires disclosure of the amount recognised as an expense in the period.

Example 1

A company makes contributions to the pension fund of employees at a rate of 5% of gross salary. The contributions made are $10,000 per month for convenience with the balance being contributed in the first month of the following accounting year. The wages and salaries for 20X6 are $2.7m.

Required:

Calculate the pension expense for 20X6 and the accrual/prepayment at the end of the year.

Example 1 answer

The charge to income should be:

$2.7m × 5% = $135,000

The statement of financial position will therefore show an accrual of $15,000, being the difference between the $135,000 and the $120,000 paid in the year.

Test your understanding 1

J operates a defined contribution scheme on which it pays 6% of employees gross salaries per annum. At the end of last year, J had accrued $10,000 for pension contributions due. Gross salaries for the current year amounted to $650,000 and J had paid contributions totalling $35,000 into the pension fund during the year.

Required:

What amounts will be recorded in the financial statements in respect of the pension plan for the current year?

Defined benefit plans: the basic principle

IAS 19 has recently been amended to clarify and simplify the accounting treatment for defined benefit pension plans.

The amended standard is effective for accounting periods commencing on or after 1 January 2013 and is therefore examinable from the May 2013 exam diet onwards.

The previous version of the standard permitted three different methods for dealing with actuarial differences whereas the revised standard contains only one method, improving consistency and comparability of accounting treatments across entities.

The entity recognises the net defined benefit liability (or asset) in the statement of financial position.

- If the liability exceeds the assets, there is a deficit (the usual situation) and a liability is reported in the statement of financial position.
- If the scheme assets exceed the liability, there is a surplus and an asset is reported in the statement of financial position.
- In simple terms, the movement in the net liability (or asset) from one reporting date to the next is reflected in the statement of comprehensive income for the year.

Measuring the liability and the assets

In practice, the actuary measures the plan assets and liabilities using a number of estimates and assumptions.

- The plan liability is measured at the present value of the defined benefit obligation. Discounting is necessary because the liability will be settled many years in the future and therefore the effect of the time value of money is material.
- Plan assets are measured at fair value at the reporting date. This is normally market value.

Recognising the amounts in the financial statements

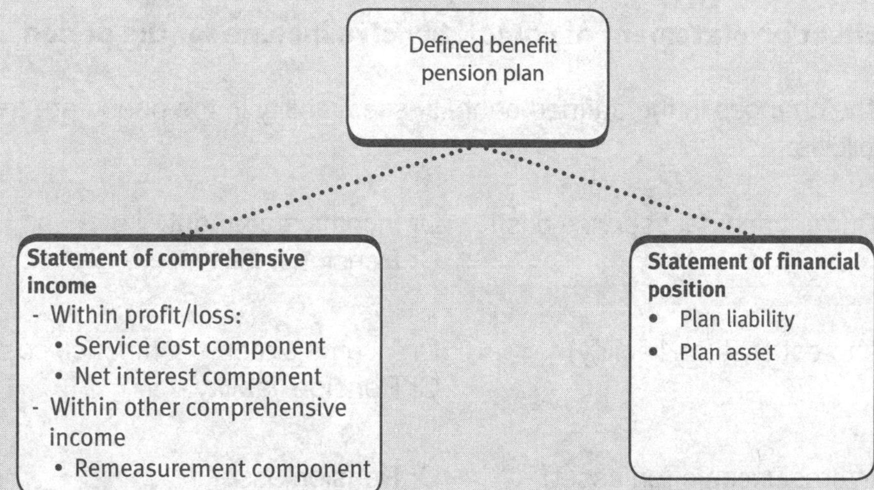

Explanation of the terms used.

- **Service cost component** includes current and past service costs, together with any gains or losses on curtailments or settlements.
  - **Current service cost** is the increase in the actuarial liability (present value of the defined benefit obligation) resulting from employee service in the current period.
  - **Past service cost** is the increase in the present value of the liability (defined benefit obligation) resulting from a plan amendment or curtailment.
  - **Curtailment and settlement gains/losses** arise when significant reductions are made to the number of employees covered by the plan or the benefits promised to them.
- **Net interest component** is determined by multiplying the net defined benefit liability (or asset) at the start of the period by the discount rate. It can be viewed as comprising interest income on the plan assets and the unwinding of the discount, creating an interest cost, on the plan obligation.
- **Remeasurement component** principally comprises actuarial gains and losses and also includes any return on plan assets not already recognised in the net interest component. The remeasurement component is recognised in other comprehensive income for the year. It cannot be reclassified to profit or loss in future periods.
  - **Actuarial gains and losses** result from increases or decreases in the pension asset or liability that occur either because the actuarial assumptions have changed or because of differences between the previous actuarial assumptions and what has actually happened (experience adjustments).

Effect on statement of comprehensive income for the period

The changes in the defined benefit asset/liability in the period are treated as follows:

Current and past service costs	Dr Income statement Cr Pension liability
Interest cost (on liability)	Dr Income statement (finance cost) Cr Pension liability
Interest income (on asset)	Dr Pension asset Cr Income statement (net off against finance cost)

Curtailments and settlements (if any)	Dr or Cr Income statement Cr or Dr Pension liability
Remeasurement component gain/loss	Dr or Cr Other comprehensive income Cr or Dr Pension asset / liability

Other entries affecting the pension assets and liabilities

There are additional changes in the defined benefit asset/liability in the period affecting only the statement of financial position:

Contributions (from the employer)	Dr Pension asset Cr Bank
Benefits paid	Dr Pension liability Cr Pension asset

Example 2

T has a defined benefit pension plan and makes up financial statements to 31 March each year. The net pension liability (i.e. obligation less plan assets) at 31 March 20X3, was $40 million ($35 million at 31 March 20X2). The following additional information is relevant for the year ended 31 March 20X3:

- The discount rate relevant to the net liability at the start of the year was 10%.
- The current service cost was $45 million.
- At the end of the year the company granted additional benefits to existing pensioners that have a present value of $10 million. These were not allowed for in the original actuarial assumptions.
- The company paid pension contributions of $40 million.

Required:

Calculate the actuarial gain or loss arising in the year ended 31 March 20X3.

Prepare extracts from the statement of comprehensive income for the year ended 31 March 20X3 and the statement of financial position at 31 March 20X3 showing how the defined benefit scheme would be presented.

Example 2 answer

	$m
Net liability brought forward	(35)
Net interest cost (10% x 35)	(3.5)
Current service cost	(45)
Additional benefits granted (past service costs)	(10)
Pension contributions paid	40
Actuarial gain (bal fig)	13.5
Net liability carried forward	(40)

You were given the net pension liability at the start and end of the year and needed to use the double entries listed above to calculate the balancing figure for the actuarial gain. This is the gap between what the actuary expected at the start of the year and what actually happened by the end of the year.

If benefits paid had been provided in the question no adjustment is required because the entries reduce pension assets and reduce pension liabilities, thereby having no effect on the net pension liability.

Statement of financial position (extract) at 31 March 20X3

	$m
Net pension liability	40

Statement of comprehensive income (extracts) for the year ended 31 March 20X3

	$m
Service cost component	(45)
Net interest component	(3.5)
Net effect on profit	(48.5)

Other comprehensive income

Items that will not be reclassified to profit or loss:

Remeasurement component – gain	13.5
Net effect on total comprehensive income	(35)

Test your understanding 2 - Alpha

Alpha operates a defined benefit pension scheme.

As at 1 January 20X6, Alpha's statement of financial position showed pension assets measured at a fair value of $1,400,000 and pension liabilities measured at a present value of $1,350,000.

The current service cost for the year was estimated at $130,000 and the discount rate used was 8%.

Alpha paid contributions totalling $120,000 into the scheme during the year and benefits were paid to scheme members totalling $110,000.

As at 31 December 20X6, the pension fund assets have been valued at $1,565,000 and the pension fund liabilities at $1,630,000.

Required:

Calculate the actuarial gains/losses arising on the pension asset and obligation in the year ended 31 December 20X6.

Prepare extracts from the statement of comprehensive income for the year ended 31 December 20X6 and the statement of financial position at 31 December 20X6 showing how the defined benefit scheme would be presented.

Test your understanding 3

The following data relates to a defined benefit scheme for the year ended 31 December 20X4.

	$000
Discount rate	10% per annum
Pension liabilities at start of year	1,030
Pension asset at start of year	1,010
Current service costs	140
Past service costs	35
Curtailment costs	15
Benefits paid out	105
Contributions paid in	110
Pension liability at year end	1,280
Pension asset at year end	1,240

Required:

Prepare extracts from the statement of comprehensive income for the year ended 31 December 20X4 and the statement of financial position at 31 December 20X4 showing how the defined benefit scheme would be presented.

Test your understanding 4

The following data relates to a defined benefit scheme for the next year ended 31 December 20X5:

	$000
Discount rate	7% per annum
Pension liabilities at start of year	1,280
Pension asset at start of year	1,240
Current service costs	150
Benefits paid out	100
Contributions paid in	130
Pension liability at year end	1,610
Pension asset at year end	1,500

Required:

Prepare extracts from the statement of comprehensive income for the year ended 31 December 20X5 and the statement of financial position at 31 December 20X5 showing how the defined benefit scheme would be presented.

Test your understanding 5

The following information is given about a defined benefit plan. To keep the computations simple, all transactions are assumed to occur at the year-end. The present value of the obligation and the market value of the plan assets were both $1 million at 1 January 20X1.

	20X1	**20X2**	**20X3**
	$000	$000	$000
Discount rate at 1 January	10%	9%	8%
Current service cost	130	140	150
Benefits paid	150	180	190
Contributions paid	90	100	110
Present value of obligations at 31 December	1,100	1,398	1,408
Market value of plan assets at 31 December	1,190	1,372	1,188

Required

Show how the defined benefit scheme would be presented in the financial statements for each of the three years ended 31 December 20X1, 20X2 and 20X3.

4 Chapter summary

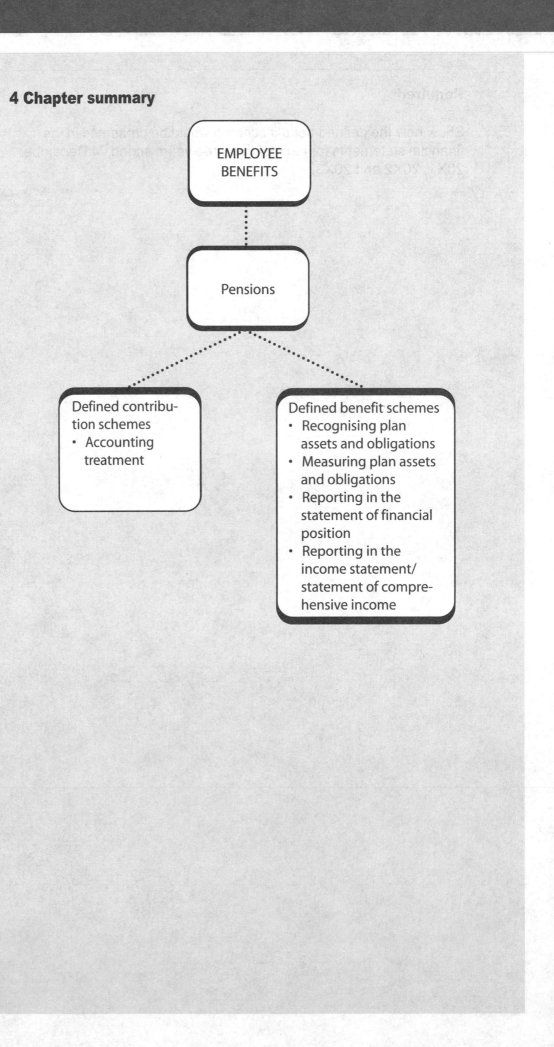

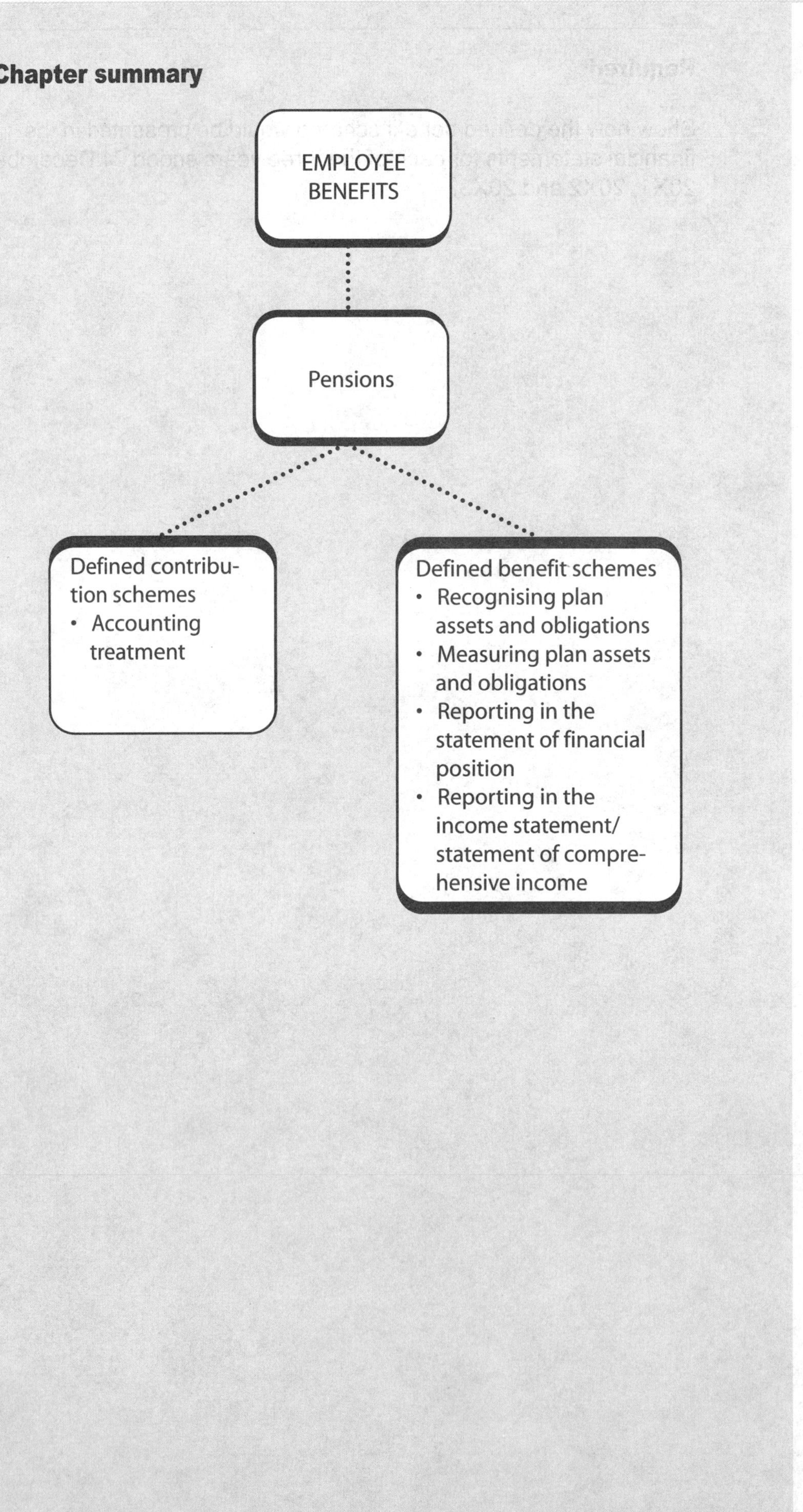

Test your understanding answers

Test your understanding 1

Statement of financial position

Current liabilities

Accrued pension contributions (10,000 + 39,000 – 35,000)	$14,000

Income statement

Pension contributions (6% × 650,000)	$39,000

Test your understanding 2 - Alpha

	Assets	Liabilities	Net
	$000	$000	$000
Brought forward at 1 January 20X6	1,400	1,350	50
Current service cost		130	(130)
Interest income / cost (8% of opening balance)	112	108	4
Contributions	120		120
Benefits	(110)	(110)	–
	1,522	1,478	44
Remeasurement component gain/loss – balance	Gain 43	Loss 152	Loss (109)
Carried forward at 31 December 20X6	1,565	1,630	(65)

Statement of financial position (extract) at 31 December 20X6

	$000
Net pension liability (1,630 – 1,565)	65

Statement of comprehensive income (extracts) for the year ended 31 March 20X3

	$000
Service cost component	(130)
Net interest component	4
Net effect on profit	(126)

Other comprehensive income

Items that will not be reclassified to profit or loss:

Net remeasurement component	(109)
Net effect on total comprehensive income	(235)

Test your understanding 3

Statement of financial position (extract) as at 31 December 20X4

	$000
Net pension liability (1,280 – 1,240)	40

Income statement (extracts) for the year ended 31 December 20X4

	$000
Service cost component (140 + 35 + 15)	(190)
Net interest component	(2)
Net expense recognised in the income statement	(192)

Other comprehensive income for the year ended 31 December 20X4

Items that will not be reclassified to profit or loss:

Net remeasurement component (W1)	62
Net impact on total comprehensive income for the year	(130)

Workings

(W1) **Remeasurement component**	**Assets**	**Liabilities**	**Net**
	$000	$000	$000
Opening net assets	1,010	1,030	(20)
Benefits paid out	(105)	(105)	–
Contributions paid in	110		110
Interest at 10% (on opening balances)	101	103	(2)
Current service cost		140	(140)
Past service cost		35	(35)
Curtailment cost		15	(15)
	1,116	1,218	(102)
Remeasurement component gain/ loss (balance)	Gain 124	Loss 62	Gain 62
Closing net assets	1,240	1,280	(40)

Test your understanding 4

Statement of financial position (extract) as at 31 December 20X5

	$000
Net pension liability (1,610 – 1,500)	110

Statement of comprehensive income (extracts) for the year ended 31 December 20X5

	$000
Service cost component	(150)
Net interest component	(3)
Net expense recognised in income statement	(153)

Other comprehensive income

Items that will not be reclassified to profit or loss:

Net remeasurement component (W1)	(47)
Net impact on total comprehensive income for the year	(200)

Workings

(W1) **Remeasurement component**	**Assets**	**Liabilities**	**Net**
	$000	$000	$000
Opening net assets	1,240	1,280	(40)
Benefits paid out	(100)	(100)	–
Contributions paid in	130		130
Interest at 7% (on opening balances)	87	90	(3)
Current service cost		150	(150)
	1,357	1,420	(63)
Remeasurement component gain/ loss (balance)	Gain 143	Loss 190	Loss (47)
Closing net assets	1,500	1,610	(110)

Test your understanding 5

Step 1 – Calculate the remeasurement component

Obligations:

	20X1	20X2	20X3
	$000	$000	$000
Obligation at start of year	1,000	1,100	1,398
Interest (10%, 9%, 8%)	100	99	112
Current service costs	130	140	150
Benefits paid	(150)	(180)	(190)
Remeasurement component (gain) loss - bal. fig.	20	239	(62)
Obligation at end of year	1,100	1,398	1,408

Assets:

	20X1	20X2	20X3
	$000	$000	$000
Fair value at start of year	1,000	1,190	1,372
Interest (10%, 9%, 8%)	100	107	110
Contribution into scheme	90	100	110
Benefits paid	(150)	(180)	(190)
Remeasurement component gain (loss) – bal. fig.	150	155	(214)
Fair value at end of year	1,190	1,372	1,188

Step 2 – The statement of financial position

	20X1	20X2	20X3
	$000	$000	$000
Pension assets	1,190	1,372	1,188
Pension obligations	(1,100)	(1,398)	(1,408)
Net pension asset (obligation)	90	(26)	(220)

Step 3 – The statement of comprehensive income

	20X1	20X2	20X3
	$000	$000	$000
Service cost component	(130)	(140)	(150)
Net interest component	–	8	(2)
Net effect on profit	(130)	(132)	(152)
Other comprehensive income			
Items that will not be reclassified to profit or loss:			
Net remeasurement component for the year on defined benefit scheme	130	(84)	(152)
Effect on total comprehensive income	–	(216)	(304)

chapter

16

Substance over form

Chapter learning objectives

On completion of their studies students should be able to:

- Discuss the principle of substance over form applied to a range of transactions.

1 Session content

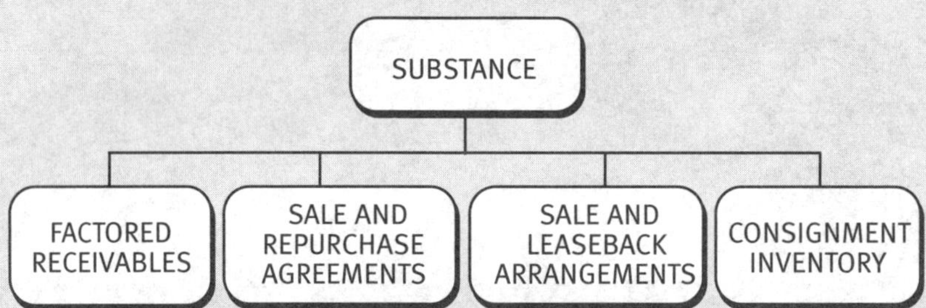

2 Reporting the substance of transactions

Introduction

IAS 1 requires that financial statements:

- must represent faithfully the transactions that have been carried out;
- must reflect the economic substance of events and transactions and not merely their legal form.

Examples of accounts reflecting economic or commercial substance which we have already met are:

- the production of consolidated accounts (chapter 4);
- recognising redeemable preference shares as liabilities (chapter 13);
- the capitalisation of a finance lease (in F1).

Determining the substance of a transaction

Common features of transactions whose substance is not readily apparent are:

- the legal title to an asset may be separated from the principal benefits and risks associated with the asset;
- a transaction may be linked with other transactions which means that the commercial effect of the individual transaction cannot be understood without an understanding of all of the transactions;
- options may be included in a transaction where the terms of the option make it highly likely that the option will be exercised.

Identifying assets and liabilities

Key to determining the substance of a transaction is to identify whether assets and liabilities arise subsequent to that transaction by considering:

- who enjoys the benefits of any asset
- who is exposed to the principal risks of any asset.

Assets are defined in the IASB Framework as resources controlled by the entity as a result of past events and from which future economic benefits are expected to flow to the entity.

Liabilities are defined in the IASB Framework as present obligations of the entity arising from past events, the settlement of which is expected to result in an outflow of resources embodying economic benefits from the entity.

Recognition and derecognition of assets/liabilities

Assets and liabilities should be **recognised** in the statement of financial position where:

- it is probable that any future economic benefit associated with the item will flow to or from the entity; and
- the item has a cost or value that can be measured with reliability.

When either of these criteria are not met the item should be **derecognised**.

With the case of assets there are two possible outcomes:

- Complete derecognition – when there is a transfer to another party of all the *significant* risks and benefits associated with the asset.
- No derecognition – no *significant* change to benefits and risks.

Off balance sheet financing

Often the motivation behind transactions that require adjustment for substance over form is the avoidance of liabilities on the statement of financial position. Motivations for keeping financing off the statement of financial position include the following:

(1) *Effect on the gearing (leverage) ratio*. If an entity is able to exclude liabilities from its statement of financial position it can manipulate the gearing ratio to the lowest possible level. High gearing levels tend to have adverse effects on share prices because the share is perceived by the market as riskier.

(2) *Borrowing capacity*. The lower the level of liabilities recorded on the statement of financial position, the greater the capacity for further borrowings.

(3) *Borrowing costs*. An entity with an already high level of borrowings will pay a risk premium for further borrowing in the form of a higher interest rate.

(4) *Management incentives*. Bonuses and performance-related pay may be based upon reported earnings for a period. If an entity is able to benefit from off-balance-sheet financing arrangements, costs may be lower, thus improving earnings.

3 IAS 18 Revenue

IAS 18 states that revenue from the sale of goods should be recognised when the entity has transferred to the buyer the significant risks and rewards of ownership.

Therefore when the entity transfers the risks and rewards the asset should be derecognised i.e. removed from the books and revenue from the sale should be recorded.

4 Examples where substance and form may differ

Examples of areas where substance and form may differ include:

- factoring of receivables;
- sale and repurchase agreements;
- sale and leaseback agreements;
- consignment inventory and goods on sale-or-return.

Securitised assets and loan transfers

These are similar in nature to factoring of receivables, where a loan asset is transferred to a third party as a way of securitising finance. The benefits associated with the asset are the future cash flows from the repayments and associated interest. The risks would include the risks of slow and non-payment or reduction in future cash flows as a result of early repayment.

5 Factored receivables

Factoring of receivables is where a company transfers its receivables balances to another organisation (a factor) for management and collection and receives an advance on the value of those receivables in return.

The receivables are legally "sold" to the factor.

The factor advances the company cash, e.g. 90% of receivables.

The factor collects receivables balance from the customer and may advance further sums to the company.

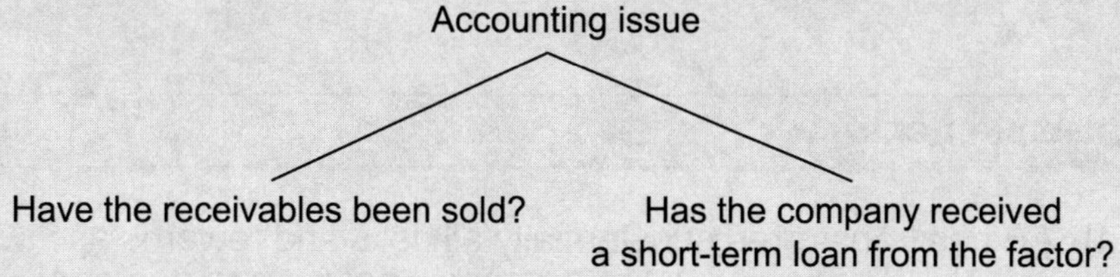
Accounting issue
Have the receivables been sold?
Has the company received a short-term loan from the factor?

Factors to consider:

- Has the company transferred the risks and benefits of the receivable to the factor?
- Will the company have to pay back the cash to the factor if the customer does not pay?
- If the company only has to pay back a fixed amount, are they still facing the majority of the risk of the bad debt?
- who bears the risk (of slow payment and irrecoverable debts)?

Example 1

The following relates to AB for the year ended 31 October 20X5.

AB supplies all its customers on credit terms. On 1 November 20X4 it entered into a factoring agreement with CD.

- It would receive 90% of its receivables total on the day of the sale.
- At the year end receivables stood at $15m.
- It would have rights to future sums, the amount would be based on when and whether the receivables paid. The faster they paid, the more AB would receive.
- CD has the right of recourse for any additional losses up to a maximum of $200,000.

Required:

(a) Explain the treatment.

(b) How would this change if there were no limit on the amount of recourse?

Example 1 answer

(a) AB has transferred substantially all risks and rewards as it will receive a minimum of $13,300,000 ((90% × $15,000,000) – $200,000 recourse). Therefore the receivables should be derecognised. A separate liability will be recognised for the potential repayment of $200,000.

Dr	Bank (90% × $15,000,000)	$13,500,000
Cr	Receivables	$15,000,000
Cr	Liability	$200,000
Dr	Finance cost (balance)	$1,700,000

The finance cost represents the cost of $1,500,000 receivables that have not been advanced and the potential cost of $200,000 repayable to the factor.

If AB receives additional sums in the future, it will:

Dr	Bank
Dr	Liability
Cr	Finance cost

(b) If the factor has full recourse then AB will not have transferred the risks and rewards since it still faces the risk of non payment entirely. Therefore, the receivables will not be derecognised and the sum advanced represents a loan secured on the receivables.

Dr Bank (90% x $15,000,000)	$13,500,000
Cr Loan	$13,500,000

The loan and receivable balance would then be derecognised when the customer pays the factor, with any difference being expensed as a finance cost.

Test your understanding 1

An entity has an outstanding receivables balance with a major customer amounting to $12 million and this was factored to FinanceCo on 1 September 20X7. The terms of the factoring were:

FinanceCo will pay 80% of the gross receivable outstanding account to the entity immediately.

- The balance will be paid (less the charges below) when the debt is collected in full. Any amount of the debt outstanding after four months will be transferred back to the entity at its full book value, with the entity having to return the funds advanced by the factor.
- FinanceCo will charge 1.0% per month of the net amount owing from the entity at the beginning of each month. FinanceCo had not collected any of the factored receivable amounts by the year-end of 30 September 20X7.
- the entity debited the cash from FinanceCo to its bank account and removed the receivable from its accounts. It has prudently charged the difference as an administration cost.

Required:

How should this arrangement have been accounted for in the financial statements for the year ended 30 September 20X7 and what are the journal entries required to correct the accounting treatment?

6 Sale and repurchase transactions

Sale and repurchase agreements are situations where an asset is sold by one party to another. The terms of the sale provide for the seller to repurchase the asset in certain circumstances at some point in the future.

Sale and repurchase agreements are common in property developments and in maturing inventories such as whisky.

The asset has been 'legally' sold, but there is either a commitment or an option to repurchase the asset at a later date.

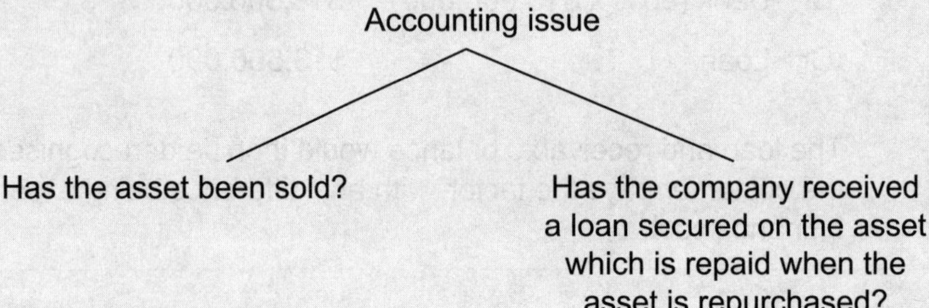
Accounting issue
Has the asset been sold?
Has the company received a loan secured on the asset which is repaid when the asset is repurchased?

Factors to consider:

- Has the company transferred the risks and benefits of the asset?

  e.g. Can the company still use the asset? Does the company bear costs associated with the asset?
- Was the asset "sold" at a price different to market value?
- Is the company obliged to repurchase the asset?
- If the company has the option to repurchase the asset are they likely to exercise this option?

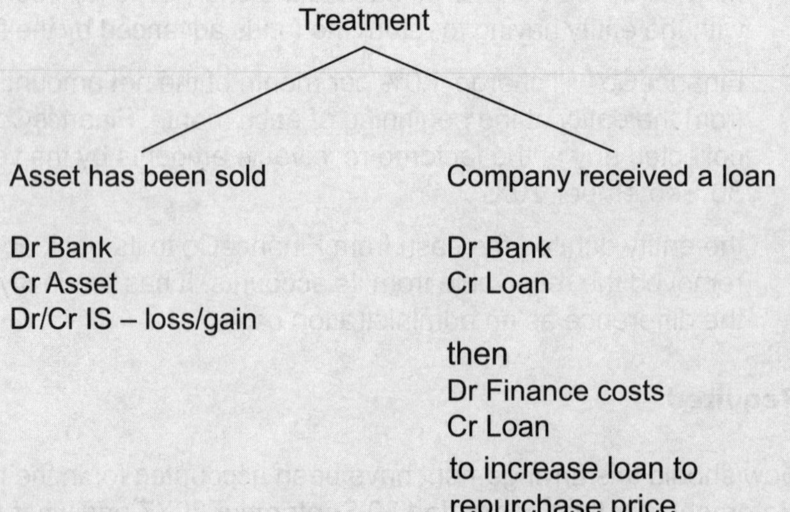
Treatment
Asset has been sold
Dr Bank
Cr Asset
Dr/Cr IS – loss/gain
Company received a loan
Dr Bank
Cr Loan
then
Dr Finance costs
Cr Loan
to increase loan to repurchase price

Example 2

Xavier sells its head office, which cost $10 million, to Yorrick, a bank, for $10 million on 1 January. Xavier has the option to repurchase the property on 31 December, four years later at $14.64 million. Xavier will continue to use the property as normal throughout the period and so is responsible for the maintenance and insurance. The head office was valued at transfer on 1 January at $18 million and is expected to rise in value throughout the four year period. The effective interest rate is 10%.

Required:

Giving reasons, show how Xavier should record the above during the first year following transfer.

Example 2 answer

Factors to consider:

- The option to repurchase is likely to be exercised as the repurchase price is lower than expected value at the repurchase date.
- Xavier continues to insure and maintain the property.
- Xavier will benefit from a rising property price.
- Xavier continues to benefit from use of the property.

Xavier should continue to recognise the head office as an asset in the statement of financial position as the risks and rewards of ownership remain with Xavier. This is a secured loan with effective interest of $4.64 million ($14.64 million – $10 million) over the four year period.

To record the secured loan:

		$m
Dr	Bank	10
Cr	Liability	10

Interest should be accrued over the four year period at the effective rate of 10%. In the first year this amounts to 10% x 10m = 1 m

		$m
Dr	Finance cost	1
Cr	Liability	1

Test your understanding 2

On 1 April 20X4 Triangle sold maturing inventory that had a carrying value of $3 million (at cost) to Factorall, a finance house, for $5 million.

Its estimated market value at this date was in excess of $5 million and is expected to be $8.5 million as at 31 March 20X8.

The inventory will not be ready for sale until 31 March 20X8 and will remain on Triangle's premises until this date.

The sale contract includes a clause allowing Triangle to repurchase the inventory at any time up to 31 March 20X8 at a price of $5 million plus interest at 10% per annum compounded from 1 April 20X4.

The inventory will incur storage costs estimated at $200,000 per annum until maturity. If Triangle chooses not to repurchase the stock, Factorall will pay the accumulated storage costs on 31 March 20X8.

The proceeds of the sale have been debited to the bank and the sale (and associated profit) have been recognised in Triangle's income statement.

Required:

Explain how the above should be treated in Triangle's financial statements for the year to 31 March 20X5.

7 Sale and leaseback transactions

A sale and repurchase agreement can be in the form of a **sale and leaseback**.

- Under a sale and leaseback transaction, an entity sells one of its own assets and immediately leases the asset back.
- This is a common way of raising finance whilst retaining the use of the related assets. The buyer / lessor is normally a bank.
- The leaseback is classified as finance or operating in accordance with the usual IAS 17 criteria.

Terminology:

A sells non-current asset to **B**

(Seller) (Buyer)

Then

A leases the non-current asset back from **B**

(Lessee) (Lessor)

Factors to consider:

- What type of lease is the asset being leased back under?
- Under an operating lease, the risks and benefits lie with the lessor, i.e. the buyer. Therefore the entity has transferred the risks and benefits to the buyer and the asset should be derecognised.
- Under a finance lease, the risks and benefits lie with the lessee, i.e. the seller. Therefore the entity has not transferred the risks and benefits. In this case IAS 17 says to record the sale but to bring the asset back in under a finance lease, with the profit/loss on disposal being initially deferred and recognised over the lease term.
- If the asset is leased back under an operating lease but the "sale proceeds" are greater or less than the market value of the asset, the excess profit or loss may need to be deferred.

Under an operating lease record the operating lease rentals through the income statement on a straight line basis.

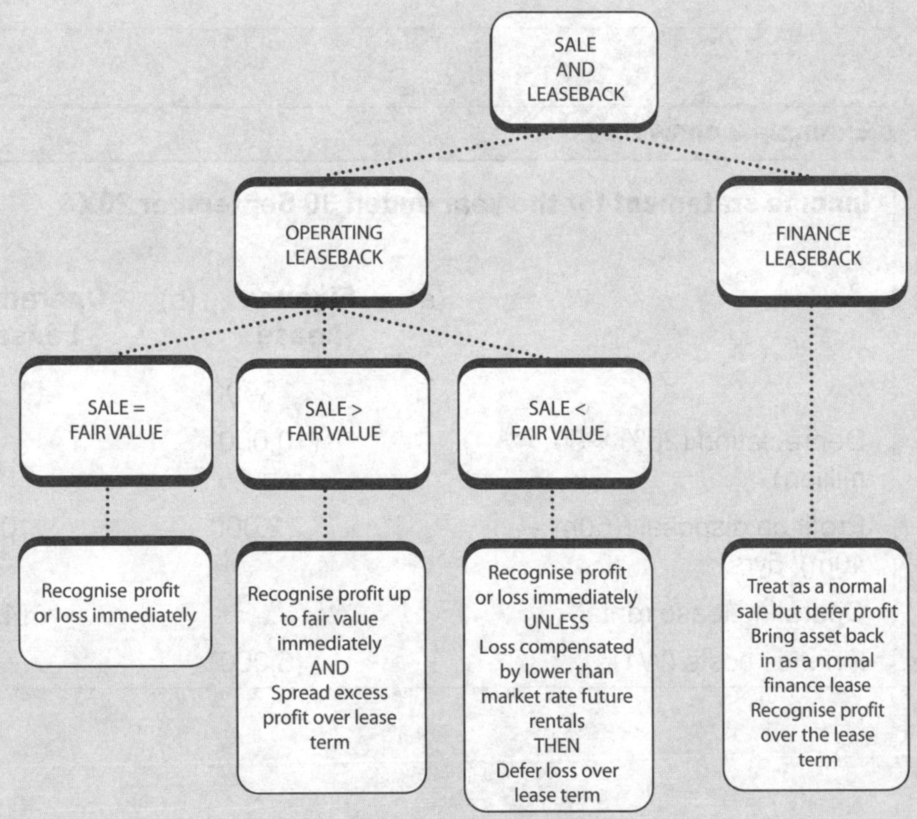

Example 3

A company sells an item of plant on 1 October 20X3 for $50 million, its fair value. The plant had a book value of $40 million at the date of the sale. The company have entered into an agreement to leaseback the plant at a cost of $14 million per annum for the next five years, payable annually in arrears. Depreciation is charged on plant at a rate of 20% per annum on the reducing balance basis. No depreciation has yet been recorded for the current year.

Required:

Prepare extracts from the income statement for the year ended 30 September 20X4 and statement of financial position as at that date assuming:

(a) the lease is a finance lease and that interest implicit in the lease is at a rate of 12% per annum;

(b) the lease is an operating lease

Example 3 answer

Income statement for the year ended 30 September 20X4

	(a) **Finance Lease**	(b) **Operating Lease**
	$000	$000
Depreciation (20% × 50 million)	(10,000)	–
Profit on disposal ((50m – 40m)/ 5yrs)	2,000	10,000
Operating lease rental	–	(14,000)
Finance costs (W1)	(6,000)	–

Statement of financial position as at 30 September 20X4

	(a) **Finance Lease**	(b) **Operating Lease**
	$000	$000
Non-current Assets		
Plant (50m – 10m dep'n)	40,000	–
Non-current liabilities		
Finance lease payable (W1)	(33,040)	–
Deferred income	(6,000)	
Current liabilities		
Finance lease payable (W1)	(8,960)	–
Deferred income	(2,000)	

Working

(W1)

	Opening	**Finance cost @ 12%**	**Cash paid**	**Closing**
Y/e Sep X4	50,000	6,000	(14,000)	42,000
Y/e Sep X5	42,000	5,040	(14,000)	33,040

Current liability = 42,000 – 33,040 = 8,960

Notes to answer – part (a)

- The plant is deemed to be sold for proceeds of $50 million, therefore there is a profit of $10 million over the book value. This profit is deferred over the lease term of 5 years so $2 million is released every year. Deferred income is a liability on the statement of financial position.
- The plant is then brought back onto the statement of financial position at its fair value of $50 million under the finance lease.
- The plant value of $50 million is depreciated over the lease term of 5 years.
- Finance costs are charged to the income statement based on the 12% interest rate implicit in the lease i.e. 12% x 50m (see (W1)).
- The total deferred income at 30 September 20X4 will be $8m ($10m – $2m) of which $2m will be treated as a current liability and $6m as a non-current liability.

Notes to answer – part (b)

- As the plant is sold at its fair value, the full profit of $10 million is recognised immediately and the operating lease rentals are recorded in the income statement every year.

Test your understanding 3

S enters into a sale and leaseback arrangement which results in an operating leaseback for 5 years from 1 January 20X7. Details at 1 January 20X7 are as follows:

	$m
Carrying amount of non-current asset	6.0
Sale proceeds	8.0
Fair value of non-current asset	7.2

The lease rentals are $4m per year.

Required:

What will be the effect on S's income statement for the year ended 31 December 20X7?

8 Consignment inventory

Consignment inventory is inventory which:

- is legally owned by one party
- is held by another party, on terms which give the holder the right to sell the inventory in the normal course of business or, at the holder's option, to return it to the legal owner.

This type of arrangement is common in the motor trade.

The manufacturer delivers inventory to the dealer which the dealer can then sell on to a customer.

Manufacturer → Dealer

Inventory is legally owned by the manufacturer until:

- Dealer sells inventory onto a third party; or
- Dealer's right to return expires and the inventory is still held

However, the inventory is actually held by the dealer.

Accounting issue

When does the manufacturer record a sale?

Who should recognise the inventory?

Factors to consider:

- Can the dealer return the goods to the manufacturer at any point in time without penalty?
- Is the price that the dealer pays to the manufacturer based on prices at the date of delivery?
- Does the dealer have to pay the manufacturer a display charge that increases over time?
- Can the manufacturer request the dealer to return the goods?
- Can the dealer use the goods e.g. for demonstration purposes?
- Who bears costs associated with the goods e.g. insurance?

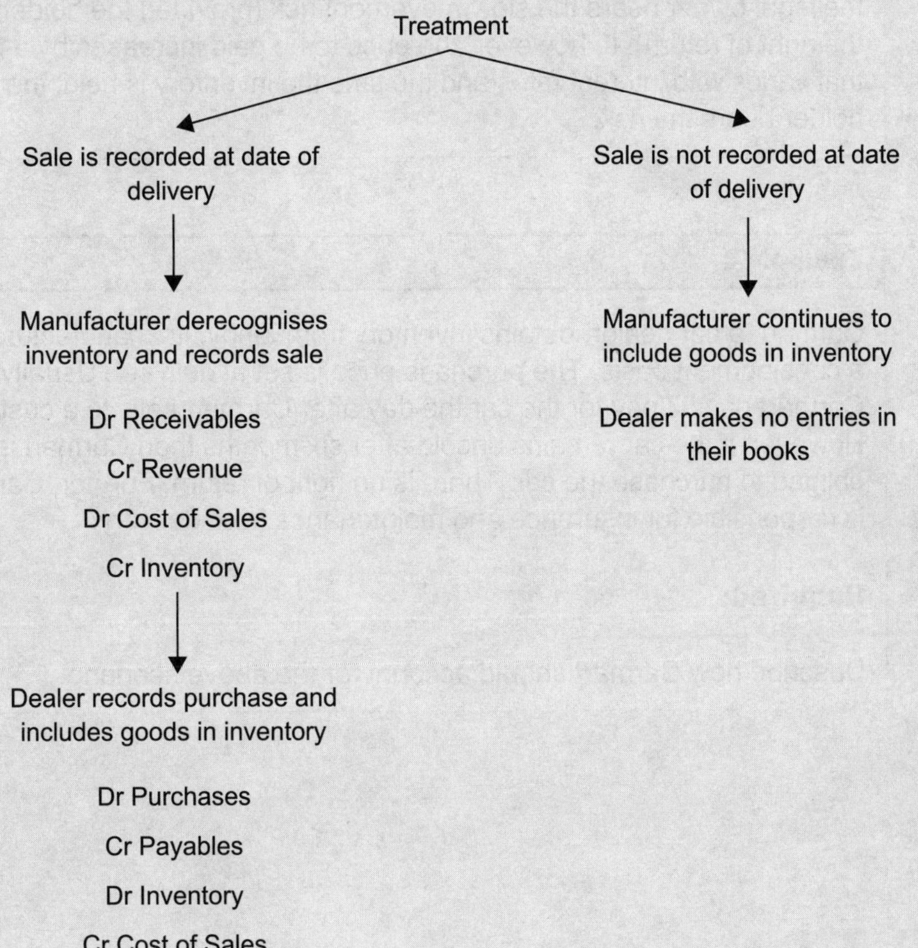

Treatment
Sale is recorded at date of delivery
Sale is not recorded at date of delivery
Manufacturer derecognises inventory and records sale
Dr Receivables
Cr Revenue
Dr Cost of Sales
Cr Inventory
Manufacturer continues to include goods in inventory
Dealer makes no entries in their books
Dealer records purchase and includes goods in inventory
Dr Purchases
Cr Payables
Dr Inventory
Cr Cost of Sales

Consignment inventory - further detail

Legal title may pass when one of a number of events has occurred, e.g. when the holder has held the inventory for a specified period such as six months, or when the holder has sold the goods.

The sales price (to the holder of the inventory) may be determined at the date of supply, or it may vary with the length of the period between supply and purchase, or it may be the legal owner's factory price at sale.

Other terms of such arrangements can include a requirement for the holder to pay a deposit, and responsibility for insurance.

The arrangement should be analysed to determine whether the holder has in substance acquired the inventory before the date of transfer of legal title.

One of the key factors will be who **bears the risk** of slow moving inventory. The risk involved is the cost of financing the inventory for the period it is held.

In a simple arrangement where inventory is supplied for a fixed price that will be charged whenever the title is transferred and there is no deposit, the legal owner bears the slow movement risk (provided the holder has the right of return). If, however, the price to be paid increases by a factor that varies with interest rates and the time the inventory is held, then the holder bears the risk.

Example 4

Carmart, a car dealer, obtains inventory from Zippy, its manufacturer, on a consignment basis. The purchase price is set at delivery. Usually, Carmart pays Zippy for the car the day after Carmart sells to a customer. However, if the car remains unsold after six months then Carmart is obliged to purchase the car. There is no right of return. Further, Carmart is responsible for insurance and maintenance from delivery.

Required:

Describe how Carmart should account for the above scenario.

Example 4 answer

Factors to consider:

- Carmart faces the risk of slow movement as it is obliged to purchase the car and has no right of return.
- Carmart insures and maintains the cars.
- Carmart faces risk of theft.
- Carmart can sell the cars to the public.

In substance there is a sale by Zippy to Carmart on the date of delivery. Zippy derecognises the cars and records the sale. Carmart recognises the cars on its statement of financial position at delivery.

Test your understanding 4

On 1 January 20X6 Gillingham, a manufacturer, entered into an agreement to provide Canterbury, a retailer, with machines for resale.

The terms of the agreement are:

- Canterbury pays a fixed rental per month for each machine that it holds.
- Canterbury pays the cost of insuring and maintaining the machines.
- Canterbury can also display the machines in its showrooms and use them as demonstration models.
- When a machine is sold to a customer, Canterbury pays Gillingham the factory price at the time the machine was originally delivered.
- All machines remaining unsold six months after their original delivery must be purchased by Canterbury at the factory price at the time of delivery.
- Gillingham can require Canterbury to return the machines at any time within the six-month period. In practice this right has never been exercised.
- Canterbury can return unsold machines to Gillingham at any time during the six-month period, without penalty. In practice, this has never happened.

At 31 December 20X6 the agreement is still in force and Canterbury holds several machines which were delivered less than six months earlier.

Required:

How should these machines be treated in the accounts of Canterbury for the year ended 31 December 20X6?

9 Linking substance and analysis of financial statements

It is likely in the examination that you will be required to explain the correct accounting treatment of a transaction and then to deal with the consequences of any required adjustments.

In order to be able to do this, you must have a sound understanding of the transactions covered in this and previous chapters:

- Factored receivables
- Sale and repurchase agreements
- Sale and leaseback agreements
- Consignment inventory
- Preference shares
- Convertible debt etc

You also need to be able to prepare the relevant double entries to record the transactions.

A question may require adjustments to draft financial statements and/or recalculation of ratios after the adjustments.

The following TYU is a good example of this type of question and some further examples can be found in the Exam Practice Kit.

Test your understanding 5 - Expand again

You are the management accountant of Expand – a large group that seeks to grow by acquisition. The directors of Expand have identified two potential target entities (A and B) and obtained copies of their financial statements. Extracts from these financial statements, together with notes providing additional information, are given below:

Statements of comprehensive income for the year ended 31 December 20X1

	A	B
	$000	$000
Revenue	68,000	66,000
Cost of sales	(42,000)	(45,950)
Gross profit	26,000	20,050
Other operating expenses	(18,000)	(14,000)
Profit from operations	8,000	6,050
Finance cost	(3,000)	(4,000)
Profit before tax	5,000	2,050
Income tax expense	(1,500)	(1,000)
Net profit for the period	3,500	1,050
Other comprehensive income		
Surplus on revaluation of properties	–	6,000
Total comprehensive income	3,500	7,050

Statements of changes in equity for the year ended 31 December 20X1

	A	B
	$000	$000
Balance at 1 January 20X1	22,000	16,000
Comprehensive income	3,500	7,050
Dividends paid	(2,000)	(1,000)
Balance at 31 December 20X1	23,500	22,050

Statements of financial position at 31 December 20X1

	A		B	
	$000	$000	$000	$000
Non-current assets				
Property, plant and equipment	32,000		35,050	
		32,000		35,050
Current assets				
Inventories	6,000		7,000	
Trade receivables	12,000		10,000	
		18,000		17,000
		50,000		52,050
Equity				
Share capital ($1 shares)		16,000		12,000
Revaluation reserve		Nil		6,000
Retained earnings		7,500		4,050
		23,500		22,050
Non-current liabilities				
Long-term borrowings		16,000		18,000
Current liabilities				
Trade payables	5,000		5,000	
Income tax	1,500		1,000	
Short-term borrowings	4,000		6,000	
		10,500		12,000
		50,000		52,050

Notes to the financial statements

(1) Sale by A to X

On 31 December 20X1, A supplied goods, at the normal selling price of $2.4 million, to another company, X. A's normal selling price is at a mark up of 60% on cost. X paid for the goods in cash on the same day. The terms of the selling agreement were that A repurchase these goods on 30 June 20X2 for $2.5 million. A has accounted for the transaction as a sale.

(2) Revaluation of non-current assets by B

B revalued its non-current assets for the first time on 1 January 20X1. The non-current assets of A are very similar in age and type to the non-current assets of B. However, A has a policy of maintaining all its non-current assets at depreciated historical cost. Both companies charge depreciation of non-current assets to cost of sales. The result of the revaluation was to increase the depreciation charge by $1 million for the year.

Expand uses ratio analysis to appraise potential investment opportunities. It is normal practice to base the appraisal on four key ratios:

- return on capital employed
- gross profit margin
- asset utilisation
- gearing (debt / debt + equity)

For the purposes of the ratio analysis, Expand compute

- capital employed as capital and reserves plus borrowings;
- borrowings as long-term borrowings plus short-term borrowings.

Your assistant has computed the four key ratios for the two enterprises from the financial statements provided and the results are summarised below:

Ratio	**A**	**B**
Return on capital employed	18.4%	13.1%
Gross profit margin	38.2%	30.4%
Asset utilisation	1.6	1.4
Gearing	46.0%	52.1%

Your assistant has informed you that, on the basis of the ratios calculated, the performance of A is superior to that of B in all respects. Therefore, Expand should carry out a more detailed review of A with a view to making a bid to acquire it. However, you are unsure whether this is necessarily the correct conclusion given the information provided in Notes 1 and 2.

Required:

(a) Explain and compute the adjustments that would be appropriate in respect of Notes 1 and 2 so as to make the financial statements of A and B comparable for analysis.

(12 marks)

(b) Recalculate the four key ratios mentioned in the question for both A and B AFTER making the adjustments you have recommended in your answer to part (a). You should provide appropriate workings to support your calculations.

(6 marks)

(c) In the light of the work that you have carried out in answer to parts (a) and (b), evaluate your assistant's conclusion that a more detailed review of A should be carried out, with a view to making a bid to acquire it.

(7 marks)

(Total: 25 marks)

10 Chapter summary

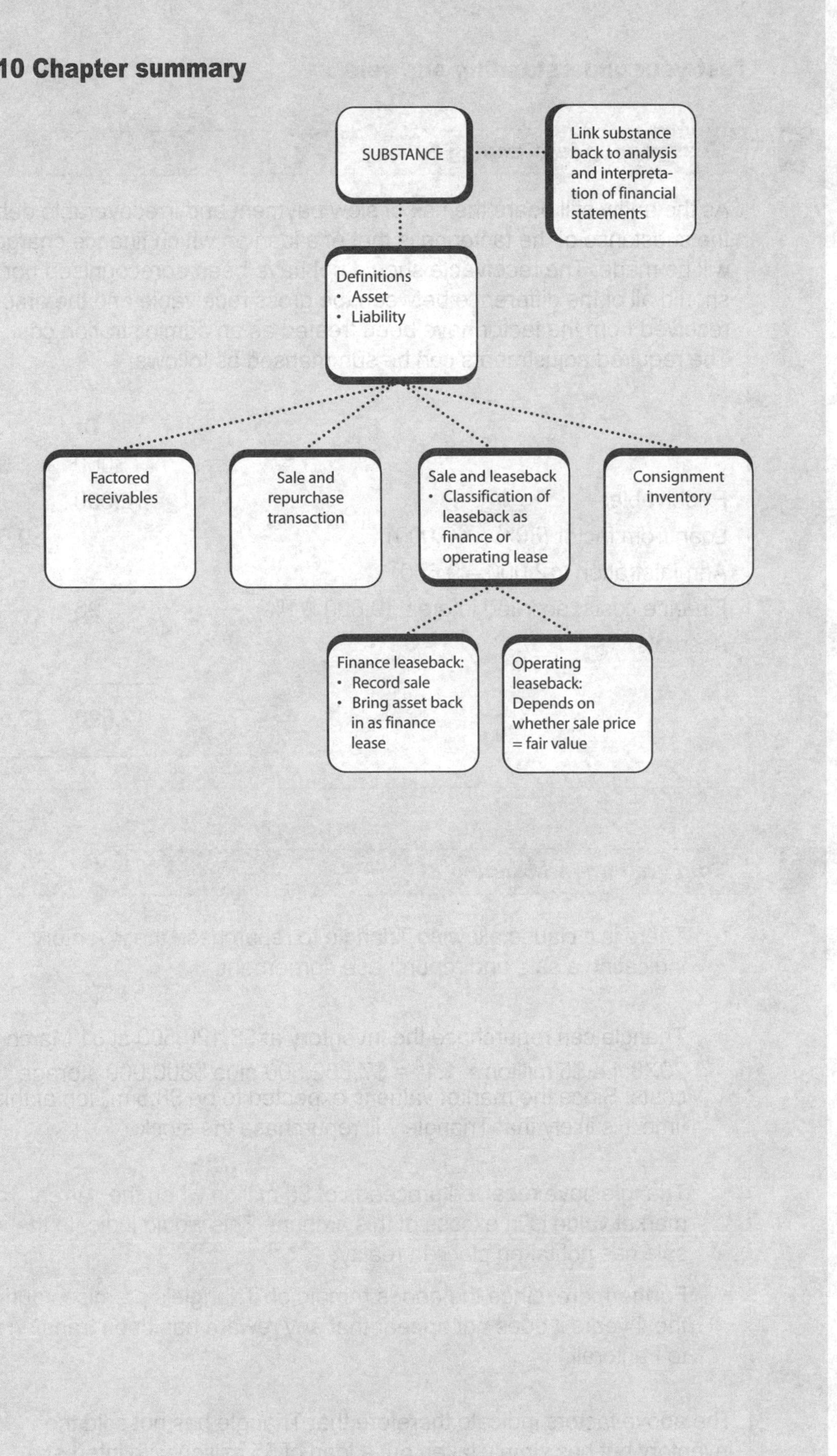

Test your understanding answers

Test your understanding 1

As the entity still bears the risk of slow payment and irrecoverable debts, the substance of the factoring is that of a loan on which finance charges will be made. The receivable should not have been derecognised nor should all of the difference between the gross receivable and the amount received from the factor have been treated as an administration cost. The required adjustments can be summarised as follows:

	Dr	Cr
	$000	$000
Receivables	12,000	
Loan from factor (80% x 12,000)		9,600
Administration (12,000 – 9,600)		2,400
Finance costs: accrued interest (9,600 x 1%)	96	
Accruals		96
	12,096	12,096

Test your understanding 2

- There is a clause allowing Triangle to repurchase the inventory, indicating a sale and repurchase agreement.

  Triangle can repurchase the inventory at $8,120,500 at 31 March 20X8, i.e.$5 million × 1.1^4 = $7,302,500 plus $800,000 storage costs. Since the market value is expected to be $8.5 million at this time it is likely that Triangle will repurchase the stock.

- Triangle have received proceeds of $5 million when the current market value is in excess of this amount. This would indicate that a sale has not taken place in reality.
- Furthermore, since the goods remain on Triangle's premises during the 4 years it does not appear that any reward has been transferred to Factorall.

The above factors indicate therefore that Triangle has not sold the inventory but has simply taken out a loan of $5 million with interest at 10% per annum that is secured on the inventory.

Therefore, Triangle should not have recorded a sale, but instead should have recorded a loan of $5 million with a finance cost of 10% per annum. The goods should remain in inventory at their cost of $3 million.

To correct the entries Triangle recorded in error:

		$m
Dr	Revenue (to reverse the sale)	5
Cr	Liability	5

Reinstate the closing inventory:

		$m
Dr	Closing inventory (SFP)	3
Cr	Closing inventory (IS)	3

Record the interest for the year at 10% x $5m = $0.5m:

		$m
Dr	Finance cost	0.5
Cr	Liability	0.5

Test your understanding 3

As the sale proceeds exceed the fair value of the non-current asset, the excess profit must be deferred over the lease term.

Profit now: 7.2 – 6.0 = $1.2m

Profit to be deferred over 5 years:

8.0 – 7.2 = $0.8m

$0.8m /5 years = $0.16m p.a.

Income statement for year ended 31 December 20X7

	$m
Operating lease rentals	(4.00)
Profit up to fair value recognised immediately	1.20
Release of deferred profit	0.16
Net effect on profit	(2.64)

Test your understanding 4

The key issue is whether Canterbury has purchased the machines from Gillingham or whether they are merely on loan.

It is necessary to determine whether Canterbury has the benefits of holding the machines and is exposed to the risks inherent in those benefits.

Gillingham can demand the return of the machines and Canterbury is able to return them without penalty. This suggests that Canterbury does not have the automatic right to retain or to use them.

Canterbury pays a rental charge for the machines, despite the fact that it may eventually purchase them outright. This suggests a financing arrangement as the rental could be seen as loan interest on the purchase price. Canterbury also incurs the costs normally associated with holding inventories.

The purchase price is the price at the date the machines were first delivered. This suggests that the sale actually takes place at the delivery date. Canterbury has to purchase any inventory still held six months after delivery. Therefore the company is exposed to slow payment and obsolescence risks. Because Canterbury can return the inventory before that time, this exposure is limited.

It appears that both parties experience the risks and benefits. However, although the agreement provides for the return of the machines, in practice this has never happened.

Conclusion: the machines are assets of Canterbury and should be included in their statement of financial position.

Test your understanding 5 - Expand again

(a) **Adjustments**

Note 1 The substance of this transaction is not a sale but a loan. Therefore the following adjustments are necessary to reverse the effect of the sale

Dr Revenue	$2,400,000
Cr Loan	$2,400,000
Dr Inventories (2,400,000 x 100/160)	$1,500,000
Cr Cost of sales	$1,500,000

Interest of $100,000 should then be accrued, but no adjustment is necessary as this would occur after the year end.

Note 2 Expand needs to be able to make meaningful comparisons between the accounts of A and B. As far as possible, both sets of accounts should be based on the same accounting policies. The only practical way of achieving this is to restate the accounts of B so that both sets of properties are stated at historic cost:

Dr Revaluation reserve	$6,000,000
Cr Property, plant and equipment	$6,000,000
Dr Property, plant and equipment (reverse excess depreciation)	$1,000,000
Cr Cost of sales	$1,000,000

These adjustments affect the accounts as follows:

	Before	Adjustment	After
	$000	$000	$000
Company A			
Revenue	68,000	(2,400)	65,600
Cost of sales	(42,000)	1,500	(40,500)
Gross profit	26,000	(900)	25,100
Profit from operations	8,000	(900)	7,100
Borrowings (4,000 + 16,000)	20,000	2,400	22,400
Capital and reserves	23,500	(900)	22,600
Capital employed	43,500		45,000
Company B			
Revenue	66,000		66,000
Cost of sales	(45,950)	1,000	(44,950)
Gross profit	20,050	1,000	21,050
Profit from operations	6,050	1,000	7,050
Borrowings (6,000 + 18,000)	24,000		24,000
Capital and reserves	22,050	(5,000)	17,050
Capital employed	46,050		41,050

(b) **Ratios**

		A		B	
Return on capital employed					
Profit from operations / Capital Employed	7,100 / 45,000	= 15.8%	7,050 / 41,050	= 17.2%	
Gross profit margin					
Gross profit / Revenue	25,100 / 65,600	= 38.3%	21,050 / 66,000	= 31.9%	
Asset utilisation					
Revenue / Capital Employed	65,600 / 45,000	= 1.5	66,000 / 41,050	= 1.6	
Gearing					
Total borrowings / Capital Employed	22,400 / 45,000	= 49.8%	24,000 / 41,050	= 58.5%	

(c) **Evaluation**

The ratios based on the adjusted accounts show that A is not necessarily the better acquisition.

The adjustments have had the effect of reducing the profits of A and slightly improving the profits of B. Although A still clearly has the better gross profit margin, B now has the better return on capital employed. There appear to be two reasons for this:

- the asset utilisation ratio shows that B is slightly better at generating sales revenue from its capital base than A; and

- A has operating expenses of $4 million more than B, although both companies have similar levels of revenue.

For these reasons B may be the better company to acquire, particularly if the operating expenses of A cannot be reduced. B has significantly higher gearing than A, but this may not be a critical factor if Expand can change the capital structure or provide the company with additional finance.

Index

Index

This book belongs to:

....

KELLY WILSON

SHOWTYM ADVENTURES

Annual

HI PONY PALS,

Welcome to our very first SHOWTYM ADVENTURES ANNUAL!

While you're all waiting for the next story in the Showtym Adventures series, I, along with my sisters Vicki and Amanda, thought this annual would be a great way to connect and share with you.

We've had so much fun filling this book with all our favourite activities, stories, games, puzzles and more.

Most of all, I would like to say a huge thank you to all our amazing fans who have enjoyed reading the stories from our childhood. It's been so inspiring for me, as an author, to hear how much our journey with horses has encouraged you to chase your dreams and pursue your own love of horses.

Happy reading, and happy riding!

Big hugs,

Kelly xx

CONTENTS

ALL ABOUT YOU

You are unique!

Fill in the boxes below to make this book your own. Use this page to map out your dreams and celebrate your favourite people, places and things – and horses, of course!

NAME: ....

BIRTHDAY: .... AGE: ....

YOUR FAVOURITE:

BREED OF HORSE: ....

EQUESTRIAN DISCIPLINE: ....

SONG: ....

BOOK: ....

MOVIE/TV SHOW: ....

FOOD: ....

FAMILY: ....

....

BEST FRIENDS: ....

....

WHY YOU LOVE HORSES: ....

....

YOUR FAVOURITE PLACE TO RIDE: ....

....

YOUR DREAM HORSE WOULD BE: ....

....

CHERISHED MEMORY: ....

....

WHEN YOU'RE NOT RIDING YOU LOVE TO: ....

....

WHEN YOU GROW UP, YOU WANT TO BE: ....

....

YOUR TOP PLACE TO TRAVEL WOULD BE: ....

....

ALL ABOUT US

Now here are some fun facts about us, as well as our proudest achievements and our all-time favourite horses!

AMANDA is one of New Zealand's top show-jumping riders, competing to Grand Prix and World Cup level. Alongside her love of horses she has an interest in filmmaking — she's directed two documentaries and filmed for our television show *Keeping Up With the Kaimanawas*. She also enjoys writing and is working on several books. In her spare time she blogs about horses and how to train them, and loves coaching young riders to improve their riding skills and confidence.

HIGHEST ACHIEVEMENT: Winning Pony of the Year

FAVOURITE WILD HORSE: Bragg, the wild Mustang

FAVOURITE SHOW JUMPER: Showtym Viking

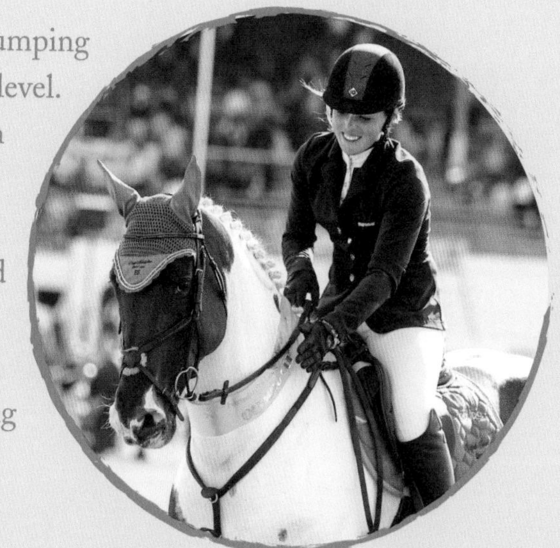

AMANDA AND SHOWTYM CASSANOVA AFTER PLACING 5TH IN THE 2015 OLYMPIC CUP.

VICKI has won countless Grand Prix, World Cup and Title classes over the past 15 years and is well-known as one of our nation's most competitive show jumpers. She also has a talent for starting young horses under saddle and in 2017 and 2018 she won Road to the Horse, the World Championships of Colt Starting, an event held in Kentucky in the USA. When she's not competing, Vicki runs equine therapy workshops and travels all around the world to help people with their horses.

HIGHEST ACHIEVEMENT: Winning Road to the Horse, the World Championships of Colt Starting

FAVOURITE WILD HORSE: Showtym Argo KH, the wild Kaimanawa stallion

FAVOURITE SHOW JUMPER: Showtym Cadet MVNZ

VICKI BEING PRESENTED WITH THE US$100,000 CHEQUE AFTER WINNING THE 2018 ROAD TO THE HORSE.

DID YOU KNOW?
The rubbery, triangular underside of a hoof is called the frog.

KELLY is an award-winning photographer and designer, as well as the author of eight bestselling books. Unlike her sisters, show jumping is just a hobby for her and although she's had a lot of success to 1.30m she prefers taming wild horses. A bold adventurer, Kelly has ticked over 100 adventures off her bucket list. One of her latest trips was a two-week expedition across the Gobi Desert, travelling on camels!

HIGHEST ACHIEVEMENT: Placing in wild horse challenges on three different continents

FAVOURITE WILD HORSE: Jackie, the wild Mustang

FAVOURITE SHOW JUMPER: Ngahiwi Showtym Dancer

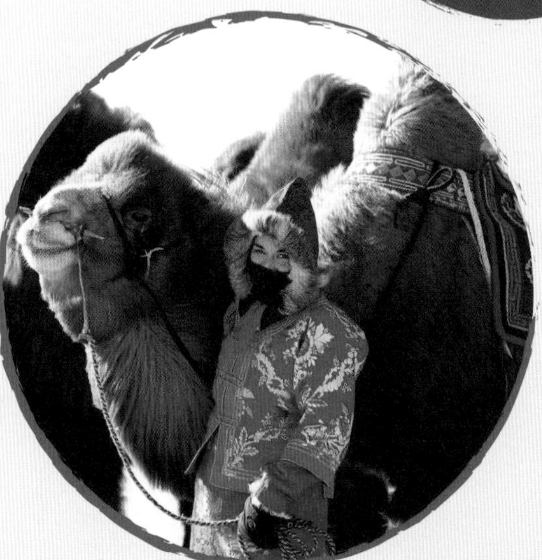

KELLY DRESSED IN TRADITIONAL MONGOLIAN CLOTHING DURING THE GOBI COLD CAMEL EXPEDITION.

A VERY DANDY QUIZ!

How well do you know the first of our Showtym Adventures books? Take the quiz to find out – but be warned that there are some tricky questions in it!

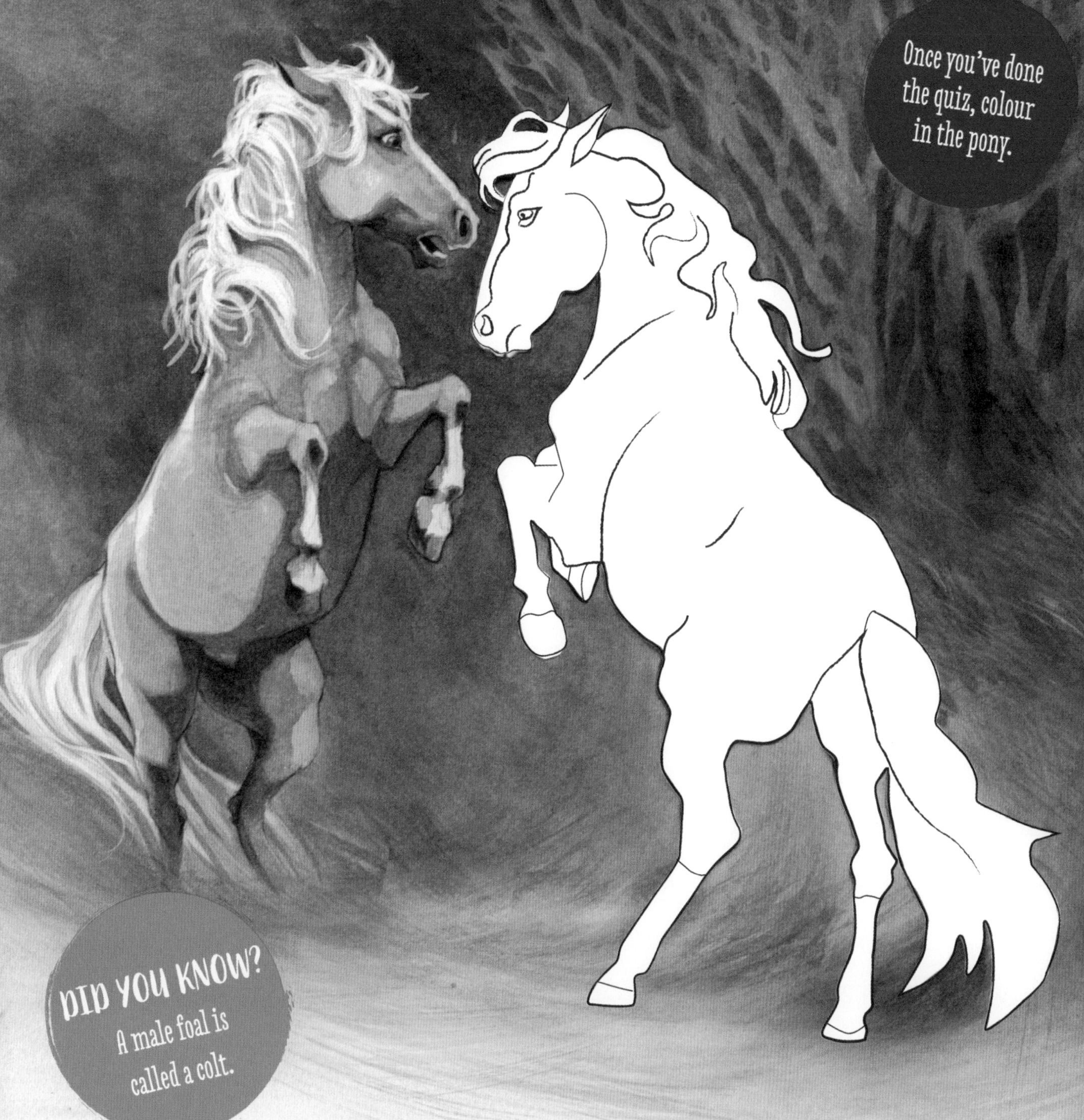

Once you've done the quiz, colour in the pony.

DID YOU KNOW?
A male foal is called a colt.

IF YOU'RE REALLY STUCK, THE ANSWERS ARE AT THE BACK OF THE BOOK.

1. WHAT COLOUR ARE VICKI'S EYES?

A. green
B. brown
C. blue
D. hazel

2. WHAT IS THE NAME OF THE LEASE PONY VICKI HAS TO GIVE UP?

A. Twinkle
B. Cardiff
C. Viking
D. Magic

3. HOW MUCH DO THE WILSONS END UP PAYING FOR THEIR FOUR WILD PONIES?

A. $175
B. $50
C. $200
D. $100

4. THE WILSONS' HORSE TRUCK IS PAINTED WITH WHICH TWO COLOURS?

A. red and black
B. white and blue
C. yellow and black
D. green and red

5. WHAT COLOUR IS DANDY'S COAT?

A. palomino
B. grey
C. black
D. chestnut

6. WHAT IS DANDY'S FULL NAME?

A. Dandelion
B. Yankee-doodle Dandy
C. Just Fine 'n' Dandy
D. Jim-Dandy

7. WHAT IS THE NAME OF MUM'S NEW MARE?

A. Jude
B. Squizzy
C. Twinkle
D. Samson

8. HOW DO THE GIRLS HELP TO FEED THE NEW PONIES?

A. by growing vegetables
B. by giving them slices of hay
C. by selling cupcakes
D. by cutting grass for them

9. WHAT IS THE FIRST THING DANDY EATS FROM VICKI'S HAND?

A. a handful of grass
B. an apple
C. a carrot
D. some hay

10. KELLY IS KICKED BY DANDY. WHEREABOUTS ON HER BODY IS SHE INJURED?

A. her ankle
B. her arm
C. her leg
D. her knees

11. WHAT COLOURS ARE THE GIRLS' PONY CLUB UNIFORMS?

A. blue and white
B. yellow and black
C. red and white
D. black and green

12. AT THE TIP 'N' OUT, WHAT IS THE HIGHEST THAT DANDY JUMPS?

A. 90cm
B. 70cm
C. 80cm
D. 60cm

PARTS OF A BRIDLE

Do you know all of the different parts of a bridle? Match the labels to the different parts below, then check the answers to see how many you got right!

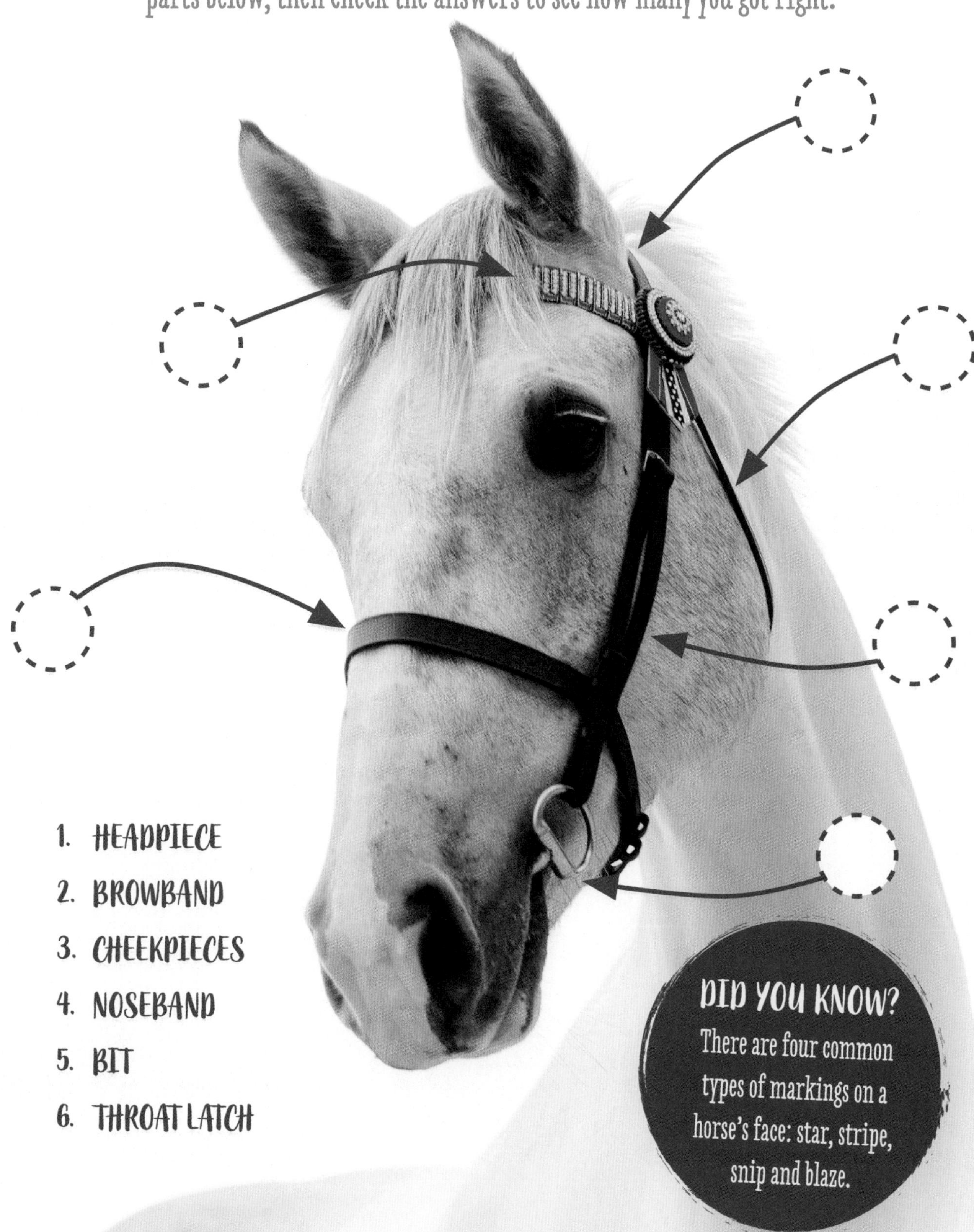

1. HEADPIECE
2. BROWBAND
3. CHEEKPIECES
4. NOSEBAND
5. BIT
6. THROAT LATCH

DID YOU KNOW?
There are four common types of markings on a horse's face: star, stripe, snip and blaze.

SECRET LANGUAGE

People's knowledge of horses goes back thousands of years – horses were first domesticated over 5000 years ago! Crack the code below to uncover an ancient name for horses.

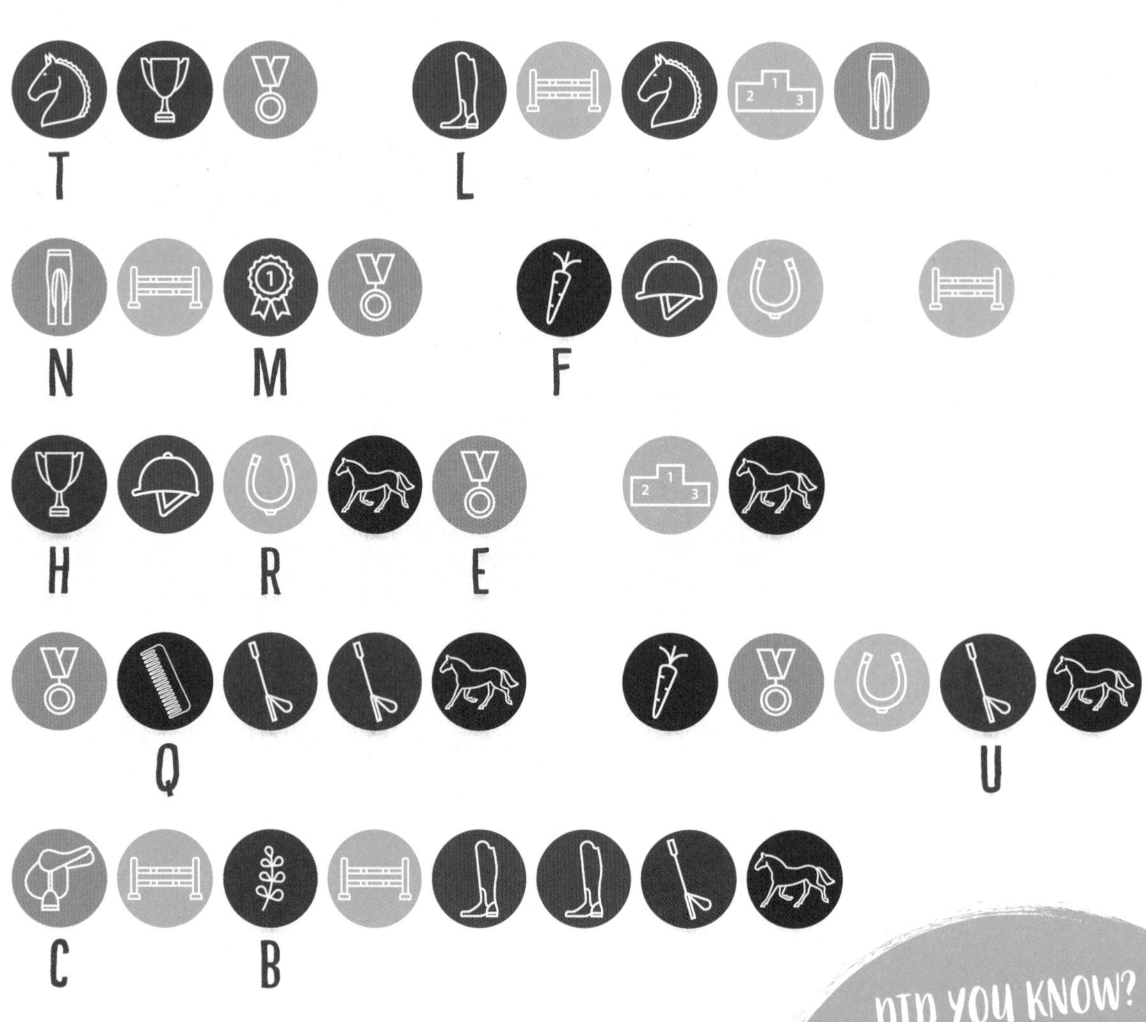

WELL DONE! YOU CAN CHECK THE ANSWER PAGE TO SEE IF YOU'VE DECODED THE MESSAGE CORRECTLY.

DID YOU KNOW?
Wild horses are often not truly wild, as they have ancestors that were domesticated. They are actually feral horses – although be careful! – they are very much wild by nature and should only be observed from a safe distance.

PLAIT LIKE A PRO

Have you always wanted to give your pony perfect plaits for competitions? We taught ourselves to plait by reading books and magazines and, after a lot of practice, we got it down to a fine art. Here we've brought all four stages together in one photo, but you can read all about this in more detail in *Cameo, the Street Pony*!

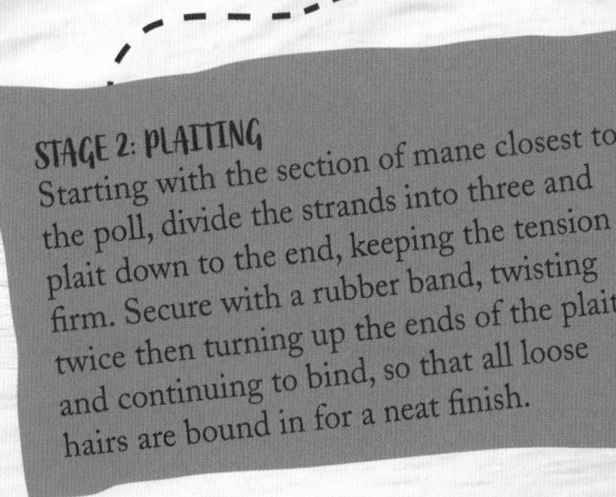

1

2

STAGE 2: PLAITTING
Starting with the section of mane closest to the poll, divide the strands into three and plait down to the end, keeping the tension firm. Secure with a rubber band, twisting twice then turning up the ends of the plait and continuing to bind, so that all loose hairs are bound in for a neat finish.

STAGE 1: SEPARATING
Wet down your pony's mane. Using the mane comb, divide the mane into equal sections and secure the sections with rubber bands.

DID YOU KNOW?
Dressage is the equestrian version of dancing.

YOU WILL NEED:

- → water (in a spray bottle or applied with a sponge)
- → mane comb
- → rubber bands matched to your pony's mane colour
- → blunt needle
- → scissors
- → thread to match the colour of the pony's mane

3

4

STAGE 3: FOLDING IN HALF AND SEWING

Pass the needle and thread through the rubber band at the base of the plait. Turn the end under and fold the plait in half, then pull the needle and thread through from underneath. Make a couple of stitches down the plait, following the zigzag so the stitches are hidden, and the needle comes out at the bottom of the plait.

STAGE 4: REPEAT FOLDING AND SEWING

Fold the plait in half again, and repeat Stage 3. Knot the thread underneath the plait and, using scissors, trim off the loose ends.

DID YOU KNOW?
Horses have outstanding memories – possibly even better than elephants'!

VOILÀ! YOU'RE ALL READY TO COMPETE. GOOD LUCK – AND HAVE FUN!

DESIGN YOUR OWN PONY & RIDER COSTUME

As children, Vicki, Amanda and I loved to dress up with our ponies – and we still do! Design your very own pony and rider costume using the illustration opposite. Maybe your pony could have wings like Pegasus, or have black and white stripes like a zebra? Go wild!

LILY POND FAIRY

MONARCH BUTTERFLY

BEACH BABES

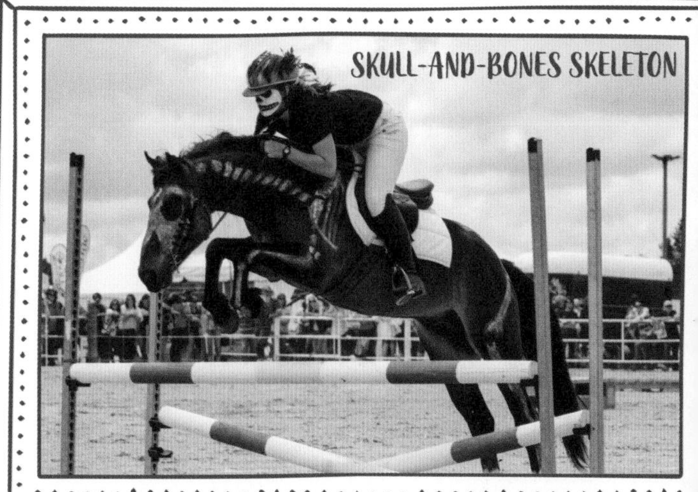
SKULL-AND-BONES SKELETON

DID YOU KNOW?
Eventing involves three phases – dressage, cross-country jumping and show jumping.

DID YOU KNOW?
The height of a horse is given in hands because, before tape measures, people would measure a horse from the ground to the top of the horse's withers using the width of a hand.

WHICH WILSON SISTER ARE YOU?

We three sisters may share the same parents and a love of horses, but that's where the similarities end. We each have a different approach to life and to riding.

Who are you most like? Answer this quiz, then add up your score to find out!

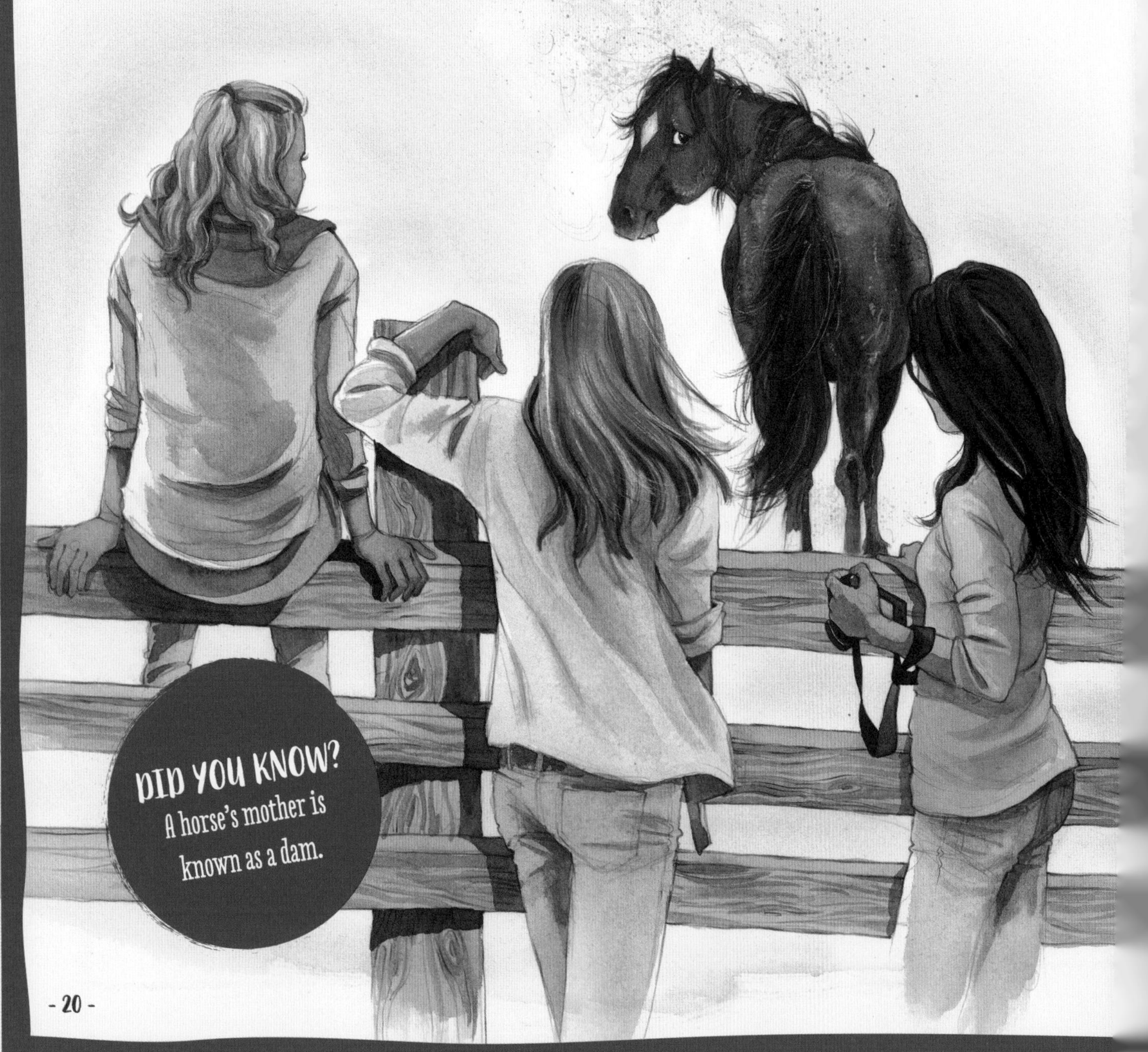

DID YOU KNOW?
A horse's mother is known as a dam.

1. YOU WOULD RATHER COMPETE AT THE:

Road to the Horse, the World Championships of Colt Starting — 1

Extreme Mustang Makeover — 2

Olympic Cup — 3

. YOUR DREAM HORSE IS:

Wild American Mustang, like Jackie — 2

Colt, started from scratch, like Kentucky — 1

Tame but green horse, like Showtym Viking — 3

3. AT AN EQUESTRIAN EVENT YOU WOULD BE:

Photographing —2

Competing in the World Cup class — 3

Performing in the Night Show — 1

4. IN BETWEEN RIDING YOU ENJOY:

Writing and filming — 3

Don't be silly, horses are everything! — 1

Travelling the world — 2

5. YOUR FAVOURITE BREED OF WILD HORSE IS:

Kaimanawa of New Zealand — 1

Mustang of the USA — 3

Brumby of Australia — 2

6. YOUR DREAM RIDE IS:

Jumping a World Cup round — 3

Galloping down the beach — 2

Starting a young horse under saddle — 1

7. YOUR FRIENDS DESCRIBE YOU AS A:

Princess — 2

Boss — 1

Comedian — 3

8. IN FRONT OF A PACKED STADIUM YOU WOULD BE:

Jumping something massive, preferably bareback and bridle-less — 1

Doing a liberty performance — 2

Hosting the show — 3

9. WHEN YOU MEET A NEW HORSE, YOU:

Can't wait to have adventures together — 3

Admire its beauty and photograph it — 2

Are determined to learn everything about it to help it reach its potential — 1

10. YOUR ATTITUDE TO COMPETITION IS:

I'm constantly striving to beat my personal best — 1

Bring it on! All forms! — 3

I can do it, but it isn't terribly important to me — 2

NOW ADD UP YOUR SCORE AND TURN THE PAGE TO FIND OUT WHICH WILSON SISTER YOU ARE MOST LIKE!

IF YOU SCORED BETWEEN 10–16
YOU ARE MOST LIKE . . .

IF YOU ARE anything like Vicki, horses are your life. You would like to spend every waking minute (and probably your dreams, too) with your pony, thinking about your pony, coming up with training plans and setting riding goals. You are super-determined, and great at solving problems because you leave no stone unturned and never give up, even on the most problematic horse. A natural leader, you're always ready to take on a new challenge. You can sometimes get a little impatient with riders who are timid or give up too quickly, but you're always there to help when someone's having difficulties. In fact, you're often the first to put your body on the line to help out with a troublesome pony. One thing's for sure: tidying your room will never be a priority — what a waste of time when there are horses needing your attention!

IF YOU SCORED BETWEEN 17–23
YOU ARE MOST LIKE . . .

A FREE-SPIRITED ADVENTURER, you adore horses and riding but you're not driven by an ambition to win prizes. You're artistic and creative at heart — you love designing games and adventures for you and your friends to have with your ponies. You're modest about your riding abilities and this means that you can sometimes feel a little unconfident when confronted with a new challenge — you might need a little push to remind you just how capable you are, and then you're more surprised than anybody when you excel. You always have a kind and encouraging word for everyone and you love socialising. But equally, you're just as happy in your own company. When not on a pony, you can usually be found tucked away somewhere peaceful, drawing, writing, painting or making plans to explore every corner of the world.

IF YOU SCORED BETWEEN 24–30 YOU ARE MOST LIKE . . .

YOU'RE THE LIFE of the party — everywhere you go, mischief and laughter are never far behind. You bubble over with energy, jokes, pranks and creative ideas. But alongside all the fun, you're also fiercely competitive — possibly because, like Amanda, you always had to keep up with your much older siblings. This is a trait that, coupled with your talent, will take you places! However, patience is not your strong suit and you sometimes need a little encouragement to stick with it and keep working on those big riding goals you've set yourself. You enjoy the closest of relationships with your pony — you're best friends. This makes it terribly tough for you to even think about trading up. But then again, you can't stand being bored — not even for a minute — and this will always help you make the tough decisions when it comes to your riding.

A GAME OF JUMPS & FALLS

Try out our Showtym Adventures version of Snakes and Ladders!
It's suitable for up to four players.

HOW TO PLAY

It's the Equestrian Extravaganza and Vicki is performing on her newly tamed Ranger, the Kaimanawa Stallion. Will Vicki and Ranger take a tumble? Or will they land all their jumps successfully?

1. Each player rolls the dice — whoever rolls highest starts.
2. Roll the dice again. If you roll 5, move along five squares on the board. If you roll 2, move along two squares.
3. If you land on a up you jump.
4. If you land on an X down you fall!

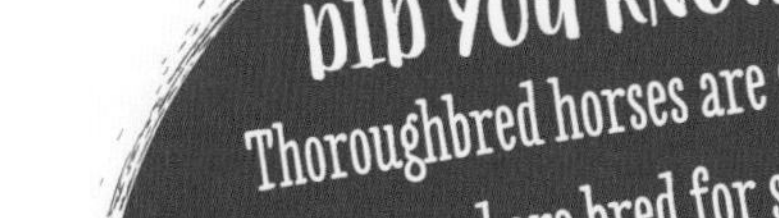

DID YOU KNOW?
Thoroughbred horses are strong but light and are bred for speed. All but light and are bred for speed. All thoroughbred horses are descendants of three famous stallions brought from North Africa to Britain in the 1700s — the Godolphin Barb, the Byerley Turk and the Darley Arabian.

YOU WILL NEED

- → A dice
- → A friend or two to play with
- → A token for each player

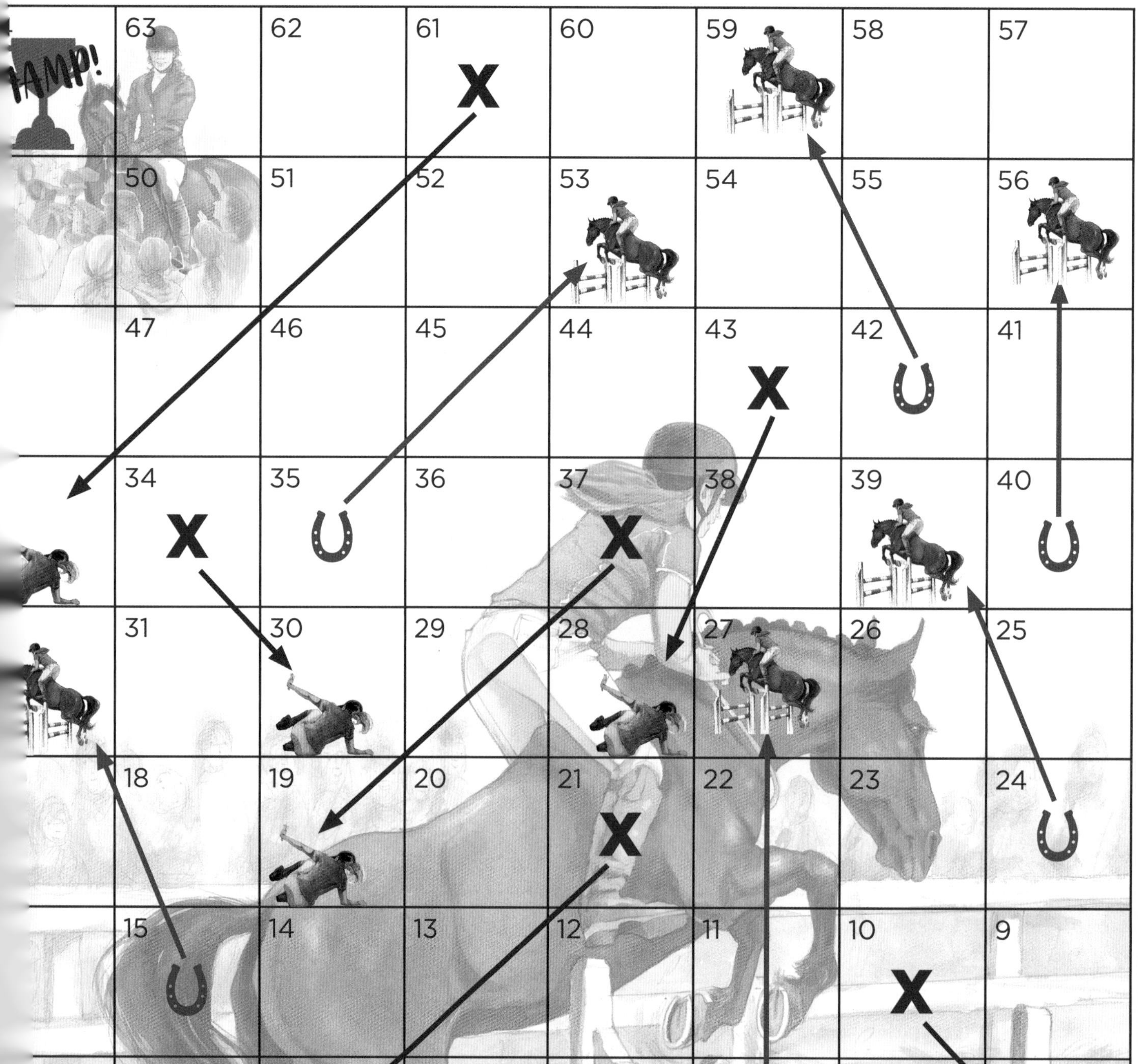

HAMP!

63	62	61	60	59	58	57
50	51	52	53	54	55	56
47	46	45	44	43	42	41
34	35	36	37	38	39	40
31	30	29	28	27	26	25
18	19	20	21	22	23	24
15	14	13	12	11	10	9
2	3	4	5	6	7	8

O!

DID YOU KNOW?
The inner framework of a saddle is called a tree.

SHOWTYM HALL OF FAME: OUR TOP 10 JUMPERS

AKA Sophie: 147cm crossbred mare. Our very first Grand Prix pony, she was sponsored by our Pony Club instructor Carol Guy. Vicki rode her for two seasons, up to Grand Prix level, with many wins and placings, and their competition highlight was winning the 2004 Speed Pony of the Year.

AKA Molly: 160cm WB mare. Molly was owned by Des Lowe in Auckland. Vicki had the ride on her in 2008 and at their first show qualified her to compete at the Horse of the Year Show. Six months later, they reunited for the biggest show of the year and, although inexperienced, they rode to victory in the Show Hunter of the Year title class.

SHOWTYM
DIVA

AKA Diva: 160cm TB mare. Showtym Diva joined our family when her owners agreed to swap her to pay for a grazing bill. This talented thoroughbred went on to show jump to Grand Prix and won the 2010 New Zealand Show Hunter Title at the National Championships before being sold to New Caledonia.

Below are some of our most successful Showtym horses and ponies! You can tell which ones were owned before 2004, or were owned by other people, as they don't carry the Showtym prefix on their names.

TB – thoroughbred
WB – warmblood
QH – quarterhorse

SHOWTYM VIKING

AKA Strider: 148cm WB x [g]elding. Showtym Viking is [a]rguably our most successful [p]ony, winning countless [G]rand Prix classes with [A]manda during their five-[y]ear partnership, including [th]e 2010 New Zealand [G]rand Prix Championships [an]d Pony of the Year. He [c]ompeted for many years [in] the Young Rider, Grand [P]rix, Super League and [W]orld Cup series before [b]eing sold to Denmark.

SHOWTYM SPOTLIGHT

AKA Texas: 148cm QH x Arab gelding. Vicki and Showtym Spotlight had their debut performance at the 2010 Horse of the Year Show, jumping bareback and bridle-less. This duo, who were adored by the public, went on to wow the crowds at New Zealand's biggest equestrian events as Pegasus.

SHOWTYM GIRL

AKA Cherry: 15.1hh TB mare. Showtym Girl started life as a racehorse. Vicki purchased her for $900 and she went on to become the most successful show-jumping mare of her era, winning almost $100,000. Most notably, Vicki competed her bareback in the Horse of the Year Puissance in 2011, jumping 1.82m and, in 2017, after four years of retirement, she made a comeback to win the $10,000 Equidays Derby.

SHOWTYM CASSANOVA

AKA Cappi: 16.1hh WB x gelding. Amanda's famed pinto has placed in just about every big show in the country with highlights including the Olympic Cup in 2015 and 2016, Equidays Grand Prix in 2016, Riding with the Stars in 2016 and the Equidays Derby in 2017.

SHOWTYM LEVADO GNZ

AKA Colt: 16hh Holstein stallion. Showtym Levado GNZ was not only a top performing Grand Prix show jumper and Champion Saddle Hunter, but also the bravest horse we've ever owned. He gained attention for his crowd-pleasing performances jumping over people, horses, cars and boats, and is also the sire of several of our current show jumpers.

NGAHIWI SHOWTYM PREMIER

AKA Ned: 16.1hh WB x gelding. Ned had a troubled beginning to ridden life and was very fearful and sore when he first arrived at our property. Vicki's love and patience paid off though, and he went on to become one of our most competitive Grand Prix show jumpers.

SHOWTYM CADET MVNZ

AKA Ollie: 16.2hh WB gelding. Although he cost just $500, Showtym Cadet MVNZ is Vicki's most successful Grand Prix and World Cup show jumper. In 2014 she rode him to victory in the Premier Stakes at the Horse of the Year Show, followed by her first World Cup win at Taupo later that year.

WHY SHOWTYM?

Here's the story behind our name!

DAD BOUGHT US a personalised number plate for our horse truck in 2003 with the letters SHOTYM. It was something of a family joke because every time we used the horse truck, it was to take us to a horse show — so it was literally showtime! Vicki loved the number plate so much she named her first show-jumping mare Showtym Girl (adding in a 'W' so it was easier to pronounce). Since then, most of our horses have carried the Showtym prefix before their names.

THE HORSE TRUCK.

DID YOU KNOW?
Horses have small stomachs, which means they need a constant supply of food, day and night.

OUR ORIGINAL PERSONALISED PLATE.

VICKI AND SHOWTYM GIRL.

WILD WORD SEARCH

Help us round up the wild horses of the world by finding all the hidden words. Can you find them all?

Words can be printed vertically, horizontally, diagonally or even backwards! Circle the words with a pen or pencil as you find them.

DID YOU KNOW?
Lunging is a way of exercising a horse in which the trainer, using a lunge line, asks the horse to move around them in a circle.

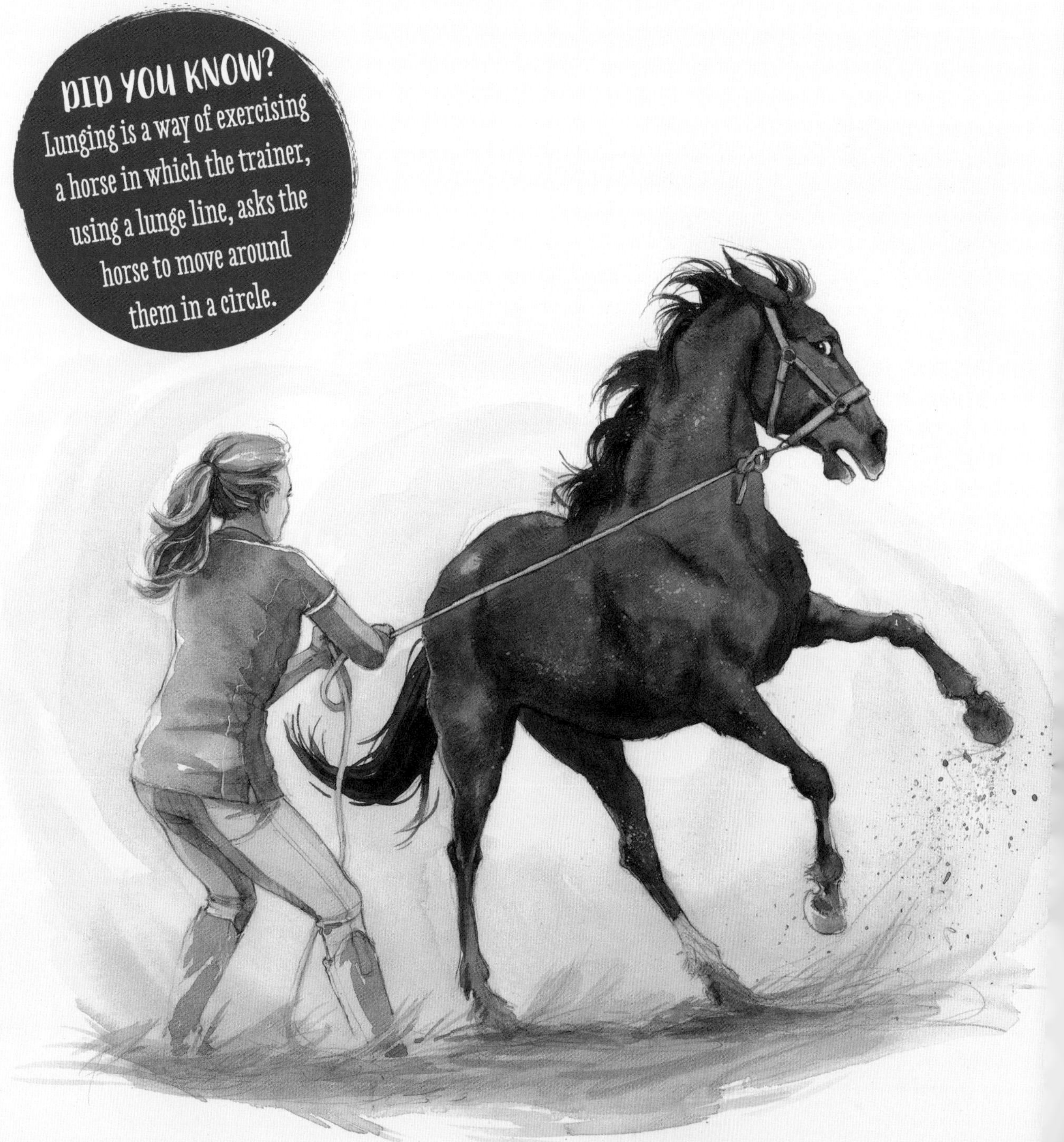

N	V	Z	J	D	T	E	H	D	S	O	R	O	N	I
S	N	O	W	Y	M	O	U	N	T	A	I	N	S	A
C	T	E	T	G	T	V	N	A	N	E	F	J	U	G
A	W	S	W	N	K	V	U	G	L	B	U	S	J	N
Z	D	U	E	Z	M	B	E	I	D	Y	T	E	A	A
N	J	M	K	W	E	R	R	W	K	R	H	D	C	T
A	O	T	A	L	D	A	V	U	A	Q	C	S	K	S
M	Y	U	I	K	Z	L	L	L	M	B	N	S	I	U
A	F	L	M	V	B	F	I	A	I	B	L	P	E	M
A	D	N	A	M	A	A	V	W	N	E	Y	J	P	L
N	U	J	N	R	P	D	I	E	S	D	Z	T	E	N
K	E	C	A	J	G	K	L	A	M	E	R	I	C	A
R	A	M	W	S	C	O	M	D	X	F	P	D	D	A
Y	C	P	A	I	B	R	T	A	R	A	L	L	A	B
I	S	L	V	K	E	L	L	Y	T	W	C	P	S	V

KAIMANAWA
MUSTANG
BRUMBY
SNOWY MOUNTAINS
JACKIE
SHYLA
BALLARAT
ANZAC
NEW ZEALAND
RANGER
MOMENTO
VICKI
KELLY
AUSTRALIA
AMANDA
ARGO
WILD WEST
AMERICA

DID YOU KNOW?
A wild horse must be haltered before it can be taught to lead.

SEE THE BACK OF THE BOOK FOR ANSWERS IF YOU GET STUCK!

CAPTAIN, THE WILD STALLION

HAVE YOU EVER WONDERED WHAT IT WOULD BE LIKE TO TAME A WILD STALLION? READ ALL ABOUT MY JOURNEY WITH CAPTAIN!

IN 2015 I SAW a striking bay stallion standing among the tussock grass in the Kaimanawa Ranges of New Zealand. He stood proud and wary as I photographed him alongside his mares. To me, these wild horses symbolised absolute freedom.

THREE YEARS PASSED before this wild stallion would come into my life again. In 2018, more wild horses were facing slaughter than ever before, with over 300 horses being mustered from the mountains. Desperate to help I applied for five stallions for myself, and then trained and mentored others to help save as many horses as possible. In total, 23 wild horses came to our property.

WHEN I SAW HIM walk off the stock truck my heart skipped a beat. I knew this stallion! He was the same bay stallion who I'd photographed in the wild.

HE SOON EARNED the name Captain. From that very first day in the yards I felt a connection with him. He was aloof and wary and my heart went out to him for all he'd lost over the past few days. Not only his freedom, but his family and the only place he'd ever called home. Everything was new for him and I could see how worried he was. At times it was hard to even get a photograph of him because he hid behind Amanda's stallion Pumba, and was too scared to even look at me. He had seemed much bolder in the wild, when he'd stood less than 20 metres away watching me.

FOR THE FIRST TWO DAYS I didn't work with Captain, so he'd have time to relax and settle in to his new surroundings. I had plenty of other wild horses to keep me busy, though. I was mentoring 10 students, aged 12 to 23 years, and we'd be at the yards from dawn till dusk. Some of the wild horses were very trusting and were eating out of our hands within minutes, and some were even being touched by the second day.

NOT CAPTAIN, THOUGH. He was very unsure about humans. Every time I worked with him I'd watch his body language to see if he was ready to trust me. If his eyes looked worried, or he pinned his ears back, o wrinkled up his nostrils, I'd know he was feeling scar so I'd slow things down. I wanted to earn his trust an friendship, not scare him or force him into submissio

THEN, THREE DAYS after he was mustered from the wild, Captain walked up to me and ate out of my hand. It was the very first step in his journey to domestication!

THE NEXT MILESTONE was smelling my hand. Captain very hesitantly stretched out his neck, cocked an ear and sniffed. I was proud of him for being so brave.

NEXT WAS OUR first touch. I held my hand up and waited patiently until Captain stepped forward and bumped my hand with his forehead. Even though he'd touched me, rather than me touching him, it gave him such a fright. He leapt backwards and gave me a baleful stare. His boldness had alarmed him and it took days before he felt ready to be touched again. But I didn't mind, Captain was worth waiting for.

SIX DAYS OUT of the wild I was able to rub Captain's head properly for the first time. My heart melted. It was one of the most special moments I've ever had with a wild horse and I was so excited to see what we would be able to achieve next!

BUT CAPTAIN HAD other ideas. For the next two weeks he decided he didn't want to be touched at all. He would flatten his ears and snake his head at me. I knew that if I expected too much of him, he had the potential to bite me, so I was very careful to give him the time and space he needed to accept all the new changes in his life.

IT WAS NOW 20 days since the muster, and in comparison to some of the other wild horses, Captain was progressing slowly. But even though Captain was the most difficult of the horses I was taming, it didn't make me love him any less. He was a special horse and I loved every minute I spent with him. Three weeks out of the wild I was able to braid Captain's forelock. He was much better to handle when he could see me properly! After that I was able to halter him straight away.

THE NEXT STEP was teaching Captain to lead so he could come out on lots of fun adventures. At first we just stayed in the paddock, in case he got loose and I'd sit with him for hours while he ate grass. My favourite moments were when he'd walk over to say hello to me.

SOON HE WAS able to go through the native forest, jumping over logs and ditches. But, even though I could do all these fun things with Captain, he was still unsure about being touched. I could only touch him on the right side of his jaw and at the top of his neck.

STILL, I COULD SEE that every day Captain was improving. Soon I was able to groom him all the way down to his hooves. He also learnt to work with obstacles and to be loaded onto the horse float.

CAPTAIN'S VERY FIRST TRIP was to the beach, which he loved. He was so relaxed he rolled in the sand nine times and we even swam in the ocean.

CAPTAIN WAS MAKING progress and was starting to really trust me. Just four weeks out of the wild he was even comfortable enough to lie down on the arena at home while I sat with him.

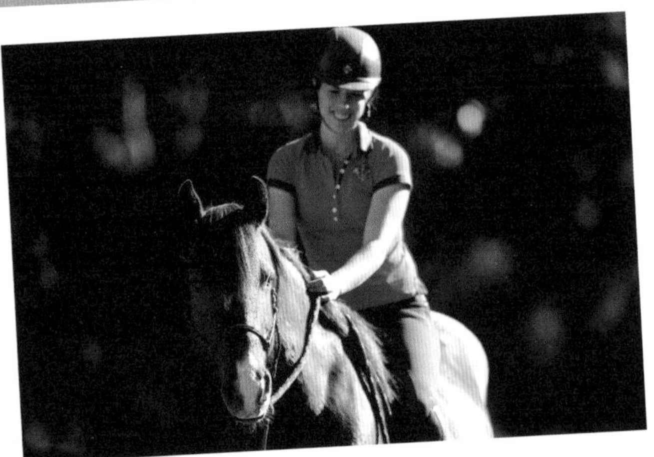

EVERY DAY I WORKED on building Captain's trust, until I could stand beside his shoulder and lean weight on his back. Finally, 10 weeks after he was mustered from the wild I was able to ride him for the first time!

SAVING CAPTAIN'S LIFE was one of the most rewarding things I've ever done. When we first started taming the wild horses in New Zealand, the majority were being slaughtered but, since 2015, every Kaimanawa suitable for rehoming has been saved. These special horses now have the love and support of an entire nation and I'm so happy that the lives of all 300 wild Kaimanawas were saved from the 2018 musters.

BONUS FACT

Captain even featured on a TV show. A film crew came to our property many times to film him and it was very special to have the first month of his journey documented.

1. THROUGH WHICH WINDOW DID MUM SPOT CAMEO TROTTING DOWN THE STREET?

A. the school office
B. her bedroom at home
C. the grocery store
D. her hospital room

2. WHY DOES KELLY NEED A NEW PONY?

A. Twinkle has been sold
B. Twinkle is now too small for her
C. Twinkle ran away
D. Twinkle is retiring

3. WHAT DID MUM FORGET TO MENTION ABOUT CAMEO?

A. she has never been ridden
B. she is lame
C. she has behavioural problems
D. she is only on loan

4. WHEN CAMEO ARRIVES AT THE WILSONS', WHICH OF THESE THINGS DOES SHE KNOW HOW TO DO?

A. how to jump over logs
B. how to be ridden in a saddle
C. how to be led
D. how to be cantered bareback

5. IN CHAPTER 4, WHERE DOES CAMEO FOLLOW KELLY?

A. to school
B. into the house
C. into the horse truck
D. to Mum's vegetable garden

6. WHY DO THE GIRLS HAVE TO WEED ALL THE RAGWORT AND BUTTERCUP PLANTS?

A. Dad doesn't like yellow flowers
B. Mum's allergic to them
C. they have a bad smell
D. they're poisonous for horses

7. WHAT DO KELLY AND CAMEO JUMP ON THEIR FIRST RIDE TOGETHER?

A. a log
B. a fence
C. a river
D. a rabbit hutch

8. WHAT COLOUR ARE AMANDA'S LUCKY GUMBOOT WHICH SHE WEARS TO THE RIBBON DAY?

A. pink
B. red
C. black
D. blue

9. WHAT IS THE NAME OF LEAH'S HORSE?

A. Superstar
B. Diva
C. Showbiz
D. Razzle Dazzle

10. WHAT PRESENTS DO DAD, GRANDAD AND UNCLE SIMON GIVE THE SISTERS?

A. homemade jump poles and stands
B. jumping boots
C. show browbands
D. riding jackets

11. WHAT RIBBON DO KELLY AND CAMEO WIN AT THEIR FIRST A&P SHOW?

A. yellow for third place
B. blue for second place
C. red for first place
D. purple for champion

12. AT THE EASTER SHOW, WHAT DO KELLY AND CA WIN FOR THE NOVICE RIDER OVER HURDLES CL

A. yellow for third place
B. blue for second place
C. red for first place
D. purple for champion

SHOW WHAT YOU KNOW ABOUT CAMEO!

How well do you know the second of our Showtym Adventures books? You could be a Cameo-whizz – take our quiz to find out!

Once you've done the quiz, colour in the pony and truck.

P5

DID YOU KNOW?
A sheepskin cloth or pad that is placed beneath the saddle is known as a numnah.

THE ANSWERS ARE AT THE BACK OF THE BOOK IF YOU NEED TO TAKE A PEEK.

DID YOU KNOW?
Ragwort, acorns, bracken, buttercup, sycamore seeds, yew and nightshades are all poisonous to horses.

THE FOREST MAZE

Amanda has found some treasure buried in the forest! She's dug it up, filled the sacks with artefacts and tied the load onto her pony Chessy. Can you help Amanda and Chessy find a path back home through the forest?

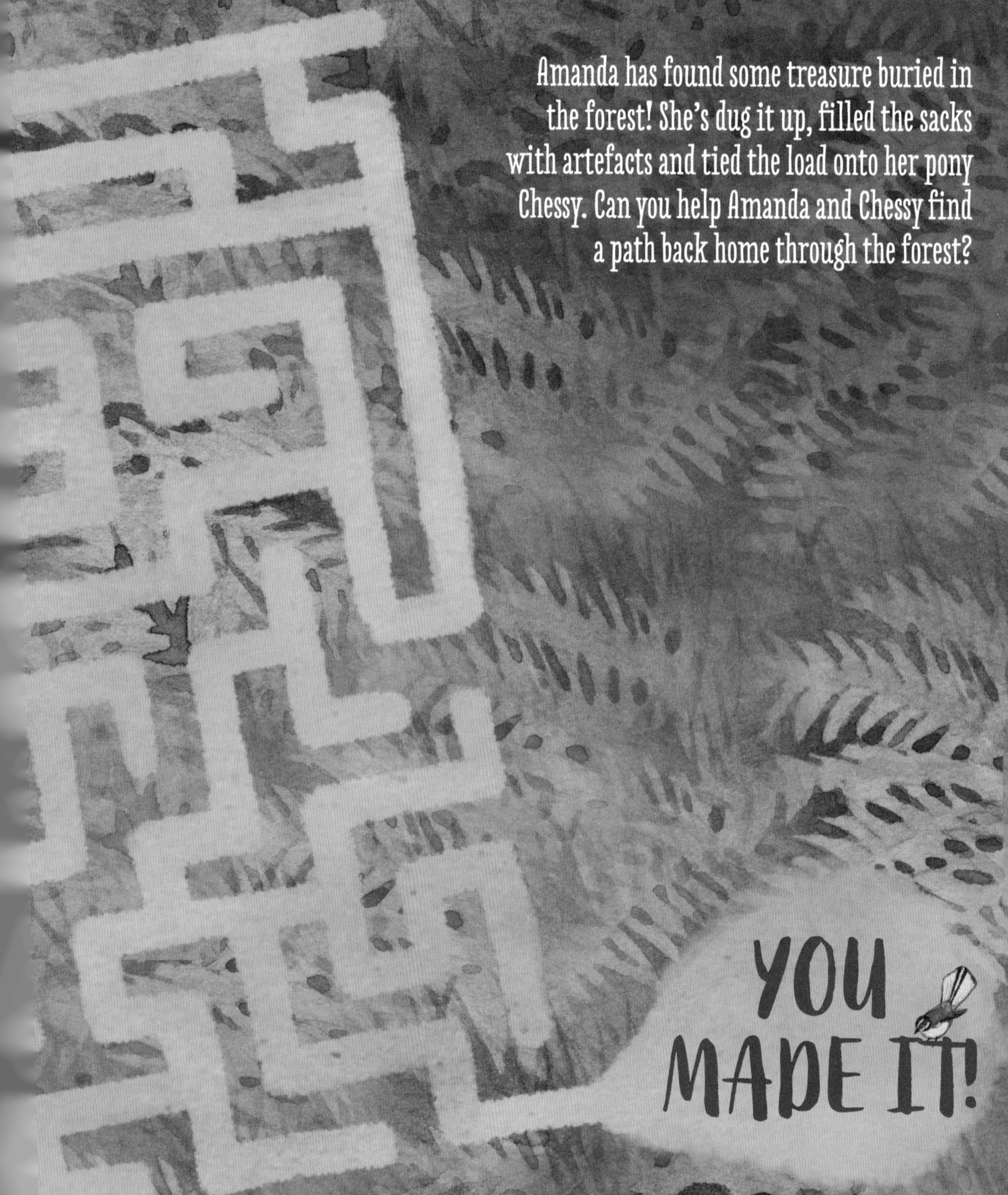

YOU MADE IT!

IF YOU GET LOST, SNEAK A LOOK AT THE ANSWER PAGE.

YOUR PERFECT PONY

Every rider is different. Use this flowchart to find the perfect Showtym Adventures pony for you!

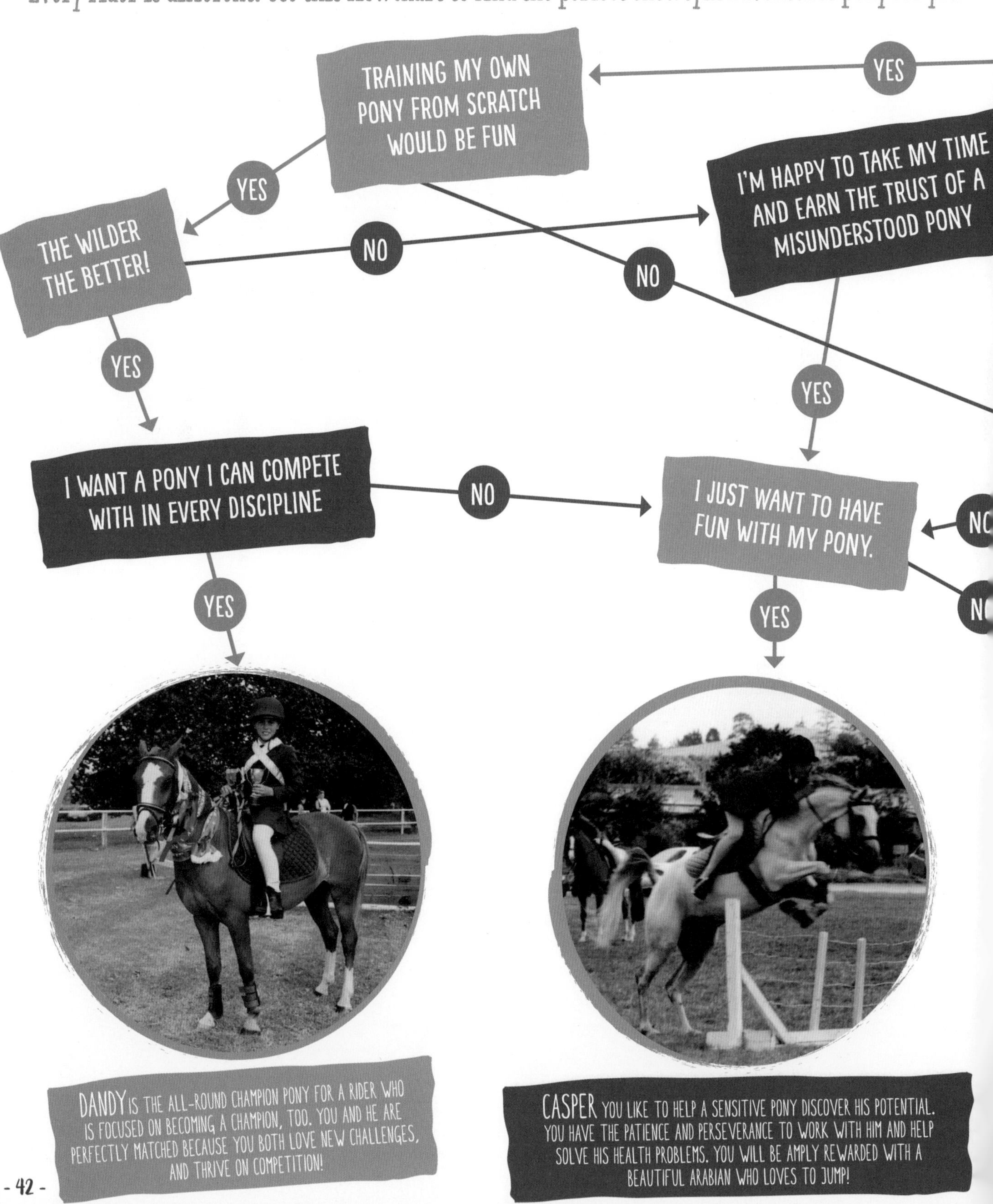

TRAINING MY OWN PONY FROM SCRATCH WOULD BE FUN
YES
YES
NO
THE WILDER THE BETTER!
NO
I'M HAPPY TO TAKE MY TIME AND EARN THE TRUST OF A MISUNDERSTOOD PONY
YES
YES
I WANT A PONY I CAN COMPETE WITH IN EVERY DISCIPLINE
NO
I JUST WANT TO HAVE FUN WITH MY PONY.
YES
YES

DANDY IS THE ALL-ROUND CHAMPION PONY FOR A RIDER WHO IS FOCUSED ON BECOMING A CHAMPION, TOO. YOU AND HE ARE PERFECTLY MATCHED BECAUSE YOU BOTH LOVE NEW CHALLENGES, AND THRIVE ON COMPETITION!

CASPER YOU LIKE TO HELP A SENSITIVE PONY DISCOVER HIS POTENTIAL. YOU HAVE THE PATIENCE AND PERSEVERANCE TO WORK WITH HIM AND HELP SOLVE HIS HEALTH PROBLEMS. YOU WILL BE AMPLY REWARDED WITH A BEAUTIFUL ARABIAN WHO LOVES TO JUMP!

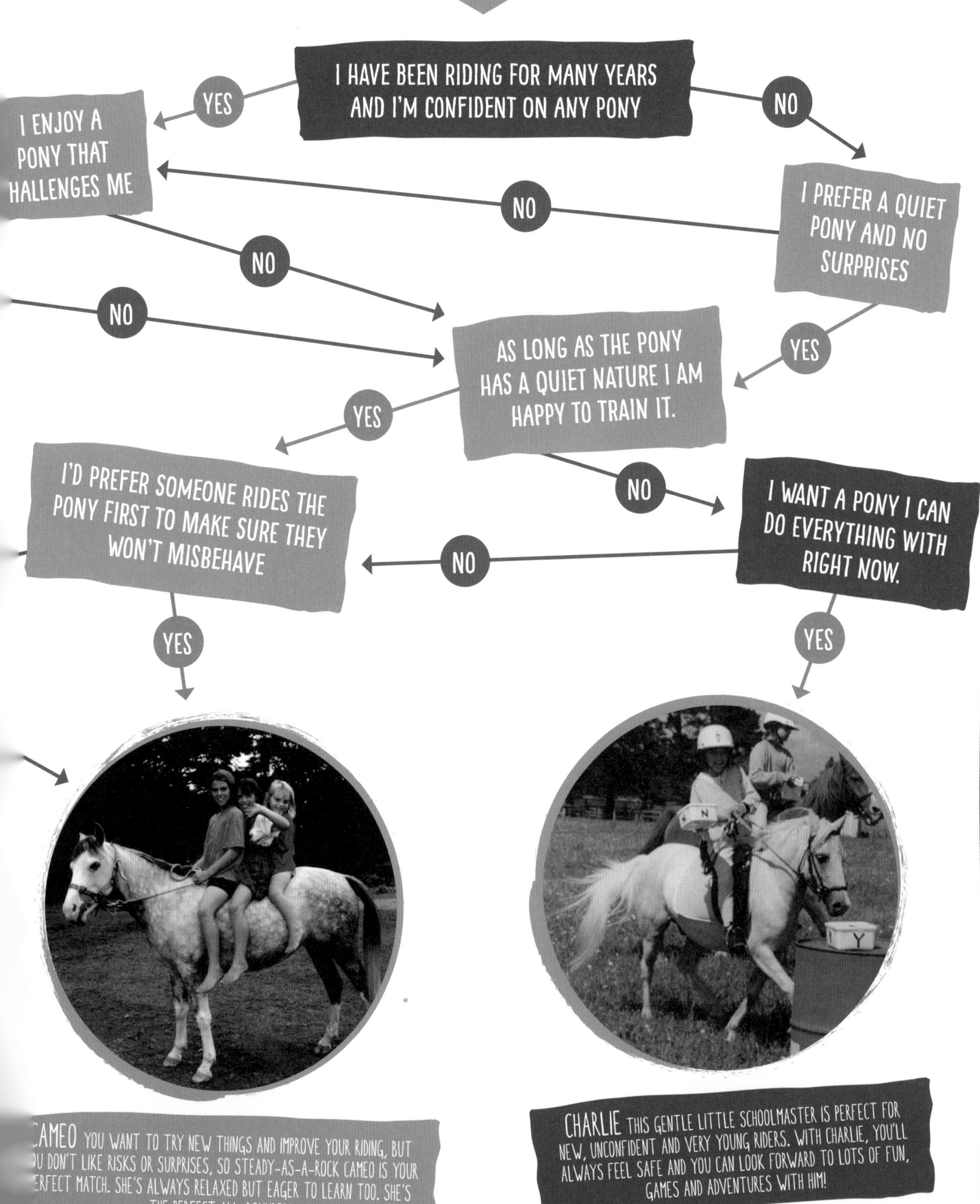
START HERE
I HAVE BEEN RIDING FOR MANY YEARS AND I'M CONFIDENT ON ANY PONY
YES
NO
I ENJOY A PONY THAT HALLENGES ME
NO
I PREFER A QUIET PONY AND NO SURPRISES
NO
NO
AS LONG AS THE PONY HAS A QUIET NATURE I AM HAPPY TO TRAIN IT.
YES
YES
I'D PREFER SOMEONE RIDES THE PONY FIRST TO MAKE SURE THEY WON'T MISBEHAVE
NO
I WANT A PONY I CAN DO EVERYTHING WITH RIGHT NOW.
NO
YES
YES
N
Y
AMEO YOU WANT TO TRY NEW THINGS AND IMPROVE YOUR RIDING, BUT U DON'T LIKE RISKS OR SURPRISES, SO STEADY-AS-A-ROCK CAMEO IS YOUR ERFECT MATCH. SHE'S ALWAYS RELAXED BUT EAGER TO LEARN TOO. SHE'S THE PERFECT ALL-ROUNDER!
CHARLIE THIS GENTLE LITTLE SCHOOLMASTER IS PERFECT FOR NEW, UNCONFIDENT AND VERY YOUNG RIDERS. WITH CHARLIE, YOU'LL ALWAYS FEEL SAFE AND YOU CAN LOOK FORWARD TO LOTS OF FUN, GAMES AND ADVENTURES WITH HIM!

CASPER'S FRIENDLY QUIZ!

Are quizzes the stuff of your dreams or your nightmares? How well do you know our spirited Arabian from the third Showtym Adventures book? Take the quiz to find out!

DID YOU KNOW?
Horses have four natural gaits – walk, trot, canter and gallop. The trot has two beats, the canter has three beats and both the walk and the gallop have four beats.

Once you've done the quiz, colour in the pony and rabbit hutch.

IF YOU NEED TO RESCUE YOUR REPUTATION, THE ANSWERS ARE ON PAGE 61.

HAT'S THE NAME OF VICKI'S FRIEND HO IS LOOKING FOR A PONY TO BUY?

A. Annabelle
B. Caitlin
C. Stella
D. Aimee

2. WHAT DOES CASPER DO WHEN HIS OWNER APPROACHES?

A. kicks
B. bares his teeth
C. gallops away
D. jumps the fence

AT BOOK DOES VICKI SAY MADE HER SPERATELY WANT AN ARABIAN?

A. *The Black Stallion*
B. *Black Beauty*
C. *War Horse*
D. *National Velvet*

4. HOW MUCH MONEY DO THE GIRLS HAVE TO RAISE TO BUY CASPER?

A. $100
B. $350
C. $400
D. $250

WHICH TWO PONIES DO THEY USE FOR PONY RIDES AT THE MARKET?

A. Dandy and Jude
B. Charlie and Cameo
C. Cameo and Jude
D. Dandy and Charlie

WHAT DOES CASPER SEEM TO HATE WEARING?

A. jumping boots
B. a halter
C. shoes
D. saddle and bridle

7. WHAT KIND OF RIDE DOES VICKI PROPOSE ON THE NIGHT OF THEIR SLEEPOVER?

A. beach ride
B. ride to buy fish and chips
C. night ride
D. river swim

8. WHICH PONY GETS SICK WITH COLIC?

A. Charlie
B. Blackie
C. Diego
D. Cameo

9. WHAT DOES MIKE SAY MIGHT BE CAUSING CASPER'S BAD BEHAVIOUR?

A. his knees
B. his teeth
C. his bony withers
D. his eyesight

10. WHICH SPICE GIRL CHARACTER DOES VICKI DRESS UP AS FOR THE DRESSAGE FORMATION RIDE?

A. Baby Spice
B. Posh Spice
C. Scary Spice
D. Sporty Spice

11. WHAT DO THE SPICE GIRLS WIN?

A. first place
B. second place
C. third place
D. fourth place

12. WHAT IDEA DOES AMANDA GET FROM VICKI AND CASPER FOR THE BEACH BABES' PERFORMANCE?

A. all white ponies
B. wearing life-jackets
C. riding bareback
D. swimsuit costumes

MY STAR HORSES!

NGAHIWI SHOWTYM DANCER

D.O.B. 2001, 15.3hh, grey TB x mare.
Dancer is the best show jumper I've ever owned, winning many classes to 1.30m before she was retired as a broodmare. She is now in foal to Daminos, our Team WS stallion.

ELDER KH

D.O.B. 2000, 15.1hh, grey Kaimanawa gelding.
Of all the wild horses I've tamed, Elder has been the most challenging. He was mustered in 2014 and it took 1000 days before I was able to touch every part of his body and pick up all four hooves.

SHOWTYM LIMELIGHT

D.O.B. 2015, 15hh, grey Kaimanawa x mare.
Lili has a line-up of star-studded relatives: her gran is Showtym Spotlight; her sire is Showtym Highligh (a Grand Prix pony); and dam is Momento KH (ou Kaimanawa from the 2012 muster).

ADMIRAL KH

CONCORD KH

ALLEGIANCE KH

Even more than the thrill of competition, I get so much joy from working with horses – especially wild horses on their journey from wild to mild. Let me take you on a tour of my stable to meet these gorgeous characters!

SHOWTYM SINATRA

).O.B. 1999, 15.3hh, bay
rossbred gelding.
got Sina as a barely-handled
-year-old stallion and he's
roving to be a top jumper!
e was named after the singer
natra, who was known as
)l Blue Eyes', because of his
ue eyes.

SHYLA, THE SNOWY BRUMBY

D.O.B. 2011, 13.2hh, chestnut Brumby mare. Shyla is the wild Brumby I tamed in 2016. She is now part-owned by 12-year-old Nina Sutherland and they have won lots of competitions including the Isuzu Off-Road Challenge at Equidays!

SHOWTYM MOONLIGHT

D.O.B. 2013, 15.2hh, palomino TB x QH gelding. Dallas is the older half-brother of Showtym Limelight and is a superstar show jumper and an amazing liberty horse! He's performed in front of thousands of people as a unicorn!

LIEUTENANT KH

CAPTAIN KH

I'VE ALSO BEEN TAMING THESE FIVE WILD STALLIONS FROM THE 2018 MUSTERS. FIND OUT ALL ABOUT THEM ON MY WEBSITE, WWW.KELLYWILSON.NZ/KELLY-LIVE

COLOUR IN THE WELSHIES

DID YOU KNOW?
A pony is an adult horse that is shorter than 148cm.

CROSS CODE

One of the Wilson sisters is on a mission!
Crack the code to find out which sister it is, and what her mission is.

To crack the code, use the crosses below. The numbers in the coded message refer to a particular cross, and the position of the lines tell you which letter it is in that particular cross. For example, the letter 'B' would be represented in the coded message like this: ⌈3

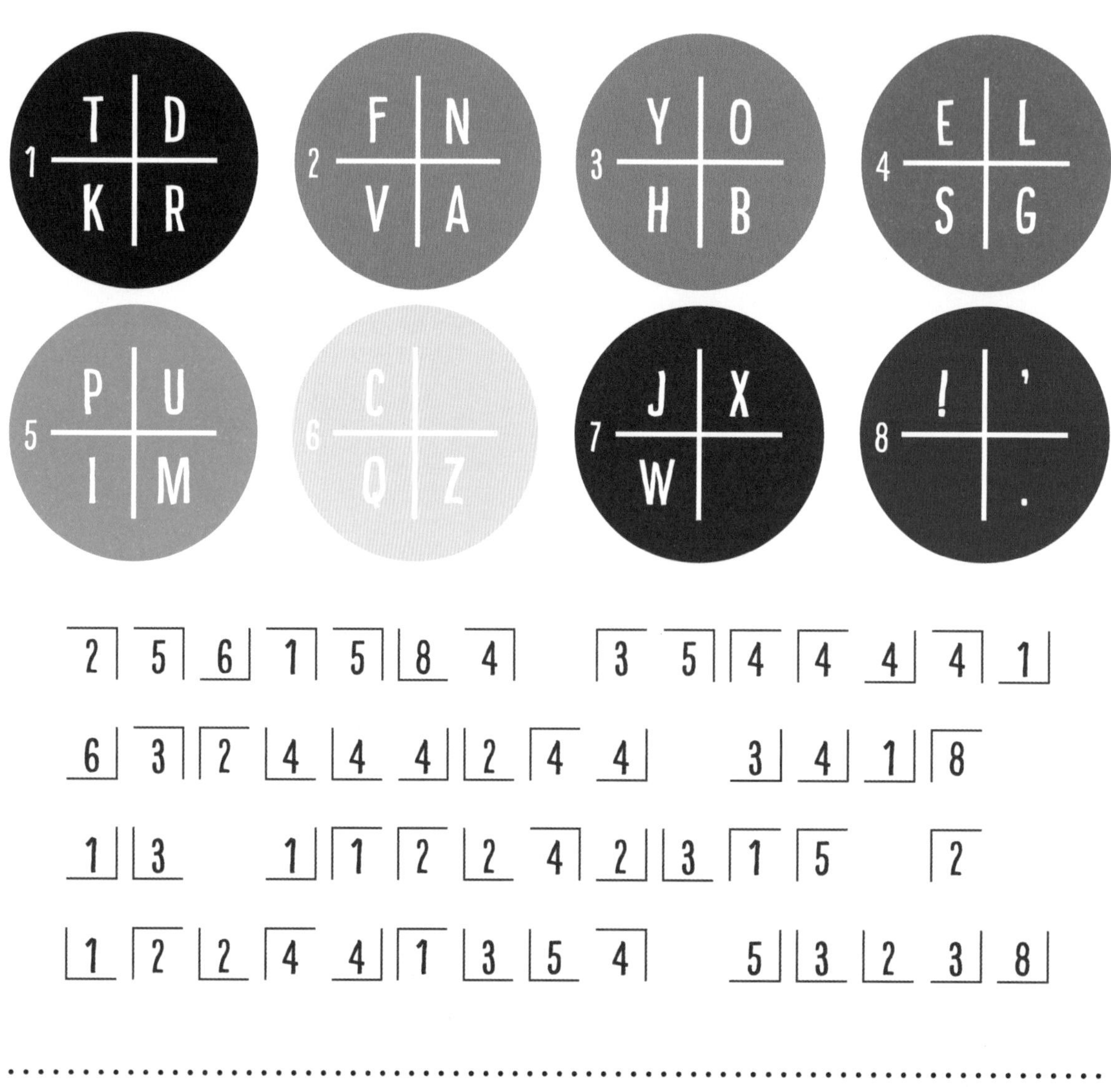

....

....

GO TO THE ANSWER PAGE AT THE BACK OF THE BOOK
TO CHECK YOUR DECODED MESSAGE.

CAN YOU CRACK THIS WEE CHESTNUT?

There's no room for wild guesses in this quiz about Chessy the wild Welshie! We're sure you'll remember sackloads of details from the fourth Showtym Adventures story.

Once you've done the quiz, colour in Amanda and Chessy.

DID YOU KNOW?
A female foal is called a filly.

THE ANSWERS ARE AT THE BACK IF YOU NEED THEM.

WHAT IS THE FULL NAME OF AMANDA'S LITTLE GREY PONY?

A. Charlie Horse
B. Prince Charles
C. Charlie Brown
D. Charlie Chaplin

2. WHAT IS AMANDA EXCITED ABOUT FINALLY BEING ALLOWED TO COMPETE IN?

A. a show-jumping class
B. a flat class
C. a hunter class
D. a lead-rein class

WHAT IS THE HIGHEST PRIZE AMANDA WINS THAT DAY?

A. a yellow ribbon for third place
B. a blue ribbon for second place
C. a red ribbon for first place
D. a purple champion's sash

AMANDA AND HER FRIEND LAURA SWAP PONIES FOR A WHILE. WHAT IS THE NAME OF LAURA'S PONY?

A. Magic
B. Voodoo
C. Alchemy
D. Hocus Pocus

OW MANY WELSH PONIES DO THE WILSONS ND BENNETTS RESCUE ALTOGETHER?

A. 100
B. 4
C. 7
D. 10

6. WHAT DOES BEN NAME A STALLION?

A. Captain Cook
B. Batman
C. Indiana Jones
D. The Lone Ranger

7. WHAT PROBLEM DOES MAESTRO, THE GREY WELSH STALLION, HAVE?

A. string-halt
B. hoof lameness
C. wolf teeth
D. a broken splint bone

8. WHAT IS SPECIAL ABOUT THE BENNETTS' NEWBORN FOAL?

A. it skips rather than walks
B. it has stripes on its legs
C. it squeaks instead of whinnies
D. it has a moustache

9. AT THE AUTUMN SHOW HUNTER SERIES, WHICH PONY DOES AMANDA WIN A BET TO RIDE?

A. Chessy
B. Casper
C. Magic
D. Charlie

10. WHAT IS THE FIRST TASK AMANDA SETS CHESSY TO BECOME A GREAT KIDS' PONY?

A. to drag a log
B. to be ridden bareback
C. to get used to other animals
D. to carry sacks

11. WHICH OF THESE ANIMALS DO THE WILSONS NOT HAVE?

A. rabbits
B. alpacas
C. calves
D. pigs

12. WHO IS THE FIRST PERSON TO RIDE CHESSY?

A. Ben
B. Vicki
C. Amanda
D. Kelly

SPOT THE DIFFERENCE

When our mum was in hospital, gazing out of the window, her keen eyes spotted a horse tied to the back of a truck as it drove slowly down the street. It was Cameo, the Street Pony!

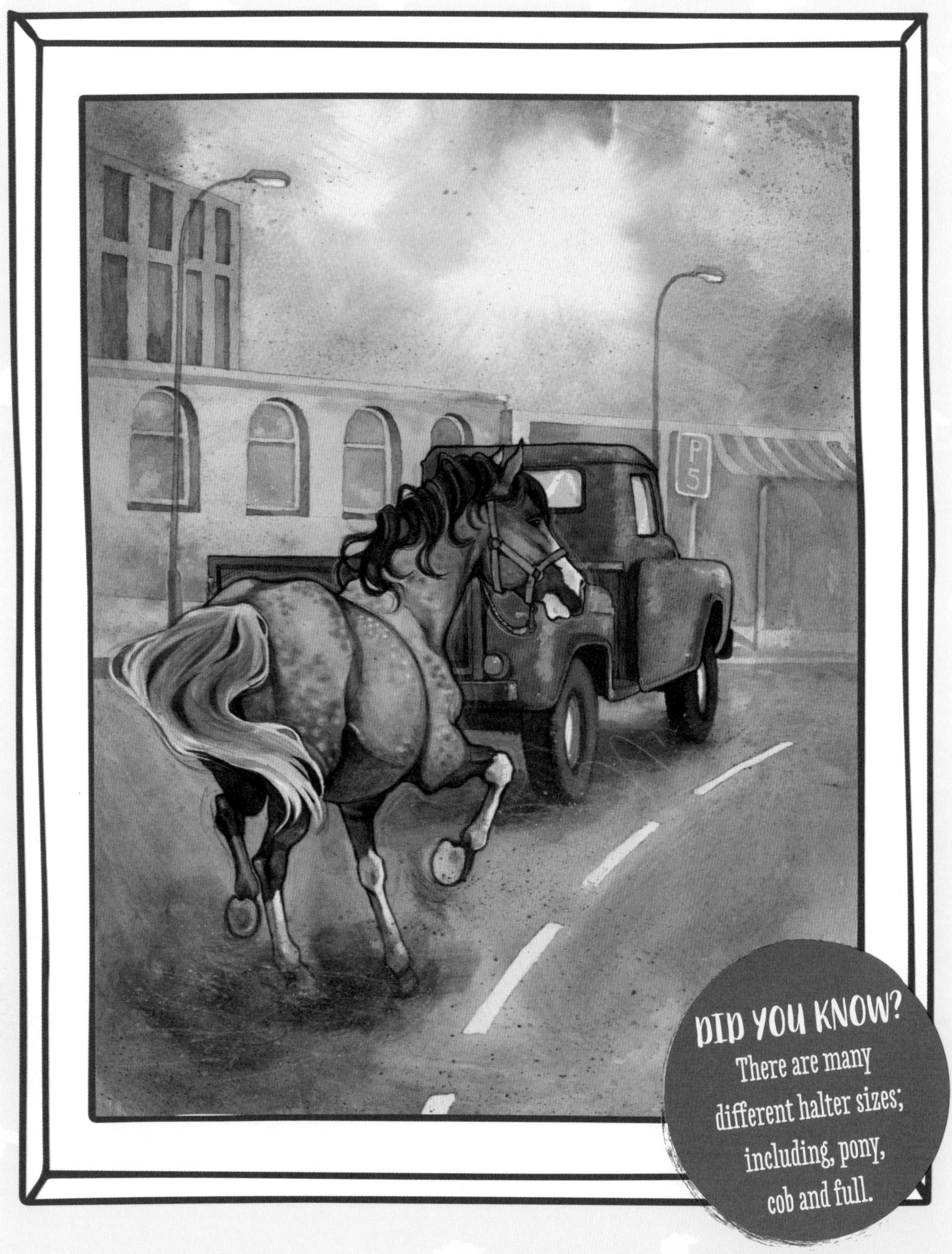

DID YOU KNOW?
There are many different halter sizes; including, pony, cob and full.

DID YOU KNOW?
A horse's father is known as a sire.

Do you also have a good eye for spotting things out of the ordinary?
Try to find the 12 differences between the illustrations below.
Can you spot them all?

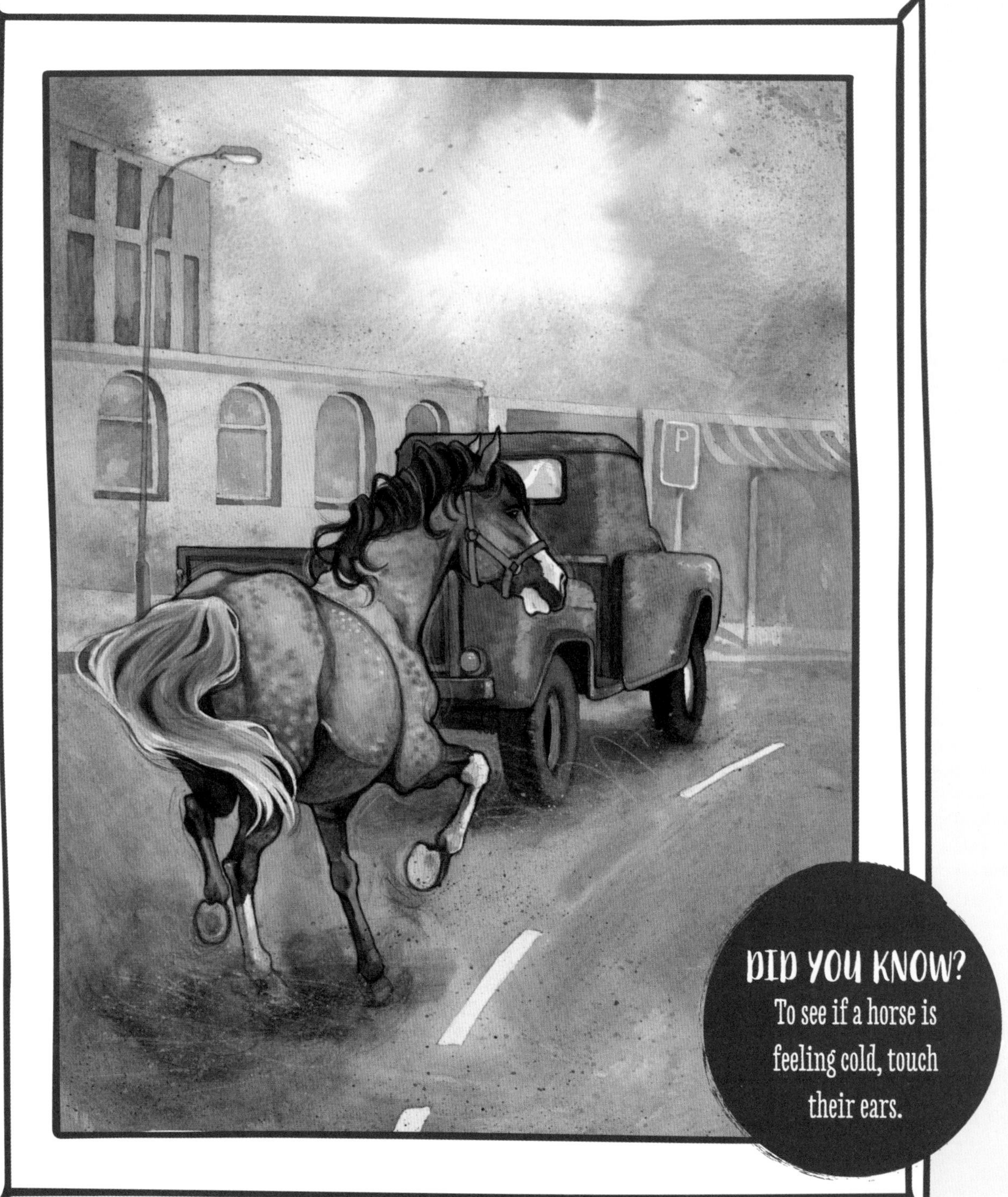

DID YOU KNOW?
To see if a horse is feeling cold, touch their ears.

TURN TO THE BACK OF THE BOOK FOR THE ANSWERS.

CROSSWORD

We've dotted interesting facts about horses throughout the book. Can you use your new knowledge to complete the crossword?

ACROSS

2. The size of a halter, between pony and full.
4. One of the four main marking shapes on a horse's face.
5. The rubbery, triangular underside of the hoof.
7. The number of beats in a walk and a gallop.
8. You touch these to see if a horse is feeling cold.
9. A horse has a small one of these, so they need a constant supply of food, day and night.
11. One of the three phases of eventing.
12. An adult horse that is shorter than 148cm.
15. This term is used for moving a horse around you in the circle.
16. The sheepskin cloth or pad beneath a saddle.
18. Before a wild horse can be taught to lead, it must first be _______.
20. Female foal.

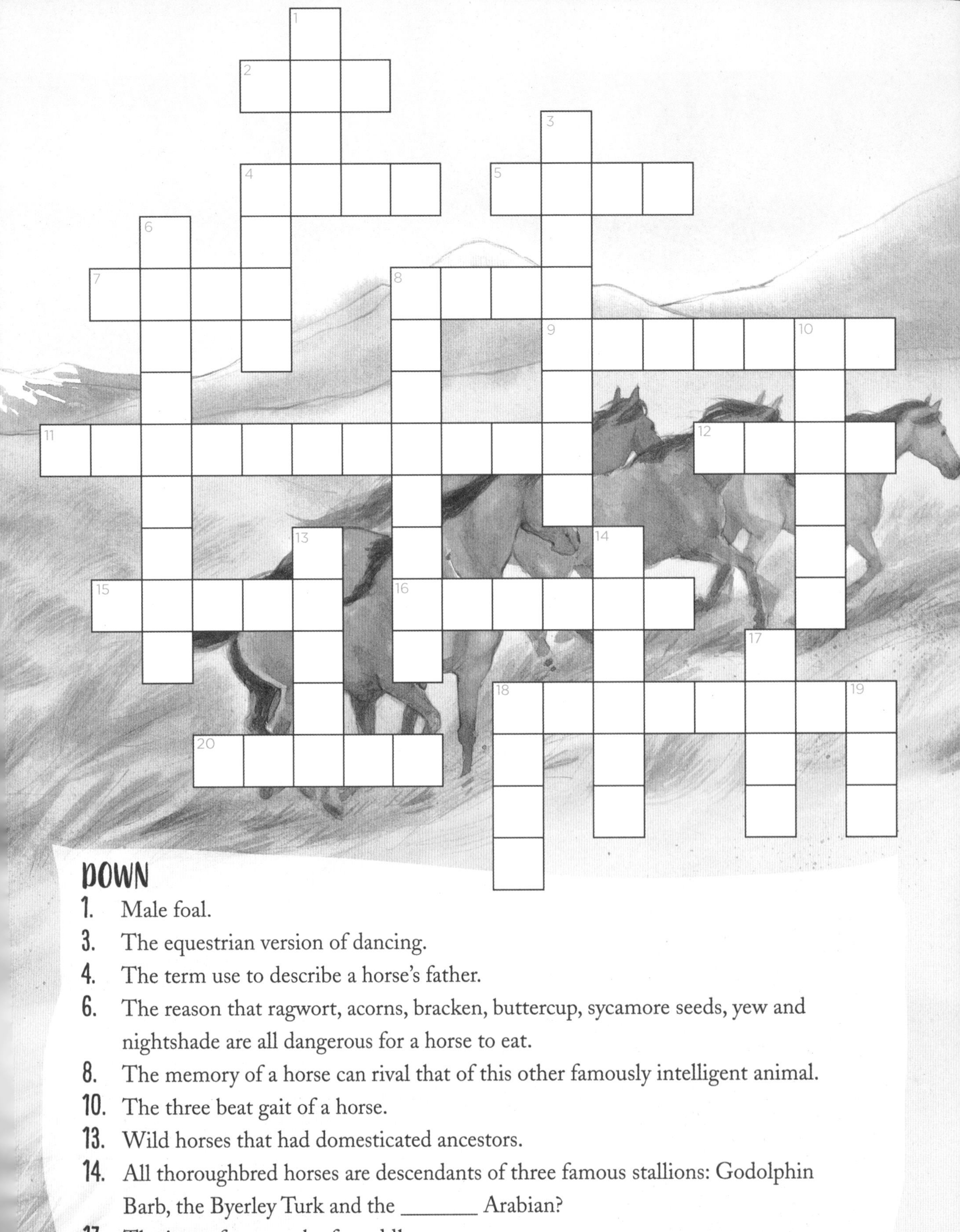

DOWN

1. Male foal.
3. The equestrian version of dancing.
4. The term use to describe a horse's father.
6. The reason that ragwort, acorns, bracken, buttercup, sycamore seeds, yew and nightshade are all dangerous for a horse to eat.
8. The memory of a horse can rival that of this other famously intelligent animal.
10. The three beat gait of a horse.
13. Wild horses that had domesticated ancestors.
14. All thoroughbred horses are descendants of three famous stallions: Godolphin Barb, the Byerley Turk and the _______ Arabian?
17. The inner framework of a saddle.
18. The term used to measure the height of a horse, from the ground to the withers.
19. The term used to describe a horse's mother.

SEE THE BACK OF THE BOOK FOR ANSWERS IF YOU GET STUCK!

MAKE A MODEL HORSE!

When we were younger, we loved playing with toy horses but funds were tight so we made our own models out of cardboard. These were brilliant when we needed to memorise our dressage tests for shows, and we always coloured our models to match the horses we would be riding! Here's how you can make your own.

YOU WILL NEED:

- → Tracing (transparent) paper
- → Pencil for tracing
- → A4 card or stiff paper suitable for your model
- → Scissors
- → Coloured pens, pencils or paints (plus glitter, stickers, feathers and anything else you'd like for decoration)

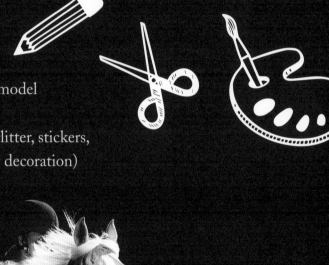

SHOWTYM SPOTLIGHT, AS PEGASUS, AT OUR RIDING WITH THE STARS SHOW IN 2016.

HOW TO MAKE YOUR MODEL

STEP 1 Place your tracing paper over the outline on page 64, and, using a pencil, trace around the shapes. If you would like to make a horse, you can simply trace the body and two plain sets of legs. If you would like to make the Pegasus model, the fore-legs will need to include wings. You should be able to fit both a horse and a Pegasus onto one sheet of A4.

STEP 2 Turn your tracing over, place it on your card or stiff paper, and draw over the back of your tracing to transfer the pencil outlines to the card.

STEP 3 Using scissors, cut out the pieces for your horse or Pegasus model. You might need to ask an adult to help with this.

STEP 4 Colour and decorate your horse any way you like. Remember to colour both sides of each piece!

STEP 5 Assemble your horse or Pegasus by inserting the legs into the slots on the body.

STEP 5 Take a picture of your finished model and send it to us. We'd love to see it!

HOW TO FIT THE HORSE AND PEGASUS ON ONE A4 SHEET

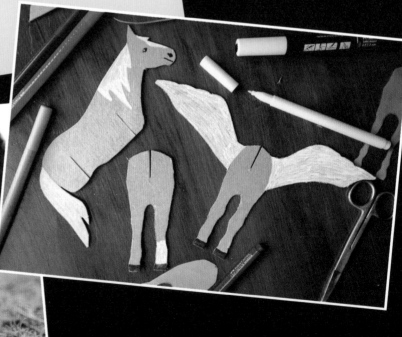

WHICH STORY WAS THAT?

See if you can match the blurb to the book to see just how much you know about our other incredible adventures! The first one has been done for you.

4

D

Vicki finally has the chance to train her own wild pony! How will she earn the trust of her beautiful new chestnut?

5

E

Kelly, Vicki and Amanda ride through the wilderness to save the American wild horses on this exciting and eventful journey.

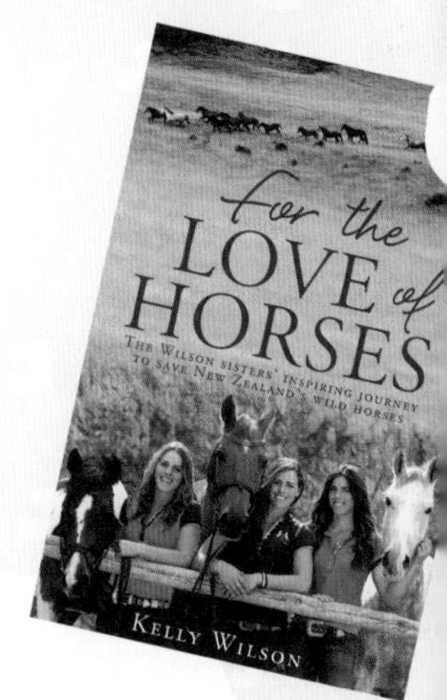

F

The true story of a wild Kaimanawa stallion who became a star performer and favourite horse of the Wilson Sisters.

6

Saving the SNOWY BRUMBIES

The Wilson sisters' adventures taming horses from Australia's Snowy Mountains

Kelly Wilson

I

Amanda dreams of training her own wild pony. When there's a muster of beautiful Welsh ponies, Amanda sees her chance, but will the striking stallion ever be safe enough to ride?

G

When Vicki hears about a difficult Arabian that no one wants, she will stop at nothing to save him. Will this pony ever trust humans again?

9
KELLY WILSON
SHOWTYM ADVENTURES
CHESSY, THE WELSH PONY

C

The Wilson Sisters' quest to train 10 wild Kaimanawa horses for a national competition. Can the sisters change the fate of these difficult and dangerous horses?

H

The Wilson Sisters travel to the mountains of Australia to rescue wild horses from an annual cull and turn them into quiet ponies for children.

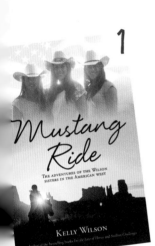

1

Mustang Ride

The adventures of the Wilson sisters in the American West

Kelly Wilson

7
KELLY WILSON
SHOWTYM ADVENTURES
VICKI'S STORY!
DANDY, THE MOUNTAIN PONY

8

Stallion Challenges

Kelly Wilson

B

story of the Wilson Sisters' humble nnings in rural New Zealand: from e trials and tears of Pony Club, the ys of riding bareback, the pressures adolescence and competitive show mping, through to the start of their courageous journey to save the wild Kaimanawas.

2
KELLY WILSON
SHOWTYM ADVENTURES
VICKI'S STORY!
CASPER, THE SPIRITED ARABIAN

A

Kelly's beautiful new steel-grey mare comes with a catch — she's never been ridden! Can Kelly face her fears on an untested pony, and go on to compete at the Royal Show?

GO TO THE ANSWER PAGE AT THE BACK OF THE BOOK TO SEE HOW WELL YOU KNOW THE WILSON SISTERS.

NEXT IN THE SERIES . . . KOOLIO, THE PROBLEM PONY

It's so exciting to share with you this preview of the fifth book in the Showtym Adventures series. In it, Vicki, Amanda and I are getting really serious about competing, but there's some tough decisions to make if we're going to pursue our dreams. For me, it means giving up my precious pony Cameo so that the family can buy a bigger horse truck. Even though I know our future is worth the sacrifice, saying goodbye is never easy!

KELLY'S STORY!

Here's a sneak peek . . .

THE NIGHT BEFORE CAMEO'S potential buyers arrived, Kelly lay awake.

She'd always thought that she and Cameo were the most perfectly matched pair in the whole world. But what if this girl also thought Cameo was perfect for *her*?

Giving up on sleep, she slipped out of bed. Pausing to check that her sisters were still fast asleep, she crept out of the room and down the hallway, and let herself outside. Then, knowing the way by heart, she ran through the darkness to Cameo's paddock.

"Come on, girl," Kelly called softly to her.

The steel-grey mare wandered over, the white highlights on her coat glowing in the moonlight. Just as she always did, she pushed her head into Kelly's arms for a hug.

"She's going to love you," Kelly whispered.

She threaded her hands through Cameo's mane and jumped onto her bare back. For more than an hour she sat quietly on her pony, watching the sky for shooting stars. Finally, when she had become so tired that her eyes would barely stay open, she slid to the ground, patted Cameo, who blinked sleepily in reply, and made her way back to bed.

The next morning, Kelly woke late and stumbled into the kitchen. No one else was around. She glanced at the clock and gasped — it was almost 11 o'clock! The family looking at Cameo were due any minute.

"Good to see you've joined the land of the living," Dad joked as Kelly came running out to the yards. Vicki already had Cameo caught and groomed. "We were beginning to think we'd have to meet these people without you."

"They're not here yet, are they?"

Vicki shook her head. "They've called to say they're running a little late. Would you like me to ride Cameo for them today?"

Kelly shot her a grateful smile. "Maybe you should, and then I can get to know the girl who's trying her. She has to be good enough for Cameo. Besides, I'll probably cry the whole time if I'm the one who has to show her off."

At that moment, a car pulled up. As her parents spoke with the family, Kelly looked hard for any faults, but they seemed friendly and genuine. Their daughter was ten years old and they were looking for a safe all-rounder for her. If they bought Cameo, she would stay in the family for years, passing to their younger daughter, who was already trading jokes and giggling with Amanda.

Once Vicki had put Cameo through her paces, the ten-year-old wanted to try riding her. Kelly watched in misery as her pony behaved impeccably. The girl brought Cameo to a halt with a radiant smile, and it was clear to everyone that she was smitten.

Kelly clung to Cameo's neck as the girl's parents again talked with her mum and dad. Tears began to trickle down her cheeks. To hide her heartbreak, she led Cameo back to her paddock, where she stayed for a while, sitting against the trunk of a tree.

Back at the house she was greeted with sympathetic looks.

"They've bought her, haven't they?"

Mum nodded and put an arm around her shoulder. "It'll be a good home for her; they'll treat her well."

"When does she go?"

"Next weekend. They live near Granny, so we'll drive Cameo there ourselves and stay with Granny for the weekend . . ." Mum's voice faded out as the news sank in for Kelly.

Just one week left with Cameo.

Blinking rapidly, she rushed to her room and flung herself on the bed.

Don't worry, I will get my smile back,
but you'll have to wait just a little longer to find out exactly how!

ANSWERS

A VERY DANDY QUIZ! – PAGE 12

1(C), 2(B), 3(A), 4(D), 5(D), 6(C), 7(A), 8(D), 9(B), 10(D), 11(B), 12(A).

PARTS OF A BRIDLE – PAGE 14

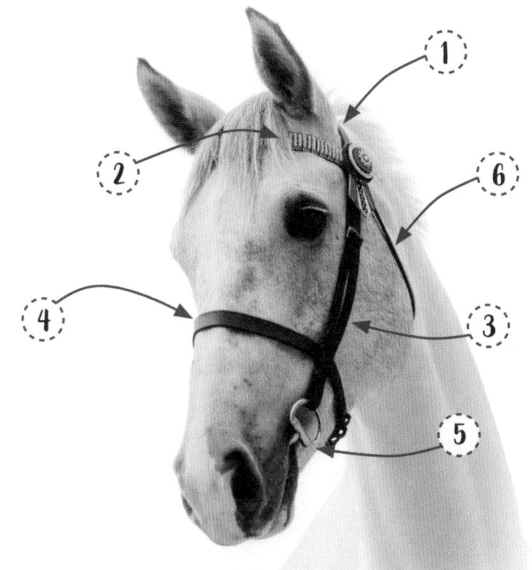

WILD WORD SEARCH – PAGE 30

N	V	Z	J	D	T	E	H	D	S	O	R	O	N	I
S	N	O	W	Y	M	O	U	N	T	A	I	N	S	A
C	T	E	T	G	T	V	N	A	N	E	F	J	U	G
A	W	S	W	N	K	V	U	G	L	B	U	S	J	N
Z	D	U	E	Z	M	B	E	I	D	Y	T	E	A	A
N	J	M	K	W	E	R	R	W	K	R	H	D	C	T
A	O	T	A	L	D	A	V	U	A	Q	C	S	K	S
M	Y	U	I	K	Z	L	L	L	M	B	N	S	I	U
A	F	L	M	V	B	F	I	A	I	B	L	P	E	M
A	D	N	A	M	A	A	V	W	N	E	Y	J	P	L
N	U	J	N	R	P	D	I	E	S	D	Z	T	E	N
K	E	C	A	J	G	K	L	A	M	E	R	I	C	A
R	A	M	W	S	C	O	M	D	X	F	P	D	D	A
Y	C	P	A	I	B	R	T	A	R	A	L	L	A	B
I	S	L	V	K	E	L	L	Y	T	W	C	P	S	V

SHOW WHAT YOU KNOW ABOUT CAMEO! – PAGE 38

1(D), 2(B), 3(A), 4(C), 5(B), 6(D), 7(A), 8(B), 9(C), 10(A), 11(B), 12(C).

SECRET LANGUAGE – PAGE 15

THE LATIN NAME FOR A HORSE IS EQUUS FERUS CABALLUS.

THE FOREST MAZE – PAGE 40

CASPER'S FRIENDLY QUIZ! – PAGE 44

1(C), 2(B), 3(A), 4(D), 5(B), 6(D), 7(C), 8(A), 9(B), 10(D), 11(B), 12(C).

CROSS CODE – PAGE 49

VICKI'S BIGGEST CHALLENGE YET
TO TRANSFORM A DANGEROUS PONY!

CAN YOU CRACK THIS WEE CHESTNUT? – PAGE 50

1(C), 2(A), 3(D), 4(A), 5(C), 6(C), 7(A), 8(D), 9(B), 10(A), 11(B), 12(C).

SPOT THE DIFFERENCE – PAGE 52

CROSSWORD – PAGE 54

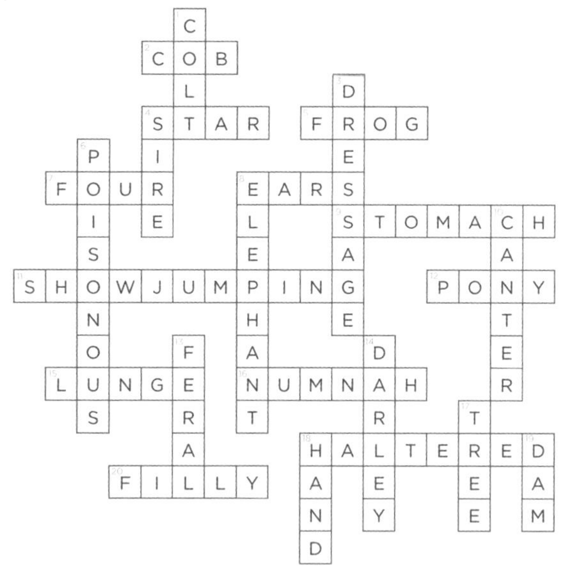

WHICH STORY WAS THAT? – PAGE 58

1(E), 2(G), 3(B), 4(F), 5(A), 6(H), 7(D), 8(C), 9(I).

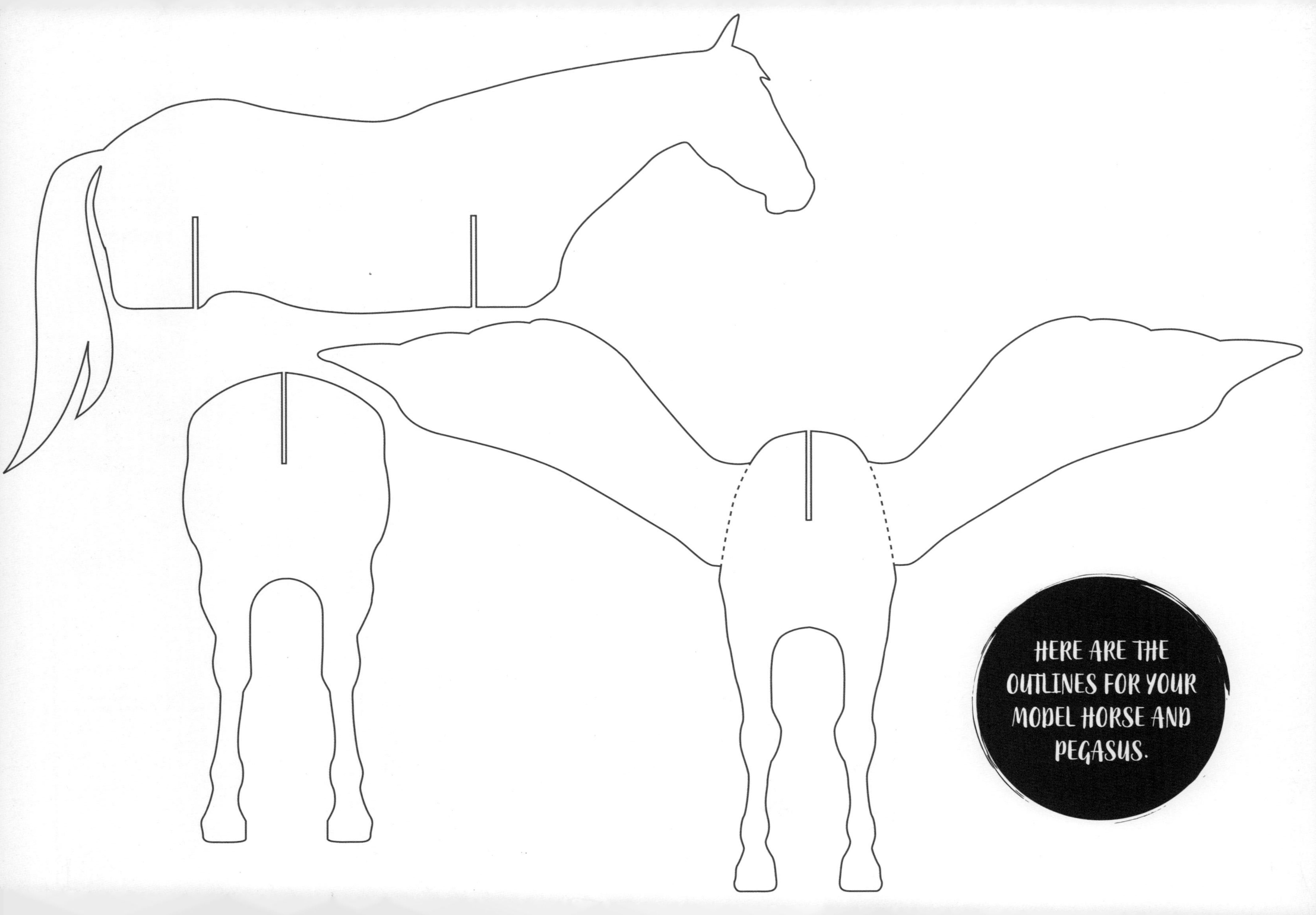
HERE ARE THE
OUTLINES FOR YOUR
MODEL HORSE AND
PEGASUS.

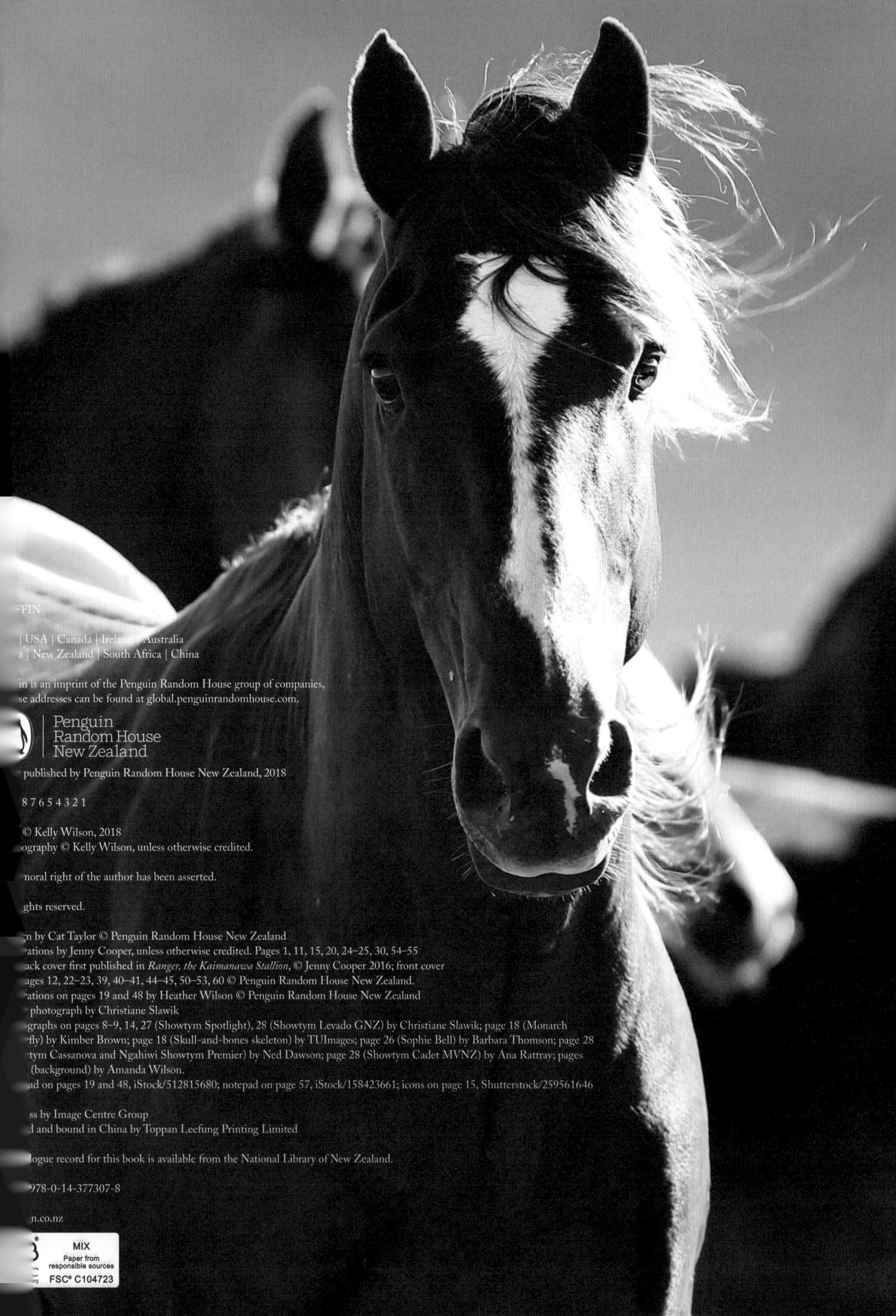

FFIN

| USA | Canada | Ireland | Australia
a | New Zealand | South Africa | China

in is an imprint of the Penguin Random House group of companies,
se addresses can be found at global.penguinrandomhouse.com.

Penguin
Random House
New Zealand

published by Penguin Random House New Zealand, 2018

8 7 6 5 4 3 2 1

n by Cat Taylor © Penguin Random House New Zealand
rations by Jenny Cooper, unless otherwise credited. Pages 1, 11, 15, 20, 24–25, 30, 54–55
ack cover first published in *Ranger, the Kaimanawa Stallion*, © Jenny Cooper 2016; front cover
ages 12, 22–23, 39, 40–41, 44–45, 50–53, 60 © Penguin Random House New Zealand.
rations on pages 19 and 48 by Heather Wilson © Penguin Random House New Zealand
photograph by Christiane Slawik
graphs on pages 8–9, 14, 27 (Showtym Spotlight), 28 (Showtym Levado GNZ) by Christiane Slawik; page 18 (Monarch
fly) by Kimber Brown; page 18 (Skull-and-bones skeleton) by TUImages; page 26 (Sophie Bell) by Barbara Thomson; page 28
tym Cassanova and Ngahiwi Showtym Premier) by Ned Dawson; page 28 (Showtym Cadet MVNZ) by Ana Rattray; pages
(background) by Amanda Wilson.
ad on pages 19 and 48, iStock/512815680; notepad on page 57, iStock/158423661; icons on page 15, Shutterstock/259561646

ss by Image Centre Group
d and bound in China by Toppan Leefung Printing Limited

logue record for this book is available from the National Library of New Zealand.

978-0-14-377307-8

n.co.nz

MIX
Paper from
responsible sources
FSC® C104723